Wars in the Third World
since 1945

Wars in the Third World since 1945

Guy Arnold

CASSELL

First published 1991 by **Cassell Publishers Limited**
Villiers House, 41/47 Strand, London WC2N 5JE, England
387 Park Avenue South, New York, NY 10016–8810, USA

British Library Cataloguing in Publication Data
Arnold, Guy *1932–*
    Wars in the Third World since 1945.
    1. Developing countries. Conflict, history
    I. Title
    909.09724

    ISBN 0-304-31671-7

    Printed and bound in Great Britain by
    Dotesios Limited, Trowbridge, Wiltshire

CONTENTS

PART II Big power intervention wars

PART III Border wars and wars between Third World countries

PART IV Israel and its neighbours

Contents

PREFACE

The difficulty about this kind of project is that it has no end. Even as I ran off the final typescript a group of West African states, led by Nigeria, decided to intervene in Liberia in the hope of bringing the civil war in that country to an end, and Iraq invaded and occupied Kuwait in a matter of twenty-four hours, triggering off what had every appearance of being a long and extremely dangerous Middle East crisis. The nature of the Third World (what in future is more likely to be called the South now that the Cold War has come to an end) – weakness derived from poverty and under-development – is likely to mean that it will continue to be a theatre of numerous small and not so small wars into the foreseeable future.

Guy Arnold
August 1990

INTRODUCTION

Ever since 1945 large areas of the Third World, whose emergence so troubled the two sides in the Cold War, have been wracked by wars: colonial liberation wars as rising nationalisms brought an end to the European empires, big power intervention wars which became an inextricable part of the Cold War, or wars between the newly independent states of the Third World. And such wars have hardly ever escaped big power interventions and complications: the two superpowers have almost always been involved and, after them, the ex-imperial powers, most especially Britain and France. The big powers have intervened directly, they have supplied arms, and they have supported one or other side depending upon the interests they wished to defend or the actions of other major powers that they wanted to counter-balance. Only occasionally has a war occurred in the Third World and been fought to a conclusion without at least some measure of big power intervention; where this has been the case the war was probably so small-scale and so quickly over that outside interests did not have time to mobilize themselves to interfere. The five-day war between Burkina Faso and Mali in December 1985 is a case in point. But, as a rule, a war in the Third World means intervention of some kind from the North, and many of these wars have been a form of proxy fighting between the opponents in the Cold War.

The Iraqi invasion of Kuwait on 2 August 1990 was swift, brutal and effective; although there was some immediate resistance and subsequent evidence that underground opposition groups, formerly banned by the Kuwaiti royal family, would take up arms against the Iraqis, the event as such could hardly be described as a war. Rather, it was the absorption in little more than 24 hours of a mini-state by a powerful neighbour possessing one of the largest standing armies in the world. But the successful invasion of Kuwait by Iraq represented only the beginning of what became one of the most severe war crises in the Third World. The international reaction was one of outrage and condemnation. There was an immediate Western response, and within days the USA and Britain had begun to deploy forces in Saudi Arabia to oppose any further Iraqi aggression in the Gulf. The Arab world was more wary: not that it supported Iraq, but it distrusted the West and this time a West which was working with the USSR rather than being opposed by it. A Saudi soldier watching the arrival of US troops at Dharhan put the point succinctly when he asked, 'Would the West be coming to guard Saudi Arabia if we did not have oil?'

The Iraqi annexation of Kuwait (even though it only turned out to be temporary) raises many of the issues which lie at the heart of North–South relations. In 1980, led by the same President Saddam Hussein, Iraq launched a war against Iran, but on that occasion there were no Western protests at violation of principle and no rush to help Iran deter aggression, for the West was then quite prepared (at least at the beginning of what turned out to be one of the longest and bloodiest wars in the Third World) to see two regimes of which it disapproved batter each other to a standstill. Principle almost never enters into big power interventions; interest is the key.

In the years immediately after the Second World War, nationalism throughout the Third World spelled the end of the European empires, and the ideological division between the capitalist West and the Communist bloc heralded the Cold War. The result has been more than four decades of violence which has been exclusively confined to the countries of the developing South. The Cold War has been the dominant factor influencing the ways in which the superpowers and their allies have reacted to a majority of all the wars in the Third World, whether or not these had anything to do with the Cold War in their origins.

Since 1945 and the coming of the Cold War, the superpowers and their allies have fought by proxy in many parts of the Third World, and the Cold War has provided a framework for intervention. This raises the question of how many wars have been needlessly prolonged because of big power interventions. The USSR has justified its interventions in the Third World on the grounds of combating the imperialist threat. President Kennedy told Belgium's Paul-Henri Spaak at the beginning of the 1960s that the real struggles were not in Europe 'but in Asia, Latin America and Africa'. And throughout this period the big powers have deliberately mobilized Third World countries to be in one or other of their camps. As a result war has become endemic to much of the Third World: in Central America, in parts of Africa and the Middle East. The superpower determination to control bases in the Middle East (to assist possible intervention in the Gulf) played a major part in the escalation of violence in the Horn of Africa. Thus in 1977 the USA and the USSR swapped surrogates in the Horn: Somalia expelled the Russians and welcomed the Americans in their place; the Ethiopians expelled the Americans and turned to the Russians.

Doctrines or pronouncements to justify interventions have been made specifically by a number of US presidents. In 1957 President Eisenhower endorsed the idea that the USA would intervene in the Middle East to prevent the spread of communism. In 1964 President Johnson justified US intervention in the Dominican Republic on the grounds of forestalling a communist dictatorship. In 1969 President Nixon at Guam enunciated the cynical doctrine that the USA would rely on its Third World allies to bear the brunt of military interventions. In 1980 President Carter said the USA would intervene in the Gulf if necessary. Under President Reagan direct US interventions have included Grenada, Lebanon, Libya and Iran, and active support for rebel forces in Nicaragua (the Contras), Angola (UNITA), Afghanistan and Cambodia.

American administrations have exaggerated the Soviet threat so as to keep in line their allies in the North and their clients in the South. By the 1980s the USA had 360 bases and 1600 military installations in 36 countries round the world. One calculation pinpoints 110 occasions when the USA has intervened in Third World countries since 1945. Certain countries, Iran under the Shah for example, have been bolstered by Western aid to act as 'policemen' for Western interests in a particular region. In 1980 US spending on military and security aid accounted for 66 per cent of its aid budget, and that year military–security aid went to 43 countries. By 1988 it went to 102 countries. The readiness of the USA to justify assistance to regimes in order that they could combat Communism, or to assist rebels in Third World countries (no matter how dubious their real cause) because they proclaimed their readiness to combat Communism, has been a recipe for instability.

The USSR may not have been as active in as many countries as the USA, but that was not through lack of will; it was due to inadequate resources on a comparable scale. However, where it did intervene, its military assistance was often massive. Between 1980 and 1984 the USSR provided sub-Saharan Africa with $2.1 billion of economic aid and $5.9 billion of military aid. In North Africa over the same years it provided $650 million in economic aid and $7.9 billion in military aid. During the decade of the 1980s it helped maintain up to 50,000 Cuban troops in Angola, more than 7000 in Ethiopia and about 1150 in Mozambique. It had a naval base at Cam Ranh in Vietnam and at Al Anad in South Yemen, while 15 foreign ports provided facilities for its warships. Between 1982 and 1985 Ethiopia received four times more aid from the Communist bloc than any other African country, 25 per cent of all Comecon's overseas aid.

Few Third World countries produce sophisticated weaponry of their own (though a number are striving to do so), but rely instead upon arms imports from the North. According to SIPRI, the six leading arms exporters to the Third World in the period 1970–9 were as follows:

Country	$ million	% of Third World Trade
USA	27,727	45.0
USSR	16,914	27.5
France	5,894	10.0
Britain	3,044	5.0
Italy	1,868	3.0
West Germany	1,444	2.3

Not all wars have been connected with the Cold War, yet it has been an inescapable fact of big power politics that the opportunity to interfere in pursuit of advantage which most wars present required some justification, if only for form's sake, and Cold War fears provided the easiest such justifications. But as the Americans discovered in Vietnam, the Russians in Afghanistan or the French in Chad, it is easier to get into a war than it is to get out again.

Part of the problem in compiling this history of wars in the Third World has been one of definition. When does civil violence become a civil war? Was the American intervention in Grenada, called for by a number of that little country's West Indian neighbours, a policing action or a mini-war? At what point does an anti-colonial insurrection turn into a war of liberation: the Algerian uprising against the French (1954–62) seems clear cut, but what of the unsuccessful uprising against the French in Madagascar in 1947?

There has been the further problem of where to place wars. The war in Vietnam began as a colonial liberation war against the French, but though the Communists led the opposition to a French return, was their primary motive nationalist or the desire to make Vietnam join the world Communist camp? Was the Korean War (1950–3) primarily a civil war between two parts of what had long been a single nation, or a big power intervention war to spread and to contain Communism? A number of the wars examined here began as nationalist revolts against imperialism and then, inexorably, were drawn into the Cold War and became something quite different.

The book is divided into five sections as follows: colonial liberation wars; big power intervention wars; border wars and wars between Third World countries; Israel and its neighbours; and civil wars: ideological. Part I, on colonial liberation

Map 1 Wars in the Third World since 1945

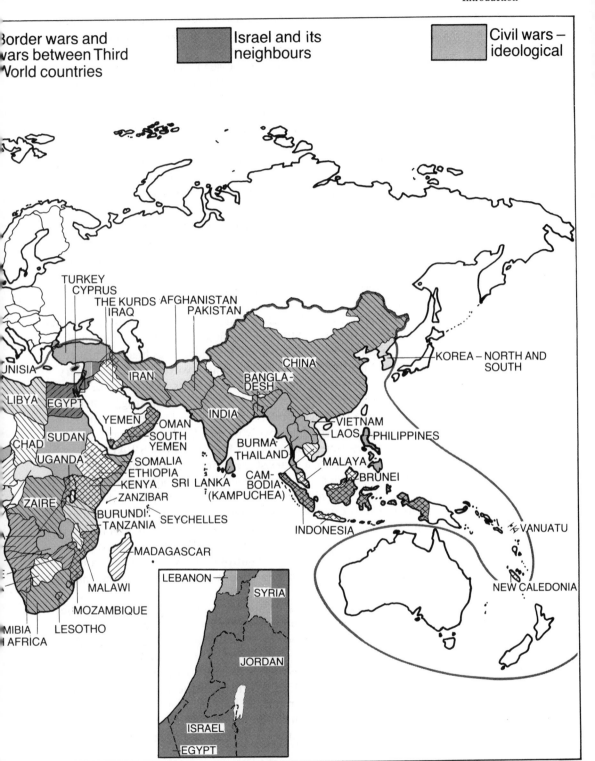

Border wars and wars between Third World countries

Israel and its neighbours

Civil wars – ideological

TURKEY
CYPRUS
THE KURDS
IRAQ
AFGHANISTAN
PAKISTAN
UNISIA
IRAN
CHINA
BANGLA-
DESH
KOREA – NORTH AND
SOUTH
LIBYA
EGYPT
YEMEN
OMAN
SOUTH
YEMEN
INDIA
VIETNAM
LAOS
PHILIPPINES
CHAD
SUDAN
UGANDA
SOMALIA
ETHIOPIA
KENYA
ZANZIBAR
BURMA
THAILAND
SRI LANKA
CAM-
BODIA
(KAMPUCHEA)
MALAYA
BRUNEI
ZAIRE
BURUNDI
TANZANIA
SEYCHELLES
INDONESIA
VANUATU
MADAGASCAR
MALAWI
MOZAMBIQUE
MIBIA
AFRICA
LESOTHO
NEW CALEDONIA

LEBANON
SYRIA
JORDAN
ISRAEL
EGYPT

wars, covers what is possibly the most straightforward area. A majority of these wars occurred in the period 1945 to 1965, although several (Angola, Mozambique, Zimbabwe) continued until the 1970s. Part II, on big power intervention wars, deals with two kinds of war: the first, what may be seen as post-imperial tidying-up operations such as the British in East Africa (1964) or the French in the Central African Republic (1979); the second, superpower ideological confrontations such as the Americans in Vietnam or the Russians in Afghanistan. Yet, though only 13 wars are listed in this section, the big powers were heavily engaged in a majority of the other wars as well, even if they did not intervene directly with their own armed forces. Some entries are multiple in nature, as for example 'China: adjustment wars' or 'South Africa: destabilizing its neighbours' in Part III. The special position of Israel, which is regarded in the Arab world as an extension of the West that has been planted in their midst, has been given a section to itself. The final section, which covers civil wars, is the longest in the book. At least to some extent the placing of a war in one section as opposed to another is arbitrary, and a number of the wars examined here partake of the qualities of several kinds of war. Angola illustrates the point.

Angola has been in a state of continuous war from 1961 to 1990, and these 30 years of war are treated in two sections (in Part I 'Angola: the liberation struggle', which covers the years 1961 to 1975; and in Part V 'The Angolan civil war 1975–1990', which is still in progress). Although the first war began as a nationalist struggle against the Portuguese, by 1975, when independence was finally achieved, the country's neighbours Zaire and Zambia had become involved on the periphery while South Africa actually invaded Angola on the eve of its independence in an effort to overthrow its new (Marxist) government. The liberation struggle merged into the civil war which had already got under way by 1975. This second Angolan war became part of a far wider struggle involving the USA (in support of the UNITA rebels), South Africa (intervening ostensibly to destroy SWAPO bases, but just as concerned to destabilize a Marxist government), and the USSR and Cuba in support of that government. The war reached an unlooked-for climax in 1988–9 when, as a result of the military stalemate if not defeat of the South Africans at the battle of Cuito Cuanavale, it suddenly became possible to achieve a settlement in Namibia and assist the process of political change that heralded a new era in South Africa under President F. W. de Klerk. For two or three years, at least, the war in Angola had become a confrontation of far wider-ranging international implications than simply a civil war between opposed factions inside the country.

Few of the wars examined in this book escape big power involvement at some level; and many would almost certainly have been far shorter in duration and less devastating in their effects had the big powers not intervened. But in a world of tensions, exemplified by the Cold War, it was perhaps unreasonable to imagine that the Third World would be permitted to get on with its own affairs without interference from the North. Most Third World countries, in any case, are exceptionally vulnerable to such interference, if for no other reason than their poverty and general weakness in relation to the major powers of the North. And the habit of interference, whether by the old imperial powers or the newer superpowers, dies hard.

The big question mark in 1990 is simply whether the end of the Cold War also means an end or at least a diminution of such big power interventions in the South. The auguries are not good, although a world in which the USA and the USSR act together as policemen rather than separately as automatic supporters of opposing factions does, possibly, offer hope of less rather than more conflict. The fact that the Cold War arms race comes to an end and the need for Cold War bases round the world disappears does not mean that big power interests in the South will also disappear. The temptation for the powerful to intervene in pursuit of their interests – however these are presented – will always be there. Thus, the fact that the Communist threat recedes in Latin America is unlikely to bring an end to US interventions in countries on America's doorstep: the USA had the habit long before the Cold War began. It is possible that the exhaustion factor will bring some wars to an end – Ethiopia, Sudan, Angola or Laos, for example – yet the signs are not good.

If the Cold War really has come to an end, then relations between North and South will provide a major international theme for the balance of the twentieth century. These relations are at present exemplified by the huge debts which the South owes the North (with little prospect of ever paying them), by the large numbers of refugee victims of the various wars that have long plagued the South, by growing North–South arguments about the environment, by the unresolved problem of Israel and its Arab neighbours, and by a growing tendency in some Third World countries to resort to extremes as their only means of standing up to the North. Such extremes include the taking of hostages and the development of chemical weapons, which are cheap and easy to manufacture but devastating in their use.

The ending of the Cold War represents a giant step forward; it would be a tragedy if it were seen to confer licence upon the big powers of the North to manipulate the South without fear of confrontation with each other.

DEVELOPMENTS 1990–1991

World tensions at all levels are liable to increase in proportion to the increase of the total world population and consequent pressures upon the world's dwindling resources. Between completion of this manuscript and receipt of the proofs a major war occurred in the Gulf, with Iraq facing a United Nations Alliance of some 30 nations led by the USA. In addition, violence continued in at least half a dozen areas where warfare of one kind or another appears to be endemic, including the Horn of Africa, Angola and Mozambique; Sri Lanka and Kashmir, where the possibility of another India–Pakistan clash is never far away; and in the several countries of Central America, where civil strife appears unending, and especially in the case of El Salvador, where one of the region's most brutal civil wars goes on unabated despite a momentary pause for elections. The signs, unfortunately, point to continuing and escalating violence in many parts of the Third World.

The Gulf War against Iraq January–February 1991

The 1991 Gulf War can be categorized under several headings: the annexation of Kuwait may be seen as a war between two Third World countries, though so uneven were the two sides that it could hardly be described as a war at all; the second, main war between Iraq and the UN-sponsored Alliance could be seen primarily as a big power intervention war (with the USA and its Western allies determined to prevent Saddam Hussein holding onto Kuwait) but complicated by the fact that Iraq was also opposed by most of the Arab world; then, when the UN operation had been completed and the Iraqis forced to relinquish Kuwait a third, civil, war erupted between the anti-Saddam forces inside Iraq and his own supporters.

The war raises a number of questions of principle and motivation. President Saddam Hussein of Iraq seized Kuwait on 2 August 1990 to increase Iraq's regional power base and assert his hegemony in the Gulf. Had he got away with it he would have posed a major threat to all the Gulf states, none of which (with the exception of Iran) was able either on its own or in combination to withstand his military might. However, the USA determined at once to oppose the annexation and if necessary force Iraq to relinquish Kuwait. On what principle did Washington act? The USA and its Western allies (especially Britain) could hardly claim to be acting on the principle that it was right to enforce a UN resolution as such since blatantly, over the years, they had ignored many UN resolutions in relation to Israel, South Africa and other parts of the world where their interests dictated inaction. Nor could they argue convincingly that they were taking action to prevent annexation *on principle* since they had remained quiescent in the case of China's annexing of Tibet in the 1950s, over Israel's annexation of the Golan Heights and that country's 'incorporation' of both the West Bank and the Gaza Strip (the occupied territories) under its control, or in the case of Turkey's annexation of the northern third of Cyprus in 1974. This relative indifference to annexation remained the case over Kuwait even though apologists (for previous Western inaction) during the course of the Gulf intervention were quick to point out that in the earlier cases Cold War antagonisms had made it far more difficult – and dangerous – to intervene. But this raises the question: even had there been no Cold War would the West have intervened in those other cases? A third possible justification for intervention was the sheer brutal nature of the Saddam Hussein regime and his possession of a range of weapons including missiles, germ warheads and possibly nuclear warheads that put the whole Middle East at risk. That justification does not hold up to serious examination. In the first place, the West has tolerated and sometimes positively encouraged brutal regimes provided they pursued policies that did not endanger Western interests (support for the Shah of Iran is a case in point). In the second place, the West in its hatred of the fundamentalist Islamic regime of the Ayatollah Khomeini was prepared to arm and support (tacitly if not too overtly) Saddam Hussein right up to his invasion of Kuwait. Moreover, once the war was over and Iraqi forces had quit Kuwait the Allies stood on the sidelines while Saddam Hussein with barbaric brutality put down the insurrections against him.

There was, in fact, only one principle of overriding importance which led the USA and the West to intervene: oil. As almost every observer, of no matter what political persuasion, has agreed: had there been no oil in Kuwait there might have been outraged denunciations of a bullying regime but there would not have been a war. It was the threat to Western economic interests inherent in the possibility that Saddam Hussein would end up controlling the largest world oil resources outside Saudi Arabia that ensured Western intervention. And that fact merely reinforces the general theme of this book: that the major powers of the North are always prepared to intervene in the affairs of the South if such intervention is perceived to be necessary to secure the interests of the North. The only principle of intervention is self-interest.

The annexation of Kuwait

On 2 August 1990, Iraqi forces invaded Kuwait in strength and within twenty-four hours had occupied the entire territory. Iraq, with nearly a million men under arms and eight years of battle experience in the earlier Gulf War against Iran (1980–8), was the most formidable military power in the region. The addition of Kuwait to Iraq meant that Baghdad now controlled about 25 per cent of the world's known oil reserves.

President George Bush of the USA and Prime Minister Margaret Thatcher of Britain (who happened to be on a visit to the USA at the time of the invasion) agreed to seek UN sanctions against Iraq.

There was in any case a long-standing quarrel between Iraq and Kuwait and at least some justification for Iraq's territorial claim to its small neighbour since Kuwait had been part of the Ottoman Empire district based upon Basrah. But the real cause of the dispute was oil. Iraq accused Kuwait of stealing oil from the Rumailia field, which lies across their joint borders, and was angry that Kuwait had been producing above its OPEC quota, thus forcing the price down to only $14 a barrel at a time when Iraq needed all the revenue it could raise in order to repair the damage that had resulted from the Gulf War. On 17 July 1990, Saddam Hussein gave a speech in which he complained of Kuwait's oil policy (overproduction), its encroachments on Iraqi territory and its demand for repayments of loans made during the Gulf War. At the same time he moved 100,000 troops up to the Kuwait border. Later in July at the Geneva OPEC meeting the price of oil – at Iraqi insistence – was raised by $3 a barrel while Kuwait promised to keep within its quota of 1.5m b/d. But it was too late and Iraq had already determined upon invasion. Even so, right up to 2 August neither US nor British intelligence believed that a war was coming; they assumed Saddam Hussein to be bluffing. (Yet in 1961 Britain had despatched troops and tanks to Kuwait to face a similar threat of invasion from Iraq which had then not materialized.)

The Iraqi army was 955,000 strong with 5000 tanks, 3500 pieces of field artillery, 513 warplanes, 160 helicopters and 330 missile launchers. On paper at least it was one of the most formidable forces in the world. Kuwait had 20,300 soldiers, 275 tanks, 92 guns, 36 warplanes and 18 helicopters. The total Kuwait population came to 2 million, of which 1.1 million were expatriate workers and their families.

World reactions

There was almost universal condemnation of the Iraqi invasion of Kuwait, and the UN Security Council at once passed a resolution condemning Iraqi aggression. The Arab world, however, was thrown into disarray: its conservative members – Saudi Arabia and the small Gulf states – knew their own safety depended upon ousting Iraq from Kuwait yet understood that this could only be done with Western – American – military assistance, which would mean the return of a neocolonial military presence to the Arab world. Israel represented a further, dangerous factor in the equation, for its proven military capacity was such that it might decide upon some form of unilateral intervention. Jordan sat uneasily between Iraq and Israel and in the event really had no option but to side, however reluctantly, with Iraq. But the most important new political factor operating at the time concerned the USSR: Moscow's readiness to co-operate with the USA to force Iraq to obey UN sanctions (even though the USSR had long been Iraq's main ally and source of military equipment) ensured that massive US intervention could be successfully carried out. Thereafter, the build-up of forces to oppose Iraq was rapid. Already by 9 August the USA had begun the despatch of 40,000 troops and 100 F-15 and F-16 fighter-bombers to the Gulf and was actively seeking UN backing for the use of its forces against Iraq. Britain had at once joined the USA in sending forces to the Gulf.

The USA now embarked upon the business of creating an anti-Iraq alliance and was faced with a number of complex problems. The first was to maintain Alliance solidarity while giving UN sanctions a chance to work. The second problem was ensuring that the USSR stayed with the Alliance in spirit if not in fact. Third was the need to reassure the Arab world, and especially Saudi Arabia (which had become the host country for the rapidly growing numbers of Allied troops that were being deployed in the Gulf), that the Western presence was to be a temporary phenomenon. Fourthly, Israel had to be persuaded to maintain a low profile since it would have been fatal to the American stand against Iraq if that stand had been portrayed as being in defence of Israeli interests in the region.

Against this background – over the months of August to December 1990 – the US-dominated Alliance was built up and held together. Britain and France provided air and ground forces; Turkey was already to do the same; and, more important, Saudi Arabia, Egypt and Syria of the major Arab states each made substantial military commitments to the Alliance. Iraqi ships or others trading with Iraq were subject to seizure or examination in the Gulf; King Hussein of Jordan made repeated but in the end fruitless attempts to negotiate a way out for Saddam Hussein; and the members of the Alliance steadily built up their military power in the region. Already by mid-August US air power based upon Saudi Arabia (with an important contribution by Britain) was enough to ensure Allied air supremacy against Iraq.

As the Alliance was built up against him Saddam Hussein played his most important diplomatic card by trying to link a solution to the Kuwait question to a solution of the Palestinian question, and though this ensured the support of the quarter-million-plus Palestinians then in Kuwait it did not succeed in splitting the Alliance. His shrewdest move was to conclude a peace with Iran, accepting the 1975 agreement concluded at Algiers with the Shah that made the border between the two countries run along the main channel of the Shatt al-Arab waterway, and agreeing to the exchange of prisoners. This enabled Saddam to move his crack troops from the border facing Iran to the south of Iraq to face the Alliance. By the end of August 1990, a military confrontation between the USA and its allies, and Iraq seemed inevitable.

During the remaining months of 1990 Alliance strength in the Gulf was built up to more than 500,000 men (and women), with the more than 400,000 US troops as the core of the Alliance in both numbers and sophisticated weaponry. As Saddam Hussein appeared intransigent and deaf to all appeals it became more and more certain that the affair could only be resolved by war. Various attempts at mediation each came to nothing, for the Alliance position was that Iraq had to quit Kuwait unconditionally while Saddam insisted – after an initial period of allowing a puppet government to operate – that Kuwait was the 19th province of Iraq.

At the time of the annexation there were present in Kuwait 300,000 Palestinians, 100,000 Egyptians, 100,000 Indians, 100,000 Pakistanis, 100,000 Sri Lankans and many thousands of other immigrant workers including large numbers of Bangladeshis and Filipinos, while in Iraq itself there were 170,000 Pakistanis, an estimated 800,000 Egyptians, and 100,000 other Asians and North Africans. One immediate result of the invasion of Kuwait was a mass exodus of refugees into Jordan and Saudi Arabia, with Jordan having to cope with an influx of 250,000. Much publicity in the West centred upon the plight of the several thousand Western migrant workers trapped in Kuwait or Iraq and the threat of Saddam Hussein to use them as a 'human shield' at installations likely to be military targets once fighting began.

A Saudi prince, Lt.-Gen. Khaled bin Sultan Abdul Aziz, was placed in charge of all Arab and Muslim troops of the Alliance (he appeared in public accompanied by a US adviser) while US general Norman Schwarzkopf commanded the US forces and, in effect, the Alliance army. By mid-September the US build-up had reached formidable proportions: four carrier battle groups, a battleship surface action group, a tactical airforce of 700 planes which included 450 strike aircraft, 4½ army divisions of approximately 70,000 men plus 45,000 marines and a further 80,000 troops on standby in the USA. Large medical units were also despatched to the Gulf in readiness for expected heavy casualties once a land war had commenced.

Moscow endorsed the US stand – the USSR's internal problems by then had become formidable – since it clearly did not wish either to pursue an independent policy of its own or to antagonize the USA. Following a summit between Bush and Gorbachev in Helsinki in early September it became clear that Iraq was almost totally isolated. By joining the Alliance and contributing substantial forces to the Gulf, Syria reversed a long period of enmity with the West to make itself acceptable once more in Washington and London. Egypt, from the beginning, took a clear stand against Iraq. By mid-September Iraq had 300,000 men in and around Kuwait and 2800 tanks dug in facing the Allies. The Palestinians in Kuwait declared for Saddam Hussein – they did not have much option – but this was to weaken their bargaining position once the war was over. By the end of September diplomats and Alliance leaders spoke of when, not if, the war would take place.

During December there was still a chance that a peaceful solution could be achieved: the UN set a deadline of 15 January for Iraq to withdraw from Kuwait. The US Secretary of State, James Baker, met the Iraqi Foreign Minister, Tariq Aziz, in Geneva in a final attempt to persuade Iraq to withdraw but it came to nothing. In the first two weeks of 1991 with no sign of compromise on either side the USSR made a final bid to persuade Saddam to back down before the deadline was reached but this, too, came to nothing. Then the UN Secretary-General, Javier Pérez de Cuéllar, made a final visit to Baghdad in an eleventh-hour attempt to prevent the war but that, too, was abortive.

Remarkably, the Alliance had held together despite fears in Washington that its disparate membership would fall apart. It was the first time since the Korean War of 1950–53 that a UN-backed alliance had been prepared to wage war according to UN Security Council resolutions but in this case with the significant difference that the two Communist giants – the USSR and China – had decided to support the UN so that no Cold War split threatened to polarize the world over the crisis.

By 15 January (the UN deadline) US forces numbered more than 400,000, British forces 30,000, French 10,000 while a further 100,000 troops had been deployed by Saudi Arabia, Egypt and Syria with small contingents from other Alliance members such as Senegal. On the eve of the war it was assumed that the Alliance – meaning its Western contingents – would have obtained air superiority almost at once and this was to prove the case.

The aerial bombardment

At 10 a.m. on Wednesday 16 January 1991, 17 hours after the UN deadline had expired, General Schwarzkopf ordered his forces into action. His strategy was to blanket Iraqi targets with non-stop air attacks, and the biggest aerial bombardment in history was unleashed on Iraq with 1000 missions being flown in the first 14 hours. Thereafter, Iraq was subjected to round-the-clock bombing with airfields, missile sites and military concentrations as the main targets. It became clear, almost at once, that Iraq was holding back or not prepared to use its air force in any major counter-offensive. Many planes were destroyed on the ground, others were believed to be in deep underground bunkers and some flew to safety in Iran, whose government said they would remain there until the end of hostilities. Iraq fired a series of Scud missiles at targets in Israel and Saudi Arabia, and after the first Israeli casualties a major concern in Washington was to persuade Israel not to retaliate unilaterally since it was feared that once it did so the Arab members of the Alliance would break ranks since they could not be seen to be fighting on the same side as the Israelis. In the event Israel did not retaliate; the US rapidly deployed Patriot anti-missile missiles in Israel. (One of the surprises of the war was the ineffective nature of the Scud missiles, which were either shot down or did relatively little damage on impact.)

The aerial bombardment continued unabated from 16 January through to 23 February, when the land war was finally launched. The great fear in Washington (a reflection of the traumas of the Vietnam war) was of large numbers of casualties once the ground war started and so the strategy was to prolong the aerial bombardment until it had done maximum damage on the ground in material terms while also undermining Iraqi morale. As it became clear that a ground war would soon have to be launched, Iraq embarked upon a scorched-earth policy in Kuwait which included firing a majority of the oil wells and releasing a huge oil slick (10 miles long) into the Gulf. The bombing of Baghdad included a target believed to be a command and control centre in which, however, 400 civilians sheltering from the raids were killed. Then in mid-February, when Moscow was making a final effort to persuade Saddam Hussein to quit Kuwait before the land war began, President Bush broke any possible deadlock by issuing an ultimatum: Iraq was to begin leaving Kuwait by 5 p.m. on 23 February or face a ground war.

The ground war

The ground war lasted 100 hours. The Iraqi forces either were demoralized by the month's aerial bombardment to which they had been subjected (in which many thousands had been killed) or were ready to surrender as soon as the opportunity presented itself so that little effective resistance was offered to the Allied advance and, contrary to all expectations, Allied casualties (dead) were in the dozens rather even than the hundreds. Many of the front-rank Iraqi troops were conscripts or immigrant workers forced into the army and held in place by special 'police' squads whose duty was to shoot deserters. This fact revealed more about the tyranny of Saddam Hussein's regime than almost anything else. Kuwait City was abandoned by the Iraqis on 26 February while, at the same time, the Iraqi defences were collapsing all along the line. Tens of thousands of Iraqi soldiers readily surrendered to the advancing Allies so that a major problem became the logistical one of handling the prisoners. The US forces outflanked the Iraqi defences north of Kuwait to cut off large numbers of troops and only Saddam Hussein's élite Republican Guards put up any real resistance. Kuwait City was found to have been devastated by looting and general destruction while the whole of Kuwait lay under a pall of smoke from about 600 burning oil wells.

The war ended on 28 February when the UN objective (of Iraq withdrawing from Kuwait and relinquishing its claim to the territory) had been achieved. This was accomplished 210 days after the Iraqi seizure of Kuwait, 43 days after the commencement of military action (aerial bombardment) and 100 hours after the launching of the ground attack.

Results

In the immediate aftermath of the war (March 1991) it is not possible to produce accurate figures of either casualties or costs but both are very high. Possibly 100,000 Iraqis were killed in the fighting, mainly as a result of the massive Allied bombing before the ground attack, while Allied casualties ran into a few hundred altogether. Kuwait estimated physical damage including looting to be in the region of $50 billion, while the damage by bombing to Baghdad and other Iraqi cities and towns and especially to water and power installations and bridges throughout the country was put at many billions of dollars. The cost of the war to the Allies came to several million dollars for every day the Allied forces were on the ground and in the end will probably be assessed in tens of billions of dollars.

The political and social costs were even greater. Basically, the defeat of Saddam Hussein was an American achievement and that fact alone meant a major Arab humiliation: the Arab world had been unable to deal with one of its own tyrants and had been obliged to rely upon a massive injection of US military might into the Gulf with the likelihood of a major US military presence in the region for years to come after the end of the war. The war itself, in which 15 Allied divisions defeated 42 Iraqi divisions in 100 hours, represented one of the most complete 'victories' in military history – in so far as the achievement of the UN objective was concerned (driving the Iraqis out of Kuwait) – yet when the fighting was over the situation that remained was hardly a victory for anyone. Saddam Hussein remained in power with formidable forces still at his disposal. Widespread uprisings in southern Iraq among Shias in Basrah and by the Kurds in the north brought the country to the brink of revolution yet by the end of March these uprisings appeared to be collapsing as Saddam deployed his loyal forces against them with great brutality and many thousands of people were slaughtered. In the south thousands more refugees fled into Iran and Saudi Arabia; in the north, after an initial success in which they had taken Kirkuk, another devastation of the Kurdish people took place and by the end of March an estimated 100,000 of them had become refugees. By early April perhaps 2 million Kurds were fleeing from government troops to become refugees in neighbouring countries or seeking safety in the mountains. Thus, the world was treated to the poignant spectacle of the Allied armies sitting on the borders of 'defeated' Iraq while the forces of Saddam Hussein were used to fight their own people in a way they had not attempted to resist the Allies while the Americans kept insisting that they would not and should not become involved in Iraq's internal affairs.

When the ruling al-Sabah family returned to Kuwait (some two weeks after its liberation) it was to preside over growing chaos including revenge killings against Palestinians, while the chances of greater democracy seemed slim despite oblique promises made to Kuwaiti opposition groups during the Iraqi occupation. The Palestinians, whose cause had been briefly – and possibly disastrously – championed by Saddam Hussein, found themselves once more the unwanted factor in the Middle East equation, although the most hopeful sign for the region as a whole was the commitment of the USA and the USSR at the end of March to hold a regional peace conference that would include discussion of the creation of a Palestinian entity.

As at the end of March 1991 Saddam Hussein remained (if precariously) in control of Iraq and appeared to have crushed the initial uprisings against him, in the process creating tens of thousands of refugees and possibly killing as many Iraqis as had been killed in the war. The USA, whether willingly or not, was in place in the Gulf as a major military force. Kuwait had been restored to the al-Sabah family but would require at least two years before its oil production could reach pre-war levels while other damage would take longer to put right. Finally, a series of uneasy questions remained of which the most important was what the West (which really meant the USA) would subsequently do about the Israel-Palestine question, for that issue would simply not disappear from the Middle East agenda and those Arab states which had maintained solidarity with the West during the period of the Alliance against Iraq expected a return in the form of real US pressures upon Israel to come to terms with the Palestinians.

What was plain at the end of March 1991 was the fact that such a massive war effort had solved few of the region's problems.

BIBLIOGRAPHICAL NOTE

A detailed bibliography which attempted to cover all the wars dealt with in this volume would be immense and uneven. In some cases – the Communist revolution in China (1946–9), the first and second Vietnam Wars or the liberation wars against the Portuguese in Africa – the literature is enormous. Some of the wars are already set in their historical context and definitive works have been written about them. In many cases, however, the war is still continuing and material has to be culled from contemporary accounts in the press or in annual publications. In such cases what appears to be of great importance at the time it is reported may have become relatively insignificant 10 years later. At the time of going to press, for example, the grim little civil war in Liberia was at its height, but only the daily press accounts were available.

The subject of modern warfare in all its ramifications is dealt with in depth by a number of research or academic institutions, such as the International Institute for Strategic Studies (IISS) in London, which produces its annual *The Military Balance*, and the Stockholm International Peace Research Institute (SIPRI). Both of these are major sources of material and publications on wars and warfare.

Generally, I have had recourse to the following kinds of source. First, I have used specific books which cover a particular war or wars, such as *Arabia without Sultans* by Fred Halliday (Penguin, 1974), which is an invaluable reference book for the wars in the Yemens and Oman, or *The Nigerian Civil War* by John de St Jorre (Hodder & Stoughton, 1972). Secondly, I have used war reference books such as Peter Janke's *Guerrilla and Terrorist Organizations: A World Directory and Bibliography* (Harvester, 1983), *Border and Territorial Disputes* edited by Alan J. Day (Keesings/Longman, 1987), or George C. Kohn's *Dictionary of Wars* (Facts on File, 1986). For more general information I have had recourse to reference books, encyclopaedias or annuals not specifically concerned with wars as such – the Europa yearbooks, for example. For wars in Africa over the crucial years of the independence struggles (for example, the Congo Crisis of 1960–5), *Africa Digest* (which appeared for more than 20 years from 1953) provides excellent factual coverage. Finally, I have built up an extensive press-clipping coverage of wars in the Third World from the mid-1980s when I first began work on this project.

PART I

Colonial Liberation Wars

Colonial liberation wars

INTRODUCTION

The 25 wars listed in Part I fall into a number of categories, although they have in common a general colonial nature: those in revolt were fighting against colonial domination of one kind or another, though not always – Ethiopia is the best example – against one of the metropolitan colonial powers of Europe.

The wars are grouped according to continent or region, but several kinds of war are represented here. The first group comprises eight countries of which seven – Algeria, Angola, Guinea-Bissau, Kenya, Mozambique, Tunisia, Zimbabwe – are in Africa and one – Indonesia – in Asia. In these countries there was a straightforward independence struggle by the indigenous peoples against the French (Algeria, Tunisia), the Portuguese (Angola, Guinea-Bissau, Mozambique), the British (Kenya, Zimbabwe) and the Dutch (Indonesia). In six of the eight cases (but not Guinea-Bissau or Indonesia) there were substantial and influential settler minorities whose interests ensured that the wars were prolonged (in Zimbabwe the settlers made a unilateral declaration of independence (UDI) against Britain; in Algeria the settlers revolted against French plans to end the war and grant independence; in Mozambique the settlers attempted a last-moment reversal of the independence process). These eight wars preceded independence and played a crucial role in hastening its arrival.

Two more revolts – those in Cameroon and Madagascar – also preceded independence and were nationalist in their basic aims, but they were complicated by ethnic rivalries between different indigenous groups, as well as opposition to continuing French rule.

There was no war in Cape Verde, but it has been included here because its fortunes and its achievement of independence were inextricably bound up with the struggle in Guinea-Bissau, while much of the leadership of the African Party for the Independence of Guinea and Cape Verde (PAIGC) came from Cape Verde.

Namibia stands on its own because, though the long war between SWAPO and South Africa was essentially an independence struggle, special features make it unique: the involvement of the United Nations, the fact that South Africa was declared to be illegally in Namibia, and the wider questions relating to South Africa's role in the region, including its use of Namibia as a base from which to destabilize Angola.

Cyprus is another unique case. The struggle on that island had three distinct features: the determination to achieve independence from Britain; the desire to achieve *enosis* (union) with Greece; and the communal rivalries between Greeks and Turks (the two ethnic components of the Cypriot population) which subsequently led to another war and partition during the 1970s.

The war in Aden (the People's Democratic Republic of Yemen) was in a sense the most imperial. There was no British settlement in Aden or the hinterland and almost no development. Britain retained Aden for strategic reasons, and as the

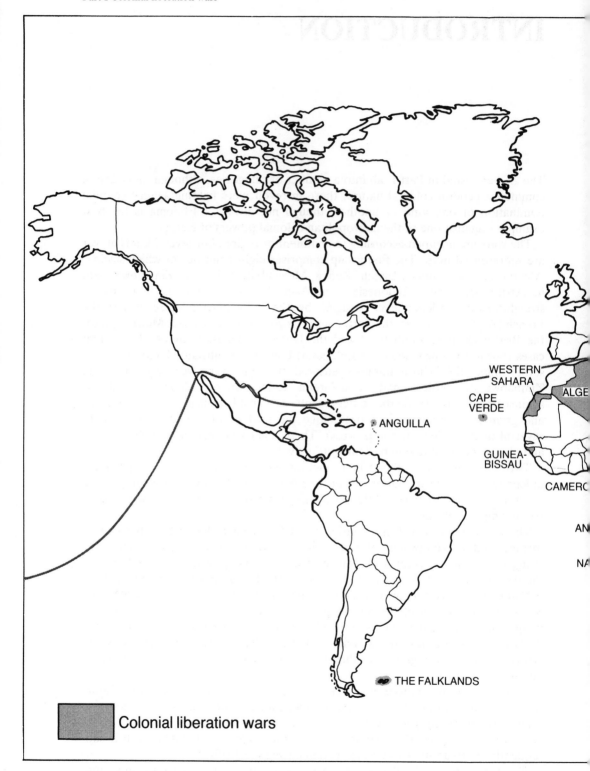

Map 2   Colonial liberation wars

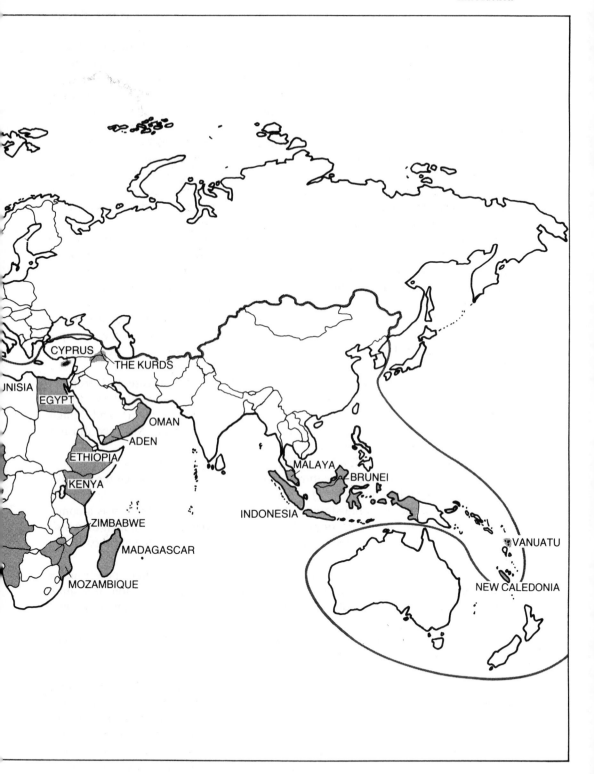

CYPRUS

THE KURDS

UNISIA

EGYPT

OMAN

ADEN

ETHIOPIA

KENYA

MALAYA

BRUNEI

ZIMBABWE

INDONESIA

MADAGASCAR

VANUATU

MOZAMBIQUE

NEW CALEDONIA

Empire disappeared so the need to hold on to Aden went too, but this did not prevent the war becoming one of the most brutal and bitter of them all.

The war in Malaya was inextricably bound up with the world-wide Cold War and was as much a part of the West's fight against Communism as an independence struggle: once it was plain that the British intended to grant independence to Malaya, the majority of the people were won over to the imperial side. In addition, there was an ethnic complication since the majority of the Communists were Chinese and not Malays.

The guerrilla war waged against the British base in the Canal Zone of Egypt was technically a post-independence affair, since Egypt had been nominally independent since 1922 and never a British colony as such. Yet from 1922 to the Suez débâcle of 1956, Egypt was very much part of the British (imperial) sphere of influence, and the guerrilla campaign of the early 1950s against the British was in essence a fight against continuing British interference in Egypt's affairs.

In Oman and Brunei a residual imperial relationship between Britain and the rulers included treaties whereby Britain would come to their defence if attacked. In these two cases the British were responding to requests for military assistance, but there were deeply entrenched colonial overtones to the relationships.

Although one of the poorest countries in Africa, Ethiopia has a long imperial tradition of its own, and in this case the separatist wars fought against Addis Ababa by Eritrea, Tigré and to a lesser extent the Oromo represent the attempts of people colonized by a Third World country either to break free entirely (Eritrea) or to achieve a greater degree of regional autonomy.

In Western (formerly Spanish) Sahara, Spain decided to extricate itself from its imperial entanglement by the expedient of recognizing the colonial claims to the territory advanced by its two neighbours – Morocco and Mauritania – and though Mauritania subsequently dropped out of the war of succession, Morocco did not and that war has yet to be resolved.

In the Pacific islands of New Caledonia a classic settler–indigenous struggle is in progress, but there are distinct features attached to this struggle since the Kanaks (the indigenous Melanesian people) no longer form the majority of the population.

In the case of the two mini-states – Anguilla and Vanuatu – there was a comic opera aspect to the little 'wars' or police actions recorded here, although they also illustrate the problems faced by tiny states which do not possess the military means to deal with uprisings.

The Falklands War falls into a curious category of its own: a major power and a middle power fighting a classic military campaign over the possession of a small colony which both claim, but whose colonial subjects wish to remain colonial subjects of the one power.

Finally, the Kurds fight an endless war in a hopeless effort to achieve nationalist recognition (and a Kurdistan state) from the five powers in whose territories their people reside. The outlook for them is dismal.

Of the 25 wars listed here, Britain is the principal colonial power in 10, France in five, Portugal in four, and Spain, the Netherlands and South Africa in one each. The principal attribute of the wars in this section is the determination of the rebels to break out of some form of colonial yoke. In a majority of cases the wars have become inextricably bound up with wider ideological considerations, and support for one side or the other in the struggle has been forthcoming from a range of outside powers or neighbours: the longer the struggle lasts, the more interests that become involved.

AFRICA

ALGERIA: THE INDEPENDENCE STRUGGLE

Origins

The roots of nationalist opposition to the French go back to the original French invasion of 1830; it took another 53 years before the whole country was subdued, while dissatisfaction with French racial and colonial policies meant that nationalism was never far beneath the surface. During the celebrations of victory in Europe (8 May 1945), Algerians displayed nationalist flags in Sétif, which sparked off an uprising in which more than 80 Frenchmen were killed. Subsequent reprisals were indiscriminate and led to thousands of deaths. Official French estimates gave the death toll as 88 Frenchmen and 1500 Algerians, but the nationalists claimed that 45,000 Algerians had been killed. Independent observers estimated a death toll between 10,000 and 15,000.

The nationalist leader, Ferhat Abbas (who in August 1944 had created a nationalist group, Les Amis du manifeste de libération(AML)), was arrested and the AML was proscribed. Further nationalist disturbances occurred in October 1945 and May 1946. Then in 1946 the Algerian People's Party, which had gone underground, reappeared as the Mouvement pour le triomphe des libertés démocratiques (MTLD), and the banned AML became a part of it. From the time of the Sétif uprising in 1945 until the outbreak of a full nationalist revolt in 1954, there was growing agitation for reform to meet nationalist aspirations.

In 1947 a faction of the nationalists formed the Organisation secrète (OS), which advocated armed struggle. In March 1954 nine members of the OS led by Ahmed Ben Bella and Belkacem Krim formed the Comité revolutionnaire d'unité et d'action (CRUA) to prepare for armed struggle. Writing in *La République algérienne* on 8 October 1954, Ferhat Abbas said:

Our people, tired of indignantly pleading its case without success before a tribunal which is ruled by racialism alone, have become silent. This silence and this calm have been interpreted as an expression of adherence. In reality, fury is at its height, and the silence is one of contempt and rebellion.

It was, in fact, the signal for the struggle which was about to be unleashed.

Outbreak and response

On 1 November 1954 CRUA, which had renamed itself the Front de libération nationale (FLN), and its armed wing, the Armée de libération nationale (ALN), launched the revolution in the city of Algiers with attacks on about a dozen targets – police stations, garages, gas works, post offices – and there were 15 deaths. In the early stages of the revolt, the journals of the main nationalist groups still advocated peaceful negotiation and opposed violence. As the violence escalated, various nationalists fled the country and pledged their support to the FLN from abroad.

During November 1954 the ALN began operations in the countryside, and the rising which had begun in the Aurès region spread quickly to other parts of the country. The French authorities increasingly resorted to the use of torture to obtain information; the nationalists responded with terrorist tactics.

Course of the struggle

The FLN was to receive substantial support from the Arab world, principally Nasser's Egypt, although after 1956, when France granted independence to Algeria's two neighbours, Morocco and Tunisia, its members were able to seek sanctuary across Algeria's borders in these countries. Probably the number of militants in the field did not exceed 8500 or 9000, but they received both active and passive support from a high proportion of the population.

The year 1957 saw the war at its most brutal. In the nine months from January to September the FLN carried out an urban terrorist campaign in the city of Algiers; possibly no more than 1200 were responsible for it. The French broke the campaign, but were only able to do so by resorting to torture on a big scale in order to obtain information. They won the immediate battle, but alienated most of the population at the same time.

Meanwhile, in the countryside, the FLN had built up a series of military and civil committees which were responsible for carrying on the war. These raised taxes for the FLN, recruited new members and acted as an alternative administration to the French (an example which was to be copied later elsewhere in Africa). Both Egypt and Syria sent arms for the FLN, while other Arab states provided money.

In April 1956 the settlers (*colons*) formed the Organisation de l'armée secrète (OAS), which in its turn was supported by sections of the French army. The OAS was to resist all peace talks with the FLN. On 1 June 1958 Charles de Gaulle came to power in France. At first it was assumed that he would support the cause of the Algerian settlers. Later that year – on 18 September – the FLN formed a government in exile based upon Tunis; Ferhat Abbas became the leader of this Gouvernement Provisoire de la République Algérienne (GPRA). In France a referendum approved a new constitution and de Gaulle offered to negotiate a ceasefire with the FLN. The following year – 16 September, 1959 – de Gaulle promised that Algeria should have self-determination within four years. A series of secret meetings were held between representatives of the French government and the FLN: June 1960 (Paris), 1961 (Geneva) and January 1962 (Rome) leading to the signing of a ceasefire at Évian-les-Bains (18 March 1962).

Meanwhile, on 22 April 1961, four generals (Raoul Salan, Maurice Challe, Edmond Jouhaud and André Zell) led a settler revolt in Algiers and attempted to seize power but de Gaulle assumed emergency powers and the revolt was crushed four days later. That year also saw disagreements in the ranks of the GPRA:

Ferhat Abbas was removed from the leadership to be replaced by Ben Khedda while two other key appointments went to Belkacem Krim as Minister of the Interior and Saad Dahlad as Foreign Minister.

A provisional government was formed in Algiers under Abderrahman Farès as President on 28 March 1962. On 1 July (as agreed at Évian-les-Bains) a referendum was carried out in which 91 per cent of the Algerian electorate voted for independence. This was proclaimed two days later (July 3) by de Gaulle.

Estimated costs and casualties

Already by the end of 1956 there were an estimated 400,000 French troops in Algeria attempting to control the revolt and that number had risen to 500,000 by the end of 1961 when the war came to an end. In addition, there was massive and costly destruction of property: schools, bridges, government buildings, medical centres, railway depots, social centres and post offices were destroyed as well as farms, while great damage was done to crops, forests and vineyards.

According to French estimates, 17,250 French officers and men were killed and 51,800 wounded from the outbreak of hostilities in November 1954 to the end of 1961. There were several thousand French civilian casualties as well. Algerian casualties came to 141,000 killed. The FLN, however, claimed that over 1 million Algerians were killed in the fighting, in the concentration camps and torture cells of Algiers and during the transfer of people to strategic centres (up to 2 million Algerians were moved) by the French authorities. At the conclusion of the war (the end of 1961) there were an estimated 5000 Algerian guerrillas in the country and a further 25,000 in Tunisia waiting to infiltrate across the border. Equipment used by the insurgents included machine-guns, mortars, recoilless rifles, bangalore torpedoes as well as captured French *matériel*.

Results: immediate and longer term

In the period immediately before independence, manoeuvres within the GPRA included the dismissal of Colonel Houari Boumédienne (the Commander-in-Chief of the ALN) for plotting a military coup. When Boumédienne's troops advanced on Algiers, the Ben Khedda faction of the FLN fled. In the general elections of 20 September 1962, the FLN faction led by Ben Bella and Houari Boumédienne won to form the government, with Ben Bella as Prime Minister and Boumédienne as Minister of National Defence. Of the two, Ben Bella was the more radical. On 19 June 1965 Boumédienne overthrew Ben Bella in a coup, and he was to rule Algeria thereafter until his death in 1978. In the years following independence Algeria had a love–hate relationship with France. At the same time, as a result of the large oil and gas deposits discovered in the Sahara, it developed as one of Africa's most advanced economies and was generally seen to belong to the radical wing of African and Arab politics.

Immediately on the heels of this devastating liberation war, Algeria and Morocco, which had not accepted the French-imposed border, were to engage in a brief but bloody border war which erupted in October 1963. A ceasefire was arranged by the newly formed OAU in February 1964. Further clashes occurred in 1967.

The impact of the Algerian war upon France was traumatic. It was a principal reason for France's intervention (with Britain) in Egypt in 1956 (the Suez crisis) because of Nasser's support for the FLN; it was also a primary cause of the downfall of the Fourth Republic in 1958, which brought de Gaulle to power. When the war ended there followed a mass exodus of *colons* from Algeria to France (of approximately 1 million *colons* present when the war began, only 100,000 remained in the newly independent country). In the immediate aftermath of the war (from July 1962 until June 1963), the OAS continued acts of revenge terrorism. The war also acted as an impetus to radical French literature from writers such as Albert Camus and Frantz Fanon.

ANGOLA: THE LIBERATION STRUGGLE

Origins

Although the Portuguese had first landed on the coast of Angola in 1483, a date which allowed them to claim four centuries of colonial rule, white settlement on any scale only took place in the twentieth century and mainly in the period immediately after the Second World War. The 400,000 white settlers who were in Angola at the beginning of the 1960s came from among the poorest people in Portugal, itself one of the poorest countries in Europe. These mainly peasant people found themselves better off in Angola than back in Portugal; inevitably, therefore, they opposed any advance of the Africans which would threaten their own economic well-being or political status.

In December 1956 various radical groups including a Communist party merged to form the Movimento Popular de Libertação de Angola (MPLA). Illido Tome Alves Machado became its President and Viriato da Cruz its Secretary-General. Later, other nationalist parties formed and merged; these included the União das Populações de Angola (UPA) and the Frente de Unidade Angolan (FUA), which was launched in 1961 by Europeans in Benguela. In 1964 Jonas Savimbi broke away from UPA to form the União Nacional para a Independência Total de Angola (UNITA), which came into being in 1966.

Outbreak and response

During the 1950s the Portuguese security police – Polícia Internacional e de Defesa do Estado (PIDE) – were quick to arrest political activists among the African population, and in the early stages of resistance organizations operated from outside the country. In 1959 Dr Agostinho Neto, whose nationalist sympathies were already known to PIDE, returned to Angola from Lisbon (where he had received training as a doctor); he was arrested in his surgery in Catete in June 1960 for his nationalist activities. As a result, many of his patients and supporters marched to Catete from Bengo to demand his release, thus sparking off a confrontation in which troops fired on the demonstrators, killing 30 and wounding more than 200. The troops then marched to Bengo and Icolo villages, which they destroyed while killing or arresting all the inhabitants. Dr Neto was imprisoned in Cape Verde and then transferred to Portugal where he was kept under house arrest. He escaped to Rabat in Morocco, and then by way of Conakry and Kinshasa he returned to Angola where he rejoined the MPLA in 1962.

The actual war of liberation was triggered by the coffee growers of Baixa, who in November 1960 stopped work and refused to pay their taxes. In January 1961 the Portuguese army embarked upon manoeuvres designed to intimidate the rural population and claimed that a few score people had been killed; the nationalists said the figure was 10,000. The MPLA dates the revolution from 4 February 1961, when the MPLA militants attacked a police station and the fortress in Luanda. Seven Portuguese police and 40 Angolans were killed, and after the funeral (of the Portuguese) groups of whites went through the streets of Luanda killing indiscriminately.

By mid-1961 an estimated 20,000 Africans had been killed, and by the end of 1961 150,000 Angolans had fled across the border into the Congo. The Portuguese settlers had suffered about 2000 dead, and most of the Africans were killed in reprisals. The Portuguese refused to negotiate any transfer of power (independence) and claimed that Angola (like Portugal's other African territories) was an overseas province of Portugal.

In April 1961 the UN debated the issue of Angola for the first time, and in December 1962 it banned the sale of arms to Angola. Angola was by far Portugal's most valuable overseas possession, and the Portuguese economy was greatly dependent upon its diamonds, coffee and iron ore, and (after 1966) oil from the Cabinda enclave.

On 15 March 1961 the UPA launched a series of attacks on government offices and plantations in the Uige District and 21 Europeans were reported killed.

Course of the struggle

The war was to be fought over a vast, sparsely populated area at great expense. Portugal, the smallest and poorest of the European imperial powers, was to fight harder and longer to hold on to its overseas possessions than any of the others. The army was to build military roads, use defoliants and establish strategic hamlets, yet by the late 1960s it only had a kill rate of 1 to 2 (according to American experts it is necessary to have a kill rate of 1 to 8 in a guerrilla war in order to win). During the course of the struggle Portugal made much of its role in NATO and received military assistance from the USA and Britain for this purpose, though diverting a major part of its military strength to fight the wars in its African colonies.

The nationalists in their turn (unlike their counterparts in Mozambique or Guinea-Bissau) were bedevilled by factions and never unified under a single independence movement. In 1962, for example, in Leopoldville (Kinshasa) in the Congo, Neto tried but without success to unite the MPLA and the UPA. In March 1962 the UPA joined with the Partido Democratico Angolano (PDA) to form the Frente Nacional de Libertacão de Angola (FNLA). The next month (April) the FNLA set up a government in exile in Leopoldville – Governo Revolucionário de Angola no Exilo (GRAE) – with Holden Roberto as Prime Minister. On 29 June

1963 the government of the Congo (Kinshasa) gave official recognition to GRAE as the government of Angola and ordered the MPLA to close its offices in Leopoldville. The OAU recognized GRAE. The MPLA, therefore, was forced to move to Brazzaville, and from there it condemned GRAE. In July 1963, in conjunction with four other groups, the MPLA launched a united front. Two more groups emerged in the Cabinda enclave of Angola: the Front pour la libération de l'Enclave de Cabinda (FLEC) and the Comité révolutionnaire de Cabinda (the enclave is sandwiched between the two French-speaking territories of Zaire and Congo (Brazzaville)). But following MPLA attacks on the Portuguese in Cabinda, the OAU extended recognition to the movement in November 1964.

Then in July 1964 a split occurred in GRAE when Savimbi resigned as its Foreign Minister. Later, in 1966, Savimbi launched the União Nacional para a Indepêndencia Total de Angola (UNITA), which organized a military wing – FALA – and began operations on six fronts.

After a number of unsuccessful attempts, the FNLA and the MPLA agreed a unified command in December 1972, with Dr Holden Roberto as President and Dr Agostinho Neto as Vice-President of the Supreme Council for the Liberation of Angola (CSLA). UNITA was then invited to become part of the CSLA. However, even before the CSLA was established, another split occurred in the ranks of the MPLA when Daniel Chipenda left the movement in protest at its projected union with the FNLA; and a third faction under Andrade also broke away. Neto was accused of 'absolute presidentialism' as opposed to fighting the enemy.

During 1972 and 1973 the Portuguese concentrated upon their policy of moving the rural people into fortified villages – *aldeamentos* – so as to control the people and prevent them providing support for the guerrillas. In February 1972 the MPLA opened a new front in the region of Moçâmedes and Huila (the Cunene region), forcing the Portuguese to move 10,000 troops there. In March 1972 the Portuguese launched 'Operation Attila' against the MPLA in eastern Angola, but by November it had failed and the Portuguese had lost control of the country's eastern border. By 1973 the MPLA was operating on six fronts, and by 1974 the war had resolved itself into a series of desultory campaigns. Then, in April 1974, the military in Portugal overthrew the country's dictator, Marcello Caetano, and General Antonio Spinola became head of state. He began negotiations to end the war in Angola and lead the country to independence.

Estimated costs and casualties

Estimates of casualties and costs are imprecise, but the war drained Portugal of resources and manpower. By 1970 there were 60,000 Portuguese troops in Angola, and the numbers were increased to 70,000 in the early 1970s as the war came to its climax. At the same time (1970) there were between 5000 and 6000 active guerrillas who were supported in the bush by between 50,000 and 70,000 peasants. There were also an estimated 400,000 refugees in the countries on the periphery of Angola – Zaire and Zambia. In 1971 the Portuguese claimed that in the previous 10 years of fighting 1071 of their soldiers had been killed as against 10,000 guerrillas. Yet by 1973, when their forces reached peak strength of 75,000 men, they were no nearer to winning the war. According to Portuguese estimates for

1972, UNITA then had 500 guerrillas in the field, the MPLA between 5000 and 6000, and the FNLA 2500.

When the Portuguese military under General Antonio Spinola overthrew the Caetano government in Lisbon, three liberation movements were operating in Angola: there was dissension both between these three (MPLA, FNLA and UNITA) and within their ranks, so that the period 1974–6, which saw the negotiations for independence, also witnessed a series of political realignments which formed the basis of the civil war that followed (see Part V, pp. 332–351). The MPLA and the FNLA insisted they would keep the war going until Portugal agreed to independence, although UNITA initially agreed to a suspension of hostilities. In May negotiations between Portugal and the guerrilla movements began while the fighting continued. A number of new parties emerged, and then in July 1974 fierce black–white rioting erupted in Luanda when 186 Africans were killed and 400 wounded. The gulf between blacks and whites widened as uncertainty as to the future continued. That October a Rhodesian-style unilateral declaration of independence (UDI) by the whites was thwarted by the Portuguese Armed Forces Movement.

Results: immediate and longer term

General Spinola was a gradualist, but in September 1974 he was replaced in Lisbon by General Francisco da Costa Gomes who determined to disentangle Portugal from its African wars as quickly as possible. The bitter rivalries between the three liberation movements meant that agreements between them were broken almost as soon as they were made. Differences were deep: part ideological; part a question of power (who was to inherit); and part tribal. These differences were at least temporarily suspended in January 1975 following a meeting between the three movements in Nairobi which enabled them to present Portugal with a united front. This led to the agreement at Alvor in the Algarve later that month. The MPLA was represented by Neto, the FNLA by Roberto and UNITA by Savimbi. Portugal agreed 11 November 1975 as the date for Angolan independence, and on 31 January 1975 a transitional government was established in Luanda.

The unity was short lived. Back in Angola on 4 February Neto was greeted by a crowd of 100,000 in Luanda where he called for unity, but from Kinshasa Roberto rejected the idea of people's power and Communism. Chipenda's wing of the MPLA staged a revolt in Luanda and then merged with Roberto's FNLA. In March fighting broke out between the MPLA and the FNLA, and dissension increased between the three movements throughout the year. In April a joint OAU–UN mission tried but failed to bring the liberation movements together. By June the fighting between the three movements had spread to the capital, but by 12 July the MPLA had driven the FNLA out of Luanda. Even Roberto had returned to Angola (for the first time since 1961) to lead the FNLA against Luanda, but without success. By August 1975 the fighting had spread to most parts of the country and South African troops had arrived in the south of Angola. Then on 19 September 1975 Portugal announced it would withdraw all its troops by 11 November, and by the end of October most of the Portuguese forces had left.

UNITA and the FNLA announced they would set up a government at Huambo until the MPLA were driven from Luanda. On 11 November 1975, when the country became independent, the MPLA proclaimed the People's Republic of Angola with Neto as President, while in Ambriz the FNLA and UNITA proclaimed the Popular and Democratic Republic of Angola with Roberto as President. But the MPLA had the decisive advantage: it had control of the capital and most of the towns, and won international recognition as the government.

It is at this point that the long liberation struggle against Portugal really comes to an end and the subsequent civil war which was to draw in the superpowers and South Africa gets under way.

Already by July 1975, with Soviet assistance, the MPLA had ousted the Western-backed FNLA and UNITA movements from Luanda and controlled 12 of the country's 15 provinces. As civil war intensified, the USA offered direct assistance to both the FNLA and UNITA, while the USSR increased the level of its assistance to the MPLA. By the time independence came in November, the USSR had airlifted approximately 16,000 Cuban troops into the country in support of the MPLA. Also during 1974 and 1975 France had supplied covert support both for FLEC in Cabinda and for UNITA. And in the south, the Republic of South Africa was preparing to intervene in a major way. As an economist reported in the *Sunday Times* (20 October 1974), 'No one knows how rich the country is going to be. But we know it is going to be very rich indeed. Possibly the richest country in the continent per head of the population after South Africa.' It was clear that Angola's independence was going to be deeply troubled, and the liberation war in fact merged into a civil war between the different nationalist factions which was to last through to the 1990s (see Part V, pp. 332–351).

CAMEROON: RADICAL OPPOSITION REVOLT

Origins

Germany established a protectorate of Kamerun in 1884 just prior to the great colonial carve-up that became known as the Scramble for Africa. Kamerun was invaded in 1916 (during the First World War) by joint British–French–Belgian forces; after the war, under the new League of Nations, it was divided between France and Britain: four-fifths of the territory became a French mandate, while two separate areas (North and South) contiguous with British Nigeria became British-mandated territories and were joined administratively to Nigeria. In 1940 French Cameroon joined the Free French, and for a time General Charles de Gaulle made Douala his headquarters.

Following the French constitutional reforms of 1946, a large number of political groups and associations flourished in Cameroon (whose League of Nations mandate had then been transferred to the United Nations), and nationalist pressures for independence mounted. Most of these groups were small and did not last long. One of the more significant was the Union des populations camerounaises (UPC), which had been established in 1948 by trade unionists under the leadership of Ruben Um Nyobe and which demanded the reunification of the British and French Cameroons. Between 1950 and 1955 the UPC was the principal nationalist opposition group, but it failed to register its growing strength in terms of votes and did not win a single seat in the elections of March 1952. As a result, and claiming that the elections were unfair, the party lost faith in the electoral process.

Um Nyobe went to New York to petition the UN Trusteeship Council and to demand independence and reunification of the British and French Cameroons. Yet neither the Trusteeship Council nor a UN mission which visited Cameroon in 1952 were convinced that Um Nyobe and the UPC represented a majority of the people. At the UPC Congress of December 1952, Félix-Roland Moumie (a Muslim from the north of the country) was elected President, while Um Nyobe remained the party's Secretary-General. Moumie, a Communist, was an advocate of violence and extreme policies. From 1952 to 1955 the UPC drifted to the left and increased its membership from an estimated 30,000 to 100,000.

At the end of 1954 a new French governor, Roland Pré, arrived in Cameroon and at first tried to make contact with the UPC. But UPC-orchestrated strikes and disturbances led him in February 1955 to adopt tough measures against the party instead. He issued orders which allowed troops to disperse unruly crowds and then said he intended to crush Communist activities. However, Pré made a mistake when he moved UPC leaders employed by the administration to posts in Yaoundé and Douala in a move to keep an eye on them. One of those moved was Moumie, who was able to give fiery anti-government speeches in the capital and in the industrial suburbs of Douala where the unions had their strongest support. In April 1955 the UPC fomented strikes in Douala and demonstrations at Yaoundé and in the Bamileke region. When Roman Catholic bishops attacked the UPC, Moumie replied that Christ had been a nationalist and that the bishops were betraying the people. But the UPC was frustrated because of the small numbers which turned out at its demonstrations and strikes, while Um Nyobe feared a decline in his popularity because of the failure to secure UN intervention.

Outbreak and response

It is not certain whether a formal decision to resort to violence was taken, but riots broke out in Douala, Yaoundé and the Moungo region on 22 May 1955 and lasted through to 27 May. They were not well co-ordinated. Um Nyobe was away in Nigeria at the time and was said to be opposed to the violence, which was blamed on Moumie. Twenty-six people (three Europeans, one gendarme and 22 Africans) were killed and more than 100 injured, and there was considerable destruction of property. The UPC was banned on 13 July and trade union leaders were arrested. Um Nyobe went into exile in British Cameroon, where in August of 1955 he was joined by other leaders including Moumie. They set up a 'government in exile'.

Course of the struggle

Later Um Nyobe returned to French Cameroon to lead a revolutionary maquis which operated in the Sanaga-Maritime region. There his activities prevented the formation of an orthodox section of the Rassemblement démocratique africain (RDA) from being formed. In 1956 the new French governor, Pierre Messmer, relaxed pressures on the UPC and some UPC militants decided to adopt legal political tactics. But the UPC as a whole took advantage of Messmer's tolerance and organized its troops in the Bassa country of Sanaga-Maritime. When elections were held in December 1956 it was clear that the UPC only had a following in the towns of Sanaga-Maritime. In Bassa Um Nyobe's followers abstained from voting and resorted to terrorist tactics. On the night of 18/19 December they cut telephone wires, destroyed bridges, tore up railway lines and burnt houses. Murders were also committed, including the assassination of Dr Délangue, a revered nationalist figure. The UPC relied upon repression as a weapon to gain support. The government was taken by surprise and reacted violently. Many French troops were drafted into the area between Douala and Yaoundé, and hundreds of Africans were shot on sight, including many who were almost certainly innocent as well as many supporters of the UPC rebellion. There were about 3000 UPC rebels, but the massive over-reaction of the government as well as its brutal methods of repression were a gift to the UPC, and as a result the newly elected Assembly was discredited from the beginning.

A new constitution was introduced on 16 April 1957 and then Ahmadou Ahidjo was elected President of the Assembly, but the UPC, which remained outside the law and unappeased, continued its terrorist tactics in the countryside. Throughout 1957 the UPC increased its terrorist tactics in Sanaga-Maritime, although on 23 September Um Nyobe said his followers would lay down their arms if the Assembly were dissolved, new elections held and an amnesty declared for political prisoners, with the country getting immediate independence. Such demands were unacceptable and on 9 November the Prime Minister, André-Marie Mbida, visited Um Nyobe's village where he made a speech denouncing the UPC and threatening 'severe measures' against those who failed 'to come out of the forests within ten days and return to their villages'. Within weeks of this speech, violence had spread to the Bamileke region where there was growing tension between peasants and chiefs as a result of land hunger and resentment at the power of the chiefs. When a young progressive chief just returned from France was deposed in favour of a more traditional chief, peasant unrest grew and was quickly seized upon by the UPC. When that December a member of the Legislative Assembly was murdered there was a fresh outbreak of guerrilla warfare. From December 1957 onwards the region was in a state of perpetual strife, with the administration in control during the day and the terrorists at night burning church property and murdering chiefs, missionaries and Europeans. France sent fresh troops to deal with the uprising.

During 1957–9 the uprising spread to Yaoundé and Douala where Bamileke immigrants formed substantial minorities. The Prime Minister, Mbida, went to Paris to ask for more French troops, although UPC forces were only estimated at 300 in the Sanaga-Maritime and 200 in the Bamileke region. France, with its hands full in Algeria, did not want to send more troops to Cameroon and hoped for a peaceful settlement instead. A new High Commissioner, Ramadier, replaced Messmer; he persuaded Ahidjo to withdraw his support from Mbida, who was forced to resign. Ahidjo became Prime Minister and adopted the UPC policy, demanding immediate independence. But he did not attempt a reconciliation with the UPC, which was angry that 'puppet politicians' had stolen its policy and were negotiating independence with de Gaulle. Then on 13 September 1958 Um Nyobe was shot by a government patrol, and became a national hero. Um Nyobe's secretary, Mayi Matip, came out of the bush claiming to be Um Nyobe's executor; he said he was ready to return to legal opposition, which he was allowed to do, and the terrorism in Sanaga-Maritime came to an end. But Matip was disowned by Moumie and other leaders of the UPC, which continued fighting in the Bamileke region.

By March 1959, after Ahidjo had won the support of the Trusteeship Council and General Assembly, he was still fighting a civil war in the Bamileke country. But his enemies were 'Communists' and so he had the support of the West. He now tried to break the UPC. In the elections in Sanaga-Maritime, Ahidjo's policy was to allow Mayi Matip and other UPC leaders who had renounced violence to win seats, even though the UPC was still not legal. Once elected these UPC members provided a noisy opposition, while at the same time condemning the violence of the revolt in Bamileke. In May 1959 Ahidjo turned his attention to the Bamileke; he took special powers, imposed a curfew and censorship, and provided for arrest on suspicion. None the less, a new outbreak of terrorism occurred on 27 June. Ahidjo then dismissed Bamileke members of his government. He toured the Bamileke region trying to convince the people of his good intentions, but loyalty to the UPC remained strong, as did fear of the government, and the violence continued.

Estimated costs and casualties

Altogether between 10,000 and 20,000 Africans (and a handful of Europeans) were killed in the years 1957 to 1962. The economic costs in general disruption in the parts of the territory where the violence occurred were very high.

Results: immediate and longer term

On 1 January 1960 Cameroon became independent. That day three Europeans and 40 Africans were killed. The next month (21 February) a new constitution was ratified by referendum, and four days later Ahidjo lifted the ban on the UPC. From then onwards there were two UPCs: the legal party inside Cameroon, which was led by Mayi Matip, and the illegal party under Moumie in exile. On 5 May 1960 Ahidjo was elected President. He enjoyed the support of most parties, although UPC supporters burnt part of Douala. In June of 1960 the UPC was attacking and burning shops, and in July the government mounted a large-scale military campaign against the rebels in the Bamileke region, killing an estimated 130 of them. Periodic violence continued until 1962.

CAPE VERDE: THE INDEPENDENCE STRUGGLE

Origins

The Cape Verde Islands had long been part of the Portuguese overseas empire; they were claimed for Portugal in 1460 and proclaimed a royal dominion in 1495. In 1836 a Governor-General was appointed to rule over both the Cape Verde Islands and the Portuguese mainland territory of Guinea (later Guinea-Bissau), although separate administrations were established in 1879. Over a long period of time, people from the mainland were taken to the islands as slaves so that close ethnic ties between the two territories were created.

The Cape Verde Islands were affected by the rising tide of nationalism that was to sweep through Africa after the Second World War. There was no actual rising against the Portuguese in the Islands nor any fighting, yet Cape Verde supplied much of the leadership for the mainland struggle which was conducted in Guinea-Bissau, and Cape Verde independence was inseparable from events in Guinea-Bissau.

The Partido Africano de Independência da Guine e Cabro Verde (PAIGC) became one of the most successful liberation movements in Africa. Its leader, Amilcar Cabral, was successful both in the field and as the enunciator of a philosophy of struggle. From 1956, when the PAIGC was formed, it claimed the right to liberate Cape Verde as well as mainland Guinea-Bissau. The majority of the PAIGC leadership were of mixed race and from the islands, and this fact held the seeds of trouble for the future.

Outbreak and response

By the mid-1960s, as the war in Guinea-Bissau intensified, Portuguese repression of nationalist activities in Cape Verde became more ruthless. The PAIGC enjoyed overwhelming support from the people of the islands to form an independent government with Guinea-Bissau. The PAIGC had a two-stage policy: to win independence for Cape Verde and Guinea-Bissau; and to bring about a federation of the two territories. In 1969 the PAIGC carried its activities into the Cape Verde Islands.

Course of the struggle

The Portuguese managed successfully to link their colonial wars in Africa with their position as a member of NATO in Europe so that, for example, Sir Alec Douglas-Home (who was Foreign Secretary in the new Conservative government which came to power in Britain in 1970) made a point of emphasizing the strategic importance to the West of the Cape Verde Islands, an emphasis which encouraged Lisbon in its determination to hold on to them.

So successful had the PAIGC campaign been on mainland Guinea-Bissau that by November 1973 the UN General Assembly had voted to recognize the Republic of Guinea-Bissau. Then, when the Lisbon coup took place in April 1974, the PAIGC welcomed it and in May of that year began discussions in London with the new Portuguese government.

Results: immediate and longer term

In July 1974 the UN Secretary-General, Kurt Waldheim, visited Portugal and made it plain that the UN backed the new (post-coup) Portuguese approach to

Africa. Portugal reaffirmed its readiness to grant independence to its African colonies, including Cape Verde. Yet in its negotiations with Lisbon the PAIGC found that the stumbling block to any agreement appeared to be the Cape Verde Islands, for at first the PAIGC insisted these had to be included as part of a single state with Guinea-Bissau. Later in the negotiations, however, the PAIGC and Portugal agreed that Guinea-Bissau should be recognized as a sovereign state (by Portugal) on 10 September 1974, and that all Portuguese military forces would be withdrawn by 31 October. A ceasefire came into force on 26 August 1974, when this agreement was signed.

The question of the Cape Verde Islands was to be resolved separately. They were to elect their own National Assembly, which would subsequently have the task of deciding whether to join in a union with Guinea-Bissau. At Algiers, where negotiations were carried out in June 1974, the leader of the PAIGC delegation said of this decision, 'The two people's national assemblies, from Guinea-Bissau and Cape Verde, will form the supreme parliament of Guinea and Cape Verde, which will set up supreme bodies of the union.' It was then assumed by the PAIGC that union would follow independence, since strong cultural ties bound the two territories to each other.

Portugal gave independence to the Cape Verde Islands on 5 July 1975 under a PAIGC government, for when pre-independence elections were held in Cape Verde on 30 June 1975, 85 per cent of those qualified to vote did so and the PAIGC was elected by 92 per cent of those voting. The first President of Cape Verde, Aristides Pereira, was a founder member of the PAIGC and had been its Secretary-General since the assassination of Amilcar Cabral in 1973. Following independence, a commission was set up to consider federation with Guinea-Bissau. On 12 January 1977 a Council of Unity was set up between the two states to search for a formula of unity, but in fact by then it was becoming increasingly clear that they would remain two separate states. Then in 1980, following the November coup in Guinea-Bissau, the concept of unity between the two collapsed, and in Cape Verde the PAIGC was renamed the Partido Africano da Independência de Cabo Verde (PAICV).

EGYPT: THE END OF BRITISH 'CONTROL'

Origins

Direct British intervention in Egypt dates from the bombardment of Alexandria in 1882, which was followed by military occupation, and from that time until the Suez crisis of the 1950s Egypt came to be regarded as within the British (imperial) sphere of influence. In 1922 Britain abolished the protectorate it had established over Egypt and recognized its full 'independence', but reserved the right to defend Egypt against outside attack and to safeguard the Suez Canal. During the years 1922–40 growing nationalist demands, articulated by the Wafd Party, aimed at a total withdrawal of British forces from Egypt. In 1936, when the young King Farouk succeeded King Fuad on the throne, the Anglo-Egyptian treaty of that year terminated British occupation of Egypt, but gave Britain the right to station forces in the Canal Zone for the next 20 years.

Egypt was a British base during the Second World War, although the population was not universally sympathetic to the British cause. In 1948 Egypt joined with other Arab states in attacking the newly formed state of Israel. The elections of January 1950 brought a Wafd government back to power, but the initial promise of social reforms did not last long. The Korean War of 1950 created a cotton boom which greatly assisted the Egyptian economy, but it was short lived and by the end of 1951 maladministration, high unemployment, corruption, bankruptcies and a balance of payments deficit produced a political crisis. King Farouk's popularity slumped and his Prime Minister, Nahas Pasha, attempted to divert attention from domestic problems by directing discontent at the British forces in the Canal Zone.

Outbreak and response

From 1951 onwards the Egyptians adopted terrorist tactics against the British forces in the Canal Zone as well as applying economic sanctions to force them to withdraw. Egypt had already referred the 1936 treaty to the UN Security Council in 1947 asking for a revision, but at that time had merely been told to continue negotiating with Britain. Then on 15 October 1951 the Egyptian Parliament voted unanimously to abrogate both the 1936 treaty and the Condominion Agreement over Sudan. As a result of this Egyptian move (it was the height of Cold War tensions), the Western powers proposed that Egypt should join a Middle East Defence Organization as an equal partner with Britain, France, the USA and Turkey. Egypt rejected this proposal and insisted on an immediate, unconditional withdrawal of British forces from the Canal Zone, and on a union of Egypt and Sudan.

Course of the struggle

A state of near guerrilla warfare now broke out along the Canal Zone between the Egyptians and the British forces stationed there. The government used skilful anti-British propaganda and intimidation tactics as well as withdrawing the entire Egyptian labour force employed by the British in the military zone. The Egyptian press and radio conducted a campaign against the British, and the government encouraged the recruitment of students and others in 'liberation units' to fight in the Canal Zone. In addition, tens of thousands of the unemployed workmen from the Canal Zone now came to swell the ranks of the unemployed in Cairo to make the situation there an explosive one.

In January 1952 the British forcibly disarmed a battalion of Egyptian auxiliary police at Ismailia after they had taken actions 'hostile' to the British forces, and in the process of doing so a number of the auxiliary police were killed. On the following day (26 January) serious anti-British rioting broke out in Cairo and twelve resident Britons were killed. The rioting became general and led to looting. The Egyptian army restored order and King Farouk dismissed the Nahas government.

Between January and July of 1952 the situation along the Canal improved until the coup of 23 July which brought the military under General Mohammed Neguib and Colonel Gamal Abdel Nasser to power. For a time after the coup the new leaders were too busy with internal reforms to wish to antagonize the British, and better Anglo-Egyptian relations followed. But Nasser's main priority (he soon replaced Neguib as the leader of the revolution) was the total withdrawal of the British from Egypt. In February 1953 his government first negotiated an agreement with Britain to allow Sudan self-determination. Then the way was clear for a final settlement with Britain.

Estimated costs and casualties

British casualties in the Canal Zone during the years 1951 to 1956 were about 30 to 40 killed and 75 wounded (British forces were finally withdrawn between March and June 1956), while there is no accurate figure for Egyptian casualties. The damage to property was far higher (e.g. the January 1952 Cairo riots), and the legacy of bitter Anglo-Egyptian relations was to emerge in the latter part of 1956 during the Anglo-French Suez invasion.

Results: immediate and longer term

Anglo-Egyptian negotiations got under way early in 1954, by which time the British High Command no longer regarded the Canal base as crucial to British military strategy, and Nasser skilfully used his control of the army and police to bring pressure to bear upon the British to force an early withdrawal. His technique was alternately to encourage sabotage groups or to restrain them. An agreement was reached on 27 July 1954 for the British to withdraw all their forces from the Canal Zone over a 20-month period. The agreement was signed on 19 October 1954. It included provisions for British forces to return in certain circumstances, but in fact the agreement meant an end of the British military presence in Egypt and full Egyptian independence of any form of British tutelage for the first time in nearly a century.

Unfortunately the evacuation did not lead to better Anglo-Egyptian relations: in the month following British withdrawal first the USA and the World Bank and then Britain withdrew their offers to finance the building of the Aswan High Dam; and then Nasser nationalized the Suez Canal (26 July 1956), which in its turn led to the Israeli attack upon Egypt (in collusion with the British and French), to be followed by the Anglo-French invasion of Suez later that year.

ETHIOPIA: THREE 'COLONIAL' WARS

Ethiopia's long history (longer than that of any other state in Africa south of the Sahara) dates back to 500 BC and the Kingdom of Aksum. Its claim to be the oldest continuous Christian state (from AD 330) and never to have been colonized (the brief Italian interregnum from 1935 to 1941 is usually ignored) between them form the basis for a number of historical myths. One result in the latter part of the nineteenth century was an attempt by the imperial rulers to reunite the component

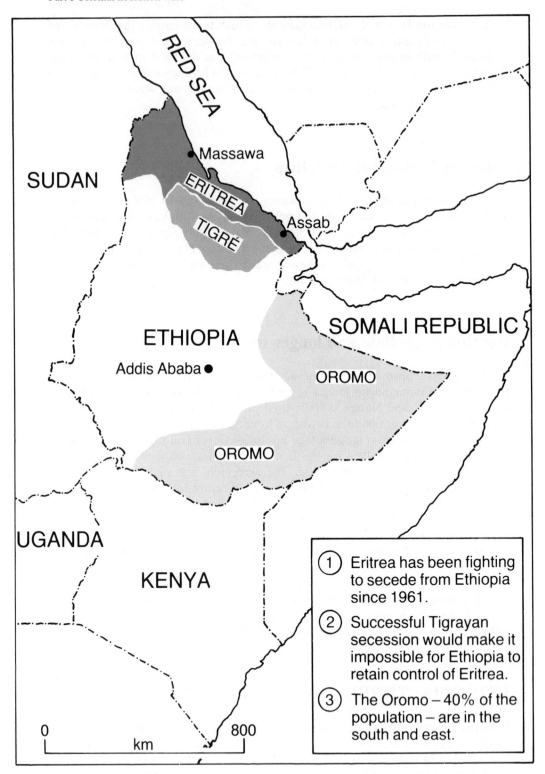

Map 3 Horn of Africa (Ethiopia)

parts of the former Ethiopian empire. In fact Ethiopia is one of the few countries of the Third World that has a recent history of colonial expansion. As a consequence, at least some of its peoples regard themselves as colonial subjects seeking independence from Ethiopia in the same way that British and French colonies sought to break away from metropolitan control in the years since 1945. (It is for this reason that Ethiopia's three 'colonial' wars are included here rather than in Part V as civil wars.)

Ethiopia has been engaged in continuous warfare of one kind or another since 1961: with the Eritreans in the north (Africa's longest war), with the Tigrayan People's Liberation Front since 1979, with the Oromo Liberation Front in the south, and with its neighbour Somalia (see Part III, pp. 190–198.) It has also played a significant role in relation to its neighbour Sudan and that country's recurring wars in the south.

In this section three wars or revolts are examined: Eritrea, Tigré and the Oromo Liberation Front.

Eritrea

Origins

In the course of the Scramble for Africa, the Italians overran northern Ethiopia and established their colony of Eritrea in 1890. However, when they attempted further colonial expansion in Ethiopia they were defeated at the hands of Menelik II at Adowa in 1896, an Ethiopian victory which marks the beginning of the modern era. On 26 October 1896, following Adowa, Menelik signed a peace with the Italians and, though the Italians recognized the independence of Ethiopia, the Emperor in his turn was obliged to accept the fact that Eritrea had become an Italian colony.

In 1941, during the Second World War, British forces liberated Eritrea from the Italians; later (1944) the British Foreign Secretary declared that the Italian empire had come to an end. The fate of Eritrea (temporarily administered by the British) was left to be decided by the big-four powers, but since they could not agree the problem was passed to the newly formed United Nations. In due course the world body decided that Eritrea should be federated with Ethiopia under the Ethiopian crown, and the federation was brought into force on 11 September 1952. The new Eritrean Assembly chose as its Chief Executive Tedla Bairu, who favoured union with Ethiopia, though he was later ousted as too moderate.

By 1958, when it had become clear that the government of Haile Selassie intended to integrate Eritrea fully into Ethiopia, the Eritrean Liberation Front (ELF) was formed in Cairo under the leadership of Osman Saleh Sabhe. Of the 10-man revolutionary council, nine were Muslims and one a Christian. The ELF claimed that integration with Ethiopia would violate the local autonomy which had been promised in 1952. Following the formation of the military wing of the ELF, the Eritrean Liberation Army (ELA), the first shots in the armed struggle were fired in September 1961. Then on 14 November 1962 the Eritrean Assembly voted for complete union with Ethiopia, and the next day Haile Selassie abolished Eritrea's autonomous status. The ELF moved its headquarters to Damascus and was always to receive substantial Arab (Muslim) backing in its struggle. For a decade the ELF was the most significant Eritrean liberation group, although others, such as the Popular Liberation Front (PLF) with Marxist leanings, came into being in the early 1960s. Both were committed to full independence for Eritrea. But by 1969 young militants in the ELF accused the leadership of feudalist or reactionary tendencies and moved towards a more socialist stance; they were supported by radical Arab governments – Iraq, Libya, Syria – as well as by Al Fatah.

Outbreak and response

Eritrean resistance to the central government was sporadic and uneven during the 1960s, although the ELF gained considerable publicity from hijackings. At the beginning of the 1970s, however, the war took a new turn when the young militants in the ELF gained control of the ELA and then from bases in Sudan developed a systematic guerrilla campaign across the border into Eritrea. At that time they numbered approximately 2500 guerrillas. They won over the rural populations and divided Eritrea into alternative (to government) administrative districts. The ELF was now stepping up its military activities, attacking targets such as bridges, police stations or government offices, and was sufficiently successful that it forced the government (1971) to place Eritrea under martial law. But a second split occurred in the ranks of the ELF during 1970 when the Marxists under Mohammed Nur broke away to form the Eritrean People's Liberation Front (EPLF).

Speaking in Tripoli in 1974, Osman Saleh Sabhe (then Secretary-General of the ELF) claimed that the Front had only resorted to armed struggle after failing to attain its ends through political means. During 1974–5 many Eritreans joined the ELF after military leaders deposed Emperor Haile Selassie and established the revolutionary Dergue in Addis Ababa. At that time of upheaval the ELF saw a real chance of victory, and by 1977 it had about 22,000 guerrilla troops in the field. Meanwhile the rival EPLF was growing in strength: during 1977 its forces captured most of the Eritrean towns and by 1978 the EPLF had an estimated 12,000 guerrillas. That year saw the two movements achieve major successes against the central government when, sometimes operating separately and sometimes together, they inflicted a series of defeats on the Ethiopian army. Yet the ELF was constantly troubled by factions: another split had occurred in 1975 when Osman Saleh Sabhe broke away to form the ELF–Popular Liberation Forces, although in 1980 when the tide had turned against the liberation movements the ELF–PLF again joined with the ELF–Revolutionary Council, only to see its support further eroded in 1981 by fresh faction fights. By 1981 the EPLF had replaced the ELF as the main Eritrean guerrilla movement, and it was to continue as the principal focus of Eritrean resistance throughout the 1980s.

Course of the struggle

The ELF had hoped that the revolution of 1974 might bring a more understanding government to power in Addis Ababa, but it soon realized that the Dergue under Mengistu was as bitterly opposed to Eritrean secession as had been Haile Selassie.

That year Sabhe demanded immediate recognition of the ELF as the sole legitimate representative of the Eritrean people, recognition of their right to self-determination and a free impartial referendum under UN auspices. Twenty-three Eritrean deputies resigned from the Parliament in Addis Ababa that August, accusing the government of taking no interest in Eritrean affairs, and though the Armed Forces Movement had initiated reforms, the ELF claimed that the army was massacring civilians in Eritrea. Parliament (minus the 23 Eritrean deputies) set up a commission to study the Eritrean problem, while the ELF issued a statement agreeing to work out a political settlement with the Ethiopian government for full national independence for Eritrea.

During November 1974, 5000 army reinforcements were sent to Eritrea to 'ensure the security of the population', while the ELF announced that US$2 million worth of Libyan-donated weapons now gave their forces superiority over the 40,000 Ethiopian troops then stationed in Eritrea. ELF forces were operating within 6 kilometres of Asmara, the capital of Eritrea, and Osman Saleh Sabhe said that, although the new regime had offered a form of self-government, the ELF insisted upon total independence. In Addis Ababa one of the top military figures, General Aman Andom, was executed for refusing to send more troops to Eritrea.

A turning point was reached in 1975 when the USSR began to provide major support for the Mengistu regime, although the effects of this were not to become apparent for some time. In January 1975 Radio Ethiopia called on the local Eritrean communities to contact the guerrillas and persuade them to end their secessionist struggle, and the government pledged itself to find a peaceful solution. But by early 1975 ELF forces, numbering between 15,000 and 25,000, controlled most of the Eritrean countryside. In February 1975 a major battle was fought outside the town of Keren, but the Ethiopian army forced the ELF to retreat and regained the initiative. Later that year, while the revolution was in full progress in Addis Ababa, ELF forces almost succeeded in taking Asmara, and in August the ELF and the PLF agreed to establish a unified democratic front in Eritrea with a single political leadership and one liberation army.

The year 1977 was climactic in the war, which by then had already lasted for 16 years. The EPLF from the north and the ELF from the west captured most of the towns, including Keren, which the EPLF saw as the future capital of an independent Eritrea. By the end of the year the Ethiopians had been confined to four towns: Barentu, Asmara, Massawa and Adi Caieh. In retrospect 1977 might have been the year when the Eritreans won their independence, but bitter strife between the EPLF and the ELF destroyed any semblance of unity in the face of the Ethiopians.

It became clear in 1978 that the Cubans, who had supported the Eritreans for 16 years, were now about to desert them. Despite public protestations to the contrary, and insistence upon continued support for the EPLF, persistent rumours suggested that the 13,000 Cuban troops in Ethiopia who had been successfully deployed against the Somalis in the Ogaden war would be switched to fight in Eritrea. In *Pravda* the Soviets, who had supported Eritrea against the government of Haile Selassie, now signalled a change of policy by denouncing the Eritrean separatist ambitions as 'helping the realization of imperialist designs'. By June 1978, after victory against the Somalis in the Ogaden, the Ethiopians counter-attacked in Eritrea with an army of 100,000, which recaptured most of the towns lost in 1977 although the Eritreans retained control of the countryside. It had been a tough struggle for the Ethiopians to achieve this result, but by the end of 1978 the character of the war had changed. A thousand Soviet military advisers and massive quantities of Soviet armoured vehicles, artillery, rockets and airpower were deployed against the guerrillas, even though the Cubans had not allowed their troops to be used against the Eritreans. The result was that the ELF had to fall back upon scattered guerrilla tactics and the EPLF retreated to the north round the town of Nacfa.

Thus by 1979 the ELF only controlled rural areas, and though it maintained its position during 1980, it was mainly destroyed in the next year in brutal battles with the EPLF. Despite attempts to resolve the ideological differences between the two groups (in Tunis, March 1981, when their representatives signed an agreement), fighting between them intensified and the EPLF emerged from it as the dominant front. The civil war between the ELF and the EPLF during 1980–1 led to the virtual expulsion of the ELF from Eritrea. It then split into more factions, and though these met in Khartoum in 1985 and agreed to form an Eritrean Unified National Council (EUNC), this fell apart within a year. In 1987 Osman Saleh Sabhe died.

In 1982, meanwhile, the Ethiopian government (hoping to take advantage of the splits in the Eritrean ranks) launched a programme of reconstruction for Eritrea – Operation Red Star – and tried to attract back to the country some of the 500,000 Eritrean refugees then in Sudan. It had little success, although the EPLF did agree to hold talks with the government. The government made it plain that it would only negotiate with representatives of a united Eritrea and that any settlement had to be in the context of a united Ethiopia. The talks were to continue through to 1985 when they finally collapsed. From 1982 onwards it was the EPLF that provided the opposition to the Ethiopian forces in Eritrea with about 8000 guerrillas. In 1982 Mengistu personally took control of an attempt to take Nacfa from the EPLF forces, but the attempt failed with an estimated 30,000 Ethiopian casualties. Even so the EPLF were hemmed into the north-west corner of Eritrea.

In January 1984 the EPLF launched a new offensive and seized Tessenai; then they gained another victory over 10,000 Ethiopians at Mersa Teklai. The following year the EPLF seized Barentu, but subsequently lost it as well as Tessenai, the Sudan border area, Mersa Teklai and the Red Sea coast to a major Ethiopian counter-attack. Yet despite these EPLF losses the Ethiopian forces abandoned the north-east coast of Eritrea in 1986, mainly because of growing reluctance on the part of their troops to serve there. The EPLF continued to mount attacks on the main towns and then in December 1987 launched a new offensive to gain a major victory over government forces at Nacfa. By March 1988 the EPLF had captured Afabet, which housed the Ethiopian army's regional headquarters, and claimed to have killed a third of the Ethiopian troops serving in Eritrea. Following that defeat, Colonel Mengistu admitted that the rebels were 'threatening the sovereignty' of the country. The EPLF claimed it had put up to 18,000 Ethiopian troops out of action. Both sides used the food weapon, the EPLF attacking food relief convoys, while victories by the Tigré People's Liberation Front (TPLF) threatened the government position still further.

EPLF successes during 1988 persuaded the Ethiopian government to improve relations with its neighbour, Somalia, so as to release troops from that border for the war in Eritrea. By early 1990, after 28 years of fighting, no end appeared to be in sight. The Mengistu government was in deep trouble throughout 1989 with both the EPLF and the TPLF mounting powerful offensives, while political change in the USSR threatened an end to Soviet material support. By mid-February 1990 Mengistu was calling on the armed forces to fight 'to the bitter end' following the

EPLF's capture of Massawa. By late March 1990 the Soviet President, Mikhail Gorbachev, was urging Mengistu to reach a negotiated settlement.

The EPLF insists a referendum should be held that allows the Eritreans to choose between regional autonomy, federation or independence. But, partly because the OAU is centred upon Addis Ababa, the Eritreans have received little support from elsewhere in Africa. The Eritreans have achieved a high degree of self-reliance since they have few sources of aid except for Sudan, which allows cross-border operations principally in the form of food aid from various Western non-government organizations (NGOs). By the end of the 1980s the EPLF had between 40,000 and 50,000 fighters, and these have consistently held at bay the second largest army in Africa, which is backed by the USSR. It is command of the air which has enabled Ethiopia to hold on to the towns.

Estimated costs and casualties

An accurate assessment of casualties in this long-lasting war is impossible, but they run into many tens of thousands. An estimate for 1974, for example, when the struggle had lasted 14 years, gave casualties as 30,000 dead and 70,000 displaced and living in poverty. Since then, however, the casualties have been vastly greater. According to the EPLF, it released 3000 Ethiopian prisoners in 1982, but those who returned to Ethiopia were either imprisoned, executed or reconscripted into the army. In June 1987 the EPLF claimed to be holding 10,000 Ethiopian prisoners of war, although the Ethiopian government refused to acknowledge that the EPLF were holding any prisoners. The guerrilla nature of the war and the constant movement of personnel as well as air attacks upon civilians and considerations of morale have each helped to blur precise casualty figures. Sometimes the need to demonstrate the ruthless nature of the enemy has persuaded the EPLF to exaggerate casualties; at other times, the need to boost the morale of its own members has worked the other way. On the government side the high rate of casualties has been consistently played down. But even taking these motives into account, the number of deaths and wounded on both sides has been very high.

Many outside interests have become involved and, though the war itself can be seen as a relatively straightforward struggle for independence by the Eritreans, most of those who have provided support to either side have done so for ideological reasons. Support for the ELF came predominantly from Islamic countries, including Syria, Libya, Egypt and Algeria. From 1974 onwards the ELF received aid from Iraq and arms from China as well as support from Cuba and the USSR (until they switched support to the Mengistu government). Up to 1972 the Ethiopian government provided support for the Anyanya rebels in the south of Sudan and in return Khartoum supported the Eritreans. Following the settlement of 1972, the Nimeiri government continued to support the Eritrean rebels. By 1986, when the war in the south of Sudan had been resumed, Addis Ababa was providing support for the Sudan People's Liberation Army (SPLA), and Sudan – largely by permitting cross-border operations – provided support for the Eritreans. The complexities of the Sudan involvement could be seen in 1988 when an estimated 300,000 refugees from the war in southern Sudan were in camps in south-western Ethiopia, while more than half a million Eritrean refugees were settled in eastern Sudan, mainly in the Kassala region and Port Sudan. Some of these Eritreans had been in Sudan for 20 years and younger ones had been born there. In mid-1988 500,000 people in Eritrea were being fed by Christian relief agencies, while a further 260,000 were being fed by Ethiopian government agencies. Thus nearly a third of Eritrea's total population were in direct receipt of relief food, and many more required help.

Results: immediate and longer term

Prospects for peace are not good (1990). The geographic importance of Eritrea, which controls Ethiopia's only seaboard, as well as the further pressures towards disintegration that would follow secession strengthen Addis Ababa's determination not to allow Eritrean independence. Peace talks were held in 1989 but broke down, and by June 1990 the Eritrean war of secession and the Tigrayan revolt (see below) had merged to provide the greatest threat in 29 years of fighting to the central government, forcing President Mengistu Haile Mariam to admit that his country was on the verge of collapse.

Arab countries led by Saudi Arabia want to see an independent Eritrea principally as a means of weakening Christian–Communist Ethiopia. The West provides a variety of humanitarian assistance to Eritrea through NGOs, but the USA is ambivalent in its attitudes. On the one hand, it sees the Eritrean war as a factor weakening the Marxist regime in Ethiopia and so welcomes it. On the other hand, it would prefer to see a more moderate (pro-Western) regime come to power in Addis Ababa, and in consequence will not commit itself to Eritrean independence since to do so would prejudice its chances of achieving better relations with a less hostile Ethiopia.

The USSR holds the key. The most likely development (mid-1990) is Soviet collaboration with the USA to force the government in Addis Ababa to a compromise peace with the Eritreans and Tigrayans, but that remains to be seen. Meanwhile the war continues.

Tigré: a war of nationalist secession

Origins

Tigré (Tigray) has long been part of the Ethiopian Empire. None the less there are bases for Tigré nationalism and in recent times these were reinforced by the Italians, who insisted, during their brief occupation of Ethiopia (1936–41), on a Tigrayan-speaking administrative area. Tigré had enjoyed virtual autonomy for 150 years prior to the nineteenth-century Tigrayan Emperor Yohannis IV (1871–89).

Outbreak and response

After the defeat of the Italians in 1941, the British supported Ras Seyoun as provincial ruler of Tigré; he had the best hereditary claims to the post. The Ethiopian Emperor, Haile Selassie, newly restored to power, believed that Britain intended to detach Tigré from Ethiopia and join it to Eritrea, so he insisted that Ras Seyoun stay in Addis Ababa. This distrust, coupled with the corruption of the Shoan officials in Tigré, sparked off the first Tigrayan revolt against the central government that year.

Haile Mariam now emerged as leader in Tigré. He appealed to past Tigrayan glories and pushed the idea that Britain would support joint Tigrayan–Eritrean independence. He opposed the Emperor's choice of governor for the province, insisting that the post went to a Tigrayan. By 1943 Haile Mariam and his supporters controlled most of Tigré, and in August of that year units of the regular Ethiopian army with their British advisers were sent to crush the revolt. The situation became sufficiently serious for Britain to employ bombers – first to drop leaflets and then to bomb Tigrayan strongholds – and the revolt collapsed. Basically a peasant movement, the revolt had also highlighted long-nourished Tigrayan resentments. Haile Mariam was most important for bringing out the idea of a Tigré–Eritrea alliance.

The Emperor, Haile Selassie, took the revolt very seriously: partly because he feared that had it appeared successful Britain might have supported the secession for its own imperial reasons, and partly because other dissident provinces might then also have revolted. But he did withdraw Shoan officials and allow the Tigrayans to provide sub-governors. Later, in 1947, when Ras Seyoun was allowed to return to Tigré, the province was given a much freer hand in ordering its affairs.

Although Tigré nationalism had long manifested itself through such revolts, it was the fall of Haile Selassie in 1974 which led to the emergence of a much more determined nationalist movement and the creation of the Tigré People's Liberation Front (TPLF). At first the TPLF was pro-Western and worked with the conservative Ethiopian Democratic Union (EDU), which opposed the military Dergue that had overthrown Haile Selassie. But then it moved to the left and received training from the EPLF in Eritrea. At the same time young militants were urging the overthrow of the existing social–political order. As a result of their radicalization, the TPLF turned on its former EDU allies and eliminated them in Tigré province.

Course of the struggle

The TPLF only became significant in the latter part of the 1970s. After the EPLF had undertaken to arm and train its forces in 1977, the TPLF fell out with the right-wing groups such as the EDU. Then, during 1977 and 1978, its existence was also threatened by the more extreme Ethiopian People's Revolutionary Party (EPRP), which had been committed to armed struggle against Addis Ababa since 1975 and now used terrorist tactics against the TPLF. It was to escape these ideological attacks that the TPLF allied itself with the EPLF. During 1978 the TPLF suffered heavy losses when the Ethiopian army, fresh from victory in the Ogaden war, moved back into Eritrea. But by 1979 the TPLF was presenting a formidable challenge to the government; it launched a guerrilla campaign against central control, captured garrison posts and killed hundreds of government troops. By August 1979 the TPLF claimed to control about 70 per cent of Tigré province. The rise of the TPLF presented the government with a double threat, since Tigré lies just south of Eritrea and a combination of the EPLF and the TPLF represented a formidable and potentially unbeatable challenge to Addis Ababa.

In the early stages of the TPLF revolt the government of Mengistu in Addis Ababa was too preoccupied with the war in Eritrea to appreciate the seriousness of the revolt in Tigré, but by the early 1980s government forces were suffering steady losses. In 1981 the TPLF went to the assistance of the EPLF in its civil war against the ELF, but later in the 1980s it was to face a number of splits in its own ranks.

During 1984, in order to attract international assistance, the TPLF moved about 200,000 'refugees' across the border into Sudan. But the tactic was unpopular and did not work out successfully: most of the Tigrayans wanted to return home, and by late 1985 the TPLF had to organize a return. This manoeuvre created bad relations with the EPLF (which had half a million of its own refugees in Sudan), and it criticized the TPLF for its opportunism. As a result there were armed clashes between the EPLF and the TPLF, and these in turn emphasized the ideological differences between them. Meanwhile, during both 1985 and 1986, Ethiopian government forces drove the TPLF from large parts of central and eastern Tigré which it controlled, while government food distribution won it friends among the local populations.

Then the position was once more reversed in 1987 and 1988. The TPLF took the offensive again after the EPLF had captured Afabet in Eritrea, forcing the government to move up troops from Tigré to Eritrea. As a result the TPLF overran garrisons in north-west and north-east Tigré. By April 1988 the government had real control only of the regional capital, Makele, while the EPLF and the TPLF had patched up their differences and were co-ordinating their military operations. At the end of May 1988 the TPLF captured the garrison town of Maychew south of Makele, thus forcing the Ethiopians to retreat south into Wolle province, and then claimed to have destroyed two Ethiopian battalions in fighting round Amba Alage in southern Tigré province. By this time the TPLF forces were estimated at 20,000 fighting men; they were supplemented by the local militia (men who take up arms for the TPLF when their own areas are threatened). Mengistu, who had dismissed TPLF activities as mere banditry, now called for a nationwide resolve to crush the rebels. By late June 1988 the Ethiopian forces had once more driven the TPLF from six of the main Tigré towns which they had been holding.

By mid-1990, when President Mengistu admitted that his country was on the verge of collapse (see above), Tigrayan forces claimed to have been victorious in a month of full-scale conventional battles only 100 miles north of the Ethiopian capital, Addis Ababa, in which they had inflicted 22,000 casualties on government forces.

Estimated costs and casualties

The costs of the TPLF uprising have been of major consequence to the government in Addis Ababa, not least because of the geographic position of Tigré province, situated as it is immediately south of Eritrea. From 1978 onwards any government move against the insurrection in Eritrea had to be made through Tigré province first, thus exposing the army to extended lines of communication and two hostile and relatively cohesive communities – the Tigrayans and the Eritreans – instead of just one. Moreover, while the EPLF and the TPLF work together, they present a sufficiently formidable combination that in recent years at least some of the Ethiopian military have said that a military victory is not possible and that the solution has to be a political one.

The scale of the operations from 1978 onwards has been very substantial. In 1978, for example, TPLF forces were able to halt an Ethiopian advance of about 12,000 troops supported by Russian tanks, armoured cars and rocket launchers with MiG aircraft supplying air cover. Ten years later much of Tigré was under TPLF control and the food weapon had become a major means of waging battle. Thus in March 1988 the TPLF had captured two important food distribution centres so that Western relief agencies reported increasing difficulty in getting supplies to drought-affected areas, while a high proportion of the whole population faced famine as a result of the war. By April 1988 there were indications that Addis Ababa intended to pursue a scorched earth policy by bombing food supply centres held by the rebels and refusing to allow Western relief agencies to distribute food in rebel-held areas. By May 1988 relief agencies were only able to operate from Makele and one other town in Tigré and yet claimed they could reach up to 400,000 people in need of food aid from these two centres. After 14 years of hostilities, the peasants in Tigré must either face starvation as a result of failed harvests and warfare or walk to find food.

No reliable figures for casualties exist, but they run into many thousands on both sides (including many civilian casualties, for example, from bombing). According to the Relief Society of Tigré (REST), about 4000 civilians were killed by bombing alone between March and November 1988, while 40 villages had also been destroyed.

Results: immediate and longer term

By mid-1990, following the heaviest fighting of the war between government forces and the Ethiopia People's Revolutionary Democratic Front (an alliance led by the Tigrayan rebels), the EPRDF claimed to have killed or wounded 22,000 government troops in a single month of fighting, while farther north the EPLF was besieging Asmara with its government garrison of 100,000 troops.

The Oromo revolt

Origins

The Oromo, who make up 40 per cent of the population of Ethiopia, are one of the two largest non-Amharic groups in Ethiopia (the other being the Eritreans); they are scattered over the south and east of the country and are not especially homogeneous. There was a significant Oromo revolt against imperial authority in

1928–9. Then, as they departed in 1941, the Italians armed the Oromo to encourage harassment of the advancing British and imperial forces, and the Oromo became involved in the 1943 Tigré revolt.

Outbreak and response

An Oromo rebellion took place in the province of Bale from 1963 to 1970; this also involved the Somalis in the province. Fighting began in Wabe district in April 1964 after a local governor (unsuccessfully) led a police force there to collect taxes. This minor defiance encouraged rebellion elsewhere in the province, and rebels captured the town of Belitu. Resistance then spread throughout the district and into the neighbouring district of Delo, so that by the end of 1965 the central area of Bale was in revolt, controlled by the rebels. In the main the revolt was a response to long-standing oppression of the peasants and was not especially nationalist. Wako Gutu, the leader of the revolt, described himself as a General of Western Somalia while the movement called itself the Liberation Front of Western Somalia, though in part this was a clear bid for Somali support.

Course of the struggle

Gutu spread the rebellion over Bale and into neighbouring Boranna, and his forces showed by their tactics that they had, apparently, received some guerrilla training: they attacked police and territorial army units. From the mid-1960s there were growing signs of an Oromo national consciousness, although divisions among the Oromo were usually greater than any unity which they achieved. The most difficult task facing the leadership was to hold the Oromo and Somalis together. Only slowly did the Oromo revolt take on nationalist characteristics, and it was never really clear to what extent the Oromo revolt was also part of the Somali revolt in the eastern (Ogaden) region. When the first Oromo revolt ended in 1970 that of the Somalis continued.

Although the revolt of the 1960s ended in 1970 when Gutu himself accepted a government appointment, the revolution of 1974 and downfall of the Emperor encouraged nationwide outbursts of dissident activity against the centre, and in 1977 the Oromo National Liberation Front (ONLF), later shortened to OLF, emerged during the Ethiopia–Somalia war. This second Oromo revolt was dependent upon Somali support; its appeal was directed to the Oromo in Bale, Sidamo and Haraghe provinces, but by the early 1980s it appeared to have petered out, although the OLF still kept an office in Mogadishu.

Estimated costs and casualties

Government repression was the principal cause of Oromo revolt. In 1986, for example, an estimated 70,000 refugees, principally Oromo, fled across the border into Somalia in order to escape a government programme of enforced resettlement in government-controlled villages. These refugees provided a potential source of recruitment for members of the Oromo Islamic Front, which was then based in northern Somalia.

Results: immediate and longer term

Of the total population of Bale province in 1970 (1,206,700), 1 million were Oromo, although the best land was owned by the Amhara, while the higher officials, such as judges, were Christian rather than Muslim. The OLF advocated self-determination for the Oromo and originally derived its support from peasants resisting government pressures to turn their peasant associations into co-operatives. In more recent years the OLF has had little military impact, although from 1984 onwards the EPLF has trained its guerrillas operating in the region of Wollega near the Sudan border. In May 1988 there were renewed hostilities in Wollega district between OLF guerrillas and government forces. But like almost every Ethiopian dissident group, the Oromo suffered from internal divisions and their defiance of central government stems more from general peasant discontent with conditions than from a sense of nationalism comparable with that of the Eritreans, for example. Although further Oromo-inspired disruptions are probable, Oromo dissidence represents one of the least of Addis Ababa's worries, at any rate in the foreseeable future. (See also Part III, pp. 190–198.)

GUINEA-BISSAU: WAR OF LIBERATION AGAINST PORTUGAL

Origins

The Guinea coast was first sighted by the Portuguese in 1446, and Guinea became a slave base between 1600 and 1800. It was ruled jointly with the Cape Verde Islands from 1836 to 1879; its land boundaries were fixed in 1891 by a series of conventions with Britain and France.

Unlike Portugal's other, larger colonies in Africa – Angola and Mozambique – Guinea-Bissau was too poor to attract many white settlers, but there had always been opposition to Portuguese rule and by the 1950s the colony was infected by the nationalism that was sweeping Africa. In 1952 Amilcar Cabral founded the Partido Africano de Independência da Guiné e Cabro Verde (PAIGC) as a discussion group, but by 1956 it had developed into a well-organized country-wide movement run by a central committee of which Cabral was Secretary-General (see also above, pp. 17–19). Both Cabral and the PAIGC can claim to be among the most successful of all independence leaders and movements, so that the struggle in Guinea-Bissau may be seen as an almost textbook example of how such a war should be waged.

By 1958 three other political movements had emerged: Movimento de Libertação da Guiné (MLG), União dos Populaçãos da Guiné (UPG) and the Rassemblement démocratique africain de la Guinée (RDAG), but they never amounted to much. The MLG was dissolved in 1964.

33

At first Cabral used peaceful tactics – demonstrations or strikes. In 1958 Portuguese troops suppressed a strike at Bafata, and then on 3 August 1959 troops fired on striking dockers in the shipyards at Bissau, killing 50 Africans. The authorities blamed the PAIGC for the troubles and banned it, but the following month, on 19 September, Cabral launched an all-out armed struggle. Early in 1960 he secretly left the country for Conakry in neighbouring Guinea, where he established a new PAIGC headquarters. Another liberation movement, Frente para Libertação e Independência de Guiné Portuguêsa (FLING), was set up under the leadership of Mario Fernandes: this advocated 'Guinea for the Guineans' and complained that the PAIGC was dominated by leadership from the Cape Verde Islands. Although FLING, like the other smaller movements, never had much influence, the claim that the PAIGC was dominated by the islanders was to be a continuing source of friction.

Outbreak and response

In July 1961 guerrilla raids were launched against administrative and military targets in the north-west of the country, forcing the Portuguese to deploy troops to guard such targets. These were the first such attacks by the PAIGC. In August 1961, from Conakry, Cabral formally announced that the PAIGC would resort to armed struggle, and from then onwards constant attacks were mounted against such targets and Portugal sent reinforcements to the colony. As early as 1962 the PAIGC held elections inside the territory; 52,000 people out of a total population of fewer than 500,000 voted to give overwhelming backing to the PAIGC. Already the movement was obtaining substantial aid from the OAU Liberation Committee as well as full support from neighbouring Guinea, and by 1963 the Portuguese admitted that the PAIGC had infiltrated 15 per cent of the countryside. In May 1963, with another ten years of fighting yet to come, the PAIGC shot down its first Portuguese plane.

The PAIGC intensified the armed struggle in 1964 when it formed its military wing – Forças Armadas Revolucionárias Populares (FARP) – which was divided into three forces: the Popular Army, the Popular Guerrillas and the Popular Militia. The army was split into groups of between 17 and 25 men to operate independently all over the country; meanwhile freedom fighters were sent for training to the USSR, China, Cuba, Algeria, Senegal, Ghana and Guinea.

Course of the struggle

By 1967 the PAIGC had established its own Radio Liberation; the movement was then directed by a politburo of 15. The political struggle (though not the military one) was extended to the Cape Verde Islands in 1969. The PAIGC worked closely with the MPLA in Angola. By 1968 a majority of the rural villages were controlled by the PAIGC, while Portuguese troops held Bissau and the other important towns. The year was a turning point. President Tomas of Portugal visited the colony in February and insisted it would remain part of Portugal. Then in May the Portuguese government sent one of its most experienced soldiers – General

Antonio de Spinola – as Governor-General and Commander-in-Chief. He was to launch a programme to 'conquer the hearts and minds of the people', yet by the end of the year the PAIGC claimed to control two-thirds of Guinea's area and 45 per cent of the population.

Under General Spinola the army provided materials and helped the people to build better houses for themselves as well as roads, bridges and schools. Some of the more educated soldiers were used as teachers in the schools, but it was far too late for such measures. Although heavy fighting took place through 1970, only in 1971 did Portugal finally admit that a state of war existed. By that time it had 30,000 troops in the country facing about 7000 guerrillas. On the nationalist side Amilcar Cabral had undisputed control of what by then was the only liberation movement in the country and had wide backing from independent Africa. He himself had come to be esteemed as one of the most successful guerrilla leaders ever.

During 1971 a UN mission visited liberated Guinea-Bissau as did other observers, and all confirmed that large areas were in the hands of the PAIGC and not the Portuguese; the next year the PAIGC claimed to have liberated two-thirds of the country. Although they denied it, the Portuguese were confined to about 100 fortified garrisons and posts in the central region between Bissau and Bafata. During September and October 1972 the PAIGC held general elections in the liberated areas for regional councils and a People's National Assembly. These elections were based on an electoral register of the liberated villages and produced some 58,000 registered voters.

On 20 January 1973 Cabral was assassinated in Conakry by dissident members of the PAIGC. He was succeeded by Aristides Pereira as Secretary-General, and the PAIGC demonstrated its strength as an organization for no collapse followed and the struggle was intensified. The PAIGC now obtained sophisticated Soviet SAM-7 ground-to-air missiles and Portugal lost its hitherto exclusive control of the air. In May, despite using savage aerial bombardment, Portugal was forced to abandon one of its important fortified military posts.

The PAIGC now lobbied intensively for international support for Guinea-Bissau's independence, and its declaration of independence on 24 September 1973 was supported by a majority of UN members including the USSR and China. On 2 November 1973 the UN voted by 93 to 7 with 30 abstentions to recognize Guinea-Bissau, which was admitted to the world body at the end of the year.

The PAIGC welcomed the April 1974 coup in Lisbon, but continued the struggle. In May it held discussions with representatives of the new Portuguese military government in London, but at that time the stumbling block to peace with Portugal appeared to be the Cape Verde Islands and the question of whether there were to be one or two successor states (see pp. 18–19). However, an agreement was signed between the two sides at a meeting in Algiers that August; Portugal agreed to recognize the independent state of Guinea-Bissau as from 10 September 1974, and all Portugal's armed forces were to be withdrawn from the country by 31 October. There were to be no reprisals. On 9 September General Spinola signed a document which brought an official end to Guinea-Bissau's status as an overseas territory of Portugal.

Estimated costs and casualties

When the conflict began in 1961 Portugal had about 5000 troops in Guinea-Bissau, but by the end of the war there were 28,000 troops in the country. An estimated 10,000 Portuguese troops were killed during the course of the war. PAIGC casualties were higher, but no accurate figures exist. By 1970, as the war reached its climax, Portugal had an army of 30,000 men in Guinea-Bissau facing approximately 7000 PAIGC guerrillas. The PAIGC had widespread international support: from the OAU Liberation Committee and a number of African countries including its neighbour, Guinea; military assistance from the USSR, China and Cuba; and non-military aid from Sweden, other Western non-government organizations (NGOs) and the World Council of Churches (WCC). In 1972 Portugal augmented its 30,000 troops with an additional 15,000 men drawn from the local black and mixed populations. By this time the Portuguese were maintaining a large number of heavily fortified posts, each containing from 150 to as many as 1000 men. They had come to rely increasingly upon air superiority. By then the PAIGC were inflicting about 300 casualties a year on the Portuguese.

The most significant single casualty suffered by the PAIGC throughout the struggle was the assassination of Cabral in January 1973, for which the PAIGC naval commander, Inocentia Canida, was responsible. In January 1974 the Portuguese Army Command released the following figures for the previous year: it claimed the PAIGC had killed 123 civilians and wounded 439; that it had launched 250 attacks, destroyed 507 huts and kidnapped 68 people. Over the same period the Portuguese claimed to have killed 959 guerrillas.

Results: immediate and longer term

Following the meeting in Algiers of 26 August 1974, the PAIGC representative, Major Pires, said that the agreement was 'the natural and logical outcome of the liberation struggle' and that the next step was to work for the liberation of the Cape Verde Islands. In fact, though the PAIGC had been the liberation movement for both Guinea-Bissau and Cape Verde, they went their separate ways (see p. 19). It had been a textbook struggle with the party mobilizing the masses rather than liberating them from above. The PAIGC instituted social reforms in the areas which it liberated during the long war. Throughout the war the PAIGC maintained remarkable unity, and this, it was agreed, owed much to the leadership of Amilcar Cabral. Following independence the greatest problem facing the new state was that of poverty. A slow *rapprochement* with Portugal took place.

KENYA: MAU MAU UPRISING

Background

The Anglo-German agreement of 1890, at the height of the Scramble for Africa, delineated the spheres of influence of the two powers in East Africa, giving Britain control over the Kenya coast, and in 1895 Britain proclaimed a protectorate of British East Africa (later Kenya). Sir Charles Eliot, one of the early British commissioners for the East African protectorate, described the interior as 'white man's country' and argued that the main object of British policy should be to found a white colony. This duly took place and much of the best land in the territory was alienated to European settlers. Land, therefore, became central to the colonial question in Kenya, and the 'White Highlands' where most of the settlers had established their farms in fact consisted of land that was traditionally claimed by the Kikuyu, the largest ethnic group in the colony. The Kikuyu became the core of the opposition to colonial–settler rule, and after a long history of campaigning about their land rights during the 1920s, 1930s and 1940s they precipitated the liberation struggle known as Mau Mau.

Origins

The term Mau Mau first occurred in 1948. There has been much controversy and confusion over the origins of Mau Mau. In fact Kikuyu resentment at European appropriation of their land in the White Highlands was its principal cause. More generally, the movement was a nationalist revolt against settler–colonial domination. The revolt was Kikuyu inspired and controlled; in any case the Kikuyu are the dominant ethnic group in Kenya. Secret oathing among the Mau Mau, the barbaric ceremonials attached to the oathing and the brutal nature of Mau Mau killings attracted great attention at the time. The aims of Mau Mau – to regain the land stolen from the Kikuyu by the white settlers and to obtain self-government – were purely nationalist. There was nothing sudden about Mau Mau; it was a final explosion of anger against long-felt oppressions and losses resulting from colonialism.

Outbreak and response

Unrest and violence directed against the colonial status quo had been developing for at least two years before 7 October 1952, when the assassination of the loyalist Chief Waruhiu precipitated the crisis. For months the government had applied pressure on the nationalist leader, Jomo Kenyatta, to denounce Mau Mau, while the white settlers had been agitating for strong government action.

The new Governor, Sir Evelyn Baring, declared a state of emergency on 20 October 1952; this in fact increased the violence, which already existed on a limited scale. The state of emergency was to last until January 1960. British troops were flown into Kenya from the Canal Zone in Egypt, and on the night of the emergency 100 of the leading nationalists of the Kenya African Union (KAU), including Kenyatta, were arrested. It soon became apparent, however, that the insurrection was only just beginning. Kenyatta and five other leading nationalists were put on trial for managing Mau Mau. The trial became a *cause célèbre*, the last of the great stage-managed colonial trials, and had the opposite effect to what had been intended: it provided enormous international publicity for the nationalist cause.

Course of the struggle

Kenyatta's trial lasted five months and focused attention on the causes of the nationalist struggle while also emphasizing its rapid spread. In March 1953, while the trial was still in progress, there occurred the Lari massacre of 97 loyalists, the worst single episode of Mau Mau. On the same night Mau Mau raided Naivasha police station to secure a stock of arms. Meanwhile the Mau Mau Nairobi Central Committee became the co-ordinating body for the whole movement and was renamed the War Council. In April 1954 government forces launched Operation 'Anvil' to arrest and screen Mau Mau suspects in Nairobi. A total of 27,000 Kikuyu were taken into detention camps for screening. The operation brought the major military aspect of the campaign to an end. Thereafter most military activity consisted of minor actions against gangs, pursuit and mopping-up operations and searches in the Aberdare forests. At the height of Mau Mau the British commander, General Erskine, had troops of divisional strength (approximately 10,000 men) under his command.

Estimated costs and casualties

To the end of 1956 11,503 Kikuyu were killed, 1035 captured wounded, 1550 captured unwounded, 26,625 arrested and 2714 surrendered. On the government and settler side, 95 Europeans were killed and 127 wounded, 29 Asians were killed and 48 wounded, and 1920 Africans were killed and 2385 wounded. This brought the total killed on both sides to 13,547. The military aspects of the emergency cost Britain £55 million. (Mau Mau is probably one of the best documented of all the anti-colonial struggles.)

Results: immediate and longer term

The Mau Mau rebellion hastened independence in Kenya, which was achieved on 12 December 1963, and more widely in East Africa as a whole and possibly further afield: Britain clearly decided it would be cheaper and more politically rewarding to grant independence rather than fight similar uprisings in each of its African colonies in turn.

The arrival of British troops in Kenya at the beginning of the emergency represented the return of the 'imperial factor' to the colony, making it impossible for the whites to make a UDI as their counterparts were to do in Rhodesia: once the troops were in Kenya, London and not Nairobi controlled the course of the struggle and, therefore, the timing of independence.

Immediately after independence Kenyatta first paid tribute to the Mau Mau freedom fighters and then made certain to deprive them of any political influence or power.

MADAGASCAR: NATIONALIST REVOLT

Origins

Towards the end of the nineteenth century Britain recognized Madagascar as part of the French sphere of influence, and Madagascar became a French colony in 1896. General Gallieni only completed his conquest of the island in 1904, and resistance continued until 1905. Gallieni, like the British Protestant missionaries, encouraged the study of the Malagasy language, thus helping to emphasize the superior–inferior relationship between the peoples of Indonesian and African origin.

Growing demands for French citizenship were part of the colonial story, while during the 1920s this widened into a demand for greater self-government. By 1946 all the Malagasies had become French citizens and sent elected representatives to the French Parliament as well as to a territorial assembly. Yet despite French 'citizenship', only a small number who had become gallicized actually had the vote.

The anti-French revolt of 1947 had its roots in ethnic divisions on the island at least as much as in nationalist antagonisms to the French. The Merina (Hova) people, of Malay–Indonesian origin, whose language was used throughout the island, had become the dominant group in Madagascar. In the nineteenth century, Protestant missionaries from Britain had converted them to Christianity and had also provided their language of Malagasy with a written form, an achievement which had the effect of emphasizing the differences between the people of the central highlands (the Merina and Betsileo) and the coastal Negroid peoples (Cotiers) who, meanwhile, had been converted to Roman Catholicism. Thus ethnic and religious divisions had a colonial background founded in British imperialism aided by Protestant missions and French imperialism abetted by the Roman Catholics (Jesuits).

Oubreak and response

In March 1947, arising out of repressed political and economic grievances, an uprising took place against the French which was essentially nationalist in character. At the time the French had only a small garrison on the island and were largely taken by surprise. The rebels created widespread troubles and much loss of life. The Merina, who regarded themselves as the original rulers of Madagascar before the advent of the French, were behind the uprising. Government reaction was brutal, and many peasants (especially Cotiers who had joined the uprising) were killed or driven from their villages to take refuge in the forests. In Paris three Malagasy deputies whose followers back in Madagascar were seen to be responsible for the uprising were first deprived of their parliamentary immunity and then arrested.

Course of the struggle

Although the Merina had inspired the uprising, it was the Cotiers who became the principal victims. Relatively few French were killed, and the main effect of the revolt was to emphasize the differences between the Merina and Cotiers. The rebels hoped to overthrow the colonial administration and attacked the French in towns and at military depots, as well as going for railways and other communications targets.

Estimated costs and casualties

Estimates of deaths vary widely between a low figure of about 11,000 and a high of 80,000.

Results: immediate and longer term

There were both external and internal effects from this uprising. In West Africa, where nationalist pressures were growing rapidly, the impact of France's brutal repression in Madagascar was to make political leaders – and especially Houphouët-Boigny of Côte d'Ivoire – even more cautious in the way they confronted the French in the years 1948–50 than would have been the case otherwise. By 1950, for example, Houphouët-Boigny had come to believe that the Communists wanted a massacre of nationalists in Côte d'Ivoire similar to that which had occurred in Madagascar, in order to polarize views against France to their (Communist) advantage.

In Madagascar the repressive measures of 1947 had a long-lasting impact upon attitudes. Not until 1956 did France pass the *loi cadre* giving universal suffrage to Madagascar, but ironically the uprising of 1947 did more to polarize Merinas and Cotiers than it did to polarize the Malagasies and French. It also helped to radicalize the country, which in the post-independence era has pursued its own policies with far less reference to the former metropolitan power than has been the case with most other Francophone states. Madagascar became independent in 1960 without further struggle, and subsequently governments maintained close relations with France.

MOZAMBIQUE: WAR OF LIBERATION AGAINST PORTUGAL

Origins

The Portuguese had established forts on the coast of Mozambique in the sixteenth century, although major settlement only occurred in the present century, much of it just prior to the outbreak of the colonial war. The territory in any case was exceptionally poor, and an added grievance to the normal nationalist resentments lay in the fact that education was minimal and jobs, even semi-skilled ones, were reserved for the Portuguese, thus preventing even quite limited African advance. Mozambique was designated an overseas province of Portugal in 1951. The year 1960, the *annus mirabilis* of African independence, gave a great boost to nationalism throughout the continent and had its impact upon Mozambique as it did in the other Portuguese African territories.

Outbreak and response

The starting point of the war was the massacre of demonstrating Africans by the Portuguese at Mueda in June 1960. Three nationalist groups were formed in exile and opened offices in Dar es Salaam. On 25 June 1962 these merged to form the Frente de Libertação de Moçambique (Frelimo) under the presidency of Dr Eduardo Mondlane, who had been a professor of anthropology at Syracuse (NY). Frelimo was fortunate in its leadership and was to be the only viable group throughout the struggle, so Mozambique was not faced with the three-way division between competing liberation groups which was to afflict Angola. On 14 December 1962 the UN passed a resolution banning the sale of arms to Portugal, thus giving its support to the anti-colonial struggle from the outset.

Frelimo was also recognized from the beginning by the Organization of African Unity and became a major recipient of OAU funds. It received military and financial support from the Soviet bloc, China, Tanzania, Algeria, Egypt, Sweden and Denmark, while certain Western organizations – the WCC and Britain's Rowntree Trust – provided funds for non-military purposes. In 1963 the Frelimo leaders went to Algeria for training. The rebellion was launched against Portugal on 25 September 1964 in the north of Mozambique, where it was possible to secure supply lines from Tanzania. A key to Frelimo's early successes undoubtedly lay in the outstanding personality of Eduardo Mondlane. He was assassinated in Dar es Salaam on 3 February 1969 and for a short while it looked as though Frelimo might fall apart. It was ruled by a triumvirate of Uria Samango, Samora Machel and Marcelino dos Santos, but after some defections and expulsions Samora Machel emerged as the supreme figure – President and Commander-in-Chief – in June 1970.

Course of the struggle

By 1968 Frelimo had grown from an initial 250 fighters to 10,000 and claimed to control one-fifth of Mozambique and 800,000 people. At that time the fighting was mainly confined to the two northern provinces – Cabo Delgado and Niassa – though there was also some fighting in Tete province. In July 1968 Frelimo held a second party congress inside liberated territory. Meanwhile the Portuguese had increased the size of their army to 50,000, brought more settlers to the country and begun to build the giant Cabora Bassa dam. The following year (1969) Frelimo claimed to control Cabo Delgado, Niassa and parts of Tete and a population of one million, while the Portuguese admitted they could not circulate freely in the northern parts of the country.

Under Samora Machel, once he had a firm grip of the leadership, guerrilla activity was intensified. By then substantial support was forthcoming from the OAU with funds being supplied for both military purposes and social, educational and economic institutions. By 1971, despite having claimed to have all but wiped out Frelimo in 1970, the Portuguese were obliged to begin all over again. By then Tete province, where the Cabora Bassa dam was sited, had become a major theatre of war and – a further complication – the Rhodesian security forces had penetrated far into the province in pursuit of guerrillas from the war across the border. International insurance companies (involved in providing cover for the dam) declared Tete to be a war risk area.

In March 1971 a confident Frelimo issued a communiqué setting forth party priorities. These were:

1. To consolidate the liberated regions.
2. To step up the work of political mobilization of the inhabitants in regions still dominated by the colonialists.
3. To extend the armed struggle to new regions.

At the end of 1971 Frelimo claimed to have launched 800 operations during the previous October and November alone; to have destroyed 107 Portuguese camps or posts; to have killed 3000 Portuguese and destroyed 344 vehicles; to have shot down 4 aircraft and 5 helicopters; to have sunk 15 warboats on the Zambezi and blown up 20 trains. Even allowing for propaganda exaggerations it was a formidable achievement.

In September 1972 Frelimo opened a new front in the Manica-Sofala area bordering Rhodesia. It was concentrating its main energies in Tete province, however, in order to disrupt the building of the Cabora Bassa dam which was ringed with triple lines of defences. As the war threatened to spread southwards the Portuguese tried to control the rural populations by the system of *aldeamentos* or fortified villages, which they rapidly extended to cover 1 million peasants. These were herded into 500 *aldeamentos*, of which 120 were in Tete province. During 1972 the Portuguese increased the size of their army in Mozambique from 50,000 to 60,000, and by that time half their forces consisted of black soldiers. Once more the High Command made extravagant claims – to have eliminated one-fifth of Frelimo.

By 1972 Frelimo was employing a variety of highly sophisticated weapons, which included Russian 122 mm rockets with a range of 7 miles and Chinese rocket launchers. The Portuguese had resorted to chemicals and defoliants, which were being sprayed by South African mercenaries using South African planes painted in the Portuguese colours.

As the war reached its climax, Tete province became the main centre of fighting, partly because of the presence of the dam and partly because the war in Rhodesia spilled over the border into this region. Rhodesian forces operated regularly in Tete province, Portuguese planes flew deep into Tanzania (about 130 miles) and South African troops were reported to be helping to guard the site of the Cabora Bassa dam (most of whose power output was destined for sale to the Republic). The dam was political from the beginning: the project was designed to mobilize Western finances to create a source of cheap power for South Africa and thereby to draw in the West to defend the Portuguese position in Mozambique.

In June 1973 Frelimo opened a fourth front north of the key Indian Ocean port of Beira. By then it had liberated between a quarter and a third of the country and 1.8 million people. At the same time Frelimo was receiving inquiries from Western commerce about ways in which it might be assisted. It turned down as immoral an offer from West Germany to provide medical supplies, since at the time West Germany was providing the Portuguese with military assistance.

After the first white farms had come under attack, early in 1974, settler appeals to Lisbon persuaded Portugal to transfer 10,000 troops from Angola to Mozambique. As the South African *Rand Daily Mail* said quite simply, 'Portugal is not winning the war in Mozambique.' The Church and the White Fathers voiced increasing doubts about the morality of the war. By this time Frelimo was operating across the Beira Corridor, which carried the vital rail and road communications from Beira to Rhodesia, while the front line had been carried to within striking distance of the Save river, only 100 miles from South Africa.

Frelimo, meanwhile, claimed that its greatest victories were to be found in the new life and freedoms that were being introduced throughout the liberated areas. The people liked their new freedom, and those still under Portuguese control were thus encouraged to join Frelimo.

Estimated costs and casualties

Frelimo training depended mainly upon Chinese instructors. By the end of the 1960s it had 10,000 armed men and a further 10,000 waiting for arms. To begin with most arms came from Czechoslovakia. By 1967 Portugal had about 50,000 troops in Mozambique deployed against 8000 to 10,000 Frelimo, who were backed by a growing militia of men without arms. The Portuguese forces used American, British, French, West German and Italian weapons, and throughout the war a growing row in Europe centred on the fact that weapons supplied by these powers for NATO purposes in Europe were used by the Portuguese in fighting their African wars. As early as 1967 a South African source claimed that Portuguese casualties (dead) since the war started then amounted to 5000.

In September 1968 (nearly half way through the war) Frelimo claimed to have killed 1000 Portuguese during the previous year's fighting, as well as shooting down 20 aircraft and destroying 100 or more military vehicles. The year 1970 witnessed a massive Portuguese offensive on three fronts in which 35,000 troops and 15,000 tons of arms and equipment were employed, while South African helicopters were used to transport the troops to battle zones. The Portuguese claimed that 651 Frelimo were killed in the operation but only 150 Portuguese, while a further 7000 Frelimo members and sympathizers had surrendered and another 1800 had been captured. Frelimo asserted that Portugal never admitted to more than 10 per cent of its casualties.

In 1972 Portugal increased its forces from 50,000 to 60,000, of whom approximately half by then were black troops. By the end of 1973 these troops were facing about 20,000 Frelimo forces in the northern provinces; as the final year of the war opened, the guerrillas effectively controlled over a third of the country.

Precise casualty figures will never be known but ran into many thousands on both sides. Although Mozambique relied upon Soviet bloc countries for most of its military support and training (a fact that was constantly hammered by the

Portuguese, South African and Western media), in the later stages of the war it obtained an increasing amount of support from Western sources. For their part the Portuguese would not have been able to sustain their long effort (the wars in Angola and Guinea-Bissau were going on simultaneously) had it not been for the massive inputs of arms they received from their NATO allies. These were supposedly for use only in the European NATO theatre, but they provided the Portuguese army with its essential military *matériel*. Once the Cabora Bassa dam had been commissioned, and as the war moved south, the South Africans became increasingly involved, especially by providing air support to the Portuguese. From 1972 onwards the guerrilla war against the white minority regime in Rhodesia constantly spilled over into the north of Mozambique, mainly Tete province.

Results: immediate and longer term

As with Portugal's other colonial wars, Mozambique helped to precipitate the Lisbon military coup of April 1974 that toppled the dictatorship of Marcello Caetano and brought General Spinola to power. Early in May 1974 the Portuguese Assembly was suspended and, as a gesture, 554 Frelimo prisoners were released. But uncertainty developed on both sides in the war as everyone waited to see what the new government in Lisbon intended. On 1 July 1974 Machel announced a new front in Zambezia province at a time when it was becoming increasingly clear that Portuguese soldiers no longer had the will to fight. Then on 27 July General Spinola gave a speech in which he recognized the right of the colonial peoples to independence. There was an immediate change of atmosphere and pro-Frelimo forces began to emerge everywhere in Mozambique. Although many whites expressed sympathy with Frelimo, others were leaving the country at the rate of 1000 a week.

The Portuguese Foreign Minister, Dr Mário Soares, reached agreement with Frelimo in Lusaka (Zambia) on 7 September 1974, and a ceasefire ended the 10-year war: independence was set for 25 June 1975. A transitional government that would be dominated by Frelimo ministers was to run the country during the intervening nine months.

Then came the white backlash. White reactionaries had begun to organize themselves following the coup in Lisbon, and 5000 whites had formed the FICO (I stay) movement; other whites in GUMO (United Group of Mozambique) hoped to prevent a UDI and come to terms with Frelimo rule. However, six hours after the Lusaka announcement of a ceasefire at which Machel made plain that Frelimo wanted the 220,000 whites to stay, groups of settlers calling themselves the 'Dragons of Death' seized the radio station and other key installations in Lourenço Marques (now Maputo), declaring they would not live under a Frelimo government but would set up an alternative of their own. Portugal, however, was determined to bring the war to an end, and after two senior emissaries had been sent out from Lisbon to assess the situation in Lourenço Marques the Portuguese army went in and retook the points in the capital that had been seized by the 'Dragons of Death'. In Dar es Salaam, where he had arrived from the Lusaka meeting, Samora Machel said Frelimo would work with the Portuguese to restore order. The rebellion was over in four days, and settlers then spoke of their desire to negotiate with Frelimo.

But the white backlash in its turn produced a black backlash: there was an explosion of African anger and rioting in which about 100 people (including nine whites) were killed and more than 350 injured. Several thousand Portuguese troops were needed to restore order in the capital, including crack units which were withdrawn from facing Frelimo in the north. By 13 September the first Frelimo troops arrived in Lourenço Marques. During this crisis South Africa remained carefully neutral and made plain that it did not intend to intervene on behalf of the whites. Then 6000 whites fled across the border into the Republic.

The provisional government consisted of six Frelimo ministers and three Portuguese, with Joaquin Chissano (Frelimo), the Prime Minister, and the Portuguese High Commissioner, Admiral Vitor Crespo, as its two principal figures. It ruled Mozambique until June 1975 with reasonable co-operation between the Portuguese and Frelimo. On 23 June 1975 Samora Machel returned to Lourenço Marques from Dar es Salaam to become President of an independent Mozambique two days later. Following independence he announced the inauguration of socialist policies for Frelimo and the country. All but a handful of the 220,000 whites emigrated, many settling in neighbouring South Africa, an exodus which was to have a devastating impact upon what in any case was an impoverished and fragile economy.

The consequences of the war were momentous. It brought an independent 'Marxist' government to power in Lourenço Marques and signalled the collapse of the 'cordon' of white-controlled territories (Mozambique, Rhodesia and Angola) which up to that time had separated South Africa from the independent black states to the north. It provided the ZANU forces fighting the illegal Smith government in Rhodesia with bases in Mozambique as well as turning the Rhodesian flank, since the long border between Rhodesia and Mozambique, which crosses terrain ideally suited for guerrilla activities, was now open to infiltration at any point by Zimbabwean guerrillas. It brought South Africa into direct contact (over a 500 km border) with a 'Marxist' African state and forced it to rethink policies that until then had been based upon supporting the white 'cordon' which divided it from independent Africa. As a result of these developments the end of white minority rule in Rhodesia was brought appreciably closer, while for the first time South Africa had to think of new options (the Soweto uprising of 1976 clearly derived some of its impetus from events in Mozambique and Angola).

One result was the development of the South African policy of destabilization, which in Mozambique took the form of massive support for the dissident Mozambique National Resistance movement, Renamo. Fifteen years after the war had ended, Mozambique still suffered from its effects: the economy remained chaotic and the country suffered deep poverty, while almost all attempts at improvement were frustrated by the brutal war with the South African-backed forces of Renamo (see Part V, pp. 364–377).

NAMIBIA: THE INDEPENDENCE STRUGGLE

Origins

South West Africa was colonized by imperial Germany during the Scramble for Africa: the area had been brought under German control by 1890, although resistance to German rule continued well into the twentieth century and included the bitter uprising (1904–7) in which 80,000 Hereros were systematically exterminated by the Germans. The colony was overrun by South African forces during the First World War and subsequently became a mandate of the League of Nations (1920) to be administered as such by the Union of South Africa.

In 1946 the mandates of the defunct League of Nations became trust territories of the newly formed United Nations, but in the case of South West Africa the Pretoria government refused to recognize UN jurdisdiction. Over no other issue of decolonization has the UN played so central a role. From 1946 onwards South African control of the territory was to be challenged every year in the UN General Assembly, leading to hundreds of meetings and resolutions. In 1949 South Africa virtually incorporated South West Africa into the Union as a province, and the Pretoria government ceased issuing annual reports of its administration to the UN. This amounted to effective annexation. Economic integration became a cloak for colonial exploitation as most of Namibia's wealth was diverted to South Africa.

At the end of 1959 (10 December) mass protests against apartheid were held in Windhoek, the capital; the police fired on a crowd of demonstrators, killing or wounding 60 people. This signalled the growth of nationalist opposition. The Ovamboland People's Organization was formed, and in June 1960 it extended its activities from Windhoek to other parts of the country. In 1964 it changed its name to the South West African People's Organization (SWAPO). A second movement, the South West African National Union (SWANU), was also formed at this time. SWAPO became the focal point of nationalist opposition both inside and outside the territory. At first SWAPO and SWANU co-operated, but the former soon outdistanced its rival in influence and, though SWANU continued throughout the 1960s and maintained representatives in a number of postings such as India, the UN, Tanzania and Egypt, and received backing from the Chinese, its influence declined sharply in the latter part of the 1960s. It was primarily a Herero organization.

SWAPO was dominated by the Ovambo people, who make up half the total population of Namibia. Except for the enduring Sam Nujoma who founded it, the early leadership of the 1960s was largely replaced at the end of the decade by a new generation including Misheck Muyongo, Moses Garoeb, Peter Katjavivi and Andreas Shipanga. In its early stages, like the ANC in South Africa, SWAPO sought change by peaceful means.

Up to 1966 SWAPO acted peacefully, petitioning the UN and otherwise attempting to persuade the South African government to move towards independence for the territory. But in 1966, after the International Court at The Hague had failed to find against South African occupation of the territory, SWAPO announced the launching of an armed struggle. Later (1971) the International Court reversed its earlier decision and found that South Africa was occupying Namibia illegally.

In 1964 the Odendaal Commission (appointed by the Pretoria government) reported on the future of South West Africa and, in effect, recommended apartheid. It suggested the division of Namibia into 10 self-governing homelands to cover 40 per cent of the territory, a form of break-up that spelt the end of a single country. In 1966 the UN General Assembly passed Resolution 2145 which terminated the mandate and stated that South West Africa was the direct responsibility of the UN. South Africa refused to withdraw from the territory and persisted in its application of apartheid there. As the UN resolution stated, South

Africa had 'consistently and relentlessly pursued a policy of racial discrimination . . . in flagrant violation of the spirit of the Mandate entrusted to it by the League of Nations'.

During the 1960s, in anticipation of the pressures which it saw mounting against it, the South African government built up Walvis Bay as a centre for training its troops in desert warfare. Since Walvis Bay is not part of Namibia, but on South African territory surrounded by Namibia, South Africa was technically not acting in violation of the mandate. At the same time South Africa also established military installations in the Caprivi Strip in north-eastern Namibia (this was in defiance of the terms of the mandate). The Pretoria government tried to persuade Britain to establish a training school for tropical warfare there and built a huge military airbase, capable of handling the largest jet aircraft, at Katima Mulilo.

Outbreak and response

From 1966 onwards, despite the UN resolution, South Africa applied all her laws to Namibia, dividing the country into 10 Bantustans or homelands and one central white area in 1968. Then, in 1969, the South West Africa Affairs Bill incorporated South West Africa into the Republic. This move was in deliberate defiance of the United Nations and aimed to perpetuate South African control over the territory and its resources. Ever since 1933 South Africa had argued to end the mandate and make South West Africa into the fifth province of the Union. From 1970 through to 1972 South Africa pressed ahead with its homeland policy, in part as a (hollow) gesture to the UN to show that it was moving the people towards independence. In 1972 South Africa held elections in the territory, but these were largely boycotted by SWAPO as well as by the Co-operative Development Party. For South Africa, Namibia's mineral wealth was always a deciding factor, and the value of its diamonds and uranium influenced British, American and EEC attitudes towards South Africa's illegal occupation of the territory since major Western mining transnationals were deeply involved in extracting this mineral wealth.

In 1958 a proposal for the partition of Namibia was rejected by the UN; in 1964 the UN voted to end South Africa's mandate; in 1968 the UN voted to change the name of South West Africa to Namibia; in 1969 the UN Security Council voted 13–0 (with two abstentions) to withdraw its administration from Namibia; in 1971 the International Court at The Hague reversed its earlier decision and ruled that South Africa's presence in Namibia was illegal. Meanwhile the UN had appointed an 11-nation Council for Namibia which announced it would visit the territory in 1968, but the South African Prime Minister, J. B. Vorster, said they would not be allowed in. In 1970 (after this defiance) the UN passed Resolution 283, requesting all states to refrain from any actions that implied a recognition of South African authority in Namibia.

UN negotiations with South Africa continued through the 1970s under the Secretary-General, Kurt Waldheim, and his special representative Dr Escher. In 1972 Waldheim visited Namibia as part of a developing UN initiative. Meanwhile SWAPO was establishing its position as the representative for all Namibia, and Sam Nujoma, President of SWAPO, told the UN Council for Namibia that SWAPO rejected further contacts with South Africa. At the OAU in May 1972 heads of state also called for a halt to further talks with Pretoria. In 1973 South

Africa convened an Advisory Council on Namibia, but this was rejected by SWAPO and by the Paramount Chief of the Herero people, Chief Clemens Kapuuo. As a result, in December 1973 the Security Council voted 15–0 to halt further talks with South Africa over Namibia, instead appointing Seán MacBride as Commissioner for Namibia and recognizing SWAPO as the 'authentic representative of the people of Namibia'. Even so, little came of these initiatives, principally because the major Western powers were not prepared for a confrontation with South Africa.

Course of the struggle

SWAPO opted for guerrilla war in 1966 at a time when access to Namibia was only possible through Zambia. Sam Nujoma had gone into exile so as to put SWAPO's case to the international community, for SWAPO never believed that it could win solely by military means. The first group of SWAPO freedom fighters had begun training in 1965, and a number of them were despatched into Namibia in August of that year and established a base in Ovamboland. The base was attacked by South African security forces in 1966, and they claimed to have wiped it out. In a major trial of 1968 a number of leading SWAPO members, including the veteran Toivo ja Toivo, were found guilty of treason. In a famous statement to the court Toivo ja Toivo said, 'We are Namibians and not South Africans. We do not now, and will not in the future, recognize your right to govern us.'

By 1968 SWAPO guerrillas were active in Eastern Caprivi, where they claimed to have killed a number of South African troops and damaged military installations. To begin with South Africa denied these claims, but it later was obliged to concede that a guerrilla war had started. At the end of 1969 at Tanga in Tanzania SWAPO held a conference at which it confirmed that 'armed struggle is the only effective way to bring about the liberation of Namibia'. A slow escalation of the guerrilla struggle took place during the early 1970s, although more spectacular resistance to the South Africans came in December 1971 with the strike of between 15,000 and 20,000 contract workers. By early 1972 the strike had all but paralysed the country and the authorities had to agree to a revised contract. SWAPO claimed that 1971 was a successful year in which its forces operated continuously inside Namibia, although at the UN the Zambian representative listed 24 border violations by the South Africans in pursuit of SWAPO and stated that Zambia was 'in a state of undeclared war with South Africa'.

The strains of the war on South Africa led it to establish (April 1972) the first fighting unit of black police armed with automatic weapons to operate in the Caprivi Strip. Later that year SWAPO attacked the South African base at Kamenga, and in April 1973 SWAPO claimed to have killed 37 out of 39 from a South African patrol. Parts of the Strip were becoming no-go areas. These SWAPO actions were militarily insignificant, but they did establish the fact that a new war of liberation was under way in southern Africa, and they forced South Africa to deploy an increasing number of troops along the northern border of Namibia. Following the Rhodesian Prime Minister Ian Smith's closure of the Rhodesian–Zambian border in January 1973, South Africa moved substantial forces into the Caprivi Strip, perhaps doubling the numbers, then 3000, which were operating in the area.

The fall of the dictatorship of Marcello Caetano in Portugal (April 1974) and the subsequent independence of Angola had major significance for the struggle in Namibia. Guerrilla activity now spread back and forth across the Angolan border, and from 1975 onwards South African troops were to make forays into Angola against SWAPO training centres and refugee camps. Although for most of the 1970s the guerrilla war was small scale with occasional escalations of activity, it had three effects: it tied down increasing numbers of South African troops in the north of Namibia; it spread the war across the border into Angola; and the publicity from it ensured continuing international pressures upon Pretoria. At the end of the decade, war incidents increased from 500 in 1978 to 900 in 1979. In May 1978, for example, the South Africans raided deep into Angola to attack the Namibian refugee camp at Cassinga: they killed 612 refugees and 63 Angolan soldiers as well as wounding a number of Angolan civilians. In March 1980 SWAPO shot down a South African plane in southern Angola.

Inevitably, the long-drawn-out struggle took its toll of SWAPO. Internal divisions surfaced in 1975 when a split occurred and some 50 SWAPO members led by Shipanga were arrested in Zambia and then detained in Tanzania. Later, after their release, Shipanga was to form the breakaway SWAPO-Democrats. Katjavivi was dismissed in 1979; Muyongo defected in 1980. Despite these setbacks, however, Nujoma remained as President of SWAPO and continued to control the majority of its forces.

South Africa's intervention in Angola at the end of 1975 to support UNITA against the MPLA government at first appeared to threaten the existence of SWAPO, but later, following the South African withdrawal, SWAPO emerged in a stronger position. By the later 1970s Cuban instructors were providing SWAPO with military training inside Angola (already by December 1976 5000 Ovambo had crossed the border to obtain military training).

Western attempts to achieve a settlement were constantly aborted by South African intransigence so that, for example, the 1981 Geneva Conference came to nothing. Under the Reagan presidency Chester Crocker worked for years to bring about a settlement that would link the withdrawal of Cuban troops from Angola with independence for Namibia. South African support for UNITA forced Angola to rely upon the Cubans, and by the mid-1980s South African forces were operating continuously inside Angola so that the Namibian war of independence had become inextricably bound up with the Angolan civil war and South African interventions on the side of UNITA.

In August 1986 a bomb explosion at a meat market in Walvis Bay killed five and injured 23. It was the first time the struggle had been brought so far south. Other bomb attacks followed. By this date the Angolan government was repeatedly accusing South Africa's forces of raids across the border into its territory. The border war escalated substantially in early 1987 with large groups of SWAPO fighters infiltrating the white farming districts in the Tsumeb region, the furthest south they had been in four years.

The war took a new turn in November 1987 when black troops of the South West Africa Territory Force (SWATF) mutinied and refused to fight in Angola alongside the South African Defence Force (SADF) and UNITA. Several hundred of these black troops from Battalion 101 (recruited from among the Ovambo) were imprisoned in Walvis Bay. Then Battlion 202, recruited from among the Oka-vango, became similarly disaffected. These were volunteer troops rather than conscripts and bore the brunt of the fighting, suffering heavy casualties. Even so, the South Africans announced 21 white deaths at this time. The mutiny of Battalion 101 followed a refusal of the troops to fight against the Angolans; they had been given UNITA uniforms to do so. One SWATF soldier who resigned accused the South Africans of cowardice and claimed that they fought behind the black SWATF units in order to keep white casualties to a minimum. A third unit, Koevet, consisted of about 2000 paramilitary police renowned for their toughness and brutality. By this time there were an estimated 100,000 South African troops and SWATF units deployed in Namibia and southern Angola, including mechanized brigades for major operations. Battalion 32, based in northern Namibia, consisted of former Angolan guerrillas from the FNLA which had been defeated by the MPLA government forces at the time of independence, and it was officered by white South Africans and American and European mercenaries.

During the second half of 1987 it became increasingly difficult to distinguish between South African military actions directed solely against SWAPO and those in support of UNITA against the Angolans and their Cuban allies. The climax was to be reached during 1988.

Estimated costs and casualties

From 1973 onwards the Caprivi Strip became a major guerrilla war zone; that year South Africa had about 8000 troops in the north of Namibia of whom 1400 were black, although South Africa only admitted the presence of army units in the region in June 1974. Troop strength was steadily increased and by 1976, following the South African invasion of Angola, 45,000 troops were stationed in Namibia, a figure that had risen to between 70,000 and 80,000 by 1980 and up to 100,000 by April 1981. These numbers testify to the effectiveness of the SWAPO threat, even if the guerrillas won few engagements on the ground. Refugee camps in Angola from 1975 onwards provided the SADF with an excuse to raid across the border.

South Africa began to recruit black troops early in the 1970s and then formed 'ethnic' units in 1980 when it created the separate SWATF to fight alongside the SADF. This was part of a deliberate policy to use Namibians against Namibians. The most notorious of the black units, Koevet, was used for counter-insurgency and regularly employed terror tactics. It was part of a divide-and-rule approach.

At the beginning of the 1960s South Africa had three bases at Windhoek, Walvis Bay and Eastern Caprivi, but by 1980 it had a total of 40 bases along the Namibia–Angola border and a further 35 elsewhere in Namibia. By that time the government had embarked upon a policy of forced removals of population and the establishment of 'protected' villages. An area along the border was cleared of 20,000 people and the Ovambo, Kavango and Caprivi districts became security areas. The South African policy inside Namibia was to cripple SWAPO by means of mass arrests, detentions without trial and bannings. The widespread use of torture has been reported and confirmed. The introduction of compulsory military service in 1980 led to a mass exodus of Namibians into Angola, where by September 1981 an estimated 73,000 (6 per cent of the population) had fled into exile.

By the late 1970s the military commander of the People's Liberation Army of Namibia (PLAN), Dimo Hamambo, with headquarters at Cassinga in Angola, controlled three sectors along the front with about 3000 guerrillas, of whom perhaps 400 were active inside Namibia at any given time. The early 1980s saw an escalation of violence, the use of police informers and atrocities against the population by the South African forces in the north of Namibia as well as a growth in the number of raids across the border into Angola. By 1986, while South Africa still only admitted to the presence of 35,000 troops in the north of Namibia, SWAPO claimed there were (with the various auxiliary units) about 100,000. South African estimates put SWAPO forces at 9000. The South Africans veiled their activities in northern Namibia in secrecy, but reports, especially from the clergy, indicated a high level of violence against the villagers to cow the local populations.

As with so many of Africa's guerrilla wars, exact casualties will never be known, but in the 20 years of fighting to mid-1986 (according to South African military estimates) 10,150 PLAN guerrillas had been killed as against 600 South African troops, with an aditional 1300 civilian fatalities. SWAPO puts the figures higher. By the late 1980s the war was costing South Africa an estimated £500,000 a day.

But there were other costs. For example, an official South African report of 1985 condemned the policies of the De Beers subsidiary in Namibia, Consolidated Diamond Mines (CDM), for stripping Namibia of its diamonds against the time when the country became independent. The diamond mines accounted for about 74 per cent of export earnings. A CDM mining technician, Gordon Brown, said there had been a plan to 'get as much out of the ground as possible before a change of government'.

At the beginning of 1988 the guerrilla war seemed set to continue indefinitely; in February, for example, a bomb killed 15 people and injured dozens more when it exploded in a crowded bank in the town of Oshakati in northern Namibia, although SWAPO denied responsibility and claimed, 'The bomb is part of the South African dirty propaganda campaign to smear the name of SWAPO.' In June the National Union of Namibian Workers, which covers mining, food, fishing, meat and public service workers, brought 60,000 members out on strike in support of 50,000 schoolchildren already on strike in protest at the actions of Koevet (especially against schoolchildren) in townships and rural areas. Koevet's tactics were basically designed to intimidate the local populations that were sympathetic to SWAPO. There was every sign that internal opposition to South Africa would escalate throughout the territory, quite apart from the activities of the SWAPO guerrillas in the north; in fact the possibility of an end to the war (see Part V, pp. 346–351) emerged in May when the South Africans decided to cut their losses and extricate their forces then besieging Cuito Cuanavale in support of UNITA deep inside Angola.

In June 1988 talks were held in Cairo on peace in Angola and Namibian independence, a process that was to continue for the rest of the year. The Cairo talks involved South Africa, Angola, Cuba and the United States, and they coincided with rising tensions inside Namibia. Several factors were at work. First, the South Africans had lost the initiative at the long-drawn-out battle of Cuito Cuanavale and wished to extricate their forces. Second, by that July a big concentration of Angolan and Cuban troops had moved south close to the Namibian border, while Cuban air and radar cover also extended to the Namibian border. And third, the Soviet Union was anxious to facilitate an agreement in the area (a move inspired by *glasnost*) with the USA. So from Cairo the talks moved to New York and, as far as Namibia was concerned, UN Resolution 435 (passed in 1978) was now to be applied to the territory: this called for a cessation of all hostilities to be followed by a series of stages supervised by the UN, including free elections to precede the implementation of a new constitution and independence.

South African determination to hold on to Namibia has been guided by several considerations: the presence of 78,000 whites whom Pretoria did not wish to desert; the huge mineral wealth of the country; and the military bases it established in the Caprivi Strip which enable it to operate in Angola and support UNITA and to threaten Zambia and Zimbabwe. On the other hand, the Republic's natural (and more easily defensible frontier) lies back on the Orange River and the surrender of control over Namibia has always been seen in Pretoria as a 'card' to be used to buy time. By November (when the talks had moved to Geneva) it did look as though agreement had at last been reached between Angola, Cuba and South Africa based on the proposals of the US mediator Chester Crocker: Namibian independence in exchange for the withdrawal of 52,000 Cuban troops from Angola within two years. The accord between the three signatory powers was confirmed in Brazzaville (Congo) early in December 1988. Then South Africa's Foreign Minister, Pik Botha, said, 'We want to be accepted by our African brothers. We need each other.'

Results: immediate and longer term

There was widespread scepticism about whether South Africa would in fact implement Resolution 435 and, for example, at the beginning of 1989 widespread protests were provoked in Namibia when the South Africans conscripted thousands of young Namibians to serve in SWATF. The move was condemned as being in bad faith following South Africa's agreement to implement Resolution 435 on Namibian independence; it was seen as a move to subject young Namibians to political propaganda prior to the elections to be held later in the year, which (if they were fair) SWAPO was widely expected to win. Later in January a second row erupted when the big five on the Security Council of the UN (the USA, the USSR, Britain, France and China) agreed for financial reasons to reduce the size of the proposed UN peace-keeping force for Namibia from 7500 soldiers to 4500. The cut was denounced by the non-aligned group of nations.

The UNTAG (United Nations Transitional Assistance Group) peace-keeping troops moved into Namibia so that by 1 April 1989 about 1000 personnel were in place on the day that a formal cessation of hostilities took effect. At once, however, the agreement appeared in danger of collapse when SWAPO guerrillas crossed the border from Angola into northern Namibia. During the first two weeks of April about 300 of these guerrillas were killed by troops of the South African Defence Force, who were brought out of their camps to police the border again. Yet despite this near-catastrophic SWAPO miscalculation, it appeared that South Africa still wanted to maintain the agreement and by early May, when most of the remaining guerrillas were reported to have returned to Angola, it seemed at least possible that the peace process would continue on target. Elections for a Constituent Assembly were held in November, followed by the withdrawal of all remaining South African troops and the closure of bases. The Constituent Assembly then met and drew up the country's independent constitution. Namibia became independent on 21 March 1990.

The implementation of the agreement and the achievement of independence by

Namibia represent a major shift in the power balance in southern Africa. The agreement removes South Africa from Angola's doorstep so that the government in Luanda is more likely to be able to overcome UNITA. It gives Namibia independence after 100 years of colonialism, although the new state remains very much subject to South African economic domination. It removes the last buffer state between South Africa and independent black Africa. And it frees South Africa to concentrate all its attention upon solving problems within the Republic.

TUNISIA: AN END TO COLONIALISM 1952–1962

Not exactly a war and yet not precisely peace: the last years of French rule saw near-civil war in the country with terrorism and counter-terrorism in the towns, while the years immediately after independence included a French aerial raid upon Tunisia (an overspill from the war in neighbouring Algeria) and the battle over the base of Bizerta which the French had retained. These confrontations, and the casualties involved, were on a substantial scale and not untypical of the end of colonialism both here and elsewhere.

Origins

North Africa was subject to the growing pressures of France, Britain and Italy during the first half of the nineteenth century as Ottoman power waned and its nominal control became more or less irrelevant. In Tunisia the Bey tried to modernize his country so as to escape the fate of neighbouring Algeria, which the French had invaded in 1830, but he only succeeded in getting deeply into debt to the Western powers. Following the Berlin Conference of 1878, which had accepted the British acquisition of Cyprus, both Britain and Germany encouraged France, which wanted to match its rival's gain in Cyprus, to regard Tunisia as its sphere of influence. Thus in 1881 France used a border violation (of Algeria) as a pretext to invade Tunisia; the French met little effective resistance and the Bey accepted protectorate status from France in 1883. A large-scale influx of settlers (both French and Italian) followed and these were given land grants.

In 1920 the Destour (Constitution) Party was formed, marking the beginning of modern Tunisian nationalism, but the party was broken up by the French in 1925. Then in 1935 the young Habib Bourguiba formed the Neo-Destour Party and initiated more radical nationalist agitation against the French so that by 1938 the party was strong enough to call a general strike. Bourguiba was exiled. The 1938 strike led to many clashes with the police and the imposition of martial law. The Neo-Destour Party was dissolved. During the Second World War Tunisia became a base first for Italian and then for German armies in North Africa until their expulsion by the Allies in 1943. Despite some French reforms at the end of the war, the nationalists demanded full independence in 1946. In 1949 Bourguiba returned to Tunisia from Cairo where he had been in exile.

Outbreak and response

In 1950 the French accepted Neo-Destour power-sharing proposals and a new government containing equal numbers of French and Tunisian ministers was appointed. More reforms followed despite opposition from the settlers, who then numbered 10 per cent of the population; but by 1952 the settler opposition to reforms which clearly signalled independence, as well as second thoughts in Paris, provoked a crisis. Strikes and anti-government protests early in 1952 were followed by the arrest of Bourguiba and other nationalist leaders, the arrests in turn producing fresh violence. A new government attempted further reforms, but there was growing terrorism on the one side and repression by the French in response. The settlers created their own counter-terrorist organization, the Red Hand, so that by 1953 the country was on the verge of civil war, with bands of Tunisian nationalists active against settlers and government in the western highlands and round Bizerta in the north and with terrorism in the towns.

These troubles were brought to an end in July 1954 after Pierre Mendès-France came to power in Paris and initiated another round of colonial reforms. He agreed full internal self-government and allowed the outlawed Neo-Destour Party of Bourguiba to come to power. This policy led to Mendès-France's downfall in February 1955, but Tunisia became fully independent in March 1956.

In the immediate aftermath of independence, relations between Tunisia and France were strained: partly because France refused to withdraw its military forces (the war in Algeria was then reaching a climax), and partly because of the Tunisian policy of nationalization, which included many French companies as well as settler-owned land.

Sakhiet Sidi Youssef

A number of clashes with the French forces fighting in Algeria had occurred in the Tunisian border village of Sakhiet Sidi Youssef, prompting the French to take retaliatory action in February 1958 when French planes attacked the village, killing 79, injuring 130 and damaging many buildings. In response Tunisia broke diplomatic relations with France, forbade the movement of French troops and demanded their evacuation from the country, and complained to the Security Council of the United Nations. The Tunisians then blockaded French troops in their barracks and expelled some 600 French citizens. Britain and the USA acted as mediators in the dispute. The French agreed to evacuate all troops except those at the Bizerta base, while recognizing Tunisian sovereignty over it. But another round of Tunisian–French clashes took place in May 1958 and again Tunisia took its complaint to the Security Council.

However, following de Gaulle's assumption of power on 1 June 1958, the French government agreed that all its forces (except for those in Bizerta) would be withdrawn from Tunisia within four months, and a fresh agreement was to be worked out to cover the French presence in Bizerta. Between 1958 and 1960 the Tunisians nationalized French interests in the country, including agricultural land belonging to the settlers for redistribution to the peasants, a policy which caused the exodus of the majority of the settlers.

The Bizerta crisis

Tunisia had requested the return of the Bizerta base a number of times since independence; on 5 July 1961 Bourguiba formally demanded its return. Demonstrations against continuing French control were mounted, and then fighting broke out between Tunisian and French troops round Bizerta. Tunisia again broke diplomatic relations with France (19 July 1961) and took its demand for Bizerta to the Security Council. More serious fighting between the Tunisians and French now took place and lasted until 22 July, by which time the Tunisians had suffered more than 800 fatalities, although the French remained in control of the base. In the south of the country the French repulsed another Tunisian attack on the fort at Garat el-Hamel.

On 28 July 1961, the French began to acknowledge the inevitable: they argued for the use of the base while international tension lasted (they meant the Algerian crisis), but agreed to negotiate over the future of the base. Talks continued into 1962 (at Rome and Paris), and the situation became less tense following the ceasefire in Algeria (March 1962). The French finally handed over the base to Tunisia at the end of June 1962.

WESTERN SAHARA: DESERT WAR

Origins

The Portuguese established a trading post on the Sahara coast in 1487, but their interests lay farther south and the territory was only to be colonized in the nineteenth century. In 1884 Spain occupied Rio de Oro (now Wad Dheheb) and Villa Cisneros (Dakhla) and proclaimed a protectorate over the coast. An agreement between France and Spain in 1900 established the frontier between Rio de Oro (Spanish Sahara) and Mauritania, but the northern border with Morocco remained ill-defined. In 1934 Spain assumed full military and administrative control of the country.

On becoming independent from France in 1956, Morocco at once laid claim to all the Spanish possessions in north-west Africa as well as to Mauritania, which was still under French rule. During the following year Moroccan irregular forces entered Spanish Sahara (now Western Sahara) to raid the principal centres of population, penetrating as far south as Villa Cisneros (Dakhla) and forcing both France and Spain to intervene with troops. In 1965 representatives of Spanish Rio de Oro (the southern part of Western Sahara) pledged their allegiance to King Hassan of Morocco, and in December of that year at the UN the Moroccan delegate said he hoped Morocco's claim to Spanish Sahara could be settled peacefully. Meanwhile in 1964 and again in 1966 Mauritania (independent since 1960) told the UN Special Committee that it wished to hold direct talks with Spain over its claim to Spanish Sahara. But in March and then October 1966 chiefs and then others in Spanish Sahara signed a memorandum in favour of union with Spain. In 1967 Spain announced that it was in favour of self-determination for its territory and created a General Assembly. In December 1967 the UN urged Spain

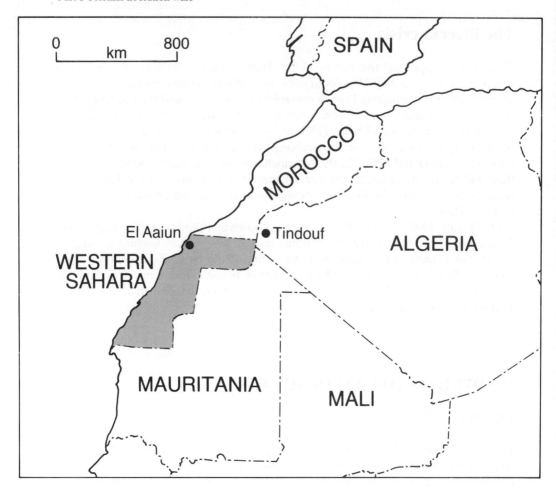

Map 4 Western Sahara

(in consultation with both Morocco and Mauritania) to hold a referendum as to the territory's future.

In June 1970 fighting broke out against the Spanish at El Aaiún and many were killed. Again the UN called for a referendum. When the UN passed a resolution in February 1973 calling on Spain to grant independence, the resolution recognized the fact that both Morocco and Mauritania had claims on the area by suggesting that the referendum should be in consultation with those two countries. King Hassan of Morocco was only prepared to agree to a referendum if it did not include the question of independence. In November 1975 Spain set up a tripartite administration for the territory with Morocco and Mauritania, and announced that it would cease to administer Spanish Sahara on 28 February 1976. The stage was set for a handover to Spanish Sahara's two neighbours.

In the meantime a number of nationalist movements had appeared, of which the most important was the Popular Front for the Liberation of Saguia al-Hamra and Rio de Oro (Polisario). A second movement – the Organization for the Liberation of Saguia al-Hamra and Oued el-Dheb (Olshod) – later changed its name to Morehob, Mouvement révolutionnaire pour la libération des hommes bleus. The nationalist movements wanted an end to Spanish rule, and their activities led Spain to declare a state of emergency in 1972. Morehob set up its headquarters across the border in Algeria, near Tindouf, while Polisario campaigned for the withdrawal of Spanish troops and a referendum. A ruling of the World Court (October 1975) laid down that when the territory had become a Spanish colony it belonged to the people who lived there, but the decisive nature of that part of the judgment was spoilt by the subsequent addition that legal ties also existed between Spanish Sahara and its two neighbours, Morocco and Mauritania. It was an invitation to trouble.

At the Arab summit held at Rabat in Morocco (October 1974), Morocco and Mauritania agreed to split Spanish Sahara between them. It was typical of colonialism in its dying phase that on his own deathbed the Spanish leader Francisco Franco (acting like a medieval king) agreed to split Spanish Sahara between Morocco and Mauritania. Once this Spanish (or Franco) decision was known, Algeria decided to arm and train the Polisario forces in the Tindouf area. The scene was set for a long desert war.

Outbreak and response

When in October 1975 the International Court decided that the former ties between Sahara, Morocco and Mauritania did not mean that the people of Sahara should not determine their own future, King Hassan of Morocco at once said he would make a claim and act upon it. Therefore on 6 November 1975 he launched the 'Green March' of 350,000 Moroccans into Sahara as a peaceful way of claiming the territory. They got as far as El-Aaiún before Spanish troops halted them. Both Morocco and Mauritania found themselves opposed by the Saharans during the last months of Spanish rule. The Djemaa (Assembly), under heavy Spanish pressure, approved a joint Moroccan–Mauritanian takeover of Sahara and then, early in 1976, Spain announced that the process of its decolonization had been completed. On the day before the Spanish departure, 27 February 1976, the

Secretary-General of Polisario (E. C. el Wali) proclaimed the Saharan Arab Democratic Republic (SADR).

Thus the Spanish handed over their 'rights' to Morocco and Mauritania, while
Polisario announced an independent state and turned to Algeria for support.
Algeria was concerned primarily to counter the growth of Moroccan power
(Algeria under Boumédienne was radical, as opposed to the conservative pro-
Western Morocco of King Hassan), while Algeria was also interested in an outlet
from Tindouf across the small border between Algeria and Sahara to the Atlantic.
King Hassan was concerned to boost his own power and prestige at a time when
his government faced growing opposition at home. The Sahara venture was to
prove very popular for years, despite the costs. On the other hand, Mauritania
soon discovered that it was too poor and too weak to sustain hostilities against
Polisario; it was soon forced out of the war (1979) and renounced its claims on the
territory.

The first major battle of the war occurred at Angala in January 1976 between
Moroccan forces and Polisario; the latter were defeated. From then onwards the
Polisario relied on guerrilla tactics rather than fixed military confrontations. In
June 1976, however, 500 Polisario guerrillas in 100 vehicles advanced to Nouakchott (capital of Mauritania) to launch an attack (they shelled the presidential
palace) and in the following year (1977) Polisario attacked the Mauritanian mining
region round Zouerate, including the railway line which carried the iron ore from
Zouerate to Nouadhibou, and kidnapped six French technicians working there.
The Mauritanian economy depended on its iron ore output, but this attack was
counter-productive since the French intervened on behalf of Mauritania and
launched air strikes against the Polisario desert columns.

Meanwhile, following the Polisario announcement of the SADR, a number of
'socialist' states in Africa such as Algeria, Angola, Benin, Congo, Guinea-Bissau,
Madagascar and Mozambique recognized it. Support widened substantially in 1979
when Mauritania dropped its claim to the territory and the post-Franco government
in Madrid repudiated the 1975 agreement to hand over Spanish Sahara to Morocco
and Mauritania.

Course of the struggle

At the beginning of the war Polisario faced two enemies – Morocco and Mauritania
– and made the tactical decision to concentrate its attacks on Mauritania, the
weaker of the two. As a direct result of Polisario activities in the north of the
country, the President of Mauritania was overthrown in a coup (July 1978);
Polisario then announced a ceasefire in the hope of inducing the new government
to give up its claim, which it did in August 1979. Polisario's very success in
knocking out one of the contestants in fact made the other claimant, Morocco,
which was by far the more powerful, all the more determined to take over the
entire territory, and it may well have ensured that in the long run Polisario could
not win. As soon as the Mauritanians withdrew, Morocco moved in troops to take
their place, occupying Dakhla and claiming the whole territory; in the fighting
which followed, losses reached the hundreds on both sides.

Fighting between Polisario and the Moroccans was at its height in the period of
1979–81, with the Polisario forces making a number of successful strikes across the

border into southern Morocco to inflict substantial casualties. The death of President Boumédienne of Algeria in 1978 did not, as the Moroccans hoped, lead Algeria to end its support for Polisario. By 1980 Polisario had about 10,000 troops, though fewer than half of these would actually be fighting inside the territory at any given time. Polisario tactics were to mount hit-and-run raids against the centres of population so that, for example, the phosphate mines at Bou Craa were forced to run at reduced capacity. At first the Moroccan response was to place garrisons in all the centres of population so as to protect these against Polisario. Even when Moroccan casualties were high and Polisario appeared to be winning the war on the ground, King Hassan continued to receive support, for by then the war had become a nationalist crusade.

In 1981 the Organization of African Unity called for a referendum, but this was not followed up and the fighting continued. That year Polisario switched its bases from Algeria to Mauritania and, following an attempted coup in Nouakchott, Mauritania broke diplomatic relations with Morocco. By 1982 Morocco had come to control the principal centres of population – El Aaiún, Smara, Bojador – and the huge phosphate deposits at Bou Craa. Morocco built defensive lines – endless sand walls – round the triangle of these towns and Bou Craa. The first phase of the walls was completed in 1982; in 1984 they were extended to the Mauritanian border and ran for more than 600 km.

By 1981 the war had become highly sophisticated. Morocco accused both Algeria and Libya of providing Polisario with the Soviet-made missiles used to shoot down Moroccan planes. Thus in October of that year Sam-6 or Sam-8 missiles brought down a Moroccan Hercules transport and a Mirage F-A jet fighter at high altitudes. The Moroccan military suggested that the missiles had been fired by either East German or Cuban 'advisers' with the Polisario guerrillas.

The war continued with varying degrees of intensity throughout the 1980s, despite OAU efforts to find a solution (which very nearly led to the collapse of the OAU – see below). In November 1987, for example, Polisario could issue a communiqué which claimed that 63 Moroccan troops had been killed and 91 wounded in a desert battle, while a Moroccan army communiqué said 245 guerrillas and 72 Moroccans had been killed in two battles. This, however, was particularly heavy fighting and occurred just before the arrival of a United Nations mission, which came to tour the area and ascertain the prospects for holding a referendum on self-determination. Later that month Polisario declared a truce. In August 1988 Morocco and Polisario accepted a United Nations plan for a ceasefire and a referendum which would give the people of Western Sahara a choice between independence and integration with Morocco. But after nine months of truce this UN peace effort broke down. At the end of September 1989 Polisario mounted a series of attacks on Moroccan positions, and on 7 and 11 October it waged substantial battles against the Moroccans at Guelta Zemmour and Hauza; both sides claimed that the other suffered heavy casualties. Thus, the possibility of an end to the war had been postponed.

Estimated costs and casualties

Given the fact that Western Sahara is mainly desert, and that its total population when the Spanish left in 1976 stood at an estimated 75,000, the war has been devastating. By the mid-1980s at least 10,000 Polisario and Moroccans had been killed, but the total casualties are likely to be much higher. Apart from the people of Sahara, Mauritania (which withdrew its claims to the territory in 1979) and Morocco, a number of other powers have become involved in the conflict, including France and Spain, Algeria and Libya. Cold War considerations have led the USA greatly to increase its supply of military equipment to Morocco for use in the Sahara war, while in the mid-1980s the question of recognition for the Sahara Arab Democratic Republic very nearly wrecked the OAU.

When Mauritania first became involved in 1975 its army stood at 1500, but by 1977 it had been expanded to 17,000; yet it was still unable to defeat Polisario even with French assistance, Arab money and a further 9000 Moroccan troops stationed in Mauritania. During 1977, for example, Mauritanian military casualties amounted to 500 dead. The war was not popular in Mauritania and did tremendous damage to what in any case was one of the poorest economies in Africa. It led directly to the coup of July 1978 which overthrew President Ould Daddah. A year later his successor, Haidallah, ended the war as far as Mauritania was concerned by renouncing its claims to Sahara, although Moroccan troops were only induced to leave Mauritania in January 1980.

Morocco did little better against Polisario in the early stages of the war, despite its immensely stronger economy, and by 1980 it was maintaining large garrisons in the south of the country (for example, 5000 troops at Zag). Early that year it launched a series of major operations against the guerrillas. Claims and counter-claims about casualties inflicted by each side make precise assessments of losses exceptionally difficult. Thus, while Polisario claimed to have put 1,357 Moroccan soldiers out of action, the Moroccans put their losses at a mere 82, even though in May 1980 they were obliged to throw an additional 10,000 troops into the field. The Moroccans then claimed that their aircraft had knocked out 60 Polisario vehicles and three rocket launchers, and subsequently that they had destroyed two motorized columns of 360 vehicles. Yet such Moroccan successes were offset by Polisario attacks deep into Morocco: in June 1980, for example, a Polisario column reached the Moroccan town of Akka, 100 miles south-east of Agadir.

Up to mid-1980 the Polisario guerrillas were better armed than the Moroccans with modern Russian and Czech equipment; their columns of between 3000 and 5000 men crossed the desert from bases in Algeria to attack Moroccan targets. But at the end of 1979 France began to supply Morocco with the advanced weapons it had been seeking and Morocco went on to the offensive. Despite its sandwalls – a policy of defensive structures which Morocco began in 1980 – the war was costing Morocco an estimated £500 million a year by 1987 and no end appeared to be in sight. The wall, which by then extended over more than 1000 miles, was designed to cut Polisario off from the rich Atlantic fishing grounds, yet the guerrillas claimed to operate up to 10 miles behind it. In 1987 Polisario accused the Moroccans of carrying out mass deportations of Sahrawis (as the Western Saharans are called) from behind the wall, while moving Moroccans in to replace them.

The position for Polisario became more difficult in 1988 when Morocco and Algeria resumed diplomatic relations (Libya meanwhile having ended its support for Polisario), although this did not mean an end to Algerian support. Polisario continued a war of attrition against the Moroccan forces, an estimated 150,000, behind their wall. Diplomats in Rabat claimed that Moroccan soldiers serving on the wall were paid double and that every bullet fired in the war against Polisario was replaced free by the USA, France and Saudi Arabia. Yet fierce battles were still being fought in the desert at the end of 1988, immediately after a UN peace plan had been conditionally approved.

Results: immediate and longer term

The Sahara war exposed the weakness of the OAU. After recognition by Cuba in 1980, SADR had been recognized by a total of 36 countries (mostly African) and, though African states pulled back from splitting the OAU over the issue (26 of its 50 members approved admission, while Morocco insisted it had to be a two-thirds majority), in 1982 SADR was admitted to full membership of the Organization. Morocco and 18 other countries then walked out of the OAU, presenting it with the worst crisis of its existence. This was apparently resolved in June 1983 when the SADR delegation voluntarily abstained from taking its seat. Morocco then ended its boycott. By 1984 Morocco had once more agreed to take part in a referendum, while reserving the right not to abide by its decisions. That year Mauritania, one of the original claimants to the territory, recognized SADR.

The question of a referendum continued through the 1980s, as did the hit-and-run war. The central question was whether the people in the refugee camps in Algeria should have a vote in the referendum. By 1988 both sides were accusing each other of cheating. Polisario accused Morocco of settling its own people in the disputed territory to ensure numerical superiority in the referendum count. In its turn Polisario was moving Malian Tuaregs into the four refugee camps round Tindouf. Algeria, which had worked consistently to obtain international recognition for SADR, did not attempt to control this new influx. In August 1988 Polisario decided not to accept the UN referendum plan unless the Moroccans first withdrew their troops and administrators from the territory. In New York, later that month, the UN Secretary-General, Pérez de Cuéllar, said he expected a referendum to be held before the end of the year, and on 30 August in Geneva representatives of Morocco and Polisario accepted UN proposals for a referendum and peace.

The referendum, to have been held by the spring of 1989, would be conducted among the 73,000 Sahrawis, but who should be included was far from clear. As the arguing about the referendum continued in September 1988, Polisario demanded that all 200,000 Moroccans should first leave Western Sahara. The Moroccans insisted they only had 80,000 in the territory; the UN suggested the figure was 150,000 (even the smallest figure was greater than the supposed total number of eligible voting Sahrawis). Polisario claimed to have 20,000 fighters; other estimates suggested the figure was no more than 6000 or 8000, although Polisario also held 3000 Moroccan prisoners.

What seems to have changed the situation was the May 1988 meeting in Algiers between King Hassan of Morocco and the other Maghreb leaders, where unity (of sorts) between the north African states had become more important than the Sahara war. In a shrewd move in August, King Hassan said he was considering turning Morocco into a federation of self-governing provinces (a political development that would make it easier to encompass SADR without Polisario losing too much face). Meanwhile both sides worked to win votes for the referendum.

Then in January 1989 meetings between King Hassan and the Polisario leaders at Marrakesh appeared to open the way to a 'complete and definitive accord'.

Following the talks, Polisario said that the talks should lead to an 'active phase' of a peace process backed by the UN and the OAU, and that both sides could now 'move on to a free and fair referendum on self-determination among the people of the Western Sahara'. However, the breakdown of the peace process in September 1989 (see above), while threatening indefinite renewed hostilities, probably depended upon Algeria, whose support is essential to any prolonged Polisario resistance. By 1990 it was clear that Algeria wished to mend its fences with Morocco, and what appeared to be taking place was a gradual withdrawal of support from Polisario. Polisario, meanwhile, was undergoing internal splits and quarrels, so the greatest likelihood was a solution that would in the end see Sahara incorporated into Morocco.

ZIMBABWE: WAR OF INDEPENDENCE

Origins

From the Unilateral Declaration of Independence (UDI) by the white minority government of Rhodesia on 11 November 1965 until independence 15 years later, the escalating guerrilla war between blacks and whites focused world attention on two problems: the racial nature of imperialism, as an intransigent white minority attempted desperately to hold on to power; and the far larger problem of white rule in southern Africa as a whole. During the first ten years of UDI (1965–1975) the Portuguese were fighting major wars in the neighbouring states of Angola and Mozambique in a doomed effort to hold on to these two colonial possessions, while from 1975 onwards (after Portugal had retired from the struggle and Angola and Mozambique had become independent) the focus shifted to South Africa and its growing readiness to intervene in the affairs of its black neighbours.

Southern Rhodesia had been settled by column of whites from the Cape who moved into the territory under the leadership of Cecil Rhodes in 1890 (hence the name); they were to fight two wars against the Ndebele in 1894 and 1896 before they secured control. Southern Rhodesia came to be regarded by Britain very much as a colony of white settlement. In 1923, following a referendum among the whites which rejected incorporation into South Africa, Britain granted the territory self-governing status, although London reserved the right to approve legislation which affected the native peoples (a right that was never exercised) and control over foreign policy. A large number of white settlers moved into the colony after the Second World War, so that by the beginning of the 1960s, when the great upsurge of African nationalism was taking place throughout the continent, there was a relatively substantial white population in relation to the black majority (1 in 20).

The roots of the struggle for Zimbabwe which followed UDI in 1965 went back to the beginning of white settlement in the 1890s under Cecil Rhodes. Three factors operated throughout Rhodesian history: white control of education to limit black advance; white control and demarcation of land; and, long before UDI, white (settler) laws which made black opposition difficult to organize and sustain.

Lines were drawn at the beginning of the 1960s when black nationalism was triumphing everywhere on the continent to the north of Rhodesia. When the Central African Federation of Northern and Southern Rhodesia and Nyasaland was dismantled at the end of 1963, Kenneth Kaunda of Zambia tried to persuade the British government not to allow the military hardware of the Federation to fall into the hands of Southern Rhodesia; his protests were ignored. Then, when Ian Smith replaced Winston Field as Prime Minister of Southern Rhodesia in 1964, he said, 'I cannot see in my lifetime that the Africans will be sufficiently mature and reasonable to take over . . . If we ever have an African majority in this country we will have failed in our policy, because our policy is one of trying to make a place for the white man.' That statement really said everything about white attitudes. Another of Smith's ministers, Clifford Dupont, said, 'We can and will halt the wind of change.'

There had been growing black agitation for universal suffrage throughout the 1950s. In 1961 Joshua Nkomo founded the Zimbabwe African People's Union (ZAPU). Two years later (1963) his lieutenant, the Revd Ndabaningi Sithole, broke away to create a more militant party, the Zimbabwe African National Union (ZANU). A few minor concessions had been made to nationalist demands in the years 1958 to 1964, but once Smith became leader of the white Rhodesia Front in 1964 it became clear that the real race clash was about to take place. From the break-up of the Central African Federation at the end of 1963 until November 1965 the Rhodesia Front, and especially Smith, prepared the ground for a unilateral declaration of independence.

As white intentions became obvious during 1965, Britain made plain that it was not prepared to coerce the white minority: first, the Commonwealth Secretary, Arthur Bottomley, said that Britain would not use force; then the Prime Minister, Harold Wilson, made a last-moment visit to Salisbury, the Rhodesian capital (now Harare), in an effort to persuade Smith not to mount a UDI. For its part the Rhodesia Front never masked its intentions, which were to maintain white minority rule.

Outbreak and response

Following the Smith regime's UDI of 11 November 1965, Britain announced limited sanctions, the United Nations called for an oil embargo and the OAU called for its members to break diplomatic relations with Britain. In Rhodesia the white minority government geared itself for siege tactics and to break sanctions. To begin with the Smith regime appeared to be entrenched in power. Sanctions were tightened in January 1966; a Commonwealth heads of government conference met in Lagos, Nigeria, to co-ordinate Commonwealth policy on Rhodesia; the Beira patrol was instituted by Britain to prevent oil shipments to Rhodesia, although for the entire period of UDI oil was supplied through South Africa by BP and Shell subsidiaries in that country.

By 1967 guerrilla action, though still on a small scale, was enough to worry the government in Salisbury, and there was every indication that the struggle would develop into a bitter racial confrontation. In August 1967 a group of ZAPU guerrillas from Zambia penetrated to within 60 miles of Bulawayo, causing a panic in Salisbury. The government there called for aid from South Africa, and from that time onwards South African paramilitary units were to be stationed in Rhodesia. The Prime Minister of South Africa, J. B. Vorster, threatened Zambia, which was applying sanctions to Rhodesia as well as permitting guerrilla bases on its territory: 'If you want violence, we will hit you so hard you will never forget it.' Also that year a ZANU spokesman said, 'The only way left open towards the achievement of this goal (independence) is an open war against settlerism.' ZAPU and the ANC of South Africa announced they would work together.

Despite internal problems (in 1970 ZAPU split into two factions), both ZANU and ZAPU had sufficient successes during this early period to prompt Rhodesia's Commissioner of Police to say in 1968, 'It would be wrong to minimize the dangers which Rhodesia faces from terrorist infiltrations; these are now employing more sophisticated tactics and are well armed.'

In May 1968 the United Nations called for mandatory sanctions. The following July South Africa experienced its first white casualty in Rhodesia when police constable Daniel du Toit was killed on the Zambezi. Meanwhile Britain's Prime Minister, Harold Wilson, had twice met Smith on board Royal Navy vessels – first HMS *Tiger* and then HMS *Fearless* off Gibraltar – but in January 1969 the Commonwealth heads of government meeting in London said that the '*Fearless*' proposals for a settlement were unacceptable. Rhodesian troops were deployed on the Rhodesia–Zambia border throughout 1969, for by that year the different guerrilla groups had set up a number of training camps inside Rhodesia.

Course of the struggle

By 1969 the Rhodesian government was regularly conducting trials of Africans accused of harbouring or otherwise assisting the guerrillas. Early in 1970 the Minister for Law and Order, Lardner-Burke, reported that the guerrillas were concentrating on quality: small bands were entering Rhodesia from widely different points – there were, for example, attacks on Victoria Falls airport and the security forces in the Zambezi valley. In June 1970 Smith claimed that 20 whites and 170 'terrorists' had been killed since the beginning of the guerrilla incursions.

The British Foreign Secretary, Sir Alec Douglas-Home, had talks with Smith in 1971 and agreed on settlement terms provided these were accepted when the Pearce Commission visited Rhodesia in 1972. In fact the terms were overwhelmingly rejected by the Africans: of 120,730 people interviewed, 107,309 Africans said no to the settlement terms, and as a result the British government dropped the proposals.

From 1965 to 1972 Rhodesia had been able to contain the insurgency: guerrilla action was spasmodic, although it kept the security forces stretched. At the end of 1972, however, the situation changed dramatically; on 21 December ZANU opened a new phase of the war by attacking Altena farm in the north-east of the country. From then onwards there were to be daily attacks on white farms. When this Zimbabwe African National Liberation Army (ZANLA) offensive was opened the guerrillas were already well entrenched in the north-east of the country, where any local support for the government had been largely destroyed by the regime's stupidity in forcibly moving the Tangwena tribe. The government now embarked on a policy of Protected Villages (PVs), collective punishments and removals of entire populations.

On 9 January 1973 Rhodesia closed the border with Zambia, a move interpreted as a sign of weakness rather than strength. In Britain Douglas-Home for the first time referred to the guerrillas as freedom fighters, rather than calling them terrorists. In February Smith reopened the border with Zambia, and President Kaunda said that the guerrillas were already inside Rhodesia. The 'maverick' white MP, Allan Savory, described collective punishments as a guerrilla leader's dream, but no one took any notice. Also that February an increasingly embattled Salisbury government warned against rumours and instituted stiff penalties for rumour-mongering, as well as introducing new racist legislation including influx control and tougher pass laws.

During 1973 it became clear that the initiative had passed to the guerrillas. Trains were derailed at Umtali (Mutari), threatening the vital Beira Corridor supply route. The government moved 8000 tribesmen in the north-east, so adding to the existing disaffection. By this time it was estimated that South Africa had between 2000 and 5000 troops in Rhodesia. The war grew in intensity throughout 1973, especially in the north-east where ZANU established a growing co-operation with Frelimo, which was fighting the Portuguese across the border in Mozambique. By the end of the year, white Rhodesians had accepted the fact that the war had become a permanency and would not be ended by any 'settlement'. In September 1973, for the first time since 1966, more whites left Rhodesia than entered it as settlers.

Allan Savory, the outspoken member of the Rhodesia Front, broke away to form his Rhodesia Party and said that 'brute force and tough talk' would lose the war. 'It is essential', he said, 'to have the active support of the African people – the side that wins this wins the war.' At the end of 1973, which in almost every respect represented a turning point in the war, the government set up Civil Defence Aid Committees throughout the country to keep civilian life running smoothly. Whites were told to watch Africans and what they said, while farmers were given instructions about wiring their houses, keeping guard dogs and varying their routines.

During 1974 the government launched a special programme to attract settlers, but it failed. In February Allan Savory provoked a furious row among whites when he suggested that ZANU and ZAPU should be invited to talks about the future of the country. By March the guerrilla threat had become the top priority for Salisbury. The Europeans were only just managing to hold on, and fewer than 25 per cent of them could claim to have been born in the country.

Then came the coup in Lisbon (April 1974) which changed the situation throughout southern Africa. Independence for Mozambique, which followed in 1975, meant that Rhodesia's eastern flank had been turned and an 800 km border would soon be in the hands of a government friendly to ZANU. It also meant that Rhodesia's value as a buffer between South Africa and independent black Africa had disappeared. The *South African Star* argued in May that the best time for a settlement in Rhodesia had already passed, and that the white minority should forget its dream of perpetual white supremacy.

In July the government began forcibly moving an entire tribe of 60,000 people from 21 villages north-east of Salisbury so as to deny the guerrillas assistance in the area. The war was coming closer to the capital all the time, and by then the security forces were fully stretched.

The year 1974 was the year of *détente*: South Africa attempted the role of 'honest broker' in the region; the Smith government released various of its detainees, including Nkomo and Robert Mugabe (a former colleague of Nkomo who had broken away to become a leading member of ZANU); and the West tried to limit the spread of the war. By that time both ZANU and ZAPU were receiving backing from the OAU Liberation Committee and help in training and arms from China, Cuba, the USSR and Algeria. In 1975 Mugabe took over the leadership of ZANU from Sithole, and after the breakdown of the *détente* exercise the war was renewed on a bigger scale than ever.

In January 1976 ZANU mounted a new offensive in the north-east of Rhodesia as well as offensives in the east and south-east. ZANLA was able to exploit Frelimo's control of the whole Rhodesia–Mozambique border for the first time. Then in April the miltary wing of ZAPU, the Zimbabwe People's Revolutionary Army (ZIPRA), began infiltrating into the west from Botswana and Zambia. In August and October the crack Rhodesian force, the Selous Scouts, raided ZANLA camps deep inside Mozambique, killing 1200 on their first raid; later they claimed to have destroyed six camps and 50 tons of amunition and equipment in camps in Tete province.

Also during 1976 ZANU and ZAPU attended peace talks in Geneva sponsored by Britain and the USA; they did so under the single banner of the Patriotic Front. From then until 1980 they were to act jointly for diplomatic purposes as the Patriotic Front, though otherwise keeping their separate identities as ZANU and ZAPU. Then in 1977, when it had become clear that the devastating cross-border raids into Mozambique (and bombing raids into Zambia) had not slowed down or altered the course of the war, the Rhodesian Commander of Combined Operations, Lt. Gen. Peter Walls, argued publicly that a political solution was essential and that the white minority could not win the war.

As a result the Smith government concluded its 'internal settlement' with Bishop Abel Muzorewa, the leader of the 'moderate' United African National Congress (UANC) on 3 March 1978. The agreement had no effect on the fighting, however, which continued while efforts to persuade the guerrillas to accept a settlement and ceasefire failed. Three days after this settlement the regime found it had to impose a dusk-to-dawn curfew over a 70 km (43 mile) belt of white farming land to the north and east of Salisbury, so serious and close by then was guerrilla infiltration. In July of that year the guerrillas were fighting gun battles in the Salisbury townships, whites were killed in the Borrowdale suburb of Salisbury, there was fighting in the centre of Gwelo and the railway between Salisbury and Bulawayo was sabotaged. In August Smith had a meeting with Nkomo to work out a possible deal, but these talks were broken off in September after ZIPRA shot down an Air Rhodesia Viscount at Kariba, killing its 40 passengers. By then ZANU had become suspicious that ZAPU was not committing its forces to the fight, but holding them back in readiness for a later power struggle with ZANU. In February 1979 a second Viscount was shot down at Kariba and Salisbury airport was mortared. None the less, Smith went ahead with April elections for the so-called internal settlement. In May the Conservative Party under Mrs Thatcher won the elections in Britain, giving rise to hopes in Salisbury of a more friendly government in London.

The war had been escalating steadily for three years, and by the time the Commonwealth heads of government meeting assembled in Lusaka at the beginning of August 1979, ZANLA had created a number of liberated zones in the rural areas of Zimbabwe; Mugabe claimed that there were between 1.5 million and 2 million people (out of a total population of 7 million) living in the liberated areas. In the west of Rhodesia ZIPRA forces, trained by Cubans in Angola, relied upon their success as guerrillas rather than consciously pursuing a 'hearts and minds' programme to win the support of the local people.

Estimated costs and casualties

From 1966 onwards the Rhodesian army was organized on a counter-insurgency basis. The air force then numbered 1200 men with 45 planes and provided the regime with air superiority. By 1969 there were some 2700 South African troops in Rhodesia to assist the army, which then numbered 3500. By 1970/71 the military budget had reached an annual figure of $17.9 million.

As the war became more difficult, young white Rhodesian men attempted to evade military service. In 1974 the government announced that it was increasing the size of the army, and (white) school leavers were to be called up as soon as possible to do their military service. At the same time the government showed little understanding towards its black majority; they were brutalized by the security forces, which used a variety of repressive measures, including torture, to obtain information. The greatest strain experienced by the whites was the constant call-up of reservists. By 1974 the white intake for military service had been doubled, while anyone over 25 was liable to a month's military service a year. Even highly qualified whites were liable to find themselves serving with the security forces for one month out of every four. That year the government lost three planes and four white South African police were killed.

In April 1974 the London *Times* speculated that, although the war in Rhodesia was not yet like those in Palestine, Cyprus or Kenya, it would be before long. From the mid-1970s onwards, despite air control and superior firepower, the regime was clearly losing the war. The whites were outnumbered 25 to 1.

When the war ended the Rhodesian army had been expanded to 20,000, of whom 14,000 were white conscripts, and compulsory military service had been extended to all white males up to 60 years old, creating a loss of job skills and leading to mounting emigration. It also meant that the regime came increasingly to rely on the indiscriminate use of air attacks on the base areas of the guerrillas in Mozambique and Zambia. The government's two élite forces were the Rhodesia Light Infantry (RLI) and the Selous Scouts (1800 strong). In addition, the regime also had the paramilitary British South Africa Police (BSAP) of 6000, a further 35,000 (mainly white) police reservists and 6000 guards who controlled the protected villages. The government was obliged to recruit more and more blacks, which reinforced the realization that white power could not hold out on its own.

At the same time the guerrilla armies contained about 40,000 men and women (two-thirds in ZANLA and one-third in ZIPRA). Thus the government simply did not possess the necessary ratio of security forces to guerrillas in order to guarantee success. By 1977, for example, ZANLA was enrolling an estimated 1000 recruits a month. Between 1976 and 1978 about 3500 ZANLA guerrillas were killed, and yet their numbers in the east of the country had grown from 1200 to 8000.

Following the shooting down by ZIPRA of the Air Rhodesia Viscount on 3 September 1978, the Rhodesian forces in October mounted air raids on ZIPRA bases in Zambia, killing 1500.

Estimates of total war casualties vary. The official government figure was 30,000 dead, although other estimates suggested a figure of 45,000. Many bush deaths undoubtedly went unrecorded.

Results: immediate and longer term

Early in 1975 Britain's Labour Foreign Secretary, James Callaghan, visited South Africa to discuss a Rhodesia solution. This demonstrated Rhodesia's isolation: it was no longer seen as of strategic use to South Africa, and Britain simply wanted to rid itself of the political embarrassment which Rhodesia represented. The war had a devastating effect on the white farmers, and by April 1979 2000 white farms had been abandoned. ZANU, meanwhile, was expending much energy in its efforts to win over the people in the liberated areas.

The Commonwealth heads of government meeting for 1979 was held – by deliberate choice – in Lusaka, and Rhodesia headed the agenda. When the heads of government assembled it was generally feared that Britain's new Prime Minister, Margaret Thatcher, would press for an accommodation with Ian Smith. On 31 July, the day before the official opening of the meeting, the Nigerian government nationalized BP assets in Nigeria, a gesture calculated to warn Britain of other vulnerable assets if any deal with Smith was attempted. In the event the Commonwealth persuaded Britain to adopt a far more radical approach to the problem, and it was agreed to hold a conference of the protagonists at Lancaster House in London, beginning on 10 September. Both President Kaunda of Zambia and President Machel of Mozambique, whose countries had suffered a great deal from the war in Rhodesia, helped to persuade Robert Mugabe and ZANU to come to the conference table (since ZANU was winning the war anyway, its leaders were reluctant to take part in a conference which they thought would work against their interests). After three months of talks a ceasefire agreement was finally signed by ZANU, ZAPU and the Smith government on 21 December 1979. As a result Britain 'resumed control' in Rhodesia and supervised nationwide elections in March 1980. Mugabe's ZANU won 57 out of 80 African seats, Nkomo's ZAPU 20 seats and the UANC 3 seats, while 20 reserved seats were held by the Rhodesia Front. To many people's surprise, the 'Marxist' Mugabe emerged the absolute victor. Rhodesia became independent as Zimbabwe on 18 April 1980.

The new government faced immense tasks of post-war reconstruction and the need to meet the expectations of a population which had long been deprived of land in the interests of the white settlers. Despite the war, however, it possessed one of the best infrastructures in Africa and there were thousands of well-qualified Zimbabweans (many of whom had been obtaining qualifications overseas during the course of the war).

In the longer term the government had two further problems to face. The first was internal, the intermittent small-scale civil war in Ndebeleland from 1980 to 1986, before 'unity' was achieved between the ruling party, ZANU, and the opposition followers of Nkomo in ZAPU. The second problem concerned Zimbabwe's position at the strategic centre of the frontline states, and the confrontation with an increasingly embattled and dangerous South Africa, which more and more during the 1980s was prepared to make cross-border raids against its neighbours in its efforts to destabilize them.

THE MIDDLE EAST

CYPRUS: *ENOSIS*, INDEPENDENCE, COMMUNAL STRIFE

Origins

In 1878, at the Berlin Conference which brought an end to the Russo-Turkish War (1876–8), the Sultan of Turkey ceded the administration, though not the sovereignty, of Cyprus to Britain. In 1914 (when Britain and Turkey went to war) Britain annexed Cyprus. *Enosis* – union with Greece – had existed prior to 1878. In 1915 Britain offered Cyprus to Greece in return for a Greek attack on Serbia, but Greece declined the offer and it was then withdrawn.

In 1931 Greek Cypriots demonstrating for *enosis* burned down Government House in Nicosia, the capital; the British reaction was increased repression to maintain law and order. By 1949 Greek Cypriots – four-fifths of the population – were united in their demand for *enosis*. Then in 1950 Makarios III became Archbishop of Cyprus and the focus of Greek demands for *enosis*. Thereafter the *enosis* movement gathered momentum and led to increasing acts of terrorism. In parallel with the *enosis* struggle, communal differences between Greek and Turk became more pronounced, leading to Turkish demands for partition.

Intense Greek nationalism expressed itself in the demand for *enosis*, while also sparking off increasingly bitter communal strife with the Turkish minority. When finally, the British gave Cyprus independence in 1960, they achieved the ironical result, in the circumstances, of persuading the Greek Cypriots to abandon *enosis* and accept independence for the island instead. Subsequently Greek–Turkish animosities split the island in two, until the Turkish invasion of 1974 was to effect this literally by imposing partition (see Part V, pp. 427–431).

Outbreak and response

Growing agitation against British rule in Cyprus over the period 1950 to 1954 was encouraged by Athens Radio. In 1954 Archbishop Makarios persuaded the Greek government to raise the question of *enosis* at the United Nations, but the attempt failed to obtain sufficient support in the world body; clashes between the British and Greek Cypriots on the island followed. A new factor which exacerbated Cypriot nationalist demands for *enosis* and independence was introduced into the problem at the end of 1954 when Britain began to transfer its huge military base from the Canal Zone in Egypt to Cyprus.

In April 1955 EOKA (the Revolutionary Organization of Cypriot Struggle) launched a campaign of sabotage and terror against the British with a series of explosions in Nicosia. The EOKA oath, administered to its followers, was purely nationalist: 'I swear by the Holy Trinity to work with all my power for the liberation of Cyprus from the British yoke, sacrificing even my life.' Although it was not apparent at the time, this marked the beginning of four years of guerrilla war. The leader of EOKA, George Grivas, signed himself as Dighenis.

Greeks, Turks and Britons were all to be victims of the war. The economy was soon in deep trouble and the British administration declared a state of emergency. Large numbers of British troops were deployed throughout the island to safeguard installations and then to pursue EOKA guerrillas in the Kyrenia and Troodos mountains. On 2 August 1955 fierce rioting in Nicosia signalled a further escalation of the war.

Course of the struggle

During the first half of 1955, while attempting to negotiate terms for Cyprus to achieve internal self-government, Britain also built up its military strength on the island, though this was more the result of closing the Suez Canal base than as a response to the coming crisis. In September 1955 members of EOKA burnt the British Institute in Nicosia. Then on 25 September a new Governor, Field Marshal Sir John Harding, was appointed to replace Sir Robert Armitage, making it clear that London regarded a military approach as necessary to combat EOKA terrorism. Following Harding's arrival in Cyprus (3 October 1955), yet more troops arrived and forces were spread all over the island. They were needed to boost the police, who by then had been infiltrated by EOKA, were subject to divided loyalties over *enosis* and, in consequence, suffered from low morale. The troops were given training in riot control. On 27 October 1955 the first British soldier was killed in Cyprus, and on 26 November Harding declared a state of emergency.

EOKA tactics were ambushes and bombs, and the killing of soldiers became a daily occurrence. Street shooting of soldiers, the police or uncooperative Cypriots were the usual form of attack. The security forces conducted anti-EOKA searches of selected houses, streets and whole villages; curfews were imposed, while large numbers of troops carried out swoops. On 8 December 1955, for example, the army carried out an island-wide search of monasteries.

More troops arrived on the island at the beginning of 1956, by which time a regular pattern of terrorist activity had emerged. Most of the EOKA terrorists were concentrated in the rugged Troodos mountains, but nationalist fervour meant that schoolchildren often defied the authorities and had to be dispersed by police or troops using anti-riot tactics. During 1956 the Radcliffe Report recommended self-government for Cyprus.

On 9 March 1956 Archbishop Makarios was arrested for complicity with EOKA and deported to the Seychelles. During the following three months killings of members of the security forces averaged about two a week. In Nicosia Ledra Street became known as 'Murder Mile'; on 10 March the tenth victim of EOKA was shot dead on it. On 18 March (a Sunday) a group of EOKA entered a Greek Orthodox Church during a service and killed a chorister. Two days later a bomb was found in the governor's bed, leading to the dismissal of all Greeks then working in Government House. Also at this time EOKA attacks on Turks increased, widening the nature of the conflict from a nationalist, anti-British one into a communal anti-Turkish one as well. More British troops were drafted into the island.

In June 1956 a huge operation was mounted to capture Grivas, the elusive EOKA leader, who by then had achieved an international reputation for his ruthless toughness. During the course of this operation EOKA started a fire in the dry bush of the mountains, trapping and killing 21 British officers and men. Although Grivas evaded capture, the operation did lead to the capture or elimination of a substantial number of EOKA activists and considerably weakened the organization as a result. The Suez Canal crisis of July 1956 led to the withdrawal of British troops at a time when their full deployment all over the island was apparently helping Harding get on top of the rebellion. In mid-August Grivas ordered a suspension of hostilities, but when his move produced no matching concessions from the British, EOKA resumed hostilities later in the year. Then, following the Suez ceasefire and subsequent withdrawal of British forces from the Canal at the end of 1956, more troops came back to Cyprus.

At the beginning of 1957 the British mounted a new campaign against the EOKA guerrillas in the Troodos mountains in which one of Grivas's principal lieutenants, Markos Drakos, was ambushed and killed. By then a number of hard-core EOKA were being caught, partly as a result of the increasing use of agents and the Special Branch. During February and March 1957 a major campaign continued against the mountain guerrillas, and by the end of February, as Grivas said in his memoirs, 'Harding had rounded up the majority of our guerrilla bands in the mountains.'

The United Nations now called for a peaceful solution to the Cyprus rebellion. On 14 March Grivas issued a statement to say he would suspend hostilities if Makarios were released. Two weeks later Britain responded by releasing Makarios, who was free to go anywhere he liked except to Cyprus. He took up residence in Athens. There was jubilation in Cyprus at the news of Makarios's release. Grivas turned down a British offer of safe conduct to Greece. More important, the Greek government now made it plain that it considered the struggle for *enosis* to be at an end and that the way was clear for an independent Cyprus.

London, meanwhile, had decided on a politcal rather than a military solution, and Field Marshal Sir John Harding was replaced as Governor by Sir Hugh Foot in November 1957. These clear signals that both sides wanted a political solution (including the more amenable attitude to come out of Athens) frightened the Turks, who believed that Britain was about to sell out their interests on the island to the Greeks. As a result there was Turkish rioting in Nicosia in January 1958, leading to 6 deaths, 50 injured and much damage to property.

But these political moves gave rise to premature expectations of peace. In May 1958 another big search for Grivas was mounted on the island. Then on 7 June Nicosia suffered from a huge fire started by Turkish Cypriots. This sparked off a period of bitter Greek–Turkish riots which lasted for the next two months; by the end of July 56 Greeks and 53 Turks had been killed. Brutal incidents took place on both sides, and after the death of two Greeks in the village of Avgorou accusations of murder were levelled at the security forces. In a huge military sweep mounted on 21 July some 1200 Greeks and 50 Turks were arrested and sub-sequently detained.

Britain's Prime Minister, Harold Macmillan, then appealed for an end to the violence. On 4 August Grivas suspended EOKA operations against the British, and the Turks said they would do the same. In Cyprus on 12 August Macmillan announced new British peace proposals, but while these satisfied the Turks they were not acceptable to the Greeks and EOKA launched a new campaign of blowing up vehicles. Athens Radio stepped up its anti-British propaganda, while the British army now resorted to a number of ruses to trap members of EOKA, with considerable success. But despite this new eruption of violence in mid-1958, a political solution now seemed possible.

Estimated costs and casualties

Like similar guerrilla wars in Algeria and Palestine, that in Cyprus led to much heartlessness and brutality. One notorious incident was the shooting in the back of the wives of two British sergeants (one fatally). Grivas denied responsibility for the incident, but it produced a brutal reaction by troops of the 29th Field Regiment and the Ulsters when they turned out all Greek males in the area of Nicosia they were searching: many were badly beaten. The last major offensive by EOKA in October 1958 caused enormous damage as mines, bombs and arson were employed. Two Canberra bombers stationed on the island were wrecked (other aircraft were also damaged). A bomb planted in a NAAFI canteen killed two airmen and wounded seven others, leading to the dismissal of 3000 Cypriots then employed by the British services.

Grivas claimed he had brought an army of 20,000 into Cyprus (from Greece), but in fighting terms his frontline EOKA forces consisted of fewer than 300 fighters sharing 100 guns and backed by 750 villagers armed with shotguns. Under Field Marshal Harding the security forces consisted of 5000 police and 25,000 troops, but it has to be remembered that most of these troops would have been in Cyprus anyway, as a result of transferring the Suez base to the island at the end of 1954, although their presence on the island ensured that the Governor had massive military strength at his disposal.

At the height of the rebellion in 1956 EOKA accounted for 416 incidents in a single month. The British virtually blockaded Cyprus – by sea and air – in the hope of containing Grivas. By the end of the hostilities official British military casualties stood at 7 officers and 72 other ranks dead and 28 officers and 386 other ranks wounded. Greek fatalities came to 218.

Results: immediate and longer term

As the struggle got under way, it aroused the fears of the Turkish minority that an *enosis* solution would swamp their interests; as a result they organized to resist *enosis* and so contributed to the alternative of an independent Cyprus with special safeguards in the constitution for the Turkish minority. At the end of 1958 the Secretary-General of NATO, Paul-Henri Spaak, launched a peace initiative which resulted in a Paris meeting between representatives of Britain, Greece and Turkey at which Britain agreed to independence for Cyprus in return for two military base facilities. Subsequently (December 1958), Grivas agreed to a ceasefire, while Sir Hugh Foot released 350 prisoners and commuted 8 death sentences. Further negotiations at Zurich led to an agreement in February 1959 (later signed in London) between Britain, Greece and Turkey: Cyprus was to become a republic in the Commonwealth with special constitutional safeguards for the Turkish minority (approximately 18 per cent), while Britain was to retain sovereignty over two military base areas.

The reaction in Cyprus was one of relief. On 1 March 1959 Archbishop Makarios was allowed to return to the island; Grivas, on the other hand, was given safe conduct and flew out to Athens, a hero. EOKA, meanwhile, had handed in its arms and disbanded itself.

Cyprus became independent on 16 August 1960, with Makarios as its first President. A Turkish Cypriot automatically held the post of Vice-President, the first to do so – Kutchuk – being the leader of the Turkish community. The 1960 Constitution reserved to the Turkish Cypriots 30 per cent of jobs in the civil service and 40 per cent of army posts, as well as providing them with certain well-defined powers of veto over important political decisions. Yet despite independence, violence as well as agitation for *enosis* were to continue; Greek resentment at the conditions in the constitution which safeguarded the Turkish minority soon manifested itself to produce a crisis in 1963 when government was brought to a standstill and communal violence between Greeks and Turks erupted once more on the island, forcing the Turks to withdraw into all-Turkish enclaves. Thereafter communal strife between Greek and Turk steadily escalated to produce the conditions which led to the Turkish invasion of 1974 (see Part V, pp. 427–431).

EOKA, whose fighting guerrillas never amounted to more than a few hundred, must be seen as one of the most successful terrorist organizations in the post-war world. It was always faced by a massive British military presence, yet still ensured earlier independence for Cyprus than otherwise would have been the case. But it did not achieve its original objective of *enosis*.

THE KURDS: AN ENDLESS WAR

Origins

The Kurds are found in north-west Iran, northern Iraq and eastern Turkey, with small enclaves in Russian Armenia and Syria. They have inhabited this region since ancient times. In Iran they have their own province of Kurdistan, but for many years the Kurds of all five countries have argued – and fought – for an independent state of Kurdistan. A mountain people (reputed to be the descendants of the Medes), they use an Indo-European language related to Persian, while a majority of them are Sunni Muslims. They possess all the attributes of a single race or ethnic group, and this reinforces their sense of nationalism. Although principally dependent upon an agricultural–pastoral economy, those in Iraq spread southwards to the region of the Kirkuk oilfields.

In 1987 there were approximately 14 million Kurds (though some estimates suggested 20 million) divided between Iraq, Iran and Turkey, but the war between Iran and Iraq and the consequent Kurdish casualties as well as refugee movements mean that figures should be treated with caution. At the beginning of the 1960s, when the Kurdish question began to attract international attention, there were 1

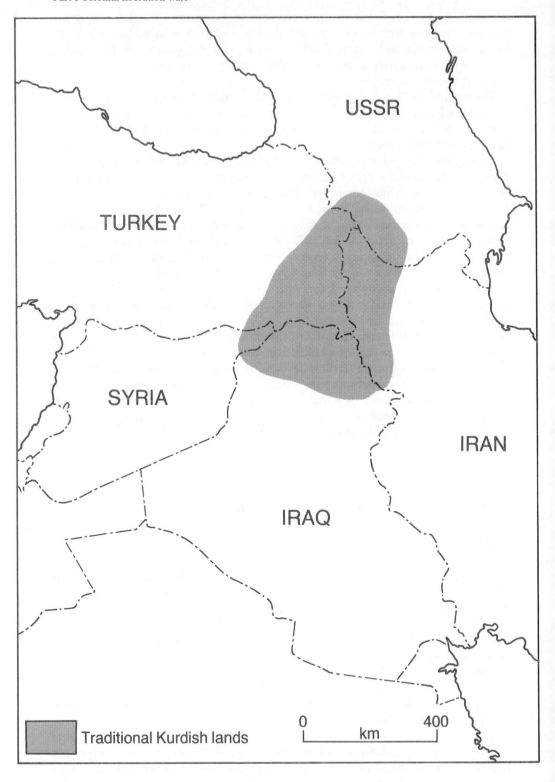

USSR

TURKEY

SYRIA

IRAN

IRAQ

0   400
km

Traditional Kurdish lands

million in Iraq, 1.2 million in Iran, 2 million in Turkey as well as small minorities in Syria and the USSR, making a total of 4.75 million Kurds altogether.

In modern times Kurdish nationalism first appeared in Ottoman Turkey where the first Kurdish newspaper was published in 1897; the first Kurdish political club was formed in Constantinople in 1909. The 1920 Treaty of Sèvres provided for the creation of a Kurdish state, but this was reversed by the 1923 Treaty of Lausanne, which recognized the revival of Turkish influence. Since that time there have been periodic Kurdish uprisings, particularly in Iraq (1922–3, 1931–2, 1944–5).

At the end of the Second World War a Kurdish republic was established with Soviet support at Mahabad in north-western Iran (1944–5), but this collapsed in 1946 when the Tehran government re-established control. The Kurds form the largest minority group in Turkey and their nationalism has been a source of periodic annoyance to Ankara, although they have been far more integrated in Turkey than in Iraq. The nationalism of the Kurds has been fed, at least in part, by the post-1945 nationalisms to be found in the region as a whole and especially in Iran and Iraq.

Outbreak and response

Since 1945 the Kurdish revolt against integration into the larger states of the region has been centred on Iraq, although the first major challenge came with the establishment of the independent Kurdistan Republic in north-western Iran, which was sponsored by the USSR. On 22 January 1946 Zaki Mohammed was elected President of this mini-state, but later in the year the Iranians re-occupied the region (which had been occupied by Soviet troops during the war) and Zaki Mohammed was arrested, tried and then hanged in March 1947.

In Iraq, where the Kurds account for between 10 and 20 per cent of the population, the Kurdish problem has been a source of instability for at least 30 years. When the Kurdish leader, Mustafa Barzani, returned home from exile in the USSR at the end of the 1950s, he effectively sparked off a decade of continual rebellion against Baghdad. The northern (Kurdish) region of Iraq – apart from its strategic significance – also includes the Kirkuk oilfields, an economic fact that greatly exacerbates the nationalist question. Roughly speaking, the Kurds have been either at war with the central government in Baghdad or maintaining an uneasy truce ever since 1958.

Course of the struggle

On a number of occasions since 1945 the Baghdad government has tried to work out a settlement with the Kurds, but it has often been blocked in its efforts by hardline nationalists – army officers and civil servants – so that each failure has contributed to deepening suspicions on both sides. The Iraqis fear that the Kurds wish to secede and take the northern oil wealth with them, and the Kurds argue that Baghdad is trying to deprive them of their fair share of that wealth.

With the fall of the monarchy in 1958 the Kurds initially collaborated with the central government, although the two sides soon fell out and armed clashes followed. In 1961 the Kurds launched an outright military offensive against the Baghdad government and then fielded an estimated 20,000 Pesh Merga (guerrillas). Mustafa Barzani, who had returned from exile in the USSR in 1958, now proclaimed an independent Kurdish state (comprising the northern Kurdish areas of Iraq). By September 1961 the rebels controlled a stretch of territory of some 250 miles along the Iraq borders with Iran and Turkey. The Kurdish guerrilla tactics continued to yield gains through 1962 and 1963, and by December of the latter year their forces had reached the area of Khanaquin, which controls the main road to Iran; government troops in the north were mainly confined to the towns.

As a result of these Kurdish successes, the government agreed to a ceasefire in February 1964: new provisions were added to the constitution which recognized certain Kurdish claims. The Kurds refused to lay down their arms, however, and before long the war had been resumed, continuing to 1966. Fighting during 1965, for example, led to border violations with Iran which fuelled Iran–Iraq enmities. The Aref government made another attempt to end the war in 1965, but without success; as a result of constant blocking of their demands, the Kurds had lost faith in the central government. In June 1966 the new Prime Minister, Dr Bazzaz, succeeded in ending the war when he produced a 12-point plan that recognized Kurdish nationalism and provided for a wide degree of regional autonomy. Bazzaz was to be removed from power before his plan could be fully implemented, and the war was resumed. None the less, in 1967 President Aref visited the Kurdish areas and stated his readiness to implement the Bazzaz proposals. During 1968 the Kurds split between the followers of Barzani, the veteran nationalist, and supporters of Jalal Talabini who was prepared to co-operate with the central government. One of the biggest obstacles to any settlement was how to determine what were Kurdish majority areas; the Kurds accused the government of deliberately encouraging non-Kurds to migrate into Kurdish areas. Even so, in 1969 the government of President al-Bakr did reach a settlement – this time a 15-point agreement (incorporating the Bazzaz proposals of 1966) – and the fighting was brought to an end.

The plan included an amnesty for all insurgents, and gave Kurdish equal status with Arabic in the Kurdish majority areas, which were to be administered by Kurds. The national government was to include a Kurdish Vice-President. This 1969 settlement came into effect in March 1970, and the fighting was brought to an end. Up to 1970 the Kurdish war had cost Iraq huge sums of money and delayed many essential developments. In October 1970 the state of emergency which had operated since 1958 was ended, as was 13 years of mail censorship, and detainees were released.

Like many nationalist movements the Kurds were plagued by breakaway groups, although in February 1971 the two wings of the Kurds – the Kurdish Revolutionary Party and the Kurdish Democratic Party (Barzani) – merged. However, unrest among the Kurds increased because of the non-implementation of the 1970 agreement. In September of 1971 the Kurds demanded representation on the Revolutionary Command Council, which was refused, and during 1972 clashes between the Kurds and central government forces occurred and the KDP talked of renewing the war. Baghdad's decision to nationalize the Iraq Petroleum Company in 1972 increased Kurdish tensions since it was seen as a move to tighten the central government grip on the oil. The Kurds also complained that the census promised in 1970 had not been held (its significance would be in determining Kurdish majority areas).

Despite these problems the 1970 settlement was the nearest that had so far been achieved to a workable solution, but by 1974 it was clear that the agreement was not going to work. In March of that year, when Saddam Hussein (then the Vice-President) made a formal offer of autonomy to the Kurds, Barzani rejected it although a minority of Kurds were prepared to accept it. Fighting was resumed: the government mounted a major military operation against the Kurds, committing 120,000 troops to the campaign, and about 130,000 Kurds fled to become refugees in Iran. Kurdish losses and privations during the winter of 1974–5 were very great, and their forces were largely confined to an area along the Iranian border.

The Pesh Merga could only fight effectively as long as the border with Iran remained open so that they could obtain assistance through Iran, but in 1975 this support was finally denied to them. At the OPEC meeting held at Algiers in March 1975 a reconciliation was effected between the Shah of Iran and Iraq's strongman, Vice-President Saddam Hussein: as a result Iran agreed to close the border and cut off further aid to the Kurds. Barzani was driven into exile (he died in the USA in 1979), Kurdish resistance collapsed and the war came to an end – but, once again, only for the time being. Barzani's sons took over the leadership of the Kurds and before long had reverted to guerrilla warfare.

In parallel with events in Iraq the Kurds of north-west Iran had also posed similar problems for Tehran. The Kurdish Democratic Party of Iran had been founded in 1945 at the time of the ill-fated and short-lived Kurdistan. Thereafter it had been forced underground, but during the 1950s had established links with the KDP of Iraq. In 1965 a radical group broke away from the KDP to form a Revolutionary Tendency which began a guerrilla campaign against the Shah in 1967, although they were soon destroyed as a cohesive force.

The Iranian government did not see the Kurdish movement as a threat in the same way that the government in Baghdad did, and in consequence was prepared to encourage the Iraqi Kurds to rebel against the Iraqi government throughout the 1960s. In 1979 the new government in Tehran accorded limited autonomy to the Kurds, but it opposed the creation of an Islamic state and another rebellion erupted. This was put down with hundreds of deaths in September 1979 when government troops retook Mahabad and an amnesty was offered to KDP members. But resistance continued and during the 1980s the Kurds took advantage of the Iran–Iraq war to pursue their claims to autonomy or independence.

Estimated costs and casualties

The costs in lives, deprivation and military activity over the period to 1979 were enormous. In the early 1960s the Pesh Merga (then at their most effective) probably numbered about 20,000; by the 1970s this figure had increased to perhaps 50,000, but by then they had to face far greater Iraqi forces, with 120,000 or more troops committed against them in 1974. When the 1960s phase of the war was concluded in 1970 it had cost Iraq many millions in money as well as delaying development, while a state of emergency had been in force for 13 years.

But the later phase of the Kurdish struggle, which might be said to have opened in 1979, was largely overshadowed by the far greater tragedy of the Iran–Iraq war of 1979–88 (see Part III, pp. 227–241).

The ongoing regional struggle

The brutal campaign launched against the Iraqi Kurds by the Baghdad government immediately the hostilities with Iran had been concluded might be seen as one result of years of Kurdish resistance and intransigence; or, as simply one more battle in a war that is unlikely to end until the Kurds obtain their independence or are annihilated. From 1969 to the Iran–Iraq agreement of 1975, for example, there was growing evidence of Iranian support for the Iraqi Kurds in their opposition to a settlement with Baghdad, and the truth of Iraqi accusations became clear once the border had been closed. Yet despite losing Iranian backing, the Kurds of Iraq were again mounting guerrilla warfare against the Iraqi government in 1976, although for the time being it did appear that Baghdad was on top of the situation. That year a new Kurdish organization – the National Union of Kurdistan – was set up in Damascus, claiming that the KDP of Iraq had become discredited. In 1977 the central government carried out a substantial reconstruction programme in the Kurdish areas, and some 40,000 Kurds were allowed to return to the north from the south where they had been temporarily settled.

But once the Iran–Iraq war had got under way the Kurds again pushed for autonomy, thus presenting Baghdad with a additional strain on resources when it was fully stretched fighting a major war. In December 1983 President Saddam Hussein held talks with the more moderate Kurds under Jellal Talibani and the Patriotic Union of Kurdistan (PUK), but excluding the KDP. The talks were broken off in 1984, but resumed later when Saddam proposed to allow Kurdish control of Kirkuk and to allot a fixed share of oil resources (between 20 and 30 per cent) to the Kurds. However, these negotiations also broke down and fighting was resumed in 1985.

Across the border in Iran the Kurds had been in revolt more or less constantly since the fall of the Shah in 1979. During 1986 the leader of the Iranian Kurds, Dr Abdorrahman Qassemlou, claimed that most of the Iranians in about 3000 military bases and outposts situated throughout Kurdistan did not wish to pursue the war against his 10,000 guerrillas. He also claimed that his forces were then holding down 200,000 Iranian troops and that Iraq, while attempting to quell its own Kurds, was providing the Iranian Kurds with assistance.

By 1987 the Kurds in eastern Turkey were also waging guerrilla warfare against their government, attacking villages along the border region with Iraq. These were members of the Kurdish Workers' Party (PKK), a Communist organization also fighting for an independent Kurdistan to include the Kurds of Iran, Iraq and Turkey. The PKK had established bases across the border in Iraq. From 1984 to early 1987 some 600 people had been killed in encounters with the PKK in eastern Turkey: 260 insurgents, 146 soldiers or policemen and 184 civilians. The PKK, under Abdullah Ocalan, came into existance in the early 1980s when it began ambushing Turkish soldiers in remote areas of eastern Turkey as well as attacking villagers who collaborated with the army. It has bases in Iraq, Syria and Lebanon. Early in March 1987 the Turkish airforce made strikes against PKK bases in Iraq, killing about 100 people in three camps. The air raid, the third Turkish incursion into Iraq since 1983, was carried out by agreement with the Iraqi government: 30 planes were employed in the raid and several thousand Turkish troops carried out an extensive operation against the PKK in eastern Turkey. (In 1984 Iraq and Turkey entered into an agreement which allows the forces of either country the right of 'hot pursuit' across their borders.) In June another raid by Kurds left 30 dead in the village of Pinarcik, but this time the insurgents had come across the border from Syria rather than Iraq. Even so, only a small number of Turkish Kurds appeared to be in sympathy with the separatist insurgents. Turkey has an estimated 8 million Kurds, and frequent political pronouncements as well as persecution have made plain the total opposition of government to any form of Kurdish autonomy.

Also in 1987 Iranian-armed Kurds attacked Iraqi forces and were estimated to be pinning down up to 35,000 Iraqi troops urgently needed to fight on the main front against Iran. In retaliation Iraqi forces launched attacks on Kurdish towns and villages, killing hundreds of civilians. By this stage in the Gulf War Iranian strategy was to bolster the Kurds who were operating behind the Iraqi lines.

In Iraq by 1987 the two Kurdish factions – the PUK under Jalal Talabini and the KDP under Barzani's son, Massoud Barzani – had formed a new alliance after an 11-year rift, and were now backed by Iran. The Iranian Kurds under Gassemlou were receiving comparable Iraqi support. Thus, towards the end of the Gulf War, each group of Kurds was being supported by the opposing government, which meanwhile was oppressing its own Kurds. By this time the joint forces of the PUK and the KDP in Iraq came to 25,000 guerrillas, using Soviet anti-aircraft missiles and US artillery and mortars supplied by Iran, Libya and Syria, and they controlled about 10,000 square miles in northern Iraq. In October 1986 some 2500 Kurds attacked Kirkuk, although it was heavily defended by Iraqi troops. In April 1987 the PUK accused the Iraqi army of using chemical weapons against villages in northern Iraq. And by June of that year heavy fighting had spilled over into the Kurdish areas of north Iraq.

In February 1988 the Kurds claimed a spectacular victory against the Iraqi army at Deeralok in northern Iraq when they killed or wounded 600, took a similar number prisoner and extended the area under their control. Yet their very success was likely to ensure the bitter enmity of the Baghdad government once the Gulf War came to an end, and it was apparent at the beginning of 1988 that the war was approaching some sort of climax. Though the Kurds had succeeded in harrying the Iraqis and tying down large numbers of their troops, they never inflicted permanent damage by taking Kirkuk or cutting the main roads. In their turn the Iraqis mounted savage attacks on the Kurds, using chemical weapons, deporting large numbers of Kurds to the south and employing terrorist tactics against the civilian populations. In March 1988, for example, Iran claimed that Iraq had killed 5000 of its Kurds in poison gas attacks, and by the end of that month there existed a growing body of evidence to substantiate such claims.

By mid-1988, as soon as the Gulf War came precariously to an end, the Iraqis – predictably – turned their full forces against their Kurdish minority of dissidents (numbering in 1988 perhaps 2.6 million). Planes and troops were moved to the north and villages were bombed, sometimes with chemical weapons (gases). The USA and Britain both claimed to have evidence of this chemical warfare. More than 100,000 Kurds fled across the border into Turkey.

As the Kurds discovered at the end of the Gulf War, they are regarded in all the countries where they live as at best a nuisance and at worst enemies to be crushed.

The savagery of the Iraqi attack on the Kurds in 1988 has to be seen in the aftermath of the Gulf War, for often when the Iraqis were most stretched the Kurds inflicted most damage on them. In Iran, where they represent a far smaller minority in relation to the total population, they are none the less regarded with deep suspicion by the central government. In Turkey they are treated as Turks and have not even been considered for potential autonomy as they were in Iraq during the 1960s and 1970s. In the USSR they are one more minority likely to cause problems. In Syria they are seen as a potential means of causing embarrassment to that country's neighbours – a group to be used but not integrated. And it was an instructive sign of government solidarity between those countries with Kurdish minorities that, despite many claims that gas and chemicals had been used, the Turkish authorities as well as the Iraqis refused to allow UN officials to examine Kurdish refugees for evidence of gas poisoning.

In October 1988, however, Syria agreed to provide both military and financial aid to Iraqi Kurds in the face of claims of continuing chemical attacks by the Iraqi army, although this was more a sign of traditional Iraq–Syria enmity at work than any fundamental Syrian commitment to the Kurds. At the same time Iraq announced an amnesty for the Kurds and small numbers of refugees in Turkey elected to return home, although far more opted to be sent to Iran. And yet, in the second week of October 1988, Kurdish guerrillas mounted an attack on Iraqi army positions to the south of Kirkuk to inflict heavy losses on the government troops. Turkey, meanwhile, managed to send 20,000 Iraqi Kurdish refugees to Iran just as the Iranian government announced it was not prepared to provide further sanctuary for refugees and closed its border. By then Tehran claimed it was housing (poorly) 32,000 refugees, a figure that was later increased to 100,000. The Turks claimed that they had received 50,000 refugees during August, although other estimates suggested very much higher figures. In both Iran and Turkey the refugees were housed in tent camps as the bitter winter set in, and their conditions were generally appalling. The Turkish authorities, though denying any moves to expel the refugees, clearly wanted to get rid of them as quickly as possible. Plenty of animosity exists between Iraqi and Iranian Kurds despite their shared desire to see an independent Kurdistan. The US Congress discussed possible sanctions against Iraq for its use of chemical weapons, but what emerged was a bill so weak that, though it condemned Iraq, it did little else.

During mid-October, despite all the publicity about chemical weapons and refugees in Turkey and Iran, the Iraqi army again used chemical weapons in attacks on Kurdish villages in the Kirkuk region (11 and 14 October). And in November thousands of Kurds attempting to flee from Iraq into Turkey (an estimated 34,000) were rounded up by the Iraqi army and held in camps. What became increasingly clear in November 1988 was that Turkey was co-operating with Iraq to control the Kurdish guerrillas. This was in line with the 1984 agreement between the two countries which allows their respective troops to cross the borders in hot pursuit. The Kurds, once more, were being crushed from two sides at once.

By the beginning of 1990 the Kurds were worse off than at any time in the preceding quarter of a century. With the Gulf War over, Iraq showed every determination to crush Kurdish resistance; Turkey was demonstrating minimum sympathy for the refugees and co-operating with Iraq, clearly determined that its own Kurds should not be given any encouragement to adopt secessionist tactics (in April 1990, for example, the Turkish government warned its own Kurdish community that it would crush any insurgency); and Iran, recovering from a devastating war, seemed as unlikely as its two neighbours to show much sympathy for any further attempts at Kurdish separatism. In April 1989 the Iraqi government had embarked on a massive programme to relocate Kurds away from their mountain homelands, and despite some resistance this went ahead. In the immediate aftermath of the war between Iraq and the (United Nations) Allies in March 1991, the Kurds took part in the widespread rebellion against Saddam Hussein. There would appear to be no prospect for an independent Kurdistan, at least during the balance of the present century.

OMAN: BRITISH TRUCIAL OBLIGATIONS

Origins

During the eighteenth century Muscat and Oman became a substantial sea power in the Indian Ocean; in the nineteenth century it extended its control to Zanzibar and Mombasa in East Africa and to parts of southern Persia in the Gulf. By the 1860s, however, its power was on the wane. Already, in 1798, the Sultan had entered into a treaty of protection with Britain and, though Muscat and Oman (later referred to simply as Oman) was never a British colony, it did become one of the peripheral states of empire with British advisers and soldiers 'assisting' the Sultan.

Sultan Said ibn Taimur came to power in 1932 and turned out to be perhaps the most reactionary figure throughout the Arab world, keeping his country completely undeveloped. When his son had completed his education in England, for example, the Sultan kept him under house restraint, fearful that he might encourage reforms.

It was under this Sultan's rule, in 1954, that the sheiks elected Ghalib ibn Ali as Imam (in the past there had been a separation of powers between Sultan and Imam) and progressives rallied to the Imam in opposition to the reactionary Sultan. The discovery of oil as well as Saudi Arabian ambitions and pressures for modernization each contributed to a series of insurgencies which troubled Oman from the mid-1950s until the early 1980s. During the 1950s the British were to be directly involved in two small military campaigns: ejecting Saudi forces from the Buraimi Oasis; and putting down the revolt of the Imam Ghalib who sought self-rule for the interior of Oman.

Outbreak and response

The frontier between the 'Empty Quarter' of southern Saudi Arabia and its two south-eastern neighbours in the peninsula – the United Arab Emirates and Oman – was ill-defined, although the Buraimi Oasis, which really consists of a series of adjoining oases, was clearly not part of Saudi Arabia. None the less, in 1952 King Saud sent a military column across the Empty Quarter to claim the Buraimi Oasis, of which part was then claimed by the Sheik of Abu Dhabi and part by the Sultan of Oman. Both rulers had protection treaties with Britain.

The Trucial Oman Levies had been formed in 1951 under British officers, although a mutiny in 1953 meant they had to be reconstituted. By 1955, however, there were four reasonably well-trained squadrons. These were used that year to regain control of the Buraimi Oasis and to expel the Saudis. In October 1955 the Levies were sent to the Oasis where they rounded up the Saudi police contingent without resistance, but they did have to fight a one-day battle through a village against the Saudi forces in which seven Saudis and two Levies were killed.

More important for the future was the revolt of the Imam Ghalib in 1955; he was based on Nizwa in the western part of Oman. His followers were forced out of Ibri and the Imam fled. The revolt was swiftly put down by the Sultan's forces: Ghalib was 'retired' to his village, and the Sultan came to Nizwa in triumph. Following these two operations (against the Saudi occupation of the Buraimi Oasis and the revolt of the Imam), the tribal leaders of Oman swore fresh allegiance to the Sultan. The Imam's brother, Talib, who had also revolted, fled to Saudi Arabia, while other dissidents made their way to Egypt whence in 1956 they mounted a propaganda campaign against the Sultan and his 'colonial' British supporters.

Course of the struggle

In 1957 Talib returned to central Oman with a small group of followers – the Oman Liberation Army – who had been recruited and trained in Saudi Arabia with financial backing from Egypt, and the rebellion of 1955 was renewed. Ghalib, supported by his brother and Sheik Suleiman, took command of the revolt, and their forces retook Nizwa and a number of villages along the Hajar mountain range about 50 miles inland from the sea. They were well equipped with arms and ammunition (Russian and American), including machine guns, mortars and anti-tank mines.

This time the Sultan formally invoked his treaty of protection with Britain and requested military assistance. As a result a few hundred British troops as well as air support were provided to assist the Sultan's forces in putting down the rebellion. Troops were sent from Kenya, Aden and Bahrain, and a British brigadier, J. A. R. Robertson, was put in command of the renamed Trucial Oman Scouts and the Cameronians. The government had control of two airfields at Ibri and Fahud (where oil had recently been discovered – no doubt the real reason for such a prompt British response), and Venom aircraft were used to attack the rebel strongholds at Nizwa, Tanuf and Izki. Then on 6 August 1957 the troops advanced on Nizwa. British forces suffered mainly from the intense heat. On 10 August after some resistance, the column entered Nizwa (one Scout was killed, four were injured). The rebels withdrew to Jebel Akhdev, a high fertile massif generally thought to be impregnable.

There did not appear to be much ground support for the revolt, and the rebel forces were soon reduced to a few guerrilla bands. However, guerrilla activity continued into 1959, mainly confined to the massif of Jebel Akhdev. It was not British policy to prolong the fighting – a UN inquiry was under way – so the British forces were withdrawn to Muscat, the airstrips were stocked up with military supplies, some forts and rebel property were destroyed and most of the troops then left the territory except for a troop of Hussars and two squadrons of Scouts; the armoured cars were used to escort oil convoys. These were increasingly hampered by mines and snipers, so in November 1957 another effort was made to take the jebel using both British and Omani forces, but again without success.

In January 1958, therefore, Britain began once more to build up its forces in Oman. Twenty-three British officers and eight Royal Marine sergeants were seconded to the Sultan's army, while the RAF sent five aircraft and pilots. The existing field force of about 450 men was not considered strong enough, so more British troops were requested; these, when they came, included 80 crack Special Armed Service (SAS) from Malaya. The force was built up through 1958, and then in January 1959 an assault was carried out on Jebel Akhdev using 1100 troops, of whom 250 were British. The operation was successful and the Sultan was once more restored to complete control.

Estimated costs and casualties

Apart from a number of British officers directly employed by the Sultan, Britain sent troops into the country from other Gulf states where they were then stationed (Aden and Bahrain) as well as from Kenya where the Mau Mau emergency was in progress. It also seconded five fighter aircraft and pilots to Oman in 1958, while at the height of the January 1959 campaign about 250 British troops were involved out of a total of 1100 men, the balance of whom were the Sultan's (British-officered) forces. Britain's costs would be treated as part of its military presence in the Gulf. The Sultan employed a substantial part of his entire income on military expenditure; the real cost could be equated with the fact that the Sultan positively opposed any development in his state, then one of the most backward in the world, so rebellion (however poorly managed) represented the only form of opposition that his regime permitted.

Results: immediate and longer term

Although the rebellion collapsed after the January 1959 military exercise, a number of Arab countries raised the question of Oman at the United Nations during 1960 and 1961. They contended that Britain with its military presence in Oman was responsible for aggression against 'the independence, sovereignty, and territorial integrity of the Imamate of Oman'. The essence of the claim was that the Imamate of Oman should be treated as a state separate from the Trucial state of Oman with which Britain had special links. It was a difficult argument to sustain and a UN Commission of Inquiry did not accept that the Sultan was guilty of oppression. At stake in real terms were two principles: the progressive Arab states wanted to force Oman into the twentieth century; and they wanted to bring an end to the military presence in Oman of Britain, which was seen to be in support of one of the most reactionary regimes in the world. Later, in 1965, the Arab states persuaded the United Nations to adopt a resolution which stated that the colonial presence of the British in Oman was preventing the people from exercising self-determination, and which called for an end to the British presence.

ADEN: OUTPOST OF EMPIRE

Origins

In 1839 Britain took Aden (with a force from Bombay) for use as an outpost on the route to its Indian Empire. Britain's involvement in Aden and later the hinterland was always dictated by reasons of strategy, and almost no development was initiated during its tenure of the territory. The opening of the Suez Canal in 1869 increased the importance of Aden, and from that time onwards Britain gradually extended its influence into the interior by concluding treaties of protection with the sheiks. In the Western Protectorate this process continued through to 1954. In the more remote Eastern Protectorate penetration was much slower and full control was only achieved in 1934. But by the 1950s, it seemed Britain had finally consolidated its hold over Aden Colony, the Western Protectorate and the Eastern Protectorate (what later became South Yemen), an area of approximately 112,000 square miles with a population of 1.5 million.

Britain made Aden a free port (thus tying its prosperity to passing trade rather than the development of the territory as a whole), and in 1954 BP opened a refinery there. By 1956 some 5400 ships called at the port each year, bringing 200,000 transit passengers and 27,000 tourists to use the duty-free shops. By 1964 Aden had become the world's fourth bunkering port, although it was badly affected by the 1956 and 1967 Suez Canal closures. When Britain quit the Suez Canal Zone (1954–6) it turned Aden into a major military base and stationed 17,000 troops there; from 1960 to 1964 it spent something like £11 million a year on the construction of a permanent base.

British interventions in its colony were minimal and were designed to keep control and exclude possible rivals rather than to develop; the result was to keep Aden and the Protectorate extremely backward. Only in 1955, when Arab nationalism was sweeping through the Middle East, did Britain finally allow 4 out of 18 Council seats to be contested in elections. There was no talk of independence.

In 1960 Aden replaced Cyprus as the headquarters for Britain's Middle East Command. In the 1962 Defence White Paper, Aden was described (along with Britain and Singapore) as one of three vital permanent bases. In 1963, when Britain abandoned its East African bases, it moved more troops to Aden.

Following the Suez débâcle of 1956, Britain decided to bring the conservative sheiks of the interior together in a federation, hoping thereby to offset the nationalist forces which were then manifesting themselves in the port of Aden. During the following 10 years of bitter struggle Britain discovered that it had left things too late. There had always been opposition to its rule: in the 1920s, for example, an early nationalist movement grew to substantial proportions in the Hadramaut; it made an appeal for Hadramaut independence in 1939, though without success.

Outbreak and response

From 1945 onwards nationalism grew in parallel with the rapid development of the port of Aden. In 1950 the Adeni Association was formed; this called for Aden's eventual independence and was constitutional in its aims and methods. Then in 1952 a more radical movement – Renaissance – came into being which argued for a single state consisting of Aden and the hinterland of the sultans, whose power should be destroyed. During 1954 and 1955 mutinies wrecked the Tribal Levies, which had been created by the British, and in 1957 (the year after Suez) tribesmen who had obtained arms from North Yemen attacked the British in Beihan and Yafai.

The nationalist, anti-British movement received major impetus in the mid-1950s from the trade union movement. Many thousands of workers came from North Yemen or from the hinterland of the Aden Protectorate, so the port was a meeting point for a wide range of views; the radical nationlist elements were encouraged by developments in the Algerian war and then by the defeat and humiliation of the British during the Suez crisis of 1956.

By December 1956 there were 21 registered unions in Aden with a total membership of 20,000. There had already (March 1956) been a pro-Nasser strike in which 7000 took part. Later in the year 18,000 came out on strike. The year 1958 witnessed a series of strikes as well as bomb explosions, and the British authorities attempted to clamp down on the unions by arresting a number of union officials. A state of emergency was declared in May and strikes were banned. But more strikes were called in 1959 and included both the port and the BP refinery. Official records listed 84 strikes for the year. In 1960 there was another 10-week strike at the refinery. In August 1960 the colonial administration introduced legislation to enforce arbitration before a strike could be called.

The strikes and other nationalist activities from 1956 onwards had the effect of undermining the economy of Aden, which was based on supplying services, and from 1960 onwards British policy was to weaken the unions by legislation and repression.

On the political front Britain had deposed the Sultan of Lahej for nationalist activities in 1958 and had then decided (1959) to organize elections for the Council, in which a majority would be elected for the first time: 12 elected, 5 ex officio and 6 nominated. Out of 180,000 adults in Aden, 21,500 were given the vote (the North Yemeni immigrant population was excluded). The nationalists boycotted the elections, however, and only 27 per cent of eligible voters actually cast a vote.

Then came the revolution across the border in North Yemen (26 September 1962), and this provided an immediate boost to the nationalists in Aden. By now the nationalists were becoming increasingly influential in the hinterland, where the sheiks who had entered into treaties with the British were discredited.

Up to this time North Yemen policy had been to encourage revolt against the federation of the hinterland, since the Imam in the North saw this as likely to weaken his influence. In 1962 Britain decided to include Aden itself in the federation, and this sparked off resistance in the hinterland by conservative elements. It was clear that the joint federation was not going to work: it had been imposed by Britain and depended on a British military presence as well as British finances, and the nationalists did not want it. In October 1962 a general strike was launched. Militants now formed the National Liberation Front (NLF). In January 1963 the British imposed stringent controls on the port of Aden; in February they decided not to recognize the newly proclaimed government of the Yemen Arab Republic (North Yemen) and later sent military assistance to the royalists (through the ruler of Beihan); in April they refused to allow a UN Mission to enter the colony to investigate conditions.

Fighting against the British (and also in support of the new revolutionary government in North Yemen) erupted in mid-1963, and in July Britain sent troops into Upper Yafai. A second revolt erupted in Haushabi during August. Then in October 1963 the NLF launched a separate campaign against the British. This month was the official beginning of the nationalist revolt; it was led by Ali Antar, who was the commander in the Radfan district.

Course of the struggle

The war for the liberation of South Yemen (which became the People's Democratic Republic of Yemen or the PDRY) divided neatly into two campaigns: that in the Radfan mountains (the hinterland of the sheiks), and the urban war in the Port of Aden itself. Guerrilla warfare broke out in the Radfan mountains in 1963. This soon turned into an armed revolution, which by 1967 had destroyed the power of the sultans so that the British-created federation also collapsed.

Over the last three months of 1963 the NLF blocked the road to Dhala, forcing the British to organize a counter-attack in January 1964, using the British-officered Federal Reserve Army (FRA). This proved a failure. It was NLF tactics not to hold ground, but to inflict maximum casualties on the British and keep them extended, and this it succeeded in doing. It was a tactic that paid maximum dividends, since it led to increasingly awkward political questions about the conduct of the war both in Britain itself and in the international community. Although Federal troops were garrisoned in two of the Radfan valleys, they were isolated and ineffective. In March 1964 the British mounted a much larger campaign; though it led to border clashes with the Yemen Arab Republic to the north, this also failed.

By this time it had become clear to London that Britain faced a substantial nationalist uprising. A further 2000 British troops were flown out to the colony and a new campaign was launched in May 1964. Yet it soon became obvious that a policy based on supporting the sheiks of the interior (and expecting their aid in fighting the revolutionaries) was not going to work. The guerrilla war, meanwhile, had switched to Aden itself to become an urban affair around the base facilities and port area. NLF strategy was to render the base useless, and, as the retired British Field Marshal, Viscount Montgomery, pointed out at the time, 'if a military base has to be defended against the local population its purpose has been defeated'. This soon became the case in Aden.

In August 1964 the NLF launched a guerrilla campaign in Aden, so the British faced two wars – one in the port and another in the hinterland. It had become clear to London that it could not hold on to the territory much longer and in June 1964 London set a date for independence: 1968. At that stage, however, Britain hoped to keep its Aden base after independence. The NLF attacked installations and made officials its targets, using arms it had captured from the sheiks. In the interior, under its leader Ali Antar, the NLF lived off the land, where it was helped by the local populations, and subverted both the police and the army. It took just four years to undermine and destroy the power of the British-backed sheiks.

The Labour Party won the 1964 election in Britain, but no change of policy towards Aden followed. By September 1965 the Governor of Aden, Sir Richard

Turnbull, was forced to suspend the constitution and impose direct rule. For another two years – in the hope of installing a friendly regime at the time of independence – Britain attempted to maintain the federation and kept its large garrison in the colony, but to little avail. Between April and June 1967 the British withdrew from the Protectorate interior. On 20 June – a sign of the total collapse of British control – the rebels seized Dhala (capital of Dhala sheikdom) and imprisoned its ruler. By August the entire interior had fallen to the revolutionaries.

Moreover, also on 20 June the FRA revolted in the Crater district of Aden and attacked British troops. The Crater rising was to last for 13 days and achieve international publicity, which did great damage to British prestige.

There were divisions, however, on the revolutionary political front. In January 1966, for example, the Organization for the Liberation of the Occupied South (OLOS) and the National Front for the Liberation of the Occupied South joined forces to form the Front for the Liberation of South Yemen (FLOSY), but FLOSY was never to be as militant as the NLF and did not have so many armed followers, although it was backed by Egypt. Its members carried out murders and sabotage. By August 1967 the entire federation had collapsed, with only one sheik remaining. The NLF had simply taken control of one sheikdom or sultanate after another.

At the end of August 1967 the chairman of the federal cabinet, Sheik Ali Musaid al-Babakri, said, 'It is a people's revolution and we cannot oppose it.' The climax came in November 1967, by which time Britain had decided to cut its losses and grant independence at the end of the month. On 2 November 500 heavily armed members of FLOSY launched an attack on the Sheik Othman district of Aden, but after five days of fighting in which about 100 were killed and 300 wounded the district declared for the NLF. On 29 November, the day before independence, NLF forces landed on the island of Socotra, which they claimed for the revolution.

Estimated costs and casualties

The rebellion forced the British to use their own 'base' troops to fight the rebellion because the Federal troops proved unreliable. Tactical fighting included the deployment of helicopters and Centurion 105 tanks. On the political front the British resorted to a policy of proscription; they forced local inhabitants out of the areas threatened by the guerrillas in order to deny the latter support. Many thousands fled to North Yemen. The British authorities employed scorched earth tactics, burning fields and villages so as to deny these areas to the enemy. The strength of the opposition to the British in the Radfan mountains during the first six months of 1964 forced them to bring into the colony a further 2000 troops (there were 17,000 at the base in any case). So successful were the rebels that in February 1966 Britain was obliged to announce in its Defence White Paper that it would abandon the base when Aden became independent the following year. This also meant a betrayal of the sultans who had supported Britain.

Over the four years 1964 to 1967 guerrilla actions have been estimated as follows: 1964 – 36; 1965 – 286; 1966 – 510; 1967 (to October) – 2900. According to the British, 290 local people were killed and 922 wounded (240 of these during the final year of fighting): these figures apply only to Aden. The British troops were guilty of a number of cases of torture and brutality against suspects.

The split between the more radical NLF and what became FLOSY in 1966 continued through to independence, but it was the NLF which always controlled the revolution and formed the post-independence government.

British military casualties, according to official army figures, were as follows:

Radfan 1964–1967
Killed: 2 officers and 22 other ranks
Wounded: 8 Officers and 180 other ranks

Aden 1964–1967
Killed: 12 officers and 56 other ranks
Wounded: 20 officers and 302 other ranks

Results: immediate and longer term

Once it became clear to the British that they could only maintain the Aden base by constant fighting, the base itself became valueless and a date was set for independence. The retreat of the British from Aden had an impact on the whole Arabian peninsula, whose conservative elements (Saudi Arabia and Oman, for example) wished the British to remain. In May 1967, while on a visit to London, King Faisal of Saudi Arabia urged the British to maintain a military presence in Aden. As a result the British Foreign Secretary announced in June that Britain would provide military support for the successor government for six months following independence (the date was then put back – though as it happened only briefly – to January 1968). The final independence negotiations between Britain and the Adenis were held at Geneva from 22 to 29 November 1967. On 27 November British troops handed over most areas of the country to the forces of South Arabia (as it was called at first), while the NLF under Qahtan al-Shaabi took over political control. British troops quit Aden on 29 November, the day before independence. When it became clear that a radical government would take over, Britain cut back its promised aid from £60 million to £12 million.

When South Arabia emerged as an independent state on 30 November 1967 this represented a major British defeat. Nowhere else in the colonial empire had the British fought a losing war up to the last days before quitting and then been succeeded by so radical, Marxist-oriented and anti-British a regime as in Aden. The extent of the British defeat can be gauged by the fact that the 1962 Defence White Paper designated Aden as one of Britain's three main world bases, whereas the 1966 Defence White Paper made it plain that on independence (then expected in 1968) the base would be transferred to Bahrain, and that Britain would not enter into post-independence defence agreements with Aden. This decision also represented the betrayal of Britain's allies in the territory, the sheiks. Thus, it had taken the revolutionaries a mere four years to defeat Britain's military purpose for the colony.

Independence got off to an uneasy start: the 1967 closure of the Suez Canal (as a result of the Six Day War) cut down Aden's entrepôt business just when the revenue was most needed, and there was a further dispute with Britain about the Kuria Muria Islands in the Red Sea, which Britain said it intended to hand over to the Sultan of Muscat. The new President, Qahtan al-Shaabi, faced discontent from the left and anti-government uprisings in May and July of 1968, as well as opposition from FLOSY, which represented the more traditional interests of the merchants and deposed sheiks who were then in the Yemen Arab Republic or Oman.

In June 1969 President al-Shaabi resigned and Salel Rubayi Ali became chairman of a five-man Presidential Committee. The country then moved sharply to the left and in November 1969 announced the nationalization of foreign firms. In November 1970 the NLF introduced a new constitution and changed the name of the country to the People's Democratic Republic of Yemen (PDRY).

Following independence the PDRY suffered a decade of troubled relations with its more conservative neighbours, including eruptions of border wars, and though the dream of unity between the two Yemens had been advanced during the 1960s, it was not then fulfilled. When the Soviet Union became involved in the Horn of Africa in 1976–8 Aden acted as a staging post for the massive airlift of military supplies that the USSR sent to the revolutionary Mengistu government in Ethiopia.

Aden represents a classic example of a colonial possession treated by the imperial power solely as an imperial convenience. Not only were few if any efforts made to improve the conditions of the people, but by and large they were treated with contempt, and even when nationalism was sweeping through the Arab world in the 1950s the British still behaved as though they only had to manipulate a few backward Arab tribes. They learnt their lesson in one of the most humiliating 'end of empire' defeats which they were to suffer. (See also Part III, pp. 241–245; and Part V, pp. 455–464.)

ASIA AND THE PACIFIC

BRUNEI: REBELLION 1962–1963

Origins

Britain had extended its protection to the much-reduced Sultanate of Brunei in 1888 after Sarawak (which had been brought under British protection by the 'White Rajahs', the Brooke family from England who ruled the territory for a century) and North Borneo (under the British North Borneo Company) had taken over large areas of the Brunei Sultan's territories during the preceding 40 years. In 1959, when Brunei produced its first written constitution, the country was described as a protected state in which Britain had responsibility for defence and foreign relations.

Outbreak and response

In December 1962 a revolt broke out in Brunei which also spread into parts of British North Borneo and Sarawak. The revolt was against the entry of Brunei into the proposed Malaysian Federation, which in its turn was part of Britain's imperial tidying-up operation prior to granting independence to its Borneo territories, and which was therfore seen as neo-colonialist. The leader of the rebellion was A. M. Azahari of the Brunei People's Party (BPP), which joined with the North Borneo Liberation Army. The rebels (briefly) proclaimed a revolutionary state of North Kalimantan. At the time of the rebellion Britain (under the auspices of the South-East Asia Treaty Organization, SEATO) still had substantial military forces stationed in Singapore and Malaya.

The rebellion broke out in the early hours of 8 December 1962 in Brunei town, and by 8 p.m. that same day two companies of the 1/2 Gurkhas had been flown into the Sultanate from Singapore. It soon became clear, however, that the rebellion was on a considerable scale, and so more Gurkhas and then other troops were brought into the territory and a temporary military headquarters was set up on the island of Labuan just off the Brunei coast. The British commander, Brigadier J. B. A. Glennie, was ordered 'to restore Brunei to the rule of the Sultan'.

Course of the struggle

The fighting lasted for 10 days from the time British troops were flown in. An emergency was declared, the BPP was banned and Azahari went into exile in Malaya. Azahari, in any case, had been an absentee politician and was thought to be in league with the President of Indonesia, Sukarno, who was shortly to launch his 'confrontation' with Malaysia's Borneo territories. This rebellion could well be seen as a trial run.

The rebellion started on 8 December with firing at the Sultan's palace in Brunei town, and attacks on the police station, power station and other similar targets. Warnings of the impending uprising had been received, and at least at the palace the Sultan's guards were prepared and held off the rebels. But elsewhere in the town the rebels captured a number of targets including the power station, enabling them to put out the lights of the capital. The rebels were more successful in other parts of Brunei, where they took a number of hostages.

In Brunei town the British Commissioner of Police (Outram) rescued the British aide-de-camp from the Residency and then led a counter-attack to recapture the power station: 11 rebels were killed in this engagement and the Police Commissioner's party took 100 prisoners.

Meanwhile the rebels had invaded the oil town of Seria (Shell were the company operators) 50 miles down the coast, where they had captured the police station and taken a number of hostages. Part of the Gurkha force (C company) were sent by road in requisitioned trucks to the relief of Seria; they had minor encounters with rebels on the way and cleared rebels out of Tutong. In Brunei town the Gurkhas and police had more fighting to do before they cleared the rebels from the main buildings, and another 24 rebels were killed. The rebels were armed with the British No. 5 jungle rifle. At this stage it was learnt that 500 rebels were advancing on Brunei town from the south, so the Gurkhas who had been sent to Seria were recalled to assist in the defence of the capital. They brought back 106 prisoners.

On 10 December a company of the Queen's Own Highlanders arrived from Singapore. In Seria hostages were used in an attack on the police station (one was killed and five wounded), but the station was not taken. Meanwhile the RAF flew the Highlanders down the coast to a point west of Seria in Twin Pioneer craft, while a Beverley transport landed 90 men and the headquarters staff at Anduki airfield east of Seria, which at the time was rebel held. The airfield was captured after a fight. More British troops were brought into Brunei by destroyer and the build-up continued. On 11 December reinforcements were flown into Anduki airfield. Following minor engagements with the rebels, the Shell employees taken hostage there were freed.

The Seria Bazaar was the main stronghold of the rebels and was to hold out for another day, but rebels were driven from the Sultan's summer palace. A detachment of the Gurkhas drove by Landrover to Kuala Belait were the police station had been taken; the Gurkhas fought their way into the town, which the rebels quit the following day. On 12 December the British troops attacked the rebels in Seria and released further numbers of Shell prisoners, while 42 Commando landed at Limbang from the river and regained control of the town after some fighting.

In the west the revolt had spread to Sarawak and some of the Gurkhas were despatched to the coast town of Miri. A further battalion of British troops (the Greenjackets) were brought by HMS *Tiger*, and these were also deployed in Sarawak. In an engagement upriver at Bekenu in Sarawak the Greenjackets killed five, wounded six and took 328 prisoners and 327 shotguns. More British troops were sent to Kuching, the capital of Sarawak. By 14 December every town had been freed of the rebels; the nature of the task now changed and it became a mopping-up operation.

The rebel leaders, however, remained in the vicinity of Brunei town and the swamps along the Brunei river, and it was not until April 1963 that the two brothers of Azahari were located: one was killed and the other captured. Then in May the Gurkhas discovered a rebel camp on the Brunei river, and in the action which followed the rebel field commander, Affandi, and his high command were captured. The revolt was then effectively over.

Estimated costs and casualties

There were thought to be about 4000 rebels at the beginning, but casualties were light – a few dozen dead, more wounded – mainly because the rebellion was met with such a prompt response. This was only possible because Britain had sufficient forces readily available in Singapore and Malaya with relatively massive air and sea back-up.

Results: immediate and longer term

The most obvious result of the rebellion was that in 1963 the Sultan decided not to join the Federation of Malaysia, which had been the ostensible reason for the rebellion, though how much he was influenced by the rebellion and how much by his growing oil wealth is another question. The task of rounding up the rebels in jungle country once the rebellion was over meant the deployment of more troops than had been needed in the actual fighting. Further troops were sent in by Britain, and on 19 December the command was given to Major-General W. C. Walker, General Officer Commanding the Gurkhas. In neighbouring Sarawak, irregulars – Iban and Kenyah – were raised by the British anthropologist Tom Harrisson to assist in rounding up the rebels. In January the 22 SAS Regiment was brought out from Britain to help in the mopping-up operations. Many of the rebels simply disappeared to their villages and buried their arms; some continued to hold out for a while in the jungle, although resistance had been broken.

It was a small, curious, nineteenth-century-style war, part of the process of 'end of empire'. It had been inspired by Indonesia's President Sukarno, who was then pursuing a virulently anti-imperialist stand and was opposed to SEATO and the concept of Malaysia, which he saw as neo-colonialist. From a British viewpoint it was a successful small war with minimal British casualties. There was soon a more dangerous conflict in the area when Sukarno embarked on full-scale 'confrontation' with Malaysia; this rebellion could be seen as a prelude to that. As a result of its intervention, Britain was to maintain good relations with both Brunei and Malaysia in the ensuing years. Gurkha battalions were to remain in Brunei, their presence paid for by the Sultan; they continued to serve in Brunei after its independence in 1984.

INDONESIA: THE INDEPENDENCE STRUGGLE

Origins

The Dutch East India Company established control of what came to be known as the Dutch East Indies in the seventeenth century, and apart from a brief interregnum during the Napoleonic Wars the Dutch retained control until the Second World War. Dutch colonialism was harsh and exploitative. In 1830 the Dutch imposed a system of forced labour in Java, the most populous and wealthy island of the archipelago. Commercial crops were grown under compulsion and shipped to Holland. By the 1870s there had been a marked development of anti-Dutch nationalism, and adherence to Islam became a symbol of this antipathy to Dutch rule. In the period 1870 to 1910 the Dutch established their authority throughout the archipelago (what came to form modern Indonesia); it was in these years that the traditional lifestyle of the people was most affected by the impact of colonialism. During the First World War the Dutch permitted a people's assembly to be formed, but they gave it few powers.

An urban intellectual élite opposed to Dutch rule began to emerge during the 1920s and 1930s and provided the core of the nationalist movement. The most important of these figures were Achmed Sukarno (the First President of Indonesia), Dr Mohammed Hatta (the first Vice-President) and Sutar Sjahrir (the first Prime Minister). In 1920 the Partai Komunis Indonesia (Communist Party of Indonesia, PKI) was formed; during 1926–7 it led an abortive revolt which was soon crushed by the Dutch authorities. Then in 1927 the Indonesian Nationalist Party (PNI) was formed under the leadership of Achmed Sukarno. It adopted the Bahasa Indonesia as its official language and began to preach a militant policy of non-cooperation with the Dutch. That year also saw the beginning of a number of All-Indonesia Nationalist Movements among youth and women, and also on a regional basis: for example, in Java, Sumatra and Ambon. As a result of these activities, Sukarno and other leaders were arrested by the Dutch authorities in 1929.

The period 1927 to 1932 saw unrest and opposition to Dutch rule. A mutiny on the Dutch warship, *De Zeven Provincien*, in 1933 was blamed on the nationalists, and a number of their leaders were arrested and exiled as a result. By 1939 the nationalists were demanding a fully fledged parliament and Indonesian National Military Service, but these and other claims were rejected in 1940 by the Dutch government.

The demands of nationalism prior to 1939 were basically moderate and not dissimilar to those being made at that time in British or French colonies. However, since the Dutch held out no encouragement to nationalist aspirations, the movement became increasingly radical. On the international front, meanwhile, growing American–Japanese rivalry in the Pacific foreshadowed the conflict to come, and the fact that the Dutch East Indies were immensely wealthy in resources made it inevitable that they would be embroiled in any Pacific war.

Following the attack on Pearl Harbor, the Japanese quickly overwhelmed the

Dutch East Indies during 1942, meeting little resistance from the Dutch, and at first many Indonesians saw them as liberators from colonialism. The Japanese encouraged a degree of Indonesian nationalism – for example, the continued use of their own national anthem and language – as well as providing military training. Their encouragement enabled the nationalist movement to become more widely known and popular. Yet, at the same time, thousands of Indonesians were sent as slave labour to build the Thai railway, and for many the Japanese were soon seen as far more oppressive than the Dutch.

The Japanese occupation lasted for three and a half years, and the nationalist leaders, Sukarno and Hatta, gave limited co-operation to the Japanese forces of occupation. Under the Japanese the civil service was Indonesianized – an important requisite for successful nationalism at a later stage. By 1945, however, there was growing unrest with insurrections occurring in a number of the islands. Japan's attempted Co-prosperity Sphere in Great East Asia was not a success.

Outbreak and response

The Japanese forces were defeated on 14 August 1945; three days later, on 17 August, Sukarno and Hatta declared independence and proclaimed a Republic of Indonesia with jurisdiction over Java, Sumatra and Madura. At the same time they enunciated five principles of nationhood, published a constitution, and proposed a Parliament and Assembly. These measures were adopted on 18 August. Sukarno was elected President of the new republic, Dr Hatta Vice-President. Then, on 5 September, a presidential cabinet was formed. The returning Dutch, however, attempted to establish separate states among the Indies as part of a federation: over the next four years of struggle (1945–9) the Dutch pushed for a looser-knit federal solution on the general principle that its separate parts would subsequently be easier to influence.

Immediately, however, British forces in south-east Asia under Earl Mountbatten's command undertook to restore the Dutch to power and were soon engaged in fighting the Indonesian nationalists. Although the official task of the British forces in Indonesia was 'the repatriation of Allied Prisoners of War and Internees and the disarming and interning of Japanese troops', they were also used to assist the returning Dutch in taking control again. But world opinion – including the then all-important American opinion – was against a resumption of Dutch imperial control. The United States, in particular, used the threat of withholding Marshall Aid from the war-torn Netherlands unless the Dutch agreed to talk with the nationalists. The process was to take four years and include substantial fighting before a settlement was finally reached. In pursuing the idea of a federation, the Dutch hoped to isolate the more revolutionary republic which Sukarno had declared over Java and Sumatra, and to strengthen the more reactionary forces in the remoter islands.

Course of the struggle

The death of the British Brigadier-General Mallaby in October 1945 led to fierce fighting in Surabaya, which culminated in attacks on the nationalists by Allied forces employing battleships, planes, tanks and armoured cars – a major assault – on 10 November. The Indonesians put up stiff resistance and did not surrender, later celebrating 10 November as Heroes Day. On 11 November Vice-President Hatta issued a manifesto which proclaimed the new Republic's aims as peace and a good neighbour policy. On 14 November the new Prime Minister, Sutar Sjahrir, inaugurated a multi-party parliamentary system.

On 22 December the Prime Minister accepted the British proposal that the Republic should disarm and intern the 25,000 Japanese troops still in the territory. This was done by the new Indonesian nationalist army, and transportation back to Japan began on 28 April 1946.

An increasing build-up of Dutch power forced the nationalist leaders – Sukarno and Hatta – to move from Jakarta to Yogjakarta on 4 January 1946, as serious fighting erupted between their forces and the Dutch. The Indonesian question was then referred to the UN by the Ukrainian SSR. As a result, a first meeting under UN auspices between the Dutch and representatives of the Republic of Indonesia was held on 10 February 1946. Meanwhile the fighting continued; there was an unsuccessful coup attempt against the Indonesian Prime Minister.

The British (under Lord Killearn) now acted as mediators, and an agreement was reached between the Indonesian government and the Dutch which recognized the Republic of Indonesia as having *de facto* sovereignty over Java, Madura and Sumatra. This Treaty of Linggadjati was initialled on 15 November 1946 and signed on 25 March 1947. But it broke down at once because the Dutch insisted that the newly recognized Republic should incorporate itself in a wider United States of Indonesia during a transitional period under Dutch control, a proposition that the nationalists rejected. They considered that the Linggadjati agreement violated their own proclamation of 1945; the fighting continued.

In July 1947 the Dutch launched a fresh military campaign; this was to last through to 17 January 1948 when a new agreement – the Renville Agreement – was signed under UN auspices. But this agreement reduced still further the territory recognized as belonging to the new Indonesian Republic, so this too did not bring peace and the fighting continued. The Dutch then mounted a second and more successful campaign which culminated in the capture of the entire republican government in December 1948; they were interned on the island of Bangka. The nationalists, however, established an emergency Indonesian cabinet in Sumatra under Dr Sjafruddin Prawiranegara.

But these Dutch successes were of little avail in the face of hostile world pressures on behalf of Indonesian independence which were expressed through the UN. In any case the guerrilla war was spreading, and the 'loyalist' Indonesian leaders who had not joined the Sukarno nationalists were becoming increasingly disenchanted with the Dutch.

A 19-nation Asia conference was held in New Delhi, India, on 20 January 1949, and appealed to the UN Security Council to make the Dutch surrender all their Indonesian prisoners as well as the territory they had seized in their two recent campaigns. The conference demanded complete sovereignty for Indonesia by 1 January 1950. As a result of this appeal, on 28 January 1949 the UN Security

Council called for a ceasefire, the release of all Indonesian government prisoners and their return to Yogjakarta.

Estimated costs and casualties

Casualties came to about 100,000 rebel (Indonesian) troops, tens of thousands of civilians and 2500 Dutch soldiers before the Netherlands accepted defeat in 1949. For the Dutch, the loss of Indonesia represented the end of the Netherlands' imperial pretensions and its control over one of the richest areas in the world in terms of both mineral resources and agriculture. According to British records for the period 1945 to early 1946, 28 British officers and 22 soldiers were killed.

Results: immediate and longer term

The Roem van Royen agreement was concluded 7 May 1949: this ended hostilities, restored the Indonesian republican government to Yogjakarta and accepted further negotiations under the UN in preparation for a Round Table conference. This was held at The Hague from 23 August to 2 November 1949: it recognized that sovereignty over all the former Dutch East Indies should be transferred to the United States of Indonesia, which was to have a federal constitution with parliament and cabinet. The new constitution – the Dutch had apparently won their battle for a federal rather than a unitary state – came into being on 27 December 1949. The question of sovereignty over Dutch New Guinea (which became Irian Jaya) was shelved for the time being, and in fact was to remain a bone of contention between the Netherlands and Indonesia for many years. Thus, in 1954, because the Netherlands still controlled Dutch New Guinea, Indonesia ended the 'union' which had been established between the two countries at independence. In 1962 the Dutch transferred their New Guinea territory to the United Nations, and in 1969 it was annexed by Indonesia.

Despite the initial success of the Dutch in obtaining a federal state, on 15 August 1950 the new government proclaimed the Unitary Republic of Indonesia. The huge, sprawling new state was to suffer years of instability, and the central government faced a number of demands for regional autonomy with revolts in Kalimantan, the Celebes and Moluccas. In the immediate post-independence period Indonesia pursued a policy of non-alignment with marked anti-imperialist characteristics. Sukarno, who had guided the nationalist movement from the 1920s, at first enjoyed tremendous popularity; his prestige was at its height in 1955 when Indonesia hosted the Bandung Conference at which non-alignment became an international movement. In 1959 presidential powers were greatly increased, and then in the early 1960s Sukarno instituted 'Guided Democracy'. He was over-thrown in 1965 when he attempted to take on the American oil companies, Caltex and Stanvac, and his successor, Suharto, led a massive anti-Communist campaign against PKI members in which an estimated 1 million Communists were massacred.

MALAYA: THE COMMUNIST EMERGENCY 1948–1960

Origins

When the main European colonial powers began to extend their influence in the Far East during the second half of the nineteenth century, Britain decided to safeguard the Straits of Malacca and its commercial interests in the area by taking control of the Malay Peninsula. Britain secured control of Perak state, the first of nine independent states, in 1874; by 1896 Britain had formed the Federated Malay States; and by 1914 British authority had been extended to all nine states of the Peninsula. The basis of Malaya's wealth was tin and rubber.

A Malayan Communist Party was formed in 1930, drawing membership almost entirely from the Chinese community. It was soon outlawed. But once Japan had overrun Malaya in the Second World War, the Communists formed a guerrilla force – the Malayan People's Anti-Japanese Army (MAPAJA) – to oppose Japanese occupation. MAPAJA was mainly composed of Chinese Communists with some Kuomintang supporters and a small number of Malays. Since MAPAJA represented the only resistance to the Japanese, the British supported the guerrillas with both officers and supplies. In 1942 MAPAJA consisted of about 3000 jungle fighters; by 1945 the numbers had increased to an estimated 10,000, including some women. They avoided large-scale actions against the Japanese. MAPAJA leaders indoctrinated their recruits to the effect that Malaya would become a Communist state after the war.

By the end of the war these guerrillas had become national heroes. They attempted to seize power during the three-week interregnum between the surrender of the Japanese forces and the arrival of a British military administration in September 1945, but the attempt failed. On 1 December 1945 MAPAJA officially disbanded, and the majority of its members, about 6000 guerrillas, handed in their weapons to the British authorities, received a bounty of £45 each and returned to civilian life. Another 4000 guerrillas took their weapons into hiding, while the leadership went underground.

By 1948, with Asian independence very much in the air, the British first proposed that Malaya should become a unitary state with a strong centre; when this was fiercely opposed by the Malays they agreed to a Federation of Malaya, and this came into force on 1 February 1948. The Communists now decided to launch their guerrilla war against the British. Their leader was a young resistance hero, Chin Peng OBE, while their military commander was Lau Yew.

Outbreak and response

Malaya in 1948 had a mixed population – Malays (the majority), Chinese, Indians, jungle aborigines and 12,000 Europeans – while the terrain consisted largely of thick jungle and mountains, perfect territory for a guerrilla war. The Communists now renamed themselves the People's Anti-British Army (though later they changed this to the Malay Races' Liberation Army), and in April 1948 they launched their war against the British. They began with acts of sabotage and intimidation, picking out as targets key workers such as foremen on the rubber estates and in the tin mines, which represented the twin pillars of the economy. The 4000 guerrillas who had secreted their arms from the war against the Japanese were now called up – in some cases forcibly – and 10 insurgent regiments (nine of which were composed entirely of Chinese) were formed. Following the killing of three Europeans on 16 June 1948, a state of emergency was declared which included the death penalty for the unauthorized possession of arms. Captured documents suggested that the Communists had intended to declare a Communist republic in August 1948.

The state of emergency meant calling in the military, for the Malayan police force, then numbering 10,000, was neither large enough nor trained to deal with such an insurrection. The bulk of the then British garrison consisted of Gurkhas, mainly new recruits, and so a build-up of British battalions commenced; before long the General Officer Commanding Malaya, Major-General C. H. Boucher, had at his disposal a brigade of Gurkhas (six battalions), a further three British battalions and the 26th Field Regiment (artillery). Air support was provided by Spitfires and Dakota transports and a squadron of Austers for reconnaissance purposes. At the beginning of the emergency the army was greatly overstretched, trying to meet demands for escorts or guards from every section of the community which was threatened or thought it was threatened by the insurgents. Furthermore, for the first few months of the insurrection Malaya was without a British governor since the High Commissioner, Sir Edward Gent, had been killed in an air crash and no immediate replacement was available. Communist tactics, in the meantime, were to paralyse the economy, which was then in the process of recovering from the war. Their principal targets were the British rubber planters, the tin miners and those Chinese who opposed the revolt.

Course of the struggle

The anti-Communist war in Malaya can be divided into four phases: the opening period (1948–50) when the guerrillas were on the offensive while the colonial authorities were learning how to cope and building up their military strength; the period of the Briggs Plan (1950–2) when major controls over the civilian population were implemented so as to deny support to the insurgents; the psychological warfare offensive under General Templer (1952–4); and the final period of mopping up, which continued to 1960 (when the state of emergency was lifted) and covered the end of British rule and the emergence of an independent Malaya in 1957.

Already by July 1948 the rebels were attacking tin mines; that month the military suffered their first casualties. Then on 16 July the police killed the rebel leader, Lau Yew. In Kelantan the Communists enjoyed a spectacular if brief success when they declared an area to be liberated. They ambushed the Malay Regiment, killing a major and six men; but then Gurkha reinforcements were brought in and the Malay Regiment regained control of the rebel-held area.

Meanwhile the British were bringing in reinforcements: troops came from Hong Kong; a 'Ferret Force' to seek out the insurgents was established; Dayak trackers were brought in from Sarawak; and the 4th Queen's Hussars arrived from Britain. In October 1948 the 2nd Guards Brigade arrived from Britain (the Grenadiers, the Coldstream and the Scots), breaking a tradition that the Guards were not used on service east of Egypt in peacetime – at that time, as the Cold War stretched military resources to the limit, Britain simply did not have enough available forces.

Gradually the British and Gurkha troops learnt new techniques of jungle warfare. In the first major offensive against the guerrillas (September 1948) 12 rebel camps were discovered and destroyed, and huge quantities of ammunition as well as Communist literature and Russian flags were found, although only 27 rebels were killed.

Chin Peng was an able leader who always followed the Maoist guerrilla principle of making sure that his forces survived: self-preservation. His men were issued with green uniforms. A key to the success and survival of the guerrillas was the Min Yuen: this 'people's movement' consisted of civilians in the border villages on the edge of the jungle. They were responsible for passing on information and orders, for obtaining supplies and recruits, and also for local acts of sabotage including murder. No figures for their numbers are available. The Min Yuen worked in small groups of 15: these controlled the jungle fringes and were the means of communication between the larger district committees and the Liberation Army.

The Communists (who reached 10,000 at their maximum and seemed able constantly to recruit new members) were well armed with weapons hidden at the end of the war and relied, when pressed, upon their ability to disappear into the jungle camps from which they operated. Their tactics were a mixture of terrorism, concentration on selected areas and vulnerable targets, ambushes and sometimes open battle.

The government introduced tough measures to control the civilian population: these included registration of the entire population, which the rebels did their best to disrupt; the power to deport unwanted people who were not citizens; and the introduction of Regulation 17D (the most unpopular measure of the entire war), under which the inhabitants of a village could be detained if it was decided they had 'aided, abetted or consorted with the bandits'.

The British military forces were always overstretched, and at first a battalion had to police an area of at least 3000 square miles. Companies established their camps on the edge of the jungle, with some troops always in readiness to respond to emergency calls. Armoured vehicles were used for this purpose. Other troops were used for local policing duties. As a result of trial and error, patrols were whittled down in size to 12 men, including two trackers. One military estimate found that 1800 man-hours of patrols were required for every contact made with the guerrillas. Guerrilla ambushes were frequent and caused mounting military losses. The year 1949 was hard for the government and military, and offensives (for example, by the Guards Brigade in August 1949) resulted in more military than guerrilla casualties. By the end of that year the guerrillas were very much on the offensive, attacking police stations and killing key civilian leaders such as foremen on the plantations. The war had become a savage, brutal affair.

A new director of operations, Lt.-Gen. Sir Harold Briggs, was appointed in April 1950, his appointment coinciding with the arrival of military reinforcements, including the 26th Gurkha Brigade, the 3rd Marine Commando and the 13th/18th Hussars. Government priority now was to make the population at large feel safer from guerrilla attacks, while also imbuing it with confidence in the security forces – which to that date had failed to establish dominance over the guerrillas. General Briggs formulated the plan which came to bear his name: its principal objective was to concentrate the squatters who lived on the edges of the jungle (and were the source of the Min Yuen) into new guarded villages. The Briggs Plan ran into many political problems since different procedures and permissions had to be obtained in each of the nine Malay states. None the less, the plan was in operation by June 1950 (just two months after Briggs' arrival in the country) and over the next two years a total of 410 new villages were created. The procedure was to build a new village without designating the people to occupy it; then squatters in a selected area would be surrounded and moved while their old village was razed and burnt; the new village would be surrounded by wire and guarded.

In June 1951 the second phase of the Briggs Plan was put into operation: starvation. A particular area would be wired off and all its inhabitants checked on leaving to ensure that food supplies were not taken out of the village to the rebels at the edge of the jungle. The effectiveness of the plan was highlighted by the intensity of the rebel response, for in June 1951 there were a total of 606 strikes by the guerrillas – the highest monthly figure recorded throughout the emergency. On 6 October 1951, a highpoint of rebel achievement, the High Commissioner, Sir Henry Gurney, was ambushed and killed, while in a new campaign in Negri Sembilan workers on plantations and in the mines were slashed by the rebels. General Briggs retired towards the end of the year, his health broken; he was replaced as General Officer Commanding operations by General Sir Rob Lockhart, the former Commander-in-Chief of the new Indian army.

The British government now appointed a soldier, General Sir Gerald Templer, as High Commissioner; he was to apply a military approach to the entire country rather than just to the guerrilla war. His primary object was to inspire the people as a whole with confidence that the battle could be won. He used a variety of techniques, some of which were to become standard practice in comparable wars in other parts of the world. On one famous occasion shortly after his arrival, he imposed a curfew on the village of Tanjong Malim (following its collaboration with the enemy), issued every householder with a sheet of paper to write down what he knew about the rebels and then had these collected the next day. In the presence of village elders, Templer himself opened the box of papers and, as a result of information supplied, the collaborators were rounded up.

Templer became famous for his 'hearts and minds' approach to the war and the determination he showed to win the co-operation of the local people. In this he largely succeeded. By the time he took control, he had under his command 24 infantry battalions and two armoured regiments. During his time as High Commissioner some Commonwealth units were drafted into Malaya, including the 1st Nyasa and 3rd Kenya African Rifles and the 1st Fijian Rifles, bringing total strength up to 10 British, 8 Gurkha, 5 Malay, 2 African and 1 Fijian unit. General Templer insisted on greater Malay participation in the campaign; he created a sixth Malay Regiment, introduced national service and strengthened the Home Guard, which reached a membership of 200,000. He demonstrated confidence that they would not side with the rebels by issuing large quantities of arms to them. He also increased the effectiveness of the police, whose numbers were raised to a total of 73,000; a campaign was mounted to improve their relations with the public, and they were provided with greater protection (which increased morale) by the provision of 970 armoured vehicles.

Under the hearts and minds campaign, voice aircraft flew over the jungle with messages to the rebels, while the soliders were employed to provide aid to the village communities among whom they operated and also to train the Home Guard. Rebel deserters were treated leniently and high rewards were given for information. Periodically, troops would be withdrawn from a specific area while instructions were broadcast to the rebels – by voice aircraft and leaflets – as to how they should surrender. Pictures were spread of prosperous ex-guerrillas in possession of bicycles after their surrender. Such tactics of psychological warfare paid dividends, and surrendered rebels were 'turned' and then used to betray or bring in other rebels from the jungle. So successful was this policy that in May 1953 a new formation of Special Operational Volunteers (rehabilitated rebels) was created; it was armed and became a highly effective anti-rebel force.

Early in 1953 General Templer abolished Regulation 17D, under which entire communities could be detained, as a sign of confidence in support for the anti-rebel campaign, and at the same time he reduced the number of detainees from 11,000 to 2000. By September 1953, for the first time, an area was declared to be 'white': that is, free of Communist terrorists (as the rebels were now called, again part of the psychological warfare). Patches of open jungle where the rebels grew food were now sprayed with acid (foreshadowing the massive defoliation which was to be carried out later in the Vietnam War), although without much effect. Deep inside the jungle SAS units were dropped by air to help the primitive jungle-dwelling tribes – the Semang and Sakai – to defend themselves from the Communist guerrillas.

On 30 May 1954 Templer's term of duty came to an end and he was replaced by a civilian High Commissioner, his deputy Sir Donald MacGillivray. Despite the success of Templer's twin policy of hearts and minds and psychological warfare, the war was far from over. The rebels were still to cause problems for years, although attacks on major targets such as the railways and buses ceased. In the first three months of 1954 further areas were declared 'white' – rebel free – and it was clear that the rebels were now on the defensive. Yet at his departure Templer said there were still between 4400 and 6000 rebels (there had been an estimated 8000-plus at the time he took over). At the end of 1954 five major operations were in progress against the rebels, and three of these were to continue through 1955.

Costs and casualties

The military costs to Britain of this war were very substantial and necessitated a major concentration of troops in Malaya for the best part of 10 years. Disruption to the economy of the colony and, still more, to its lifestyle was of major proportions, so that under the state of emergency large areas were either militarized or operating under stringent security conditions. By and large the people of Malaya came to support the British against the Communist insurgents, but only when the scale of the British military effort as well as the civilian – hearts and minds – measures had made it plain that the Communists could be defeated.

From an initial colonial garrison of six Gurkha battalions there was a steady build-up of British troops until at the height of the emergency under Templer there were 26 infantry battalions in the country as well as various support units. Britain sent 500 police sergeants to Malaya (many with experience in Palestine); air reinforcements were supplied by the Royal Australian Air Force (a squadron of Lincoln bombers); Kenya, Nyasaland and Fiji each sent a battalion of troops; and Malaya steadily built up its own forces through the emergency, so that at the end the single original Malay Regiment had expanded to six, the police force to

73,000 and the Home Guard to 200,000. At the end of 1950 a new unit – the Malayan Scouts – was formed for long-range jungle penetration; they were to be joined by a squadron of the Special Armed Services (SAS) in 1951 (and became SAS themselves), while a third detachment came from Rhodesia. The SAS would be dropped into the jungle by parachute and were supplied with rations to last them 10 days.

The Royal Navy was to be used on occasion for offshore bombardment and, more important, employed its American-supplied Sikorsky helicopters to lift troops into the jungle. The RAF used Whirlwind helicopters, while the army developed the Sterling sub-machine-gun as the most efficient jungle weapon. Many of the rubber estates became armed camps, and a Special Constabulary was formed which at the end of the war numbered 28,700.

Up to March 1950 (which covered the period of the first, most effective rebel offensive) civilian casualties (dead) were estimated at 863, police at 323 and soldiers at 154, and half those civilian and police casualties were killed in the six-month period ending in March 1950. Over this same period the rebels were reported to have lost 1138 dead, 645 captured and 359 surrendered. Assessments of rebel strength appeared constantly to be too low: estimated at 3000 in April 1950, they turned out to be far stronger and could obtain reinforcements from across the Thai border, which would have required a force of 100,000 to police effectively.

During 1950 the police lost 222 dead and 381 wounded, the army 72 dead and 108 wounded; the rate of civilian casualties declined that year. The principal justification for the Briggs Plan was that it forced the rebels out of the jungle to fight. Thus in 1950 a total of 369 rebels were killed and 294 captured (of whom 147 surrendered voluntarily); in 1951, however, rebels lost 1025 killed and 322 captured (201 surrendered voluntarily). Estimates at the end put total civilian casualties at 2473 dead and 810 missing; Malay police casualties were put at 1346 dead, and Malay soldiers at 128 dead. British army fatalities were 70 officers (including 10 from Gurkha battalions), 280 British soldiers and 159 Gurkhas.

Rebels killed were estimated at 6710; but many more perished as a result of starvation, disease or strafing in the jungle. A total of 1287 rebels were captured and 2702 surrendered. By the end of the emergency about 500 rebels were believed to roam the jungle near the Thai border.

Results: immediate and longer term

The back of the rebellion was broken during the two years when General Templer was High Commissioner (1952–4), yet a hard core of rebels were still very much in business in July 1955 when elections were held for the 52 unofficial seats in the federal legislative assembly: 51 of these were won by the Alliance Party led by Tungku Abdul Rahman, who became the country's Chief Minister. Following his victory, Tungku Abdul Rahman declared (9 September 1955) an amnesty for the Communists provided they laid down their arms and surrendered as a body. He met the Communist leader, Chin Peng, at Baling, 32 km (20 miles) from the Thai border, but the talks broke down and the offer was rejected. On 26 February 1956 the amnesty was withdrawn. Yet the rebels were clearly weakening in resolve, and from that time onwards the military, once they had surrounded or made contact with the enemy, were under instructions to call upon them to surrender first before engaging in battle.

Meanwhile Malaya was moving rapidly towards independence. In December 1955 Tungku Abdul Rahman visited London, where he obtained a promise of independence for August 1957. July 1957 was the first month since the emergency had begun in which there was not a single killing, and the following month, at independence, the Tungku again offered an amnesty, but insisted that in the meantime operations against the rebels would continue. These tactics began to pay off that October when the Communist political commissar of South Perak first surrendered and then, over the succeeding six months, brought in every branch in his district. Other surrenders became more frequent and rebel morale dropped; at the same time the British began to withdraw their troops, so that by the end of 1958 there were only three British battalions in the country. Finally, on 31 July 1960, the state of emergency was ended, three years after Malaya had achieved independence.

The rebellion took place during the early years of the Cold War when world tensions were at their height. The successful resistance to Communist subversion in Malaya at a time when China had just become Communist under Mao Zedong clearly had an important psychological impact on the Cold War in the Far East, and independent Malaya (later the Federation of Malaysia) became a centre of stability and economic growth. Malaya thereafter could be counted among the most conservative states in the region, although maintaining a non-aligned stance.

The impact of the military lessons were equally far reaching, and successful British resistance to Communism in Malaya undoubtedly influenced the stands taken by the US Secretary of State John Foster Dulles during the 1950s in relation to French Indo-China, and must also have affected the concept of the 'domino' theory which became popular at that time in Washington.

The military campaign was later regarded as a textbook case, and it came to be accepted that a guerrilla war had to be opposed by psychological warfare and winning the 'hearts and minds' of the local people quite as much as by actual fighting. And though General Templer got great credit for his approach, he did not hesitate to acknowledge his debt to Mao Zedong. The British tactics in Malaya were to be studied in many subsequent wars, such as Vietnam and Rhodesia, and almost 40 years later were to be referred to by the South African military as they conducted their war against SWAPO in the north of Namibia.

NEW CALEDONIA: SETTLER COLONIALISM

Origins

At the heart of the confrontation that has troubled New Caledonia through the 1980s is the fact that the Kanaks (indigenous Melanesians) are no longer a majority in their own country. Kanaks now represent 43 per cent of the population of 150,000, the Europeans 37 per cent, while the balance consists of incomers – Asians and other Pacific islanders. The roots of this problem go back to the settler arrival in New Caledonia, the alienation of Melanesian land and the French decision of 1856 to create separate administrations for settlers and Melanesians. Land alienation created its own repressive legislation and sparked off a number of

Melanesian revolts against the French, the last of these in 1917. Long-standing enmities between settlers and Kanaks resurfaced in the 1970s when demands for independence had become general in the Pacific region. In 1974 there were anti-French demonstrations and then a general strike.

Kanak demands for self-determination produced a French response in 1976: the Council of Government was increased in size and given more responsibilities. However, three years later in 1979, the French government dismissed the Council when it refused to support French proposals for a 10-year 'contract' between France and New Caledonia since the contract contained nothing about independence. As a result, France placed New Caledonia under direct rule of the High Commissioner. Subsequent rigged elections excluded the pro-independence parties and allowed the two parties in favour of continuing colonial status to win 22 out of 36 seats in the Assembly.

Tensions between settlers and Kanaks now increased, and so in January 1982 a series of reforms to defuse the growing crisis were passed: these included measures designed to allow greater Melanesian participation in government, and land and economic reforms. At the same time France announced it would rule New Caledonia for a year by decree.

In November 1983 the French Minister for Overseas Territories, Georges Lemoine, visited New Caledonia, where he advanced proposals for reform over the period 1984–9 to culminate in 'an act of self-determination' in 1989 when one of the options available would be independence. The Kanaks rejected these proposals on the grounds that the wait was too long; they were opposed by the settlers and thrown out of the territorial assembly in April 1984.

Outbreak and response

The Kanaks boycotted the elections to the territorial assembly in November 1984, and the parties seeking independence formed the Front de libération nationale kanake socialiste (FLNKS), whose congress then formed a 'provisional government' on 1 December 1984 under the leadership of Jean-Marie Tjibaou. In the same elections the anti-independence Rassemblement pour la Calédonie dans la République (RPCR) took 34 out of 42 seats. Already during November there had been violence and both French and Melanesian deaths. Then on 5 December in the Hienghene valley 400 km (250 miles) north-east of Nouméa, the capital, a massacre of Kanaks by settlers took place; the repercussions of the massacre, in which ten died, became far more important two years later.

In January 1985 the new High Commissioner, Edgard Pisani, presented a new plan under which he envisaged independence in association with France in 1986 after a mid-year referendum. It was a return to the politics of de Gaulle in Africa in 1958. The Pisani plan was greeted by further violence. Then, following the police shooting of a leading member of the FLNKS, a state of emergency was declared. President Mitterrand visited the territory briefly in February 1985.

New, more radical plans were put forward in April 1985; these were designed to produce a pro-independence Melanesian majority, but the Assembly, which was controlled by the settlers, rejected the proposals in June 1985, although they were accepted by the French National Assembly in July of that year.

An ongoing problem

By mid-1986 France was coming under increasing regional criticism for its New Caledonia policies, and in August of that year the French Prime Minister, Jacques Chirac, visited the territory to explain France's plans for its future. Meanwhile, earlier in the month, the 13 members of the South Pacific Forum, including Australia and New Zealand, had called for New Caledonia to be placed on the United Nations' list of territories to be decolonized. The conservative government of Chirac had scrapped the socialist plan of the previous year – 'independence in association with France' – and proposed instead to hold a vote giving a direct choice: independence or to remain part of France. The Kanaks demanded that only the original indigenous people – themselves – should be allowed to vote.

A bitter row erupted between France and Australia, whose stand in the South Pacific Forum had infuriated Chirac. He described the Australian Prime Minister, Bob Hawke, as 'very stupid' and said he would welcome a change of government in Canberra. Australia insisted that its stand on New Caledonia was related to legitimate regional concerns.

The situation took on a far grimmer aspect in October 1986 when, following 21 months of investigations, the examining magistrate dismissed all charges against the settlers involved in the December 1984 massacre, saying they had acted in self-defence. The release of the seven defendants stunned diplomats in the country, but in settler-dominated Nouméa the seven killers appeared on television and their release was greeted with jubilation. The League of Human Rights described the dismissal of the charges as 'a perfect illustration of French colonial justice in the Pacific'. Other settlers named in the affair were not even questioned, while the dead Kanaks were described as 'aggressors and terrorists'. The magistrate ruled that the shooting had been carried out in the 'exceptional circumstances of a war situation'. Kanak reaction to this judgment was deeply hostile; the Kanak leader, Jean-Marie Tjibaou, said, 'There will be no justice in New Caledonia before independence.'

In September 1987 another referendum was held – boycotted entirely by the Kanaks – in which 98 per cent of those who voted, the settlers, rejected independence in favour of remaining French. The Kanaks insisted that their opposition to French rule would continue; by this time they were convinced that France did not intend to allow New Caledonia to achieve independence because Paris regarded the territory as vital to French strategic interests in the Pacific region, using a neighbouring area for its nuclear testing. France has a garrison of 8000 troops in New Caledonia.

In April 1988 further violence erupted during the French presidential elections, which the Kanaks called upon their followers to boycott. On the remote island of Ouvéa hooded separatists hacked three gendarmes to death and kidnapped 27 others. A fourth gendarme died, eight others were wounded and further attacks were mounted against polling stations; ballot papers were burnt and illegal road blocks erected. As a result, Bernard Pons, the Minister for Overseas Territories, flew to New Caledonia and General Antonio Jerome was sent out with reinforcements to take command of the gendarmes. Yet the situation was already out of control in many parts of the territory. The violence and consequent low poll represented a setback to the Chirac policy of full integration for New Caledonia with France.

The drama of the kidnapped gendarmes on the island of Ouvéa escalated as they were surrounded by 500 French infantry, including 250 crack commandos. Meanwhile a French patrol boat shelled a Kanak separatist camp at Pouobo, 400 km (250 miles) north-east of Nouméa. President Mitterrand called on the Kanaks to release the hostages; they regard him more favourably than any other French politician. When, in early May 1988, the cave in which the hostages were held was eventually stormed, 19 Kanaks lost their lives. But then at Paris on 26 June 1988 a reconciliation was effected and peace accords were agreed between the FLNKS led by Jean-Marie Tjibaou, the French loyalists led by Jacques Lafleur and the French Prime Minister, Michel Rocard. New Caledonia was to be divided into three autonomous provinces, and a referendum on self-determination was scheduled for 1998.

This agreement just might have worked, but early in May 1989, when Tjibaou and his right-hand man, Yeiwene Yeiwene, visited the island of Ouvéa on the anniversary of the hostage taking and shoot-out of 1988, both were assassinated by Djubelly Wea, who himself was subsequently gunned down by Tjibaou's body-guards. Wea was the militant Kanak who had been responsible for the hostage-taking a year earlier; he had been imprisoned briefly in Paris but had then returned to New Caledonia. He was an implacable enemy of Tjibaou's path of reconciliation.

These assassinations threw the entire future of New Caledonia into doubt again and indicated the likelihood of a return to violence, despite urgent calls for calm and the arrival in New Caledonia, for the funeral, of the French Premier, Michel Rocard.

It was already apparent early in 1988 that the Kanak leadership had managed to politicize the entire Melanesian population of New Caledonia. At the same time the dominance of settler interests is clearly emphasized by the fact that there are few Kanak graduates, only 36 primary teachers out of 800 and six senior officials out of 1000.

In October 1989 the French Prime Minister, Michel Rocard, released a number of Kanaks held for kidnapping, which helped lower tensions. The provincial elections returned 27 members of the RPCR, while the FLNKS won 19 seats.

Small as New Caledonia is in terms of total population, there is every indication (especially after the May 1989 assassinations) that the troubles will escalate, as will the bitterness, until independence is achieved.

VANUATU: A SMALL DISTURBANCE

A crisis in a mini-state, such as Vanuatu (formerly New Hebrides), may offer matter for jest elsewhere, but its potential for violence can be proportionately as great as in a far larger country. Moreover, most mini-states simply do not have the police or military required to restore order in such situations, so they are obliged to call on friendly outside powers to intervene and do the policing for them.

The Anglo-French condominium of the New Hebrides was set up in 1906 to replace a joint British–French naval commission. Subsequently, the administration of the islands was run on dual lines with both British and French national services as well as condominium or joint departments. Indigenous New Hebrideans could not claim either British or French citizenship. The result was a society divided.

Elections were held in 1979: these were won by the Vanuaaku Party (VP), which was largely composed of the Anglophile elements supported by British interests and Protestant missions; the VP won 26 out of 39 seats, and their victory sparked off riots in the island of Espiritu Santo by supporters of the rival party, Na-Griamel. The British and French authorities on the islands could not agree as to what should be done; given their constant inability to work together effectively in the years preceding independence, this was not surprising.

On 29 November 1979 Walter Lini, the leader of the VP, was elected Chief Minister. Then, in June 1980 (a month before independence was scheduled for all the islands), the leader of Na-Griamel, Jimmy Stevens, declared the island of Espiritu Santo to be independent of the rest of New Hebrides. He named the island the 'Independent State of Vemarana'.

On 30 July 1980 the New Hebrides became independent as Vanuatu, and at once its new Prime Minister, Walter Lini, appealed to Papua New Guinea for help in dealing with the rebellion on Santo. With logistical support from Australia and New Zealand, Papua New Guinea sent 300 troops. These landed on Santo and arrested the ringleaders of the revolt, who were mainly French and mixed-race supporters. There were a number of deaths before the rebellion was put down. Most of those arrested were released the following year.

This tiny insurrection in a mini-state required 300 troops from neighbouring Papua New Guinea, supported by Australia and New Zealand, to put it down and regain control for the elected government.

THE AMERICAS

ANGUILLA: COMIC OPERA

Background

As part of its 'end of empire' tidying-up operations, Britain linked the little West Indian island of Anguilla (with a population of 6000) to its larger neighbours, St Christopher and Nevis, in February 1967. The Anguillans, however, resented what they considered to be a takeover by St Christopher and Nevis, and therefore, three months after the mini-federation had been launched, the Anguillans ejected the St Christopher police from their island and insisted they would rule themselves, although still as part of the federation.

Discussions concerning the rights and wrongs of the Anguillan action were to take place between the government of the federation, Anguilla and Britain over the next two years without the three participants finding any solution: while Anguilla maintained its opposition to federation, Britain insisted that federation was the right answer to Anguilla's problems as a mini-state.

Declaration of independence

Finally exasperated, Anguilla declared independence in January 1969, and the British representative on the island was withdrawn. Britain refused to recognize that Ronald Webster, the Anguillan leader, represented the wishes of the 6000 islanders. In March 1969 a junior minister from the Foreign Office, William Whitlock, was sent to Anguilla, but on arrival the Anguillan authorities refused to talk with him and put him back on the inter-island boat on which he had come.

At this point the drama descended into pure farce. On 14 March Harold Wilson, Britain's Prime Minister, called an emergency cabinet meeting to decide on action (including military options) needed to regain control of the island. The key British ministers were Wilson, Denis Healey (Minister of Defence) and Michael Stewart (Foreign Secretary). On 18 March British paratroopers took the island; no resistance was offered and the only weapon discovered was one old rifle. The paratroopers were withdrawn to be replaced by a detachment of London policemen (who were no doubt happy to have a holiday in the Caribbean sun), and British administration was re-established in Anguilla. In his book *Life and Labour*, Michael Stewart, the Foreign Secretary responsible for this extraordinary action, explained: 'I was told the island might be seized by desperadoes who would turn it into a centre for tax-dodgers, drug-pushers, even gun runners.'

At the time of the Anguilla farce, UDI in Rhodesia under Ian Smith and his

Rhodesia Front had been running for four years and the British government had resolutely ruled out any use of force to bring this rebellion to an end; in consequence the Anguilla 'invasion' provoked many ribald comparisons about what Britain was prepared and able to do in colonial situations for which it still claimed responsibility.

THE FALKLANDS WAR

Origins

Between 1690 and 1766 various British and French groups settled temporarily on the Falkland Islands, but none stayed permanently. The French ceded their claims to Spain in 1767, so the territory could be said to have a Spanish colonial background similar to that of Argentina when that country became independent in 1816. There were no inhabitants on the islands when colonists from Argentina settled there in 1826. In 1832 the British, forever searching for convenient ports of call upon which to base their world-wide naval power, expelled the Argentinian settlers and took over the islands, which they made a Crown Colony in 1833. Ever since that time Argentina has claimed the Falkland Islands, which Argentinians call the Islas Malvinas.

Periodic demands for a settlement of their claim over the years met little response from Britain and, though negotiations about the future of the Falklands were opened between Argentina and Britain in 1966, they made slow progress. In 1982 the Argentinian government of the military junta under General Galtieri announced that it would seek other means to resolve the dispute with Britain, clearly implying the use of force. At that time the military government in Argentina was extremely unpopular, and undoubtedly one calculation in its seizure of the Falkland Islands was to divert attention away from this unpopularity at home by uniting the country behind a popular nationalist cause. Moreover, the Argentinian military did not believe that Britain would fight if the islands were occupied, and they had been encouraged in this belief by Britain's withdrawal of the one naval vessel which had been based on the Falklands, in consequence leaving only a token detachment of Royal Marines in the territory.

Outbreak and response

On 2 April 1982 Argentinian forces invaded the islands, expelled the Governor, Sir Rex Hunt, and established a military government. A British task force was sent to the South Atlantic in response to the invasion, and after six weeks' fighting the Argentinian forces on the islands surrendered. British submarines (the number involved was not made public) bottled up the Argentinian surface fleet in port, forcing the Argentinians to rely on their naval air force and one or two submarines: these came close to doing fatal damage to the British force.

The Argentinian air force had 51 old Skyhawks, 14 Mirage 111 fighter bombers and 6 Dagger interceptors armed with conventional high-explosive bombs. They were operating at maximum range, so on arrival in the area of the British task force they could only make one run over their targets before returning to base.

The British forces were composed of extremely efficient professionals; even so, the margin for error was small and the logistics for operating 13,000 km (about 8000 miles) from Britain presented formidable problems. The task force included two aircraft carriers (one of which, *Hermes*, was 30 years old) carrying 20 short-range Sea Harriers, and the loss of one carrier could have crippled the expedition and made the invasion impossible. There were, then, elements of luck involved for both sides.

Course of the struggle

Following the landing on the Falklands (2 April) of the original 2000 Argentinian troops who forced the token garrison of Royal Marines to surrender, a further 18,000 Argentinian troops were brought in from mainland Argentina. They were lacking in armour and were poorly equipped to face the oncoming winter, and a majority of them were one-year conscripts with indifferent training.

The British government took an immediate decision on 2 April to send a task force to regain the islands, and this was assembled in time to sail from Portsmouth over the weekend of 5–6 April. The British force commander was Rear-Admiral John Woodward and the landforce commander Major-General Jeremy Moore. For refuelling and re-equipping the British forces, the RAF built up its Ascension Island base in the South Atlantic – still at a distance of 6440 km (4000 miles) from the Falkland Islands. On 25–26 April the British reoccupied the island of South Georgia, first to have been seized by the Argentinians, and, as a result of surprise, also captured an old Argentinian submarine still in port.

The first phase of the short war lasted from 1 to 21 May, and consisted of the land-based Argentinian air force attacking the approaching task force. On 2 May the British submarine *Conqueror* sank the old Argentinian battleship *General Belgrano* and 368 sailors were drowned. Britain's two carriers had to be protected by a radar screen provided by the accompanying destroyers and frigates. During this phase of the fighting, the Argentinians lost between 15 and 20 of their planes, while HMS *Sheffield* was destroyed by an Exocet missile.

On 21 May British forces landed at Port San Carlos; the strategy was to mount an overland attack on Port Stanley in the hope of minimizing British military and civilian casualties. The initial landing at Port Carlos was unopposed, but the Argentinians soon brought up 5000 troops and some heavy fighting then followed. The Argentinian air force sank two frigates, *Antelope* and *Ardent*, the destroyer *Coventry*, and (by Exocet missile) the container ship *Atlantic Conveyor*, which was bringing supplies, including 20 Harriers. Two landing ships – *Sir Galahad* and *Sir Tristram* – were also sunk with considerable loss of life when the British made a second landing to create a bridgehead 5 miles south-west of Port Stanley. From Port San Carlos the British advanced rapidly across the island, taking the settlements at Darwin and Goose Green on the way, with the result that the Argentinians were cut off in Port Stanley and General Mario Menendez surrendered on 14 June.

Costs and casualties

In a sense the biggest cost of the war was the sad incongruity of Britain sending a naval task force, reminiscent of the Second World War, 13,000 km (8000 miles) across the Atlantic to fight the Argentinians over a group of semi-barren islands because the politicians had been unable to come up,with a reasonable formula to settle long-standing but not insuperable differences. Between 2 April and 14 June 1982 the British lost a total of 255 dead, the Argentinians more than 650. The biggest single death toll came from the sinking of the *General Belgrano* (368 Argentinian sailors drowned), an event that caused controversy then and later, since it was argued that the *Belgrano* was steaming away from the battle zone which implied that the orders to sink it were deliberate in order to scupper the chances of a peace settlement. Whatever the truth of the accusations, the controversy continued for years and did no good to the reputation of Britain's Prime Minister, Margaret Thatcher.

The Argentinians lost between a third and half their operational planes; Britain lost six of its task force fleet.

Results: immediate and longer term

Immediately after the military victory the British Governor, Sir Rex Hunt, returned to the Falklands as Civil Commissioner and Britain established a military garrison of 4000 troops on the islands – the 'Fortress Falklands' policy. In Argentina the military government refused to declare a formal end to the hostilities until Britain would agree to negotiate about sovereignty, but London argued that this was not negotiable. Then, as a direct result of their defeat, the military were forced to step down and Argentina returned to democratic rule in December 1983 with the election of President Raúl Alfonsín.

Talks were held between Britain and Argentina in July 1984, but these broke down on Britain's refusal to discuss sovereignty. The United Nations continued to press for fresh talks. At the time of the war Britain had received widespread international backing for its action, largely because of the unpopularity of the military dictatorship in Argentina and its unilateral attempt to solve the problem by force of arms, but in the years that followed much of this support disappeared as Britain refused to negotiate about the future of the islands and maintained its Fortress Falklands policy.

On the political front there were important results in both countries. Many Argentinians were delighted at the downfall of the military junta and the return to civilian rule which were directly attributable to the war. In Britain the position of the Prime Minister, Margaret Thatcher, which had been precarious before the war, was immeasurably strengthened by its outcome – this became known as the Falklands factor in her Conservative Party's victory in the elections of 1983.

On the military front a number of lessons were learned, and most military observers were agreed on the precarious nature of operating such a task force at such long range. A great deal of luck was on the side of the British. Had more Argentine bombs exploded on target, including one or two more Exocet missiles, and had one of the carriers or troop carriers been sunk, it would have been a very different story. Britain, in any case, received massive intelligence as well as equipment support from the USA.

The war did not solve anything. At the end of the 1980s Argentina still claimed the Falklands, Britain was still maintaining its Fortress Falklands policy and neither side was talking to the other. Britain, moreover, was finding itself increasingly isolated over the issue at the United Nations, where year after year it was overwhelmingly defeated when Argentinian motions were proposed calling for negotiations. A new 240 km (150 mile) fishing zone was implemented by Britain round the Falklands, coming into effect on 1 February 1987.

PART II

Big Power Intervention Wars

Big power intervention wars

INTRODUCTION

The interventions dealt with here were each carried out by one or other of the two superpowers or, in Africa, by either Britain or France, the two principal ex-colonial powers. There is no easy way to classify these interventions, which fall into several categories.

Africa

The British intervention in East Africa in 1964 has the greatest legitimacy: Britain was requested by the governments of Tanganyika, Kenya and Uganda in turn to provide military assistance when their armies mutinied, and though there was a 'neo-colonial' flavour to the operation – the three countries had only recently become independent from Britain – the request for intervention came from those who had the authority to make it in the three capital cities concerned.

French intervention in Gabon, also in 1964, was not quite in the same category since the government had been overthrown in a coup and the ousted President Leon M'ba only got back to power after France had used military force on his behalf. French intervention in the Central African Republic (then an empire) was altogether different. By 1979 the Emperor, Jean Bédel Bokassa, had become notorious for his brutalities and an embarrassment to the French who, until shortly before the coup which overthrew him, had supported Bokassa despite his many excesses. There is considerable evidence to suggest that the coup which overthrew Bokassa was entirely masterminded in Paris, while its success was ensured only by the arrival of French troops in Bangui.

The 1986 American bombing raid on Libya remains a unique example of a major power deciding on punitive measures to 'teach a lesson' to a minor country. The long-standing Libyan–American quarrel, and the American belief that Colonel Gaddafi was behind anti-American terrorist activities, produced such frustration in Washington that the USA finally chose to punish Gaddafi by a so-called pinpoint bombing raid against military targets, as well as against Gaddafi himself.

Asia

Three wars are listed under Asia – Afghanistan, Korea and Vietnam – and in these three cases the intervention was on a massive scale. Soviet pressures persuaded North Korea to invade South Korea; subsequently the conflict became a Cold War trial of strength with massive allied forces (principally from the USA) on the one

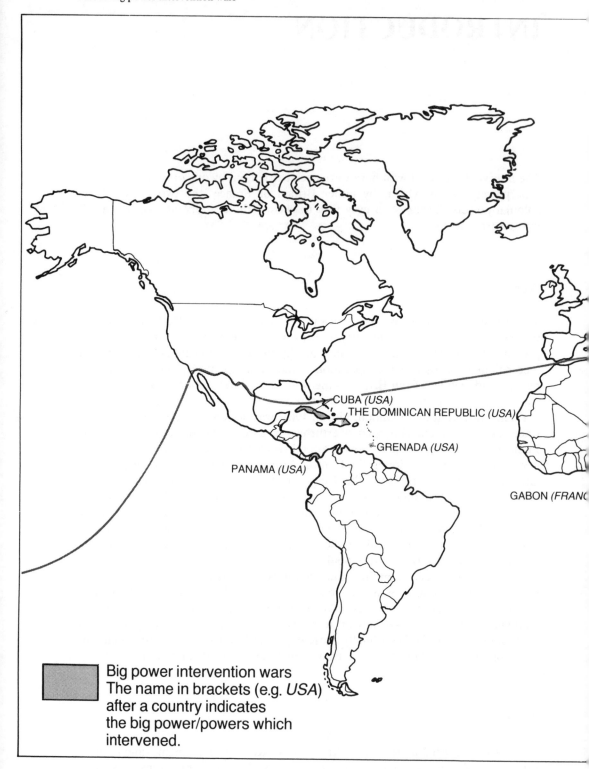

Big power intervention wars
The name in brackets (e.g. *USA*)
after a country indicates
the big power/powers which
intervened.

Map 6   Big power intervention wars

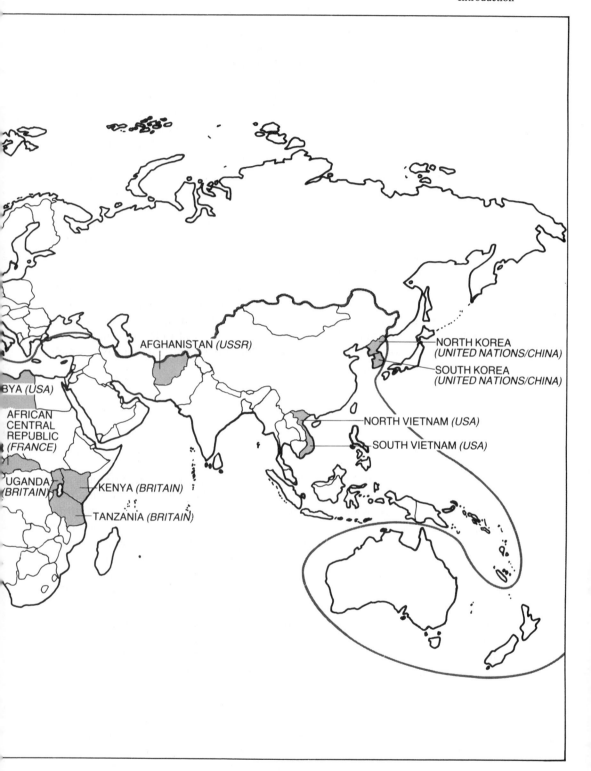

AFGHANISTAN *(USSR)*

BYA *(USA)*

AFRICAN
CENTRAL
REPUBLIC
(FRANCE)

UGANDA
(BRITAIN)
KENYA *(BRITAIN)*

TANZANIA *(BRITAIN)*

NORTH KOREA
(UNITED NATIONS/CHINA)

SOUTH KOREA
(UNITED NATIONS/CHINA)

NORTH VIETNAM *(USA)*

SOUTH VIETNAM *(USA)*

side and major Chinese military commitment on the other side. Two of the wars (those in Afghanistan and Vietnam) lasted for many years. There are many similarities between the American involvement in Vietnam and the Soviet involvement in Afghanistan. In each case the superpower went to the support of a government of doubtful legitimacy for ideological reasons. In each case it committed major military resources in wars where the enemy consisted largely of poor peasants with apparently minimal military capacity. In each case Cold War considerations were what had brought about the intervention in the first place. In each case the superpower found it had taken on more than it had bargained for and was constrained, in the end, to withdraw without having achieved its objective, the Soviets managing to save considerably more face in extricating themselves from a war they found they could not win than did the Americans. In each case the superpowers left behind governments that had relied upon them for their survival and seemed unlikely long to survive their departure. These two intervention wars are prime examples of the limitations (even defeats) that determined peoples can inflict on the most powerful nations in the world.

The difficulty of assigning these wars to categories is illustrated in the case of Vietnam, where two wars are dealt with. The first (from 1946 to 1954), between the French (returning to the country at the end of the Second World War, hoping to resume colonial control) and the Vietnamese, began as a colonial war of independence but turned into an ideological Cold War confrontation. The Americans subsequently took over from the French and the second Vietnam War which followed was wholly ideological.

The Americas

The four interventions listed here – Cuba, the Dominican Republic, Grenada and Panama – are similar in that they each represented the same general American principle: that the USA would interfere, if necessary with force, in the countries of the region if in Washington's terms they were perceived to be moving too far or dangerously to the political left, although the reasons for intervention in Panama were rather different. The 1962 missile crisis in Cuba is a case on its own: it was a confrontation between the two superpowers at the height of the Cold War over a Third World country, Cuba, and that country's right (disputed successfully by the USA) to allow the USSR to station missiles on its soil. The confrontation was resolved by the two superpowers without reference to Fidel Castro or Cuba.

American intervention in the Dominican Republic, which was widely condemned in Latin America, probably had the least justification and fell into an older pattern of big power interference: that designed to secure the kind of government the big power saw as most favourable to its own interests. The American intervention in Grenada, on the other hand, was generally popular in the Caribbean, even though it was condemned by Margaret Thatcher's government in London as interference in Grenada's internal affairs. The Panama intervention is extraordinary in the sense that the corrupt figure of Noriega whom the intervention was designed to overthrow was to a remarkable degree an American creation who got out of hand.

*

Whatever the justifications for their interventions put forward by the big powers, these were generally condemned by the Third World as a whole: they were seen, at best, as exercises in neo-colonialism, the continuing post-independence manipulation of power and control; at worst, as wholly unjustified attempts by the big power concerned to force Third World countries to adopt policies that Washington, Moscow, London or Paris deemed to be in their interests.

AFRICA

CENTRAL AFRICAN REPUBLIC 1979

Background

Following the coup which brought Jean Bédel Bokassa to power at the end of 1965, relations between the Central African Republic and France entered a period of alternating confrontation and accommodation. This was partly the result of Bokassa's unpredictability, and partly because of French determination to maintain its neo-colonial grip on Central African political and economic affairs. At the end of the decade, for example, several French diamond-mining companies were expelled, while in 1971 the Central African Republic tried to transfer the headquarters of its Central Bank from Paris to Bangui and to cease participation in Air Afrique, moves which were opposed by France. In 1973 Bokassa accused the French of destabilizing his country, although later in the year, following a meeting between Bokassa and President Pompidou, France increased its aid to the Central African Republic.

These ups and downs in relations between the two countries had all the characteristics of an unequal contest: in effect, whatever Bokassa's personal failings, he was trying to break free of French tutelage, while the French were determined to maintain the virtual stranglehold they had on the economy and much else of the country's life. Thus, in 1974 Bokassa again threatened French interests when he forbade the sale of French newspapers, closed down the French Consulate-General and nationalized a number of French companies.

There was an upturn in relations in 1975, following President Giscard d'Estaing's visit to the Central African Republic for the Franco-African summit of that year, but the relationship was always an unhealthy one, France pushing its position of dominance and the Central African Republic remaining heavily dependent on Paris for aid.

In the second half of the 1970s Bokassa's excesses – highlighted by his extravagant self-coronation as Emperor in 1977 (when he renamed the CAR as an empire) – made him an increasing embarrassment to France since he was dependent upon it for aid. Opposition to his rule came to a head in 1979. There were extensive student demonstrations in January against wearing new uniforms which had to be purchased from Bokassa's own factory. Others joined the student demonstrations, leading to pitched battles with the police. Order was only restored with the help of troops from Zaire (though both countries denied this) and at the cost of between 50 and 400 deaths. Unrest continued, and in May an international scandal followed the reported murder in April of up to 100 teenagers arrested for protest activities who were beaten to death. France, as a gesture of protest, cut off military but not other aid.

French intervention

The CAE Ambassador in Paris, Sylvestre Bangui, resigned to set up a rival party in exile: Front de libération des Oubanguiens. Other opposition movements now came into being, and at a meeting in Cotonou (Benin) on 9 July 1979 these groups formed a common anti-Bokassa front. There was a steady escalation of anti-Bokassa sentiments through August and September, and then on 20 September (following the announcement by Paris that it was ending budgetary aid to the CAE) when Bokassa had flown to Libya to seek aid, a bloodless coup was effected. The former President, David Dacko, was flown into the country in a French air force plane direct from France to form a government of 'salvation'. At the same time about 1000 French troops from Gabon and Chad were also airlifted into the country and Dacko proclaimed himself President.

The French troops also had the specific task of securing the Bouar military base for French use as headquarters for its activities in the region, including intervention in Chad, Congo or Zaire.

The French action could hardly be justified in international law; it was an example of big power manipulation to ensure a change of government that suited French regional interests. President Dacko did not have an easy start to his second presidency: the student protests continued and Dacko, understandably in the circumstances, was regarded as a French stooge. Bokassa succeeded in embarrassing the French by insisting on his right as a French citizen and property owner to take up residence in France until Paris persuaded the President of Côte d'Ivoire, Félix Houphouët-Boigny, to allow Bokassa residence in his country on compassionate grounds.

Dacko was ousted in another coup in 1981, which brought the military Chief of Staff, General André Kolingba, to power as head of state. In 1986, for reasons that remain unclear, Bokassa returned to the CAR from exile. Although he had been sentenced to death in his absence, the government ordered a retrial in the presence of international observers; Bokassa was again sentenced to death for his crimes, but in 1988 the sentence was commuted to labour for life.

GABON: A FRENCH MILITARY BASE

Gabon became independent on 17 August 1960, and Leon M'Ba, leader of the Bloc démocratique gabonais (BDG) became the country's first President in February 1961. His principal rival was Jean-Hilaire Aubame, leader of the main opposition party (Union démocratique et sociale gabonaise, UDSG), whom M'Ba made Foreign Minister in the coalition government but then sacked in 1963 when he appointed Aubame President of the Supreme Court. Continuing differences between the two men, whose rival parties (the BDG and the UDSG) were still joined in an uneasy coalition, led M'Ba to dissolve the National Assembly in January 1964 and call elections for February.

But on 18 February the military, led by Major Daniel M'bane, overthrew the government in a coup and invited Aubame to form a provisional government. Within 24 hours of the announcement of the coup over Libreville Radio French paratroopers had been used to restore M'Ba to power. The de Gaulle government in Paris justified the intervention in terms of the bilateral defence agreement signed between France and Gabon at independence. Nineteen Gabonese and two French soldiers were killed in the fighting. In the elections which were held on 12 April M'Ba's BDG won 31 of the 47 seats. Aubame was sentenced to 10 years' hard labour followed by 10 years' banishment, although he had not initiated the coup. He was finally released in 1972 by M'Ba's successor, President Bongo.

The French intervention had at best dubious justification, but was a clear instance of preferring their man. Fifteen years later (1979) there were still French troops in Gabon, and some of these were used to ensure that Dacko became President of the Central African Empire in place of Bokassa (see above, pp. 120–121).

THE EAST AFRICAN ARMY MUTINIES 1964

Origins

Army mutinies occurred in the three newly independent (ex-British) territories of Kenya, Tanganyika and Uganda in January 1964, and these mutinies and British military assistance in putting them down are treated together since the three events were closely interrelated. A week before the mutinies took place a far more serious and bloody revolt had occurred on 12 January in the island of Zanzibar (see Part V, pp. 419–421), leading to the overthrow of the ruling Arab minority and its replacement by a left-wing revolutionary African government. This clearly influenced events on the mainland. These upheavals may be seen as part of a post-independence adjustment process.

Kenya had only become independent in December 1963, Uganda the previous year and Tanganyika in 1961; the military structure in each case was based on British models and so was familiar to the troops sent in to reverse the mutinies. Moreover, a fact of significance which may, ironically, have been a contributory cause of mutiny was that the three small armies were still largely led by British officers. Thus, for the soldiers independence may have appeared to have meant no more than a continuation of an apparently unchanged colonial situation.

In this immediate post-independence period Britain was ready to assist 'stability' by interventions at the request of the successor governments. In any case, as a result of the build-up of troops in Kenya during the Mau Mau emergency that country had come to be regarded as a possible military base by Britain (troops from Kenya had been despatched to Arabia in 1956 and to Aden in 1958), and at independence Kenya had agreed that British troops should remain stationed in the country for a further year. Thus, at the time of the mutinies, the British Land Forces Kenya, at brigade strength, were readily available for intervention purposes.

Outbreak and response

Tanganyika

Early on the morning of 20 January 1964 the 1st Battalion Tanganyika Rifles mutinied in protest against pay and conditions, although there was clearly an anti-colonialist element to the mutiny as well. They locked up their British officers, seized the airport and arrested the acting British High Commissioner. They later sent the British officers and NCOs with their families to safety in Nairobi. The Tanganyikan President, Julius Nyerere, appealed for British assistance; in a broadcast to the nation he said, 'My hope is that we shall never see such a disgrace repeated in Tanganyika.'

The British response was to embark troops on HMS *Centaur* at Aden and despatch them to the capital, Dar es Salaam. They included 45 Commando, 815 Naval Helicopter Squadron and escort cars of the 16th/5th Lancers. They sailed at midnight of 20 January and were off Dar es Salaam by 24 January. Meanwhile, on 21 January the 2nd Battalion Tanganyika Rifles had also mutinied at Tabora. On 25 January the government requested British intervention and 600 Marines were landed to put down the mutiny.

Brigadier Sholto Douglas, who had been in command of the Tanganyikan troops and had been in hiding since the revolt, was picked up by launch from the mainland and later accompanied 45 Commando when it was lifted by helicopter to a field next to the barracks held by the mutineers. To distract attention from the helicopter lift the gunboat put down a barrage. The marines seized the entrance to the barracks, Brigadier Douglas called on the troops to surrender and when they resisted the marines stormed the barracks using anti-tank rockets, and the mutineers surrendered. Total casualties came to three dead and six wounded. A longer exercise followed: the remainder of the marines were landed to dominate Dar es Salaam and round up those mutineers who had escaped and fled into the town.

Uganda

By 23 January the news of the mutiny had spread its effects and a second mutiny of Ugandan troops appeared imminent. The Ugandan Prime Minister, Milton Obote, also called for British aid, and by 11 p.m. of that evening British troops had been airlifted into Entebbe from Nairobi. The British troops were placed under the command of the local British commander, Colonel J. M. A. Tillet. The trouble was located at Jinja, 110 km (70 miles) from Entebbe, where the 1st Battalion Uganda Rifles and the newly formed 2nd Battalion mutinied. They took control of the armoury and drove off the British personnel. Some British troops (Scots Guards) were left to hold Entebbe airport, while a contingent of the Staffords set off by road for Jinja. They reached the Jinja camp in the early hours of 24 January, and at dawn the mutineers found themselves surrounded and surrendered without a fight. Their weapons were removed.

Kenya

A comparable mutiny also occurred in Kenya on the evening of 23 Janury when the Commanding Officer of the 11th Kenya Rifles at Lanet called for help. British troops, the 3rd Royal Horse Artillery, were 32 km (20 miles) away at Gilgil camp, and on the next day D Battery (75 men) moved in to capture the guardroom and armoury, from which, however, some arms had already been removed. There was some fighting and one mutineer was killed. The Battery took the officers' mess and the telephone exchange, while African officers attempted to persuade the men to surrender. The British commander decided to contain the mutineers for the night so as not to risk killing wives and children who were with them. The next day the men said they would only surrender to African officers. This was allowed, but when most of them had surrendered and handed in their arms a few tried to reverse the situation; they recaptured the armoury and D Battery had to attack it for a second time. It was a short, sharp affair.

But in the meantime the whole of the British 24 Brigade was deployed to handle any possible escalation with troops out in Mombasa and Nairobi as well as at the mutineers' barracks. After a week the situation was judged to be under control and 41 Commando (flown out from Britain) was sent to Dar es Salaam to relieve 45 Commando.

In the Kenya case, faced with an immediate threat to his country's newly won independence, Jomo Kenyatta did not hesitate (as did Nyerere) to turn to Britain for help, and British troops were at once deployed to crush the mutiny. As a direct result of this mutiny and the prompt British response, Kenya and Britain signed a formal defence treaty the following March.

Estimated costs and casualties

Actual casualties were minimal – half a dozen dead and a handful wounded – while costs were relatively light since Britain had troops in the region, either in Kenya itself or in Aden, and their deployment could be treated as part of their regional duties.

Results: immediate and longer term

The psychological cost of these mutinies was considerable and caused the three heads of state to show a subsequent wariness in relation to their armed forces which was to have varying repercussions in the succeeding years. More generally, African nationalists were shocked and their pride hurt that, so soon after independence, three new states were each obliged to turn to the former colonial power to ensure the safety of their governments from their own military. The reactions in Kenya and Tanganyika were diametrically different.

In Kenya Jomo Kenyatta entered into a defence agreement with Britain and allowed British army units to train in his country thereafter. At the same time he built up the paramilitary General Service Unit (GSU) as a powerful counter-balance to the army, which he never really trusted, and was quite ready to call in the British again should the need arise.

In Tanganyika the reaction of Nyerere was so to revamp and reorganize his armed forces that the need to turn to the British would never arise again. The mutiny, indeed, acted as a spur towards more radical policies which helped move Tanganyika in an ideological direction further from the former colonial power. This was the opposite to what happened in Kenya. The army was disbanded (most of the soldiers were discharged ignominiously, although certain leaders were charged before a special court) and a new one recruited mainly from the ranks of the Tanganyika African National Union (TANU) Youth League.

LIBYA: AN AMERICAN ATTACK

Origins

Colonel Muammar Gaddafi became President of Libya in 1969 following the coup which ousted King Idris. His determination to take effective control of the country's oil resources began the process which gave the Organization of Petroleum Exporting Countries (OPEC) 'teeth' in the 1970s. Always controversial, Gaddafi has used Libya's oil wealth to support many nationalist and more dubious causes round the world, although his defiance of the United States has been generally popular among many Third World countries. Indeed, Gaddafi became to Washington what a generation earlier Nasser had been to London – a permanent thorn in the flesh – with the result that Washington was on the look-out for an excuse both to punish Gaddafi and, if possible, to topple him from power.

The excuse came in 1986 with the terrorist bomb that killed a US serviceman in a Berlin discothèque. The bomb was blamed on Gaddafi terrorists and the raid on Libya which followed was the culmination of a long period of deep US frustration at the tactics of Libya's leader in support of 'terrorism' and the difficulty of doing anything about it. Earlier in the year US Sixth Fleet manoeuvres off the coast of Libya were seen by many (apart from Gaddafi and the Libyans) as being deliberately and unnecessarily provocative.

The raid

On the night of 14–15 April 1986 US bombers flying from bases in Britain and from aircraft carriers of the US Sixth Fleet in the Mediterranean bombed targets in Tripoli and Benghazi in Libya, including Gaddafi's home.

Estimated costs and casualties

Total casualties (dead) came to 130, both civilian and military, and included Gaddafi's adopted daughter. If the purpose of the raid had been to topple Gaddafi, it failed. He was regarded as the only Arab leader to 'stand up' to the USA. Moreover, during the furore of world reaction which followed the raid, no Arab leader could be seen to support or condone the raid no matter what the state of their relations with Gaddafi – and many detested him. Following the raid, Colonel Gaddafi was able to describe President Reagan as 'the world's number one terrorist'.

Results: immediate and longer term

The raid polarized world opinion with a majority, including all countries of the Third World, condemning the US action and only a small minority led by Britain supporting the raid. It was claimed both at the time and later that Britain's Prime Minister, Margaret Thatcher, supported the American action and sanctioned (at very short notice) the use of the British-based US bombers which supposedly were in Britain solely for NATO duties as a return favour for the very substantial support Britain had received from the USA during the Falklands War four years earlier. She was widely criticized in Britain as well as further afield for her decision.

Following the raid and Gaddafi's subsequent subdued international demeanour, the USA called on Libyans to overthrow him, but these calls had no effect. Many Libyans who may have opposed Gaddafi were none the less outraged at the American action. Even so, despite the unfavourable image presented by the world's leading power bombing a relatively defenceless Third World country and killing civilians in the process, Gaddafi himself was generally so unpopular that the immediate sympathy he received did not last. The Americans maintained pressure throughout 1986 to persuade Gaddafi to abandon support for terrorism, and his reputation was sufficiently damaged that opponents predicted he would lose control in Libya. However, they were wrong. Thus in an August NBC-TV interview (recorded on 28 July 1986) Gaddafi said that Libya was at the disposal of the Palestinian people because there was no more sacred struggle than theirs. And by September at the Non-Aligned Summit in Harare, Zimbabwe, Gaddafi was sufficiently back to his old form to tell its members that most were aligned to the West and that the movement was irrelevant.

The raid, however, raised awkward and embarrassing questions about US behaviour and use of its power. It was suggested that the USA had attacked Libya – as opposed to Syria or Iran, both of which could also be accused of supporting anti-Western terrorism – because Libya could not retaliate. The raid demonstrated the comparative helplessness of a superpower against the pinpricks of a minor but determined opponent: short of invading Libya or imposing sanctions, such action appeared as bullying rather than as considered and justifiable policy. Further, the USA had claimed that the bombing was precise, on military targets, when in fact it damaged civilian targets and killed civilians. In the end the raids did more damage to the USA than to Libya and showed how impotent a great power may be in relation to the provocations of a small one.

ASIA

AFGHANISTAN: STRATEGY VERSUS ISLAM

Origins

In a sense Afghanistan was a nineteenth century creation of Britain (operating from its imperial base in India) and Czarist Russia (equally imperialist and expansionist). Afghanistan sat between the two empires and acted uneasily as a buffer state over which they intrigued. Britain fought two wars against the Afghans in the nineteenth century, one with disastrous results.

In the 1960s slow and cautious efforts at modernization inevitably clashed with traditionalist Islam and once the modernizers had been equated with Communism and Marxism an ideological struggle was bound to follow. In any case the USSR had long regarded Afghanistan as a cockpit of immense strategic importance over which it would like to obtain influence and if possible control. The opportunity came in 1979.

In 1964 Afghanistan experimented in constitutional monarchy and held elections for two chambers the following year. But in the period 1965 to 1972, during which there were five different prime ministers, the King refused to pass into law a series of Acts which would have made the experiment in constitutionalism effective. The result was the coup of July 17, 1973, when Mohammad Daud Khan, who had been Prime Minister and was King Zahir Shah's brother-in-law, seized power to abolish the 1964 constitution and make Afghanistan a republic with himself as Prime Minister and Chairman of the Central Committee of the Republic. Although he began with a series of socialist policies and was at that time heavily dependent upon aid from both the USA and the USSR Daud soon moved to the right and sought better relations with other Islamic countries.

By 1977, when he introduced a new constitution, Daud had alienated the two main left-wing groups – Khalq (People's Party) and Parcham (The Flag) – and for the first time in a decade these two united to oppose him. As a result, 1977 and 1978 became years of increasing violence – with assassinations, violent demonstrations and repression – until, following the arrest of PDPA leaders, the military staged another coup (27 April 1978) in which Daud Khan and his family were killed. The new Democratic Republic of Afghanistan was proclaimed: Nur Mohammad Taraki (the leader of the People's Democratic Party of Afghanistan, PDPA) became President and Prime Minister, while Babrak Karmal of Parcham and Hafizullah Amin became Deputy Prime Ministers.

The new government announced nationalist and Islamic policies and proclaimed a policy of non-alignment. Khalq emerged as the dominant force and almost at once the tenuous unity established with Parcham collapsed. Members of Parcham were purged from the government, others were sent abroad to diplomatic posts.

Reforms announced by the Taraki government were seen as Communist and pro-Moscow by the great majority of the traditionalists of the countryside. The PDPA programme of land reform was designed to break the power of the landowning classes in favour of the landless peasants. In fact the PDPA derived most of its support from a small intellectual minority; as a result, both the land and reform and adult literacy campaigns collapsed in the face of widespread opposition and uprisings in most provinces.

Outbreak and response

An anti-government uprising occurred in the Nurestan region bordering on Pakistan late in the summer of 1978. Other uprisings followed, and there were bomb explosions in the capital Kabul. Then, following the assassination of the US Ambassador, Adolph Dubs, on 14 February 1979, American aid to Afghanistan was abruptly ended. On 18 March Amin was promoted to Prime Minister. Taraki kept his post as President, but he was losing support. Meanwhile revolts in the countryside spread and the army was unable to cope with them. Amin requested Soviet military aid. A confrontation between Amin and Taraki on 14 September led to the death of the latter. Amin attempted to mend fences with the USA and Pakistan, but to little avail. He then launched a new series of campaigns against the rebels after offers of amnesty had been rejected or ignored. As the fighting grew, so too did the flood of refugees into Pakistan and Iran.

During 1979 the Soviet Union counselled moderate policies on Amin; then on 24 December Soviet forces invaded Afghanistan, and on 27 December Amin and many of his close followers were killed. Babrak Karmal, who had been in exile in Moscow, returned to become Prime Minister, President of the Revolutionary Council and Secretary-General of the PDPA. The new government attempted a more conciliatory line, promising respect for Islam and Afghan tribal customs. But the Soviet forces were regarded with almost universal hostility, and Islamic groups became increasingly influential in opposing both them and the Karmal government. Moscow defended its intervention in terms of the November 1978 Treaty of Friendship between the two countries, and claimed that Amin had been over-thrown in an internal revolution and that the USSR was responding to requests for assistance from the new government.

The Soviet invasion of Afghanistan fitted into a historical pattern. For more than a century Russia had wanted to break the ring of hostile states on its southern periphery, and in 1979 the old Communist orthodoxy – of spreading revolution – still prevailed. There was nothing new about the Russian move. Moscow thought it saw an opportunity to benefit from the revolutionary situation inside Afghanistan, but its forces soon ran into trouble; by the end of 1980 the original 30,000 or so Soviet troops in Afghanistan had been more than doubled to over 80,000. Anti-Soviet resentment ran deep inside Afghanistan, whose people, united in little else, were steadfast in their almost total opposition to the invaders. The USSR also soon found that its intervention was denounced by most of the world. Apart from opposition from the West and its allies, which was to be expected, the USSR found it had also incurred the enmity of the Islamic world and most non-aligned nations as well; the UN, the OIC, ASEAN and the Non-Aligned Movement all called for

Soviet withdrawal. Only the Communist bloc and a few non-aligned nations supported the invasion.

During 1980 the Soviet forces took over more and more responsibility from the Afghan army, which became progressively demoralized as its ranks were depleted by wholesale desertions of troops to the peasant opposition, reducing it within a year from 80,000 to an estimated 32,000. The Karmal government became more isolated, with growing feuding between the Khalq and Parcham factions. Soviet propaganda suggested an imminent withdrawal would take place as soon as peace had been restored, but by Ocotber 1980, after Karmal had visited Moscow, it was apparent that his government was little more than a Soviet puppet. Although Soviet forces kept open the supply line from the USSR to Kabul, roads to the east and south from the capital were closed by the rebels for lengthy periods, and it became clear that a long war between government and rebels would follow. By September 1980 there were already 900,000 Afghan refugees in Pakistan.

Course of the struggle

The impact of the Soviet intervention on international politics soon became clear as the USSR found itself under pressure from the West, the United Nations, the Islamic world and a majority of the Non-Aligned Movement to quit Afghanistan, while Western pressures for a boycott reduced the number of countries attending the 1980 Moscow Olympics to 81. Throughout the 1980s, with varying fortunes, there was determined Mujaheddin resistance to the Soviet forces in Afghanistan, while the war was to force up to a third of the total Afghan population of about 15 million to become refugees in Pakistan and Iran. Various attempts to find a peaceful solution failed, while the Afghan economy deteriorated sharply, production slumped and exports were lost. At the same time the country became more and more dependent on the Soviet Union and at government level, at least, appeared to be little more than a Moscow satellite.

The year 1981 was one of stalemate as the USSR became entrenched while UN attempts to find an acceptable solution came to nothing. Provisional Basic Principles were published, and in June a Supreme Council of Afghan Tribes was formed; later this became the National Fatherland Front under the umbrella of the PDPA. There was a modification of the land reforms. A Defence Council was formed in August of 1981 with power to control all military matters, and eight military zones now covered the whole country. Steadily, despite much-publicized 'withdrawals', the size of the Soviet military commitment was increased. The anti-government guerrilla (Mujaheddin) groups, despite their lack of co-ordination, none the less disrupted public installations, making roads, bridges and schools their targets. They operated from among the refugees in both Iran and Pakistan, and were active over most of the country. The government forces began to take reprisals for Mujaheddin attacks on villages, and these in turn led to counter-reprisals and a general growth of brutality on both sides. Heavy Soviet casualties were reported, though no figures were released, and as early as March 1981 the UNHCR reported 1.7 million refugees in Pakistan and 400,000 in Iran. Pakistan was believed to be supplying the Mujaheddin with weapons, while both Egypt and Saudi Arabia were backing them with supplies and money. The USSR, meanwhile, began to make available civil advisers to the government, and young Afghans were sent to the Soviet Union for training.

During 1982 the government did somewhat better, while the insurgents were less active and had fewer successes. On the political front President Babrak Karmal managed to eliminate most of the Khalq members of the government. The UN continued its peace efforts, which were designed to achieve the withdrawal of the Soviet forces, to resettle the refugees (who then numbered an estimated 3 million) and to obtain long-term international guarantees safeguarding the future of Afghanistan. In March 1983 talks between UN representatives and the Soviet government were held in Moscow, but they came to nothing. Then in 1984 the fighting escalated again, with key battles being fought in the Panjsher valley to the north of Kabul, and round Kandahar, the second city of Afghanistan, in the south, leading to increased government dependence on Soviet support. That year the government softened its approach to land reform by allowing middle-income peasants to hold 4 hectares (10 acres) of land instead of only 2. It was, if anything, a sign of weakness as the Karmal regime faced continuing party disunity and a steadily weakening economy, while it also tried to bolster an army demoralized by purges and desertions.

By 1984 the guerrillas were well armed with weapons supplied mainly by the USA and China. Government tactics were to hold the towns and main roads, to attack concentrations of guerrillas and to carry out retaliatory raids against villages known to harbour or assist the rebels. In September government forces, assisted by Soviet troops, sealed the border with Pakistan. By this time the civil war had produced wide areas of famine and a mass exodus of refugees – 3 million to Pakistan and 1.5 million to Iran.

The situation continued much the same in 1985 without either side gaining a decisive advantage; precise information about the course of the war or the rate of casualties was always difficult to obtain except for the outcome of spectacular engagements – as, for example, when the guerrillas destroyed more than 20 Afghan air force planes at Shindad air base on 12 June. UN peace efforts were maintained all through the year without result.

By 1986 Babrak Karmal was in deep trouble because of his failure to get on top of the war, and on 4 May he resigned as Secretary-General of the PDPA, supposedly for health reasons, but in fact as a result of Soviet pressure; later, in November, he also resigned as President. He was replaced by Mohammad Najibullah, the former head of the secret police. That December Najibullah visited Moscow to work out how to end the conflict, which by then was costing the USSR a vast amount of money and continuing world hostility without yielding any tangible gains. However, the emergence of the new Soviet leader, Mikhail Gorbachev, was soon to have an impact on the war in Afghanistan. The announcement in October 1986 that six Soviet regiments were to be withdrawn was probably a feeler on Moscow's part; it was greeted with scepticism in the West.

More peace talks took place in 1987, and their focus was on a timetable for Soviet withdrawal. The government offered the rebels a ceasefire but got no response. In July Najibullah visited Moscow to work out a fresh initiative after the failure of the ceasefire, and in August Kabul itself was threatened by the rebels, then at their most aggressive and successful. Najibullah's political star was already waning both at home and in Moscow – or so it seemed – and his claim that 15,000 rebels had laid down their weapons was not believed. Despite this, on 30 November

1987 Najibullah was elected President (head of state), which was a new post under the new constitution. There was heavy fighting throughout the year and there were high casualties on both sides.

Estimated costs and casualties

At the beginning of 1982 Western estimates of casualties already stood at 20,000 Afghan dead and 10,000 Soviet dead and wounded, although, as the war continued, accurate information was hard to obtain. For most of the 1980s after the initial build-up, the Russians maintained approximately 110,000 troops in Afghanistan, though the figure could vary and was to reach 125,000 before the Soviet withdrawal. Pakistan became deeply involved in the war: as the host to more than 3 million refugees (and these, of course, were a changing population depending upon the fortunes of the war); as a determined backer of the Islamic Mujaheddin and the principal conduit for arms and other assistance to them; and in its own geopolitical terms, quite apart from its overt sympathies with the Mujaheddin, because Pakistan regarded any Soviet presence in Afghanistan as a threat to its position. Iran also became involved, although throughout the 1980s it was deep in the throes of its own internal revolution and fighting a war against Iraq in the west. Iran, like Pakistan, became host to Afghan refugees – about 1.5 million at the peak; it supported the Mujaheddin for ideological (Islamic) reasons and opposed any Soviet presence in Afghanistan.

By 1983, and for the balance of the 1980s, the Afghan economy had become overwhelmingly dependent on that of the USSR, which was its main source of supply and took 70 per cent or more of its exports.

The escalation of the war led to a growth of atrocities on both sides. The United Nations, for example, accused the USSR of bombing villages, massacring civilians and ignoring human rights as laid down in the Geneva Convention. It also accused the Soviet forces of holding up to 50,000 political prisoners and using torture to obtain information.

Damage to military installations and other buildings and then, as the war intensified, to whole villages and towns as a result of shelling or bombing became widespread. The population of Kabul increased from about 700,000 when the war began to more than 2 million by 1986 as refugees from the countryside crowded into it, while over 5 million people (out of 15 million) were uprooted by war, the greater part of these becoming refugees.

According to American estimates, Soviet losses by the end of 1986 came to 500 aircraft and helicopters and 25,000 casualties, of whom 10,000 were killed and the rest wounded. The estimated financial costs to the USSR came to more than £1 billion a year. In January 1987 revised US estimates suggested Soviet casualties had then reached 35,000, including 12,000 dead. One factor of growing importance in the USSR was the unpopularity of the war at home, especially with parents whose conscript sons were likely to be sent to Afghanistan.

As usual in such a war an ever-increasing number of countries supplied arms and other military equipment. The USA and China were the principal sources of arms for the Mujaheddin, yet the latter also obtained British equipment, including Blowpipe missiles. In 1987, for example, a senior Soviet diplomat attacked the role of the USA in prolonging the war by supplying the Mujaheddin with Stinger missiles, providing training for 50,000 insurgents a year and voting $600 million in support funds. At the same time, he said, the USA was exerting pressure on Pakistan not to negotiate with the government in Kabul for a peace settlement.

The numbers of Afghan rebels actually fighting varied, according to the season of the year, from a low of about 35,000 to a maximum of about 175,000, and one US estimate suggested that over the whole period of the war following the Soviet invasion an average of 46 Russians had been killed every week. Although Soviet military performance was good in terms of the statistics of counter-insurgency (the kill rate), the Soviets manifestly failed to win the hearts and minds of the majority of the Afghan people. Nor, on the other hand, did the Mujaheddin unite behind a single leader comparable to Ho Chi Minh in Vietnam, and (see below) once the Soviet forces had withdrawn the divisions in the ranks of the Mujaheddin played into the hands of the Kabul government. None the less, despite the collapse of the army (through desertion) to a mere 30,000 in 1980, it had been rebuilt to a respectable 120,000 by 1986.

Breaking the silence which it had maintained throughout the years it was in Afghanistan, the Soviet Union released figures for casualties in May 1988 (as it was withdrawing the first quarter of its 120,000 troops from the country). It claimed that 13,310 soldiers had been killed, 35,478 had been wounded and 311 were still missing. (Western intelligence estimates had been extremely accurate, putting Soviet dead between 12,000 and 15,000 and wounded at 35,000.)

Approximately 250,000 Afghans on the government side were estimated to have been killed, and more than 1 million on the insurgent side.

Results: immediate and longer term

The coming to power of Gorbachev in the USSR led to a different perception of Soviet international interests. While Moscow had always claimed that its forces would be withdrawn from Afghanistan as soon as they could leave behind them a stable government, hardly anyone in the West or elsewhere had believed them. But during 1986 it became clear that the USSR really was seeking a way out of its Afghan intervention, provided it could find a suitable formula to enable it to withdraw without too great a loss of face.

By December 1986 the UN mediator, Diego Cordovez, who had been shuttling between Afghanistan, Pakistan, Iran and the USSR since 1982, claimed that 'forward movement' had been achieved and that the key issue was a timetable for the withdrawal of Soviet troops, then estimated at 115,000, with UN teams overseeing their departure and checking a halt to the flow of supplies to the insurgents from Pakistan. At that point Moscow was refusing any withdrawal as long as arms and supplies continued to flow to the insurgents from the West, the conservative Arab states and Iran. Pakistan maintained its refusal to deal directly with the Kabul government, which it claimed was no more than a puppet of Moscow.

Increasingly, at this time, Afghanistan came to be seen as the test of Soviet sincerity in relation to its new *glasnost* policies; for both the Islamic world and the Non-Aligned Movement, what happened in Afghanistan was the key to Moscow's 'good neighbour' policy. More important from Moscow's point of view, intervention to prop up a Marxist government that appeared to be universally detested had been a costly failure. At the same time the long war had done considerable damage to Western interests in the region: the 3 million refugees in Pakistan had become a major source of friction as well as of arms for subversive groups. And American support for the Mujaheddin provided through Pakistan, which Washington built up with massive military assistance, had far more to do with old Cold War attitudes than with sympathy for the Mujaheddin cause. Pakistan had become an arsenal of weapons supplied by the USA, China and others, and the insurgents were selling these (guns, missiles, rocket-propelled grenade-launchers, anti-tank mines) openly throughout the country; some, for example, were getting into the hands of Sikh extremists in the Punjab. The result was to turn Pakistan into something of a US military satellite: not only had it come to depend on huge American military subventions and to act as the principal conduit of arms into Afghanistan, but American forces were using airstrips and ports along its Makran coast in Baluchistan at the entrance to the Gulf, while their listening posts monitored Soviet missile tests. Pakistan's sympathy for the Afghan cause was beginning to disappear as the strain of the huge refugee presence affected most aspects of the country's life.

Early in 1987 the Soviet Foreign Minister, Eduard Shevardnadze, and Anatoly Dobrynin, the Kremlin foreign policy adviser, visited Kabul for talks with Dr Najibullah and his colleagues about a Soviet withdrawal, which the Soviets insisted had to be linked to the stability of the regime it would leave behind. By then there were growing signs that Moscow believed the Afghan leadership could survive its withdrawal, not least by dividing the opposition and wooing to its support centrists and those most disillusioned by the course of the war. But while such talks were in progress, the guerrillas were acquiring new weapons, including Swiss 20 mm anti-aircraft guns and Chinese 107 mm rockets, especially as American supplies appeared – at least temporarily – to have dried up in the wake of the Irangate scandal. At the same time the war had become more of an embarrassment to Pakistan, where 3 million refugees had come to be regarded as a destabilizing factor. Thus, in the middle of January the government of Kabul instituted a unilateral ceasefire, although the insurgents ignored it and stepped up their attacks. Negotiations for a Soviet withdrawal were slow, however, and by the end of February (although agreement over the repatriation of the then estimated 5 million refugees as well as international guarantees had been settled) the timetable for the Soviet withdrawal remained outstanding, with Moscow insisting that there had to be a stable Afghanistan before its forces left the country for good. By the end of March Afghan air raids across the Pakistan border threatened an escalation of hostilities, reducing the peace efforts to a much slower, more problematic pace, at least for the time being. By October 1987 the Iranians had become much more active on behalf of the insurgents, for the first time supplying weapons for the guerrillas operating from Pakistan and wooing individual field commanders inside Afghanistan with cash. Iran also succeeded in uniting a number of warring factions into a single new alliance. In Peshawar seven Afghan guerrilla parties – four fundamentalist and three moderate – chose Maulvi Younis Khalis as their representative for the coming year.

In February 1988 Moscow forced the pace when Gorbachev set 15 May as the date for the start of Soviet troop withdrawals, with 10 months for completion whether or not agreement was reached in Kabul as to the membership of a new ruling coalition. And though the withdrawal was made dependent on the agreement between Afghanistan and Pakistan then being worked out in Geneva under UN auspices, it had become abundantly clear that Moscow wished to end as soon as possible an involvement which had done it major damage on the international front and caused deep resentment at home. Afghanistan and Pakistan agreed to the terms of the withdrawal shortly afterwards, and the first 30,000 Soviet troops had been withdrawn by June 1988.

In October 1988 the USSR promised to donate US$600 million in humanitarian aid to Afghanistan for distribution by the UN, which had launched an international appeal for aid and had then received promises of $700 million. The Soviet money was to be used to help every province and was in effect a Soviet gesture of reparation. Given that an estimated 10 to 20 million mines then needed to be cleared, the problems of national rehabilitation were clearly on a massive scale. In the end, ironically, it appeared that Moscow was pushing for peace while both the Mujaheddin and their principal ally, Pakistan, were stalling on the assumption that, once the Soviets had withdrawn, the insurgents would rapidly take over control of the country and government.

By February 1989, as the last Soviet troops were preparing to meet their 15 February deadline for quitting Afghanistan, President Najibullah summoned 30,000 civilians to arms for the 'life-and-death struggle' for Kabul. With an estimated 150,000 troops, paramilitary forces and militias, the ruling PDPA prepared for what appeared to be a last-ditch struggle as most diplomats predicted the rapid collapse of the Najibullah government once all the Soviets had gone. But it became increasingly clear even as the Soviets finally departed that the various Mujaheddin groups were deeply divided, while the representatives of the nearly 2 million Shia Muslims in Iran were refusing to co-operate with the Pakistan-based groups of the east.

The swift collapse of the Najibullah government did not take place. In March the insurgents began their assault on the main eastern town of Jalalabad, but although they penetrated some parts of the city and 30,000 refugees fled the area, they did not succeed in taking it. By May 1989 government forces were having considerable success in repulsing the attack on Jalalabad, the insurgents were still disunited and the Najibullah government was showing new signs of confidence. The people as a whole were demonstrably war weary; at that point the UNDP estimated that in Kabul alone 40,000 people were in urgent need of food aid.

In the year following the Soviet withdrawal, the two superpowers maintained their support for the opposite sides in the continuing Afghan confrontation, with the USSR providing the Kabul government with up to £120 million a month in aid, and the USA continuing to back the Mujaheddin guerrillas. The years 1989 and 1990 became two of the bloodiest of the entire conflict as rival warlords fought for control. By mid-1990 a stalemate had been reached: the USSR was unwilling to withdraw support from President Najibullah, who had been a loyal ally of the Kremlin; and President Bush was not prepared to cut US support for the Mujaheddin. There was every indication that a messy guerrilla war was set to continue indefinitely. However, contrary to earlier Western expectations, President Najibullah appeared to be consolidating his hold on the country without a Soviet presence.

KOREA 1950–1953: COLD WAR PAWNS

Origins

Despite having a unique culture of its own, Korea was destined to play a buffer role between China and Japan. In 1895, following the Peace of Shimoneseki which concluded the Sino–Japanese War, Korea was declared independent, but fifteen years later, in 1910, it was brought under 'permanent' Japanese suzerainty. Not only did Japan take control of the entire Korean peninsula, but it administered it solely in its own interests and was to continue to do so up to its defeat in 1945 at the end of the Second World War. At the July 1945 Potsdam Conference the Allied leaders agreed that, on the defeat of Japan, Korea should recover the independence it had lost to Japan in 1910: the Russians were to accept the surrender of the Japanese north of latitude 38, the Americans the areas south of that line. It was not the intention of the West that the 38th parallel of latitude should become a permanent frontier between two Koreas but, given the rapid development of the Cold War, this is what happened, one state becoming Communist, the other pro-West.

During the period 1945–8 the Russians provided assistance in implementing Communism in 'North' Korea and also supervised the creation of a large army. In 'South' Korea the Americans fostered the growth of Western-style politics. The United Nations tried but failed to re-establish a united Korea. In 1947, for example, when neither side would agree to unification, the USA turned the problem over to the UN. But when the question of unification was referred to the General Assembly of the United Nations, the USSR refused to discuss the issue and claimed that it was outside UN jurisdiction.

The following year (1948) a United Nations Commission supervised general elections in South Korea, from which Syngman Rhee emerged as President of a Republic of South Korea with an elected government which was subsequently recognized as the lawful Korean government by most independent states, except for the USSR and its Bloc allies. Following these elections, the USA in 1949 withdrew the troops which it had maintained in South Korea since the end of the war, although it did leave behind some military advisers. In North Korea the administration announced elections and subsequently proclaimed the formation of the Democratic People's Republic of North Korea (3 September 1948). The Soviets then also withdrew their wartime forces, but left a number of technicians behind.

In the years 1948–50, following the formation of the two Koreas, an increasing number of border incidents and confrontations occurred for which both sides were to blame. Neither of the new states was economically self-supporting, and both governments used the border incidents to distract attention from internal problems. In June 1950 a United Nations Commission met with representatives of North Korea on the 38th parallel to discuss unification, which the North Koreans insisted they wished to attain peacefully. This meeting took place two weeks before the North Koreans invaded South Korea.

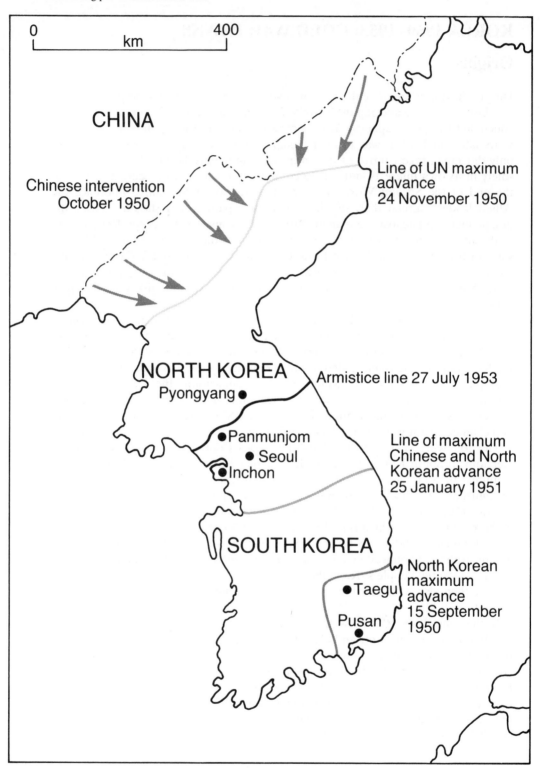

0 400 km

CHINA

Chinese intervention
October 1950

Line of UN maximum
advance
24 November 1950

NORTH KOREA

Pyongyang ●

Armistice line 27 July 1953

● Panmunjom

● Seoul

●Inchon

Line of maximum
Chinese and North
Korean advance
25 January 1951

SOUTH KOREA

North Korean
maximum
advance
15 September
1950

● Taegu

Pusan
●

Map 7   Korea

Outbreak and response

There was never to be any official declaration of war. On 25 June 1950 North Korean forces crossed the 38th parallel to invade South Korea in an attempt to unify the two Koreas on their terms. Fighting was to last from that date until 27 July 1953 when an armistice was signed at Panmunjon. The Soviets must have known of the impending attack, but the Chinese almost certainly did not: that was to prove a factor of prime importance later.

The United Nations Security Council met in emergency session and passed a resolution (27 July) which called on all members to provide the world body with assistance to halt the invasion and on the North Koreans to withdraw behind the 38th parallel. Although the members of the Communist bloc dissented, the USSR was boycotting the Security Council at the time and so was not present to exercise its veto. The American President, Harry S. Truman, then announced the immediate despatch of American troops to Korea, and the British Prime Minister, Clement Attlee, promised full British support. Truman, however, did not ask Congress to declare war, rather ordering US troops to assist the UN with its 'police action'. At the same time the US 7th Fleet was moved into the area to protect the island of Taiwan, a move which ensured that China would become involved in the conflict since Beijing saw the US move as a threat to its interests in the region.

The war may be divided conveniently into four phases.

Phase 1

When war broke out the North Korean army consisted of seven full-strength divisions and four independent brigades; they were well armed with Russian tanks and had good artillery. Their initial attack, in which 60,000 troops were launched across the border, was well co-ordinated and achieved total surprise. South Korea had eight divisions, but these had only been maintained at brigade strength; they had little artillery or armour. The South Korean defences were breached at once and they fell back rapidly, suffering heavy losses in the process but also inflicting heavy casualties on the North Koreans. The North Korean army entered the South Korean capital, Seoul, on 30 June just five days after launching its attack. The same day American troops were landed in South Korea: these initial four divisions were poorly trained and equipped, and were to be driven back with the South Koreans to the Pusan bridgehead. On 7 July the US General Douglas MacArthur was named Supreme Commander of the UN Korean forces.

Once committed the Americans rapidly built up their forces; North Korea soon lost air superiority to the Americans and was not to regain it for the remainder of the war. The USA then enforced a naval blockade of the Korean coast. British troops arrived in Korea on 29 August. None the less, during this first phase of the war the UN forces were pushed back to the bridgehead round Pusan on the west coast of South Korea. On 1 September the attacking North Korean forces launched a major offensive against the Pusan perimeter, but the UN forces held their ground and the attack slowed down and then ended in mid-September. Up to this point in the war the North Korean forces had been on the offensive and had made remarkable early gains, but in the process of their rapid advances they had also clearly overstretched their resources and communications. The first phase of the war ended when the North Korean attack on the Pusan perimeter petered out.

Phase 2

On 15 September General MacArthur launched his first counter-offensive: he made a surprise landing of US forces at the Inchon beachhead 160 km (100 miles) below the 38th parallel to cut the North Korean line of communications to its forces further south round the Pusan perimeter, and to move 32 km (20 miles) inland to recapture Seoul. The Inchon landing achieved total surprise and the following day (16 September) the UN forces broke out of the Pusan perimeter in another successful offensive. It was now the turn of the North Korean army to experience defeat, and in a few days of fighting the UN forces were to capture large numbers of North Korean troops. The 1st US Marine Division moved inland from Inchon to recapture Seoul on 28 September, but only after heavy fighting. By 1 October the North Koreans were falling back, partly in rout, to the 38th parallel, but six North Korean divisions had been trapped in South Korea by the MacArthur manoeuvre and their army had suffered enormous casualties and losses of equipment. The mass surrenders of North Korean troops also suggested a loss of morale.

At this point in the conflict, as the UN forces drove the North Koreans back to the 38th parallel, China warned that it would regard an invasion of North Korea as a direct threat which would be likely to bring China into the war, a warning that General MacArthur was to discount. By October, apart from the South Korean army, the UN forces consisted of the US 8th Army and contingents from Britain, Australia, Canada, Turkey and the Philippines (by the end of the war there would be 21 national contingents under UN command).

Cold War politics now came to the fore. General MacArthur wished to push forward at once into North Korea. On 7 October the United Nations General Assembly authorized the continuation of the war into North Korea 'if necessary', and two days later (9 October) the UN forces crossed the 38th parallel to enter North Korea and (presumably) reunite the two Koreas. On 19 October Pyongyang, the North Korean capital, fell to the UN forces; the city had already been heavily bombed by the US air force and was devastated. On 24 November General MacArthur announced a major offensive with the propaganda slogan 'home by Christmas', and the next day, as the UN forces headed for the Yalu river which formed the boundary between North Korea and China, 180,000 Chinese 'volunteers' entered the war.

Phase 3

China's Premier, Zhou Enlai, had already warned the United Nations that his country would not be passive should the UN forces invade North Korea; his warning was supported by huge concentrations of Chinese troops north of the Yalu. Despite this, General MacArthur had worked on the assumption that China would intervene only if his forces actually crossed the Yalu. This thinking led

MacArthur into a military miscalculation, for when his forces had conquered North Korea he allowed them to be widely dispersed without any defensive depth. The initial Chinese response to the invasion of North Korea was to use Soviet MiG 15s, which attacked UN bases from airfields in Manchuria. There was also some patrol probing. But then, on 26–27 November, some 14 Chinese divisions attacked the UN line across North Korea, which was broken at Tokchen. Soon the entire UN army, which was greatly outnumbered, came under threat from the Chinese offensive. In one thrust the Chinese and North Koreans drove southwards to recapture Pyongyang on 4 December; a second Chinese thrust using six divisions bottled up the US 10th Corps in an enclave near the east coast at Wonsan. Later the 10th Corps managed to fight its way to Hungham on the coast, from whence it was evacuated to Pusan (11–24 December). By 15 December the UN forces had been driven back to the 38th parallel, but although the North Koreans and their Chinese ally announced the invasion of South Korea at the end of the year, this in fact petered out and lines were established by both sides along the 38th parallel.

The Chinese were handicapped by supply problems and were not always able to follow up their successes. This allowed the UN forces to disengage and retreat below latitude 38, although they suffered very heavy losses of equipment. During December General Matthew B. Ridgway succeeded General Walker as the US Commander, his predecessor having been killed in a road accident.

Phase 4

On 1 January 1951 the Chinese launched a new offensive along the entire UN line (the 38th parallel); after three days' fighting they recaptured Seoul, and by mid-January they were 110 km (70 miles) into South Korea across a broad front. Then, on 21 January, the UN forces counter-attacked: first the Chinese were forced back across the Han river; then, on 14 March, Seoul was recaptured for the second time in the war. By 8 April South Korea to the east of the Imjin river was once more under UN control.

During this stage of the war, when the UN was reeling before the Chinese offensive, General MacArthur had publicly quarrelled with President Truman and urged the bombing of mainland China in order to halt the Chinese offensive. He provoked deep fears in the West (Britain, for example) that such action would lead to a wider conflict which would draw in the USSR, and President Truman was obliged to relieve him of his command on 11 April 1951.

On 23 April the Chinese launched another major offensive. It was during this that the 1st Battalion of the British Gloucester Regiment distinguished itself at the Battle of Imjin River when its effective strength was reduced to 100 men during a three-day battle that held up the rapid Chinese advance. By early May the Chinese offensive had slowed down, and a renewed offensive lauched on 16 May did not break through the UN lines. On 21 May the UN forces counter-attacked and the Chinese were driven back to the 38th parallel.

Peace negotiations

In June 1951 the Russian delegate at the UN indicated that the Communists were prepared to discuss a truce, and talks between the two sides began at Kaesong on 10 July. These talks were to drag on for two years, periodically interrupted by outbreaks of fighting, although the battles lines between the two sides were to remain static. In the USA General Eisenhower, who was running for President, promised he would end the war if elected.

The first break in the talks occurred in August 1951 when each side accused the other of infringing the neutrality of the talks zone. In October the talks were resumed at Panmunjon, and by December the two sides had got as far as exchanging lists of prisoners of war. The talks continued throughout 1952 with prisoners providing the main stumbling block to a settlement. The Communist side wanted all prisoners to be returned, but the United Nations was opposed to the repatriation of unwilling prisoners and claimed that large numbers of both North Koreans and Chinese did not wish to be repatriated. These opposing stands produced stalemate. Then, in mid-1952, pro-Communist prisoners held in South Korea revolted, and in October the talks were again adjourned. At the end of the year India proposed a compromise for a ceasefire; this however, was turned down. General Eisenhower, as he had promised, visited Korea.

Only in April 1953 did the two sides agree to exchange sick and wounded prisoners. Then, on 8 June, a complicated plan was agreed whereby prisoners who did not wish to be repatriated would be handed over to a third, neutral power. President Rhee of South Korea turned down the armistice terms on 18 June and then allowed 25,000 North Korean prisoners to 'escape'; in retaliation the Chinese mounted heavy artillery bombardments against the South Korean-held sectors of the line, and these were to continue until the armistice was finally signed. There were heavy casualties on both sides. Finally an armistice agreement was signed on 27 July 1953: the two sides accepted the battle lines of the 38th parallel as the boundary between the two Koreas. A political conference to discuss reunification was to follow 90 days after the armistice; this soon broke down and subsequent efforts to bring about reunification came to nothing.

Estimated costs and casualties

By May 1951 Communist military casualties were estimated at 250,000 dead, material losses were enormous and North Korea had been devastated by bombing. The figure of 250,000 included Chinese dead, but casualties may have been much higher. The main United Nations forces in support of the South Koreans were first the Americans, then the Commonwealth Division (Britain, Australia and Canada), and Turkey. Principal casualties on the UN side were: USA 33,600 dead and 108,400 wounded; Britain 1000 dead and 3500 wounded. South Korean casualties were proportionately much higher, though no firm figures exist.

In the end the UN repatriated 77,000 prisoners, while 22,500 refused repatriation. The Communists repatriated 12,700 prisoners, of whom 3,597 were American and 945 British. Approximately 400 UN prisoners held in North Korea (mainly

South Koreans) refused repatriation. Of those refusing repatriation, 15,000 anti-Communist Chinese were sent to Formosa and 7500 North Koreans were handed over to South Korea. The Communists agreed to help the 400 UN troops who refused repatriation.

The civilian populations on both sides suffered even higher casualties than did the military (including deaths from malnutrition), and an estimated 5 million people lost their lives. Both North and South Korea suffered enormous physical devastation.

One particular result of the war was to publicize the concept of brainwashing. Crude Chinese attempts at brainwashing prisoners, especially those from the USA and Britain, received much attention at the time and went far to build up Western stereotypes of Communist techniques. The techniques of brainwashing supposedly used were popularized in Richard Condon's novel *The Manchurian Candidate*, which was made into a highly successful film.

Results: immediate and longer term

The conclusion of the war could be described as a victory for the United Nations in so far as it had prevented North Korean aggression from succeeding, although this would not have been the case without the willingness of the USA to intervene on a massive scale. The USA always had equipment superiority and was also able to maintain air superiority throughout the war. The defeat of North Korea represented the first holding of the line against Communist expansion since 1945. The war also saw the emergence of China as a formidable power in the region, capable of fielding large numbers of tough combat troops.

The war was fought along entirely conventional lines – in the end with both sides dug in along the 38th parallel it was more reminiscent of the First World War than the Second – although the UN forces did use helicopters effectively for fighting in difficult terrain, foreshadowing their use by Americans in Vietnam.

At the end of the war there were still two Koreas so, given the terrible suffering and loss of life that had been endured on both sides, the war could be seen as an exercise in futility. It was, however, a landmark in the formation of Cold War attitudes and fears which were to last for a generation. The main combatants – apart from the Koreans – were the Chinese on the one side and the Americans and British on the other, while the USSR supported North Korea in the background. The fears raised by General MacArthur that the war could escalate into a nuclear conflict led Britain's Prime Minister, Clement Attlee, to journey to Washington in an effort to persuade President Truman not to allow the bomb to be used. The two-man meeting between President and Prime Minister demonstrated to Attlee the limitations of British power as well as the justification for Britain having its own bomb!

The war also saw the emergence of India as the leader of non-alignment. Following the armistice of July 1953, the United Nations voted 27 for, 21 against with 11 abstentions (India did not vote) on 27 August for India's inclusion in the UN Political Conference on Korea. The invitation to India to take part, opposed by the USA in particular, was a vital admission of principle: that non-aligned countries had as much right to a say in matters pertaining to peace as did those who had taken part in the fighting.

VIETNAM: THE THIRTY YEARS' WAR

Introduction

Two wars are dealt with here. The first began in 1946 as a nationalist war of liberation against the French and ended with the settlement reached at Geneva in 1954 following the French defeat at Dien Bien Phu. The second war started almost at once, although there was a certain gradualness to begin with before the terrible escalation of the 1960s. This second war continued until the withdrawal of the Americans in 1972–3 and the subsequent collapse of resistance by South Vietnam in face of the dual onslaught of the North Vietnamese and their South Vietnamese allies (the Viet Cong). It could be said to have ended with the formal reunification of the two Vietnams in 1976.

But the seeds of the second war were all sown during the first one, and long before Dien Bien Phu the French had turned what was essentially an end of empire colonial struggle into an ideological one in which they represented themselves as guardians of Western values and 'democracy' fighting against the onslaught of world Communism. They did this in order to enlist American support, which they then obtained on a massive scale. The French were finally defeated, but by then the USA was already so committed to the concept of preventing South Vietnam falling to Communism that Washington hardly even made a pretence at adhering to the Geneva settlement; instead, the USA built up its own client ruler in South Vietnam (President Ngo Dinh Diem) and then, inexorably, became more and more involved in a war that it could not win. By 1973, when the USA finally withdrew from Vietnam, the ideological aspects of the war had become irrelevant.

The first Vietnam War: 1946–1954

Origins

By 1884 Indo-China (comprising Cambodia, Laos and Vietnam) had been brought under French colonial control. The territory was a storehouse of potential wealth, and French exploitation meant that Indo-China as a whole became the third largest exporter of rice and rubber in the world. One result was that per capita consumption of rice inside Indo-China fell by 30 per cent between 1900 and 1939, while the people were heavily taxed to pay for the French occupation. The French colonial administration controlled the sale of four key commodities – opium, alcohol, tobacco and salt – and taxes on these provided 60 per cent of revenues. Nationalist uprisings against the French and pressures for an end to colonial rule became constant from the 1920s onwards. French colonial exploitation increased the poverty of the people, while providing minimal education or development in return.

The Japanese invaded Indo-China in 1940, and the French colonial authorities (on instructions from the Vichy government in France) collaborated with the Japanese and continued to administer the territory on behalf of the new rulers. Towards the end of the war (1945) the Japanese dispensed with their French collaborators and appointed a local aristocrat, Bao Dai, as 'Emperor'.

Map 8   Vietnam

During the period of the Japanese occupation the Vietnamese nationalists had united behind the Communist leader Ho Chi Minh, who as Nguyen Ai Quoc was a founder member of the Communist Party of Indo-China. He returned to Indo-China as the Comintern-appointed leader from Moscow, and in May 1941 he called a Vietnamese nationalist conference in south China at which the Viet Minh (League for the Independence of Vietnam) was created. Vo Nguyen Giap was given responsibility for creating a military organization. Under Ho Chi Minh the nationalists were prepared to co-operate with the Americans or the French who had rejected Vichy in order to fight the Japanese. Then, on 14 August 1945, the Japanese surrendered and the nationalists assumed that at last the moment of their independence had arrived. According to agreements reached at Potsdam, the Nationalist Chinese were to occupy North Vietnam and the British the south; as they surrendered the Japanese ignored the Vietnamese nationalists and handed over control to the incoming forces of these two powers.

The French now returned to resume colonial control – their first troops arrived in October 1945 – and the British handed over the south to them by the end of 1945, with the Nationalist Chinese ceding the north during 1946. The Viet Minh, therefore, reactivated their guerrilla forces ready for a renewed struggle. Giap was an able guerrilla commander who had served with Mao Zedong in China; by 1945 he had 10,000 guerrillas under his command. Ho Chi Minh set up a Vietnamese People's Liberation Committee, and immediately following the Japanese surrender the Committee appealed to Bao Dai to abdicate in favour of the Nationalists. He did so and on 19 August the Indo-China Communist Party (ICP) seized control in Hanoi, although there was greater opposition to the Communists in the south of the country. On 28 August Ho Chi Minh dissolved the Liberation Committee and established a provisional government in its place with most posts going to members of the ICP. A great deal of bloodletting followed (the August Revolution) as ideological opponents of the Communists were eliminated. An estimated 10,000 people were killed in Hanoi alone and many thousands more elsewhere.

On 2 September 1945 in Hanoi Ho Chi Minh proclaimed the Declaration of Independence of the Democratic Republic of Vietnam. At that point the USA urged France to accept Ho Chi Minh as the new head of state, but the French were determined to reassert their colonial control and were only prepared to recognize Vietnam as a state within the French Union.

Outbreak and response

The Vietnamese people were determined to oppose any efforts at recolonization, whether by the French or anyone else, and when Ho Chi Minh declared Vietnam independent at Hanoi on 2 September he assumed that the new republic covered the entire territory of Vietnam. But even as he made his proclamation the British were accepting the Japanese surrender in the south, where they released the French who had been imprisoned by the Vietnamese for collaborating with the Japanese. When British troops under General Lacey arrived in Saigon (the capital) they were welcomed by the Viet Minh, but the British ousted them at once in favour of the French, so Vietnamese independence in Saigon lasted a mere three weeks.

In the north, however, the French were obliged to proceed with greater caution.

Thus, on 6 March 1946 they signed an agreement with Ho Chi Minh under which Vietnam gained 'independence' within the French Union. This did not satisfy the Vietnamese, and negotiations with the French for full independence continued until September. Ho Chi Minh then made a call to arms to defend the newly independent Republic of Vietnam and appealed to the world community for support. Giap launched a full-scale offensive against the French – by then he had 60,000 badly equipped men under his command – and the fighting began. That November the French bombarded the northern seaport of Haiphong in a series of military manoeuvres designed to regain total control. The Giap offensive did not succeed and the French forces drove the Vietnamese army into the hills in the north of the country near the Chinese border, where they were to remain for three years. So began the first Vietnam War. By the time it came to an end in 1954 the French had 250,000 troops in the country.

During eight years of warfare the French fought the nationalists to regain control of what they still regarded as an imperial fief, but the era of Western domination in Asia was over: in 1947 British India became independent, in 1948 Burma, in 1949 the Dutch recognized Indonesia as the successor state to their East Indies empire, and the same year saw the triumph of the Communists under Mao Zedong throughout mainland China. Also in 1949 the French appointed the durable Bao Dai as emperor of a Free Associated State of Vietnam, although keeping the real power in their own hands. From that point onwards the war went against them.

Course of the struggle

Even though the French came increasingly to represent the Viet Minh simply as Communists (at a time when the Cold War was at its height), in fact the other, non-Communist, nationalists were just as determined to have independence. From 1947 to 1954 the French escalated their military effort to regain total colonial control over Vietnam, yet despite a massive military input they failed to win the war, a lesson which the Americans subsequently discounted.

At the beginning of 1947 – after Giap's first offensive had been defeated – the French moved their troops into Hanoi. The Vietnamese, who had made the mistake of confronting the French in conventional military battles and had lost heavily, now reverted to guerrilla tactics. In the north of Vietnam the French built a series of forts along the border with China; they assumed these would enable them to control the border and the region, but Giap's forces ignored the forts and infiltrated south.

In April 1948 Ho Chi Minh issued a series of orders to his forces in the form of Twelve Recommendations which insisted on close identification by the Viet Minh with the peasants – in essence a 'hearts and minds' approach to the struggle. A turning point was reached in November 1949 when all China had fallen to the Communists under Mao Zedong. As a result, Communist China was now able to provide cross-border sanctuary and logistical support for the Viet Minh forces.

The Chinese Communist victory also had a profound influence on US policy, which now sought to 'contain' the spread of Communism; as a result, Washington became increasingly anxious to support the French in Vietnam as a bastion against the spread of Communism, a role the French were quick to adopt in return for

American money and arms. The Viet Minh, meanwhile, began to spread south-wards again and ensured their control of the countryside by eliminating village headmen unsympathetic to their cause. The French now granted 'independence' to Vietnam with the puppet Bao Dai once more elevated, this time as President, although real control remained in French hands. The move was designed to attract much-needed American military assistance since the USA, with its in-built opposition to colonialism, did not wish to appear to be helping France hold on to a colony. From 1950 onwards the French represented themselves as fighting a war against Communism and defending Bao Dai's free Vietnam against Communist aggression. On May Day of that year the French–American strategy was made more plausible when the Viet Minh acknowledged that their Democratic Republic of Vietnam was in the Soviet ideological camp. The USA now established a Military and Advisory Group (MAAG) in Vietnam, and the first American arms were delivered in August 1950. In October the Viet Minh moved against the French forts along the country's northern border – they had already cut them off from the main French forces in the south – and captured them all over a period of 17 days.

In January 1951 the Viet Minh began a drive on Hanoi, but their troops were heavily defeated at Vinh Yen, where they lost 6000 dead and 500 captured. They had again made the mistake of confronting the French in major military engage-ments. This defeat was followed by a period of relatively small-scale guerrilla warfare. The ideological nature of the struggle was coming more and more into the open; on 3 March 1951 the Viet Minh formally dissolved itself in favour of the ICP (although the term 'Viet Minh' continued to be used).

By April 1953 the Viet Minh had extended the war across the border into Laos. To counter this development the French determined to pin down the Viet Minh forces in the area close to the Laos border, and they chose Dien Bien Phu as the focal point for a confrontation. They hoped once more to force the Vietnamese into a pitched battle (they had always won in such circumstances previously), but on this occasion the French army was surrounded and trapped. The siege of Dien Bien Phu lasted from 13 March to 7 May 1954, during which time all supplies had to be airlifted into the French. On 7 May, however, after eight weeks of bitter fighting, the French garrison surrendered. This defeat effectively ended French military power in south-east Asia and led Paris to abandon any further pretensions to political control in Indo-China.

Estimated costs and casualties

For France the war meant the end of its Asian empire, leaving it free to fight its last colonial war in Algeria, which was lost in a not dissimilar manner. For Vietnam the war was the beginning of 30 years of strife which was to grow far more terrible during the 1960s, although there were many thousands of casualties in this first war. The French would have been obliged to give up much sooner than they did had it not been for massive American military aid: for the last four years of the war the USA bore 80 per cent of the costs, while also supplying most of the military equipment. Washington was not interested in preserving the French empire, but only in extending American power and influence in the region in order, as American policy makers believed, to prevent Communist expansion.

Following the Geneva Conference of 1954, about 900,000 Vietnamese (Roman Catholics and those who had supported the French) moved south from North Vietnam, while between 30,000 and 100,000 from the south moved north.

Results: immediate and longer term

The Americans saw Vietnam as the key to south-east Asia and in terms of the Cold War, which was then moving towards a climax, believed its retention in the Western camp was a stategic necessity: that was the principal reason for their involvement. As Secretary of State John Foster Dulles said in March 1954 (before the fall of Dien Bien Phu), 'It is rich in many raw materials such as tin, oil, rubber and iron ore . . . The area has great strategic value . . . It has major naval and air bases.'

Nine nations took part in the Geneva Conference of May 1954, which arranged a ceasefire between France and the Viet Minh and designated the 17th parallel as the dividing line (including a demilitarized zone) between the Viet Minh to the north and the French and their Vietnamese allies to the south. The agreement of 21 July effectively created two Vietnams: the Communist, Soviet-backed north; and the pro-Western, American-supported south. Vietnam was separated into two (temporary) zones largely as a result of American opposition to a single Vietnam, which would have been in the Communist camp rather than that of the West. The agreement stipulated that free elections were to be held throughout Vietnam in 1956.

The outcome of the Geneva Conference was unacceptable to the USA, which had invested very heavily in the French military effort and did not wish even North Vietnam to end up as a Communist state. The terms of the agreement were soon ignored by the United States, while the French continued to recognize the discredited Bao Dai. At best the Geneva Conference brought a temporary lull in the fighting and allowed the French to extricate themselves from an impossible situation. At worst it simply delayed the coming battle for control of all Vietnam and allowed both sides time to prepare for a renewed and, as it turned out, far more bloody struggle.

The second Vietnam War: 1955–1975

Origins

The second Vietnam War was essentially an attempt by South Vietnam (supported by the USA, which was determined to prevent the spread of Communism in south-east Asia) to stop North Vietnam and the Viet Cong from uniting north and south. The Geneva Conference had recognized that Vietnam was one country and one people; it was the USA which, for Cold War reasons, ensured that an absolute divide along the 17th parallel of latitude should be maintained. By rejecting elections in the two Vietnams during the immediate post-Geneva period, the American protégé, Diem, sabotaged the settlement. On 17 November 1954 General Collins, President Eisenhower's special representative in South Vietnam, forced the appointment of Diem on the south by threatening to end all further American military aid unless he was accepted. So Bao Dai, himself a puppet, appointed Ngo Dinh Diem as Prime Minister, and the following year Diem held what was regarded as a farcical referendum to abolish the monarchy. South Vietnam became a republic on 26 October 1955, and Diem its first President.

As a result of forcing their candidate on the South Vietnamese, the Americans found themselves drawn inexorably into defending his position and fighting a war which was to prove one of the most costly forays into international affairs in the history of the USA.

Opponents of the Diem regime were automatically labelled as Communists, and his rule became increasingly dictatorial and repressive. He refused to take part in all-Vietnam elections in 1956 (as agreed at Geneva), and early in his presidency he offended the powerful Buddhist sects by appointing Roman Catholics to most of the key posts. Meanwhile guerrilla actions against the government intensified, and Vietnamese from the south who had received training in the north now returned to join the Communist resistance movement (what became the Viet Cong), which grew steadily stronger and more effective). Diem appealed to the USA for ever more assistance in building up the Army of the Republic of Vietnam (ARVN).

Between 1955 and 1960 a number of requests by Hanoi to South Vietnam to allow elections were turned down by Saigon, where it was believed that as many as 80 per cent of the people would then vote for Ho Chi Minh. Although for a few years after Geneva an uneasy truce was maintained between North and South Vietnam, everything indicated that an outbreak of hostilities between the two was inevitable.

Outbreak and response

Although there is no obvious date, the second Vietnam War might be said to have commenced in 1958 when the Communists began attacking government officials in the south. The National Liberation Front (NLF) was established in South Vietnam in December 1960 (its military wing was the Viet Cong) to resist the Diem government. It obtained immediate and widespread support and within two years had control of 80 per cent of the countryside, where it built schools and provided rudimentary health services. The NLF issued a 10-point programme of reforms in which it called for reunification with the north in stages. In October 1961 President John F. Kennedy sent a mission to Saigon which recommended massive American military aid. An original 800 military 'advisers' had soon increased to 15,000. Under the new American initiative the following steps were taken: the ARVN was increased to 600,000 men; 16,000 strategic hamlets were created so as to deny support to the Viet Cong; trees were defoliated to destroy cover for the guerrillas; and the American military advisers were given operational control. By 1962 American advisers were fighting alongside the South Vietnamese.

Growing discontent with the government of Diem led the Americans to withdraw their support from him, and he was assassinated on 1 November 1963. Attempts by the United Nations Secretary-General, U Thant, to negotiate a settlement were rejected by the new US President, Lyndon B. Johnson. Then in August 1964 North Vietnamese patrol boats were reported to have fired on the US destroyer *Maddox*, and in retaliation President Johnson ordered the bombing of the north from naval vessels in the Gulf of Tonkin. The action was endorsed by Congress. It was in the political vacuum which followed the fall of Diem (it was not until 1967 that Thieu became President) that Washington decided on a far greater American participation in the war and sharply increased the number of troops in the country as well as the supply of weapons. The USA also pressured its allies to become involved militarily, and US forces were joined in Vietnam by 50,000 South Korean troops and smaller contingents from Australia, New Zealand and Thailand.

Course of the struggle

Despite massive military superiority, the US forces were constantly baffled by a jungle war they found they could not win. The American forces experimented during this war in 'the ready-made laboratory of South Viet Nam', as the *Wall Street Journal* described it. Units of the North Vietnamese army now began to use the 'Ho Chi Minh' trail, which lay to the west of the border with Cambodia, to come south and join the Viet Cong. In Saigon the government became increasingly unstable, while dependence on the USA became ever more apparent. Air Vice-Marshal Nguyen Cao Ky, Diem's successor, was unable to check a deteriorating political and military situation.

A rapid escalation of the war took place during 1965. On 7 February the Viet Cong attacked the American base at Pleiku, killing eight and wounding 126. President Johnson ordered reprisal bombing on Hanoi, which took place at the time when the Soviet President, Aleksei Kosygin, was there to discuss a new peace initiative. On 6 March two battalions of marines were landed on beaches near Da Nang to relieve the city, which was then under siege. By June 1965 there were 50,000 US troops in South Vietnam fully operational in support of the ARVN. Yet despite the evidence, much ignorance or wilful misreading of the situation was demonstrated in the USA. Thus, on 23 April 1965 the Secretary of State, Dean Rusk, said, 'There is little evidence that the Viet Cong has any significant popular following in South Vietnam.'

By the end of 1965 there were some 250,000 US troops in Vietnam (though one estimate suggests no more than 188,000) under the command of General William C. Westmoreland. But these land troops were backed up by a further 60,000 men of the 7th Fleet, which was operating off Vietnam, as well as 600,000 troops of the South Vietnam army (largely equipped and paid for by the USA) and the USAAF based in Guam, which carried out an increasing number of strikes against the north. Bombing missions against North Vietnam were intensified through 1965 and came to a total of 20,000 sorties (averaging 70 a day). The rate was doubled during 1966, although the two principal cities of the north – Hanoi and Haiphong – were not bombed regularly. The USAAF planned to drop 638,000 tons of bombs during 1966, half the total tonnage used by the USA against the Germans in Europe and North Africa throughout the Second World War.

In mid-1966 the US Command and the ARVN adopted new tactics as follows: pacification campaigns in which villages were isolated in order to protect them from the guerrillas; search and destroy missions designed to force the guerrillas out into the open; the creation of 'free fire' zones where the local populations were forcibly evacuated; and massive defoliant spraying to destroy tree cover. Heavy bombing of the north was alternated with pauses in the hope of persuading North Vietnam to negotiate.

During 1967 US military strength in Vietnam was increased to about 389,000, while more North Vietnamese troops came south to join the Viet Cong, whom the Americans found they could neither destroy nor dislodge. In September elections were held in South Vietnam for President – those favouring negotiations were banned from taking part – and General Nguyen Van Thieu became President. Massive American superiority in the air as well as the huge firepower and sophisticated weapons at the disposal of its troops on the ground gave the impression that the south was getting on top of the war, but the relative optimism of 1967 was shattered by the Tet offensive at the beginning of 1968.

The Viet Cong and North Vietnamese troops launched the Tet (New Year) offensive on 30 January 1968. Their forces infiltrated Saigon, Danang, Hue and other cities and struck at both military and civilian targets. They seized the imperial palace in Hue, which they held for 26 days. They did enormous damage, and although they did not succeed in sparking off a general uprising as they had hoped, the fighting capacity which the troops from the north displayed clearly took the Americans by surprise. The year 1968, indeed, proved to be a turning point in the war. Despite round-the-clock bombing of the north – by then more bombs had been dropped on Vietnam than the total in the Second World War – the infiltration of South Vietnam continued unabated and no American tactics seemed to make much difference. General Westmoreland requested more troops.

But in the USA growing public opposition to the war forced a major reappraisal in Washington and on 31 March President Johnson announced a halt to bombing north of parallel 20 and said that he would not seek re-election at the end of the year. In October President Johnson ordered a halt to all bombing, and Hanoi responded by reducing the level of its attacks in the south. Washington and Hanoi then agreed to hold preliminary peace talks in Paris, and General Westmoreland was replaced by General Creighton Abrams. The long process of de-escalating the war had begun.

Military action in 1969 was lower key. In June 1969 President Richard M. Nixon met President Nguyen Van Thieu at Midway and announced the first withdrawal of US troops – 25,000 – although by then there were 500,000 in Vietnam. The US also began a programme of 'Vietnamization' and – a clear response to home political pressures – US commanders in the field were told to keep casualties to a minimum. In September Ho Chi Minh died. But the Paris peace talks continued and South Vietnam agreed to negotiate directly with the NLF. The North Vietnam delegation, however, insisted that the 'puppet' regime in Saigon should be dissolved. The NLF now proclaimed a Provisional Revolutionary Government (PRG), which, it said, was the legitimate government of South Vietnam. The position of President Thieu steadily became more precarious.

A new escalation of fighting took place in the spring of 1970 when US and ARVN forces crossed the Cambodian border in an effort to destroy Viet Cong staging posts. The USA also carried out a series of bombing raids against northern Laos where North Vietnamese and Pathet Lao forces were fighting the government forces, which were pro-South Vietnam. At the same time it stepped up bombing attacks on the Ho Chi Minh trail. This escalation of bombing, however, led to increased anti-war demonstrations in the USA.

Despite these developments, the decision to pull out of the war and ultimately to leave South Vietnam to its fate had already been taken. The numbers of

American troops were reduced through 1971 even though the peace talks in Paris had stalled over the issue of POWs. By the end of 1971 it was agreed in Saigon that the South Vietnamese forces were to be responsible from then on for all ground fighting, although they would continue to receive US air support. In March 1972 the North Vietnamese felt strong enough to invade the demilitarized zone and captured Quang Tri province; in retaliation President Nixon ordered the mining of Haiphong and other North Vietnam ports. But from the American point of view, the war was all but over.

Estimated costs and casualties

In the early days of American involvement in Vietnam, propaganda presented Diem as an upholder of democratic values when he was nothing of the sort. And one of the great costs of this most brutal war is to be found in the many distortions of the truth which surrounded it. All war breeds distortion, but few in modern times have been responsible for quite so much double-speak.

The huge expenditure by US military personnel in Vietnam came to $200 million a year, but very little of this benefited the ordinary people. Instead it helped turn Saigon into a gigantic military brothel and fuelled corruption and the black market.

A whole people became both politicized and militarized by the war. For example, 'self-defence' units of Vietnamese would fire from their villages at American planes, while many became guerrillas. A report to Congress in the mid-1960s claimed that some military actions resulted in a death rate of six civilians for every guerrilla killed. For its part the NLF estimated in 1965 that up to that date 170,000 civilians had been killed and 800,000 wounded or disabled. When it became clear early in 1965 that the war in the south was being lost, the Americans decided to carry the fighting to North Vietnam with round-the-clock bombing, thus greatly extending the total area subjected to warfare and vastly increasing the number of casualties.

The brutalities of the war, which has been described as the first 'sitting-room war' because it could be followed nightly on television, had a traumatic effect on the American people. Through the 1960s growing anger and widespread anti-war campaigns in the USA had a major impact on the American political scene, one effect being to persuade President Johnson not to seek a second term, while his successor, President Nixon, came to power committed to a withdrawal from Vietnam.

The build-up of American forces in Vietnam continued through the 1960s from 15,000 military 'advisers' in 1961, to 330,000 troops in 1966, to more than half a million in 1968. In addition, Washington involved as many other powers as it was able, so contingents of 50,000 South Koreans, 8000 Australians, 2000 Filipinos, 5000 Thais and 540 New Zealanders also served in Vietnam (although, for example, 50,190 Australians served in Vietnam altogether), while Britain's Prime Minister, Harold Wilson, only just managed to resist President Johnson's pressures for a British force to participate in the war. South Korean, Australian, New Zealand and Thai forces together lost 5,226 dead. The arsenal of weapons used by the Americans included toxic sprays to destroy rice fields, defoliants, noxious gases against civilians, napalm fire bombs on villages and anti-personnel bombs. The results were horrendous.

In the south the Viet Cong played down the fact that they were Communists and played up their nationalism. When the Viet Cong became operational in 1961 it numbered 6000 guerrillas; this number had risen to 50,000 by 1966, with a further 100,000 part-time guerrillas to be called upon when needed. Most of the weapons captured from the guerrillas turned out to be of Western rather than Communist origin.

American combat deaths came to 45,941, although a further 10,000 troops died of other causes while in Vietnam. In addition, 150,000 wounded required hospitalization. Total costs were estimated to be in the region of US $200,000,000,000. At least 1 million Vietnamese – soldiers and civilians – were killed on both sides, but the true figure is probably significantly higher; the wounded and maimed accounted for an even higher figure.

Results: immediate and longer term

Talks between the USA, North Vietnam and South Vietnam continued from July to December 1972, but when they broke down the USA carried out 10 days of intensive bombing as a reminder of the damage it could inflict should it continue fighting. The talks were resumed in the new year, and an agreement was finally reached on 27 January 1973. Under its terms a truce was to go into effect at once; all US forces were to be withdrawn; all US bases were to be dismantled; all prisoners of war were to be released; an international force was to keep the peace; the South Vietnamese were to determine their own future; North Vietnamese forces already in the south were to remain, but not be reinforced; the 17th parallel was to remain the boundary between the two Vietnams until they could be united by peaceful means.

In fact, once the US forces had fully withdrawn – in August 1973 a war-weary Congress proscribed further US military action in Vietnam – the war between north and south resumed as both sides violated the terms of the truce, the ARVN abandoned more and more outposts and the Viet Cong captured one provincial capital after another. In January 1975 the Communists mounted a full offensive until, following Thieu's abandonment of Quang Tri and Hue, panic swept the south. The army then disintegrated, and the remaining Americans as well as some Vietnamese with special influence escaped by sea or air. On 21 April President Thieu resigned, the government surrendered unconditionally and Saigon fell to the advancing North Vietnamese and Viet Cong without putting up any resistance. A military government was appointed on 30 April and ruled South Vietnam for a year until, on 2 July 1976, the two Vietnams were reunited as the Socialist Republic of Vietnam. Saigon was renamed Ho Chi Minh City.

The new Socialist Republic rapidly made its influence felt and became an important power in south-east Asia. The Vietnam revolution and nationalist struggle, however it is described, succeeded against the massive power of the USA because the Communist revolutionaries won the hearts and minds of the people. Subsequent persecutions of Roman Catholics, the pro-French and pro-Americans or anti-Communists caused tens of thousands to flee by sea – the 'boat people' of the next decade.

Ten years before the end of the war the UN Secretary-General, U Thant, said of the fighting, 'Twenty years of outside intervention and the pressure of foreign armies have so profoundly affected Vietnamese political life that it seems illusory to represent it as a mere contest between Communism and liberal democracy.' That judgment made as much sense at the end. Argument about the Vietnam War will continue indefinitely: it focused world attention on the ideological confrontations of the Cold War, but it also highlighted the power of nationalism. In the end it was the tenacity of a peasant people that triumphed against the might of the world's greatest power.

Indeed, despite the awful human suffering of the people of Vietnam, arguably the greatest casualty of the war was the United States. Vietnam represented the first ever defeat suffered by the USA, and the effects on a whole generation were traumatic. Further – a lesson that the USSR had to learn a decade later in Afghanistan – Vietnam demonstrated the limits of a superpower's ability to control small nations, despite the formidable forces which it could deploy. Moreover, it showed that nationalism rather than any other ideology remains the strongest force at work in the world.

THE AMERICAS

CUBA: A VERY CLOSE THING

Origins

For the first half of the twentieth century until Dr Fidel Castro Ruz came to power the United States regarded Cuba as its protégé. The USA had intervened against the colonial power, Spain, in 1898 and following the blowing up of the US battleship *Maine* in Havana harbour had fought a brief war – the Spanish–American War of 1898 – which led to Cuban independence. However, from 1899 to 1902 the newly freed colony was under American occupation. Cuba became a republic in 1901 and was granted independence by the USA in 1902, although, according to the terms of the Platt Amendment, the USA gave to itself the right to intervene in Cuban affairs, a right that Washington invoked a number of times over the years. Further, from this time until the overthrow of Fulgencio Batista y Zaldívar by Castro in 1959 the Cuban economy was dominated by American business interests, dependent on the USA for investment, tourists and a market for its main crop, sugar.

In 1940 Batista came to power in Cuba and presided over a corrupt, inefficient and unpleasant dictatorship until his final overthrow in 1959. During the 1950s (1953–9) Castro led several unsuccessful attempts to overthrow Batista (see Part V, pp. 535–539). He finally succeeded in 1959. Unfortunately, American opposition to Castro and his increasingly left-wing or 'socialist' government was to grow rapidly in the period immediately after he came to power; this opposition, at times virulent, was as much as anything a reflex reaction at the height of the Cold War to any government of the left. As a result, perhaps inevitably, Castro turned to the USSR as an alternative to Cuba's long-standing 'big brother', the USA. Over the two years 1959–60 the Castro government moved steadily to the left and inaugurated a series of socialist reforms. These reforms – land reform to the advantage of the peasants, nationalization, expropriation of foreign assets – accompanied by the development of increasingly close ties with the USSR, had the effect of alienating the Cuban middle classes. In addition, pressures from his more radical brother Raúl and Che Guevara, both of whom had accompanied him from the time of the 1956 landing and were now his closest advisers, as well as the exigencies of government led Castro to adopt and use the small Cuban Communist Party. This move fuelled US and middle-class fears, and some 700,000 middle-class Cubans fled the country with most of them ending up, at least to begin with, in Florida. Castro, unburdened by middle-class opposition, implemented his socialist revolution, and by the end of 1960 his government was in complete control of the political and economic life of Cuba.

The Bay of Pigs

Among the Cubans who had fled to the USA were a number who planned a counter-revolution against Castro. These would-be coup makers were encouraged and helped by the US Central Intelligence Agency (CIA), while left-wing exiles (those whose extreme views had led them to quarrel with the Castro line from the other side of the political spectrum) were excluded from joining the counter-revolutionaries and were actually locked up briefly in Florida when the attempt was made. In April 1961 the anti-Castro Cubans invaded Cuba by boat from Florida. They landed at the Bay of Pigs, but the attempt turned into a fiasco. The invaders were rapidly rounded up, there was no popular uprising as the counter-revolutionaries had hoped, and Castro's hand was greatly strengthened, allowing him to turn on and crush other dissidents in the country. The other most obvious result of the Bay of Pigs fiasco was a rapid deterioration of the already bad Cuban–American relations.

Thus, by mid-1961 the Americans, who had seen themselves as the original liberators of Cuba, now found themselves standing by at the height of the Cold War while their protégé became Communist. In February 1962 the USA applied an economic embargo to Cuba.

The missile crisis of 1962

As early as May 1960 the Soviet leader, Nikita Khrushchev, had promised to defend Cuba with Soviet arms; in July 1962 US intelligence learned that the USSR was shipping missiles to Cuba and by 29 August Soviet technicians were in Cuba constructing missile launching sites. On 14 October US intelligence verified that a first ballistic missile had been installed on a Cuban launching site and President Kennedy began to consider his alternatives: one possibility was a US invasion of Cuba, another to continue diplomatic pressures on the USSR to change course. On 22 October President Kennedy first made public the fact that Soviet offensive missile sites were being constructed in Cuba (which is only 145 km (90 miles) off the coast of Florida) and then declared a naval quarantine of the island, a move which the Organization of American States (OAS) sanctioned on 23 October. The President warned that the USA would seize all offensive weapons.

The week of 22–28 October was one in which the USA prepared for war and the rest of the world stood by helpless, wondering whether the two superpowers would unleash a nuclear catastrophe upon them. But then, on 28 October, Khrushchev announced that the USSR would dismantle its missile sites and return the weapons to the USSR, while its approaching fleet did an about-turn in mid-Atlantic. The two superpowers reached their agreement without consulting Castro, a fact that created intense Cuban anger and humiliation, although the following year Castro appeared as the guest of honour at the Moscow May Day parade, a gesture of reconciliation. The Soviet withdrawal had been carried out sufficiently to Washington's satisfaction that the naval blockade was lifted on 20 November. Castro refused to allow a UN inspection of the sites which had been agreed by the two powers, but the USA felt it could monitor Cuba adequately with its U2 spyplanes; when Castro threatened to shoot these down he was cautioned not to do so by Khrushchev.

Many years later (during *glasnost*) revelations from the three principal protagonists – the USA, the USSR, and Cuba – made it clear that the Soviet Ambassador in Washington, Anatoly Dobrynin, had not known that the missiles were being installed, so secret was the whole affair. At the same time the Cuban leaders thought Washington intended to use the incident as an excuse for a full-scale invasion of Cuba and had placed 270,000 men under arms in readiness 'to fight the invaders to the death'. There were 100,000 troops standing by, plus 40,000 Soviet soldiers, although the Americans had estimated that no more than 10,000 to 12,000 Soviet troops were on the island. The Havana government estimated a possible death toll of 800,000 people. Cuban hostility to the USA continued, and according to Jorge Risquet Valdes, a member of the Cuban Politburo in 1989, 'If the US had understood that mighty nations cannot impose their will upon smaller ones there would have been no crisis in 1962. And that philosophy remains.'

Results: immediate and longer term

The immediate results of the missile crisis were to heighten world tensions between the two sides in the Cold War and to entrench for another generation Cuban mistrust of the USA. The crisis probably also played a part in the downfall of Khrushchev in 1964 and influenced Cuba turning somewhat away from the USSR and veering towards China in the following years. Undoubtedly, as well, the apparent nearness of a nuclear war gave impetus to anti-nuclear movements round the world, while driving home to all the smaller powers their ineffectiveness when faced with a possible superpower confrontation. (See also Part V, pp. 535–539.)

THE DOMINICAN REPUBLIC: AMERICAN INTERVENTION

Origins

The Dominican Republic, which shares the West Indian island of Hispaniola with Haiti, had a troubled history of alternating Spanish, French and slave control until in 1844 the Spanish colonists founded the Republic of Santo Domingo. During the 50 years from 1865 to 1915 there were no fewer than 25 revolutions and 35 governments. The United States intervened in the Dominican Republic in 1916 in the hope of recovering US loans, and the Marines were to remain on the island until 1924, thus establishing a precedent for intervention.

In 1924 an elected government came to power, replacing the provisional government set up two years earlier under American auspices, but the instability of the following years enabled Rafael Trujillo to take power in 1930 and remain in control as dictator until his assassination in 1961.

During the 1960s several left-wing movements emerged, though none was especially influential. In the elections of 1962 the left-of-centre Partido Revolucionario Dominicano (PRD), led by Juan Bosch, came to power, but seven months later Bosch, who was regarded as too liberal by a powerful section of the military, was overthrown in a coup led by Colonel (later General) Elias Wessin y Wessin. Bosch went into exile, but the military who had ousted him and the PRD were inefficient and unpopular. In 1965 a counter-revolution was launched by members of the deposed PRD and a number of junior officers under Francisco Caamano: their object was to restore constitutional government and they became known as the Constitutionalists.

The 1965 revolution and American intervention

The revolution of 1965 called for the return to power of Bosch, and it appeared as though it might have succeeded had it not been for American intervention. The insurrection was launched on Saturday, 24 April 1965 and led at once to fierce fighting with the forces of the junta. In a sense the outbreak was forced by circumstances, although it would have come anyway. A group of army officers suspected of plotting against the government, which had replaced the military junta that overthrew Bosch in 1963 and was then headed by Donald Reid Cabral, were summoned by the Chief of Staff, General Marcos Rivera Cuesta, to the 27 February military camp across the Rio Ozamo from Santo Domingo. The officers, however, seized their opportunity by arresting the Chief of Staff and summoning other plotters to their aid, and the revolt spread rapidly. The news of the insurrection brought thousands on to the streets. The following day Cabral resigned and a 'Constitutional' government took over.

On the Sunday the US Navy Caribbean Task Force was ordered from Puerto Rico to the vicinity of the Dominican Republic; the force consisted of six ships with 1700 Marines on board. By then there was fighting in Santo Domingo between the Constitutionalists and the anti-Bosch forces led by General Wessin y Wessin (the man originally responsible for Bosch's overthrow). It appears that early in the insurrection Wessin appealed to the USA for military support. By Tuesday, 27 April there was considerable bloodshed in the city: Wessin had ordered aircraft from San Isidro, where his headquarters were situated, to bomb rebel centres in the city. A number of foreign journalists who had collected in a hotel to await evacuation were reportedly terrorized for some hours by rebels, while Marines at the US Embassy were fired on with the result that a Marine rifle platoon was landed by helicopter at the US Embassy on 28 April. Meanwhile large quantities of arms had been handed out in the city to supporters of the Constitutionalists.

The US Embassy over-reacted and advised Washington that the revolt had been taken over by pro-Cuban Marxists (three years after the Cuban missile crisis this was likely to precipitate American intervention). Two leaders of the revolt – Colonel Francisco Caamano Deno and his deputy, Héctor Aristy – were regarded as dangerously left-wing. Therefore, in addition to the platoon of Marines sent to guard the embassy, President Lyndon B. Johnson ordered in 500 Marines to protect American lives. Shortly afterwards the decision was taken to send in a further 1000 Marines both to prevent a bloodbath (which seemed likely) and to prevent the Constitutionalists regaining control. This decision was taken at a time when Wessin's forces were in difficulties and the city was in the hands of the Constitutionalists. At least some military commanders outside the city had yet to decide whom to support and remained neutral.

The USA then decided to support Wessin and his forces directly, and increased its military participation dramatically. The Marines now landed armoured vehicles, and paratroopers of the 82nd Airborne Division were flown to the Dominican Republic from North Carolina. They arrived at San Isidro on 30 April. The Marines and paratroopers established a military corridor across the centre of the capital, thus breaking and isolating the Constitutionalist forces. The numbers of American troops were steadily increased until they reached a total of 22,000. Serious fighting continued well into May, and the Constitutionalists were not finally defeated until the end of June.

The Organization of American States (OAS) had only just agreed to ratify the American intervention; then, on 25 May, it created an 'Inter-American Peace Force'. These troops now landed in the Dominican Republic. The OAS, working with the Papal Nuncio in Santo Domingo, arranged a ceasefire between the two sides in the revolution, but the Marines remained for the time being so as to 'guarantee' an acceptable form of government. The United Nations Security Council sent a fact-finding mission to the country.

After the Constitutionalists had been defeated and their leaders had gone into exile, a provisional President, Héctor García Godoy, took control in September pending elections which were set for 1966.

The rebels always denied that the Communists would take over, although one of Washington's justifications for its intervention was to forestall such a possibility, for the USA was determined to prevent another 'Cuba' in the Caribbean region.

Results: immediate and longer term

The American Marines left the Dominican Republic by 6 June, although some units of the 82nd Airborne Division remained and with the OAS force helped 'contain' both the left and the right. The Americans, working through their special ambassador Ellsworth Bunker, organized the provisional government under García Godoy which supervised the elections of June 1966. During the period which followed, the Americans threatened to use their troops against the Dominican military if they attempted to overthrow the provisional government of García Godoy or to frustrate the 1966 elections. The threat worked; the elections were held and won by the Partido Reformista (PR) led by Joaquín Balaguer, who was to remain in power until 1978. Bosch contested the elections but lost. Balaguer was the American candidate and also had good relations with the military. This persuaded the Americans that he could handle the situation, and in September 1966 they withdrew the remainder of their forces from the country. Balaguer went on to win the elections of 1970 and 1974, although the left refused to take part in them. There was some further violence but it was 'contained', and Balaguer steadily reduced Cuban or revolutionary influence, which was manifested through the Revolutionary Movement of 14 June (MR-14) and through the Dominican Popular Movement (MPD). Neither was able to mount violent opposition and the left became discredited, although there were to be a number of unsuccessful coup attempts.

The US intervention was widely criticized in the Americas: it had prevented the Constitutionalists (who had been the legitimate government ousted by the military) from regaining power. The USA, however, claimed that following the events of

1965 its intervention had prevented both the extreme left and the extreme right from taking power. At least the USA could point to the fact that a series of democratic elections under centrist politicians followed the 1965 intervention and that no further coups took place.

GRENADA: MINI-STATE REVOLUTION AND US INVASION

Origins

The Grenada United Labour Party, which under Sir Eric Gairy ruled the island prior to 1979, was corrupt and brutal; its strong-arm men beat up political opponents and both Maurice Bishop in 1973 and his father (who was killed mysteriously in 1974) were victims of these tactics. Maurice Bishop determined to oust Gairy. He became a champion of the poor and created the radical New Jewel Movement; then in 1979 Bishop carried out a coup against Gairy to become Prime Minister. His People's Revolutionary Government (PRG) suspended the constitution, while promising to hold elections at a later date.

Grenada is a tiny impoverished island (in 1983 the population was 111,000) dependent on tourism and the export of cocoa, bananas and nutmeg. It has always suffered from high unemployment. Bishop was a popular Marxist, but his party failed to hold the elections it had promised; its left-wing policies also meant a steady deterioration of relations with the USA (always wary of Communism in the Caribbean) and the conservative member states of the Caribbean Community and Common Market (Caricom). Bishop in fact allowed Grenada to continue as a mixed economy because he had little choice in the matter, although he accepted increasing aid from socialist sources – the USSR and Cuba. By 1983 a new airport was being built at Point Salines: this was financed by the EEC and OPEC, but construction was by Cuban engineers and labour.

The coup

In October 1983 a power struggle occurred within the leadership of the New Jewel Movement. Bernard Coard, Bishop's colleague, who was more radical than the Prime Minister, resisted Bishop's attempt to mend fences with the USA, which was bitterly opposed to Grenada taking aid from the USSR and Cuba. Although Coard was responsible for toppling Bishop on 14 October, he himself was quickly removed by the army commander, General Hudson Austin, and disappeared (presumed killed). The PRG was replaced by a Revolutionary Military Council, and Bishop and other members of his government were arrested (Bishop was put under house arrest).

On 19 October supporters of the Prime Minister freed him and other colleagues, and then they went to the army compound at Fort Rupert to protest. Troops fired on the crowd, while Bishop and other cabinet colleagues were seized and taken into the compound where they were executed. The other ministers executed with

Bishop were Unison Whiteman (foreign affairs), Jacqueline Cruft (education) and Norris Bain (housing). Some 60 people altogether were killed.

The invasion

The USA regarded the use of Cubans in the construction of the Point Salines airport as provocative; in any case they thought the new airport might be used as a Cuban–Soviet base. The murder of Bishop and his colleagues by General Hudson Austin provided an excuse for intervention, especially as the Organization of Eastern Caribbean States (OECS) requested American assistance. On 25 October, therefore, 1200 US Marines accompanied by additional Army Rangers and Navy Seal Commandos (1900 men altogether) invaded Grenada. They were assisted by an OECS force of 300 soldiers and police, who had been raised from the nearby islands of Antigua and Barbuda, Barbados, Dominica, St Lucia, St Vincent and the Grenadines. Later the same day the USA brought further paratroopers into Grenada, so by the end of October the total force had been increased to 7000. The invaders met considerable resistance from the Grenada army, joined by Cuban construction workers, but in November the USA felt able to reduce the number of troops to 4000 and by December there was only occasional sniper action from the jungle against the invaders. All US combat forces had been withdrawn from the island by mid-December, although 300 non-combat advisory personnel were left behind to assist the Caribbean peace-keeping force.

Results

Following the invasion the Revolutionary Military Council was disbanded and General Austin was arrested. The Cuban construction workers were sent home, and though Castro protested, he maintained an unusually low profile over the affair (Bishop had been his friend and he disapproved of the coup against him). There was controversy at the time – and later – as to whether the Governor-General of Grenada, Sir Paul Scoon, had requested aid from OECS before it arrived or only did so after the event. Now, however, he assumed control of the government. When the US forces withdrew, the OECS force was increased from 300 to 500. An interim non-political council was appointed, while elections were set for December 1984; then the old politician, Herbert Blaize, and his New National Party were voted into power, winning 14 out of 15 seats. Grenada had returned, more or less, to normal.

The USA justified its intervention as a response to a Soviet–Cuban threat, and insisted that the Point Salines airport being constructed by the Cubans was being built as a military base. The crisis in Grenada and American–OECS intervention highlighted some of the problems faced by mini-states: when their governments are taken over violently or when they are manipulated by outside powers, to whom do they turn for assistance? Whatever the rights and wrongs of the American intervention, which was widely welcomed by OECS and in Grenada itself, it belonged to a long-standing tradition of American intervention against left-wing governments. It is, for example, at least open to question whether the USA would have intervened had there been no Cubans on Grenada. The intervention led, briefly, to strained relations between the USA and Britain (the former colonial power), which publicly opposed the intervention on the grounds that events in Grenada were an internal affair only. Gairy stood in the 1990 elections but was defeated.

PANAMA: EXIT NORIEGA

Introduction

More than any other country of the region Panama has always been subject to US manipulation. It was carved out of the national territory of Colombia in 1903 at the instigation of the USA and began its existence as a US protectorate, while the Panama Canal was dug to link the Atlantic and Pacific oceans. During the early years of Panama's existence American military intervention was the norm. Deep resentment of the US presence in Panama has always been a fact of political and social life. Washington responded to growing anti-American feelings under the leadership of General Omar Torrijos by agreeing to a new Panama Canal treaty in 1977, under which control of the Canal will revert to Panama on 31 December 1999.

General Manuel Noriega had been associated with the campaign to regain sovereignty over the Canal that began in the late 1950s, although from that time onwards he was also regarded as a CIA asset.

Origins

Noriega manipulated his way to supreme power following the death of Torrijos in an air crash in 1981. At that time he was offered the command of the military in return for supporting Colonel Ruben Dario Paredes to win the 1984 presidential election; General Noriega reneged on his bargain, put his own man in and transformed the National Guard into the much more powerful Panama Defence Force (PDF). The USA then encouraged Noriega to expand the army (aiming at 20,000 by the end of the century) and train it to defend the Canal. From 1984 onwards Noriega was involved in playing off the CIA (on whose payroll he remained) and the drug traffickers. He handed over drug traffickers who would not share their profits with him, but gave protection and laundered money for those who gave him a cut. His fortune is estimated to have reached hundreds of millions of dollars. At the same time the PDF became involved in gambling and prostitution rackets. Noriega's power was based on corruption that was certain to rebound on him. Things began to go wrong in 1987.

In June 1987 Colonel Roberto Diaz Herrera, who had been second-in-command of the PDF, accused Noriega of involvement in the death of Torrijos in 1981, causing three months of protests and strikes against Noriega. Then, on 5 February 1988, Noriega was indicted on drug trafficking charges in the USA. On 26 February the Panamanian National Assembly appointed Manuel Solis Palma as President in place of Eric Delvalle, who had been ousted after trying to dismiss Noriega, but the USA refused to recognize the appointment and the opposition called for a general strike. On 3 March the USA imposed economic sanctions, blocked $60 million of Panama funds in US banks and announced it would stop payments of Canal dues (worth about $15 million a month). On 15 March, after violent confrontations between police and anti-Noriega demonstrators, President Reagan called on Noriega to step down. The following day an uprising was attempted by Colonel Leónidas Macias, head of the National Police, and on 18 March Panama declared a state of emergency.

The presidential elections of 7 May 1989 were nullified by the government, which declared its candidate, Carlos Duque, the winner; both the opposition and independent observers claimed that the opposition candidate, Guillermo Endara, was the winner. Violent protests followed on 8 May and US President George Bush called on Noriega to step down. On 10 May an electoral tribunal annulled the election results, sparking off protests in which five people died. The next day the USA reinforced its Canal Zone garrison of 10,000 troops and recalled its ambassador. Washington now made it plain that it would only relax its pressures after new elections had been held. On 1 September Noriega appointed Francisco Rodríguez (a former Treasury Department official) as acting President. On 3 October a group of 200 officers led by Major Moisés Giroldi Vega seized military headquarters and announced the overthrow of Noriega. Loyal troops then reversed the situation and most of the leaders of the coup were killed; a purge of the PDF followed. It appeared that the USA had been involved in the October coup attempt. The government passed emergency measures which included the curtailment of human rights.

On 3 November the US Justice Department ruled that the US military had the right to arrest wanted criminals in foreign countries. Events now moved to a climax, and on 15 December the Panama Assembly named Noriega head of government and 'maximum leader' and declared a state of war with the USA. The next day a US Marine lieutenant was shot dead by Panamanian troops and US forces in Panama were put on extra alert. On 18 December Panamanian policemen wounded a US soldier; on 19 December Washington warned Noriega against attacks on US citizens in Panama and refused to rule out military action. For Washington the main problem by then was to bring Noriega to court in the USA to face drug trafficking charges.

The invasion

The USA invaded Panama on 20 December 1989 with 14,000 troops (to add to the 12,700 already present in the Canal Zone). A government headed by Endara was sworn in by a judge at the US military base. The fighting was to last several days, with both the Panama Defence Force and the special 'Dignity Battalions' which had been formed of Noriega loyalists resisting in a battle that resulted in great damage to parts of Panama City. Noriega took refuge in the Vatican Nunciature, where he was to be besieged by US troops over the Christmas period and into the New Year.

The spearhead of the US forces consisted of about 2500 troops of the 193rd Light Infantry Brigade, a US Marines tank company and the 'Green Berets' of the 3rd Battalion of the 7th Special Forces Group. They were backed by a further

10,000 men airlifted in at the last moment in an effort to maintain surprise. The Pentagon claimed that most resistance had ceased 24 hours after the attack, although the claim turned out to be somewhat premature. The Panama Defence Forces had about 7300 troops. Three days after the invasion paramilitary groups loyal to Noriega bombarded the US command headquarters in Panama City, while members of the Dignity Battalions nearly succeeded in killing the newly installed Vice-President, Arias Calderón. General Maxwell Thurman, the head of the US command in Panama, had to concede that resistance from an estimated 2000 members of the Dignity Battalions might continue for another five days. In an effort to bring an end to two days of looting, 1500 US military police made a sweep of Panama City; they were resisted by the Dignity Battalions and the looting continued. By 23 December it was estimated that about 1000 members of the PDF had taken refuge across the border in Costa Rica. Five days after the US invasion, fighting in Panama City was still heavy and several embassies had been attacked and looted. The US forces were reinforced to bring their numbers up to 30,000. The whereabouts of Noriega were unknown for several days before it was learnt he had taken refuge in the Papal Nunciature. Altogether it took a week before opposition collapsed and the Americans settled down to the awkward business of besieging the Nunciature in order to force Noriega to surrender. Two weeks after the invasion Noriega surrendered and was flown to Miami to stand trial in the USA for his drug trafficking offences; the object of the mission had been accomplished.

Estimated costs and casualties

Early estimates of casualties were 23 US and 500 Panamanians dead, of whom about half were civilians. Other estimates suggested a much higher figure. Later Noriega (awaiting trial in Miami) claimed that the death toll had in fact been between 3000 and 4000, mainly civilians, which was far higher than the American estimate. Then in May 1990 the US human rights group, Americas Watch, produced a report which claimed that 15,000 people were rendered homeless in the attack, dismissed the official US Southern Command figure of 202 deaths as an underestimate and suggested that 300 civilians had been killed. Americas Watch also accused the US military of handing over Panamanian prisoners to the new government, which was carrying out a purge of Noriega supporters. There were many more wounded (including about 250 US servicemen) and there was major damage to Panama City itself.

Results: immediate and longer term

Two weeks after the invasion the USA could claim success in its objectives: General Noriega had been handed over to a Florida courtroom to stand trial, and an elected government had been restored to office in Panama. Whether a subsequent trial of Noriega – given the likelihood under the US legal system of years of court wrangling – would prove beneficial either to the US image or to US–Panamanian relations remained to be seen.

Other results are more difficult to assess. Whether or not Noriega is proved to have been trafficking in drugs to the USA does not solve the problems which have created the massive drugs problem in the USA in the first place. International reaction to the invasion was mixed: at a time when upheaval in eastern Europe was being met by restraint from Moscow, the USA was seen to be using 'big stick' tactics in Central America. US action was generally criticized by Latin American states, and at the UN only Britain and Canada supported the invasion, whose legitimacy in international law was seen as extremely doubtful. An emergency debate of the Organization of American States (OAS) which called for immediate US withdrawl from Panama was passed by 20 votes with six abstentions and only one (the USA) against.

None the less, Operation Just Cause had succeeded in its objectives and the departure from power of Noriega was lamented by almost no one. President Endara came to power courtesy of the USA; he will have to oppose continuing US interference in the affairs of Panama or he is likely to lose power at the next elections. The basic relationship between the USA and Panama has not changed; rather, the client status of the latter has been reinforced by the events of December 1989.

PART III

Border Wars and Wars between Third World Countries

Border wars and wars between Third World countries

INTRODUCTION

A feature of almost every war in this section is either overt big power involvement or a situation whose genesis lay in the colonial past. Three wars – the civil wars in Chad, the Gulf War and the 20-year saga of Cambodia – are among the longest and bloodiest that have taken place in the Third World.

Africa

A further three wars covered here – Burkina Faso, the Ogaden war and the Shifta war between Kenya and Somalia – represent post-independence attempts to adjust borders inherited from colonial days, and only one of them – the Ogaden war between Ethiopia and Somalia – was on a major scale. In the case of South Africa and its neighbours we are really examining an uneasy state of tension rather than actual wars, with South Africa using its superior military and economic power to overawe and threaten its weaker neighbours, sometimes to the extent of cross-border raids, and always with the effect of keeping them uneasily geared for intervention. Although all of South Africa's immediate neighbours are listed here, the major wars in Angola and Mozambique are only touched on in order to round off the picture; South African involvement in those two countries is dealt with in depth in Part V.

The long-lasting civil war in Chad, with its racial and religious overtones between north and south, was complicated by the role of Libya, which annexed the mineral-rich Aozou Strip in the north, and by the periodic interventions of France.

Perhaps only in the case of the Tanzania–Uganda wars that led to the downfall of Idi Amin can it be argued that big power activity or external support was relatively minimal, despite the fact that Amin relied increasingly on Libyan assistance.

The Seychelles affair is an illustration of how easily tiny countries may be threatened.

The Middle East

There are only two wars or series dealt with in this region: the Gulf War between Iran and Iraq, and the series of border wars between the two Yemens. With the possible exception of Vietnam, the Gulf War rates as perhaps the grimmest and bloodiest of any war fought in the Third World. It involved all the major powers

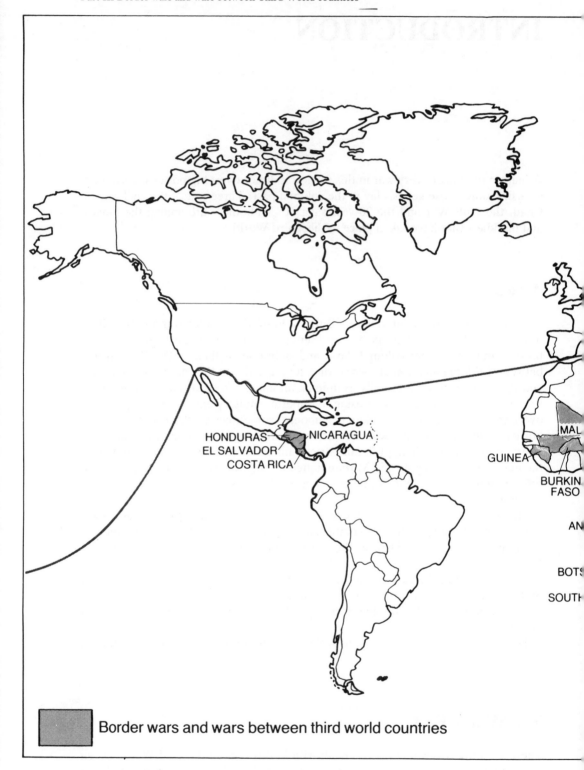

Map 9 Border wars and wars between Third World countries

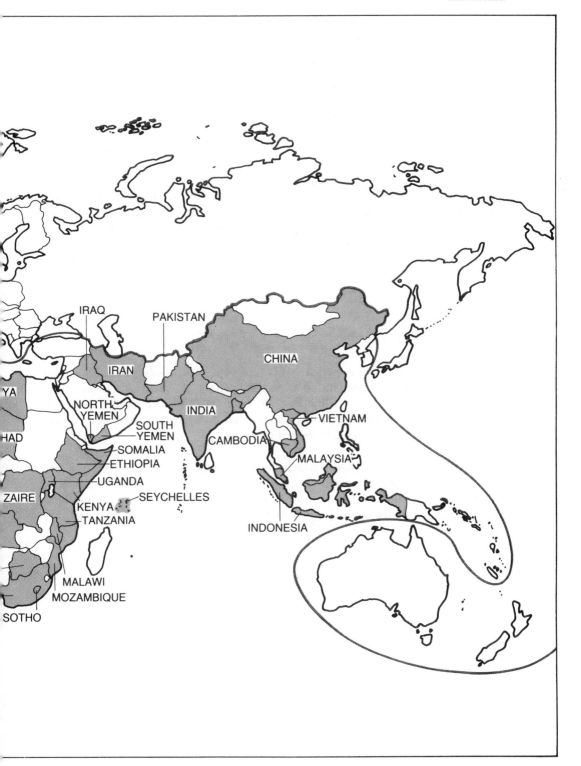

and threatened the vital oil supplies of the region; it represented a confrontation between Arabs and Iranians, the Shatt al-Arab (the waterway formed by the union of the Euphrates and Tigris rivers) acting as an ethnic as well as a geographic border; and it demonstrated how hard it is for the major powers to stop a war even when (as at the end) the USA and the USSR were prepared to work in concert.

Asia

These Asian wars were primarily about post-colonial adjustments, especially in the case of China and its neighbours, and India and Pakistan. At the same time they were inextricably bound up with the Cold War. The case of Cambodia is the most complex, including civil war, border war with Vietnam, the Pol Pot devastations and the Vietnamese invasion, which only ended with Vietnamese withdrawal in 1989.

The Americas

The three wars in Central America involving Costa Rica, Nicaragua, El Salvador and Honduras cannot be separated from the exercise of American power in the region. American pressures on these small, poor states to endorse and assist US policies towards Sandinista-controlled Nicaragua ensured that they were drawn into a conflict they would have preferred to avoid.

The monotonous regularity with which the big powers become involved in Third World wars – whether the excuse is the Cold War, oil or some other 'principle' – illustrates above all how, during the period since 1945, the Third World has provided the means for the major powers to play out their antagonisms by proxy.

AFRICA

BURKINA FASO: THE FIVE-DAY WAR, DECEMBER 1985

Background

Upper Volta (or Burkina Faso, as it has been known since 1984) was originally created by the French in 1919. Then, in 1932, it was divided between its three colonial neighbours, Côte d'Ivoire, Mali and Niger. However, it was reconstituted once more as a separate territory in 1947. One result of this history was that Upper Volta's neighbours each had its own interpretation of the border regions. From independence in 1960 onwards Mali claimed the Agacher Strip, which had been allotted to Upper Volta and was believed to be rich in minerals. At the end of 1974 a border dispute erupted between the two countries, diplomatic relations were broken off and Mali sent troops to occupy the Strip. During 1975 the Organization of African Unity (OAU) acted as mediator and apparently settled the dispute – to Upper Volta's satisfaction. But the quarrel festered for years and the two countries did not resume diplomatic relations with each other. In 1983 the dispute was referred to the International Court of Justice at The Hague.

Then in 1985 the quarrel came to a head once more. As tension mounted between the two countries, the Non-Aggression and Defence Aid Agreement (ANAD) of the Communauté économique de l'Afrique de l'ouest (CEAO) sent delegations to each of the adversaries to hear both sides of the dispute and urge them to keep the peace. Algeria and Nigeria (not members of ANAD) also attempted mediation. But the two countries prepared for war. Mali moved troops from Bamako to the disputed area, and a top official of the Democratic Party of the Malian People (UDPM) then claimed that 'our armed forces have done their duty' and that no Burkinabe soldier remained on Malian soil. At the same time UDPM militants in Bamako insisted that Burkina Faso was illegally occupying Mali villages and pledged their support to President Moussa Traore.

Outbreak and response

On 25 December 1985 fighting between troops of the two countries broke out on the border, with both sides claiming the Agacher Strip; although the fighting was sporadic in nature, there was an estimated total of 300 casualties (dead) on both sides. The war only lasted for five days, but during its course Burkina Faso announced that it had bombed the Malian town of Sikaso and that its troops had destroyed four Malian tanks and routed Malian infantry. Burkina Faso also

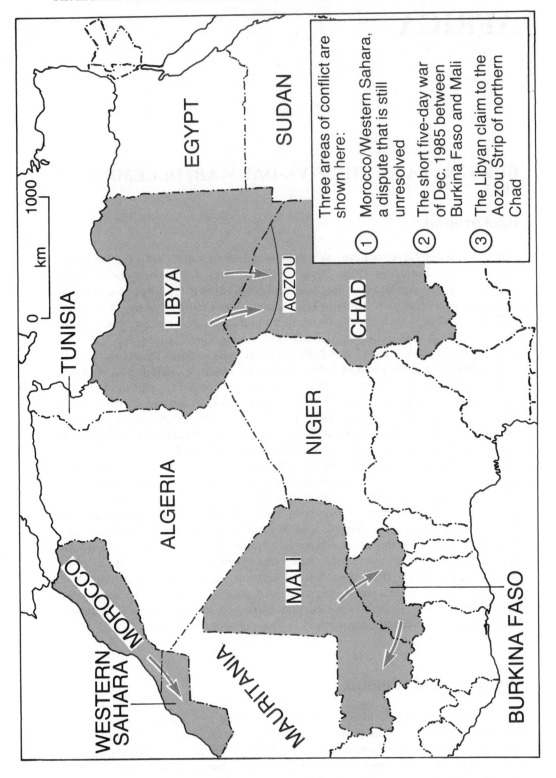

Three areas of conflict are shown here:

(1) Morocco/Western Sahara, a dispute that is still unresolved

(2) The short five-day war of Dec. 1985 between Burkina Faso and Mali

(3) The Libyan claim to the Aozou Strip of northern Chad

Map 10   North Africa

suffered a Malian air raid on Ouahigouya, with 13 killed and 35 wounded. Burkina Faso claimed that a 'European imperialist power', (France) was helping Mali. Libya's Muammar Gaddafi offered to mediate the dispute, and though Mali turned down his offer at first, both Libya and Nigeria maintained their pressures to bring an end to the war.

Results: immediate and longer term

On 30 December the two heads of state (Moussa Traore of Mali and Thomas Sankara of Burkina Faso) signed a document brought to them by the Ivorian foreign Minister, Simeon Ake, and Minister of Defence, Jean Kouan Banny, and ANAD's Secretary-General, General Jean Gounis of Senegal. Under its terms they agreed to a ceasefire and to receive an observation team which would monitor troop withdrawals and, later, an exchange of prisoners. Several ceasefires – by Libya, Nigeria and the OAU – had been attempted, but it was the ANAD mission that succeeded; the ceasefire came into effect on 31 December 1985.

Although the two sides welcomed the ceasefire and ANAD's help, neither pretended that the dispute which had marred relations between them since independence had been solved. Burkina Faso, for example, suggested that Mali aggression had been a French-backed effort designed to destabilize Sankara's revolutionary government. In fact neither country (both among the poorest on the continent) could afford to make war, although land claims and national pride had made the clash inevitable.

Both sides in fact claimed a victory. Burkina Faso argued that it had won, despite the superior military equipment of the Malians, because of the revolutionary determination of its troops. Mali, on the other hand, had held land up to 100 km (62 miles) inside Burkina Faso.

However, in January 1986 Sankara and Traore were reconciled at an ANAD summit held in Yamoussoukro, the designated political capital of Côte d'Ivoire, where the heads of state of Niger, Mauritania, Senegal and Togo were present in addition to Côte d'Ivoire's President, Félix Houphouët-Boigny, the two combatant presidents and Benin (as an observer) The two countries agreed to withdraw their troops from the border region. At a rally in Ouagadougou Sankara told Malian prisoners that they were free to go home: 'We are all Africans and our common cause is peace and development.' Both heads of state agreed to a monitoring force of Nigerian and Libyan troops. Prisoners were exchanged in February, and then in June the two countries exchanged ambassadors for the first time since 1974.

Part of the disputed territory was administered by Mali and part by Burkina Faso while they waited for the judgment of the International Court. This was finally delivered in December 1986; the Court ruled that the Agacher Strip be divided equally between the two countries, and each claimed to be satisfied.

It was a small-scale war, but it came as the culmination of a quarter-century of enmity and tensions which might have been avoided had more care been exercised by France in dividing its colonial territories before giving them independence. The credit for confining the war and bringing about a rapid peace goes to the neighbours of the two combatants, who acted with commendable speed.

CHAD: CIVIL WARS AND LIBYAN EXPANSIONISM

Introduction

Two wars extended over many years became so inextricably intertwined that it is easier to treat them together and almost impossible not to do so. Since the mid-1960s Chad had been bedevilled by a series of civil wars between the north (Arab-Muslim) and the south (Black-Christian), though they might be regarded as a single war with a number of uneasy breaks; only in 1989 did it appear – precariously – that perhaps the two groups were at least prepared to try to live peaceably with each other.

At the same time Libya became deeply involved: first, as an ally of the northern groups, which were in revolt against the southern-dominated government in the capital, N'Djamena; and then as a territorial claimant for the Aozou Strip, the slice of territory along the southern border of Libya, which forms the northernmost area of Chad. Libya's principal motive for intervention has undoubtedly been to annex the Aozou Strip, and in pursuit of this claim Gaddafi has been prepared to switch his support between the various internal contenders for power in Chad. When this annexation was effected in 1973 no objections were forthcoming either from Chad's President, François Tombalbaye, or from neighbouring states. But following Tombalbaye's fall in 1975, his successor as President, General Felix Malloum, did raise the question of the annexation. Later, in 1980, at the invitation of the acting President of the provisional government, Goukouni Oueddei, Libyan forces occupied most of Chad. While Goukouni, then and later, appeared ready to accept the Libyan claim to the Strip, Hissène Habré and other leaders repudiated it. When Habré came to power in 1982 he reopened the question of the Strip with Libya but got no satisfaction; in 1987 his army retook the greater part of it after inflicting a major defeat on the Libyans.

Origins

Chad became independent from France in 1960 and, like the other countries in the Sahel region that stretches across northern Africa, it suffered from the problem of a land divided between a black, 'Christian' south (in this case the most prosperous section of the population) and a poorer north which was mainly inhabited by nomadic, Arab or Arabicized peoples who were Muslim. There was a deep cultural divide between the conservative, sparsely populated north and the more populous, Westernized and advanced south.

In 1962 the country's first President, François Tombalbaye, took steps to turn the country into a one-party state under the Parti progressiste tchadien (PPT), and though representatives of both groups – southerners and northerners – were members, Tombalbaye was its dominant force. A French garrison had remained in the north of Chad at independence, but in 1964 these French troops were withdrawn to be replaced by elements of the Chad national army, which soon became embroiled in local disputes. Although the one-party state was accepted in the south, this was not the case in the north. A first revolt, partly in reaction to heavy taxes, took place in 1966 at Ouaddai and was supported from across the

Sudanese border. This and other early rebellions were haphazard: in part against taxation and the southern civil service; and in part the result of long-standing northern suspicion of and antipathy to the people of the south. Gradually the northern rebels organized themselves to form the Chad Liberation Front (Frolinat). A coup attempt in 1971 was supposedly backed by Libya, which later recognized Frolinat and provided it with offices in Tripoli.

In the meantime the question of the Chad–Libyan border surfaced to add a new dimension to an already complicated situation. The border had first been defined by France and Britain in 1898 in a typical 'Scramble' agreement to define respective spheres of influence as the powers completed the carve-up of Africa. Italy accepted the border agreement in 1902, and at the conclusion of the First World War Britain and France again agreed on the frontier. Back in 1911, however, Italy had occupied Tripoli, which until then had been part of the Ottoman Empire; its colonial possession became known as Libya in 1934. In 1955 independent Libya agreed by treaty with France the border between Libya and what was still French Equatorial Africa.

Libya based its 1973 annexation of the Aozou Strip on a protocol that had been entered into by France and Italy in 1935, in which 111,370 square kilometres (43,000 square miles) of the Strip, including the towns of Aozou and Guezendi, had been recognized as part of Italian Libya. Subsequently France had not ratified the protocol. Thus Libya had some basis for its claim. The Libyan annexation was influenced by the fact that the Strip was known to contain considerable deposits of uranium.

Outbreak and response

Frolinat was founded in 1966 and became the spearhead of a revolt which up to that time had been sporadic and without obvious purpose. Another anti-government outbreak occurred in 1966 at Salamat in the south, while in the far north the Toubou nomads, acting as government guards at Aozou, mutinied in sympathy with northern aspirations. The first leader of Frolinat, Dr Abba Siddick, was soon replaced by Goukouni Oueddei, who was prepared to rely on Libyan support.

At this stage France stepped up its involvement. In August 1968 the French air force transported government troops to Aozou; then in 1969 1600 French troops were sent to Chad in support of Tombalbaye. This number was reduced in 1971, and the troops were removed altogether in 1972 without having made much difference to the growing power of Frolinat, which remained undefeated. But in accordance with the 1960 and 1964 defence agreements between France and Chad, French troops were stationed at Fort Lamy (later N'Djamena) and Fort Archambault.

In its early stages Frolinat obtained arms and money from Algeria, but in 1971 Libya became its principal ally and source of military equipment. Although Tombalbaye tried to contain the revolt by taking northerners into the cabinet, Frolinat rejected the move. Then, following a coup attempt against him, Tombalbaye broke diplomatic relations with Libya, which he accused of complicity; as a result, Gaddafi openly recognized Frolinat and provided it with tanks and anti-aircraft missiles. The fighting escalated and Frolinat captured a number of key northern positions, including the towns of Bardai and Faya Largeau. Frolinat still had no recognizable ideology; rather, it was based on race and religion, and a sense that the people of the north ought to dominate those of the south.

It was part of the nature of Frolinat to splinter into rival factions. Before long Goukouni (and his Popular Armed Forces, FAP) proved too independent for Libya, so Gaddafi switched his support to a rival Frolinat group (the Common Action Front, FAC) led by Ahmat Acyl. But then a third faction, the Northern Armed Forces (FAN) surfaced in the north-east of the country under Hissène Habré.

The Nigerians then took a hand; in June 1972 a Nigerian commando unit was arrested outside the capital. In November of that year the government renewed diplomatic relations with Libya, and the two countries signed a pact of friendship. Yet in 1973 Libya moved its forces into the Aozou Strip, which it annexed. In 1975 the army overthrew the Tombalbaye regime. Tombalbaye was replaced by General Félix Malloum, who became President of a Supreme Military Council; yet Malloum was no more able than had been his predecessor to subdue the north or persuade the Libyans to quit the Aozou Strip.

In 1975 a crisis developed with France over the government's handling of the seizure by Frolinat of three French hostages, and Malloum therefore terminated the French base facilities at N'Djamena (September). These, however, were restored in 1976. Meanwhile a Frolinat split favoured Goukouni at the expense of Habré, and with Libyan military aid his forces were able to capture the town of Bardai in July.

Course of the struggle

1978

In January 1978 Malloum and Habré met in Khartoum where they signed an agreement which included a ceasefire and a new government that would contain members of Frolinat. But almost immediately Frolinat settled its internal differences and launched a new offensive against the government. The Chad army suffered major defeats, and Frolinat forces captured Fada and Faya-Largeau in the north. Malloum was forced to appeal to France and Libya to intervene. For the time being the country was split, with Frolinat holding the north and the government the south.

That April, however, Frolinat broke the ceasefire and its army advanced on the capital. France then sent a force of 2500 Legionnaires as well as several squadrons of fighter-bombers in support of the government, and at first their presence led to violent demonstrations against France. Later, the French launched a major offensive against Frolinat: early in June French and Chad forces supported by French Jaguar fighter-bombers attacked a rebel force of about 1000 equipped with heavy Soviet tanks around the strategic town of Ati, which lies 180 miles to the north of the capital. The rebels suffered heavy losses. Malloum's government had appeared to be on the point of collapse until this defeat was inflicted on the rebels.

At the same time between 2000 and 3000 Libyan troops were estimated to be supporting the Frolinat rebels. Thus, by mid-1978 both France and Libya had become substantially militarily involved on opposite sides in Chad's civil war. The French victory halted the advance of Frolinat, but it did not defeat them, and by

July the country was effectively partitioned between government forces holding the south and backed by the French military presence and Frolinat forces holding the north and backed by Libya.

Hissène Habré, the former leader of Frolinat, had joined up with the Chad government forces earlier in the year. Now, following the military stalemate, he reached an agreement with Malloum: the latter was to remain President while Habré became Prime Minister. A new *charte fondamentale* was promulgated. Muslims now had a slight majority in the cabinet. Habré's army, FAN, was to be abolished and its members integrated in the national army. France at this stage decided to back Habré, whom it preferred to Goukouni as Muslim leader.

By December the limited co-operation which had been achieved between Malloum and Habré had collapsed. Habré would not disband FAN, and by January 1979 his forces were clashing with the government army in the capital; in February they captured the radio station. Habré's forces showed themselves to be far superior to those of the regular army. Then Goukouni's Frolinat forces, in yet another volte-face, advanced to N'Djamena to fight alongside Habré's FAN.

1979

In February 1979 Habré ousted Malloum in a coup, but general civil war ensued with Muslims massacring blacks and blacks slaughtering Muslims in retaliation. Some military order was restored by Colonel Abdelkadar Kamougue (the former Foreign Minister), who rallied the Chad Armed Forces (FAT). Then Nigeria intervened in an attempt to curtail Libyan ambitions. Conferences were held in Kano, Nigeria, during March and again in April; those taking part were Habré, Goukouni, Malloum and a pro-Nigeria faction, as well as Libya, Cameroon, Niger and Sudan. A ceasefire followed by the demilitarization of the capital, N'Djamena, was agreed and a transitional government of national unity (GUNT) was set up. The armies were to be integrated. Malloum and Habré resigned and Goukouni became President of GUNT. Nigeria agreed to send a neutral force to maintain security. But Nigerian determination to impose its own candidate on Chad – Mahamat Abba – led Goukouni and Habré to quit the conference and return to N'Djamena, where they agreed to form a government of national unity. This soon broke down, however, and for the balance of the year GUNT was rendered inoperative by factional squabbles, while agreements entered into by the factions were never kept.

1980

In March 1980 fighting broke out again in N'Djamena between Malloum's FAP, now commanded by Kamougue, and Habré's FAN. The fighting between the two sides continued all year. The French declared themselves neutral; they had decided to get out of Chad and by May had withdrawn all their troops from the country.

In June Goukouni signed a treaty of friendship with Libya (without consulting GUNT). The treaty included a clause which allowed Libya to intervene if Chad's internal security was at risk, and following an October offensive in the north by

FAN, Libyan aircraft bombed Faya and N'Djamena and the whole northern area was captured from Habré's FAN by Goukouni and his Libyan allies. This phase of the civil war was a triumph for Goukouni and a revitalized GUNT. By December 1980 an estimated 5000 Libyan troops were in N'Djamena in support of Goukouni, and temporary peace returned to the capital.

1981

On 6 January 1981 Goukouni and Gaddafi reached an agreement in Tripoli for an eventual political union of Chad and Libya. This agreement had not been discussed with members of GUNT and there was an angry reaction in N'Djamena. This led to a weakening of Goukouni's authority, while Habré, who had sustained a major defeat in the capital the previous year, none the less continued fighting in the north-east of the country, where he had retired.

Other African countries of the region were becoming increasingly anxious at Libyan expansionist ambitions. At a meeting in Lomé, Togo, 11 heads of state condemned Libyan activities and called for an Inter-African Force (IAF) to be sent to keep the peace in Chad. Nigeria, in particular, was opposed to Libyan activities in Chad. Following renewed and fierce fighting in N'Djamena during April, the Libyan forces intervened to restore order and many casualties resulted. Goukouni then persuaded the Libyans to withdraw from N'Djamena airport and a conference was called. This was attended by Presidents Shehu Shagari of Nigeria and Siaka Stevens of Sierra Leone, who 'thanked' Libya for restoring the peace. Under strong French pressure the Libyans began to withdraw their forces in mid-1981.

At their June meeting in Nairobi the OAU again agreed on a peace-keeping force for Chad, which both France and the USA now promised to support financially, the USA entering the picture mainly in its determination to thwart Gaddafi. In mid-December a substantial African force arrived in Chad; led by a Nigerian, Major-General Ejiga, it included 2000 Nigerian, 2000 Zairean and 800 Senegalese troops. But controversy followed at once: while the IAF saw its role as a neutral one of keeping the peace, Goukouni saw it as a means finally to destroy Habré and FAN. By the end of the year, as a result of great OAU pressures, the Libyans finally withdrew. Habré was the main beneficiary of their withdrawal since he managed to capture most of the military equipment which they left behind, and the stage was set for a new FAN offensive.

1982

By mid-January FAN had captured a number of northern towns in the wake of the Libyan withdrawal. Both the OAU and the IAF (its instrument) called for reconciliation between Goukouni and Habré, the latter having significantly reversed his earlier misfortunes. In June FAN forces entered N'Djamena unop-posed; Kamougue fled from the capital, and his influence in the south, which had always been the source of his support, now appeared to have fallen away; Goukouni fled to Algeria.

Habré, however, faced a variety of international pressures from France, Libya, Nigeria, Sudan and the OAU. None the less by September, when his army also captured the key towns of Sarh and Moundou, Habré appeared to have control of the greater part of Chad. His victory could be attributed to two main causes: the greater discipline and efficiency of his army (FAN); and the endless in-fighting which was a feature of GUNT under Goukouni, whose overt support of Libyan claims had eroded his standing with the fiercely nationalistic Chadians of all groups. In October Habré was able to set up a government which was widely representative, and by the end of the year the various pro-Habré military groups had merged to form FANT (Forces armées nationales tchadiennes).

1983

A number of reversals occurred during 1983 with Goukouni's forces retaking the greater part of the north and a series of revenge killings and massacres in the south. By March, affected by defeats in the north, Habré's FAN was also suffering from internal tribal factions. Even so, Habré had gained international recognition as Chad's head of state, and in March Chad complained at the UN that Libya was still in occupation of the Aozou Strip. Habré's negotiations with the Libyans broke down on their insistence that he recognize their claim to the Aozou Strip and make Chad an Islamic country.

A new source of friction now arose. In April fighting broke out between the forces of Chad and Nigeria over the sovereignty of a number of islands in the south-east corner of Lake Chad. Here the Nigerians allied themselves with the anti-Habré rebels. On 16 May the Nigerians claimed that more than 300 Chad soldiers had been killed in the clashes of the previous weeks. There followed a Chad counter-attack with French mercenaries in support, while Nigerian MiGs bombed Chad villages. In July, however, the two countries agreed to end the fighting and reopen their joint border, although it was later closed again until May 1984.

In June Gaddafi decided to intervene once more, providing Goukouni with substantial fresh supplies of military hardware. France, under pressure from both the USA and Francophone leaders deeply distrustful of Gaddafi, decided once more on military intervention. A French force of 2800 men was airlifted into Chad from the Central African Republic during August; its object was to separate the two sides by occupying an east–west line across the country from Salal to Arada. Its presence was sufficient to prevent Goukouni and his Libyan allies from coming further south. France and Libya both manoeuvred carefully in their efforts to avoid a full-scale confrontation. Meanwhile widespread and growing violence in the extreme south of the country emphasized the inability of the central government to maintain control. And from the north Goukouni claimed that his GUNT was now at war with France. Libyan planes bombed the government-held town of Oum Chalouba (5 September), causing numbers of casualties; the town had been the site of a fierce battle a week earlier in which the Goukouni–Libyan forces had been repulsed with heavy losses. Meanwhile, a new stream of southerners fled as refugees into neighbouring countries; according to Kamougue, the former Vice-President under Goukouni, they fled because life had become impossible under the Habré government.

At the end of September, for the first time in more than a decade, President Habré visited France in order to take part in the Franco-African summit; his presence sealed a *rapprochement* with France, which earlier had regarded him as an enemy. Habré, however, was critical of the French for not fighting the Libyans; so far they had not fired a single shot.

1984

In late January France accused Libya of resuming hostilities and at once sent air reinforcements to Chad from both France and Gabon. A French Jaguar fighter-bomber had been shot down by missile from a column which had penetrated south of the 'Red Line' which divided Chad between the rebel-held north and govern-ment-held territory. Following this incident, the French moved the Red Line limit a further 100 km (60 miles) north.

At the beginning of February government sources claimed to have wiped out a column of 600 rebels: several hundred had been killed or wounded and 234 taken prisoner. The Goukouni forces claimed to have killed 358 government troops.

At the end of April, Gaddafi announced that he would be willing to withdraw his troops from Chad so as to remove any pretext for the French to maintain their troops in the country. It was a new move in a complex game designed to get the French out of Chad.

By the middle of the year an increasingly confident Habré dissolved Frolinat and replaced it with a new party, the Union nationale pour l'indépendance et la révolution (UNIR) It was a conscious move towards unity, with a more even division of government posts between Habré supporters and southerners. But, despite this move, by the end of August the south had collapsed into civil war again; government repression was brutal and there was much suffering among the civilian population, sending a wave of refugees across the border into the Central African Republic. This fighting was to continue to April 1985.

In September 1984 France and Libya reached an agreement that both would withdraw their forces from Chad. The French, clearly relieved to have a way out of a military commitment which was costing £250,000 a day, had removed all their troops (3300) by 10 November; but the Libyans remained, forcing President Mitterrand to admit that he had been fooled. Later he said that France would not use force to drive out the Libyans, but would intervene again if they advanced on N'Djamena. He recognized that Aozou belonged to Chad, yet suggested Habré should concentrate on ending civil strife – a backhanded way of saying 'leave Aozou to Libya'.

Zaire also had about 1000 troops in Chad in support of Habré, and President Mobutu said he might now withdraw these as well. In December, when it had become clear that Libya had not withdrawn simultaneously with the French and still retained about 3000 troops in northern Chad, President Habré none the less refused an offer by France to send troops back again. Thus by the end of the year the French were out, the Libyans remained in the north, Habré had a deep distrust for French motives and the military stalemate waited to be broken.

1985

During 1985 Habré consolidated his grip on the central government and secured growing international recognition. In October the Libyans began to reinforce their units in the north, bringing the total of their troops up to about 4000. Meanwhile, the government had largely brought the rebellion in the south under control, while the opposition appeared to have become increasingly fragmented, both developments which strengthened Habré's position.

1986

In February 1986 the Libyans launched an offensive across the 16th parallel of latitude, the dividing line between north and south Chad. Gaddafi had calculated, incorrectly, that France would not intervene again. Habré's forces repulsed the Libyan–GUNT attack; then Habré appealed to France for aid. French bombers from their base in the Central African Republic now bombed the Libyan airstrip at Ouadi Doum north-east of Faya-Largeau, and following a Libyan air strike on the airport at N'Djamena, the French set up their own air strike force in the Chad capital. The USA now assisted with the provision of $10 million military aid for Habré.

During the course of the year Goukouni's GUNT largely disintegrated, with many GUNT forces going over to Habré in the south. By mid-November US arms for Habré were arriving in Douala, Cameroon. The French now sent 1000 troops to Chad in support of their air units which were already in the country; the troops were again deployed along the 16th parallel. It was now Habré's turn to go on to the offensive. In December FAP troops, now loyal to Habré, fought Libyan troops near Bardai in the extreme north and in the Tibesti mountains. Habré's forces crossed the Red Line and advanced northwards, supported by French aircraft which dropped supplies.

In December Habré claimed that the Libyan forces were employing genocide tactics in the north. The Libyans also directed their attacks against the FAP forces of their former GUNT allies who had switched to Habré's side. At this stage the French appeared unwilling to become engaged if it meant a direct confrontation with Libyan forces; Habré was desperate for France to provide him with anti-aircraft and anti-tank guns and to help him drive the Libyans out. Apart from the 1200 French troops along the 16th parallel, a further 4000 were in the Central African Republic. Libya was then estimated to have between 6000 and 8000 troops in northern Chad.

President Habré complained that he could not obtain help from either France or the USA, although he had asked for weapons and vehicles; he said Chad's economy was wrecked after 20 years of war and the country was unable to face Libya on its own. The French did then assist to the extent of dropping supplies to Habré's forces in the north, and the USA promised $15 million worth of military equipment. Libya now threatened to invade the southern half of the country, and the French said publicly that they were not encouraging Habré to send his troops into the north where the Libyan troops were stationed. But in mid-December, shortly after these exchanges, the Libyans suffered a major defeat at the hands of

Goukouni's supporters, who had switched to the government side the previous October.

Libyan troops backed by tanks were routed at Bardai; 400 Libyans were killed and 17 tanks destroyed. A result of this new twist in the war was to put pressure on France to provide President Habré with air cover so that he could send his forces north to assist the Goukouni Popular Armed Forces, then estimated to be 3000 strong. The *rapprochement* between Habré and Goukouni (or at least Habré and Goukouni's forces, for Goukouni himself remained an apparent prisoner in Tripoli), if it could be made to last, appeared to offer the best chance yet for Chad to end the civil war and oust the Libyan invaders from the north.

1987

At the beginning of the new year Libya sent reinforcements to Chad. While the Libyans fought a defensive action at the oasis of Zouar, their planes bombed the town of Arada in the south and there was every indication that the war would escalate sharply. In retaliation for the Libyan raid on Arada – a deliberate Libyan affront to the French, since the town is south of the 16th parallel – the French destroyed the Libyan radar station at Ouadi Doum. Now Habré's FANT moved north at speed – they were lightly armed – to launch attacks on the Libyans, who were forced to retreat from most of the towns they were occupying. FANT captured the main Libyan stronghold of Ouadi Doum after fierce fighting. It was the first time government forces had fought the Libyans that far north, and they had emerged successful in the encounter.

Libya now began to assemble large numbers of combat aircraft in southern Libya and northern Chad, and its planes began to fly over targets well to the south of the 16th parallel. But the defeat by Habré forces of the Libyans holding Fada – only a small number escaped and the majority were either killed (784) or captured, while more than 100 Soviet tanks were destroyed – was seen as a turning point in the war. In N'Djamena about 130 Libyan prisoners were displayed to the diplomatic corps in order finally to refute repeated Libyan claims that it had no troops in Chad. By mid-January French transport planes were bringing new military supplies to Kalait, the northernmost French military outpost, ready for the main push by Habré.

Then in mid-January Gaddafi sent messages to African heads of state to say he wanted an end to the war in Chad; by then both Fada and Zouar had fallen to Habré's forces, which were poised for an all-out attack on the Libyan military base at Faya-Largeau. But Libya continued to build up its forces, reaching an estimated 15,000, while an additional 2000 to 3000 were across the border in Sudan's Darfur province. So, early in February, France decided to reinforce its garrison in Chad and rushed an additional 1000 men to the country from the Central African Republic. Thereafter, in the curious fashion of wars, there was a lull. Then, in mid-March, came the biggest victory of the war when Hissène Habré's FANT, led by Hassan Djamous, captured Ouadi Doum, which was the main base for Libya's strike aircraft and was protected by more than 5000 Libyans. It is estimated that about 3600 Libyans were killed, 700 were captured and 2000 died of thirst in the desert as they fled northwards.

Following the fall of Ouadi Doum, the Libyans gave up their last major base at

Faya-Largeau without a fight and retreated to the north. For the first time it looked as though Habré was at last in a position to assert his authority over the whole country. Many of the Libyan troops turned out not to be Libyans at all, but members of the Islamic Pan-African Legion, often mercenaries press-ganged from among those who had gone to seek work in Libya. The war in Chad was reported to be deeply unpopular in Libya and became more so as the defeats and casualties mounted. The successful drive to the north by FANT had also had the effect of isolating the Libyan forces in the Darfur province of Sudan.

At the beginning of April government forces drove the Libyans from the small outpost of Gouro, which is only 90 miles south of the Aozou Strip and this raised a new question: both France and President Abdou Diouf of Senegal, the current chairman of the OAU, tried to dissuade Habré from attempting to retake the Aozou Strip and to persuade him instead to refer the matter to arbitration at the International Court of Justice. But the Chad government ruled out arbitration and repeated the government's determination to recapture the Strip.

The next serious fighting was to come in August when FANT forces were ready to take on the Libyans in the Aozou Strip itself. On 8 August, under Mahamet Nouri, FANT first took Aozou town but were then forced to retreat by heavy Libyan air attacks. A month later they attacked and occupied Maater es Sarra in south-east Libya, where they destroyed 22 aircraft and 100 tanks, and killed 1700 Libyans. This was the first time that Chad forces had crossed into Libyan territory. On 11 September the two countries agreed to a ceasefire.

1988

The ceasefire of September 1987 was followed by a form of stalemate, despite the spectacular victories of FANT over the Libyans. The French refused to extend their air cover to enable the Chad army to take permanent control of the Aozou Strip, which the Libyans had heavily fortified. None the less, despite periodic clashes, there was a growing improvement in relations between the two countries: in May, just before the OAU summit, Gaddafi announced his willingness to recognize the government of Habré and launch a 'Marshall Plan' to reconstruct war-damaged areas in Chad. For the time being, at least, it appeared that Chad recognized Libyan *de facto* control of the Aozou Strip, and that Gaddafi was prepared to recognize Habré and not attempt any more to overthrow him.

Estimated costs and casualties

Casualty figures for such a long-drawn-out war are notoriously difficult to estimate. During 1980, at the height of the fighting in the capital, for example, it is estimated that between 3000 and 4000 civilians were killed. Between 1965, when the civil conflict first got under way, and the end of the 1970s an estimated 20,000 people were killed. During the 1980s repeated heavy fighting possibly accounted for another 30,000 deaths. In the short conflict between Chad and Nigeria over the Lake Chad islands in 1983 perhaps 500 Chadians alone were killed. During the battle of Oum Chalouba in 1983, whereas the government claimed to have killed

800 rebels and captured 600, other sources suggested that no more than 30 rebels had been killed and about the same number wounded. There were very heavy casualties during the fighting against the Libyans in 1987, yet while Chad inflated the number of Libyans killed, the Libyans played down their losses: one estimate in April 1987 put Libyan losses for the preceding few months at 4000 dead, with 200 tanks and 45 aircraft destroyed.

Libyan intervention must have cost that country an enormous sum, yet it had the oil wealth to pay for its invasion; Chad, on the other hand, was one of the poorest countries in Africa and was heavily dependent throughout the struggle on aid from outside. That assistance came principally from France, whose troops came and went on three major occasions, although they were always in the background across the border in the Central African Republic. When France had 1600 or more men stationed in Chad, which was an average figure for a good many years during the fighting, the cost to Paris was somewhere in the region of £250,000 a day. French casualties were few, though great publicity attached to those which occurred. French politicians discovered that the war in Chad was not popular, and much French effort was directed at not being drawn in too far. The maximum number of Libyan troops reported to be operating inside Chad at any time was 15,000, though more usually the figure was half that; the maximum number of French troops was in the region of 3300. Zaire sent paratroopers and planes to assist the Habré government in 1983, and at one stage had 2000 troops in Chad.

At various stages of the war Chadian refugees crossed into neighbouring countries, mainly the Central African Republic and Sudan, and for some years in the 1980s, for example, the UN High Commissioner for Refugees figure for Chadian refugees in the Darfur province of Sudan stood at or near 25,000.

The USA became involved as a periodic supplier of arms to the Chad government during the 1980s, providing $25 million worth in 1983, and $15 million worth in early 1987; more important was its role in exerting pressure on France to remain involved and so thwart the designs of Libya's Gaddafi.

The Chad war appeared on the annual agenda of OAU summits for years and led to two attempts to find a solution by providing an inter-African force to keep the peace.

Results: immediate and longer term

The announcement by Gaddafi in May 1988 that he was prepared to recognize the government of Habré in N'Djamena must be seen as a triumph for Habré himself, his FANT forces and the French, whose troops had ensured that Libya did not attempt an offensive south of the 16th parallel. On 3 October 1988 the two countries resumed diplomatic relations, although Libya still retained the Aozou Strip and Chad had not renounced its claim.

However, on 31 August 1989 Libya and Chad signed an agreement in Algiers to give them a year to resolve their differences over the Aozou Strip before going to arbitration, and in the interim it was agreed that the Strip should be administered by an African observer force. Following this agreement, which France had worked to bring about, the French government announced that it would reduce the number of its troops in Chad. France and Libya then agreed to withdraw all their troops on a stage-by-stage basis (though this did not include Libyan troops in the Aozou Strip, which Libya had held since 1973).

GUINEA: A MINI-INVASION

On 22 November 1970 approximately 350 troops led by Portuguese officers came by sea to invade Conakry, the capital of Guinea; the attempt failed and 48 hours later had been defeated. The reasons for this invasion were complex.

Origins

Guinea became independent in 1958 after Sékou Touré, alone of Francophone leaders, urged the people of Guinea to vote against de Gaulle's proposed community of overseas territories. Thereafter his country became largely isolated in Francophone Africa and heavily dependent in its early years on Soviet and other Communist bloc sources of aid. Over the years there had been a number of threats of possible coups or invasions against the regime.

During the first 10 months of 1970 Guinea's relations with its neighbours and France (although not Portugal, which was then the colonial power in neighbouring Portuguese Guinea) had improved dramatically. Guinea, however, had allowed the Partido Africano da Independência da Guiné e Cabo Verde (PAIGC) from neighbouring Portuguese Guinea to establish its headquarters in Conakry. By then the PAIGC was fighting a bitter war against the Portuguese, who had an estimated 35,000 troops in the country yet were clearly beginning to lose the war.

The 1970 invasion was one in a series of attempted coups. A plot of March 1969 by former ministers and army officers also included the army commander; an assassination attempt against the President in June of that year was only just foiled. The result of these plots was a certain sense of paranoia in Conakry, while accusations of imperialism were levelled against outside powers, usually France.

Sékou Touré's socialist policies had driven an increasing number of the country's élite into exile, either to Paris or to the nearby states of Côte d'Ivoire and Senegal, both of which tended to be close supporters of France's African policies. By 1970 there were an estimated 500,000 Guineans abroad, and though many were only seeking material improvement, a significant proportion were dissidents opposed to the regime in Conakry.

Opponents of the regime established the National Front for the Liberation of Guinea (FLNG): there were branches of FLNG in both Côte d'Ivoire and Senegal, their presence contributing to the poor relations between those two countries and Guinea. Another group calling itself the Regrouping of Guineans in Europe was based in Paris.

The improvement of relations between Guinea and its neighbours meant that the governments in Abidjan and Dakar began to curtail the activities of the FLNG, which in consequence sought a new base. The Portuguese allowed FLNG to establish a base in Portuguese Guinea. Touré himself had close personal relations with the PAIGC leader, Amilcar Cabral. The Portuguese, reportedly, had been making overtures to the FLNG since 1967.

The invasion

Early on the morning of 22 November 1970 President Sékou Touré went on the radio to announce that foreign ships were offshore in Guinean waters and that hundreds of mercenaries of many nationalities were landing in Conakry. Touré then sent messages to all African heads of state appealing for help in repelling the invaders, whose forces included Europeans as well as Africans. He also sent a message to the United Nations asking for airborne troops to be sent to fight the invaders.

Fighting in Conakry lasted for two days, but by 24 November the situation was under control and the people returned to work: they were enjoined to stay 'armed and vigilant'. On 28 November it was reported that a further 200 soldiers from the regular Portuguese army in Portuguese Guinea had attempted an invasion across the border, but had been repulsed. It was not at once clear how responsibility for the invasion could be divided between internal dissidents, Guinean exiles and Portugal and other foreign powers.

Estimated costs and casualties

Losses were estimated at 100 Guineans killed and 200 invaders dead, with many more taken prisoner. Between 350 and 400 men carried out the invasion; they were brought to the waters off Conakry in two troop transports and three or four smaller patrol boats. The men were equipped with infantry small arms. They were divided into groups, each of which was assigned a particular target: the army camp, the airport, the power station, the presidential palace (which was destroyed) and the PAIGC headquarters. The ships used were Portuguese, with Portuguese crews drawn from the Portuguese armed forces. The invaders, moreover, were commanded by Portuguese officers, although most of the men were either dissident Guineans or African troops from the Portuguese army in Portuguese Guinea. In January 1971 91 people were sentenced to death and 66 to life imprisonment for the parts they had played in the invasion. Those sentenced to life imprisonment included 12 Lebanese, 18 Frenchmen and 6 West Germans.

Results: immediate and longer term

This Portuguese-controlled invasion of Guinea was a bold attempt to overthrow an African government. But many others were clearly implicated: on 24 January Guinea broke diplomatic relations with Senegal for its alleged complicity in the plot, and later that year – 29 July – with West Germany for the same reason.

General Spinola (the Governor and Commander-in-Chief of the Armed Forces in Portuguese Guinea) and the Portuguese government in Lisbon denied any involvement and claimed that the invasion had been conducted solely by Guinean dissidents. But a UN fact-finding mission which visited Guinea shortly after the invasion found that the invaders had been either Guinean dissidents or Africans of the Portuguese army from neighbouring Portuguese Guinea commanded by

Portuguese officers. At home the government found that others implicated in the invasion plot included seven former ministers, the Roman Catholic Archbishop of Conakry, three senior civil servants and a former police commissioner. Following the invasion, Touré ordered the party to arm the people.

A quite different result of the invasion was a temporary demonstration of African unity. For a short period there was near unanimity among all African states in their expressions of support for Guinea, with offers of financial and military assistance. This solidarity with Guinea, not a popular country in Africa, did not last long, although ranks had been firmly closed against outside interference in the continent.

At the United Nations in December 1970 the Security Council adopted a resolution 'strongly condemning the Portuguese Government for its invasion of Guinea' and asking for full compensation to be paid. The USA, Britain, France and Spain abstained.

Guinea accused NATO countries, and most specifically France, of complicity with the Portuguese in the invasion. A special OAU meeting called to consider the invasion met in Lagos, Nigeria, and promised aid to Guinea. The invasion prompted the OAU to raise the issue of a permanent OAU joint military high command (or intervention force), but discussion of this was postponed to 1971.

Touré used the invasion as a pretext to clamp down on internal dissidents and arrest opponents on unspecified charges of complicity. Relations with Guinea's neighbours Côte d'Ivoire and Senegal were to deteriorate as a result of the invasion, and Guinea accused Senegal of harbouring mercenary troops in readiness for a second invasion. Touré also accused West Germany of espionage in Guinea as well as complicity in the invasion, and insisted on the withdrawal of the West German Ambassador and the expulsion of 100 West German residents.

It may have been a small-scale affair, but the invasion raised a number of awkward political questions: about NATO activities in support of Portugal in Africa; about Western destabilization tactics in a country whose policy they opposed; and, for a small African state, the clear difficulty of pursuing a policy which was out of line with those of its neighbours.

KENYA–SOMALIA: THE SHIFTA WAR

Origins

The conflict between Kenya and Somalia has its roots in the same claims of the Somalis to a Greater Somalia (the area over which traditionally their nomadic peoples have ranged with their herds) as operated in the case of the Somali conflict with Ethiopia (see the Ogaden war, pp. 190–198). In the case of Kenya the Somali claim was twofold: that the north-east corner of Kenya was part of the area over which Somalia's people had long been used to range; and that the 129,500 square kilometres (50,000 square miles) of the area which eventually became the North-Eastern province of independent Kenya contained a population that was mainly Somali – about 200,000 in 1963. This region of Kenya to which Somalia laid claim was represented by one of the five points of the star that formed the centrepiece of the flag that the new state of Somalia flew at its independence in 1960.

The British colonial administration of Kenya had constant problems with the nomadic Somalis, who moved freely back and forth across the border into this area of their colony. Between 1948 and 1960 the British made the Northern Frontier District (NFD), as the region was then designated, a closed area where politics were not allowed, an area that required entry and exit permits for its relations with the rest of Kenya. Between 1960 (Somali independence) and 1963 (Kenyan independence) a number of pressures were mounted by the new government in Mogadishu in the hope of persuading the British to allow the NFD to become part of Greater Somalia. The result was a classic British compromise which recognized the special 'Somali' features of the region while, none the less, passing on control to Kenya. Thus, in 1963 the Commonwealth Secretary, Duncan Sandys, laid down that the Somali-dominated NFD could not secede, but that it should have the status of a seventh (North-East) province in an independent Kenya.

Outbreak and response

Once the British stand was clear, Somalia broke diplomatic relations with Britain (12 March 1963). Two days later, on 14 March, still nine months before Kenya's independence, the Prime Minister, Jomo Kenyatta, said that he would not contemplate 'any secession or handing over of one inch of our territory'. Kenya, then and later, resolutely opposed Somali claims to North-East Kenya and made it plain that its territory was not negotiable.

Following Kenya's independence in December 1963, the Somali claims became a recurring feature of Nairobi's foreign relations, on one occasion provoking a Kenyan statement to the effect that Kenya would go to any lengths to protect the north-eastern part of the country against Somali aggression. There was talk of secession in the north-east during the 1963 elections in Kenya, and since the dispute continued after independence the government felt obliged to commit a substantial part of its limited defence force to the area. Following independence Kenya held Somalia to blame for the rebel – Shifta – activity in the North-East Province and, on 25 December 1963, declared a state of emergency over the area which was to last for over five years.

Course of the struggle

Border hostilities between Kenya and Somalia and, most particularly, the activities of the Shiftas continued for four years from 1963 to 1967 when a reconciliation between the two countries was effected.

One of the first resolutions of the newly formed OAU, taken at its Cairo Summit of July 1964, was that member states pledged themselves 'to respect the borders existing on their achievement of independence'. Somalia refused to accept this resolution. Several attempts to mediate between the two states during the period 1964 to 1966 failed. Then at the 1967 OAU Summit held in Kinshasa, Zaire (then known as Congo Kinshasa), a Kenya–Somalia *rapprochement* was achieved to bring an end to the four-year war. Zambia's President, Kenneth Kaunda, was asked to act as mediator at a subsequent meeting held in October 1967 at Arusha,

Tanzania; the meeting was also attended by Presidents Kenyatta of Kenya, Nyerere of Tanzania and Obote of Uganda, as well as Prime Minister Egal of Somalia. As a result it appeared, at least for the time being, that an apparently intractable conflict, which had been responsible for a dangerous little war, had been resolved.

Estimated costs and casualties

At the end of 1966 the Kenyan government estimated that over the previous three years casualties (killed) had amounted to the following: 1650 Shifta bandits, 69 Kenyan military and police personnel; and 500 Kenyan civilians. The economic burden for Kenya of policing the area over the three years following independence had been considerable.

Ten years later (from 1976 onwards), when the Ogaden conflict erupted, Kenyan defence expenditure was substantially increased in order to deal with threatened or actual Somali border incursions.

Results: immediate and longer term

Kenya lifted its trade ban on Somalia following the Arusha meeting and later Kenyatta was to refer to the border war as a 'little quarrel'. In January 1968 the two countries restored diplomatic relations, and in March 1969 Kenya raised the state of emergency which had been imposed in the North-East Province in December 1963 and relaxed restrictions on Somali herdsmen. But over the years 1969 to 1977 the border question lay dormant; it had not been resolved.

Tensions erupted once more at the time of the major Ogaden war between Somalia and Ethiopia, although they were largely contained: Somalia had enough on its hands in Ethiopia and did not wish to face fighting with Kenya at the same time. Kenya backed the Ethiopian position. At one point in the war Kenya forced down an Egyptian plane which was carrying military supplies to Somalia and went on record condemning US support for Mogadishu. In 1977 when the British Foreign Secretary, David Owen, visited Kenya and saw the President, Kenyatta's main concern was to know where Britain stood in terms of the Ogaden conflict.

Early in 1979 President Daniel arap Moi, who had succeeded Kenyatta on the latter's death the previous year, toured the North-East Province where the Kenya Somalis lived. The province had long been the target of Somali propaganda suggesting its eventual incorporation in Greater Somalia. As a result of Shifta activities over the years, the province had suffered from lack of economic development. Moi was determined to reinforce Kenya nationalism in the area and make plain – as had his predecessor – that Somali claims would be resisted. Later that year (September) President Moi met President Barre of Somalia at Taif in Saudi Arabia, but no agreement was reached. Kenya pressed for Somalia to renounce its claims to the North-East Province, but Somalia insisted on self-determination for the people.

During this period Kenya became a firm ally of Ethiopia (although their basic political ideologies were far apart), so reinforcing its opposition to Somali claims; in 1979 the two countries concluded a treaty of friendship, and at the beginning of

December 1980 Colonel Mengistu Haile Mariam visited Nairobi. On 7 December President Barre reacted to Mengistu's Nairobi visit, describing the joint communiqué issued by the two heads of state as provocative.

Border clashes in late 1980 led to six Kenyan deaths, although President Barre denied any Somali responsibility and said that his country did not seek to obtain Kenyan territory. Slowly during the 1980s relations between Kenya and Somalia improved. The two Presidents held talks in Nairobi following the OAU Summit of September 1981, after which President Barre said, 'We in Somalia have no claim whatsoever on any part of Kenya's territory.' Further clashes were to occur in 1984, although by December of that year a Somali delegation was to visit Nairobi to sign a border security agreement.

THE OGADEN WAR 1977–1978

Origins

The Ogaden war of 1977–8 was not a sudden affair, but the culmination of long-standing antagonisms bound up in the complex history of the region, with its many territorial claims and counter-claims. When the war finally erupted it threatened to make the Horn of Africa as explosive as the south of the continent, for all the major powers were involved and continuing instability in the Horn threatened the oil-rich Gulf at a time when the influence of the Organization of Petroleum Exporting Countries (OPEC) was at its greatest. By supporting the new revolutionary government of Colonel Mengistu Haile Mariam in Ethiopia, the USSR was making a bid to oust the USA as the major power in the region.

The Ogaden is a rocky desert region in south-eastern Ethiopia whose waterholes are the focal points for nomads. The Somalis, who are the principal nomadic people of the Horn, have long regarded the region as their own. They probably moved into the Ogaden about 500 years ago when they displaced the Galla, driving them westwards into the Ethiopian highlands. Thereafter they moved across the Ogaden as they chose until, in the nineteenth century, they first encountered the expanding power of the Ethopian Empire under Emperor Menelik and then found themselves divided between the European imperialists during the 'Scramble' and carve-up of Africa at the end of the nineteenth century.

In 1888 an Anglo-French treaty recognized French control of Djibouti and Britain's 'interest' in British Somaliland, which was regarded in London as a safeguard for Aden and the route to India. Then in 1891 Emperor Menelik sent a letter to the European powers in which he denounced all other claims on his territory and laid claim in his turn to a number of surrounding places, including Khartoum in Sudan and the Ogaden. Britain then agreed that Ethiopia should be regarded as part of the Italian sphere of influence. The Italians subsequently occupied Eritrea, but when they advanced into Tigré they were defeated by the Ethiopians at the battle of Adowa in 1896. It was the one place in all Africa where European partition was blocked by an African military victory. The next year an Anglo-Ethiopian treaty set the border between Ethiopia and British Somaliland and cut across the traditional Somali grazing lands of the Haud (the plateau now spanning the Somali–Ethiopian border). However, it was agreed that the Somalis could move their cattle into this Ethiopian territory to graze during the wet season – a decision that created the basis for later claims and counter-claims.

In 1898 Menelik sent an expedition into the Ogaden to expand his empire. By 1908 the Emperor of Ethiopia had agreed his borders in the east with the French (in what is now Djibouti, then the Territory of the Afars and Issas or French Somaliland) and the British and Italians in British and Italian Somaliland respectively, and these agreements recognized all of the Ogaden province as part of Ethiopia.

Violent upheaval came to the region again with the Italian invasion of Ethiopia in 1936, although the previous year the British and French Foreign Ministers, Samuel Hoare and Pierre Laval, had attempted to prevent war by suggesting that the Ogaden be awarded to Italy. British imperial forces liberated Ethiopia and Eritrea in 1941, and from 1942 to 1947 British and Italian Somaliland and the Ogaden were united under a single British military administration. Britain hoped to create a new, permanent territory consisting of these three under its control, but the Ethiopian Emperor Haile Selassie wanted the British out of the Ogaden and distrusted British intentions in the whole region. In 1946 Britain's Foreign Secretary, Ernest Bevin, put forward the idea of a 'Greater Somalia' to cover the area of grazing lands over which the Somali nomads traditionally moved; this included the Ogaden. British ambitions in the area were thwarted by the UN and other great power pressures, and in 1955 Britain conceded Somali control of the Ogaden to Ethiopia. Yet in 1956, when Anthony Eden was Prime Minister, Britain again tried to persuade Ethiopia to return the Ogaden to Somalia, causing Haile Selassie to say, 'You British made all the frontiers. How can you ask us to change them now?'

In 1960 Italian-administered Somalia became independent and was joined with British Somaliland to form the new state of Somalia. Ethiopia was angered by this union, which created an enlarged Somalia that was seen in Addis Ababa as a threat to Ethiopian control in the Ogaden – as indeed it was to prove. The flag of the new state included a five-pointed star: two points represented Italian and British Somaliland, which had been united; the other three represented Somali claims to the surrounding territories of Djibouti, then still under French control, the Ogaden and the north-east corner of Kenya (then still a British colony). When the Organization of African Unity (OAU) was formed in 1963 Somalia refused to accept one of its first resolutions: that all members should agree to accept their inherited colonial boundaries.

Border clashes were to occur throughout the 1960s. In 1964 these developed into an undeclared war, and though both sides accepted an OAU-imposed ceasefire, the clashes continued, erupting again in 1973 at the time of the tenth OAU Summit, which was held in Mogadishu, the capital of Somalia. Thus the Somalis claimed the Ogaden as part of Greater Somalia, and in the mid-1970s a liberation movement, the Western Somali Liberation Front (WSLF), was formed. This found allies in the Ogaden (Oromo tribesmen who were disenchanted with rule from Addis Ababa), while discontent in Ethiopia led the Somalis to believe they could count on a great deal of support.

When, during 1975 and 1976, the revolution in Ethiopia produced growing internal upheavals Somalia increased the level of its support and training for the WSLF as well as for Afar dissidents in eastern Ethiopia. By early 1977 Somalia was sending an increasing number of WSLF groups into the Ogaden, where they were gaining control of a growing area of land. In March 1977 Cuba's Fidel Castro attempted to mediate between the two states, but to no avail. In May 1977, once the Ethiopians had expelled the Americans, the USSR made plain its support for the new regime. This persuaded the WSLF that the time had come for quick action. In June the French gave independence to the Territory of the Afars and Issas (as Djibouti), a development which further stimulated the liberation movement to action. By the middle of 1977 the WSLF was receiving substantial if unofficial assistance from the Somali armed forces.

Outbreak and response

As a result of sympathy for the Somali cause in the Ogaden region as well as Ethiopian weakness, the WSLF achieved startling successes in the period June to November 1977, virtually driving the Ethiopians out of the Ogaden. In July units of the Somali army crossed into the Ogaden in large numbers to support the WSLF. At the end of July the Ethiopian government claimed heavy civilian casualties had been inflicted by Somali aircraft, which, it said, had bombed Aware and Degahbur in eastern Ogaden. By early August the Somali guerrillas said they had killed thousands of Soviet-backed Ethiopian troops and controlled 60 per cent of the 259,000 square kilometre (100,000 square mile) Ogaden region. Both sides accused each other of atrocities against the civilian population. When in early August Ethiopia called for an emergency meeting of the OAU this was tantamount to an admission that its forces were losing the escalating war in the Ogaden. At the specially convened OAU Summit in Gabon, Ethiopia accused Somalia of a full-scale invasion and called on the OAU to 'make every possible effort to secure the immediate withdrawal' of regular Somali troops, who, it claimed, were occupying parts of the Ogaden. The OAU upheld the OAU Charter on the inviolability of borders and repudiated Somali claims to the Ogaden. At this stage in the fighting Ethiopia was clearly giving priority to its other war in Eritrea (see Part 1, pp. 23–28); should it lose that, it would be deprived of its entire Red Sea coastline.

Course of the struggle

By mid-August there was heavy fighting around the desert stronghold of Dire Dawa; civilian refugees poured into Djibouti and Somalia; the Ethiopians brought in heavy mechanized units from the north to bolster their Ogaden defences, while diplomatic sources claimed that Soviet T54 and T34 tanks were arriving in the country. The Somali guerrillas, meanwhile, now claimed to have killed 1088 Ethiopian soldiers in fighting for the towns of Gota and Errer situated 64 km (40 miles) west of Dire Dawa. Ethiopian forces also suffered heavy casualties at Mieso, only 240 km (150 miles) from Addis Ababa and the deepest the guerrillas had penetrated into the country. Between June and mid-August the Somalis had escalated the guerrilla conflict into a full-scale war and were besieging the towns on the edge of the mountains that marked the end of the Ogaden plain.

Their onslaught had taken the Ethiopians by surprise, and tens of thousands of casualties, killed and wounded, were reported on both sides, though no accurate figures were available. By then an estimated 70,000 Ethiopian troops were attempting to stem the Somali advance. On 28 August Mengistu called for national mobilization and created a National Operations Council with wide-ranging powers to direct people for the war effort; he took personal command of the fighting to hold the strategic towns of Dire Dawa and Jijiga.

Ethiopia now formally accused Somalia of using its army and air force in support of the WSLF inside the Ogaden, and the two countries broke diplomatic relations on 8 September. In a decisive battle at the end of the month, the Somalis captured Jijiga and defeated the Ethiopian ground forces at Gara Marda pass, opening the way to the city of Harer. A mutiny in the Ethiopian Third Division at Jijiga made the Somali victory possible. The Ethiopian air force, however, maintained its air superiority, halting the Somali advance with round-the-clock bombing. By early October massive supplies of Soviet equipment – new T55 tanks and armoured personnel carriers – were reaching the front from Assab, as well as long-range artillery (185 mm and 155 mm guns) to give the Ethiopian army parity with the Somali artillery. MiG replacements for the Ethiopian air force were also arriving at the battlefront. By mid-October the pending battle for Harer and Dire Dawa appeared likely to settle the conflict. At the same time Addis Ababa was reported to be full of freshly arrived Soviet equipment that had come up by convoy from Assab. Soviet military experts were in the city supervising the assembly of new MiG fighters, delivering new equipment and training personnel in its use. In addition, Cuban instructors were training army recruits. During the last week of October Mengistu made a secret visit to Cuba, then on to East Germany and the Soviet Union. His visit to Cuba was followed by the arrival of more Cuban advisers.

By mid-November the Somalis were in control of all the Somali-speaking areas of the Ogaden and were besieging Harer. Later, when it appeared Harer would fall to the Somalis, Soviet and Cuban advisers were evacuated from the city. Then, in a fierce counter-attack, the Ethiopians held on to Harer, and that success was perhaps the real turning point of the war. In any case, by then, Soviet armour and Cuban troops were being deployed to reinforce the Ethiopian army and boost its low morale. December was a month of regrouping as Ethiopia built up its forces preparatory to a major counter-attack and the Somalis found themselves to be over-extended, the outskirts of Harer being the farthest into Ethiopia they were to penetrate.

Ethiopia was saved from a major defeat and permanent loss of territory because of a massive airlift of military supplies from the USSR – hundreds of tanks and MiG fighters – as well as the arrival of about 16,000 Cuban troops. On the other side, Saudi Arabia promised Somalia large-scale financial aid for military supplies provided Mogadishu broke its close relations with the USSR. As a result, that November, Somalia broke diplomatic relations with Cuba and abrogated its treaty of friendship with the USSR, withdrawing the military facilities which it had made available to Moscow and expelling the 6000 Soviet personnel who were then in Somalia. Saudi Arabia then offered Somalia £170 million to purchase Western arms.

Once it had expelled the Soviets, Somalia assumed it would receive large-scale support from the West, an expectation that was reinforced by Western acclaim for the way it had handled the October hijacking of a Lufthansa plane. Somalia made urgent pleas for military aid, but although some was forthcoming from Arab sources, almost nothing materialized from the West, which only offered civil aid and warned the Cubans and Soviets against intervention. The West also criticized Somali aggression and insisted that the colonial inherited boundaries should be respected. China, however, gave full backing to the Somali position.

The end of 1977 saw the Ethiopians, supported by Cuban forces and led by Soviet officers with Soviet equipment, launch their counter-offensive. By mid-January 1978, when the Soviet and Cuban Defence Ministers (Marshal Dmitry Ustinov and General Raúl Castro respectively) made a secret visit to Addis Ababa, the position had been sufficiently turned round to elicit from the Somalis the accusation that the USSR and its allies were about to invade Somalia. Yet a week after this accusation Somali forces had again penetrated the city of Harer, where fierce fighting took place after several weeks of inactivity. The Somalis reported the capture of their first Cuban prisoners, although Addis Ababa denied that any Cubans were involved in the fighting.

By the end of January 1978 evidence of the Soviet–Cuban build-up in support of an Ethiopian counter-offensive was mounting: US and other Western sources reported a large influx of Cuban and Soviet military personnel. At the same time the big influx of Soviet military equipment (by airlift) continued, using South Yemen as a staging post. By early February the Ethiopian air force was carrying out a series of intense raids on Somali positions; the Somalis had no effective air defences.

The expected Ethiopian counter-attack began at the end of the first week in February with a two-pronged assault towards the north-eastern corner of Somalia near the border with Djibouti. The first prong aimed at the Somali-held town of Jijiga and on towards Hargeisa; the second towards the Somali port of Zeyla, a short distance from the Djibouti border. The Ethiopians, however, insisted that they did not intend to invade Somalia, but only to drive the Somalis out of Ethiopian territory. Meanwhile several thousand more Cubans were reported to be *en route* for Ethiopia, and Ethiopian planes attacked Berbera and Hargeisa. In Addis Ababa open hatred for the Western powers became a dominant theme because of their perceived opposition to Ethiopia and its revolution and their refusal to condemn Somali aggression. By mid-February, for the first time since the war began, the Somali Ministry of Information announced that units of the Somali regular army were being sent into the Ogaden against the Soviet and Cuban-backed Ethiopian forces (by then the Ethiopians claimed to have been fighting against Somali regular troops for several months). At the same time the government in Mogadishu called for mass mobilization and declared a state of emergency. Large numbers of volunteers (one figure given was 30,000) subsequently enlisted. The government claimed that their priority was to defend the national borders, although if necessary they would be sent to the Ogaden.

Bitter fighting through February saw the Ethiopians gain the upper hand in the war, driving back the Somalis round the city of Harer and advancing to within 40 km (25 miles) of Jijiga ready for the crucial battle to retake the city. The Ethiopians were then able to reopen the railway line to Djibouti. Colonel Mengistu threatened to expand the peasant militia of 500,000 into a force of 6 million.

The first stage of the Ethiopian counter-offensive, completed by mid-February, was to remove the Somali threat from the towns of Harer and Dire Dawa. Before they embarked on the second phase – to drive to the Somali border – the Ethiopians waited for further Cuban reinforcements. Meanwhile, there were growing pressures in the West to supply at least limited amounts of arms to the

Somalis, despite the official Western position of not supplying weapons to either side and of denouncing Soviet support for Ethiopia. By the end of the month a Soviet General was in command at Harer and three Russian major-generals were reported to be masterminding the Ethiopian counter-offensive. The number of Soviet advisers had increased to 1000 and Cuban troops to 10,000 or 11,000, while Cuban pilots were also reported to be flying missions against the Somalis. About 400 Soviet tanks and 50 MiG fighters were involved in the fighting. Soviet equipment supplied to Ethiopia up to that date was estimated to be worth £512 million.

Early in March, after fierce fighting, the Ethiopians recaptured Jijiga and the surrounding area, opening up the way for an advance to the Somali border. An estimated 15,000 Cuban, Russian and Ethiopian forces took part in the fighting, which involved the use of long-range artillery and missiles, T55 and T62 tanks, and MiG 21s and 23s. There were heavy casualties. The Ethiopians reiterated that they did not intend to invade Somalia, only to drive its forces from Ethiopian territory. For the first time Mengistu admitted publicly that Cuban forces were fighting alongside those of Ethiopia. By the second week of March the Ethiopians, led by Cuban and Soviet troops, had reached the Somali border and the Mogadishu government admitted the loss of Jijiga.

On 8 March the Somali government announced that it would withdraw its regular troops from the Ogaden region (in response to a US ceasefire proposal), and Ethiopia responded positively on 11 March, but insisted that Somalia had to abandon the Ogaden unconditionally. On that day rail services resumed between Addis Ababa and Dire Dawa, while restoration work on the remaining 320 km (200 miles) of line to Djibouti was said to be progressing.

Thus, by mid-March 1978 the Somali army had lost the crucial series of battles for the key cities (Harer, Dire Dawa and Jijiga) and had been forced to pull its forces out of Ethiopia. Having done so, Somalia called for a Cuban–Soviet withdrawal to match its own. But for the rest of 1978 the WSLF and the Somali Abo Liberation Front (SALF) continued to wage guerrilla warfare, and by February 1979 these liberation groups were still in control of most of the Ogaden countryside.

Estimated costs and casualties

Colonel Mengistu ordered general mobilization in August 1977. In support of Somalia, Arab states and Iran flew in tonnes of small arms and medical supplies, whereas the USSR, which had been Somalia's main ally and source of military supplies, ceased to provide small arms by June 1977 in an attempt to prevent Somalia using them or supplying them to WSLF in the Ogaden. On a visit to the USSR Somalia's President Siad Barre failed to persuade the Soviet Union to reverse its policy of arming Ethiopia while slowing down the supply of arms to Somalia. Ethiopia had only four allies at this stage: the USSR (at a time when it was still the principal arms supplier to Somalia) and Cuba, Libya (despite its Arab-Islamic status) and Israel, the odd combination emphasizing the complex nature of the situation in the Horn.

By September Ethiopia claimed to have shot down 23 of Somalia's 50 MiGs since the war had escalated six weeks earlier. At the same time it had moved approximately 40,000 newly trained militiamen to reinforce the regular army of 10,000 in the towns of Jijiga, Harer and Dire Dawa. And Somalia began openly wooing Arab support when President Siad Barre described the Red Sea as an Arab sea and said, 'The responsibility for its security falls on Arab shoulders alone.'

When in November Somalia broke diplomatic relations with both Cuba and the USSR the costs were very high: while Somalia ended its treaty of friendship with the USSR and withdrew all naval, air and ground military facilities, it also expelled 6000 Soviet military and civilian advisers (up to June 1977 the USSR supplied all Somalia's weapons). By January 1978 President Barre was appealing for aid to the USA, Britain, France, West Germany and Italy to defend Somalia against an invasion by Ethiopian and Soviet bloc forces.

In February 1978 Israel's Foreign Minister, Moshe Dayan, admitted that his country was selling arms to Ethiopia on the grounds that Israel had an interest in maintaining good relations with countries that bordered the Red Sea, which was vital to its shipping, and that for years Israel had co-operated with Ethiopia and never with Somalia. The same month Somalia (with an army of 30,000) decided to mobilize the civilian population ready to meet an expected invasion.

By June 1978, according to US intelligence sources, Russian war material supplied to Ethiopia amounted to 61,000 tons, which had been transported to the country by freighters and an air ferry involving 59 planes. The total number of Cubans involved was variously estimated between a low of 11,000 and a high of 19,000; these numbers were reduced to between 2000 and 3000 once the Ogaden war had been successfully concluded.

However, though the main war could be said to have ended by mid-March 1978, guerrilla activity, supported by Somalia, was to continue in the Ogaden; it was not until 1980 that Ethiopia regained effective control of the entire Ogaden region. One result was a massive influx of refugees into Somalia during 1979 and 1980, possibly reaching a high figure of 1 million in the latter year, although relief agencies suggested that 700,000 was more realistic. These refugees were to remain in border camps for years to come.

Casualties – dead and wounded – on both sides are far more difficult to determine since propaganda and morale considerations meant that neither government was either forthcoming or consistent in supplying reliable details. Each side tended to claim large numbers of enemies killed while playing down its own losses, and at the height of the fighting both sides claimed very heavy casualties running into many thousands dead and more wounded. Given the ferocity of the fighting as well as bombardment and bombing of civilian targets, the final toll must have come to tens of thousands dead and many more wounded on each side.

Results: immediate and longer term

The immediate effect of the war was to turn upside down the system of regional alliances involving outside powers: the USSR, which had been Siad Barre's principal external aid donor, switched to become the military backer of Ethiopia and supplied, at the height of the war, both the weapons and the generals to ensure a successful Ethiopian counter-attack. The West found itself in a dilemma: only too anxious to limit Russian and Cuban influence in Ethiopia, it none the less found difficulty in providing outright support for Somalia, which had so clearly been the aggressor in the war.

The conservative Arab states, led by Saudi Arabia, fell in behind Somalia, which, in an astute insurance move as it turned out, had applied to join the Arab League in 1974. And Cuba, whose forces had already played a significant role in Angola, now emerged with considerable kudos as a result of the successful deployment of its forces in Ethiopia.

Once the main war was over by mid-1978, the geopolitical situation in the Horn had been changed almost beyond recognition, with the USSR and its Cuban ally entrenched in Ethiopia and the West uneasily coming to terms with a Somalia that even in defeat was no easy or subservient ally, having abandoned none of its claims. In the immediate aftermath of the Somali defeat, Siad Barre was confronted by overtures from East and West, Arabs and non-aligned states, and he avoided making commitments to any of them. The American refusal to supply Somalia with arms during the war made the Somali government bitter towards the West; and despite the Soviet support for Ethiopia, overtures were tentatively made by Mogadishu towards a *rapprochement*. At the same time in Ethiopia a series of summary executions were reported. On 24 March 1978 Ethiopia and Cuba issued a joint statement that Somalia must publicly renounce its territorial claims on Ethiopia, Djibouti and Kenya to ensure a lasting peace in the Horn.

But the war did not end with the defeat and retreat from the Ogaden of the Somali army. Somalia refused to make peace, accept the international boundary or withdraw its support for the WSLF. As early as April 1978 the WSLF and SALF were claiming big successes against the Ethiopians, while the Somali government continued to support their claims, provoking Ethiopia into threatening to attack Somalia.

Once the main war had been concluded, the Ethiopian government was able to move forces to the north for a renewed campaign against the Eritrean guerrillas and – after considerable pressures – to involve some of the Cuban forces as well. By June an American delegation was visiting Mogadishu to survey Somalia's defence needs, although being careful to make no undertakings. At the same time the WSLF guerrillas claimed to have inflicted major casualties – 2000 dead – on the Ethiopians and Cubans.

In November 1978 Mengistu visited Moscow, where he signed a treaty of friendship and co-operation with the USSR, thus recognizing the reality which had emerged from the war and the massive support which Moscow had provided. It meant, at least for the time being, that Ethiopia was firmly in the Soviet camp.

Siad Barre survived the disaster of the Ogaden war. He crushed an attempted coup in April, and dissidents fled to Kenya and Ethiopia to form the Somalia Salvation Front. By December 1978 Somalia was complaining to the UN of Ethiopian air strikes against refugee camps and villages inside Somalia, although the government continued in its policy of supporting the WSLF and SALF. In January 1979 President Daniel arap Moi of Kenya visited Addis Ababa and signed a treaty of friendship and co-operation aimed, in part, at countering Somali expansionism.

After the main fighting, when a majority of the Cubans were withdrawn, two brigades were to remain in the Ogaden to guarantee the frontier. During both 1978 and 1979 the Ethiopian air force bombed villages across the border.

The Ogaden war polarized the always complex politics of the Horn to an even greater extent than normal. Saudi Arabia, Iran, Egypt and Sudan supported

Somalia; Libya, Yemen PDR and Kenya backed Ethiopia. The massive support provided for Ethiopia by both the USSR and Cuba ensured that the Cold War came to the Horn. Kenya, which was always deeply suspicious of Somali intentions and claims, agreed in 1980 to allow US forces to have military facilities at Mombasa, but also maintained its treaty of friendship with Ethiopia.

A major result of the war was the huge flood of ethnic Somalis from the Ogaden as refugees into Somalia, where they were to remain for years in a series of bleak camps along the border. Thus, by 1980 the United Nations High Commissioner for Refugees (UNHCR) could describe the situation in Somalia as 'the worst refugee problem in the world'. At that point there were an estimated 1.5 million refugees in Somalia, of whom 743,000 were in camps and about 800,000 scattered among the population. There was widespread malnutrition, and only massive aid from the international community prevented the situation from deteriorating still further.

The guerrilla war was to continue in the Ogaden with the WSLF controlling much of the countryside, although the Ethiopian and Cuban forces held all the towns. Border incidents between Ethiopia and Somalia occurred spasmodically through the 1980s (see Part V, pp. 387–391).

THE SEYCHELLES: A BOTCHED COUP

Introduction

The British colony of the Seychelles became independent in 1976 with James Mancham, who had the reputation of being a 'playboy', as its first President. The islands, which had a tiny population of about 60,000, depended on fishing and tourism for their existence, but their position in the centre of the Indian Ocean, lying on important sea routes, gave them a strategic importance that was further enhanced at the time the Seychelles became independent because both sides in the Cold War were then looking for potential bases in the Indian Ocean.

In 1977, just a year after independence, France-Albert René seized the armoury on Mahe Island and then in a coup ousted Mancham, who was on a visit to London. The new President was a left-wing socialist, very different from his outgoing predecessor. Tanzanian forces are credited with leading the 1977 coup for René; they were to remain in the Seychelles to train the army, and, it was suggested, René could not thereafter afford to get rid of them. He and his government were regarded with caution if not misgivings by the West.

On 25 November 1981 a commercial flight arriving in the Seychelles disgorged some 50 white mercenaries who attempted to topple the government of René. The attempt failed.

Origins

According to the Johannesburg *Star*, the mercenaries who took part in the coup attempt were recruited in South Africa over an 18-month period prior to November 1981; they were offered Rand 1000 each, with the promise of a further 10,000 if the coup succeeded. Those taking part included South Africans, white Zimbabweans, Australians, Britons and one or two Americans.

Several originators of the coup were suggested at the time: Mancham and other of the wealthy old guard who had fled when he was ousted and who were in London with him; the CIA, which was assumed to want René ousted because of his left-wing leanings and which wanted to ensure that the strategic islands were in the Western camp (even though the US already had a satellite station in the Seychelles and about 100 personnel with it).

All the mercenaries were recruited in South Africa. Later, one of the mercenaries captured in the Seychelles admitted that he was a senior South African intelligence officer. About 20 of the total number of mercenaries turned out to be South Africans. The Seychelles government was to accuse South Africa of being behind the coup, whose leaders claimed to have mounted it on behalf of the former president, Mancham.

According to exiles in London, the coup was the work of the banished Seychelles aristocrats who were financed by rich Arabs. Known as the *grands blancs*, they hoped to overthrow René and reverse the socialism he had introduced into the islands.

The coup attempt

Early on the morning of 25 November the mercenaries took a coach to Swaziland airport at Manzini, carrying their guns and other weapons in their luggage. They boarded a scheduled Royal Swazi Airlines flight to the Seychelles, their armoury of weapons undetected. They arrived in the Seychelles at 5.30 p.m. that day, claiming to be rugby players coming to sample the local beer. Other conspirators already on the island as tourists were to join with them. They nearly got through customs undetected, but a gun was discovered. Fierce fighting between the mercenaries and the Seychelles police and militia then followed. The mercenaries were armed with rocket-propelled grenades and sub-machine guns. They took hostage about 100 people at Pointe Larne International Airport, and then seized the terminal buildings. Surprisingly, in the shoot-out that followed, there were hardly any casualties (only one Seychellois was killed).

When it became clear that they were outgunned and would be defeated, 44 of the mercenaries under the leadership of 'Mad Mike' Hoare (already notorious from his exploits in the Congo during the 1960s) hijacked an Indian airliner that had landed to refuel and forced it to take them back to Durban. Seven of the mercenaries were captured.

Estimated costs and casualties

The 44 mercenaries who forced the Air India plane to take them to Durban found the airport sealed off by the South African police. After five hours of negotiations they first let the crew and passengers go and then gave themselves up. Immediately, the South Africans let 39 of the 44 go free (though saying they might later be charged) and kept five, including Hoare. Subsequently, all 44 were made to stand trial, but only on the hijacking charge; they received sentences – in a number of cases suspended – ranging from 6 months to 10 years for Hoare.

In the Seychelles the government announced that it had captured five mercenaries and that three were still at large. Later seven were brought to trial in the capital, Victoria; of these, four were South Africans, two white Zimbabweans and one a Briton.

Estimates of the cost of the attempt differ: the lowest is about £500,000; the highest about £2.5 million.

Results: immediate and longer term

By 4 December things had returned to normal in the Seychelles and stranded tourists were allowed to leave, although a dusk-to-dawn curfew was maintained. One soldier had been killed, so the charges against the seven mercenaries were expected to be murder or conspiracy to murder. In February 1982, however, the six men and one woman were charged with treason. In South Africa, meanwhile, the 44 captured mercenaries had been warned not to co-operate with the UN commission which had been set up to investigate the aborted coup. The seven in the Seychelles were not finally brought to court until June 1982. Counsel for six of them was Nicholas Fairbairn MP from Britain, who persuaded his clients to plead guilty. As a result, there was effectively no trial and no witnesses were called. The seventh, the South African, Martin Dolinchek, defended himself. Four of the seven were sentenced to death, Dolinchek to 20 years. They had acted as the advance party of the group that came by plane.

Of those who flew back to South Africa, about 20 were South Africans. A deeply embarrassed South African government denied any involvement in the coup, arguing instead that there existed two dissident groups which hoped to overthrow René. The government claimed that the mercenaries had approached it for help and been refused. South African denials of any knowledge or complicity looked fragile, however, especially in view of the fact that a South African intelligence officer was one of the group. Even so, the Seychellois exiles in London claimed responsibility; René himself put the blame on Mancham, although he later alleged that the Kenya government had also been involved.

Although at first South Africa had only kept five of the 44 and had allowed the others to go free, there was such an outcry – both internationally and from the opposition in South Africa, which claimed that the decision would fuel the suspicion that South Africa had backed the coup – that later the government decided to charge all 44 with kidnapping and hijacking. The UN Secretary-General, Kurt Waldheim, expressed amazement at South Africa's releasing of the hostages and said it would encourage others who contemplated similar illegal actions. The South African government was obliged to admit that some of the mercenaries were recruits who had only recently been discharged from the country's regular armed services.

In March 1982 43 mercenaries were charged with hijacking an aircraft. One of the mercenaries, a journalist called Peter Duffy, claimed that seven or eight senior members of the South African government had been involved in the coup. Charges against two of the mercenaries were dropped since they agreed to be state witnesses. The failure of the coup demonstrated South Africa's ability to 'shoot itself in the foot', as one newspaper put it, and few observers believed that the authorities did not know about the projected coup. The government admitted that members of the South African Defence Force (SADF) had supplied Hoare and his mercenaries with weapons. In December 1982 the UN commission which had been set up to investigate the coup attempt found that the SADF as well as South African intelligence were aware of the forthcoming coup.

Gestures of solidarity with the René government were made shortly after the coup attempt by both Britain and France; they offered financial help to restore the damage which the airport had suffered in the fighting.

In August 1982, in an incident apparently unconnected with the previous year's coup attempt, about 100 soldiers of the Seychelles army mutinied. The revolt lasted for 36 hours and was crushed by the Tanzanians on the island. The official death toll was put at eight. The rebels offered the four mercenaries sentenced to death their freedom if they would join the revolt, but they refused to do so.

Then in October 1982 the British Foreign Office alerted the René government to a second coup attempt that was being planned in London; this, apparently, was being masterminded by James Mancham and Gerard Hoareau (President of the right-wing Seychelles Resistance Movement).

In July 1983 the six mercenaries then in jail, including the four originally sentenced to death, were freed by President René as an act of clemency. One of them, Jerry Puren, who was a South African, once back in his country described the whole coup attempt as a shambles.

In December 1983 British and South African private detectives uncovered yet another coup being planned in South Africa, organized by Seychellois exiles (Paul Chow, Eddie Camille and Gerard Hoareau) who had also been behind the 1981 attempt. This time the South African government arrested five would-be coup makers, not wishing to look foolish a second time round. By then most of the 43 had finished their sentences, though Hoare was still in prison.

Although the coup attempt ended satisfactorily for René, the Seychelles were, none the less, partially destabilized by it; in mid-1983 the government was still dependent on the Tanzanian soldiers who had put down the 1982 mutiny and on 60 North Korean advisers. These developments in the Seychelles over this three-year period demonstrated just how easy it is to destabilize or overthrow the government of a small country. They also appeared to demonstrate how much the South Africans had come to accept the idea of destabilization taking place from their territory.

SOUTH AFRICA: DESTABILIZING ITS NEIGHBOURS

In this section the minor border wars and the impact of South African destabilization tactics on most of its neighbours – Botswana, Lesotho, Malawi, Swaziland, Zambia and Zimbabwe – are treated in a single narrative. This seemed the best way to convey a sense of South Africa's pervasive power in the region as a whole, although extensive cross-reference is made to entries in other sections of the book. In the case of two neighbours – Angola and Mozambique – where South African intervention has been of major proportions, only brief mention is made here, with more detailed consideration of the ongoing civil wars in those countries being given in Part V. Similarly, a brief reference to Namibia is appropriate here,

Map 11   Southern Africa

although South Africa's involvement in that country is dealt with in depth in Part I.

Background

South Africa's policy of apartheid, which has been consistently denounced in the United Nations ever since that body's inception after the Second World War, was bound to become a principal focus of increasing violence once black African colonies achieved their independence. For a number of years after 1945, however, South Africa played its part on the world stage as a middle power, a member of the United Nations and the Commonwealth, a country the racial policies of which might be frowned upon but were tacitly ignored by most Western countries, until the break-up of the European African empires brought a large number of new African states on to the world stage.

The years 1960 and 1961 proved the turning point. In February 1960 Britain's Prime Minister, Harold Macmillan, gave his 'wind of change' speech in Cape Town; in March the Sharpeville massacre focused world attention on apartheid; and by the end of the year 17 new black African states had emerged. In 1961 South Africa left the Commonwealth after its African and Asian members, led by Malaya's Tunku Abdul Rahman, had made it plain that the policy of apartheid was not compatible with continued membership of the Commonwealth association. Thereafter, slowly yet inexorably, South Africa withdrew into itself, preparing for a confrontation with its black neighbours to the north.

Even so, South Africa was to have another 15 years of prosperity and relative immunity from pressures: as long as the Portuguese controlled the two neighbouring territories of Angola and Mozambique, and the white minority did the same in Rhodesia (Zimbabwe), South Africa was protected from the rest of independent black Africa by a cordon of white-controlled states whose ideology was similar to its own. There were, it is true, the three small black states – Botswana (which became independent in 1966), Lesotho (1966) and Swaziland (1968), formerly known as the (British) High Commission Territories – which were inside the cordon, but they were far too weak to pose any threat to South African hegemony over the region.

Ian Smith's Unilateral Declaration of Independence (UDI) for Rhodesia in 1965 was an unwelcome embarrassment to Pretoria since it focused world attention on white racial policies in the region, but it was the collapse of Portuguese power that altered the southern African geopolitical situation and forced the Republic to rethink its policies in relation to its northern neighbours. In April 1974 Marcello Caetano, the right-wing President of Portugal, was overthrown in a military coup; this was followed in 1975 by the withdrawal of Portugal's two armies from Angola and Mozambique and independence for those two countries during the second half of 1975. The consequences were to prove momentous.

In the first place Rhodesia was left so exposed that it was only a matter of another five years before it, too, became independent as Zimbabwe, under a tough 'Marxist' leader who was totally opposed to apartheid. In the second place South Africa now found that it had an eastern border of 800 km (500 miles) with a revolutionary Mozambique whose sole political party, Frelimo, also proclaimed its Marxist sympathies. Thirdly, Angola now posed a threat to South Africa's continued hold over Namibia since it was prepared to allow the South West Africa People's Organization (SWAPO) guerrillas to operate from bases on its soil.

In response to these new pressures South Africa embarked on a policy of destabilizing its African neighbours. This policy had four main aims: first, to keep them in turmoil (Angola and Mozambique) so that they did not become an overt threat; second, to wreck the transport lines (most notably the railways) that passed through those countries and served the landlocked states of Malawi, Zambia and Zimbabwe, so that they would be obliged to trade through the Republic; third, to dissuade them from assisting the African National Congress (ANC) guerrillas (and to a lesser extent the Pan African Congress (PAC) guerrillas) either with bases and arms or with passage through their territories to South Africa; and finally, to demonstrate South African power and create a sense of permanent threat.

Angola

It took Pretoria some time to decide on the parameters of its new policy, although there was no doubt as to the general aim: destabilization. Thus, in October 1975, when the Portuguese had all but withdrawn and independence was scheduled for 11 November of that year, a strong South African military column invaded Angola with the apparent intention of driving to Luanda and overthrowing the Movimento Popular de Libertação de Angola (MPLA) government, which was then clearly going to succeed the departing Portuguese. By the beginning of November the South Africans had overrun Moçâmedes, Lobito and Benguela and looked set to take the capital. This swift threat brought rapid reactions, most notably the 5 November decision of Cuba to despatch substantial numbers of troops to Angola to assist the MPLA government, thus bringing Cuba into the southern African scene as a major factor for years to come (for a detailed account of South African interventions in Angola, see Part V, pp. 332–351).

The South Africans withdrew from Angola at the end of January 1976, more as a result of US pressures and the threat that they would be left isolated than as the result of a military defeat. But a pattern of military intervention had been established and from then onwards (until the agreements of 1988 and 1989) South Africa was to interfere frequently in Angola. At first its excuse for such incursions was to take out SWAPO bases as the liberation war in northern Namibia and the Caprivi Strip slowly escalated (see Part 1, pp. 45–53). But later, and especially from the early 1980s, South African incursions were designed to destabilize the Angolan government and provide support for Jonas Savimbi's rebel União Nacional para a Independência Total de Angola (UNITA) (see Part V, pp. 332–351) as much as they were directed against SWAPO.

It was the military stalemate at the important strategic base of Cuito Cuanavale in south-eastern Angola in 1988 (close to being a military defeat for South Africa) which signalled a major change in the region, including South Africa's reluctant agreement to implement the UN independence process in Namibia; and the recognition (which was perhaps as important) of the extent to which the whole region had become militarized. When South Africa agreed to implement UN Resolution 435 and quit Namibia, it also agreed to end its support for UNITA; in return Angola agreed to deny any future base rights to the ANC, whose estimated 1000 members then in Angola were forced to leave.

Following the implementation of UN Resolution 435 which led to Namibian independence in March 1990, South Africa no longer had direct border contact with Angola, and the possibilities for intervention were commensurately lessened.

Botswana

Introduction

For many years prior to Bechuanaland's independence as Botswana in 1966, South Africa had attempted to persuade Britain to hand over control of the territory to Pretoria. And though Britain had refused to do so, it had been prepared to appease South Africa on a number of issues, most notably in 1950 when the Commonwealth Relations Secretary exiled the young hereditary Chief of the Bamangwato, Seretse Khama (who was later to become Botswana's first President), from Bechuanaland for marrying a white woman, since this was offensive to the racial policies prevalent in South Africa.

When Botswana did achieve independence, apart from the fact that it was landlocked, its economy was inextricably tied into that of the Republic (Botswana is a member of the South African Customs Union, SACU), so that it was constantly subject to pressures from its powerful neighbour. In consequence, all Botswana's policies thereafter were to be bound up with the South Africa question. Indeed, so exposed and weak was Botswana that South African refugees felt afraid to remain in that country. As a high-ranking Botswana civil servant said, 'To be landlocked is difficult enough. To be black and landlocked in southern Africa is a lonely and expensive experience.'

In the early days after independence South Africa countered Seretse Khama's refusal to enter into diplomatic relations with his neighbour and his pronouncements against apartheid by hitting at the economy. Thus there would be a sudden dearth of refrigerated trucks on the railway just when Botswana needed to ship its meat exports; or a cable breakdown that prevented long-distance telephone connections since all Botswana's were routed through Johannesburg. In 1970 the South African Prime Minister, B. J. Vorster, tried to prevent Botswana from building a 290 km (180 mile) all-weather road to the Kazungulu ferry crossing to Zambia, as later he was to exert pressures when Botswana wished to open diplomatic relations with the USSR.

In 1974 a black South African student activist, Onkgopotse Tiro, took refuge in Gaborone, where he was killed by a terrorist bomb, almost certainly the work of South Africa's Bureau of State Security (BOSS). After the 1976 uprising in the South African township of Soweto, an increase in South African refugees through Botswana led to more difficult relations, with South African secret police infiltrating into the country. Botswana was to be subject to pressures from two directions: UDI in Rhodesia led to border violations that stretched Botswana's limited 'defence' or policing capacities to the full; and South African destabilization tactics created an uneasy state of permanent tension.

Border confrontations

From 1965, when Rhodesia made its unilateral declaration of independence (UDI), until 1980 Botswana was subject to border problems with its neighbour; subsequently it continued to face problems with independent Zimbabwe until at the end of 1987 the achievement of 'unity' between the two main parties, the Zimbabwe African National Union (ZANU) and the Zimbabwe African People's Union (ZAPU), led to easier relations.

UDI in Rhodesia forced Botswana to expand its paramilitary police for border patrol duties. Later the increasing border threats and incursions from Rhodesia during UDI (when guerrillas fighting the Smith regime came back and forth across the border) and during the 'dissidents' war (see Part V, pp. 421–426), and then the destabilization activities of South Africa, persuaded Botswana to create a permanent defence force in 1977. Relations with Smith's Rhodesia and then Mugabe's Zimbabwe produced border tensions which led to periodic incidents. When in 1982 the strains between ZANU and ZAPU erupted in violence, large numbers of ZAPU supporters crossed into Botswana as refugees. In 1983 the Botswana government was deeply embarrassed when the ZAPU leader, Joshua Nkomo, fled Zimbabwe and came to Botswana as a political refugee; his presence in the country threatened to involve Botswana in Zimbabwe's political feuds.

More important was growing tension with South Africa following Botswana's independence in 1966. The collapse of Portuguese power in Angola and Mozambique in 1975 made Pretoria increasingly sensitive about activities in neighbouring states; the result was its policy of 'destabilization', which for Botswana meant an increasing state of uncertainty induced by threats, border incursions and occasional raids on South African refugee groups in the country, including the capital, Gaborone.

Part of a wider conflict

In 1980 Botswana was embarrassed at the revelations that Basarwa (bushmen) from Botswana were being recruited as trackers for the South African Defence Force (SADF) in its war against the South West Africa People's Organization (SWAPO) in Namibia. In 1981 South Africa became verbally threatening – the newspaper *Beeld* spoke of 'our own Cuba' – when the Botswana Defence Force (BDF) purchased Soviet equipment and then, in October 1981, Soviet military advisers came to train the BDF in the use of the equipment. Botswana's President, Quett Masire, described the South African pressures as deliberate destabilization tactics. In essence Botswana was expanding the capacity of the BDF the better to patrol its long borders in order to prevent African National Congress (ANC) insurgents from crossing into South Africa, thus removing any excuse for South African incursions.

Botswana insisted that it would receive refugees from South Africa, but also made it plain that it would not allow them – or other groups – to use its territory as a base for operations against South Africa. During 1984 South Africa exerted strong pressures on Botswana to enter into a non-aggression pact with it, hinting that otherwise it might station troops along the border and disrupt normal border traffic. As a result of these pressures, President Masire, while on an official visit to the USA in May 1984, stressed that Botswana would never allow subversive activities to be mounted from its territory.

In February 1985 Botswana accused South Africa (and the 'homeland', Bophu-thatswana) of threatening to invade its territory in 'hot pursuit' of terrorists. South Africa claimed that ANC guerrillas were then infiltrating the Republic across the Botswana border. Fresh threats followed during 1986, and though both the USA and Britain promised military aid to Botswana, this was not sufficient to deter South Africa. Thus, in March 1986 Botswana felt obliged to expel ANC represen-tatives from the country. Prior to the May 1987 elections in South Africa, Pretoria warned its frontline neighbours that, if necessary, it would launch attacks on them in order to prevent the ANC from disrupting the elections. In 1988 a British military team arrived in Botswana to train the BDF, and Britain sold Botswana nine second-hand Strikemasters.

Course of events

When Rhodesia became independent as Zimbabwe in 1980 there were approxi-mately 25,000 Rhodesian refugees in Botswana; these were now able to return home, relieving Botswana of the burden of their presence and giving rise to the hope that Botswana–Zimbabwe relations would be normalized.

During April 1982 cross-border exchanges of fire between the BDF and South African units were an indication of rising border tensions between the two countries.

In March 1983, when Joshua Nkomo fled Zimbabwe and asked for political asylum in Botswana, tensions between the two countries rose sharply. Zimbabwe accused Botswana of providing guerrilla bases for Nkomo and his ZAPU followers, and of sending them to South Africa for training. A determined effort was then made to improve relations with Zimbabwe. For example, Botswana expelled 200 refugees (mainly Zimbabweans) who were described as dissidents. Border inci-dents between the two countries continued, however. Late in 1983 Botswana and Zimbabwe held security talks, and thereafter relations improved.

The year 1985 was a bad one for Botswana–South Africa relations. In February a bomb exploded in Gaborone with ANC refugees as the target. Talks between the two governments appeared briefly to have defused the crisis, but not for long. On 14 June 1985 members of the SADF raided Gaborone, where they 'attacked' ANC bases, and at least 15 people were killed. This raid was the culmination of several months of mounting pressures. Later that year (November) a car bomb killed four people outside Mochudi hospital, although there was doubt as to whether the bomb was placed by the South Africans.

There was also renewed tension with Zimbabwe following the elections of July 1985, which, among other things, led to a new flow of refugees into Botswana. By February 1986, however, the two countries were able to express their joint satisfaction at stopping what they called South African-sponsored attacks along the Botswana–Zimbabwe border.

South Africa mounted pressures on Botswana through 1986 to curb the activities of ANC guerrillas, whom it claimed operated from Botswana territory. In May South Africa mounted a military campaign against three of its neighbours in a deliberate effort to nullify the positive impact which the Commonwealth Eminent Persons' Group (EPG) was then having in its talks with leading South Africans. The SADF launched attacks on three of its neighbours – Botswana, Zambia and Zimbabwe. There were land and air attacks on buildings at Mogaditsane near Gaborone, which resulted in one death. Pretoria claimed that these attacks were on ANC targets, but widespread international condemnation followed. The attacks achieved their purpose, however, which was the collapse of the EPG talks.

In 1987, after another warning from Pretoria that Botswana was harbouring members of the ANC, a bomb explosion in Gaborone killed four people. In August of the same year a former British soldier was sentenced to five years in prison for the attempted murder in Gaborone of a South African who was prominent in the anti-apartheid movement. South Africa was now insisting that responsibility for policing the huge border between the two countries in order to check ANC infiltration lay with Botswana. At the same time South Africa opposed Botswana's policy of receiving South African refugees because Pretoria insisted that these were all terrorists.

In March 1988 South Africa admitted responsibility for a commando raid on a house in Gaborone in which four people (allegedly members of the ANC) were killed. In June President Masire announced that two South African soldiers had been captured from a group which had penetrated into the country to a town south of the capital, where they had fired on the BDF. There was also another car bomb attack in Gaborone. Botswana's casualties included three policemen hurt in the June raid, and three women and a baby killed in the March raid. President Masire accused South Africa of state terrorism.

A changing climate?

Following the unity agreement of December 1987 in Zimbabwe, it seemed that Botswana and Zimbabwe could enjoy reasonable border relations thereafter. And following South African President F. W. de Klerk's speech of 2 February 1990 in which he unbanned the ANC, and his subsequent release of Nelson Mandela, the possibility of a new, more friendly policy from Pretoria and an end to 'destabilization' appeared likely, though time was needed to see if this would actually take place.

Lesotho

Background

Lesotho (formerly the British colony of Basutoland) became independent in 1966. For many years before that date South Africa had exerted pressures on Britain to hand over control of its colony to Pretoria, but London had resisted such demands. When it became clear that Basutoland would become independent, South Africa was obliged to devise other means of exerting controls or pressures on an unwanted enclave of black independence in the midst of the apartheid state.

A tiny landlocked country entirely surrounded by the territory of South Africa,

Lesotho in consequence would in any circumstances be vulnerable to pressures from its powerful neighbour. Given the nature of the South African apartheid regime and the opposition to it which has been expressed by all independent black African countries, the 'captive states' – Botswana, Lesotho and Swaziland, which are wholly or predominantly surrounded by South Africa and are obliged for survival to belong to the South African Customs Union – are easily subject to economic or other pressures mounted by Pretoria.

In the case of Lesotho, which is by far the poorest of the three, as many as 150,000 of its adult males are liable to be working in the mines or on the farms of South Africa at any given time, their remittances home accounting for 40 per cent or more of total GDP. Further, as a result of its geographic situation, Lesotho has acted as a natural magnet for those South Africans who wished to flee their own country. By 1980, for example, there were an estimated 11,500 refugees from the Republic in Lesotho, at least a proportion of whom belonged to the banned African National Congress (ANC), and at that time new arrivals were being registered at the rate of 100 a month.

In 1976, following the uprising in the Soweto township outside Johannesburg, the Prime Minister of Lesotho, Chief Lebua Jonathan, strongly condemned apartheid; also that year, despite strong pressures to do so, he refused to recognize the South African Bantustan ('homeland') of Transkei as an independent state. By the end of that decade, as South Africa itself came increasingly under world pressures, Pretoria devised a growing number of ways to destabilize its neighbours. In the case of Lesotho, the Pretoria government decided to work through the exiled faction of the Basutoland Congress Party (BCP) led by Ntsu Mokhehle and created the Lesotho Liberation Army (LLA).

In May 1979 the LLA launched its first attacks in Maseru, the capital of Lesotho, when it bombed the central post office and two high-tension electricity pylons as well as the headquarters of the electricity corporation. Later it carried out further bombings in the northern part of the country, its targets being bridges and telephone and electricity poles. Although no great damage was done, the attacks served to stretch the tiny security forces to the limit. These LLA attacks were supported by a campaign of disinformation mounted from South Africa. They had sufficient impact to oblige Jonathan to meet President Botha in August 1980, after which there was a temporary halt to LLA activities.

Destabilization

Early in 1981 the LLA attacks were resumed with greater intensity, while Pretoria asserted that there were ANC military bases inside Lesotho. In the course of the next two years a number of attacks were mounted on houses in Lesotho which were known to be used by members of the ANC. On 31 July 1981 the Lesotho government protested to Pretoria that a mortar attack had been carried out on a petrol depot near Maseru.

Then, on 9 December 1982, South African commandos carried out a pre-dawn raid on a number of homes in Maseru, which lies a mere 3 km (2 miles) from the South African border, and a total of 42 people were killed. They included 30 South African refugees, while the rest, including women and children, were Basotho. South Africa claimed that the people whom its forces had killed were trained terrorists, but this was denied both by the exile representatives and by the Lesotho government. As a Lesotho minister described the event, the raid 'destabilized us psychologically'.

Between 1982 and January 1986, when the South African blockade led to his downfall, Prime Minister Jonathan attempted increasingly to obtain international – often socialist – support against South African destabilization pressures. Relations between Lesotho and South Africa deteriorated sharply during 1983; early in the year the Maseru abattoir and water storage tank were attacked. Later a helicopter attack was mounted on oil depots with the support of the South African Defence Force (SADF). It was the first time it was possible to prove that an attack had involved South African military personnel. In April Jonathan accused South Africa of carrying out a number of attacks on his country.

Pretoria steadily escalated the pressure, and the Lesotho security forces clashed with 'bandits' from South Africa. Then South Africa demanded the expulsion of 3000 South African refugees, while giving support to the Basotho Democratic Alliance under the former Lesotho Foreign Minister, C. D. Molapo. Jonathan was forced to make concessions and in September agreed to expel a number of named members of the ANC. Sixty South African refugees were voluntarily deported, and South Africa then eased up on its pressure tactics. But though the Foreign Ministers of the two countries met and agreed that neither country would allow its territory to be used as a base for attacks on the other, the tensions continued to mount.

During 1984 South Africa exerted economic pressures to force Lesotho to follow the example of Mozambique, which had entered into the Nkomati Accord with Pretoria that year (Part V, pp. 364–367), leading Jonathan to accuse Pretoria that August of attempting to bribe him into signing a non-aggression pact. In 1985 President Botha threatened to repatriate the estimated 100,000 Basotho then working in the Republic should sanctions be applied to his country, a threat that highlighted both Lesotho's vulnerability and South Africa's readiness to use bullying tactics. Even so, Lesotho affirmed its belief that sanctions ought to be mounted against South Africa.

Then, in December 1985, South African commandos again raided Maseru, killing nine people, of whom six were South African refugees. At the beginning of 1986 South Africa mounted an economic blockade of Lesotho and maintained it for three weeks; it contributed directly to the coup of 20 January, effectively ensuring that Jonathan was ousted. He was replaced by Major-General Justin Metsino Lekhanya. South Africa's Foreign Minister, 'Pik' Botha, said of Jonathan at this time that he was the 'greatest destabilizing factor in Lesotho'. The South African blockade undoubtedly precipitated the coup; it is possible that Pretoria also masterminded it, although by then Jonathan had more than enough Basotho enemies of his own at home.

Results: ongoing

The new government of Lekhanya did not hand over the South African refugees as Pretoria had demanded, but deported them instead to Zambia. South Africa then lifted the blockade. It soon became clear that as far as Pretoria was concerned Lekhanya was far more pliable than Jonathan had ever been. He established good relations with South Africa and concluded an agreement on mutual security. Then, on 24 October 1986, a treaty between the two countries led to the commencement of the Highlands Water Project to export water from Lesotho to South Africa; South Africa had previously repeatedly blocked the implementation of the project as a means of exerting economic pressures on the Jonathan government.

Given the fact that it is totally enclosed within the territory of South Africa, Lesotho will always be vulnerable to pressures from its neighbour; however if, as at least seemed possible in mid-1990, South Africa can resolve its racial and political problems without major bloodshed, then the future prospects for Lesotho become far less threatening.

Malawi

Under President Hastings Banda, Malawi has pursued a unique policy with regard to South Africa. It was the only country on the entire continent to have entered into diplomatic relations with the Republic, which it did the year after independence (1967). Then, in 1968, Malawi accepted substantial financial aid from South Africa to assist with the construction of the new capital at Lilongwe. Banda has constantly argued, isolating himself in the process, that South Africa should not be boycotted and that dialogue rather than sanctions would one day lead to a change of policy (over apartheid) in South Africa. As late as 1987, when conditions in the region had changed fundamentally from the days in which this Malawi policy had first been enunciated, President Banda insisted, in a speech in February, that Malawi would not boycott South Africa either diplomatically or economically.

In the circumstances Malawi has not been subjected to South African cross-border activities as have the other frontline states. Yet, in the late 1980s, it became a major victim of South African destabilization tactics. This was the direct result of South African-backed rebel Renamo activities in Mozambique. Malawi's shortest and cheapest route to the sea is the 600 km (373 mile) railway from Blantyre to the Mozambique port of Nacala on the Indian Ocean. That line has been out of serious action for years, with the result that almost all Malawi's imports and exports have to use the southern route through the Tete corridor, then across Zimbabwe to Durban. This adds 50 per cent in costs to import and export transit charges.

Border skirmishes with Mozambique

The endless lawlessness in Mozambique, which resulted from the activities of the Mozambique National Resistance (MNR) movement, or Renamo, was increasingly to spill across the country's borders during the 1980s to affect its neighbours: either in the form of large influxes of refugees – Malawi, Zambia, Zimbabwe and Swaziland were all to receive varying numbers of these refugees, with Malawi taking by far the largest number – or in violence, including border clashes and minor battles.

Evidence of a minor border war in the south-east of Malawi between its forces and the regular Mozambican army came to light in 1986. The problem was not made easier by the fact that the government of Mozambique accused Malawi's President Banda of both harbouring and training Renamo guerrillas.

Minor confrontations

In August 1986 a detachment of Mozambican soldiers pursued a group of Renamo rebels into the south-east of Malawi, but they were met by Malawi soldiers near the small town of Chikwawa, where the two groups fought a battle in which at least seven men were killed. On another occasion four Malawi civilians were killed by anti-personnel mines on the border near Mount Mlanje. This time, according to Malawi officials, the mines had been planted by Mozambican troops to prevent refugees crossing into Malawi. In a battle between Mozambican troops and MNR guerrillas for control of the forests round Mount Mlanje, a total of 47 were reported to have been killed. Subsequently, 25 of the Mozambicans, including officers, were captured by Malawian forces and imprisoned in Blantyre. The Mozambican Security Minister, Colonel Sergio Viera, claimed that the 25 had merely strayed across the border by accident and denied that the Mozambique army had been involved in cross-border raids.

Malawi in its turn denied that the government was working in collusion with the MNR or allowing the transit of arms from South Africa to the MNR through Malawi. A Malawi official said, 'We would be foolhardy to sustain a movement which has cut our vital routes to the sea'; he was referring to the Nacala railway, which is Malawi's only direct route to the sea. Yet at one border post, at least, the Malawian commander openly admitted to fraternizing with members of the MNR from just inside Mozambique.

Evidence of anxiety about Banda's policies became more evident in September 1986. At the Harare Non-Aligned Summit at the beginning of the month President Machel of Mozambique accused South Africa of obtaining bases for Renamo in a member state of the Organization of African Unity (OAU), an obvious reference to Malawi. Subsequently, he threatened to close the border with Malawi and place missiles along it unless Malawi ended its aid to the Renamo rebels. The following week, however, a more diplomatic approach to Banda was attempted when three of the frontline leaders most open to the pressures of destabilization from South Africa – Machel of Mozambique, Kaunda of Zambia and Mugabe of Zimbabwe – travelled to Blantyre for a summit with Banda. Their object was to persuade Banda to co-operate with them in their opposition to South Africa and their attempts to impose sanctions. Thereafter, the border 'war' appeared to fizzle out.

Indeed, there was an apparent reversal of Malawi policy the following year, for by then Malawi had become involved in the work to rehabilitate the railway line from Blantyre to Nacala on the Indian Ocean, its shortest route to the sea. In April 1987 Malawi sent troops to guard part of the Nacala railway, which its workers were then helping to reconstruct, and between 400 and 500 Malawi troops were reported to be stationed along the line of rail. On 25 May a group of over 100 Renamo rebels attacked a gang of Malawi railway workers and their Malawi and Mozambican army guards near the town of Malema, which is 150 km (93 miles) inside Mozambique. Four Malawian and seven Mozambican soldiers were killed as well as five Malawi railway workers, while a further 17 were wounded. The number of Renamo casualties was not known. This incident soured relations beteen Malawi and South Africa, which backs Renamo, although it did not lead to a break.

Despite years in which Banda is reported to have supported a number of groups in Mozambique that were hostile to its Frelimo government, by 1987 it had become clear that Malawi's best interest lay in assisting the rehabilitation of the Nacala line, which by then had been out of action for three years as a result of Renamo sabotage. Malawi and Mozambique became reconciled and signed a joint security pact.

By the end of 1987 Britain agreed to supply the Malawi army with £750,000 worth of non-lethal military equipment to help protect the railway line to Nacala; at the same time the British Minister of State at the Foreign Office, Lynda Chalker, said British military personnel might be sent to Malawi to advise on security for the line. The death of Machel in December 1986 probably made it easier for Banda to change his policy towards Mozambique; certainly, by December 1987, relations between the two countries had been transformed, largely as a result of their co-operation over the rebuilding of the Nacala railway. Malawi had come to view the MNR as their common enemy and was then facing the rapidly growing problem of incoming refugees fleeing MNR depredations in their own country.

Mozambique

South African destabilization tactics have been most damaging in Mozambique. Pretoria's policy was possibly more defined in relation to Mozambique than anywhere else and was designed to achieve three things: to undermine the economy; to wreck the transport system (the three railway lines to Nacala, Beira and Maputo which serve the landlocked countries of the interior and formerly provided Mozambique with 40 per cent of its revenues); and to force Mozambique to deny passage to the ANC.

During the last stages of the Portuguese war (1972–5) South Africa provided an increasing amount of logistical and other support to the hard-pressed Portuguese army. Then, following Mozambique's independence in 1975, Smith's security adviser, Ken Flower, proposed the Mozambique National Resistance (Renamo): a resistance movement that would oppose Frelimo and, by creating civil disturbances, hamper the efforts of the Frelimo government to assist the Zimbabwe African National Union (ZANU), which then had its bases in Mozambique. Renamo, originally financed from Smith's Rhodesia, made spectacular progress as a wrecker. Then in 1981, following Zimbabwe's independence (at a time when Renamo seemed to have run its course), South Africa took over the role of providing support and Renamo once more became so successfully active that by 1984 President Machel was forced to enter into the Nkomati Accord with South Africa. Under the Accord Mozambique agreed to banish the ANC from its territory and South Africa agreed to stop supporting Renamo. Mozambique kept its side of the Accord; South Africa did not.

Towards the end of 1986, following the air crash which killed President Machel, Renamo increased its campaigns so effectively that it threatened to cut Mozambique in two, and Zimbabwe considered sending three more brigades of troops to assist Mozambique in the war. By then it had become increasingly obvious that a fourth South African objective was to draw Zimbabwe more and more into the task of fighting Renamo in Mozambique, so as to over-extend its resources.

By 1989, as a result of Pretoria's Mozambique policy, Zimbabwe was maintaining about 10,000 troops in that country to guard the Beira Corridor, the Limpopo line and the Tete Corridor, as well as providing patrols for other affected areas. Tanzania had a further 3000 troops deployed in Mozambique, while even Malawi had 300 soldiers deployed along the Nacala railway. Perhaps the greatest irony of all was the fact that Britain had undertaken to train units of the Mozambique army in Zimbabwe at Nyanga, using its British Military Advisory Training Team (BMATT) to do so (see Part V, pp. 364–367).

Namibia

The long fight to hold on to Namibia against official world condemnation of its presence in the territory formed one more part of South Africa's ongoing battle with its neighbours (see Part I, pp. 45–53). From 1975 onwards South Africa used northern Namibia and the Caprivi Strip as jumping-off points for raids into Angola and Zambia. The bitter struggle waged by SWAPO ever since 1966 had cost many lives, but in 1990 South Africa finally quit the territory, which became independent under the terms of UN Resolution 435. Namibia, therefore, entered the 1990s as an independent state, albeit one economically heavily dependent on South Africa.

Swaziland

Swaziland was the third of the British High Commission Territories, three-quarters surrounded by South Africa and sharing its fourth border with Mozambique. A deeply conservative society, Swaziland found difficulty in accepting either neighbour: racist South Africa or Marxist Mozambique. Following the achievement of independence in 1968, Swaziland kept a low profile and was helped in this by a versatile economy which gave it a degree of independence impossible for Lesotho. But it was still a member of the South African Customs Union and a potential captive of its South African neighbour.

Yet Swaziland also was to suffer from cross-border raids and periodic kidnapping incidents involving South African police or the South African Defence Force (SADF) in search of ANC personnel. In 1982 Swaziland entered into a secret agreement with South Africa: the two countries began negotiating about Swazi 'lost lands'; meanwhile the Swaziland government increased its harassment of the ANC. In 1984 the proposals for the land transfer (of so-called Swazi lands then a part of the Republic and adjacent to Swaziland) were opposed by both black and white in South Africa and were dropped, although the Swazi authorities continued their harassment of the ANC. Then, following the Nkomati Accord of 1984 between South Africa and Mozambique (see above), Swaziland revealed its own secret agreement with Pretoria and in the course of the following year deported more than 200 members of the ANC; and it continued to do so, despite efforts by the OAU to bring about a reconciliation between Swaziland and the ANC.

At the end of 1985, despite this apparently ready co-operation, elements of the SADF crossed into Swaziland to threaten villagers in order to force them to expel resident members of the ANC. Further raids during the months of June, July and August 1986 resulted in the deaths of a number of ANC supporters, some in the industrial centre of Manzini. The raiding continued in 1987: four ANC were killed in Mbabane in January, three more in May, three in July and two more in August, and the South African police were implicated. A South African refugee was shot dead in Manzini in January 1988. Deportations of the ANC continued through 1988.

More important to South Africa than the ANC deportations, perhaps, were the public statements of opposition to sanctions expressed by Swazi leaders, and it seemed at least likely that Swaziland was preparing to act as a conduit for sanctions-breaking in the event of their application to the Republic. Even so, Swaziland did not escape some of the more unpleasant effects of South Africa's destabilization activities and by 1988, for example, was obliged to play host to an estimated 25,000 refugees from the war in Mozambique.

Zambia

Zambia, like Malawi, is geographically removed from direct contact with South Africa, although that fact has not saved it from the effects of destabilization. During the long years of UDI in Rhodesia, Zambia arguably suffered more from the application of sanctions to that country than Rhodesia itself, and many of the South African troops committed to helping Ian Smith's regime were stationed along the Zambezi facing Zambia. More than once during those years South Africa's Prime Minister, J. B. Vorster, threatened Zambia with reprisals for its role as a host to most of the region's liberation movements.

From 1966 onwards the South West Africa People's Organization (SWAPO) had headquarters in Zambia, and the United Nations Namibia Institute was located in Lusaka; more than once South African forces raided into Zambia from the Caprivi Strip. Zambia suffered as a result of the civil war in Angola since the cutting of the Benguela railway had a disastrous impact on the cost of transporting out its major export, copper. There were also UNITA incursions into Zambia.

In May 1986 the South African Defence Force (SADF) raided alleged ANC houses in Lusaka, although the principal reason for that raid was to scupper the talks then being conducted in South Africa by the Commonwealth's Eminent Persons' Group (EPG). In October 1986 South Africa's Defence Minister, General Magnus Malan, gave a public warning to President Kaunda that if he continued to grant the ANC refuge he could expect South African military reprisals. Further bomb attacks in Lusaka in October 1987 and in January and June 1988 were attributed to South Africa.

On Julius Nyerere's retirement as President of Tanzania in 1985, President Kaunda became the chairman of the frontline states, and by 1989 he was unrivalled in his knowledge of the region's problems. Kaunda knew more of the leading actors in the confrontations of the region than anyone else, and in August 1989 he had a first meeting with the new South African leader, F. W. de Klerk, at Livingstone in southern Zambia.

Zimbabwe

Although South Africa was opposed to UDI in Rhodesia, once it had been declared Pretoria was obliged to support the white minority stand there: white solidarity demanded such support; and it was imperative that sanctions should not be seen to work or the example of Rhodesia would encourage the enemies of South Africa to demand sanctions against the Republic as well. As the UDI years passed, Rhodesia became more and more dependent in both economic and military terms on South Africa.

Already by 1968 about 300 South Africans were serving with the Rhodesian forces, and by 1973 there were estimated to be anything from 2000 to 5000 South African troops in Rhodesia, mainly stationed along the Zambezi facing Zambia. The river had come to be regarded in Pretoria as South Africa's front-line. By 1979, when it was clear that the white minority had lost and that black majority rule would shortly be achieved in Rhodesia, South Africa played a role in exerting pressure on the Smith government to come to terms with its black opponents. This had nothing to do with any change of heart in Pretoria; the South African government wanted stability to the north and, if possible, a government in Harare (formerly Salisbury) over which it could exert some influence (see Part 1, pp. 62–68).

From 1980 onwards (after Rhodesia had become an independent black Zimbabwe) an uneasy relationship developed between Pretoria and Harare. As a result of the UDI years, Zimbabwe's economy remained heavily dependent on that of South Africa, and some years would be needed before this state of affairs could be changed. South Africa, for its part, saw Zimbabwe, with its tough integrated army, sophisticated infrastructure and relatively strong economy, as the most formidable of the frontline states; as a result, the Pretoria government pursued a policy of destabilization which had two separate approaches. On the one hand, bomb outrages against so-called ANC targets, spying activities and occasional cross-border raids maintained a suitable level of tension designed to remind the new government of its vulnerability. On the other hand, the civil war in Mozambique, by threatening Zimbabwe's only alternative transport routes to those through the Republic itself, ensured that Zimbabwe was increasingly drawn into the task of guarding lines of communication such as the Beira Corridor with a substantial part of its armed forces at considerable expense.

In May 1986 (when the Commonwealth Eminent Persons' Group was visiting South Africa) SADF units carried out a raid against ANC 'bases' in Zimbabwe; there were further raids and bomb outrages in Harare in 1987 and Bulawayo in January 1988. In 1987 Renamo announced that it was at war with Zimbabwe and in June of that year attacked an army base across the border at Dukosa when 17 Zimbabwe soldiers were killed. Between that raid and December an estimated 80 civilians were also killed by Renamo in cross-border attacks. In June 1988 the Zimbabwe government foiled a South African attempt to rescue five alleged South African agents then imprisoned in Harare; by August of that year there were 11 alleged South African saboteurs in Zimbabwe prisons.

President Robert Mugabe of Zimbabwe attracted particular venom in Pretoria because of his repeated demands for sanctions against South Africa, his efforts to change Zimbabwe trade patterns away from the south, the growing success of the Beira Corridor rehabilitation exercise and the fact that Zimbabwe appears as a relative multi-racial success story across the Limpopo. When the Non-Aligned Movement met in Harare in September 1986 (and President Mugabe became its new chairman) he opened the summit by calling for positive action on South Africa.

The Southern African Development Co-ordination Conference (SADCC)

Formed in 1979, its members originally consisted of the nine frontline states (Angola, Botswana, Lesotho, Malawi, Mozambique, Swaziland, Tanzania, Zambia and Zimbabwe); Namibia was invited to join on achieving independence in 1990. SADCC was created to develop the regional policies of its members in order to make them less dependent on South Africa. It concentrates on transport and communications (SADCC initiatives are responsible for the major efforts that began in 1986 to rehabilitate the Beira Corridor, Limpopo and Nacala railways in Mozambique), food security and, wherever possible, increasing trade between members. It is seen in Pretoria as the frontline answer to South African destabilization efforts and economic domination of the region.

The Commonwealth

Seven of the nine frontline states most concerned with South African destabilization tactics – Botswana, Lesotho, Malawi, Swaziland, Tanzania, Zambia and Zimbabwe – are members of the Commonwealth; as a result, the Commonwealth has become deeply involved in the whole South Africa question, not least because South Africa itself was formerly a member of the Commonwealth. The ANC has said that its members (the black majority) were not consulted about South Africa leaving the association in 1961 and would like to rejoin after majority rule has been achieved.

The Commonwealth, therefore, has become one of the most important international organizations mounting pressure on Pretoria and, in its turn, has come in for major denigration from the South African government. Ever since 1985 South Africa has been the most important issue on the agenda of Commonwealth heads of government meetings (CHOGMs), which are held every two years.

Conclusions

When F. W. de Klerk became President of South Africa in 1989 he inaugurated a new era; his speech of 2 February 1990, in which he announced the unbanning of the ANC and other opposition parties, and the subsequent release of ANC leaders including Nelson Mandela were clear indications that the ruling National Party was determined upon a new course of political action. One of the earliest fruits of this new direction was Namibian independence in 1990, which, despite many predictions to the contrary, Pretoria did not attempt to sabotage at the last moment. How South Africa behaves towards its northern neighbours – the countries it 'destabilized' during the 1980s – remains to be seen.

TANZANIA AND UGANDA: THE FALL OF AMIN 1978–1979

Introduction

The first full Commonwealth heads of government meeting (CHOGM) to be held outside London met in Singapore in January 1971 and was to be dominated by the issue of South Africa. The new British Conservative government of Edward Heath had announced its intention of resuming the sale of arms to the Republic. President Julius Nyerere of Tanzania led the opposition to this change of British policy; when he discovered that President Milton Obote of Uganda did not intend to attend the Singapore meeting he managed to persuade him to change his mind since he wanted his support in any argument with Prime Minister Heath about the arms for South Africa issue. As a result of Nyerere's pressure, President Obote left Uganda at a time when he had already warned the head of his army, Idi Amin, that he was to be investigated for illegally smuggling gold across the border into Zaire and when the head of his security forces was also absent from the country. Once Obote was safely out of Uganda in Singapore, Amin wasted no time in mounting a successful coup and took over as head of state.

Initially, Amin's seizure of power appeared to have substantial popular support, at least among the Buganda people, who had never forgiven Obote for his 'coup' of 15 April 1966 when he had established a republican form of government. In May 1966 the Buganda had attempted to secede from the central government (see Part V, pp. 406–410); Obote had introduced a state of emergency and sent troops against the Buganda and their Kabaka (hereditary ruler). Subsequently, the Kabaka (King Frederick Mutesa II) went into exile in Britain, where he died in 1969. Buganda was deprived of its regional autonomy, and the kingdoms of Buganda, Bunyoro, Toro and Ankole were abolished.

At the conclusion of the Commonwealth Conference ex-President Obote returned to Tanzania to take up residence in Dar es Salaam as the exile guest of President Nyerere; the latter clearly felt a degree of responsibility for his guest since he had persuaded him to leave Uganda in the first place, thus giving Amin his opportunity to seize power.

Origins

Britain had been increasingly uneasy at what it considered to be the 'left-wing' policies of Obote, while Israel, which was then supporting the struggle by the southern Sudanese against domination from Khartoum, also wanted a more pliant government in Kampala. Both countries, therefore, had an interest in the overthrow of Obote and were remarkably quick to recognize the new Amin government. On coming to power Amin made a series of populist gestures: he released a number of detainees and had the body of the Kabaka brought back from Britain for burial, giving rise to false hopes among the Buganda that he was about to restore their power. He then went on a tour of Uganda and subsequently overseas to visit Britain and Israel. But at home Amin was already demonstrating his ruthlessness: for example, troops considered to be a threat to him (about 1000 Langi and Acholi) were massacred during 1971. New soldiers were recruited from the West Nile region.

On 7 July 1971 Uganda closed its borders with Tanzania because, it alleged, some 700 Ugandans had been killed in fighting with pro-Obote guerrillas who had crossed into the country from Tanzania. This was the first pro-Obote, anti-Amin incursion from that country.

A year later, in August 1972, about 1000 Obote supporters began a second 'invasion' of Uganda from Tanzania, and though they had been defeated by 20 September, Ugandan planes bombed the Tanzanian town of Bukoba in retaliation, killing 9 and injuring 11. Tanzania then sent 1000 troops to the border and the little war gave every appearance of escalating into something more serious. Tanzania protested to the OAU about the bombing. On 22 September the Uganda air force raided Tanzania again, this time bombing Mwanza on Lake Nyanza. A ceasefire was then agreed, with Somalia acting as mediator. Libya, meanwhile, had sent (20 September) five air force transport planes with 399 military technicians and equipment to assist Amin. The planes were delayed *en route* in Khartoum and so only arrived at Entebbe on 22 September, by which time Uganda and Tanzania had agreed a ceasefire. The ceasefire was ratified in the October Mogadishu Agreement.

Those who had taken part in the pro-Obote invasion consisted mainly of members of the Uganda army and police who had fled to Tanzania during 1971. The adventure was a total failure and also a humiliation for both Obote and Nyerere. Following the Mogadishu Agreement, Obote was to lie low for a time in Tanzania.

Amin, meanwhile, had embarked on his populist anti-Asian policy, which led to the expulsion of the 30,000 Asian community, mainly to Britain, in the period August to December 1972. At the same time Amin also nationalized all British companies in Uganda without offering compensation. By the end of that year the basis of Amin's rule had become clear as an alternating mixture of populist measures and terrorist tactics.

Between 1972 and 1975 the size of the Ugandan army was increased from 7000 to 20,000. A coup attempt in 1974 led to heavy fighting, and by 1976 the regime was in deep trouble. The army used its position to plunder the country, and though some elements believed that such behaviour was undermining their credibility, others behaved as though the plundering could continue indefinitely. Then in June 1976 the Palestine Liberation Organization (PLO) hijacking of an Israeli plane to Entebbe and its subsequent successful rescue by the Israelis did considerable further damage to Amin's reputation. By 1978 Amin's regime had become a byword for tyranny and an embarrassment to Africa, while threats to his regime became increasingly frequent and dangerous. In August 1978 an abortive coup attempt led to the massacre of pro-Amin troops. It is generally believed that this persuaded Amin to embark on diversionary tactics.

He had already amassed troops on the Tanzanian border and in October these crossed the border into the Kagera salient. They withdrew again almost at once, but this was in the nature of a probing operation. Ugandan air force planes now bombed Bukoba; then, on 30 October, Amin's army invaded in earnest to advance as far as the Kagera river, occupying 1840 square kilometres (710 square miles) of territory before withdrawing at the end of November. Uganda claimed that it had first been invaded by Tanzania, but the real reason for the Ugandan action was to cover up army mutinies which had taken place at Mbabara. The Libyans were already involved in assisting Amin, and some Libyan prisoners were reportedly taken by the Tanzanians during the November action. The Ugandans left considerable devastation in their wake.

In January 1979 the Tanzanians in their turn invaded Uganda. They expected to stimulate a popular uprising against Amin, but when this failed to occur they still continued to advance in the hope of bringing about Amin's downfall. Only slowly did the Tanzanians commit themselves to a full-scale invasion that – it was hoped' – would lead to Amin's collapse. Initially, the Tanzanian People's Defence Force (TPDF) came in the wake of two small armies of Ugandan exiles (pro-Obote forces) who were volunteers.

Course of the struggle

The two volunteer Ugandan armies were led by Lt.-Col. David Oyite-Ojok (a staunch Obote man) and Yoweri Museveni. By February 1979 the TPDF had captured the towns of Mbabara and Masaka and found that it was encountering little resistance as Amin's army fled to the north. In March 1500 Libyan troops were flown into Entebbe to support Amin, but their arrival did not alter the pace of the Tanzanian advance and many of them were to perish during the battle for the capital. Amin's forces put up real resistance at Mutukula and Lukaya. Then, on 7 April, Entebbe and the international airport fell to the invaders after major fighting and heavy casualties. The battle for Kampala followed; Tanzanian troops entered the city three days later and were to be joined by citizens in looting the capital (10 and 11 April). The next week Jinja fell to the invaders and Amin then fled to Libya. Later he took refuge in Saudi Arabia. The West Nile region (the heartland of Amin support) was occupied during May and did not put up much resistance.

When it came to the point the two-pronged Tanzanian attack through Masaka and Mbabara met with little resistance, though the reasons for this are not entirely clear. On the one hand, it has been suggested that Amin's forces ran out of ammunition; on the other, it is said that he did not dare trust his forces in battle. And even the presence of up to 3000 Libyan troops did not stiffen his resistance against the Uganda National Liberation Army (UNLA). The Ugandan army had become one of the most mechanized in Africa and did not rely on infantry; in fact its armoured vehicles became easy targets for the invaders, and the Amin forces collapsed as much as anything because of low morale.

Estimated costs and casualties

During the 1978 phase of the war – the Ugandan invasion of the Kagera salient – some 10,000 Tanzanians who lived in the region were displaced and unaccounted for; the area suffered from much destruction as the local people fled before the advancing Ugandans, and much damage was done to property and installations.

In the second phase of the war – in 1979 – the Tanzanian forces (TPDF) numbered between 4000 and 5000. They came in the rear of the Ugandan exiles, who numbered 1000 to begin with, although as they advanced their numbers were soon swollen to 3000 – with either deserters from Amin's forces or opponents of his rule. By March, as he appeared to be losing control over his own troops, Amin came to rely increasingly on the Libyans (various estimates have put their numbers between 1000 and 3000), 1000 Moroccan troops sent to his support from Zaire and (according to one report) 1000 Palestinians. The Libyans brought substantial military supplies, including ammunition, small arms, shells, anti-tank guns and long-range artillery.

Gaddafi had vowed that he would not permit the Amin government to be overthrown. Libya had made substantial investments in Uganda; it saw the country as a PLO base as long as Amin was in control (he had in any case become a convert to Islam). More than 400 Libyans were killed in the fighting and many more were cut off as they fled into the bush.

Results: immediate and longer term

A period of uncertainty was now to follow, with several rulers – Lule, Binaisa, Muwanga – in quick succession before Obote came back to power again. Although Nyerere did not wish to appear overtly to force Obote back on to the Ugandan people, the ex-President was in fact his choice, while the continuing presence in the capital of Tanzanian troops acted as a political factor of crucial importance. They were to play a role in ousting both Lule and Binaisa before Obote returned to power. Uganda was to suffer from the effects of Amin's rule throughout the 1980s. The people had learnt the lesson of lawlessness from the top and were to be deeply affected by it thereafter.

Immediately on the fall of Amin, Dr Yusuf Lule, an academic whose sympathies were with the Buganda, became head of state. He had led the Uganda National Liberation Front (UNLF), but was a largely unknown, compromise candidate. He lasted from 13 April until 19 June when pressure from the Tanzanians (whose military forces were to remain in the country until 1981) led to his replacement by Godfrey Binaisa, a former Obote minister. Binaisa did not last quite a year. In February 1980 he dismissed Paulo Muwanga (then Minister of the Interior), who was an Obote man. This drew from Nyerere the threat to withdraw Tanzanian troops if law and order were not restored, a roundabout way of supporting Muwanga. In April Binaisa persuaded the National Consultative Council that political parties should not contest the forthcoming elections and that candidates should only represent the UNLF. Then, on 10 May, he attempted to dismiss the army commander, Brigadier David Oyite-Ojok (another Obote man), but instead Oyite-Ojok and Muwanga combined to dismiss Binaisa and set up an interim government. On 27 May, Milton Obote returned to Uganda from Tanzania and announced his intention of taking part in the elections. These were not finally held until December 1982 (the first in the country since 1962). Obote won 68 out of 126 seats, and he was inaugurated as President of Uganda for a five-year term on 17 December.

The Obote government faced mammoth tasks of national rehabilitation. There was indiscipline in the army and a high degree of general lawlessness, while the economy was in ruins. The 1980s were to see another breakdown of law and order and the eventual ousting of Obote after further brutal factional divisions. Yoweri Museveni then emerged as head of state (see Part V, pp. 406–410).

ZAIRE: THE TWO SHABA WARS 1977 and 1978

Introduction

From its independence in 1960 the Belgian Congo or Congo-Kinshasa (renamed Zaire in 1971) had a troubled history: this resulted in part from its colonial past and almost total lack of preparation for independence; in part from the giant size of the country and its many ethnic divisions; and in part from international intrigues. Thus the Western powers, although either indifferent to the way Mobutu Sese Sheko, President from 1965, ran the country – largely as though it were a personal fiefdom – or positively hostile to his rule, were none the less always prepared to support him rather than risk any alternative regime whose policies might be anti-Western. The USA, moreover, used Zaire as a conduit for CIA assistance to the anti-government liberation movements in Angola, while Mobutu himself supported first the Frente Nacional de Libertação de Angola (FNLA) and subsequently the União Nacional para a Independência Total de Angola (UNITA), so there were hardly ever reasonable relations between the Kinshasa government and the government in Luanda.

The reason for Western ambiguity over a regime that has often been rated among the worst in Africa results from Zaire's vast wealth: the country is a storehouse of minerals – cobalt (67 per cent of Western supplies), copper, lead, uranium and industrial diamonds to name but a few; it possesses vast agricultural possibilities (rubber, coffee, tea, cocoa, palm oil, cotton) and can tap (from its huge river system) an estimated 13 per cent of world hydro-electric potential. In addition to these advantages its position in the geographic centre of Africa, with borders on nine other countries, gives it an almost unrivalled strategic importance.

In these circumstances the Western powers have repeatedly overlooked behaviour on the part of Mobutu's government that they might have condemned had it occurred in countries not blessed with Zaire's resources. Moreover, directly or indirectly (through interlocking transnational mining corporations), the West has major interests locked up in the huge mineral resources of Shaba province (the former Katanga). Thus, an embattled Mobutu has found that he can obtain assistance from the West if threats to Shaba are also seen as threats to Western investments and strategic interests.

In March 1977 and again in May 1978 dissidents from Zaire – the National Front for the Liberation of the Congo (FNLC) – invaded Shaba from northern Angola.

On the first occasion France provided indirect assistance to the Mobutu government; on the second it intervened directly, while the USA put the 82nd Airborne Division on special alert and an emergency NATO meeting was called to consider possible military intervention in Zaire. Thus in May 1978 – the more serious of the two wars – after consulting with the American President, Jimmy Carter – President Giscard d'Estaing of France sent in troops of the Foreign Legion, while Belgium sent in paratroopers. Subsequently, President Carter accused the Cubans of masterminding the invasion, although President Castro of Cuba claimed that he had warned Washington of what was going to happen. The fact is that Zaire has always been seen as of such strategic importance that any upheaval in that country has led to Western intervention or readiness to intervene so as to maintain a pro-Western status quo – and that, since 1965, has meant supporting Mobutu.

Origins

During the struggle against the Portuguese in Angola, Zaire had always provided a base for the FNLA; as a consequence, when the MPLA emerged as the new government of Angola in 1975 there was anger and suspicion at Zaire's motives, although a reconciliation was effected between Angola's President, Agostinho Neto, and Zaire's Mobutu in 1976 at Brazzaville (Congo). It was then agreed that refugees in Zaire could return to Angola and that several thousands of Katangese soldiers then in Angola should return to Zaire. These latter had been part of Moise Tshombe's army at the time of his attempted secession from the Congo at the beginning of the 1960s (see Part V, pp. 411–417).

At this time – the mid-1970s – Shaba province was still being 'punished' for the attempted secession of 1960–3 and was not receiving anything like its share of revenues, although contributing something like 80 per cent of the national income from its mineral wealth. There was, in consequence, great discontent in Shaba, so the invaders were readily welcomed. They, however, hesitated to follow up their initial success, even though Mobutu's own army melted away in panic.

On 24 February 1977 President Neto addressed diplomats in Luanda and detailed Angolan aircraft and military vehicles which, he claimed, had been hijacked by Zaire. He also claimed that Zaire intended an invasion of the Cabinda enclave the following October. This was the background for the first Shaba war.

Shaba 1

On 8 March 1977 about 1500 ex-Katanga gendarmes crossed the border from Angola into the south-east of Shaba with the apparent objective of controlling the railway line along which the minerals were sent from the Shaba mines to Lobito on the Atlantic. They occupied a number of towns in western Shaba, including Kasaji, Mutshatsha and Kisenje (the centre of manganese mining). They met little resistance from the Zaire army and got to within 40 km (25 miles) of the major mining centre of Kolwezi. Their leader was General Nathaniel Mbumba and they called themselves the Front national pour la libération du Congo (FNLC). They were at least passively supported by Angola in the sense that it took no steps to prevent them launching their cross-border attack.

Mobutu blamed Angola and claimed that the force was receiving help from the USSR, the DDR and Cuba and that Soviet and Cuban mercenaries were leading them. He was clearly appealing to Western fears of Communism. The USA responded by providing $15 million worth of non-lethal military equipment. Mobutu appealed to France and Morocco for help and on 7 April King Hassan of Morocco agreed to send 1500 troops to Zaire, which President Giscard d'Estaing of France agreed to transport in 11 military planes to Kolwezi. Some French military instructors were also sent. The French motive for intervention was clear enough – to increase French influence in Zaire – but King Hassan's reasons for providing military assistance were not so obvious. Egypt and China also made offers of help. Nigeria attempted – unsuccessfully – to mediate. Government control was restored in Shaba once the Moroccan troops had arrived, and no major confrontation took place. The FNLC forces faded away, while many of the local people also fled into the bush to avoid reprisals. By May the first Shaba war had collapsed

The government instituted purges in Shaba, and the Lunda in particular were penalized for not having shown sufficient hostility towards the invaders. The result of this government behaviour was simply to increase general resentment against the central authorities so that the people were even more prepared to revolt the following year. The Mobutu government had suffered a loss of face. The FNLC – undefeated – had disappeared ready to fight another day, so the crisis remained unresolved. In part it represented a wider problem of bad relations between Zaire and Angola, resulting from Zairean support for the FNLA in the years prior to the MPLA victory in 1975.

Shaba 2

On 11 May 1978, fourteen months after the first Shaba invasion, a second attack by several thousand men was launched across the border from Angola; on this occasion the invaders at once occupied Kolwezi and established control of the railway from there to the Angolan border. They seemed to have much clearer objectives in mind. As before, the Zaire army melted away and Mobutu had to appeal for international assistance to save his regime. The FNLC forces were again led by General Nathaniel Mbumba and were both better trained and better armed, with weapons originating from Warsaw Pact countries. The FNLC forces, numbering about 4000, had infiltrated into Shaba over several months, some in civilian clothes. They were Lunda and came from Lunda bases in both Angola and Zambia. Kolwezi, their main objective, is a centre of the Lunda in Shaba. For the first few days the FNLC maintained discipline and appeared a potentially threatening force, their officers talking of overthrowing Mobutu and his government. But after about four days discipline broke down among both the Zaire troops and the FNLC, and looting and killing followed, including many of the white mineworkers round Kolwezi. Other whites were taken hostage.

President Mobutu accused the Cubans, the Angolan government and the USSR of responsibility, though they denied involvement. Forty-four whites were massacred in Kolwezi, another 16 were killed elsewhere and 40 were taken hostage, later to be killed. Both Belgium and France intervened directly. On 19 May some 400 Foreign Legion paratroopers were dropped on Kolwezi by the French; two days later (21 May) 1000 Belgian paratroopers were landed at Kamina in order to rescue the European population. During the fight for Kolwezi the French paratroopers killed an estimated 300 members of the FNLC, and by 23 May the FNLC were in retreat either to Angola or Zambia.

This second Shaba war was considerably more serious than the first one and, had the FNLC maintained discipline beyond the first few days, could have had quite different consequences. By June a Pan-African peace force had been installed in Shaba, while countries sympathetic to Zaire sent military instructors to retrain its army. By the end of the year Zaire and Angola had been reconciled.

Estimated costs and casualties

About 2000 whites of the mining communities were airlifted out of Shaba and back to Europe, and their disappearance represented a major disruption to the mining operations of the province. Apart from the whites and FNLC killed (see above), several hundreds of the citizens in the towns affected were probably also killed in the looting and massacring that took place.

Results: immediate and longer term

The FNLC claimed that France and Belgium had intervened to save Mobutu, although those two countries insisted they had only come to safeguard their own nationals or other whites. The second Shaba war illustrated the general weakness of Zaire, the almost total unreliability of its army and the determination of the Western powers to prop up the Mobutu government. It also illustrated the extent to which the newly independent government of Angola was dependent on the Eastern (Communist) powers and increased distrust between Angola and Zaire.

Much of 1979 was devoted to sorting out the aftermath of the war. When the French and Belgian troops were withdrawn at the end of 1978 the USA, France and Belgium jointly financed the logistics for the Pan-African force of 1500 troops, consisting of 1000 Moroccans and smaller contingents from Côte d'Ivoire, Senegal and Togo. This force remained in Shaba until mid-1979 when the main contingent (the Moroccans) was withdrawn to be followed by the smaller contingents. At that time (July 1979) President Neto of Angola undertook to prevent any further FNLC cross-border activities on condition that Mobutu stopped providing support for anti-MPLA forces in Angola. The two Presidents met that August and relations between them appeared to have improved.

France, Belgium and China each made offers to retrain and rebuild the Zaire army. President Carter accused the Cubans of helping the FNLC invade Shaba; this was denied by Havana, although it did admit to foreknowledge of the FNLC attack. There was at least circumstantial evidence that the DDR had helped train the FNLC forces for the second Shaba invasion.

The immediate effect of the war was to undermine still further Mobutu's credibility – although he was later to recover – and to damage Zaire's economy by disrupting the Shaba mining sector and causing an exodus of the white miners and technicians. In consequence Mobutu was obliged to appeal to the international community for further aid; although this was provided, the donors insisted on attaching stiff reform conditions to their loans.

THE MIDDLE EAST

THE GULF WAR: IRAN AND IRAQ 1980–1988

Origins

Although the Gulf War was ostensibly caused by the dispute over control of the Shatt al-Arab river, formed by the confluence of the Tigris and Euphrates, the rivalries between Iran and Iraq were deep-seated and long-lasting in their nature; they might be traced as far back as the third century, when the present boundaries roughly coincided with the meeting points for the Persian and Roman Empires. Iraq regarded itself as the successor of the Ottoman Empire and, as such, claimed jurisdiction over the entire Shatt al-Arab waterway up to its eastern (Iranian) bank. Iran had always argued that such a claim was unjust and insisted on the application of the Thalweg principle – that a river boundary should be delineated along the median line of the deepest channel.

A number of attempts had been made during the twentieth century to secure mutually acceptable recognition of the boundaries between the two countries: the position of the inland port of Khorramshahr had been agreed in 1914, while another Shatt al-Arab Treaty that settled the position of Abadan had been concluded in 1937. In 1969, however, the Shah of Iran abrogated the 1937 treaty; and in 1971 Iran seized the islands of Abu Musa, and the Greater and Lesser Tumbs, which controlled the entrance to the Gulf and so, potentially, the whole Gulf oil trade.

A turning point appeared to have been reached in 1975 when the Shah of Iran and Vice-President Saddam Hussein of Iraq met in Algiers and came to a new agreement. Iraq had blamed Iran for fuelling the long-lasting Kurdish war in its northern region, and Iran now agreed to end its support for the rebellious Kurds as part of an overall settlement of differences. The two countries accepted that the boundary of the Shatt al-Arab should be delineated along the median line as Iran had always claimed. But four years later the Shia revolution in Iran led to the downfall of the Shah and everything was once more in the melting pot. The war which followed was not really about the Shatt al-Arab, although that was the *casus belli*; the causes went much deeper and included Arab racial suspicions of the Iranians and resentment at the Shah's efforts to make Iran into the regional superpower. The underlying causes of the war were twofold: religious–nationalist rivalry as to which power should wield political hegemony in the Gulf; and economic rivalry, for by 1980 Iraq's oil resources were known to be greater than those of Iran and second only to those of Saudi Arabia, although Iraq had not much more than a quarter of Iran's population. Another complicating factor was Western attitudes. The West had encouraged the Shah to make Iran the local superpower, yet once he had been overthrown in the religious revolution of the

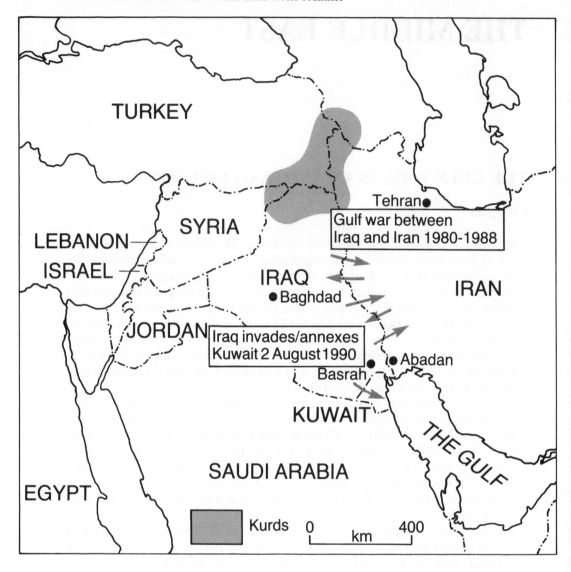

TURKEY

SYRIA

LEBANON

ISRAEL

Tehran●

Gulf war between
Iraq and Iran 1980-1988

IRAQ
●Baghdad

IRAN

JORDAN

Iraq invades/annexes
Kuwait 2 August 1990

●Abadan

Basrah

KUWAIT

THE GULF

EGYPT

SAUDI ARABIA

Kurds   0   400
                km

Ayatollahs, the West lost its enthusiasm for Iran as local superpower even as Tehran began consciously to throw off Western influences.

Outbreak and response

On 15 January 1979 the Shah left Iran never to return and real power passed to Ayatollah Khomeini and the 15-man Islamic Revolutionary Council. This Shia revolution in its more powerful neighbour reactivated Iraqi suspicions of Iran (they had never been far beneath the surface) with the result that Iraq revived its claims to the whole Shatt al-Arab, although nearly two years were to elapse between the Shah's departure and the Iraqi demands which sparked off the war in September 1980. The Iraqi government made the classic mistake of assuming that it could take advantage of revolution inside Iran to achieve its objectives at Tehran's expense, underestimating the nationalist weapon it was placing in the hands of the new revolutionary government – a war against an external aggressor – while calculating that the disparity in power between the two countries would be compensated for (in Iraq's case) by Arab support.

In April 1980 guerrillas who claimed allegiance to Ayatollah Khomeini attempted to assassinate the Deputy Prime Minister of Iraq, Tariq Aziz, a cause of anger which accentuated the deteriorating relations between the two countries. Finally, at the beginning of September 1980, Iraq presented Iran with four demands: to withdraw from the islands of Abu Musa and the Greater and Lesser Tumb; to renegotiate the agreement of March 1975 which had been signed in Algiers with the Shah; to grant autonomy to the Arabs of Khuzestan in Iran; and to undertake not to interfere in the internal affairs of Arab countries. These conditions were designed at least in part to provoke, and on 17 September, after Iran had refused to agree to such terms, Iraq abrogated the Algiers Agreement and claimed the entire Shatt al-Arab waterway up to the east (Iranian) bank.

Although neither side declared war formally, Iraqi troops now entered Kurdistan; on 22 September they entered Khuzestan. Iraqi planes then bombed Tehran, and Iran retaliated by bombing Baghdad, Basra and Kirkuk. Fighting rapidly escalated into a full-scale war. Iraq achieved a number of early successes, such as the capture of Khorramshahr and the territory surrounding Abadan; yet, to the surprise of most international observers, Iranian resistance rapidly stiffened and it soon became clear that Iraq was not going to have a walkover.

At first Iraq's war objectives appeared to be threefold: to take control of the Shatt al-Arab; to inflict maximum damage on the revolutionary government in Tehran; and to destabilize the south-western region of Iran, which included a substantial Arab-speaking population. But Iranian morale did not collapse under the Iraqi onslaught and it was found to possess better (US) weapons than Iraq, most of whose weaponry came from the USSR. Both the United Nations and the Islamic Conference attempted to mediate, but without any success.

When the war began in 1980 Iran's armed forces numbered 240,000; they were equipped with Western weapons, but needed assistance from Western technicians, most of whom had been withdrawn as a result of the anti-Western stance of the revolutionaries (although their withdrawal had not weakened Iran as much as Iraq had calculated would be the case). At the same time Iraq's armed forces numbered 242,000, of whom 200,000 were army.

During the first months of the war to the end of 1980 Iran suffered a great deal of physical damage: oil exports from Kharg Island had to be halted; the huge refinery at Abadan was largely destroyed or at any rate rendered inoperable; further damage was done to the refineries at Tehran and Tabriz, severely reducing the country's oil output; and the ports of Khorramshahr and Bandar Khomeini were brought to a standstill. Furthermore, up to 1 million people were displaced and turned into refugees. Yet by December 1980 the original Iraqi offensive had been brought to a halt and hostilities – for a time – were reduced to artillery exchanges across the Shatt al-Arab.

The Iranian government, meanwhile, had announced its intention of pursuing the war until all Iraqi forces had been expelled from Iranian territory and the government of Saddam Hussein in Baghdad had been brought down. Fears that the war would spread proved groundless – at least for the time being – although the three Western powers (the USA, Britain and France) increased their naval forces in the region, while Saudi Arabia was careful to preserve its neutrality. During these first months of war Iraq lost between 30 and 50 fighters and fighter-bombers; Iran between 60 and 100. By December the conflict had settled down into a form of stalemate not unlike the trench warfare of the First World War, a comparison that was to be made frequently over the next few years.

Course of the Struggle

Throughout the course of the Gulf War Iran was also in the throes of its internal revolution, which turned out to be one of the most radical of its kind anywhere in the Third World. Thus, the war became a nationalist cause and was used by Tehran to rally the people, who in any case both felt themselves to be isolated and gloried in their isolation. Whatever calculations Baghdad may have made about Iranian revolutionary instability when it launched the war turned out to be false.

A second crucial factor throughout most of the war years was Western antipathy to Tehran. In part the Shia Islamic revolution was fuelled by deep antagonism to Western values and resentment at what had come to be seen as Western penetration of Iran and subversion of Islam during the reign of the Shah. This was given concrete form in 1979 with the seizure of the American hostages, the bungled attempt to rescue them and the subsequent long negotiations for their release. Washington did not forgive Khomeini for this episode, and though the West did not look on the Baghdad regime with much favour and regarded Saddam as a hard man of the left and an ally of Moscow, it preferred Iraq – marginally – to Iran.

As it happened, both Middle East powers were major sources of oil and so, even *in extremis*, could always sell enough oil to pay for minimal military requirements. Moreover, when it came to the point, dislike for either or both regimes did not prevent the major arms suppliers from providing crucial weaponry – at a price – and the USA, the USSR, Britain, France and China each provided arms at different times. So did others.

1981

At the beginning of 1981 the Iraqi army was in occupation in parts of Kurdestan and had established a bridgehead to the east of Abadan; though it failed to take the oil town, the Iraqi bombardment destroyed much of it, including the vital refinery. Indeed, the initial Iraqi impact had been sufficiently devastating to create an estimated 1.5 million Iranian refugees. Yet by mid-1981 the war had evened out into a balanced state, fortunes see-sawing from side to side, with heavy casualties on both. Iranian artillery, for example, at an early stage shelled Basra, which was to suffer a great deal from then onwards.

Both sides were to carry out a series of air strikes against each other. Iran bombed oil installations at Basra in January, Kirkuk in the summer and power stations in the south during October. Iraq carried out air strikes against Iran's southern ports, the oil terminal at Kharg Island and the oil pumping station at Gurreh, reducing Iran's oil exports to a trickle in the process. In September, the first anniversary of the war's beginning, Iraq launched a new offensive, but by the end of the month its troops had been forced to withdraw to the left bank of the Karun river.

Throughout the war Iraq was always to be conscious of its relatively small population compared with Iran's, and one consequence of this was that Baghdad constantly played down casualties, although the government gave generous benefits to widows and orphans. Iran, on the other hand, was still in revolutionary crisis, and at one level the war might almost have been seen as a relief since it acted as a rallying cause. At the beginning of the year the negotiations for the release of the American hostages who had been held at the embassy in Tehran since their seizure in 1979 – in return for the unfreezing of blocked funds held in the USA – were successfully concluded. In June a bomb explosion in the headquarters of the Islamic Revolutionary Party killed 72. For most of the year the war continued at a relatively low level of intensity.

Iraq was still enjoying remarkable economic prosperity from her huge oil revenues and was spending more than any other Arab state on development projects. Baghdad still expected to play host to the Non-Aligned Movement Summit in 1982. But the economic danger signals were piling up, and crude oil output dropped from a daily average of 3.4 million barrels before the war to just 900,000. By the end of the year the Iraqis had been forced out of their bridgehead to the east of Abadan, while in December the Iranians also broke through the Iraqi lines at Susangerd.

1982

In 1982 Iran took the offensive and on 22 March its armies forced the Iraqis to retreat on the Khuzestan front. Then in April Iranian forces crossed the Karun river to establish a bridgehead. In May the Iraqis were forced out of Khorram-shahr. At that stage in the war, clearly reflecting revised fortunes, Iraq announced its readiness to withdraw from any remaining Iranian territory and seek a peace through the good offices of the Organization of Islamic Conference (OIC). On 14 July, however, the Iranians invaded Iraq in a drive on Basra. Despite early gains, this offensive was repulsed with heavy losses. On 1 October the Iranians launched another offensive on the Iraqi town of Mandali and then attempted a drive towards Baghdad, but Iraq succeeded in halting this by mid-November.

The political repercussions of the war spread far afield. Once the Iranians had invaded Iraqi (Arab) soil, they found that relations with other Arab countries were to deteriorate sharply. At home the Iranian revolution made targets of left-wing groups. Iraq, meanwhile, was obliged to cancel the Non-Aligned Movement Summit which had been scheduled for Baghdad that September. Having performed better on the military front during 1982, Iran stiffened its conditions for peace: it demanded that Saddam Hussein be removed from office, that an independent commission be appointed to apportion blame for the war and that Iraq be made to pay reparations. At the same time the Iranian economy was under growing pressure; the demand for Iranian oil had dropped, with oil output averaging only 1.5 million barrels per day for the first half of the year, though it had risen to 1.7 million barrels in November. On the other hand, it was a year of military setbacks for Iraq, which in its turn had a lower oil production and faced greater austerity.

Officially, the two superpowers maintained neutrality and refused to provide military equipment, yet both combatants obtained embargoed materials without difficulty. Iraq now found itself relying increasingly on other rich Arab states for financial aid, while its oil output was down to 600,000 barrels per day, with only the pipeline through Turkey in operation. President Saddam insisted that the war should take priority over everything else.

1983

By 1983 both sides had suffered heavy casualties – dead and wounded – as well as huge losses of equipment and increasing damage to the towns in which the fighting took place or which were subjected to bombardment. In many respects the war had bogged down into a trench confrontation in the style of the First World War, although there was an escalation of fighting through the year. Iran's strategy was to maximize its advantage in manpower by attacking across a wide front. It launched a series of offensives in February, April, July and October, although these failed to break through the Iraqi lines. On the whole the Iranians were poorly equipped, while Iraq had better equipment and was able to build up and increase its air superiority. In October Iraq launched a series of missile attacks on Iranian cities and mined the Gulf approaches to the port of Bandar Khomeini.

An international row erupted following the French agreement in October to supply Iraq with five Super Étendard aircraft armed with Exocet missiles, since it was feared that these would be deployed against Gulf shipping. Even so the international community was generally more favourable to Iraq than Iran: this was the result of the anti-Western and isolationist stands taken in Tehran and the generally unsympathetic view taken of the revolution from outside Iran.

1984

During 1984 Iraq demonstrated the advantages of air superiority; it used this especially to harass Iranian oil tankers in the Gulf, and the 'tanker war' became increasingly threatening to international interests. By June the tanker war was endangering the entire oil business of the Gulf; in one engagement Saudi Arabia shot down an Iranian plane. At the same time Iran suffered heavy losses in its land offensives, which failed to make any real headway except in the south, where the Iranians broke the Iraqi lines to take the Majnoon oilfield. Iran mobilized huge numbers – possibly 400,000 – during the year, many of them boys in their early teens. Late in the year Iran abandoned the tactic of human wave attacks, which simply proved too costly in manpower.

When the war entered its fifth year in September it appeared to be in stalemate, although the shipping war in the Gulf escalated dangerously. Further attempts at mediation came to nothing, with Iran still insisting that Saddam should be ousted from power in Baghdad. The international line-up of support increasingly favoured Iraq: thus, while Iran only had support from Iraq's sworn enemy Syria, most other Arab states lined up behind Iraq and the USSR gave it substantial support. Although the USA remained officially neutral, its policy included close support for Saudi Arabia and it also re-established diplomatic relations with Iraq – for the first time since 1967. Moreover, in April 1984 the US Vice-President, George Bush, said publicly that an Iranian victory in the Gulf War would represent a major threat to the whole region. The USA also accused Iraq of employing chemical weapons.

1985

During 1985 public life in Iran was dominated by the war and the country found itself increasingly isolated: the Arab world, apart from Syria and Libya, supported Iraq, as did the USSR, and though much of the West professed neutrality, much also supported Iraq. Antagonism to Iran was as much a judgment on the excesses and cruelties of the Islamic revolution as a judgment on the rights and wrongs of the war. Arab opposition to Iran had two causes: the first arose from a sense of solidarity with another Arab state (even though Iraq was hardly popular with the rest of the Arab world); the second from fear in the Gulf states that Iran would spread its revolution and upset the status quo of established regimes.

In March, briefly, the Iranians managed to cut the road between Baghdad and Basra. However, the year was mainly noteworthy for what became known as the 'war of the cities'. Although early in the war the two protagonists had agreed not to attack civilian targets, this pledge was abandoned following an Iranian attack on Basra in March. Iraq then launched the war of the cities and bombed some 30 Iranian towns and cities, including Tehran, Isfahan, Tabriz and Shiraz. In return Iran shelled Baghdad and Basra during April. In June Iraq mounted a series of intense air raids on Tehran.

Iran now switched tactics in the hope of extending Iraq's more limited manpower resources and launched a series of small-scale attacks the length of the 900 mile front. From mid-July to the end of the year Iraq concentrated a series of air raids on the oil terminal of Kharg Island. Both sides, however, were now demonstrating unmistakable war-weariness, which emerged in Iran in the form of an open debate about the war and the desirability for peace. There was also a clear desire for peace manifest in Iraq, yet all efforts at mediation continued to fail. Both countries faced growing economic hardships: the Iranian economy deteriorated as foreign reserves fell and demand for oil remained static; Iraq found increasing difficulty in meeting its debts.

1986

The war created some odd alliances, with conservative Arab states including Saudi Arabia joining the USSR in support of Iraq, with Libya and Israel supporting Iran, with the USA now supplying arms secretly to Iran (what became the Irangate scandal), and with China and France selling arms to both sides. In 1986 a political scandal rocked the US administration when it became known that there had been a secret American deal with Tehran to sell arms to Iran and that part of the payments received had subsequently been diverted to the Contras fighting the Sandinista government in Nicaragua (see also Part V, pp. 551–559). Lt.-Col. Oliver L. North of the White House staff, the central figure in this scandal, was 'relieved' of his duties (he subsequently stood trial) for his part in the affair, the repercussions of which continued in Washington for several years.

In Iran the leadership said it would launch a final offensive (one estimate suggested that more than 750,000 men had been mobilized). On 10 February the Iranians crossed the Shatt al-Arab to capture the disused Iraqi port of Fao. For most of the year Iraq concentrated its efforts on bombing the Iranian oil terminals, while Iran launched a series of missile strikes at Kirkuk, Baghdad and Basra, and also carried out a series of raids on neutral tankers in the Gulf. As in 1985 the demand for peace grew in both countries. Iraq's Saddam Hussein called for peace in August, as did the Freedom Movement inside Iran.

An Iraqi air force raid on the oil-loading terminal at Sirri Island in the Gulf in August was so serious – two supertankers were destroyed and 20 seamen killed – that Iran was forced to abandon the facility and transfer its oil export terminal to Larak Island 120 miles further east. The raid led to a fall in Iran's oil production from 1.6 million barrels per day to 1.2 million. At Kharg Island 11 of the 14 oil-loading berths had to be abandoned. Deep concern was expressed by foreign and oil ministers meeting at Abha in Saudi Arabia at the escalating threat to the whole Gulf; the ministers worked out a new set of peace proposals to place before the Non-Aligned Movement Summit that was due to take place in Harare, Zimbabwe, that September.

By the end of August Iran had massed up to 650,000 men along the southern sector of the front ready for their 'final' offensive. At the same time Tehran Radio waged a propaganda battle to claim that the war would be over by the following spring. The indications suggested an all-out assault on Basra. At the same time persistent reports suggested that a state of low morale existed in the Iraqi army. In Baghdad diplomats believed that Iran had mobilized up to 1 million men. An Iranian victory was viewed with growing fear by the Arab states of the Gulf, which turned with increasing desperation to Washington to stop the war; should its forces capture Basra, the Gulf would effectively became an Iranian lake. Yet it was some time before a major advance took place. Then, in December, an Iranian thrust on the southern front was halted in a two-day battle in which Iran lost 10,000 men. Tehran played down the battle, but in Baghdad it was claimed that the push had been intended as the 'decisive offensive' that had long been promised by Iranian leaders. Tehran radio claimed that 3000 Iraqi troops had been killed and 6500 wounded in an Iranian attack on four islands in the Shatt al-Arab. Meanwhile Iraqi opponents of Saddam Hussein met in Tehran, in the Supreme Assembly of the Islamic Revolution of Iraq to call upon all ethnic groups in Iraq to reject the Saddam government.

It was a curious period, for despite the massive mobilization no commensurate offensive was launched, although expectations of one remained high. Iran, in any case, had difficulties during the year with one of its few allies, Syria, over the latter's policies in Lebanon, although in the end the differences were resolved. The USSR agreed to purchase natural gas from Iran, but it did not alter its opposition to Tehran's war posture. Also during the year US officials visited Tehran secretly and arranged for spare parts to be provided. American hostages in Lebanon were released, although US officials explained their visits to Tehran by saying they were merely trying to make contact with moderates!

Iraq's position became increasingly precarious during the year. Although its forces regained territory in the north, it lost Fao in the south. None the less, the Iranian attack in the south that December was repulsed. The war was then costing Iraq an estimated $1 billion a month.

1987

By 1987 the greater national resources that Iran could call upon – a population of 50 million and a GNP of $188,000 million – were beginning to tell. Iran's regular forces then numbered 654,000 men, but its equipment was commensurately far less than that of Iraq. Thus Iran had an estimated 1000 tanks, 750 artillery pieces and only about 60 combat aircraft. On the other hand, Iraq, with a population of 16.5 million and a GNP of $34,000 million, by then had armed forces of 1 million men, 4500 tanks, 3000 artillery pieces and 500 combat aircraft. But while the war effort was costing Iran approximately 12.3 per cent of GNP, it was costing Iraq 51.1 per cent. Such a disparity was bound to wear Iraq down before its larger opponent, and during 1987 Iranian offensives did bring Iraq near to collapse.

In January Iran launched major offensives against Iraqi positions between Khorramshahr and to the east of Basra. Much of Iraq's superiority in aircraft was nullified by missiles which Iran had obtained (secretly) from the USA, part of whose policy at this time was to maintain a balance by ensuring that neither side came out on top. The January offensive brought Iranian forces within a few miles of Basra, and they lost an estimated 45,000 dead before the attack faltered and got bogged down. Iraqi dead were fewer in number, but still ran into many thousands. World fears for international shipping led to the suggestion that the UN might establish a UN naval patrol force to deter attacks on ships in the Gulf.

Many of the Iranian casualties were 'Baseej', volunteers from schools and colleges, many of them young boys, who were given a month's training before being sent to the front for human wave attacks. In the air the Iraqis now deployed Soviet F29 Fulcrums, a fighter with the ability to locate and then track and shoot down enemy aircraft using its own radar. On the other hand, with its air force much reduced, Iran had come to rely far more on the effects of long-range missiles which it fired on Baghdad. The January offensive was certainly one of the bloodiest of the war.

Then, in late February, the seven-week Kerbala-5 Iranian offensive, as it had been called, was brought to an end. In part this was due to Soviet and Syrian pressures and a trade-off whereby Iraq agreed to halt its bombing raids on Iranian towns. Suddenly there were signs that a truce might be accepted by both sides. The Soviets informed the Iranian Foreign Minister, Ali Akbar Velayati, then on a visit to Moscow, that they would persuade Iraq to stop the bombing if the offensive were called off, but that if it were not they would let Iraq increase its attacks on Iranian cities by allowing it to use SS-12 missiles with a range of 870 km (540 miles). At the same time the Syrians warned Iran that should it take Basra this would only have the effect of increasing general Arab hostility. Iran was probably also influenced to call off its offensive when the UN Secretary-General, Pérez de Cuéllar, proposed to set up an international panel to determine whether Iraq or Iran was to blame for the war, something Iran had been insisting upon.

The Islamic Republic News Agency (IRNA), clearly preparing the way for an end to the offensive, claimed that Iran had captured 160 square kilometres (62 square miles) of territory and described the seven-week offensive as one of the most severe blows dealt Iraq throughout the war. Iran, it suggested, had achieved its goal of destroying the Iraqi war machine: some 700 Iraqi armoured vehicles, 7500 other vehicles, 80 planes and seven helicopter gunships had been destroyed, as well as 56,000 Iraqi soldiers killed or wounded. Iran then called off its offensive, although it had not taken Basra.

A lull followed with both sides recuperating after the bloodiest offensive of the war. In April, however, Iran launched another offensive against Basra, though on a smaller scale. Iraq claimed at once to have defeated it, and both sides said they had killed 2000 enemy. But this (the eighth offensive against the city) did not succeed any better than its predecessors, and early in May Tehran announced that it would declare a ceasefire if the UN Security Council were to identify Baghdad as the aggressor.

By June the emphasis of the war had shifted to the Gulf, where Iraqi attacks on vessels bound for Iranian ports and the announcement of more American warships being assigned to the Gulf indicated a possible escalation into crisis. Kuwait, neutral in theory but in fact a firm supporter of Iraq, pursued a policy to involve the superpowers in the conflict in the belief that between them they would not permit an Iranian victory, something the rest of the Gulf states feared but were afraid they could not prevent. At any rate, at the end of June, the USA announced that it would send the battleship *Missouri* to the Gulf to protect Kuwaiti tankers, where it would join an international force consisting of two British frigates and a destroyer, one French frigate, four Soviet minesweepers and a guided-missile cruiser, and five other US warships (with three more to come), between them making up the most formidable international fleet since the Second World War.

In July the five permanent members of the Security Council – the USA, the USSR, Britain, France and China – agreed to support a mandatory resolution calling for a ceasefire in the Gulf War, a resolution upon which the USA and USSR co-operated closely. It became increasingly clear during the year that Iran was becoming more isolated. Libya ceased to support it and the death in Mecca (31 July) of 275 Iranians led Tehran to accuse Saudi Arabia of killing its pilgrims on behalf of the USA, while France broke diplomatic relations with Iran and Britain closed its consulate in Manchester. In mid-October 19 US warships destroyed two Iranian production platforms in retaliation for an Iranian attack on a US-registered tanker in Kuwait waters, yet despite these apparent escalations, war-weariness and world pressures were coming together towards the end of 1987 to bring about a ceasefire if not a peace.

During the last two months of 1987 Iran engaged in a curious game of bluff and counter-bluff: on the one hand, it appeared ready to discuss UN Resolution 598, which called for an immediate ceasefire; at the same time the Supreme War Support Council asked Ayatollah Khomeini to approve fresh mobilization for a 'chain of successive and effective operations along all the warfronts'. Iraq, meanwhile, kept up its attacks on tankers in the Gulf. Satellite photographs showed extensive Iranian preparations for a new offensive: troops were massed on the southern front, probing attacks were launched elsewhere to keep the Iraqis guessing, and arms factories were reported to be increasing production. All the indications were for another assault on Basra.

But world attention remained focused on the Gulf, which was what Iran wanted; with minimal effort – a handful of Revolutionary Guards using speedboats – it had succeeded in drawing something like 70 naval vessels – from the USA, its allies and the USSR – into the Gulf. Thus, if the new land offensive against Basra failed, Iran would still be able to negotiate the sort of peace it wanted. As the year came to an end, hopes were still being placed on UN Resolution 598 and the possibility that, however reluctantly, Iran would be prepared to accept a ceasefire.

1988

During 1988 Iraq recovered from its near collapse of the previous year and managed to inflict growing losses on Iran in the 'war of the cities', using missiles against Tehran, Qom and other cities from February onwards. Iran was unable to respond in kind. In January Arab diplomats from Oman, Syria and Saudi Arabia appeared to think Iran would, at last, be prepared to sit down with leaders of the Gulf states to discuss a ceasefire. Yet at the same time Iran extended the period of conscription for its soldiers from 24 to 28 months and amassed 500,000 troops for another offensive on the southern front. It was reliably reported, however, that the use of chemical weapons by Iraq had undermined the morale of Iranian troops, as the bombardment of Tehran had undermined the civilian will to resist.

In March China's Foreign Minister, Wu Xueqian, told President Reagan that Peking was prepared to support the proposed UN arms embargo in the war, although at that time the USSR vetoed the proposal. The supply of Chinese Silkworm missiles to Iran was helping prolong the war. But then, 17–18 April, the Iraqis overran the Iranians holding the port of Fao. The Americans, meanwhile, by openly siding with Iraq, torpedoed the UN Security Council initiative to end the war by mediation. China then announced its intention of vetoing the proposed arms embargo because of US clashes with the Iranian navy, so the Security Council became split between the USA, Britain and France in favour of an arms embargo and the USSR and China against. In May and June the Iraqis again advanced to reclaim other territories taken by Iran – first the area of Fish Lake north-east of Basra, then the Majnoon oilfield.

But both sides needed peace and at last, on 20 August 1988, Iran accepted UN Resolution 598 and a ceasefire came into effect. The eight-year war, one of the bloodiest ever to have been fought in the Third World, came to an end. Periodic meetings through 1989 and into 1990 between Iranian and Iraqi representatives did not bring the two sides any closer to a definitive peace treaty. But on 3 July 1990, for the first time since the ending of the Gulf War, the Foreign Ministers of Iran and Iraq met at the United Nations in a preliminary meeting to what could be substantive peace talks.

Estimated costs and casualties

Casualties in dead and wounded, damage to cities and the oil installations of the Gulf, and the massive write-off of military equipment were each immense. Not only did the war cut back the oil production of the two combatants and do great damage to their oilfields and installations, but it drastically retarded their development as well. For political propaganda reasons, each side exaggerated its opponent's casualties and played down its own. Even allowing for this they were on a major scale. Thus in 1981 Iranian casualties were estimated variously as between 10,000 and 20,000 dead with many more wounded. In 1982 Iraqi casualties were estimated at 40,000 dead, 70,000 wounded and 40,000 captured. In 1983 Iranian dead came to not less than 50,000. Moreover, as the war continued and threatened world oil supplies, so more and more outside powers were drawn into it as arms suppliers to one or other (or both) sides (the French, for example, supplying Iraq with Super Étendard aircraft in 1983), or because they feared what would happen to their interests in the area. Thus, in 1983, when Iran threatened to close the Straits of Hormuz, the USA made a specific pledge that its forces would keep the Straits open (at the time it had a huge naval task force in the Indian Ocean).

By 1983 the war was costing Iraq $1 billion a month, while its export earnings (mainly oil) had dropped from the high of $26 billion a year in 1979 to $10 billion in 1983 and its oil exports (now only through the Turkey pipeline) were reduced to 800,000 barrels per day. As a result Iraq was obliged to seek more and more international loans: that year it obtained $500 million from a syndicate of Western banks, $1.6 billion from a French syndicate and $1.8 billion from Japan. Even so, it was obliged to apply increasingly stringent financial economy measures. A 1985 Iraqi assessment showed that in five years of war Iraq had suffered 70,000 dead and 150,000 wounded, and had lost 50,000 prisoners. At the same time it had spent $35 billion of foreign currency reserves on the war and run up $40 billion of war debts.

By 1986 China had become the largest source of arms for Iran, supplying $300 million worth of missiles and other equipment in the first six months of the year. Deals by China to supply Iran were made in London, Hong Kong and Beijing. By then they were also preparing to deliver heavy tanks and a Chinese version of the MiG21 fighter. Chinese missiles shipped to Iran through North Korea were judged to be the equivalent of Soviet Scuds with a range of 300 km. At the same time, in defiance of the US embargo, Iran was obtaining European help with its missile programme. European manufacturers defied the US embargo, partly out of resentment at the way the USA had virtually monopolized the market in the

Shah's time and partly to ensure that they secured a large part of the post-war reconstruction work. Thus rocket guidance systems of the US design manufactured in West Germany under licence were reaching Iran through Yugoslavia.

There was a sameness about reports of war engagements: always both sides claiming enemy dead in thousands, and the language of the war became increasingly macabre. Thus in December 1986 one Iraqi report claimed to have smashed an Iranian attack, killing 10,000 and turning the Shatt al-Arab waterway 'red with blood'.

By 1987 war imports were costing Iraq $5 billion, and while the country required a war chest of $15 billion, it only received oil revenues of $8.5 billion. Yet by September the oil export position had improved with 500,000 barrels per day exported via the Turkey pipeline and 1.5 million barrels via Saudi Arabia. Conflicting estimates of casualties make a precise final figure an impossibility, but one reasonable estimate at the beginning of 1987 put Iraqi dead at 250,000 men and Iranian dead at 500,000.

Conflicting political interests produced many doubtful interventions. According to the *New York Times*, for example, the USA provided both sides with deliberately distorted and inaccurate intelligence information in an effort to ensure that neither side would be victorious. It appeared that the USA sold arms to the Ayatollah at the same time that it provided help to Iranian *emigré* groups attempting to overthrow him. Moreover, it seems that the sale of American weapons to Iran (approved by President Reagan in 1985 and in fact the beginning of the Irangate scandal) was on the basis of information supplied by the Israelis. In 1987 the Belgian government obtained 'irrefutable' evidence that its ports and airports had been used as staging posts in American embargo-breaking operations to sell arms to Iran.

During the course of the war the Western powers, the USSR, the UN, the Gulf Arab states (the Gulf Co-operation Council) and the Organization of Islamic Conference each tried and failed to mediate a settlement between the two sides. Kuwait, one of the richest states on earth but powerless on its own, played a major role in bringing the full force of US power into the Gulf War by seeking to place its tankers under the protection of the American flag. Subsequently, it became a target for Iranian anger and missile attacks during the latter half of 1987.

The major arms-producing powers either directly or through proxies ensured that both sides obtained at least a proportion of the weapons they sought. By 1987 the USA, the USSR, Britain, France and China – the big five of the UN Security Council – each had a presence in the Gulf or were supplying arms to one or both sides openly or clandestinely. This huge outside involvement in the war reflected both the vital strategic importance of the Gulf as a region and the fact that the two combatants were each major oil producers. One cynical calculation of outsiders must undoubtedly have been that when the war did eventually come to an end both countries possessed the wherewithal (in oil revenue potential) to finance massive reconstruction programmes.

Other powers were also sucked into the war. By 1987 Pakistan, for example, was in danger of becoming involved in the Gulf War because of the 50,000 military personnel it supplied to some 22 Middle East and East African countries; the Kuwaiti and Saudi navies were almost entirely manned by Pakistani sailors; the Saudi naval school at Jubail, which trains Gulf naval crews, was run by Pakistani officers; and two divisions of the Pakistan army were stationed in Saudi Arabia, one of them protecting the oilfields along the Gulf coast.

A summary of war costs made by the Stockholm International Peace Research Institute (SIPRI) in 1988 claimed that total casualties came to 1.5 million dead and that the two combatants had purchased $27 billion in major arms (excluding small arms, ammunition and parts) during the preceding eight years. Total military expenditure over the eight-year period came to between $168.5 billion and $203.6 billion, with Iran spending between $9 billion and $10 billion a year (5 to 6 per cent of the GNP) and Iraq spending between $11 billion and $13 billion a year (25 to 30 per cent of GNP). Iraq was most dependent on the purchase of arms, buying $24 billion worth in eight years, with $11.5 billion coming from the USSR and $6.8 billion from France. Iran, on the other hand, relied more on 'labour-intensive war technology', although it purchased $3 billion worth of arms from China (53 per cent of its total).

A knock-on effect of the war was the huge increase of military expenditure (an additional $20 billion) by the Gulf states, which strengthened their armed forces as a precaution in the years 1980 to 1988. Their principal suppliers were the USA, France, Britain and West Germany. Few wars anywhere since 1945 involved so many interests or cost so much in wealth and lives.

Results: immediate and longer term

The immediate result of the war at the time of the ceasefire might be seen as a return to the *status quo ante*, with neither combatant having apparently altered its territorial position and both having suffered grievous material and human losses. In fact the results are momentous. In the first place the war created a surge of Shia self-confidence throughout the Middle East. Once seen as the downtrodden of Islamic society, the Shias have now taken on a new militancy that has, for example, come out in terrorist activities, especially in Lebanon. More than that, however, the war has led to an increase in Islamic fundamentalism throughout the Arab world.

Second, the Arabs have now come to see themselves as being under pressure from two enemies instead of only one in their midst: Israel has been joined by Iran. Both these countries are thought to demonstrate a contempt for international pressures in pursuit of what they see as their national objectives.

Third, the war demonstrated just how little the major powers are able to contain regional violence when it occurs. All the powers became involved in efforts to bring about a peace, but this was to little avail despite the extent of the pressures which in theory and practice they could, and sometimes did, try to bring to bear upon the combatants. This apparent inability to bring an end to the fighting raises a quite different question: the extent to which the external powers used the Gulf War for their own purposes, whether these were selling arms, manoeuvring for economic advantage or in other ways using the shield of war activities to further their own ambitions in the region. The Irangate scandal and other revelations of American (and other power) readiness to provide support for both sides did little to encourage international confidence in big power motives and a good deal to engender heightened distrust for their international stands.

In the subsequent uneasy truce that followed the war – meetings between the two sides have brought no real moves towards a lasting peace – what has emerged perhaps more clearly than anything else is the radicalization of the Islamic world.

All the Gulf states felt threatened by the war, and the insistence on fundamentalism that has been Iran's great contribution to Islam will continue to have an impact and influence far into the twenty-first century.

Iran's insistence on a renewed fundamentalism represents the positive side of a policy the other aspect of which has been a determined rejection of the Western values that seemed increasingly to permeate Iranian society during the reign of the Shah. This Iranian reaction to Western penetration raises another question of potentially momentous importance for the future: how far can a relatively underdeveloped society buy or otherwise import the modernization it requires without also allowing its traditional values to be subverted in the process? Since the Gulf War finally came to an end just as *glasnost* and *perestroika* also appeared to herald an end to the Communist development path in the Soviet bloc, the question has especial relevance: must the values associated with Western capitalist materialism permeate world society in its entirety?

When through *force majeure* – war-weariness and massive external pressures – Iran finally accepted UN Resolution 598 on 20 August 1988 Ayatollah Khomeini described taking that decision as 'more deadly than taking poison'. Nor were the Iraqis any happier, for Saddam Hussein and many Iraqis have always considered that they were forced into conceding joint control of the Shatt al-Arab in the 1975 agreement with the Shah in Algiers and wish to return to the position held prior to that concession. Thus it may be said that the war has done nothing whatever to solve the immediate arguments between the two combatants, a fact that subsequent peace meetings simply reinforced when no agreement could be reached over questions relating to the clearing of the Shatt al-Arab. Moreover, since the agreement of 1975 was mainly brought about because of Iranian and CIA support for the Kurdish rebellion in the north of Iraq (which the Shah called off in return for the 1975 agreement), one result of the 1988 ceasefire was an immediate and savage Iraqi assault on its Kurds (see Part I, pp. 73–81).

NORTH YEMEN AND SOUTH YEMEN: BORDER WARS

Introduction

Yemen in south-west Arabia was brought under Ottoman rule in 1517 when the Turks were expanding throughout the Arab world and Middle East; Yemen, however, was on the periphery of the Ottoman Empire, and it was not until 1872 that the Ottoman Turks occupied the area fully and put their own governor over it. In 1911 the Yemenis revolted against Turkish power; as a result the Imam Yahya obtained control of the mountain region, while the Turks retained control over the coastal areas. A consequence of this deal was the willingness of the Imam Yahya to support Turkey during the First World War.

A series of regional realignments followed the end of the First World War: the Imam Yahya was opposed both to Ibn Saud, who became the King of Saudi Arabia in 1926, and to the British, who held Aden (which they had acquired in 1839) and the Aden protectorate (South Yemen). Yemeni hostility to the new Kingdom of Saudi Arabia led King Ibn Saud to invade Yemen (later the Yemen Arab Republic – YAR) in 1934 when his forces drove the Yemeni troops back to the capital, Sana. In the subsequent peace treaty agreed at Taif, King Saud took Tihama and Najran for Saudi Arabia; otherwise he withdrew from Yemen and left it to its own devices. But this Saudi incursion of 1934 left open questions about Saudi claims for the future.

Over the same period (1919 to 1934) YAR forces had occupied several border areas belonging to the Aden protectorate, but in 1934 Britain and Yemen concluded a 40-year treaty of peace and friendship. Border adjustments carried out at the time were slightly more favourable to YAR than those in existence in 1914 under nominal Turkish suzerainty. By this 1934 treaty Britain formally recognized the independence of YAR and the border dispute between the two territories was considered settled.

The old Imam Yahya was killed during an attempted coup in 1948; there was a month's interregnum when the country was ruled by Abdullah al-Wazir before the succession passed to the Imam's son, Saif al-Islam Ahmed. In 1951 YAR began to seek and obtained international aid from Britain, the USA and France; at the same time it established full diplomatic relations with Britain, the USA and Egypt.

In the period since 1945 both Yemens have had deeply troubled histories. The YAR, or North Yemen, claimed Aden and the Aden protectorate when these were still part of the British Empire, and during the 1950s, for example, Yemeni tribesmen attacked villages in the protectorate from across the YAR border. During the 1960s YAR was ravaged by a brutal civil war that also brought in outsiders, with Egypt supporting the republicans and Saudi Arabia the monarchists. At the end of the 1970s the country suffered from rebellions – first in the north (1977), then in the south (1978) – before border clashes with the People's Democratic Republic of Yemen (PDRY, South Yemen) in 1979 again developed into a full-scale war.

The Aden claim

The new Imam Ahmed reasserted the old claim for Aden. Anglo-Yemeni talks were held in London in 1950, and it was these talks which led to the establishment of diplomatic relations. At the same time the two countries agreed to set up a commission to look at existing border disputes. But the new accord soon broke down with the resumption of border incidents. YAR opposed the British plan to federate the sheikdoms and sultanates of the Aden protectorate, and the Imam now adopted a policy of bribery and infiltration among the border tribes. In 1953 YAR put forward its claim to Aden and the Aden protectorate through the United Nations. Border incidents now increased.

The border war of the 1950s

Negotiations with Britain did not lead to any agreement and so the border incidents continued. The international climate favoured YAR claims against Britain and Aden: in the first place, colonialism in all its forms was under attack, while nationalist claims were likely to receive sympathetic attention at the United Nations; in the second place, the Cold War was approaching a climax, so any regime with a grievance was assured of support from one or other side – YAR was to receive arms from Communist states, although the Arab League did no more than endorse YAR's anti-British stand.

In April 1956 YAR entered into a mutual defence pact with Egypt, Saudi Arabia and Syria, while the Arab League supported the YAR claim to the Aden protectorate as part of historic Yemen. Imam Ahmed now also turned to the USSR (with which he established diplomatic relations) and Eastern Europe for support, and in 1956 recognized Communist China as well.

The border dispute with Aden, then still a British colony, was at its height in 1956 and 1957; during the latter year Yemeni tribesmen attacked villages in the Aden protectorate. For Britain the dispute was an irritant, especially in 1957 (the year after Suez), when London was concerned to repair relations with the Arab world and when in any case internal pressures for independence were beginning to build up in Aden colony. The violence died down towards the end of 1957, but flared up again early in 1958. That year the prestige of the Egyptian President, Colonel Nasser, throughout the Arab world was probably at its greatest, and he was prepared to lend his support to any movement that opposed British 'colonialism' in the region. The Arab League denounced Britain's position in Aden colony and the protectorate.

In February 1958 a Yemeni delegation visited Cairo, where it was agreed that YAR should join the recently formed United Arab Republic (UAR) of Egypt and Syria, and this was ratified in Damascus on 8 March. Later that year (July) and again in May 1959 talks were held between YAR and Britain to resolve the dispute; no firm settlement followed, although the border incidents died down. In the meantime little was done to implement the federal union with the UAR and this was finally dissolved in December 1961.

The second border war

None of the borders between the states and sheikdoms of the southern Arabian peninsula had been adequately demarcated, so when these states became independent during the 1960s and 1970s there were many grounds for dispute. The British colony comprising Aden and the protectorate became independent in 1967 as the People's Democratic Republic of Yemen (PDRY) or South Yemen, and there were to be occasional border clashes between its forces and those of YAR. For most of the 1960s, however, YAR was too busy with its internal rebellion to pay much attention to the border dispute, although the PDRY backed the rebels in YAR. But towards the end of the 1970s the border dispute between the two countries became dangerous once more.

In October 1978 an attempted coup against President Ali Abdullah Saleh of YAR was said to have the backing of the PDRY. The result was a rapid deterioration of relations between the two countries, and on several occasions from October 1978 to January 1979 the YAR government accused the PDRY of border violations and acts of sabotage. Then in February 1979 border incidents escalated into fighting. A guerrilla group, the National Democratic Front (NDF), which was based in the PDRY, now carried out a series of raids on YAR border towns, some of which its forces held on to. On 2 March a ceasefire was arranged through the mediation efforts of Iraq, Jordan and Syria, but this soon broke down and fighting increased until the Arab League managed to intervene successfully and supervised NDF withdrawals at the end of March.

One of those sudden about-faces for which the Arab world is famous then occurred when in Kuwait, on 29 March, representatives of the two Yemens agreed to work for an eventual union. The following May the two countries agreed to set up joint economic projects and co-ordinate their development with unification as the guiding principle. Saudi Arabia, the main power of the peninsula, opposed Yemeni union, which it saw as a threat to its interests. None the less, moves towards union proceeded and in 1981 the two Yemens agreed to form a Yemen Council as a prelude to unification. This and other joint bodies were given the task of preparing for a unified state – a Yemeni Republic. But once the gestures had been made, little subsequent progress followed.

At the same time that unification talks were taking place the fighting continued, albeit spasmodically. In October 1980, for example, the PDRY increased the level of its support to the NDF. A series of guerrilla engagements against the YAR government were launched in April 1981 and culminated in some bitter fighting in August. The NDF invested the town of Ibb, which it attempted to seize, but its forces were repulsed with big losses after some heavy fighting. A ceasefire was agreed in November, and relations between the two Yemens had become sufficiently relaxed to allow President Saleh to visit Aden in December of that year for talks about the proposed unification. As a consequence a draft constitution (of 136 articles) for a united Yemen was agreed in January 1982.

Once more the NDF, which was clearly acting under PDRY instructions, broke the ceasefire and new fighting took place. In April the NDF captured the town of Juban some 10 km (6 miles) inside YAR. The next month the YAR armed forces mounted a counter-offensive, but the PDRY continued to support the NDF through the year. Further talks were held between the two countries in November 1982 when YAR pressed for the PDRY to withdraw its support from the NDF. By the end of that year it must have been clear that a merger of the two Yemens was unlikely to take place.

Costs and casualties

The costs of these border clashes are difficult to quantify. They formed the backdrop to other political manoeuvres in the region or to much more intense internal rebellions. Between 1967, when the PDRY emerged as the successor to Aden colony, and 1982, one estimate puts the loss of life in the border clashes at about 1000.

In 1979 the war was reckoned to have cost YAR a considerable loss in revenues because there was a fall-off in remittances from its citizens working in the Gulf and Saudi Arabia. In October 1981 President Saleh visited Moscow and rescheduled his country's debt of $400 million in loans for military hardware.

Results: immediate and longer term

The PDRY finally withdrew its support from the NDF in late 1982. Further unification talks were held in August 1983 in the joint Yemeni Supreme Council, but no union followed. In January 1986 a bloody coup took place in the PDRY, yet on 25 February of that year the Prime Minister,of YAR, Abdel Aziz Abdel Ghani, said his country still wished to pursue the possibility of a union. In October there were reports of border clashes, but these were denied. In July 1987 President Saleh held talks with the PDRY which aimed to achieve a more modest goal of national reconciliation between the two Yemens, but little came of the talks. Then, once more, on 4 May 1988 a unity accord was signed between the two Yemens under which they would pursue economic co-operation, abolish travel restrictions between the two countries and work to set up a joint constitution. The two Yemens united to form a single Republic of Yemen (capital Sana) on 22 May 1990. Implementation of unification (over the following 30 months) was to be overseen by a presidential council. (See also Part V, pp. 455–463).

ASIA

CHINA: ADJUSTMENT WARS IN TIBET, INDIA AND VIETNAM 1950–1989

Introduction

The triumph of the Communists under Mao Zedong in 1949 produced a strong unified China for the first time in generations, and it was inevitable that the new government would re-examine relations with its neighbours and, where necessary, insist on border adjustments. China did this in relation to Burma, India, Korea, Pakistan and Vietnam, and in the case of both India and Vietnam this led to wars, albeit on a limited scale. The case of Tibet was quite different from that of the others since China claimed suzerainty over it. However, in the course of asserting its control over Tibet, China clashed with India since the borders between the two countries had been settled during the period of British rule in India. This raised the question of 'unequal treaties' because while newly independent India was prepared to accept the borders inherited from the time of British rule, China was not. This fact produced the clash of 1962.

China and Tibet

Introduction

Tibet had been conquered in 1253 by Kublai Khan, who instituted government by the Lamas. The country was not brought under full Chinese control, however, until 1720. A Nepalese invasion of Tibet in 1792 was thought to have been instigated by the British in India; in consequence the Tibetans remained deeply suspicious of the British throughout the nineteenth century. In the second half of the nineteenth century three attempts to open up trade between British India and Tibet ended in failure. Then, in 1888, the Chinese invaded the little kingdom of Sikkim on the north-east border of India, leading Britain to send an expedition to drive them out. An Anglo-Chinese Treaty of 1893 was concluded without consulting the Lamas, so producing further Anglo-Tibetan antagonisms. At the beginning of the twentieth century the British Viceroy in India, Lord Curzon, sent Colonel F. E. Younghusband to attempt to negotiate a peace with Tibet, but when this failed Younghusband went back (1903) with a military expedition to Lhasa, which he only reached in August 1904 after tough fighting. The Dalai Lama fled. The subsequent treaty dictated by the British forbade further Tibetan incursions into Sikkim, established a number of British trading rights in Tibet and forbade

Tibet to give trading or other concessions to any other power. In 1906, however, an Anglo-Russian Treaty recognized Chinese suzerainty over Tibet, and in 1908 the Dalai Lama was reinstated by Chinese authority, thus emphasizing China's position. He was deposed in 1910 and fled to India.

Following the Chinese revolution of 1911, China agreed (1912) to leave Tibet and the Dalai Lama again returned. Later that same year, however, China sent an army to reconquer Tibet; this withdrew under pressure from Britain. Britain then called a conference at Simla in northern India (1913–14) between the three interested parties – Britain, China and Tibet – which produced a convention that recognized Tibetan autonomy. Tibet was divided into an inner and an outer zone, with China excluded from interfering in the administration of the outer zone. Britain recognized that Tibet was a part of Chinese territory and China agreed not to turn the territory into a province. Subsequently, however, China refused to ratify the convention.

Sir Henry McMahon was the leader of the British delegation at Simla. In an attempt to resolve border problems he appended a letter to the convention in which he defined the border between British India and Tibet as the watershed of the Himalayas in a line approximately 160 km (100 miles) north of the Assam plains in what were then known as the North East Frontier Agency (NEFA) territories. The proposed border became known as the McMahon Line. There has been controversy about this line ever since 1914, and about whether or not McMahon had any authority to make such a demarcation.

When Tibet allowed a commission from China into the country in 1939 (it remained in Tibet thereafter), this amounted to an admission of some form of Chinese suzerainty. During the final years of its rule in India (between 1944 and 1947) Britain extended control up to the McMahon Line (something it had not previously done), only to discover that people in the areas it now took under its control were paying taxes to Tibet. Thus, when the Chinese decided to reassert their authority over Tibet in 1950, there were numerous precedents to support their claims and a number of dubious border claims to be settled as well.

Reassertion of control 1950

Following the triumph of Mao Zedong and the establishment of the People's Republic of China in 1949, Beijing sent an army from Sichuan to reconquer Tibet (1950). They invaded eastern Tibet, overwhelming the ill-equipped Tibetan forces opposed to them, but then halted on the border of western or outer Tibet. Tibet appealed to the UN, India and Britain for help, but none was forthcoming. So in 1951 a Tibetan delegation led by the Panchen Lama journeyed to Beijing where it pledged loyalty to the new China. Tibet was made into an autonomous region (May 1951), but China was to control defence and foreign policy.

In 1954 the Dalai Lama and the Panchen Lama went to Beijing as representatives to the National People's Congress and were elected vice-chairmen of the Congress. This might be taken to have sealed the new relationship between Tibet and China. At that time the Tibetan leaders had little option since 1954 was the year when India and China agreed a treaty over the status of Tibet under which India recognized China's control of the territory. That was the high point of Chinese–Indian relations when the two countries enunciated the Five Principles of

Peaceful Co-existence or the Panchsila: 'The principles and considerations which govern our mutual relations and the approach of the two countries to each other are as follows: (1) mutual respect for each other's territorial integrity and sovereignty; (2) mutual non-aggression; (3) mutual non-interference in each other's internal affairs; (4) equality and mutual benefit; and (5) peaceful co-existence.'

In 1956 the Dalai Lama and the Panchen Lama toured India on a goodwill visit. There was an ambiguity about their stance, and clearly they wished to ensure good relations with their other great neighbour, India, in case of possible problems with China in the future. Indeed, resentment against China grew during the 1950s: there was an influx of Chinese soldiers and civilians into Tibet and, following a revolt against Chinese authority in upper Chiang Jiang (Yangtze) valley in 1956, a number of refugees fled into Tibet to augment anti-Chinese sentiments.

The 1959 uprising against China

Towards the end of the 1950s China began to tighten its grip on Tibet. In the capital, Lhasa, simmering discontents exploded in March 1959 into a full-scale uprising against Chinese occupation. The Chinese military invited the Dalai Lama to attend a theatre performance in their headquarters on 10 March 1959. A trap was feared and the inner cabinet advised the Dalai Lama to escape. With most of his ministers and about 1000 followers he fled the capital and crossed the border to seek refuge in India. Two days later the Chinese shelled the Dalai Lama's summer residence, the Norbulingka, sparking off a general panic. Fighting lasted for 10 days and an estimated 40,000 Tibetans were killed. A further 87,000 were killed in central Tibet during the course of the year. Some escaped to southern Tibet, but by the end of 1960 the whole of Tibet was under Chinese military control.

In 1965 China 'absorbed' Tibet, depriving it of its special autonomous status. During 1966 and 1967 Tibet suffered from the excesses of the Red Guard and then of the Cultural Revolution, and full Chinese military control was not reasserted again until 1969. Tibetan guerrillas fought the Chinese throughout the 1960s; they were supplied by the CIA and some of their leaders were trained in Colorado (USA), until 1971 when US support was withdrawn on the eve of President Nixon's visit to China. During this period (the 1960s) foreigners were excluded from Tibet.

The Tibet rebellion of 1989: 30 years on

Riots in September 1987 marked an increase in anti-Chinese unrest in Tibet, with a new generation of young Tibetans ready to revolt at Chinese rule and the restrictions which it placed on them. By 1989 there were approximately 115,000 Tibetans in exile who did not accept Chinese occupation of their country. These exiles demonstrated their anger following the 1988 visit to China by India's Prime Minister, Rajiv Gandhi, during which he assured his hosts that India regarded Tibet as an autonomous region of China and would not permit anti-Chinese activity by Tibetans then living in India. Still in exile in India, the Dalai Lama argued for self-rule, although accepting that China should continue to be responsible for foreign affairs and defence; when this concessionary statement was rejected by China, younger radicals reacted by denouncing the Dalai Lama's position as too compromising.

Chinese policy at the time of the Cultural Revolution had been to destroy all vestiges of religion. Later, the policy was partly reversed as a mistake, but the reversal did not end the bitter anti-Chinese sentiments and these culminated in a number of riots in the 18 months before the March 1989 anniversary. The death in January 1989 of the Panchen Lama, who had collaborated with the Chinese and condemned separatism, deprived the Chinese of their principal Tibetan ally.

At the approach of 10 March, 1989 (the thirtieth anniversary of the 1959 uprising that had driven the Dalai Lama into exile), demonstrations in Lhasa led to some of the worst bloodshed in 30 years when the Chinese police opened fire and killed at least 30 – and possibly many more – protesters. The Chinese then decided to expel foreigners from Tibet and restrict communications with the region. They claimed that 'the separatist clique based abroad' was responsible for fomenting the troubles. From Dharamsala in India the Dalai Lama then issued a statement in which he voiced his fear that the Chinese would turn Lhasa into a slaughterhouse: 'Now no foreigners. That means no witnesses, so the Chinese now feel completely free to do whatever they want.'

Three days before 10 March (and following three successive days of rioting) 2000 Chinese troops were moved into the centre of Lhasa following the declaration of martial law. By then Tibetan estimates suggested that 100 had been killed. The Chinese had abandoned the pretext that the troubles were only stirred up by a handful of troublemakers and admitted that the security forces had to shoot as the only means of stopping the rioters. Then all non-resident foreigners were ordered out of the area as part of the martial law restrictions; it was largely their accounts which had kept the outside world informed of what was happening. Both the USA and Britain registered strong protests at Chinese repression.

In the course of the 1989 uprising it became clear that the younger Tibetans had rejected the Dalai Lama's policy of passive resistance, and China found itself facing an 'occupied territory' situation. But at the same time there was little evidence of any organization or training: most of the resistance was spontaneous and apparently unplanned. China denounced what it described as foreign interference in its affairs, but at the same time said it was prepared to negotiate with the Dalai Lama about his return to Tibet provided he renounced any talk of independence. At the end of March the Chinese general responsible for martial law in Lhasa, General Zhang Shaosong, warned of growing anti-Chinese feelings in Tibet and admitted that more than 600 members of the Chinese security forces had been killed or wounded in the region over the preceding eighteen months.

China and India

Introduction

The Bandung Conference of 1955 was dominated by the figures of Zhou Enlai for China and Pandit Nehru for India; the conference was deeply concerned with the issue of non-alignment and whether or not peaceful co-existence with Communist

China was possible and practicable. But it must also have been apparent to any discerning observer that future rivalry for influence between the two giants of Asia – China and India – was an emerging possibility. Nehru had shown real sympathy for the new China during the 1950s until, at the end of the decade, China made plain its repudiation of a number of existing boundaries, including those between Tibet and India which had been determined in colonial times. Beijing considered these to have been imposed upon it by 'unequal treaties'.

When in March 1959 the Dalai Lama fled into India with a number of his followers, his presence in the Himalayan border town of Dharamsala alone was enough to cause tension between the two countries. China accused India of interfering in its internal affairs. It then took the opportunity to suggest that the two powers should review their joint frontiers. The immediate Indian reaction was to assert the validity of the McMahon Line and to claim that, at the time the line was fixed, Tibet had had the right to enter into an agreement or treaty.

In August 1959, in what turned out to be a prelude to 1962, a Chinese force occupied the Indian frontier post at Lonju and expelled its garrison. Between that incident and the war of 1962 Nehru and Zhou Enlai were to hold bilateral talks about their frontier, but these always foundered on the Indian insistence on the validity of the McMahon Line. In an astute move which bolstered its later claims China (1959 and 1960) did succeed in peacefully settling border disputes with Burma and Pakistan in a way that altered borders which had formerly been defined by the British. India was particularly angered at the settlement with Pakistan, which accepted its occupation of part of Kashmir. When the Chinese, whose occupation of Tibet (now Xizang) had brought them up to the Indian border, again proposed negotiations to settle the joint boundary India once more insisted that the McMahon Line was the only valid border. The result was an escalation of border hostility. In 1960 China repudiated the India–Tibet boundaries as imposed by Britain, and a number of border clashes followed.

The 1962 Chinese 'invasion' of northern India

In the autumn of 1962 India ordered its forces to occupy a number of forward areas along the McMahon Line, and Indian troops attempted to drive the Chinese out of positions which India claimed to be part of its territory. Clashes occurred on 20 September and again on 10 October near the meeting place of the Tibet–Bhutan–India border, and there were some casualties on both sides. Then the Chinese retaliated with a major offensive (at least in the sense of moving substantial forces forward into Indian territory) when on 20 October they advanced into both Ladakh and the NEFA territories. The Chinese advanced as much as 160 km (100 miles) south of the McMahon Line. In Ladakh they overran a series of India army posts; farther east they occupied Tawang, so the plains of Assam lay open to them.

It appeared that the two Asian giants were on the verge of a full-scale war. The immediate effect was a humiliation for Nehru. In the first place, it did not appear as though the Indian army was strong enough to prevent a Chinese advance into India; in the second place, Nehru had made a point of defending the Chinese revolution during the 1950s, and the necessity to go to war was the reverse of everything for which, supposedly, he stood.

Nehru appealed urgently to Britain, the Commonwealth, the USA and the USSR to support India in its confrontation with China. Britain rushed guns to India; the USA sent bombers. Then, as suddenly as they had come, the Chinese withdrew. On 7 November they announced that they would withdraw their forces in the north-east to the lines they had held prior to their advance of 20 October. At the same time they insisted that India should observe a neutral buffer zone. The Chinese, however, did not withdrdaw from the positions they had taken in Ladakh, where they held on to the border road.

Six non-aligned nations – Burma, Cambodia, Ceylon (Sri Lanka), Ghana, Indonesia and the UAR – led by the Prime Minister of Ceylon, Mrs Sirimavo Bandaranaike, attempted to mediate between the two powers. A meeting was held in Colombo, Ceylon, from 10 to 12 December 1962. Both China and India accepted its proposals, but since subsequently each placed its own, different interpretation on the proposals no progress was achieved, with the result that suspicions between the two countries were to continue unallayed.

China did not relinquish the areas which it retained in November 1962, and occasional border incidents were to occur periodically in subsequent years (the most recent in 1986). None of these has been serious, but the quarrel remains unresolved.

At the time of the war – 1962 – China was almost totally isolated. The Soviet Union had recently withdrawn its aid and the quarrel between the two had come out into the open, leaving China without friends either inside the Communist camp or outside it. And so, although the clash with India was ostensibly about border adjustments, it was in fact about a great deal more. By humiliating India militarily, China served notice on Asia that, of the two, China had to be reckoned with as the more powerful and influential. It was a crude display of power, but it undoubtedly had an effect. Beijing had made it plain that China was not to be overlooked or ignored.

China and Vietnam

Introduction

China's support for the Viet Cong and the north during the long struggle of the Vietnam War was partly ideological; still more was it dictated by China's fear of American power and its determination to see an end to American intervention on its doorstep. But when the war came to an end, long-held suspicions on both sides threatened the wartime alliance of expediency. China's new fear was encirclement by the USSR – at the time the quarrel between the two Communist giants was very bitter – while Vietnam, in its turn, shifted away from dependence on China towards the USSR.

Vietnam was now set on a course of intervention in Kampuchea (Cambodia) against the Pol Pot government. It was supported in this by the USSR, while China supported Pol Pot. Chinese fears were enhanced because of the build-up of Soviet troops along their joint borders, and China suspected that Vietnam was aiming to establish hegemony over the whole Indo-Chinese peninsula, perhaps by fostering federal links with Laos and Kampuchea. Such a development would create a powerful state on China's southern border, a possibility which Beijing regarded with hostility. If, in addition, such a Vietnamese-dominated combination were to be backed by the USSR, it would be downright dangerous.

There were other reasons for concern in Beijing. The Vietnamese shift towards the Soviet camp which began in 1977 had several causes, including disagreements over the long Sino-Vietnamese border and the deterioriating position of the considerable Chinese community in South Vietnam, which now found itself adversely affected by the socialist measures introduced by the new Communist government. The Chinese were no longer allowed to carry on private trading and lost their shops. The result was a major exodus, with an estimated 160,000 Chinese fleeing from Vietnam to China before Beijing closed the border.

When, in June 1978, Vietnam became a full member of the Soviet-dominated Council for Mutual Economic Assistance (CMEA) this was seen by China as a repudiation of Chinese friendship, although already that May the Chinese had begun to withdraw their aid technicians from Vietnam (the process was completed in July) and to close down their development projects. In December 1978, when the Vietnamese invaded Kampuchea to oust the Pol Pot government and replace it with a pro-Vietnamese one under Heng Sampin, the two countries – China and Vietnam – became totally estranged. Essentially China supported the Pol Pot regime in Kampuchea because it was opposed to Vietnam, and Beijing wished to prevent Vietnam becoming over-powerful in the region.

The border war of 1979

Vietnam invaded Kampuchea on 25 December 1978. Two weeks later – 8 January – it had driven the Pol Pot government out of Phnom Penh and replaced it with a pro-Vietnamese regime. Relations with China promptly collapsed, and then, during January and February, the Chinese launched a series of cross-border attacks before their troops invaded Vietnam along the whole frontier on 17 February. There was a fortnight of heavy fighting, and while the Chinese forces did not acquit themselves particularly well, they did capture Lang Son 18 km (11 miles) inside Vietnam. Prior to this full-scale invasion the Vietnamese Foreign Ministry had claimed that there had been 583 armed incursions by the Chinese in 1978 and a further 240 in the first six weeks of 1979, which resulted in 40 deaths and several hundred wounded.

On 1 March 1979 the Chinese halted their attack and proposed negotiations. Vietnam refused any meetings until the Chinese had withdrawn behind the border; this China claimed to have done by 16 March, although the Vietnamese insisted that the Chinese were still in a number of positions in their territory as late as 27 March. Negotiations began on 18 April and were to continue for two years without results. Chinese tactics – a cross-border invasion in force and a limited advance, followed by a call for negotiations and withdrawal – were similar to those it had followed with India in 1962 (see above).

From 1979 through the 1980s the border was to remain 'active'. Vietnam claimed that there were many Chinese incursions in 1980, while other incidents – some of battle proportions – were to take place during the rest of the decade as long as the Vietnamese were in Kampuchea (see pp. 262–273).

The 1980s: border hostilities

China and Vietnam were to accuse one another of border violations throughout 1980: that September, for example, China claimed that Vietnamese incursions had become so serious that it was not possible to resume the peace talks which had been broken off in March. China insisted on linking talks about their border dispute with the Vietnam invasion of Kampuchea, but Vietnam refused to discuss this. Chinese policy during 1981 was designed to keep up pressures the length of the border with Vietnam so as to stretch Vietnamese resources to the maximum and take some of the pressure off the Pol Pot guerrillas; this was achieved by frequent border incidents all year.

In heavy fighting during a Vietnamese incursion of May 1981 an estimated 150 Vietnamese were killed, while China evacuated civilians from the border area. There were further substantial clashes in June and August, and it was China's turn to protest at incursions. Half-way through the year Vietnam reduced its armed forces in Kampuchea from 200,000 to 170,000 in order to reinforce its northern border with China.

In April 1983 China carried out a series of heavy artillery bombardments across the border, the most dangerous escalation of the war in two years, and that July Vietnam accused China of stepping up border activities. In April 1984, after Vietnamese forces had pursued Khmer Rouge guerrillas into Thailand, China launched a series of raids across the border. There was a fall-off in border activity during 1985, and Vietnam then said it would attach no preconditions to talks with China about normalizing their relations; China insisted that first Vietnam had to withdraw from Kampuchea, a condition which it reiterated through to 1987.

By the end of the decade Sino-Soviet tensions were gradually lessening as a result of the Soviet Union's policy of *glasnost*, so a *rapprochement* between the two powers at last appeared to be a real possibility. At the same time Vietnam had finally decided to withdraw from Kampuchea. In this way the two principal Chinese fears – encirclement by the USSR and a Vietnamese-dominated Indo-Chinese peninsula – were both receding.

Results

By 1989 Vietnam had become heavily dependent on the USSR just when Moscow was changing its policies and seeking general *détente*; China, on the other hand, had built up its relations with Thailand and to some extent with the Association of South East Asian Nations (ASEAN) as well, a reversal of the situation at the beginning of the decade.

Although there was a good deal of military activity across the border during the 10 years 1979–89, the level of casualties is hard to gauge with any accuracy. Following a Chinese offensive in 1984, for example, the Vietnamese claimed there had been 100 Chinese casualties – killed or wounded. Then in January 1987, after a Chinese attack on the Vietnamese position at Ha Tuyen, the Vietnamese claimed to have killed 1500 Chinese; the Chinese, on the other hand, claimed to have killed 500 Vietnamese while only losing a few dozen of their own men.

By late 1989, following the Vietnamese withdrawal from Kampuchea, a settlement between China and Vietnam appeared as a genuine possibility for the early 1990s.

INDIA–PAKISTAN: WARS 1948, 1965 AND 1971

Introduction

The state of Pakistan came into being as a result of the break-up of the British Indian Empire, and the partition, which led to half a million deaths (see Part V, pp. 485–491), was deeply resented by Indians of all parties. The principal reason for a separate state was religious: Pakistan was to be a home for the Muslims of the Indian subcontinent. In itself this aim hardly made geopolitical sense since the two major centres of Muslim population – the north-west of India centred on the Punjab, and Bengal in the east – were separated from each other by 1770 km (1100 miles) of Hindu-dominated India. Thus from its birth in 1947 Pakistan was in a weak position with regard to its far more powerful neighbour, and this fact coloured all its subsequent foreign policy decisions. One result was the suspicion and fear that over the years led to three wars between the two powers: in 1948 over Kashmir; in 1965 over the disputed area of the Rann of Kutch as well as Kashmir; and in 1971 (perhaps the war which ought most obviously to have been foreseen) over the secession of East Pakistan to form the new state of Bangladesh.

When, on 15 August 1947, the two independent successor states to British India emerged, both faced the immediate problem of incorporating the 500 princely states scattered throughout the subcontinent. It had been decided that these could join either India or Pakistan according to the choice of their rulers, provided that their boundaries matched those of the partition boundaries as these had already been agreed.

The war of 1948

The British created the state of Jammu and Kashmir (generally referred to simply as Kashmir) in 1846 during a period of major imperial expansion. Its rulers were Hindu, but a majority of its people were Muslim (although in Jammu a majority were Hindus and Sikhs). At independence a majority of all the people were Muslim, but according to the agreed formula it was up to the ruler, the Hindu Maharajah, to decide whether he should join India or Pakistan. He asked the two countries for a standstill arrangement to allow him to decide. This was granted, but during September tribesmen from neighbouring areas of Pakistan infiltrated into Kashmir and Pakistan exerted pressure by a partial blockade. By 22 October the tribesmen were advancing on the capital, Srinagar, and this forced the Maharajah to make a decision. He appealed to India for help and, after he had agreed to accede to the Union of India, troops were airlifted from Delhi to Srinagar on 27 October and the tribesmen were turned back from the capital. Fighting continued to the end of the year, and although the Indian forces succeeded in driving the tribesmen out of the Kashmir valley during November 1947, the

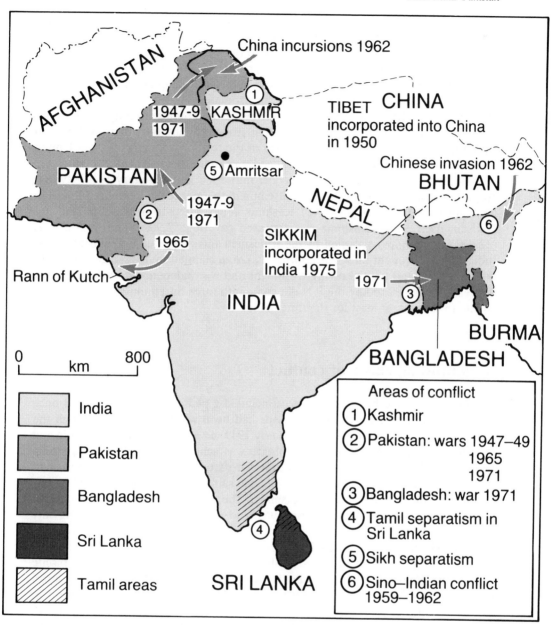

Map 13   India and its neighbours

tribesmen then opened a second front in the south-west of Kashmir, where heavy fighting was to continue until March 1948.

In January 1948 India took the problem to the United Nations, where it accused Pakistan of assisting the tribesmen. Although at first this had been denied, Pakistan later admitted that its regular troops were involved in helping them. At the UN India complained that, in addition to an estimated 50,000 tribesmen who had already invaded Kashmir, a further 100,000 were undergoing training in Pakistan.

In May 1948 Pakistan committed regular troops to Kashmir; then in August a fresh offensive was launched in the north of the territory. Meanwhile, the United Nations Commission on Kashmir arranged a ceasefire between the two sides (13 August 1948), although this did not come into effect until January 1949. By that August, when the United Nations attempted to impose its ceasefire, Pakistan maintained that only Azad (free) Kashmir could agree to a ceasefire and not Pakistan itself. Azad Kashmir was the area covering 82,900 square kilometres (32,000 square miles) occupied by the tribesmen and supported by Pakistan which India had not brought under its control. Pakistan claimed that Azad Kashmir was not a province but had its own government and was independent. None the less, the ceasefire sponsored by the UN did come into force on 1 January 1949 to bring an end to the war, at least for the time being.

A continuing cause of conflict

The original United Nations proposals included a plebiscite for all Kashmir once the Pakistani and then the Indian troops had been withdrawn, but although the ceasefire had come into effect on 1 January 1949, no agreement between India and Pakistan as to withdrawal and a plebiscite was achieved through to 1952. India maintained that Pakistan had not withdrawn its troops and, indeed, that it had reinforced them. On the other hand, Pakistan said that no plebiscite would be fair as long as India had troops in Kashmir. The two countries attempted direct negotiations over the issue during 1953 and 1954, but without reaching any agreement. In 1953, meanwhile, India imprisoned Sheik Mohammed Abdullah, the man Delhi had appointed Prime Minister of Kashmir, for by then he was opposing full integration in India. Delhi now abandoned the idea of a plebiscite and the two countries – India and Pakistan – in effect settled down to keep control of their respective parts of Kashmir. United Nations attempts at mediation in 1957, 1962 and 1963 proved abortive. In 1963 India declared that the parts of Jammu–Kashmir which it controlled were a state of India.

The war of 1965

Boundaries between India and Pakistan in the area of the Rann of Kutch were ill-defined, and in April 1965 a number of border skirmishes occurred between Indian and Pakistani troops. Pakistan got the better of the exchanges (Britain's Prime Minister, Harold Wilson, suggested arbitration), which encouraged it to exert greater pressures in Kashmir. India's Prime Minister, Pandit Nehru, had died the previous year and India was now ruled by Lal Bahadur Shastri. Pakistan's Foreign

Minister, Zulfikar Ali Bhutto, decided to take advantage of an India weakened by the loss of its first great independence leader and raised the Kashmir question once more. Pakistani forces were infiltrated into the Indian part of Kashmir in order to launch a new guerrilla offensive and bring the United Nations once more into a mediating role. But the guerrilla offensive failed to take off, and India retaliated with actions against Pakistani positions along the 1949 ceasefire line. Pakistan then mobilized an armoured force to cut Indian communications in Kashmir, and in order to force the Pakistanis to call off their actions in Kashmir India launched a three-pronged attack across the Pakistan border into Lahore on 6 September. China came to Pakistan's relief by creating incidents along the Sikkim border, thus threatening India with a possible repeat of the 1962 invasion (see above, pp. 250–251). Big power pressures were then exerted and India and Pakistan were persuaded to agree a ceasefire on 22 September. In the subsequent debate at the United Nations India discovered itself to be relatively isolated, with most Muslim states as well as other non-aligned nations siding with Pakistan.

The USSR now acted as the principal peacebroker, and President Ayub Khan of Pakistan and Prime Minister Shastri of India agreed to meet under Soviet auspices at Tashkent in January 1966 with Soviet Premier Aleksei Kosygin in the chair. After arduous negotiations the Russians persuaded the two sides to agree a peace which in fact was no more than a return to the status quo which had existed prior to the hostilities of the previous year. Unexpectedly, Shastri died while still in Tashkent.

No solution

Nothing had been resolved by the war of 1965, and further clashes over Kashmir were to take place periodically thereafter. The next war between the two countries came in 1971 over the formation of Bangladesh (see below), but apart from that Kashmir continued as a source of potential conflict between the two countries.

The war of 1971: the creation of Bangladesh

The next major Indo-Pakistani crisis came in 1971 when the Pakistan government in West Pakistan (where the power lay) decided to use the army to prevent a breakaway by East Pakistan (see Part V, pp. 465–468). India had to handle an estimated 7 million refugees who flooded into West Bengal from East Pakistan. It was in India's interest to weaken Pakistan, and the crisis in East Pakistan gave it the opportunity to do so. India acted with great skill and carefully prepared the way for intervention.

First, India appealed to the international community for assistance in dealing with the huge influx of refugees, and in the process was able to publicize its own humanity and suggest that the fault lay with the policies pursued by Pakistan. Second – a crucial precaution before becoming embroiled in any major war with Pakistan – India secured its rear. On 21 August 1971 India entered into a treaty with the USSR 'in support of non-alignment', in which each state promised to help the other (short of military intervention) if either were to be attacked by a third party. Third, after having ensured benevolent neutrality from the USSR, India first sheltered and trained Bangladeshi guerrillas, then gave them arms and supported them back in East Pakistan in their struggle against the Pakistan army.

Indian support for the secessionists in East Pakistan was a crucial factor in their struggle for independence and led to full-scale war with Pakistan. This was launched by Pakistan on 6 December 1971. In the west the Pakistanis raided Indian airfields in the hope of neutralizing their airpower. The war lasted a mere 12 days. In the west Pakistan held its own, but in the east India defeated the Pakistani army in a lightning campaign. A ceasefire was agreed on 17 December 1971, and the ceasefire line was subsequently endorsed at Simla in India the following June by Prime Minister Indira Gandhi of India and President Zulfikar Ali Bhutto of Pakistan.

Results

This third Indo-Pakistani war was the most momentous in its results. It led to the creation of a new state, Bangladesh. It halved Pakistani power on the subcontinent and left India in an even more dominant position than it had been up until that time. And finally, perhaps, it established the most likely – and enduring – pattern for the subcontinent in the post-imperial age, though only time will show whether that judgment is correct.

The Commonwealth

When Britain relinquished its imperial position in India both the successor states – India and Pakistan – became members of the Commonwealth, while the formula worked out in 1949, which recognized the British monarch as head of the association but not necessarily as monarch of its individual member states, enabled republican India to remain in the Commonwealth. Pakistan left the Commonwealth in 1972 when Britain and other members recognized the new state of Bangladesh. Although General Zia attempted to rejoin the association, Pakistan was to remain outside for 17 years until it finally rejoined in 1989 under Prime Minister Benazir Bhutto. It was generally felt that India acted as the main obstacle to Pakistan rejoining, but during the second half of the 1980s Prime Minister Rajiv Gandhi embarked on a policy of reconciliation with his neighbours and in particular Pakistan. In 1988 he visited the Pakistani capital, Islamabad, for a meeting of the South Asian Association for Regional Co-operation (SAARC) and used the occasion to encourage reconciliation between his country and Pakistan. In any case Pakistan's first woman Prime Minister, Benazir Bhutto, who took office in 1988, faced more than enough political problems and so was anxious to take her country back into the Commonwealth: having recognized Bangladesh and achieved a level of reconciliation with India, the way was clear for a Pakistani application to rejoin. This was accepted without opposition at the 1989 Kuala Lumpur Commonwealth heads of government meeting, allowing Pakistan to rejoin the Commonwealth and, hopefully, heralding a period of better India–Pakistan relations.

Kashmir 1990

Pakistan was to raise the Kashmir issue in 1980 and 1981 at meetings of the Islamic Conference. Then, in February 1987, India was forced to evacuate 100 villages along the joint India–Pakistan Kashmir border following shelling by the Pakistani army. The degree of tension and the military costs involved can be gauged from the fact that after the shelling episode of 1987, when the two countries agreed to withdraw their troops from the border area in stages, this involved an initial 50,000 men on either side.

Then, just as India and Pakistan appeared to be nearing a *rapprochement* after 40 years of tensions, a wave of anti-Indian agitation among Kashmir's Muslim militants threatened to destroy the progress achieved, forcing India to rush thousands of extra troops to Srinagar in January 1990 to face extremists demanding separation from India. Demonstrations lasted through January and February, and militants called on Pakistan's Prime Minister, Bhutto, to provide arms for 100,000 Kashmiri commandos so that they could bring about an independent Kashmir. In March, Prime Minister Bhutto said that India should allow Kashmiris to decide their own future by plebiscite. By mid-April, as tension steadily increased, India brought the number of its troops in Kashmir up to 200,000. Following Indian attempts to seal the border between Indian- and Pakistan-held Kashmir, about 5000 refugees crossed into Azad Kashmir where they demanded arms. By May there were growing fears in Pakistan that India might order a pre-emptive military strike against refugee camps in Azad Kashmir, and by mid-1990 the situation was so explosive that it seemed at least possible that militant Muslim demands for an independent Kashmir could spark off another India–Pakistan war.

INDONESIA: CONFRONTATION WITH MALAYSIA 1963–1966

Origins

Confrontation between Indonesia led by Ahmed Sukarno and Malaysia under Tunku Abdul Rahman supported by Britain has to be seen in the context both of the Cold War, at its height in the 1960s, and of Indonesian nationalism. Between 1957 and 1965 Sukarno was at the height of his power and influence. He maintained a balance between the Indonesian army and the Partai Komunis Indonesia (PKI), which were then the two main centres of power in the country. This was the period of so-called 'Guided Democracy'.

In 1961 Malaya's Prime Minister, Tunku Abdul Rahman, put forward the idea of a federation to cover Malaya and Singapore and the British Borneo territories of Brunei, North Borneo (later Sabah) and Sarawak. In part the object was to incorporate Singapore in a wider political grouping in order to forestall an extreme left-wing government from taking over in that territory. Although at first Sukarno appeared to be indifferent to the idea of the Federation of Malaysia, he later changed his mind: this was partly a response to the unsuccessful rebellion in Brunei at the end of 1962 when the Party Ra'ayat under Azahari (see Part I, pp. 90–93) revolted against the oil-rich government of the Sultan. Brunei in any case had refused to join the proposed federation. Azahari fled first to Manila, but later went on to Jakarta, the Indonesian capital, where he proclaimed a government-in-exile for North Kalimantan (to incorporate Brunei and parts of Sarawak that had been taken from the Sultan during the nineteenth century by the White Rajahs of Sarawak). The PKI supported Azahari and his Party Ra'ayat and called on the government of Sukarno to support the rebels.

Sukarno now changed his position and denounced the proposed federation as a neo-colonialist plot designed to perpetuate Western (British) influence in the area. The British, for their part, lent a certain credence to such an accusation by the way in which they speeded up the process of 'persuading' their colonies of Sarawak and North Borneo to join the federation. They did not hold plebiscites among the people of these colonies, who would probably have opted for full independence had they had the chance to do so.

Sukarno decided to oppose the Federation of Malaysia on three broad grounds: first, that rebels in Sulawesi and Sumatra had received aid from Malaya and Singapore; second, though this was not stated, that the economic achievements of Malaya and Singapore far outstripped the economic performance of Indonesia at that time; and third, that the federation was a British neo-colonial creation designed to prolong British influence in the area. This last reason fitted in well with Indonesia's stand as a non-aligned country.

The PKI was most insistent in pushing for confrontation and demanded all-out war against Malaya and Singapore, which the PKI described as stooges of Western (British) colonialism. And so, in order to prevent the territories of British Borneo – Sabah and Sarawak – from joining the Federation of Malaysia, Sukarno launched an aggressive policy of confrontation (*konfrontasi*). Confrontation as seen in Jakarta represented opposition to neo-colonialism; there was at least some justification for this deriving from the manner in which Britain had pressed its Borneo colonies to join the federation and its prompt military response to the 1962 uprising in Brunei.

Outbreak and response

Malaysia came into being in September 1963, and in response Sukarno increased his 'Crush Malaysia Campaign'. In Jakarta, meanwhile, the PKI organized a mob which attacked and burned the British Embassy, while other mobs were organized to sack or take over British firms and estates. At the United Nations, however, Indonesia (which up to that time had been treated as a favoured member for its role in the struggle for independence) found its policy of confrontation condemned; in November 1964, moreover, Malaysia was admitted to the world body and in angry reaction Indonesia cancelled its membership.

Once the Federation of Malaysia had been proclaimed, Sukarno ordered all-out confrontation; yet at the same time he insisted that what was occurring was a revolt by Malays against the policy of Tunku Abdul Rahman and not an Indonesian intervention.

Confrontation led Sukarno into closer contact with Communist China, which was one of the few countries to support his policy. In November 1964 Sukarno went to Beijing to confer with Zhou Enlai; probably it was this growing liaison with China and the apparent dependence on Chinese aid that led to the downfall of both Sukarno and the PKI in 1965. In the early stages of confrontation Dipa Nusantara Aidit, the PKI chairman, called for the creation of an army of workers and peasants, a liberation force which, apparently, was to help in the Crush Malaysia Campaign. But this was seen by the Indonesian army as a direct threat to its own position. Although the army mounted a military campaign against Malaysia, its operations were largely token because in reality the High Command was waiting to cope with the domestic explosion which it rightly saw to be coming.

Both confrontation and the takeover of Western businesses in Indonesia at that time were, as much as anything else, a working out of nationalism during a period when most states in the region, including Indonesia itself, had only recently achieved independence and were still deeply suspicious of Western motives.

Course of the struggle

Only Communist China, then at its most isolated, backed the Indonesian policy of confrontation; as a result, relations between Beijing and Jakarta became very close, which ultimately ensured the downfall of both Sukarno and the PKI. The Indonesian army was in any case wary of the Crush Malaysia Campaign and did not wish to become over-involved in it, especially as it was increasingly doubtful of the policies which Sukarno was following. Confrontation was often as much political rhetoric as it was military action, and the Crush Malaysia Campaign became a military and diplomatic stalemate which did nothing for Indonesia's international standing, although it was threat enough to its small neighbours, Sabah and Sarawak.

Volunteers (often Communist) from Indonesia made forays across the border into Sarawak. They were met on the other side by the deployment of British and Commonwealth troops in support of Malaysian forces, and although the Indonesian army was only lukewarm about confrontation, the guerrilla war none the less rapidly expanded. The British and Commonwealth forces (many of them Gurkhas) were already highly experienced in guerrilla warfare from the long jungle campaign against the Communists in Malaya and, though only a relatively small force, proved more than a match for their far more numerous Indonesian opponents.

On the international stage – at the United Nations, for example – Indonesia found itself largely outmanoeuvred and obtained support only from the Communist powers. China, however, supplied military equipment and indicated that it might come to Indonesia's assistance should the latter be attacked by Britain. Indonesian raiding parties attacked the Malay peninsula, and Indonesian skirmishers became active across the border into Sabah, where they were opposed by British and Australian troops. The long Sarawak border with the Indonesian province of Kalimantan was patrolled by British troops. On the whole the Indonesian regular forces, despite being well armed, largely with Chinese and Soviet equipment, seemed reluctant to engage the British and Commonwealth forces that had been deployed in Malaysia. Operations launched against the peninsula ended in failure and surrender.

At one stage in the war Sukarno called for 20 million volunteers to liquidate the Tunku's 'puppet state', but Malaysia stood firm in the face of apparently far greater force and its government ruled out any talks with Indonesia until confrontation had been brought to an end. At the annual Independence Day ceremony of 17 August 1965, Sukarno referred to the idea that had been put forward earlier by Aidit, the chairman of the PKI, that an army of workers and peasants should be raised to fight Malaysia. That September he sent a secret mission to Beijing to discuss the supply of 100,000 small arms, apparently for use by the army of workers and peasants in its confrontation with Malaysia. It was at this point that the Indonesian army – or a part of it – took a hand and mounted the coup attempt of 30 September 1965. Although this was unsuccessful – Sukarno remained head of state – his power was shorn and the policy of confrontation was effectively abandoned, although it was not officially ended until August 1966.

Estimated costs and casualties

At the peak of confrontation Britain had 17,000 servicemen deployed in Borneo. British and Commonwealth casualties came to 114 killed and 181 wounded (many of these were from the Gurkha battalions), while civilian casualties among the local people came to 36 killed, 53 wounded and four taken prisoner. Indonesian casualties were an estimated 590 killed, 222 wounded and 771 captured.

Results: immediate and longer term

The army used the abortive coup attempt of September 1965 as an excuse to destroy the Communists, who were massacred in tens of thousands (no accurate figures have ever been given for these massacres, but the numbers killed may have exceeded a million), and to proscribe the PKI. In the course of the next year Sukarno was reduced to a figurehead and General Sukarto became the real power, though at first operating as a member of a triumvirate. By July 1966 Sukarno had lost his remaining powers and in August the military High Command, which had never been in favour of it anyway, ended confrontation. Then, in a volte-face, the Indonesian army co-operated with Malaysian forces across the border in Sarawak to track down Communist bands then operating along the Sarawak–Kalimantan border. Once confrontation had been brought to an end, it became easier for Britain to accelerate its military withdrawal from east of Suez.

KAMPUCHEA/CAMBODIA: BORDER WAR, CIVIL WAR, VIETNAM INVASION

Introduction

The history of Cambodia (which has changed its name several times) has been deeply troubled ever since the Japanese invasion of 1941. The country, inevitably, was drawn into the war in Vietnam (see Part II, pp. 142–153) so that by 1970 it was suffering from border incursions by the North Vietnamese and Viet Cong, and bombing by the Americans. In the mid-1970s it was rent by civil war and the victors, under their Prime Minister Pol Pot, imposed on the entire people one of the most brutal and murderous regimes to be found anywhere in the world. This miserable period was only brought to an end in 1979 following a full-scale invasion and occupation by Vietnam, although the Vietnamese occupation was deeply resented and resisted by the Khmer Rouge and other non-Communist groups, while the world community refused to give legitimacy to the Vietnam-supported government in Phnom Penh. Despite this, Vietnamese withdrawal in 1989 appeared to have sparked off yet another period of civil war.

Cambodia was incorporated in the French Indo-Chinese Empire in 1864, and the French retained the Khmer monarchy. Strong anti-French nationalism developed during the 1930s, in part as a protest against the clear preference which the French demonstrated for the Vietnamese. In 1941 Prince Norodom Sihanouk came to the throne under French colonial auspices, but later in the year the whole peninsula was invaded and occupied by the Japanese. They were content to leave King Sihanouk as the nominal ruler of Cambodia. When they departed in 1945, however, the Japanese encouraged the Cambodians to revolt against the returning French and declare their independence. In Cambodia the revolt was contained, although the French soon faced serious fighting in the neighbouring territory of Vietnam. Sihanouk remained as constitutional monarch.

At the time when French colonial power disintegrated (1950–3) Cambodia became independent (9 November 1953), and this independence was recognized by the great powers during the Geneva Conference of July 1954. Meanwhile, the Free Khmer party in Cambodia allied itself with the Viet Minh against the French, and some of the Khmer Communists either stayed in the jungle to form a core of guerrillas against the new government or went to North Vietnam.

In 1955 Prince Sihanouk abdicated as monarch in order to form his own political party – the Popular Socialist Community (Sangkum) – which was to win all the seats in the assembly in the elections of 1955, 1958, 1962 and 1966.

By 1963, as it became increasingly clear that North Vietnam would eventually win the war, Sihanouk – always a political weathervane – veered towards the left and renounced American aid. At the same time, however, he also attempted to destroy the Khmer Rouge guerrillas then operating in the rural areas. But in this he was less successful and in 1967 the Khmer Rouge organized a major uprising against him. Although the uprising was brought under control, it did demonstrate the growing strength of the Khmer Rouge.

Border incursions 1965–1973: the Vietnam War

From 1965 onwards the North Vietnamese and the Viet Cong forces established bases in east Cambodia from which they operated into South Vietnam. Sihanouk was unwilling to do anything about them, with the result that both US and South Vietnamese forces began to raid across the border into Cambodia in efforts to knock out these Communist bases. In the circumstances Sihanouk's bloody repression of the 1967 uprising in Battambang was a shortsighted reaction, for it had the effect of driving large numbers of anti-government peasants into joining the Khmer Rouge.

By 1970 Sihanouk's complaisance towards the Vietnamese bases in Cambodia led the Americans to seek an alternative ruler for the country, and so they encouraged General Lon Nol, who mounted a coup in March of that year while Sihanouk was on a visit to Paris. Lon Nol then tried to do what Sihanouk had known he was unable to achieve and expel the Vietnamese Communists from the country. He began by expelling the Communist Vietnamese diplomatic mission from Phnom Penh and ordering the Vietnamese army units to leave Cambodia. In response the North Vietnamese invaded Cambodia, whose army was weak and ill-prepared for major resistance, and by April the Vietnamese were threatening the capital, Phnom Penh. The situation was saved by the South Vietnamese and the Americans, whose forces moved in to prevent the North Vietnamese seizing the Cambodian capital.

In exile Sihanouk allied himself with his former enemies, the Khmer Rouge, a move which greatly strengthened their standing in Cambodia and led to an increase of overall opposition to Lon Nol. Sihanouk and his new allies formed the National United Front of Cambodia (FUNC), which in turn set up a government in exile – GRUNC – operating from Beijing.

Although the Lon Nol government survived the Vietnamese invasion of 1970, it faced increasing problems thereafter. Cambodia found itself permanently on the fringes of the Vietnam War and subject to cross-border military actions which the government could not control. Ironically, it was the Khmer Rouge guerrillas who were to assume increasing responsibility for protecting Cambodia from foreign incursions, and the opposition groups, represented by GRUNC in Beijing, grew in importance as the Lon Nol government found itself less and less in charge of events.

In October 1970 the government changed the name of the country from Cambodia to the Khmer Republic, bringing an end to the constitutional monarchy. In March 1972 Lon Nol made himself President, subsequently 'legitimizing' his position by referendum.

The war in Vietnam came to an end in January 1973, by which time Lon Nol was losing his grip on most of Cambodia except for the cities. The USA, meanwhile, had continued to bomb the Khmer Rouge forces which were then fighting against the Lon Nol government, but the settlement in Vietnam also brought this activity to an end. Lon Nol launched an offensive against the Khmer Rouge in 1973 (with American aid), but it failed and his authority remained confined, increasingly precariously, to the towns. Massive US bombing of Cambodia in the period 1970–3, supposedly against supporters of the North Vietnamese, in fact had been indiscriminate. While it failed to stop the Vietnamese, it turned many people into supporters of the Khmer Rouge Communists.

Civil war 1973–1975

At one level the civil war of 1973–5 was a prelude to the Vietnamese intervention at the end of the decade. The Khmer Rouge gathered support, not least because of the mistakes and shortcomings of those they wished to overthrow. By 1974 Lon Nol found himself isolated; major American aid had come to an end with the US withdrawal from Vietnam, and he found that he only really controlled the capital city, Phnom Penh. Early in 1975 (the dry season runs from December to April) the Khmer Rouge launched a major offensive; they cut links to the capital so that the government was dependent on US airlifts for supplies. On 1 April Lon Nol left

Phnom Penh and flew into exile in the USA, and on 17 April Phnom Penh fell to the Khmer Rouge forces.

There followed a grim episode of Cambodian history – associated with the idea of the 'killing fields' – when supporters of the defeated government or of other anti-Khmer Rouge groups, intellectuals or others who were deemed a threat to Khmer Rouge policies were liquidated or sent to rural areas to do forced labour in collective farms. The towns were depopulated and huge numbers were killed or died of malnutrition. Although Prince Sihanouk was initially restored as head of state, he remained outside the country until the end of 1975, returned briefly but left again in 1976.

Despite the fact that Lon Nol enjoyed American support – or perhaps because of it – the Khmer Rouge overthrew his regime in 1975 with comparative ease. The Republic of Democratic Kampuchea was proclaimed and Pol Pot became Prime Minister. In 1976 the new regime was given the formal support of the People's Republic of China. In 1977 the Kampuchea Communist Party became the official governing body of the country.

The Pol Pot years 1976–1979

As soon as they had taken Phnom Penh in 1975 the Khmer Rouge began the programme (see above) under which large numbers of urban dwellers were sent into the rural areas. Conditions were appalling and led to many deaths, while others – political enemies, the middle classes or intellectuals – were eliminated in purges. Also, at this time, the Khmer Rouge expelled a number of ethnic minorities including Vietnamese, Cham-Malays and Europeans, although the ethnic Chinese were permitted to stay.

A new constitution was promulgated in January 1976 and the country was renamed Democratic Kampuchea. Elections to the new assembly were held in March 1976 – only approved revolutionary candidates were permitted to stand – and Sihanouk then resigned as head of state while GRUNC was dissolved. The new assembly appointed Khieu Samphan as head of state and, more important politically, the new Council of Ministers appointed Pol Pot as Prime Minister.

In 1977 Pol Pot emerged victorious in a factional political fight, so his position as Prime Minister was strengthened. He made public the fact that the Communist Party of Kampuchea (CPK) had existed since 1960 and that he was Secretary of its Central Committee. Despite claims to neutrality or non-alignment, the Pol Pot government in fact demonstrated increasing antagonism to Vietnam – foolishly in the circumstances since it did not have the military power to match that of its neighbour. These tensions contributed to the Vietnamese decision to invade and oust the Pol Pot regime at the end of 1978, although other Vietnamese ambitions also played a part.

War with Vietnam 1977–1979

From May 1975 onwards increasing border clashes occurred between Kampuchea and Vietnam, and these escalated into a full-scale border war at the end of 1977.

In April 1977 there was an attempted coup against Pol Pot which had the backing of Vietnam. At the very end of 1977 – 31 December – Pol Pot publicly accused Vietnam of trying to incorporate Kampuchea into a Vietnam-dominated federation and he broke diplomatic relations with his neighbour. In May 1978 an uprising against Pol Pot was supported by Vietnam, but it failed to dislodge the regime.

At the end of 1978 – 2 December – Vietnam assisted in the formation of an anti-Pol Pot Kampuchea National United Front for National Salvation (KNUFNS). Then, on 25 December, regular forces of the Vietnamese army with Kampuchea rebels invaded Kampuchea in a determined bid to overthrow the Pol Pot government. The Khmer Rouge simply did not have sufficient strength to hold a full-scale Vietnam invasion at bay and Phnom Penh fell to the Vietnamese on 7 January 1979. Vietnam now installed its own choice of government.

A Vietnam puppet government 1979–1989

The war of December 1978–January 1979 was swiftly concluded once the Vietnamese occupied Phnom Penh, and on 11 January the People's Republic of Kampuchea (PRK) was proclaimed and Heng Samrin became President of the People's Revolutionary Council. Then, on 18 February, Kampuchea concluded a peace treaty with Vietnam. In March Vietnam admitted publicly that its troops were in Kampuchea.

The KNUFNS held elections in May 1981 – approved candidates only – and at the end of that month the first congress of the ruling Kampuchea People's Revolutionary Party was held. The Khmer Rouge, meanwhile, had reverted to what they did best, and their guerrillas waged a constant war against the Vietnamese, who needed to bring in 200,000 troops to maintain control of the country.

The Kampuchea question was to remain highly complex throughout the 1980s. It was not simply that there were both Communist and non-Communist opposition groups operating against the puppet government which Vietnam had installed and supported; there was also the question of legitimacy and international recognition, for despite the excesses of the Pol Pot regime, Vietnam had few international backers; the United Nations still recognized the ousted Pol Pot government as the legitimate representative of the country and most neighbouring states represented by the Association of South East Asian Nations (ASEAN) were determined that Vietnam should quit Kampuchea. One result of the long Vietnam War had been to ensure that Vietnam itself possessed one of the largest, most formidable armies in the region.

During the 1980s (beginning with their defeat in 1979) the Khmer Rouge forces, which numbered about 30,000 and had taken to the jungle, waged continuous if sporadic guerrilla warfare against the occupying Vietnamese troops. Other guerrillas representing non-Communist groups which also opposed the Heng Samrin government and its Vietnamese backers were also active. The annual dry season saw most of the fighting.

On the international front a United Nations vote of October 1980 still recognized the ousted Pol Pot regime as the legitimate government of Kampuchea, while south-east Asian countries refused to accord Heng Samrin's government either recognition or legitimacy. This state of affairs was to continue through the 1980s, with the ousted government retaining its seat at the UN and the Samrin govern-ment only obtaining recognition from a limited number of countries. For its part Vietnam insisted that the change it had brought about in Kampuchea was permanent. Following its invasion of Kampuchea, the number of Vietnamese in the country rose to between 4 and 8 per cent of the population. The Khmer Rouge now attempted to revamp their image as information about the extent of the atrocities which had been carried out under their auspices – the killing fields – became more widespread. Meanwhile, ASEAN tried to promote an alternative to both Pol Pot and the Vietnam-backed Samrin government.

1981

When Samrin's most powerful minister, Pen Sovan, who was secretary-general of the party and chairman of the Council of Ministers, began to act too independently of the Vietnamese, he was ousted in December and Samrin became party leader. During 1981 the Chinese increased their support for the Khmer Rouge: in May, for example, Beijing announced that it was prepared to supply aid for all 'patriotic' forces in Kampuchea, by which it meant any groups oppposed to Vietnam. Later in the year (September) the Khmer Rouge leader, Khieu Samphan, led a deputation to Singapore to meet Prince Sihanouk. They were under pressure from China to form an anti-Vietnam coalition. At the United Nations that September the General Assembly voted to continue recognizing the Khmer Rouge govern-ment, with 77 votes for, 37 against and 31 abstaining.

1982

This was notable as the year in which the anti-Vietnamese factions came together in a coalition. Meeting in Kuala Lumpur in June, the Khmer Rouge (Communist), the Khmer People's National Liberation Front (KPNLF) (non-Communist) and the Armée nationale sihanoukist (ANS) formed the government of Democratic Kampuchea with Sihanouk as President, the former head of state Khieu Samphan as Vice-President and Son Sann of the KPNLF as Premier. The new coalition was given the backing of ASEAN and as a matter of tactics played down the role of the Khmer Rouge. It demanded the withdrawal from Kampuchea of the Vietnam-ese, who were sufficiently disturbed by the publicity which the 'government' of Democratic Kampuchea received, especially that resulting from the endorsement of Sihanouk whose influence and charisma remained remarkably strong, that they felt the need to make a conciliatory move. In a gesture aimed at winning ASEAN goodwill Vietnam announced the withdrawal of 10,000 of its troops, then estimated at 180,000. The gesture was not appreciated.

1983

During 1983 both sides – the Heng Samrin government and the coalition in exile – made determined propaganda efforts to win international support. Prince Sihanouk made a much-publicized visit – through Thailand – to western Kampuchea to attend a cabinet meeting with his Khmer Rouge allies. The Vietnamese launched a major offensive in an effort to destroy the Khmer Rouge jungle camps and break their resistance. In fact the resistance became tougher and had the counter-effect of producing defections on the government side, which sparked off purges in the administration. At the end of the year and into 1984 the anti-Vietnamese guerrillas launched a series of attacks on urban centres in western Kampuchea near the Thai border.

1984

The 1984 offensive against towns carried out by the forces of Democratic Kampuchea (with new weapons supplied by China) was relatively successful. The Vietnamese, who were then estimated to have 160,000 troops in the country, launched major counter-attacks, but by then Vietnam appeared to be losing the propaganda war. Moreover, following an attack on Khmer bases in Thailand, the Thai army counter-attacked and in a small battle killed 70 Vietnamese. Vietnam made efforts to improve the Kampuchean forces of Samrin, but had little success because the morale of these troops was not high. In October, for the sixth year running, the United Nations General Assembly called for the withdrawal of foreign troops from Kampuchea. The relatively successful anti-Vietnamese guerrilla campaigns of this year led the Vietnamese to improve their access to the Thai border regions ready for a major offensive at the beginning of 1985.

1985

This turned out to be a crucial year for Kampuchea in a number of respects: China supplied the coalition alliance rather than just the Khmer Rouge with arms; Vietnam announced 1990 as the year when all its troops would be out of Kampuchea; and Pol Pot retired to an advisory position, though this announcement gave rise to much scepticism. At the end of 1984 and into 1985 the Vietnamese forces launched a series of successful counter-attacks on the Khmer and other guerrillas. In January some 4000 Vietnamese troops overran the KPNLF headquarters camp at Ampil; in February they captured the Khmer Rouge camp at Phnom Malai; and in March they took Tatum (the Sihanouk camp). Altogether they drove about 250,000 Khmer Rouge supporters into Thailand as refugees. Subsequent Vietnamese strikes across the border brought them into conflict with the Thai army. China supported its allies (the coalition) by exerting pressure along the Sino-Vietnamese border, although its activities were restrained, possibly because Beijing was seeking a *rapprochement* with the USSR, which was Vietnam's most important ally.

It was also a year of intense diplomatic activity. In July ASEAN called for talks between the exiled coalition government and the Vietnamese including the Phnom Penh government (an initiative which was supported by the USA), although the proposal was turned down by the Vietnamese.

1986

During 1986 the Samrin government began to erect a defensive line along part of the Thai border; yet guerrilla resistance increased and the exiled Democratic Kampuchea won growing support. The coalition established a joint military command.

1987

Slowly during 1987 the signs of a coming settlement increased. Vietnam no longer ruled out any peace talks which also included the Khmer Rouge, and it withdrew some more troops – perhaps 20,000 – although still retaining 140,000 in Kampuchea. The Vietnamese tried to build up the Kampuchean army of 35,000, but it was poorly led and poorly fed. Meanwhile, Sihanouk's forces of about 10,000 men were growing, partly as a result of desertion from Samrin's army. Pol Pot was said to be ill and no one was prepared to negotiate with him. In June 1987, addressing a foreign ministers' meeting of ASEAN, the Prime Minister of Singapore, Lee Kuan Yew, said, 'There have been reassessments of positions in Moscow and Hanoi. Both have put the revival of their economies at the top of their priorities. An eventual Cambodian settlement . . . is more likely than continued Vietnamese defiance. Hanoi knows her isolation is the direct result of her present policies, and this isolation has inflicted too heavy a burden on her economy.' The USSR put pressure on its Vietnamese ally to compromise, and in December Sihanouk met the Prime Minister of the Samrin government, Hun Sen, for three days of talks in Paris.

1988

Diplomatic efforts to find a solution continued throughout 1988. Talks were held in Indonesia between the various Kampuchean factions and their allies, although splits in the coalition were becoming more marked. There was fighting along the Thai border as a result of efforts by the Khmer Rouge to improve its position, and in December Vietnam withdrew a further 20,000 men, reducing its total strength in the country to between 100,000 and 120,000.

At the beginning of the year the Prime Minister of Kampuchea, Hun Sen, went to Paris for reconciliation talks with Prince Norodom Sihanouk. He insisted that neither Pol Pot nor certain other Khmer Rouge leaders should take part in any future quadripartite government; he would then be ready to set out a schedule for

Vietnamese withdrawal. The most controversial question in all talks of reconciliation was that of the Khmer Rouge and the role they would play; with 20,000 well-trained troops armed by the Chinese they were a factor that could not be ignored. And to underline the point the Khmer Rouge mounted an offensive during January when Prime Minister Hun Sen was holding his talks with Prince Sihanouk in Paris. While the Vietnamese Foreign Minister, Nguyen Co Thach, said the Paris talks could lead to a breakthrough, he also insisted that there could be no return to power of the Khmer Rouge.

By June it had become clear that Vietnam was indeed going to withdraw, and a further 40,000 troops were pulled out. The run-down of the Vietnamese presence was generally welcomed, but in Kampuchea (increasingly referred to as Cambodia once more) fears were growing that Pol Pot and the Khmer Rouge would come to power again. This was based on the assessment that the West and the non-Communist south-east Asian states were so anxious to see the Vietnamese withdraw that they would be prepared to allow the Khmer Rouge back into power. At the same time the Khmer Rouge were increasing their recruitment and receiving more arms from China. Moreover, the Khmer Rouge adopted a new strategy: instead of confronting the Vietnamese forces with their superior weaponry, they were moving into the villages to settle down and wait until all the Vietnamese had withdrawn. At the end of June, as Vietnamese troops left the country, the battle became increasingly political as the various factions prepared to fight for future control of Cambodia, with the indications becoming clearer that the Khmer Rouge would be a major part of any political solution.

The three coalition leaders – Prince Sihanouk of ANS, Khieu Samphan of Khmer Rouge and Son Sann of the KPNLF – agreed that the PRK government would have to be dismantled after the Vietnamese withdrawal and that a four-party coalition (in which it would be one member only) would then be headed by Sihanouk. President Heng Samrin rejected this.

One result of the long Vietnamese occupation was the presence in Cambodia of between 500,000 and 700,000 Vietnamese civilians who had settled under the military. They became a fifth column for Vietnamese interests in a country whose total population is only about 8 million.

In November the Khmer Rouge issue was raised in a different form when the Cambodian Prime Minister, Hun Sen, accused the Chinese of sabotaging the peace efforts by insisting that the Khmer Rouge had to be a part of any solution and that Deng Xiaoping had told Sihanouk he had to include the Khmer Rouge in any future government. Despite these manoeuvres, the Vietnamese withdrawal continued and in December a further 18,000 troops returned home.

As far as the international community was concerned, the issue of the Khmer Rouge was clearly less important than that relating to the Vietnamese. The 1979 Vietnamese occupation of Cambodia ended the infamous Pol Pot regime, but their invasion was seen as an attempt, funded by the USSR, to annex Cambodia. As long as the Vietnamese remained in occupation, a *rapprochement* between China and the USSR was impossible since China was the chief supporter of the Khmer Rouge. At the same time the USA was not prepared to restore relations with Vietnam. By 1988, however, new policies in Moscow led the Soviet government to exert pressure on Vietnam to withdraw so that the USSR could pursue its policy of *glasnost* and achieve an understanding with China. By December 1988 the revitalized Khmer Rouge had an estimated 40,000 well-armed troops whose leadership showed no signs of changing its earlier fanatical ideology, while China had made it plain that it would not cut off military aid to the Khmer Rouge until the Vietnamese had withdrawn completely. Prince Sihanouk appeared to have resigned himself to a solution which included the Khmer Rouge.

1989

Early in 1989 it began to look as though a solution – at least as far as total Vietnamese withdrawal was concerned – would soon be achieved. The basic questions to be resolved were the continuing Soviet supply of arms and finance to Vietnam, consequent Chinese support for the Khmer Rouge and other support for the coalition opponents of the Vietnam-backed government in Phnom Penh. The Chinese indicated a readiness to phase out their support for the coalition if the Russians did the same in relation to Vietnam and if the Vietnamese completed their withdrawal from Cambodia during 1989. In Cambodia the key person remained Prince Sihanouk, whose main demand was that all factions should be disarmed.

By the end of January 1989, when Vietnam had 50,000 troops remaining in Cambodia, the Prime Minister, Hun Sen, promised to pull them out by September if agreement could be reached on an interim government that would subsequently supervise elections, and if China stopped providing military support to the Khmer Rouge. Thailand, which to that point had been a firm supporter of the Cambodian opposition, began to act as mediator once it became clear that the USSR and China wished to remove the irritant of Cambodia from their own attempts at *rapprochement*. When in February 1989 China and the USSR agreed to a summit meeting in Peking, this followed Beijing's acceptance that the USSR was exerting enough pressure on Vietnam to secure total withdrawal later in the year: China had always seen Soviet support for Vietnam in Cambodia as part of a policy aimed at encircling China.

A year of apparently endless negotiations came to a climax in September as Vietnam's military presence in Cambodia at last came to an end. During the final withdrawals a new guerrilla offensive was launched in the west, and the Khmer Rouge and their non-Communist allies, the Khmer People's Liberation Front as well as ANS, made some substantial immediate advances and claimed a number of victories. At first the Hun Sen government appeared firmly in control and argued that it faced no more than the sort of protracted border war that its neighbours, Burma (now Myanmar) and Thailand, had dealt with for years, but this reaction had to be altered almost at once: the President of the National Assembly in Phnom Penh, Chea Sim, warned the country that it faced civil war as the border town of Pailin came under steady Khmer Rouge bombardment.

What had become clear by September was the genuine desire of Vietnam to withdraw from Cambodia. This arose not because its ideology had changed, but because its poverty and need for development would be helped best by economic aid and ties with the West, and these would only be forthcoming after the withdrawal had been completed. All the signs were for a showdown between the Hun Sen government and the Khmer Rouge – a civil war for political control. The Hun Sen government saw such a civil war as inevitable, with the Khmer Rouge as the principal antagonists conducting low-intensity guerrilla warfare throughout the country.

271

Once the last Vietnamese troops had left the country, Thailand alleged that in fact thousands of Vietnamese had been left behind: as regulars in the Cambodian army, as settlers or as military advisers. Similar accusations were made by the Chinese. At the same time two of the three coalition groups – the KPNLF and ANS – were receiving training from Thailand, the USA and Britain, while the Khmer Rouge, the most formidable still of the guerrilla groups, continued to receive Chinese arms and backing. Thus, by the end of September 1989, the indications were that Cambodia would settle down into an uneasy state of guerrilla warfare not dissimilar to that in Afghanistan following the Soviet withdrawal.

This guerrilla warfare was being waged (October 1989) by the KPNLF and ANS as well as the Khmer Rouge, with the former (non-Communist) groups needing to demonstrate their military capacities and ability to attract people to their banners in a way that the Khmer Rouge no longer needed to do. Despite endless denunciations of their record, the Khmer Rouge emerged after the Vietnamese withdrawal as a major factor that had to be taken into account in any permanent Cambodian solution. Moreover, their leadership remained remarkably consistent: largely the same men have run the movement for 20 years. Once it was clear that the Vietnamese really had departed, the West was shown to be in disarray, finding itself supporting the anti-Phnom Penh government coalition which includes the Khmer Rouge whom previously the West had consistently denounced. The indications for the 1990s were a continuing civil war, with the major powers sitting on the sidelines rather than intervening more openly.

Estimated costs and casualties

Few countries anywhere in the Third World have experienced as much violence and as many casualties since 1945 as has Cambodia. In the first phase of its civil war – 1972 to the end of 1978 – although estimates vary widely, it is believed that a minimum of 1 million lost their lives, while the maximum estimate suggests as many as 3 million. During the second phase of Pol Pot 'national resistance' to the Vietnamese occupation the casualties have been much lower. In the first five years – 1979 to 1984 – following the defeat of the Pol Pot forces and the Vietnamese occupation, deaths of Pol Pot rebels were put at about 3000.

The most consistent figure for deaths under the Pol Pot revolution is one in the region of 2 million, and even the most conservative estimates suggest that one-fifth of the total population met their deaths during this period. By the beginning of the 1980s only 14 per cent of the people lived in towns: many towns had been wholly or partly destroyed by US bombing up to 1973; and many people had been forcibly resettled in the countryside during the Pol Pot years. Also at this date there were an estimated 330,000 Khmer refugees in Thailand, although that figure fluctuated through the 1980s. For example, at the beginning of 1987 about 250,000 Cambodian refugees were receiving international aid in Thailand.

Bald figures are insufficient to quantify the costs in terms of human suffering. Thus, at least 1 million residents in Phnom Penh in 1975 were forced to leave the capital and work the land in conditions little short of slavery, and many did not return. Stories of the brutalities committed have already gone into folk legend, and the name of the Khmer Rouge remains deeply feared by large sections of the population. The economy has been reduced to one of the poorest in the world.

Results

At the end of 1989 (November) the United Nations General Assembly, in a motion on 'the situation in Kampuchea', voted 124 to 17 in favour of the coalition – that is, the Khmer Rouge, the KPNLF and ANS – as opposed to the sitting government of Hun Sen (formerly backed by Vietnam). It did so, moreover, despite protestations from the West in particular that no one wished to have anything to do with the Khmer Rouge. Thus the British Minister of State at the Foreign Office, William Waldegrave, said, 'We, like all other civilized people in the world, wholly denounce the Khmer Rouge and all their actions.' (Britain, none the less, voted for the resolution.) Despite such pronouncements, the indications for the 1990s were that a Cambodian government would sooner or later include the Khmer Rouge. Moreover, until that happened there appeared to be little chance that Cambodia would enjoy a settled peace. However, by February 1991 the Phnom Penh army was using helicopter gunships against the Khmer Rouge in a new escalation of the fighting. The fighting was aimed at controlling the population rather than territory as such and solutions remained open-ended.

THE AMERICAS

COSTA RICA: THE NICARAGUA WAR

Like Nicaragua's other neighbours, Costa Rica found it increasingly difficult during the decade of the 1980s to keep free of entanglement in that country's debilitating civil war, not least because of the US determination to use the surrounding countries as springboards from which the rebels (Contras) could operate against the Sandinista Nicaraguan government. In November 1983, therefore, in an attempt to keep clear of such entanglements, Costa Rica proclaimed its neutrality in the Nicaragua conflict; the government insisted that Costa Rican territory would not be used as a base for operations against its neighbours. Such a policy did not meet with US approval, although generally Costa Rican–US relations are good. Costa Rica was the only country in the region without a standing army, and it now found that, at a time when its civil police had to deal with an increasing amount of internal anti-government action from rival factions, it also had to face growing border problems with Nicaragua.

Clashes occurred along the border with Nicaragua during 1983 and 1984 and led Costa Rica to protest in May 1984 that Nicaraguans had attacked a border guard post. In reply the Nicaraguan government claimed that members of the civil guard assisted by Contras were to blame, so the two countries agreed to set up a joint commission to monitor the border.

In 1983 the USA provided Costa Rica with $4.6 million in security assistance, but the next year the figure was doubled to $9.2 million. In addition the USA provided the relatively huge amount of $180 million in aid, a gift which provoked fears that Washington was attempting by bribery to buy over Costa Rica as a base for Contra operations against the Sandinista government. These fears sparked off a mass demonstration in May 1984 when between 20,000 and 30,000 marched through the capital, San José, to insist on the country's neutrality. In a clear bid to find alternative sources of aid, President Monge visited 12 European countries to seek assistance and raised $135 million. However, it was becoming more and more difficult for Costa Rica to maintain the pretence of neutrality, while border skirmishes increased in intensity and numbers.

By 1985 not only were there reports of Contra bases in the mountain regions of the north of the country, but the rebels had established an office in San José. Earlier the government had deported the Contra leader, Edén Pastora Gómez. Moreover, the first half of the year saw skirmishes between the Costa Rican Civil Guards and units of the Nicaraguan armed forces patrolling the border region, so relations between the two countries became increasingly strained. By 1985 there were some 8100 Nicaraguan refugees registered in Costa Rica.

Costa Rica's neutrality in relation to the Nicaraguan war came increasingly into question. Since the government had been obliged to turn to the USA for aid during its economic crisis of 1983–4, it became harder to resist US pressures in relation to the Contras, while the extent of the US aid response was indicative of Washington's determination to put an end to Costa Rica's neutrality. By 1985 relations with the USA, which effectively meant aid dependence, had grown stronger, so relations with the Sandinista government inevitably became more strained. The USA now provided military advisers to train the Costa Rican Civil Guard, a form of aid which the region interpreted as evidence that Costa Rica had abandoned its neutrality.

Presidential elections in 1986, however, brought Oscar Arias Sánchez to power, and he insisted that he would prevent the Contras from using Costa Rica as a base. Then, in July of that year, the Sandinista government filed an action at the International Court of Justice at The Hague to restrain Costa Rica from harbouring Contra forces. This action followed border fighting when for the first time Costa Rica admitted publicly that Contra forces were operating from bases in the north of the country.

President Sánchez made determined efforts to help the peace process in Nicaragua. In July 1987 he turned an airstrip on the border with Nicaragua which had been used by the Contras into a national park. It was later revealed that the airstrip had been used on the authority of the former US National Security Council aide, Colonel Oliver North, for the delivery of US aid in the form of arms to the Contras (see above, pp. 234–235 and Part V, pp. 551–559). More important than such a gesture, President Sánchez was the author of the Central American Peace Plan, which was signed on 7 August, 1987 by five countries of the region: Costa Rica, El Salvador, Guatemala, Honduras and Nicaragua. This peace plan acted to re-emphasize Costa Rican neutrality, and as a result Nicaragua dropped its action against Costa Rica at the International Court of Justice. But Costa Rica's ability to pursue an independent policy remained limited by the extent of its international debts, which in 1987 reached the huge figure (for such a small economy) of $4.5 billion.

In January 1988 the International Verification and Monitoring Commission visited Costa Rica to verify the border peace agreement. President Sánchez was facing growing internal unrest and was accused of paying more attention to solving external problems than to dealing with his own country's difficulties at home. However, the elections of February 1990 in Nicaragua (see Part V, pp. 551–559), which saw the defeat of the Sandinistas under President Daniel Ortega and the election of Violeta Barrios de Chamorro as President, greatly altered the regional political situation. Costa Rica could now expect an end of Contra/US activity on its soil, making it easier for the government to concentrate on internal problems.

EL SALVADOR–HONDURAS: THE SOCCER WAR 1969

Origins

Although the pretext for the short Soccer War of 1969 was a disputed decision in the World Cup soccer play-offs, the reasons behind it were deep-seated resentments arising out of the position of Salvadorean immigrants in Honduras. From as early as 1920 Salvadoreans had escaped the poverty of their own overcrowded country (El Salvador is the most densely populated country of Central America) by moving into Honduras, where they had taken over empty lands as settlers. Unemployment and scarcity of land forced some 300,000 migrants into Honduras during the 1950s and 1960s. Then, in 1965, an agreement between the two countries allowed the Salvadoreans the chance to regularize their position in Honduras. However, only about 1 per cent did so, and as a result, when Honduras passed agrarian reform measures in January 1969, a majority of the Salvadorean farmers found themselves to be illegal squatters liable to eviction from their land and expulsion from the country. An increasing flow of Salvadoreans back into their own overcrowded country – about 15,000 of them with tales of hardship and bad treatment – coincided with the World Cup soccer play-offs and contributed to the explosion which followed. In any case tensions between the two countries had been growing for some time. The sporting incident was merely the pretext on which El Salvador broke off diplomatic relations with its neighbour in June 1969. At this point each side complained of atrocities committed against its citizens by the other, and the Organization of American States (OAS) began an investigation.

The war

In the brief war which followed Honduras was humiliatingly defeated; the fighting lasted only four days and the better trained and equipped Salvadorean army crossed the border to wreak considerable havoc. During the first two weeks of July 1969 there had been a growing number of border incidents. Then, on 14 July, Salvadorean forces crossed the border to occupy part of Honduran territory, while the army and air force bombarded a number of towns and border areas. The Honduran air force retaliated with raids on Salvadorean targets, although Honduran troops remained on the defensive.

The OAS called for an end to the hostilities and the unconditional withdrawal of Salvadorean forces from Honduran soil. Although the fighting ended on 18 July, El Salvador did not withdraw all its forces until 27 July.

Costs and casualties

An estimated 5000 people were killed in this brief war. El Salvador's oil refinery was put out of action and much other material damage was done by air raids and bombardments. A number of refugees were also created. In the longer term El Salvador suffered considerable damage to its economy as a result of its aggression since its three neighbours – Honduras, Nicaragua and Costa Rica – all cut back their trade with the country.

Results: immediate and longer term

The OAS negotiated the truce of 18 July which ended the fighting. Later that year – 27 October – the OAS passed a series of resolutions which covered bilateral relations between the two countries, although these were not finally agreed and incorporated into a treaty until 1980. Honduras refused to sign the peace treaty and in addition brought to an end regional co-operation over the period 1969 to 1980; Honduras would make no concessions to El Salvador until a clearly defined boundary between the two countries had been agreed.

The first stage in what turned out to be a decade of manoeuvres and bargaining came with the agreement of 4 June 1970, which established a demilitarized zone along the border – 3 km (2 miles) on either side – to be monitored by OAS observers and guaranteed by Costa Rica, Guatemala and Nicaragua. A number of efforts to reach agreement were made during the 1970s. Border incidents in 1976 led to a meeting of the foreign ministers of the guarantor nations; they produced the Act and Protocol of Managua (9 August 1976), which led to the stationing of OAS military observers on the frontier and the appointment of a mediator. The work of this mediator – Dr José Luis Bustamante y Rivero (a former President of Peru) – finally produced an agreement which was formalized in the Lima Peace Treaty of 30 October 1980. As a result the border between the two countries was re-opened on 11 December 1980.

The Treaty of Lima terminated the state of war which had lasted since 1969 and settled two-thirds of the 343 km (213 mile) border between El Salvador and Honduras to the satisfaction of both sides. However, some areas remained in dispute (*bolsones territoriales*, territorial pockets), so border differences were to persist through the 1980s until the two countries agreed to submit their differences to the International Court of Justice at The Hague in 1986. Furthermore, other subjects of dispute – increased Honduran taxes on regional imports, which affected El Salvador, and the presence in Honduras of 40,000 Salvadorean refugees – meant that tensions between the two countries persisted through the 1980s.

HONDURAS: THE USA AND CONTRA BASES

Introduction

When the Sandinista government came to power in Nicaragua in 1979 relations with Honduras became increasingly strained, especially as former members of the Nicaragua National Guard (loyal to the deposed Nicaraguan President Somoza, or to the kind of government he had represented) infiltrated across the border into Honduras where they set up bases. Diplomatic relations between the two countries were temporarily broken in 1979, although they were restored again in 1980. From that year onwards the Contras in Honduras began to use the country as a base from which to launch attacks on the Sandinista government in Nicaragua; and by 1981 the Honduran army was already said to be providing support to the Contras. The Contra presence in Honduras during the 1980s, encouraged and supplied by Washington, posed the government of Honduras with a growing and increasingly unwelcome problem since it feared it would not be able to control the Contras on its own. Casualty figures are uncertain, but although these were probably low, hostilities along the border gradually intensified during the decade, while both geography and politics made Honduras the natural US forward base in Central America.

The situation became relatively fixed in 1981 when three things happened: the Contras used Honduras as a base area for attacks on the Sandinista regime across the border; the Honduran army (according to Nicaragua) began to assist the Contras; and the USA increased the level of its military assistance to Honduras. As a result, it appeared possible that war between Honduras and Nicaragua might follow. To complicate matters further Honduras had to face internal opposition from a number of left-wing groups: the Cinchonero Popular Liberation Movement (MPL), which had been formed in November 1979 and launched an armed struggle against the government in 1980; the People's Revolutionary Union (URP), which had also been formed in 1979; and the Workers' Revolutionary Party, which in 1980 was responsible for the kidnapping of an American executive of Texaco. This latter movement was especially opposed to the US military presence in Honduras.

These left-wing terrorist organizations were the response to gross inequality and great poverty; they inspired a savage reaction from the government and the right established vigilante groups to counter their activities. Thus 1982 became a year of internal turmoil for Honduras, which had to face a further influx of refugees from its other troubled neighbour, El Salvador, while the Contras continued to operate from its territory with impunity and the USA sent additional military advisers. The Honduran army, at this time under the command of General Alvarez, was accused of conducting a dirty war against 'subversives'. By the end of 1982 there were an estimated 10,000 Nicaraguan refugees in Honduras and a further 25,000 from El Salvador.

The following year border tensions mounted and further undermined government authority, while the so-called Nicaraguan Democratic Force rebels, backed by the USA, intensified the number of their raids into Nicaragua. Washington had clearly come to regard Honduras as the key to its Central American policies: the USA sent more military advisers to Honduras and established a training base for the military from El Salvador at Puerto Castilla. By August 1983 there were some 4000 US troops in Honduras, and later these took part in a six-month military exercise with 6000 Honduran troops – Operation Big Pine II – which continued through into 1984; the exercise inevitably deepened Nicaraguan suspicions of both US intentions and the Honduran role in relation to them. Although these large-scale military manoeuvres came to an end in March 1984, another exercise was started in June 1984 and they became part of a series which continued through to 1988.

The American military presence created a Honduran backlash since the scale of US military operations caused resentment in the Honduran military High Command. In addition, there was resentment against the Salvadoreans who came to train at the US base which had been established at Puerto Castilla in 1983, for the two countries had long been at loggerheads (see above, pp. 245–277). Financial assistance made a difference, however, and Honduran anger was assuaged in October 1984 when Washington agreed an aid package for Honduras of $141 million.

The presence of the Contras in Honduras and their escalating operations increased tensions with Nicaragua during 1985, even though the government did not admit that the Contras operated from its territory. The Honduran government, in any case, had become increasingly dependent on Washington and was loath to take any action that would offend the US administration. Even so, by May 1985 the Honduran government was talking of disarming the Contras and expelling them. The situation did not improve in 1986; indeed, there was growing controversy over both the Contras and the US role in Honduras, while the newly elected Honduran President, José Ascona, publicly admitted the presence of Contras for the first time, as well as the fact that he allowed them to receive aid. On a visit to Washington that May he told President Reagan that he would allow US aid to the 15,000 or more Contras because otherwise he believed they would be uncontrollable. At the same time he said that Honduras was not to be used as a launching pad for attacks against its neighbours. The USA agreed a further aid package of $61.2 million. By December 1985 US helicopters were being used to ferry Honduran troops to areas where Nicaraguan troops had entered Honduran territory in pursuit of the Contras.

The effect of US backing for the Contras over the period 1982 to 1986 was to transform the position of the American Ambassador in Tegucigalpa (the Honduran capital) from that of a diplomat in a post of minor importance into one of major political influence. By the end of 1986 there were more than 15,000 well-armed Contras in camps along the 800 km (500 mile) border between Honduras and Nicaragua, almost entirely financed from Washington. At the same time there was growing unease in Honduras at its increasing dependence on American aid and at the US–Contra relationship on its soil that seemed to be entirely divorced from Honduran interests. Honduras discovered that it no longer had an independent foreign policy, that it had an increasing number of displaced people on its territory and a permanent border conflict with Nicaragua, and that it was internationally isolated. In addition, the Honduran military had become increasingly corrupted by what became known as the 'write-off racket'. The huge joint US–Honduran military exercises, involving thousands of troops, meant that vast amounts of equipment from clothing to weapons were 'written-off' and sold by the Honduran generals to the Contras. By the mid-1980s the Hondurans had come increasingly to see themselves as pawns in a power game controlled by the United States.

In 1987, despite being one of the signatories of the Central American Peace Plan of President Oscar Arias Sánchez of Costa Rica, Honduras expressed doubts. In reality it feared that an end to the war would leave it exposed, with thousands of well-armed and uncontrollable Contras on its hands. At the same time, and equally worrying, the US military presence in Honduras seemed to have become a permanency. Between 1982 and 1987 Washington had provided Honduras with a staggering $1 billion in aid, a sum Honduras could not have hoped to receive except as a result of the Contra presence and the war across the border with Nicaragua. What Honduras sought in 1987 was an American assurance that its assistance would continue if aid to the Contras was cut off, for by then the Irangate scandal had broken and the Iran–Contra hearings were in full spate in Washington. This concern continued through 1988 when it did begin to look as though the USA would eventually abandon its support for the Contras.

By 1989 Central America, like half the rest of the world, was waiting to see how the reverberations of *glasnost* would affect its complex relations and whether, as a result of accommodations between the USA and the USSR, Central America would be left to work out a peace formula of its own. (See also Part V, pp. 551–559.)

PART IV

Israel and its Neighbours

Israel and its neighbours

INTRODUCTION

The apparently endless and unstoppable nature of the Middle East conflict between Israel and its Arab neighbours, which has gone on more or less without pause since 1948, must continue as long as the objectives of the two sides are seen to be irreconcilable. Israel has come to be regarded by the Arabs as an outpost of Western interests forcibly planted in their midst and largely maintained by American power, while the Arabs are treated by the Israelis as being unreasonable for insisting that the tiny area covered by the state of Israel none the less belongs to the Arabs and should be Palestinian. If the Jews can feel so passionately about a land from which they had been absent for 18 centuries, they have yet to understand the feeling of loss experienced by the Palestinian Arabs who have been deprived of it. There can be no resolution of the Middle East question until the Israelis are prepared to negotiate with the Palestine Liberation Organization (PLO) about an Arab Palestine – and that, inevitably, must mean the surrender of at least a portion of the territories they now hold.

The key to the conflict in the Middle East between Jews and Arabs or Israel and its neighbours is the denial by the Arabs of the legitimacy of the Jewish claims on which the state of Israel was founded in 1948: namely, that historical possession of the territory up to the diaspora under the Romans in AD 135 justified the subsequent repossession of Palestine by the Jews 1800 years later. On the other hand, the Jews, or a substantial proportion of them (though by no means all), who had been without a homeland of their own since the dispersion and to a greater or lesser degree had been integrated – or not – in the various lands of their adoption, wanted a homeland of their own and claimed Palestine. Expulsions and persecutions in Europe and elsewhere over the centuries had emphasized their homelessness, while their religion pointed explicitly to Palestine (or Israel) as the homeland given by God to the Jews. The fact that Palestine was an Arab land when at the end of the nineteenth century Zionism began to grow into an important political force was – for Jews – beside the point.

The Austrian Jew, Theodor Herzl (1860–1905), became the leader of Zionism and the chief advocate of a modern Jewish state in Israel. And as Jewish immigration into Palestine and subsequent settlement grew during the 1880s, when the territory was still part of the Ottoman Empire, so too did Arab hostility. In 1880 there were approximately 25,000 Jews in Palestine; by 1914 the figure had risen to 90,000 (there were then about 450,000 Arabs in the territory). But up to the First World War, despite Herzl and the developing attraction to international Jewry of the concept of Zionism, the pace of immigration remained relatively slow. It was to be given a major boost in 1917 by what came to be known as the Balfour Declaration, made by Britain's then Foreign Secretary. At the time (1917 was the worst year of the war) Britain was in urgent need of allies, and the Balfour

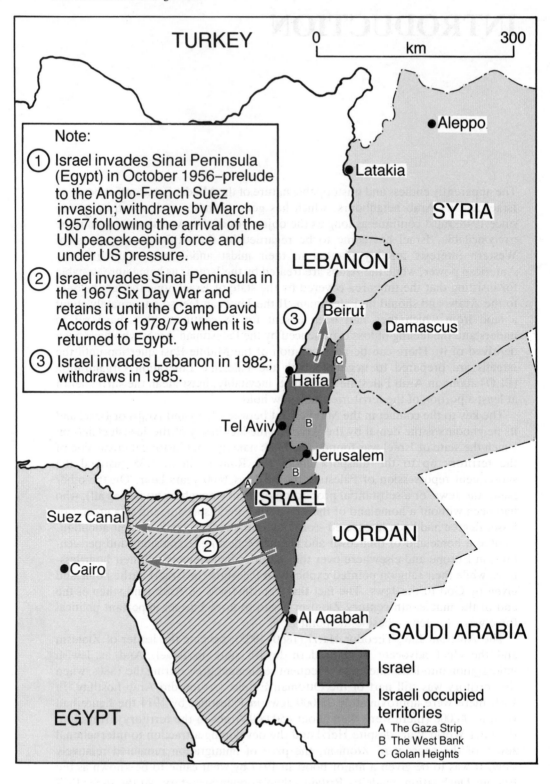

TURKEY

0   km   300

●Aleppo

●Latakia

SYRIA

LEBANON

Note:

① Israel invades Sinai Peninsula (Egypt) in October 1956–prelude to the Anglo-French Suez invasion; withdraws by March 1957 following the arrival of the UN peacekeeping force and under US pressure.

② Israel invades Sinai Peninsula in the 1967 Six Day War and retains it until the Camp David Accords of 1978/79 when it is returned to Egypt.

③ Israel invades Lebanon in 1982; withdraws in 1985.

③ Beirut ●Damascus

Haifa

C

Tel Aviv   B

Jerusalem

B

A

ISRAEL

JORDAN

Suez Canal ① ←

② ←

●Cairo

Al Aqabah

SAUDI ARABIA

Israel

Israeli occupied territories
A The Gaza Strip
B The West Bank
C Golan Heights

EGYPT

Declaration was designed to attract the support of the international Jewish community to the allied (British) war cause.

Originally, the Zionists appealed to Istanbul for permission to settle in Palestine, but as the Ottoman empire declined they turned to Britain and France, believing that these two leading Western powers would be more likely to help. The Balfour Declaration was made on 2 November 1917, in a letter to a leading British Jew, Lord Rothschild. Balfour said that 'His Majesty's government view with favour the establishment in Palestine of a national home for the Jewish people, and will use their best endeavours to facilitate the achievement of this object.' But while, from then onwards, the Jews argued that the Declaration placed a seal of legitimacy on their claims, the Arabs rejected it both at the time and later.

Indeed, as the First World War drew towards its climax and the Ottoman Empire was dismembered, three sets of claims and promises had to be faced: first, the Zionist claims to a Jewish homeland in Palestine, now reinforced by the Declaration made by the Foreign Secretary of the world's greatest imperial power; second, Arab hostility to such a claim, backed by the promise of the Allies (principally Britain again) that there should be Arab self-determination and the creation of an Arab state to comprise (loosely) those Ottoman lands then occupied by the Arabs; and third, and most likely to triumph in the short run, the imperial ambitions of Britain and France, which saw themselves as the natural imperial successors to the Ottoman Empire. In May 1916, a year and a half before the Balfour Declaration, the British and French had reached a secret understanding (the Sykes–Picot Agreement between Sir Mark Sykes for Britain and Georges Picot for France) under which they effectively divided the Ottoman Empire of the eastern Mediterranean between their two countries. The mandate system of the League of Nations (however it may have been interpreted subsequently) was seen by the two imperial powers as a means of extending their power and influence in the region.

At San Remo in April 1920 Britain and France agreed on the division of the spoils (as mandates), taking under their control large areas that the Arabs had seen as part of an independent Arab state or nation. The British mandates covered Palestine, Transjordan, the Negev desert to Eilat, and Iraq. In addition, by means of a series of protectorates and the treaties with the 'trucial' states of the Gulf, Britain virtually ringed the Arabian peninsula, which it saw as part of its sphere of influence. France had the mandates over Syria and Lebanon.

However, the mandate over Palestine, which was approved by the League of Nations on 24 July 1922, committed Britain to secure the establishment of a Jewish national home in Palestine, 'provided it did not prejudice the civil and religious rights of non-Jewish communities' – a condition that was clearly unworkable and indicated right from the beginning the double standards that the League, Britain as the mandatory power and subsequently the United Nations were to apply to this question. At the time the mandate was granted, 92 per cent of the inhabitants of Palestine were Arab and they owned 98 per cent of the land; this ratio of people and land ownership was to be changed fundamentally under the British mandate to the advantage of the Jews and to the detriment of the Arabs. The Arabs argued that, no matter how small the area given over to the Jews (out of all the Arab lands of the Ottoman Empire), it was still Arab land and had been promised to the Arabs as part of an eventual independent Arab nation.

Historically, Britain has to take responsibility for much of the bitterness and the divisions which have bedevilled Middle East politics ever since that time, for it made two incompatible promises: a homeland for the Jews in an Arab territory and self-determination for the Arabs. At the same time, in concert with the French, it acted in true imperial style and carved out spheres of influence for itself. Unsurprisingly, therefore, the region was to witness endless and escalating divisions, and the growth of mistrust and hatred between Arab and Jew. Already by 1920 the Arabs had begun to attack Jewish settlements in Palestine.

The mandate

The years of the British mandate were to be troubled throughout with mounting Arab–Jewish hostility, Arab attacks on Jewish settlements, periodic British attempts to stop Jewish immigration and mounting hatred between the two sides. The British sat on this developing volcano with growing unease; every attempt by the mandatory power to obtain any form of Arab–Jewish co-operation or agreement always foundered on totally opposed objectives which admitted no common ground. By 1928 there were 150,000 Jews in Palestine and 600,000 Arabs, and the year witnessed major clashes between the two groups.

The accession to power in Germany of Adolf Hitler in 1933 accelerated the pace of Jewish immigration into Palestine; at the same time the Arabs formed an Arab High Committee to oppose further Jewish immigration. The British, meanwhile, found that the task of policing Palestine had become increasingly difficult, and more and more British soldiers were killed or wounded in clashes with militant Arabs. A British Royal Commission of 1936 reported the following year that the answer to the growing violence and Arab–Jewish hostility was partition. Reluctantly, the Jews were prepared to accept this as a solution, but the Arabs rejected it and instead launched the Arab revolt of 1937 against both Jews and British in Palestine. The Arab position was unswerving: total opposition to any legitimization of Jewish control over any Arab land. Britain, faced with mounting violence, was forced to abandon the idea of partition at least for the time being. Instead, in a White Paper of May 1939 Britain put forward a new solution: that Palestine should be neither Jewish nor Arab and that it should become independent after 10 years with both groups playing a part in government. This White Paper solution was rejected by both Arabs and Jews. Meanwhile, the persecution of Jews under the Nazis led to ever more determined demands for unrestricted immigration into Palestine since a majority of countries at that time were partially or wholly closed to Jewish immigration. By the outbreak of the Second World War there were 445,000 Jews in Palestine, then accounting for 30 per cent of the population. During the course of the war (1939–45) Jewish immigration into Palestine was cut back by the British, while the extermination of Jews under the Nazis in Europe (the Holocaust) proceeded apace.

Already in 1937 the more extreme Jews had formed the Irgun Zvai Leumi (National Military Organization); they believed that Britain had betrayed the Zionist cause and as the war came to an end they resorted increasingly to terrorist tactics against the British in Palestine. Irgun Zvai Leumi was joined by the Stern Gang, another terrorist organization. In 1942 leading Zionists met at the Biltmore Hotel in New York and announced what came to be known as the Biltmore Programme (11 May 1942), under which they demanded that Palestine should be opened to unrestricted Jewish immigration, that the Jewish Agency should control immigration and that Palestine should be turned into a Jewish commonwealth. At the end of the war a reluctant British army allowed the formation of a Jewish Volunteer Brigade. More important, by then the Jews had won over substantial and influential American support for the creation of a Jewish state.

The Creation of Israel 1945–1948

The Nazi persecution of the Jews before and still more during the Second World War, and the horrendous revelations that followed the allied opening up of the concentration camps at the war's end, acted as a major impetus to the Jewish determination to establish a homeland at all costs. The revelations also increased international sympathy for the Jewish cause. By 1945 Britain had come to accept that a compromise between the Jews and Arabs in Palestine was not possible: terrorism was increasing rapidly and pressures from the USA were mounting to persuade Britain to permit unfettered Jewish immigration into Palestine. By 1946 the Jewish population of Palestine had reached 608,000 and then represented 40 per cent of the total population. It was to reach 650,000 on the eve of the birth of Israel.

The Jewish Agency, meanwhile, had formed a military wing, Haganah, which included units of shock troops or Palmach. This was reinforced by the two terrorist organizations, Irgun Zvai Leumi and the Stern Gang. Even before the end of the war the Jewish extremists had turned to terrorist tactics which were making the mandate increasingly unworkable. When the war in Japan came to an end in August 1945, Haganah, Irgun Zvai Leumi and the Stern Gang formed a united front against the British, while the Jewish Agency proclaimed its readiness to establish a provisional government. Britain now found itself maintaining major forces in Palestine at a time when war-weariness and the general demand for demobilization made it increasingly politically difficult to keep large numbers of men under arms. It was fighting both Jewish and Arab terrorists and facing mounting costs and casualties in order to maintain a mandate that was unpopular at home, attacked internationally (especially by the United States) and becoming unworkable in Palestine itself.

In April 1946 an Anglo-American Committee of Inquiry recommended the immediate admission of 100,000 Jewish refugees from Europe as well as an end to the restrictions on Jews buying land. Britain was not then prepared to admit Jews to Palestine in such numbers. Throughout this period, however, Jews continued to arrive illegally in Palestine.

The United Nations

Early in 1947 Britain decided to refer the question of Palestine to the United Nations, and also made it plain that Britain intended to bring its mandate to an end and to withdraw its troops by 15 May 1948. On 2 April 1947 Britain referred the question of Palestine to the United Nations, and subsequently a UN Special Commission on Palestine (UNSCOP) went to Palestine where it was boycotted by the Arabs but assisted by the Jews. It reported to the General Assembly (31

August 1947), proposing partition (the majority proposal) or a form of federation. A modified scheme for partition of Palestine between Arabs and Jews was agreed by 29 November 1947 and passed by the United Nations General Assembly. Under this plan 56 per cent of Palestine was reserved for the Jewish state, while Jerusalem, the Holy City for three religions, was to be an international zone administered by the United Nations. In the voting Britain abstained and made it plain that it would not accept a solution that had to be imposed by force (Britain was the power with the forces in Palestine and would be responsible for implementation).

The impasse between Britain and the United Nations in fact led to the result Britain was trying to avoid – a general escalation of violence both between Arab and Jew and between the Jews and the British. The Arabs refused to accept this United Nations solution and said they would oppose it by force. In the riots and disorders which followed an estimated 1700 people were killed. The decision represented a victory for the Jews since it both affirmed the right of the Jews to establish a homeland in Palestine and assigned to them slightly more than half the territory. By January 1948 Arab volunteers were arriving in the territory to help the Palestinian Arabs oppose the establishment of a Jewish state, although these volunteers were dealt with relatively easily by the Jewish forces. In April 1948 the Jewish forces went on the offensive against the Arabs, so already by the time the mandate ended 400,000 Arabs had evacuated Palestine to become refugees.

The birth of Israel: 15 May 1948

Already by 13 May Zionist forces had gained control of all the areas of Palestine that had been assigned to the Jews; they had also captured important positions in the areas set aside for the Arabs. Then the Irgun Zvai Leumi stormed the Arab village of Deir Yassin and massacred part of the population in an act of terror that led to a mass exodus of Arabs. The British formally brought their mandate to an end at midnight on 14 May 1948 and the state of Israel was then proclaimed. Within a few minutes after midnight both the USA and the USSR had recognized the new state. Immediately on 15 May the regular forces of Palestine's Arab neighbours – Egypt, Transjordan, Iraq and Lebanon – moved into Palestine, but while the Arab Legion of Transjordan was well trained, the other Arab forces were poorly trained and badly co-ordinated, and despite having superiority of both numbers and armaments, they scored few successes except in Jerusalem itself. It was now that against great odds the Jews were to win: they did so by virtue of a determination that was fuelled in part by desperation and in part by the motivation of at last achieving a homeland back in Palestine which was seen as the fulfilment of their history.

The war of 1948

The invasion of 15 May 1948 led to eight months of fighting – it did not come to an end until January 1949 – although there were two partly observed truces. A series of armistice agreements between Israel and its antagonists were then enacted in the period January to July 1949. The Arab states which invaded Israel in 1948 saw themselves as coming to the assistance of the Palestinian Arabs, but they were ill-prepared and poorly motivated and found themselves fighting in unfamiliar terrain far from their home bases. The Jews, on the other hand, were exceptionally highly motivated, fighting for their new homeland and their survival. In the fighting which followed, the Jews managed to occupy and hold 20 per cent of the territory which the United Nations had assigned to the Arabs.

Only the Jordanian forces – the Arab Legion then commanded by the British soldier, John Glubb Pasha – achieved any military success. At the end of the war some 400,000 Palestinian Arabs became Jordanian citizens when the West Bank of the Jordan was joined to Transjordan and the country was renamed the Hashemite Kingdom of Jordan. The other Arab forces involved in the war included an Egyptian armoured brigade of 4000, three regiments of the Syrian army, an Iraqi mechanized brigade which fought alongside the Arab Legion, and the tiny Lebanese army. There was also the Arab Liberation Army inside Palestine led by Fawz el-Kawkji.

The Jewish militia then numbered 35,000, of whom about 18,000 were armed; they could also call on a further 15,000 on the farms and settlements, who would play a defensive role. The Jewish leadership said that all the country's public and private transport had to be placed at the disposal of the army, that every Jew with any military training had to enlist no matter what his job might be, and that all firearms throughout the land were 'nationalized'. The tiny state of Israel was completely open to Arab attack and by virtue of its oddly drawn geographic shape was immensely vulnerable, so at the beginning of the war the Jewish position appeared precarious in the extreme. The Arabs occupied areas in the south and east and initiated a blockade of Jerusalem. Their advances, however, were quickly halted by the Israelis, who then counter-attacked to obtain and maintain control of all the territory that had been assigned to them according to the United Nations partition, as well as taking over a fifth of the territory assigned to the Arabs. The Arab League announced its aim at the beginning of the hostilities as the safeguarding of an independent Palestine for its lawful (Arab) inhabitants – in effect, majority rule. Had majority rule then been applied, it would have spelt the end of the state of Israel. The United Nations condemned the Arab invasion as soon as it was launched.

Estimated costs and casualties

Casualties resulting from Arab–Jewish clashes during 1946 were estimated by the British as 212 killed and 428 wounded, of whom 45 were British forces, 29 members of the Palestine police and 138 civilians (14 British, 60 Arabs, 63 Jews and one other). The wounded included 122 British forces, 43 Palestine police and 263 civilians. Casualties recorded for the period between the announcement of the UN Partition Plan (29 November 1947) and 1 February 1948 were 989 killed, of whom 427 were Arabs, 381 Jews and 181 British; there were 1941 wounded. On 1 March 1948 the British announced that casualties since 30 November 1947 came to 3000 killed and wounded.

The Jews estimated that their casualties between 30 November 1947 and the end of the war in January 1949 came to 4000 Jewish soldiers and 2000 Jewish civilians killed. No figures are available for Arab casualties over the same period.

One major international casualty was the United Nations mediator, Count Folke Bernadotte of Sweden, who was assassinated on 17 September 1948 by a Jewish terrorist. He had been appointed on 20 May and had been responsible for negotiating the two short-lived ceasefires of June and July.

As a result of the fighting, 400,000 Arabs from the territory that the Jews had conquered and a further 300,000 from the West bank who fled into Transjordan became refugees. These formed the nucleus of the Palestine refugee problem that was to continue thereafter, and they would later provide the hard core for membership of the PLO.

On 11 December 1948, the United Nations passed a resolution to the effect that Arab refugees should be free to return to their homes in Israel, but this was never to be effectively implemented since the Israelis insisted that any such return of the Arabs must be related to a general settlement.

Results: immediate and longer term

When the war of 1948 came to an end the Jews had won convincingly, a victory that ensured Arab hostility for years to come. They had also won control of more than a quarter of the mandated territory over and above what had been assigned to them, a fact which added to the Arabs' humiliation at their defeat. Although a series of armistices were agreed between the new state of Israel and its Arab opponents (with Egypt, 24 February 1949; Lebanon, 23 March; Transjordan, 3 April; Syria, 10 July; Iraq did not make an armistice), none of the Arab states was prepared to recognize the new Jewish state.

Israel surrendered some of the territory it had gained, but was to keep two-thirds of what had been Palestine: Galilee, the whole coast except for part of Gaza under Egypt, the Negev, a strip of territory from the coast to Jerusalem and the western part of the city. But the rest of Jerusalem, including the Old City and what had been the Arab share of Palestine, were taken over by Transjordan. No Palestine as such any longer remained.

The departure of the Arabs from what had been Palestine to form refugee communities in the territories round Israel (by 1949 there were an estimated 900,000 of them altogether) was the commencement of one of the most intractable of all subsequent problems, a problem that still existed at the beginning of the 1990s. This departure, however, meant that for the first time the majority of the population of the state of Israel were Jews.

Emerging desperately triumphant against apparently enormous odds and with the bitter memories of the Holocaust so recent, it is understandable that the new state made defence and the military capacity to defend itself against any combination of its Arab neighbours its first priority. Moreover, as part of this defensive stance Israel thereafter became aggressive in the sense that it was ready to raid its neighbours if by doing so it thought it could persuade them to leave it alone.

The new state immediately embarked on a programme to attract Jewish immigration, and in the three years 1948–51 its Jewish population was doubled. Ironically, Iraq helped this process by expelling its old Jewish community.

Once Israel was established, the big powers of the West – the USA, Britain and France – attempted to stabilize the situation with their Tripartite Declaration of 1950 that they would supply arms to both Arabs and Jews for internal security reasons and to prevent a violation of the armistice by force. In November 1950 the Arab League decided that the wartime blockade of Israel should be continued since an armistice did not constitute a peace. In Transjordan King Abdullah held a referendum for the Arabs of the West Bank; they agreed to become part of Transjordan, which was then renamed Jordan.

More generally, the establishment of Israel led the Arabs to regard the USA and Britain as its main backers, a fact which contributed to growing anti-Western feelings throughout the Arab world. The USA, indeed, became the main source of external finance for Israel, which drew enormous funds thereafter from both official and private American sources. Israel was rapidly developed as a modern state with an economic system more akin to those of the West than to those of its Arab neighbours, another fact that emphasized Jewish–Arab differences. The new state embarked on a precarious existence surrounded by hostile Arab states which in combination had vastly superior populations, so it was to be constantly in a state of siege. It was heavily dependent on external finance and for years continued to seek immigrants to build up its strength. At the same time its population was highly motivated.

The results of the war of 1948 might be summarized as follows: it confirmed the existence of the state of Israel; it left what was to be a continuing 'state of war' with Israel's Arab neighbours, who refused to see the Jewish victory of 1948 as final; it created the huge Palestine refugee problem; and it left a number of problems, such as the impossible Israeli frontiers and the divided status of Jerusalem, that were bound to lead to further disturbances in the future. At the end of the war there were approximately 660,000 Jews in Israel and only 150,000 Arabs.

THE SUEZ WAR 1956

Introduction

In the years following the war of 1948 the focus of attention for the new state of Israel was on the 900,000 Palestinian refugees on its borders. They were claimants to the area occupied by Israel, which they persisted in calling Palestine and refused to recognize. These refugees were also the source of the *fedayeen* or guerrillas who raided Israel and kept its borders in a state of constant tension. When in 1950 King Abdullah incorporated into Jordan both the West Bank and the Old City of Jerusalem his action was opposed by other Arab hardliners since such a move was seen to undermine the idea of a Palestinian state which had to be regained. In an attempt to stabilize a situation that their earlier actions (in supporting the creation of the state of Israel) had made inherently unstable, the Western powers – the USA, Britain and France – tried with their 1950 Tripartite Declaration, which limited arms supplies to both sides in the region, to ensure that there was no arms race to fuel future confrontations. It was, in fact a situation that was almost certain to explode a second time.

As memory of their defeat of 1948 receded, the Arabs' bitterness increased; and from 1953 onwards tensions between Israel and Jordan became acute. In October 1953, for example, Israeli forces massacred 50 people in the village of Qibya. In 1955 there were frontier clashes along the Gaza Strip and in the demilitarized area facing the Sinai peninsula, in the region of Huleh and on the shores of Lake Galilee; in fact Israel faced tensions on virtually every front with its Arab neighbours. Further, the Syrians objected to Israeli plans to divert the waters of the Jordan for irrigation purposes. The north-east of Israel came under more or less constant bombardment from the Syrians in the Golan Heights, while from the Gaza Strip the *fedayeen* mounted repeated attacks across the border into Israel.

In February 1955 the Israelis mounted a raid on the Egyptian garrison in Gaza as a reprisal whose object was to discourage cross-border harassments. The result, however, was the opposite to what Israel had intended, for it drove Egypt's ruler, Colonel Nasser, to seek greater military strength by a major increase of armaments. In August he entered into negotiations with Czechoslovakia and agreed to make large purchases of military equipment – both heavy armaments and aircraft – from that country. This agreement, completed in September, altered the whole perspective of Middle East politics: it ensured a much greater Soviet involvement in the region, which was now to be drawn inexorably into Cold War confrontations; and it sparked off an Arab–Israeli arms race which up to this point the West had attempted to hold in check.

The immediate Western response to Israeli fears was a refusal by both the USA and Britain to sell equivalent arms (to those supplied by Czechoslovakia to Egypt) to Israel, although France provided Israel with jet aircraft. At the same time Egypt maintained a strict blockade of the Suez Canal and the Gulf of Aqaba against both Israeli vessels and any others carrying cargo to or from Israel. It did so on the grounds that it was in a state of war with Israel, even though the blockade was contrary to a 1951 UN Security Council resolution.

Nasser's international position was greatly strengthened during 1955, for he was one of the leading figures at the Bandung Conference which launched the concept of non-alignment. But Nasser's economic situation was weak and as a matter of urgency he wanted to build the Aswan High Dam so as to bring new land under irrigation for agriculture and to provide electricity for industrialization in order to meet the demands of a rapidly growing population. In February 1956 the World Bank offered a loan of $200 million provided that the USA and Britain between them provided a further $70 million, and that Egypt put up the equivalent of $900 million to cover local costs and also obtained the agreement of the riparian states – essentially Sudan – to the construction of the dam.

But the climate for such an agreement was marred by the growing antagonisms and suspicions of the Cold War. The last British troops in Egypt were finally withdrawn (under the terms of the 1954 agreement) in June 1956. Egypt, however, chose to denounce the Western-backed Baghdad pact as well as American and British Middle East policies generally, while the US Secretary of State, John Foster Dulles, opposed the Egyptian decision to take arms from Czechoslovakia. As a result of these conflicting interests, the American offer to finance the Aswan High Dam was withdrawn on 20 July to be followed by Britain two days later, and this led to the withdrawal of the World Bank offer as well; in retaliation Nasser announced the nationalization of the Suez Canal Company on 26 July, so sparking off a major international crisis. Nasser said he would use the revenues from the Canal to finance the construction of the dam.

Britain, France and the USA protested at the nationalization of the Suez Canal and in August held a conference in London to consider their response to Nasser. A committee under Prime Minister Robert Menzies of Australia went to Cairo with proposals for the international operation of the Canal, but these were rejected by Egypt.

In retrospect it seems clear that Britain's Prime Minister, Sir Anthony Eden, was determined to use punitive measures to bring President Nasser to heel; the question was how and in what circumstances. The British motives for intervention in Egypt were complex. Eden believed that Nasser fell into the same mould as Hitler and Mussolini. There was also the actual loss of Britain's stake in the Canal (42 per cent). But probably most important was the psychological reaction of a declining imperial power to a visible snub by a country which until very recently Britain had in part controlled (the last British troops to be stationed in Egypt had only left a month before Nasser nationalized the Canal). Essentially Suez was an 'end of empire' problem for Britain.

France's motive for intervention was more precise and practical: Nasser was providing major support for the Fronte de libération nationale (FLN) in Algeria, who were then demanding independence and waging a bitter and increasingly successful war against the French (the subsequent failure of the Suez intervention led to a growth in support for the FLN from among the newly independent and non-aligned nations).

A second conference was held in London during September at which a Canal Users' Association was formed. On 13 October the United Nations Security Council adopted an Anglo-French resolution on the principles for a settlement. But a second resolution, which invited Egypt to put forward proposals for users of the Canal, was vetoed by the USSR. The next day (14 October) Eden was visited by the French Minister of Labour, Albert Gazier, who was a confidant of Prime Minister Guy Mollet, and General Maurice Challe. They put forward the plan for Israel to invade Sinai and then for Britain and France to call for an end to the fighting, and to intervene if this did not happen. A secret pact along these lines was now agreed at Sèvres (in what became known as the Treaty of Sèvres) between the British Foreign Secretary, Selwyn Lloyd, the French Prime Minister, Guy Mollet, and the Israeli Prime Minister, David Ben-Gurion. Later the French Foreign Minister, Christian Pineau, who was also at the Sèvres meeting, flew to London to confirm arrangements with Eden. The Israelis were to attack on 29 October.

When hostilities did take place following the Israeli invasion of the Sinai peninsula, two wars rather than one occurred: the Israeli–Egyptian campaign; and the Anglo-French invasion of Egypt. The first war between Israel and Egypt could be seen as the second round in the confrontation between the new state of Israel and its Arab neighbours; the second war, which became an international *cause célèbre*, was a last British exercise in old-fashioned imperial gunboat diplomacy and became inextricably mixed up in escalating Cold War confrontations in the region.

In the October 1956 elections to the Jordan Parliament the pan-Arab parties emerged victorious; this led to a growth of anti-Israeli sentiment. Immediately after these elections Egypt, Syria and Jordan established a unified military command. This was seen as a growing threat by Israel, so even without the complications of Nasser's nationalization of the Suez Canal Israel might well have gone to war with its neighbours. In any case, ever since 26 July Britain had been preparing a battle fleet at Malta and assembling troops ready for an invasion of Egypt.

The Israeli invasion of the Sinai Peninsula

On 29 October Israeli forces crossed the borders into the Sinai peninsula and advanced rapidly on all fronts; within five days they had taken Gaza, Rafa and El Arish as well as occupying most of the Sinai peninsula to the east of the Suez Canal. They took prisoner the Egyptian garrison at Sharm al-Sheikh and the island of Tiran, which commands the Gulf of Aqaba. Israel had its own objectives which were independent of any agreements it had made with Britain and France: to destroy Egyptian bases in the Sinai desert; to open sea communications from Eilat through the Gulf of Aqaba; and to take over the Gaza Strip. This second Israeli–Arab war cannot, however, be divorced from the wider Suez question, even though, from Israel's point of view, Suez only provided the occasion for action.

The Anglo-French invasion of Suez

A major British war fleet had been assembled at Malta ready to sail for Egypt, and the fact that it could do so immediately after the Israeli invasion of Sinai meant that Britain either had already planned such action independently of any Arab–Israeli hostilities or had foreknowledge of Israeli intentions. In the event 22,000 men were to be landed in the Canal Zone, of whom 13,500 were British and the remainder French. On 30 October, the day after the Israeli invasion of Sinai, Britain and France presented their ultimatum to Israel and Egypt, calling on them to cease warlike actions and to withdraw 32 km (20 miles) from either side of the Canal. In addition they asked Egypt to agree to the temporary stationing of Anglo-French forces at Port Said, Ismailia and Suez. Israel agreed to comply with the terms of the ultimatum; Egypt refused, not least because it was being asked to withdraw from parts of its own territory. At the United Nations Britain and France vetoed a US–Soviet resolution which called for an immediate Israeli withdrawal and for all members of the United Nations to refrain from the use of force.

On 31 October, following the Egyptian rejection of their ultimatum, Anglo-French air operations were launched against Egyptian airfields; these continued until 4 November. Then, on 5 November, British and French paratroopers and seaborne troops were landed at Port Said and began an immediate advance down the Canal. By this time the Israelis had overrun the Gaza Strip and most of Sinai.

The intervention met with widespread condemnation. On 2 November a United Nations resolution called for a ceasefire, and on 4 November the General Assembly adopted a Canadian resolution to create a United Nations Emergency Force (UNEF). Then, on 6 November (acting in response to heavy pressure from US President Eisenhower), Britain's Prime Minister, Sir Anthony Eden, announced that provided Egypt and Israel had accepted an unconditional ceasefire the conflict would be terminated by midnight of that day.

Estimated costs and casualties

In the Sinai campaign Israeli losses came to 180 dead and four captured; Egyptian losses came to 1000 dead and 6000 captured. A number of other Egyptians were killed in the desert by unfriendly Bedouin.

In the Canal invasion British casualties came to 16 dead and 96 wounded; French casualties came to 10 dead and 36 wounded. Egyptian casualties (according to British sources) came to 650 dead and 900 wounded.

The Suez Canal was blocked by the Egyptians, but was cleared by a United Nations salvage fleet by the end of March 1957. Other costs are more difficult to estimate, but include the damage by bombing to the Egyptian airfields, loss of *matériel* and the economic effects of closing the Canal. The Canal was blocked by the Egyptians until it was cleared by a United Nations salvage fleet at the end of March 1957.

Results: immediate and longer term

There were two sets of consequences arising out of the war: those relating to Israel and its Arab neighbours; and the much greater international consequences affecting Britain, France and the Cold War.

On 7 November the Israeli Prime Minister, David Ben-Gurion, said that Israel would hold on to its conquests until Egypt came to a settlement. But the following day, under pressure from both President Eisenhower of the USA and the Soviet Premier, Nicolai Bulganin, Israel agreed to withdraw from Egyptian territory once the UNEF had arrived in Egypt. Israel sent two frigates to the Gulf of Aqaba to safeguard the approach to Eilat. By January it had evacuated most of Sinai, although on 23 January 1957 the Knesset voted to keep control of the Gaza Strip, to prevent its continued use as a base against Israel, as well as Sharm al-Sheikh at the entrance to the Gulf of Aqaba. Both the Gaza Strip and Sharm al-Sheikh were returned to Egypt in March 1957 as a result of American pressure. Israel reserved the right to self-defence if its ships were attacked in the Gulf of Aqaba.

The Sinai campaign resulted in a number of advantages for Israel: it meant a direct sea route from Aqaba to east Africa; new collaboration with France and a move towards closer relations with Europe (though not with Britain); and an end to Arab infiltration from Sinai and Gaza. The war marked the beginning of a conscious Israeli policy of seeking allies in Africa and elsewhere – leaping over the barrier of Arab states that surrounded it.

Despite being defeated by the Israelis and invaded by Britain and France, Egypt also gained substantial advantages from the war. Paradoxically, the failure of the Suez invasion resulted in Nasser emerging with immense prestige throughout the Arab world, almost as though he rather than world opinion and the superpowers had forced the British and French to call off their invasion. For the next 10 years his influence and the impact of the Voice of Cairo radio in subsequent Arab and African independence struggles were to be among the most important political factors in the Middle East. When the Suez Canal was reopened it was under full Egyptian control for the first time, run by the Egyptian Canal Authority according to the terms of the 1888 Constantinople Convention that it should be open to vessels of all nationalities in both war and peace.

The first units of the UNEF reached Egypt on 15 November; the British and French forces had all been withdrawn by the end of December. In Britain the failure of Suez had momentous political consequences. It was a traumatic turning point in post-war perceptions of British power and the role of Britain in the world, and it split the nation in two. It marked the end of Eden's political career and the rise of Harold Macmillan, who succeeded him as Prime Minister. After Suez Britain did not again attempt to use old-fashioned gunboat diplomacy in its relations with what was coming to be called the Third World. Anglo-French relations were also harmed by Suez, the French believing that American pressure had led Britain to drop them in favour of toeing the Washington line. The war may well be taken as the beginning of the deep French suspicion of the Anglo-Saxons that was soon to be so marked an aspect of de Gaulle's policy. On becoming Prime Minister in January 1957, in succession to Eden, Macmillan made his first priority that of restoring Anglo-American relations. Perhaps most clearly, the failure of Anglo-French intervention made plain the decline in power terms of these two major European nations to the second rank.

It was one of the ironies of the Suez War that the failure did far more damage to Britain's international standing than to that of France. The Anglo-French withdrawal was also regarded as a setback by Israel, which had hoped to see them establish a buffer between itself and Egypt.

Another major result of the Suez War was an increase in Soviet influence in the region. During 1957 the USSR was to take 50 per cent of Egyptian exports, and in 1958 it finalized its agreement to finance the building of the Aswan High Dam. It rearmed Egypt and from that time onwards became markedly pro-Arab at the expense of Israel. In January 1957, in response to the developing Communist interest in the region, President Eisenhower set forth what came to be known as the Eisenhower Doctrine: that US forces would defend any Middle East state threatened by any other state controlled by international Communism.

In summary the war saw a decline of British influence in the Middle East, the growth of Franco-Israeli ties, an increase in Soviet influence in the Arab world and a commensurate growth of American support for Israel. The Arab–Israeli question, moreover, had become still more complicated and enmeshed in Cold War and superpower diplomacy.

THE SIX DAY WAR 1967

Introduction

In the years following the Suez War of 1956 there were hopes that a more stable Arab–Israeli relationship would emerge. Israel worked to improve relations with Europe, especially France and also West Germany, which completed the payment of agreed reparations to Israel in 1962. At the same time Israel embarked on a policy of providing aid (as a result of immigration it had a surplus of people with technical skills) to developing countries in Africa and Asia. It concentrated especially on Africa, leaping over its Arab neighbours to offer assistance to the newly independent countries on the African continent, where only Mauritania and

Somalia refused to recognize Israel on achieving their independence. Many heads of state from newly independent countries visited Israel during this period. Although between 1956 and 1967 there were some border incidents with Egypt, these on the whole remained low key, mainly as a result of the continuing presence of UNEF in the Gaza Strip and at Sharm al-Sheikh. In 1959, however, Egypt stepped up its sea blockade of Israel. In 1960 Israel celebrated the arrival of the one millionth Jewish immigrant.

At their summit of January 1964 Arab leaders endorsed the creation of the Palestine National Council (PNC), which held its first meeting in May of that year in the Jordanian sector of Jerusalem. The PNC was responsible for setting up the Palestine Liberation Organization (PLO). On 2 June the PNC adopted the Palestine National Charter, which stated that 'Palestine is the homeland of the Palestinian Arab people' and went on to state that the territory of Palestine as under the mandate was indivisible. The Charter also laid down that the Palestinian people had the right to possess their homeland when they had achieved its liberation, and further stated that Palestinian Arabs were those who normally had resided in Palestine until 1947 (in other words, the huge numbers of refugees then in camps around the periphery of Israel). The newly formed guerrilla arm of the PLO, Al Fatah under Yasser Arafat, began to mount an increasing number of attacks on Israel from both Jordan and Syria. From 1964 onwards tension between Israel and Syria mounted after the latter had opposed Israel's plans to use the waters of Lake Tiberias for irrigation.

During 1966 the Israeli Foreign Minister, Abba Eban, began efforts to improve relations with the Communist world, although he achieved little. The year saw increasing tensions with Syria as new groups of Arab commandos infiltrated across the border into Israel. Then and at other times Arab backing for such activities was uneven. Serious fighting broke out along the border in July 1966, which gave the Israelis the opportunity to destroy most of the diversion works on the Jordan which the Syrians had been carrying out. At the same time Palestinian commando leaders increased their activities along the Israel–Jordan border, and the Israeli attack on the village of Samua in October 1966 further escalated the general tension. That month Israel complained to the UN Security Council about Syrian border violations.

Prelude to war

In November 1966 President Nasser of Egypt agreed an Egyptian–Syrian defence pact. Immediately following this Israel launched attacks on three villages near Hebron in Jordan, which in turn led to disturbances in the West Bank as the local Arabs demanded arms with which to defend themselves. By the end of the year both Jordan and Israel were anticipating war. Then, early in 1967, tension along the Israeli–Syrian border mounted again. Paradoxically, disunity in the Arab camp was a contributory cause of the Six Day War. King Hussein, whose attitude towards Israel could be described as moderate, had become a target for Cairo Radio; King Faisal of Saudi Arabia and President Bourguiba of Tunisia were also targets for such attacks. Hussein responded by suggesting that Egypt should recall its army from Yemen to face Israel instead. Other Arab leaders asked why Egypt, which claimed to have the strongest military forces in the Arab world and to be the leading Arab nation, did not ask the UNEF to withdraw from Sinai instead of sheltering behind it and then close the Straits of Tiran to Israel. Such Arab provocations certainly played a part in persuading Nasser to prepare for war.

During April 1967 Syria began systematic shelling of Israeli cultivation in the demilitarized zone, and then Syria lost a number of MiGs in action against the Israelis, who raided deep into its territory. Two of the Syrian planes came down in Jordan. The USSR now warned Egypt of an impending Israeli attack on Syria. During May pressures on both sides escalated rapidly. On 12 May Prime Minister Eshkol of Israel threatened Syria with reprisals if terrorist activities were not stopped. Egypt moved large forces to the Israeli border (15 May) and the following day declared a state of emergency. Then both Syria and Jordan announced mobilization. On 18 May Egypt requested the United Nations to remove the UNEF from its territory. Iraq and Kuwait mobilized. Following the withdrawal of the UNEF, both Egypt and Israel called up their reservists and the PLO placed its guerrilla forces under Arab command in Egypt, Syria and Iraq. On 22 May President Nasser accepted the Iraqi offer of military assistance if Egypt were attacked; the following day he closed the Straits of Tiran to Israeli shipping. This was seen by Israel as the prelude to war. Britain and the USA protested at the closure, but all Arab leaders expressed their support for Egypt. On 24 May Egypt claimed that the Gulf of Aqaba had been sealed. Israel's Foreign Minister, Abba Eban, visited London, Paris and Washington in quick succession to warn the maritime powers that Israel believed it had the right to break the blockade. Now Sudan mobilized, Algeria sent military units to fight with Egypt and (30 May) King Hussein of Jordan flew to Cairo where he signed a defence pact with Egypt under which each country would go to the assistance of the other if it were attacked.

Thus, on the eve of the war Egypt had defence agreements with both Jordan and Syria, though neither of those countries had an agreement with the other and a joint Arab military command did not exist. At the very end of May Iraqi troops moved into Jordan and through to the frontier with Israel. Early in June (2 and 3 June) 20 maritime states signed a British–US draft declaration which affirmed the right of free passage through the Gulf of Aqaba, although the draft did not lay down any means of enforcing such free passage. On 4 June Nasser said that such a declaration transgressed Egyptian sovereignty. Libya now pledged troops to the coming war and Iraq became a member of the Egypt–Jordan Pact.

The course of the war

The Six Day War was a classic example of military precision and planning which allowed Israel to defeat the far larger forces of its three neighbours – Egypt, Jordan and Syria – which in turn had the backing of other Arab states. At dawn on 5 June Israel launched a series of simultaneous air attacks on 25 airfields of Egypt, Jordan, Syria and Iraq, putting large numbers of their aircraft out of action and immobilizing the runways. The bulk of Egypt's aircraft were destroyed on the ground at 17 military airfields. These air strikes were the key to Israel's success, for they destroyed the best part of the opposing Arab air forces right at the beginning of hostilities, thus depriving their ground forces of air cover. On 6 June Israeli forces advanced into Sinai and defeated or put to flight a total of seven

Egyptian divisions. That day Nasser broke diplomatic relations with Britain and the USA (for their support for Israel) and expelled their citizens from Egypt. On 7 June the Israelis occupied Sharm al-Sheikh and the Old City of Jerusalem and reached the Jordan river; Israeli forces also occupied the Gaza Strip. At the same time there was fierce fighting with the Syrians along the border below the Golan Heights.

The Israeli attacks had been so swift and effective that on 8 June, when Israeli forces reached the Canal, both Egypt and Jordan agreed to a ceasefire. After Jordan had been defeated the Israelis launched a costly attack on the Golan Heights and penetrated an average of 19 km (12 miles) into Syria, taking the Heights and then moving along the road to Damascus to take the town of Quneitra. Syria agreed to accept the UN ceasefire proposals on 10 June. Meanwhile, on 9 June President Nasser announced his resignation on Cairo Radio; his First Vice-President and Deputy Commander-in-Chief, Marshal Abdul Hakim Amer, also resigned.

At the close of the war Israel was in control of the Sinai peninsula to the Canal, Sharm al-Sheikh on the Gulf of Aqaba, the whole of Jerusalem and the West Bank of Jordan, the Gaza Strip, a 19 km (12 mile) strip of Syria and the town of Quneitra. The Six Day War represented a brilliant Israeli victory over all its Arab enemies and raised Israel's military prestige to an all-time high. Israel now held three times as much territory as at independence in 1948.

Estimated costs and casualties

Israeli dead on all fronts came to 766. Egyptian dead came to 10,000 soldiers, who were either killed or died from lack of water in the Sinai peninsula as they tried to get back to the Canal. Jordan lost 6000 dead. Almost all the 60,000 Syrian Arabs living on the Golan Heights fled deeper into Syria, leaving the heights virtually uninhabited.

At the same time (representing a different problem for the future) the number of Palestinian Arabs under Jewish control increased from 300,000 to 1,200,000 as compared with a total of 2,500,000 Israeli Jews: for though 200,000 Arabs fled the West Bank into Jordan, a further 600,000 remained, while Israel had also taken over responsibility for 300,000 Arabs in the Gaza Strip.

Egypt suffered severe economic consequences from the war. It had again blocked the Canal and lost revenues from this; it also lost oil in the Sinai desert and tourism estimated to be worth £E12.5 million a month.

Results: immediate and longer term

At the end of the war Israel controlled 69,930 square kilometres (27,000 square miles) of territory as opposed to 20,720 square kilometres (8000 square miles) in 1949, and now made it plain that Israel would retain the Old City, the Gaza Strip, the Golan Heights and part of the West Bank. In order to strengthen its hold on these newly conquered territories Israel embarked on a policy of settlements; its aim was greater security, to exclude from Israel (if possible) those areas where there were too many Arabs and to swing the demographic balance in favour of the Jews. In July, despite a UN resolution, the Israelis made it plain that they would not return any part of Jerusalem to the Arabs; effectively, Israel annexed the whole city.

Israeli policy now was to demand direct negotiations with its Arab neighbours, but following an Arab summit held that August in Khartoum, the capital of Sudan, the Arab states determined against either recognition of Israel or negotiations with it. The ceasefires that had been arranged between Israel and its three neighbours were subsequently violated by both sides.

On 22 November the UN General Assembly accepted Resolution 242, which became the basis for the UN stand for years to come. A UN special representative, Dr Gunnar Jarring, was appointed to attempt to bring the two sides together. Israel said that it would not return to the boundaries of 1949, but would hold on to its newly acquired territory: it reiterated this stand both at the United Nations and in the Knesset, and said further that any adjustments to the territory which it held would have to depend on a permanent settlement being accepted by the Arabs.

The results of the war for Egypt were an immediate disaster: its air force had been destroyed; huge amounts of armaments had been written off; and its army had been shown up as wholly inadequate with low morale in face of the Israeli onslaught. The Suez Canal had once more been closed, and half the country's total oil output which came from Sinai was lost – at least for as long as Israel held on to the Sinai peninsula.

Although President Nasser resigned on 9 June, there was an overwhelming and mainly spontaneous Egyptian reaction in his favour and on 10 June he was recalled by the unanimous vote of the National Assembly. None the less Egypt's shattering defeat at the hands of Israel had done damage to Nasser's image as the leading figure in the Arab world from which he was not to recover. Immediately, however, he set about the task of post-defeat reconstruction; the Soviets were willing at once to replace a large proportion of the aircraft and other arms that had been written off. Discontent in the army led to a plot to reinstate Hakim Amer, the Deputy Commander-in-Chief, but this was put down without difficulty.

At the Arab summit in Khartoum that August, Egypt agreed to lift its pressures on the Arab oil states (Kuwait, Libya and Saudi Arabia) to boycott Britain and the United States, in return for financial aid for reconstruction; they agreed to pay a total of £135 million a year (£95 million to Egypt and £40 million to Jordan). Nasser also came to an agreement with King Faisal of Saudi Arabia to withdraw Egypt's 40,000 troops from North Yemen. In October 1967 Egypt did a little to regain its lost prestige when its navy sank the *Eilat*, Israel's flagship. The Israeli response was to launch a series of attacks and bombardments on the Canal cities, forcing the Egyptians to evacuate the civilians from them. A war of attrition then developed along the Canal with frequent bombardments and raids. Nasser, it became clear after his defeat, had been brought round to favouring a political solution. He accepted Resolution 242 of November, which called for an Israeli withdrawal in return for a *de facto* recognition of Israel.

The last years of Nasser (to his death in 1970) were to be troubled. In February 1968 a military court passed sentences ranging between 15 and 20 years on the senior air force officers for their conduct in the war. After providing replacements for about half Egypt's lost armaments the Soviets also produced substantial economic help in 1968, including the offer to build a steel mill at Helwan.

However, Egypt's defeat and the wider defeat of the Arabs adversely affected Soviet prestige in the Middle East since Moscow was seen as their main supporter.

For Jordan the war meant the loss of the West Bank and the move across the river into Jordan of some 200,000 Arab refugees. King Hussein had hesitated to enter the war, but in the end had been forced to do so by general Arab pressures and the strength of the war party. Throughout 1968 there were to be artillery duels along the Jordan valley between the Israelis and Jordanians. In the longer term, however, defeat in the war threatened Jordan's internal stability, while the growing strength and prestige of the Palestinian guerrillas on his territory led to the war of 1970 between Hussein's government and the Palestinians, which threatened to destroy Jordan.

Syria alone of the combatants rejected the idea of any compromise with Israel and was to remain its bitter opponent from then on. In general terms the Arab reaction to the defeat of 1967 was to renew the policy of non-recognition, so the scene was set more or less at once for the next round of Arab–Israeli hostilities. Although UN Resolution 242 had been accepted by both sides, they read it differently, for the clause about Israeli withdrawal from all territories occupied was open to more than one interpretation. For the Arabs the period 1967 to 1973 was concerned with the question of recovering their lost lands, while the PLO became increasingly powerful and influential. During this period the Israelis again turned to the USA as their principal military backer following an arms embargo imposed by France under de Gaulle.

In 1970 there was an American initiative under President Richard Nixon's Secretary of State, William Rogers, who put forward a new peace plan. Both Egypt and Jordan accepted the plan, which brought an end to the shooting along the Canal. Once more, however, nothing had been solved.

THE YOM KIPPUR WAR 1973

Introduction

Although Nasser never really recovered his pre-1967 prestige, his death in 1970 none the less brought to an end an era in Arab rejuvenation. He was succeeded by his only Vice-President, Anwar el Sadat, who at least outwardly continued Nasser's policies. In April 1971 the proposed Confederation of Arab Republics – Egypt, Libya and Syria (Sudan dropped out of the negotiations) – caused a political crisis; Sadat feared a coup and carried out a pre-emptive purge, and a number of leading figures, including his Vice-President, Ali Sabry, were arrested. Sadat replaced them with people loyal to himself and overcame the crisis. Since Sabry had been pro-USSR, there were fears in Moscow that Sadat was shifting towards the West. However, in June 1971 Egypt signed a 15-year treaty of friendship and co-operation with the USSR; there was no obvious alternative at that time, and Sadat wished to maintain his ties with Moscow, whose support would be essential in any confrontation with Israel.

Sadat had inherited from Nasser a difficult 'no war, no peace' approach to Israel that sooner or later was likely to produce its own escalation and crisis. During the first three years of his presidency (1970–3) Sadat was feeling his way: first, he had to establish his political authority at home in the aftermath of the charismatic

Nasser; and then he had to decide how to tackle the Israel question. He sought help from Washington to enforce an Israeli withdrawal from Sinai, but none was forthcoming. At the same time the Soviets were reluctant to provide him with the modern military equipment he would need if Egypt were to take on the Israelis in another war.

These difficulties were greatly increased by pressures from the political left and students, from the Palestinians, who were becoming both more vociferous and more confident, and from the army, which was restless as it remained immobile along the banks of the Suez Canal. Furthermore, about 1 million refugees from the Canal towns had been dispersed into Cairo and elsewhere in Egypt, greatly adding to the country's already formidable social problems. The result of these pressures was to make Sadat appear dangerously isolated. His action in expelling Soviet advisers in mid-1972, although immediately popular, left Egypt exposed and vulnerable since it appeared to demonstrate that Sadat had no policy. There was no source of military aid other than the USSR: France would not supply arms, Britain would only provide very limited amounts and the USA was firmly committed to Israel.

However, Sadat did possess one advantage which he used with considerable diplomatic skill. He did not overawe other Arab leaders with his charisma as had Nasser from his position of popular dominance; as a result, they were prepared to plan a new Arab strategy with him. He brought about a *rapprochement* with Saudi Arabia, which was to be crucial in the war of 1973 and its aftermath, and at the same time he managed to appear far more 'reasonable' to the West, and to the USA in particular. In May 1973 Israel celebrated the twenty-fifth anniversary of its establishment as a state and gave considerable offence with its military parades in Jerusalem and its air of belligerence: hubris had set in.

Thus, by mid-1973 there was no sign of any solution to the Arab–Israeli confrontation: the Israelis had not returned any of the territories taken in 1967 and, moreover, had established some 50 civilian or para-military settlements in those territories. Despite the fact that both Egypt and Jordan had signalled their willingness to recognize the state of Israel, provided that a peace settlement included the return of the occupied territories, Israel showed no comparable readiness to negotiate. Indeed, despite annual UN resolutions calling on Israel to restore the occupied territories, it refused to give up any of its 1967 conquests.

The USA in fact held the key to a solution; it was the only country that had the power to break the deadlock, but it could only do so by forcing Israel to compromise and in 1973 seemed quite unwilling even to attempt such a policy. But though the USA was the major external support of Israel, the US economy was becoming increasingly dependent on imports of Middle East – Arab – oil. American policy at this time appeared too simplistic: to ensure Israel's continuing military superiority over its neighbours without extracting any political concessions in return. In March 1973 the USA supplied Israel with 48 jet fighters. Then in the summer the USA was obliged to use its veto in the United Nations to block the passage of a resolution which called on Israel to return the occupied territories. Another factor of importance during 1973 was the growing *détente* between the USA and the USSR, which persuaded the Arab states that neither superpower was prepared to risk war over the Middle East question.

Prior to 1973 the Israelis had persuaded themselves that Egypt feared to go to war against them again and that the Bar-Lev Line (the fortifications they had built facing the Egyptians along the east bank of the Suez Canal) would effectively prevent any Egyptian penetration of Sinai. But Sadat was busy on the diplomatic front: he brought about a complete *rapprochement* with Faisal of Saudi Arabia, who provided the funds for military equipment; he concluded an agreement with Syria's President Assad for close military co-operation in a limited war against Israel; and he made Egypt's peace with King Hussein of Jordan. Then he obtained sophisticated weapons from the USSR.

Meanwhile, during 1972 and 1973, concerted pressures by a number of Arab leaders persuaded a growing number of African states to break diplomatic relations with Israel, so undermining its 'leapfrog' policy of the preceding years (to secure friends in black Africa). Up to 1972 the collective African policy towards the Middle East had been to support UN Resolution 242, but at the 1972 OAU Rabat Summit African states for the first time were persuaded to take a far tougher line towards Israel. Then, in 1973, at the Non-Aligned Movement Summit in Algiers, Africans were prepared to endorse a resolution which pledged full support to Egypt, Jordan and Syria in their efforts to recover the occupied territories. Just before the outbreak of the Yom Kippur War, Zaire, which had been a close supporter of Israel, delivered a bitter blow to its position by breaking off diplomatic relations.

Outbreak and response

In great secrecy for over a year before October 1973, Sadat had been planning a war to reverse the defeat of 1967. Almost no one knew of his plans in Egypt and he successfully fooled both Israeli and American intelligence, neither of which believed that the Egyptians had the military capacity to cross the Canal in sufficient force to take on the Israelis effectively. In fact when Egypt launched the war it got some 500 tanks across the Canal on pontoon bridges and breached the Bar-Lev line with powerful hoses. The Egyptian military performance of 1973 was in marked contrast to its lamentable showing six years before: the army showed sophistication and intelligence in its planning, and once engaged the troops fought with both tenacity and bravery.

Sadat's objective was not to regain the lost lands, although that was the declared war aim of both Egypt and Syria, for he was realistic enough to know that result to be most unlikely: it was to inflict high casualties on the Israelis and to force the superpowers once more to look at a lasting peace plan for the region.

In a carefully co-ordinated operation Egypt and Syria launched their joint attack on 6 October 1973, taking Israel completely by surprise. That date was the Jewish Day of Atonement (Yom Kippur) when all public services were suspended. On the first crucial day Egypt destroyed 100 Israeli tanks, while the Syrians launched a major tank attack the length of the Golan Heights where they also broke through the Israeli lines.

The Israelis responded with very rapid mobilization of their reserves, but by the third day of the fighting the Egyptians had occupied the east bank of the Suez Canal to a depth of several miles and were approaching the strategic Mitla Pass in Sinai. By then the Syrians were within 8 km (5 miles) of the Israeli frontier.

Meanwhile, other Arab countries mobilized and were to send between 10,000 and 15,000 troops to the war front. These came from Algeria, Libya, Kuwait, Morocco, Sudan and Tunisia. Iraq sent air units to the front. The units from

Algeria and Morocco as well as Iraqi air force units went to Egypt; the others went to the Syrian front. This time Jordan did not go to war with Israel, although it sent units of the army to fight on the Syrian front. But although Jordan had not opened a front against Israel, the fact that it had mobilized forced the latter to keep troops facing Jordan since it could have intervened at any time during the fighting.

Course of the war

The tank battles fought in Sinai were estimated to have been larger than any fought during the Second World War. On the Golan Heights the Israelis managed to halt the Syrian advance and then counter-attack successfully, but they only did so with massive and costly air attacks and because of a brilliant rearguard action. The war was to last for three weeks. The Syrians were finally driven back behind the previous ceasefire line. On the Suez front a small Israeli commando unit managed to cross the Canal on the twelfth day of the fighting to establish a bridgehead (15–16 October) on the West Bank at the north end of the Great Bitter Lake near the Nile Delta. This was heavily reinforced, enabling the Israelis to isolate the town of Suez and 10,000 men of the Egyptian Third Army, and to cut the Cairo–Suez road. After the ceasefire arranged by the UN (22–5 October) the Israelis extended the land under their control to 1200 square kilometres down to Port Adabiya south of Suez.

On 17 October, at the height of the fighting, the Arab oil producers met in Kuwait and agreed to reduce their oil production. On 19 October Abu Dhabi stopped all exports to the USA. Arab solidarity over the supply of oil to the West (see below) profoundly altered Western attitudes to the Arab–Israel question and led to a new set of responses. The oil states banned the supply of oil to the USA and the Netherlands, and reduced supplies to the other European countries while at the same time increasing the price. The result was greatly to weaken Israel's bargaining position.

The determination of the Egyptian and Syrian troops, which had been so clearly lacking in 1967, was a new factor of major importance that took the Israelis as well as other observers of the war by surprise. It brought to the Middle East question a new dimension that upset the military dominance which the Israelis had exercised in the three previous wars (1948, 1956 and 1967) and had by 1973 come to take for granted.

Estimated costs and casualties

The fighting was heavy and losses were high on both sides. Israel suffered 3000 dead or missing; this was the highest number in any of its wars and had a profound impact upon public opinion. Egyptian casualties were lower than those in the 1967 war: about 7700 dead. Between 15 and 22 November Egypt exchanged 245 Israeli prisoners of war for 8400 Egyptians. During the course of the three-week war Soviet arms deliveries to Egypt came to between 700 and 800 tons a day. Egypt lost an estimated 242 aircraft and 880 tanks. No official figures for Arab casualties were issued, but losses suffered by Syria must have come to several thousand dead. Following the war, Syria received large new shipments of Soviet arms to replace those it had lost.

Results: immediate and longer term

By the end of the war Israel had regained the military advantage, had obtained further land in Syria and was threatening Damascus itself. Yet despite Israel's having ended the war in a position of military superiority over Egypt and Syria, the war had changed fundamentally the whole Middle East balance of power. The most important immediate result lay in the initiative which the Arab oil-producing states had taken in calling for a boycott of those states which supported Israel. A second result which was almost equally momentous was the fact that the Egyptians and Syrians had broken the myth of Israeli military invincibility. After 1967 the Israelis had come to believe (and behave) as though they were absolutely and permanently superior to the Arabs in matters military, and this belief had now been shattered.

A third new factor concerned Africa: when Israeli forces crossed the Suez Canal on to *African* Egyptian soil they changed the African line-up. Until then African leaders had avoided too close an involvement in the Middle East question by arguing that it was not an African affair, but after the Suez crossing it became a question of an outside invasion of Africa. As a result virtually every African state, including in the end Ethiopia and Kenya, which had been among its close allies, broke diplomatic relations with Israel.

In the immediate aftermath of the UN-arranged ceasefire of 25 October, which both sides frequently broke, the US Secretary of State, Dr Henry Kissinger, began his shuttle diplomacy between the two sides. On 17 January 1974 he secured an agreement between Israel and Egypt whereby the Israelis withdrew to a line 32 km (20 miles) east of the Canal in return for a reduction of Egyptian troops on the east bank. A UN force was then inserted between the two as a buffer. Kissinger obtained an Israeli–Syrian agreement only on 31 May 1974: under this both sides withdrew to the 1967 ceasefire lines and Israel gave up Quneitra.

The war led directly to the emergence of a strong Organization of Petroleum Exporting Countries (OPEC), which was to dominate the world oil scene for the succeeding 10 years: immediately it meant the use of the oil weapon (boycotts or the reduction of output in order to exert political pressure on the USA and the European countries); later, this new economic power of the Arab oil states (joined by the other principal Third World producers, such as Indonesia, Iran, Nigeria and Venezuela) led to the demand for a new international economic order and to the 1975 Conference on International Economic Co-operation (CIEC) in Paris, where the concept of North and South was to emerge.

Another effect of the war was to encourage the rise of the PLO in both influence and impact so that, commensurate with the period of OPEC's pre-eminence, the PLO became the crucial 'swing' factor in Middle East political calculations.

A change of emphasis in the West became apparent on 6 November when, in response to Arab oil pressures, the nine member states of the EEC called for Israel to withdraw from the territories it had occupied in 1967, and argued that the rights of the Palestinians should be taken into account in any Middle East settlement. It became clear that at last Europe was losing patience with Israel. The

Arab states reinforced this new EEC approach by emphasizing that neither would Israel be safe from further attack nor would the oil supply to Europe be assured until a settlement had been reached.

In June 1974 the US President, Richard Nixon, went on a peace mission to the Middle East, and this, coupled with the efforts of Henry Kissinger to bring about a settlement, led to a reconciliation between the Arab states and the USA. Following Nixon's trip the Israeli Finance Minister, Shimon Peres, visited Washington, where he succeeded in having a $500 million loan converted into a gift. But Israel was not to regain its pre-eminent influence in Washington, mainly, though not exclusively, because the USA and the rest of the world had come to realize the extent to which it depended on Arab oil.

Yet despite the united Arab front and the new attitudes which the oil weapon had induced in both Europe and the USA, the Israelis did not respond by surrendering the annexed territories and through 1974 the initiative for a peace settlement became increasingly bogged down. United Nations forces were stationed between the two sides in both Sinai and the Golan Heights. There were bitter Israeli–Syrian recriminations over the treatment of prisoners, and the Israelis destroyed Quneitra before they evacuated it.

Military equipment on both sides was soon restored by respective allies, although the Egyptians complained at their treatment by the USSR, which replaced all Syria's losses but only part of Egypt's. The USA supplied Israel with $3000 million worth of military equipment. In the immediate aftermath of the war the two superpowers escalated the supply of arms to their respective allies, but when this appeared to endanger growing *détente* between the USA and the USSR Washington pulled back and told Israel that it was only prepared to supply arms provided that this did not endanger the *détente* then taking place.

One result of the war in Israel itself was to cause a split between those who placed their faith in military might as the surest means of holding the Arabs at bay and a growing peace lobby who wanted to make greater attempts at real negotiations with Israel's neighbours. Dissatisfaction with the government was another result of the war: General Dayan's popularity slumped, while that of another general, Ariel Sharon, who had successfully crossed Suez, was in the ascendant. He left the army to lead right-wing hawks in the Likud Party. A generally troubled Israel entered 1974, and in April the Prime Minister, Golda Meir, resigned; after a period of political bargaining Yitzhak Rabin became Prime Minister. He dropped Moshe Dayan as Defence Minister and Abba Eban, who had been Foreign Minister since 1966. Both Rabin and his new Foreign Minister, Yigal Allon, were prepared to concede land to the Arabs in order to obtain a working peace. Thus in September 1975 Israel concluded a Second Disengagement Agreement with Egypt and then withdrew from another area of Sinai. From 1975 onwards Egypt's primary concern was to recover the remainder of Sinai, and when it succeeded in recovering all of Sinai following the Camp David Accords of 1978 (signed in 1979) it also found that it had become isolated in the Arab world. The Arab judgment of Egypt was that it had abandoned the wider Arab and Palestinian cause in its more selfish determination to recover its own lost territories.

Perhaps the most important result of the 1973 war was to reduce Israel to more manageable proportions: the mystique of its military invincibility had been destroyed, and, with the development of OPEC and the oil weapon, Western countries which had previously supported Israel were now far readier to criticize its actions and take the part of the Arabs.

JORDAN: THE PALESTINIAN UPRISING 1970

Introduction

Jordan was always the least defensible and most vulnerable of the Arab states surrounding Israel. The addition to its limited population of large numbers of Palestinian refugees was not so much a source of added strength as a cause of anxiety, for the Palestinians, who came to outnumber the original population of Transjordan, owed no allegiance to the Hashemites and were far more likely to see their citizenship of Jordan as a temporary expedient than to regard it as anything more binding. Following the first Arab–Israeli war of 1948–9, Transjordan annexed the West Bank (21 per cent of the original Palestine) and became the Hashemite Kingdom of Jordan. The Palestinian Arabs became a majority of the Jordan population. They regarded themselves, moreover, as more advanced than the Jordanians, and therein lay the seeds of further problems.

But though from 1949 onwards the population of Jordan included more than half a million refugees, many of whom were destitute, it was also largely due to the enterprise and capacities of the Palestinians that Amman was transformed into a modern city. A further complication for Jordan lay in the fact that the Palestinian part of the population wanted confrontation with Israel, so it was impossible, even apart from geography, for Jordan to keep clear of Israeli entanglements. At least until the early 1970s King Hussein was to see himself as speaking on behalf of the Palestinians.

The Six Day War of 1967 proved a disaster for Jordan, which lost the West Bank and gained 200,000 refugees across the river on the east bank; the tourist industry collapsed, while closure of the Suez Canal rendered Jordan's only port at Aqaba virtually useless. For the next three years, moreover, Jordan found itself constantly engaged in artillery barrages with Israel across the ceasefire lines, and subject to repeated Israeli raids mounted in retaliation for Palestinian commando raids from Jordan that Hussein's government, in any case, was unable to control. These Israeli retaliatory tactics, which caused heavy casualties in towns such as Irbid and Salt, led to a depopulation of the east bank.

Thus, between 1968 and 1970 the government of Jordan faced a growing dilemma: to allow free movement to the Palestinian guerrillas, in which case these crossed the border to attack Israel and invited retaliation; or to attempt to curtail the guerrilla activities, which would lead to an internal confrontation between the government and the Palestinian guerrillas. King Hussein, who over the years became a supremely adroit politician, was obliged to vary his tactics, sometimes clamping down on the activities of the guerrillas, at other times allowing them much freer rein. In the end, however, Jordan's stability depended on a political settlement.

During this period the Palestinian guerrilla movements led by Al Fatah emerged as rivals in power to the government itself. In November 1968, on the anniversary of the Balfour Declaration, a major confrontation took place in Amman between government and guerrillas which produced street fighting and brought the capital close to civil war. There were further similar confrontations in February and June 1970, and it appeared only a matter of time before one of these explosions produced a full-scale civil war. An agreement between King Hussein and Yasser Arafat in 1970 bought the government time, but only by the expedient of Hussein sacking his Commander-in-Chief and a cabinet minister, who were regarded as antagonistic to the *fedayeen* (commandos). Then on 7 August 1970, Hussein followed President Nasser's lead and accepted the settlement plan of the American Secretary of State, William Rogers, under which Egypt and Israel agreed to a 90-day Canal Zone ceasefire. This was interpreted by the Palestinian Arabs as tantamount to a declaration of war since the Rogers Plan recognized the existence of Israel.

The rise of the PLO

In 1964 King Hussein, along with other Arab leaders, had agreed to the establishment of the Palestine Liberation Organization (PLO), but he was not prepared to allow its army – the PLA – to train on Jordanian soil, and nor would he permit the PLO headquarters to be in Jordan. His political instincts in this were absolutely correct, yet even so the rising influence and prestige of the PLO over the second half of the 1960s threatened to undermine the Jordanian government, which in any case at that time was seen as a moderate in the Arab world and had few friends. In Jordan the Palestinian guerrilla groups acted more and more as a law unto themselves, so a head-on clash with government appeared inevitable. When agreements were made they broke down almost at once.

The guerrilla organizations controlled the refugee camps, where they had no problem in recruiting the young to train in their turn as guerrillas. In addition they enjoyed widespread support among the people of Jordan as a whole since many of these were Palestinians. Thus the guerrillas formed a virtual state within a state. Al Fatah received assistance in the form of military training and arms from the Arab states, particularly Syria, and money from the Gulf states. It was an explosive mix.

The uprising of September 1970

The acceptance by Jordan of the Rogers Plan with its ceasefire for the Middle East was the spark which set off the explosion of 1970 since it ignored the Palestinians' state of war with Israel. Fighting broke out between government forces and the guerrillas at the end of August; and then there was an assassination attempt against the King. On 6 September Palestine guerrillas of the Popular Front for the Liberation of Palestine (PFLP) hijacked two Western airliners, which they flew to a deserted airfield in Jordan near Zeraq; later, two more airliners were hijacked and, though some of the passengers were released, several hundred were held in order to secure the release of guerrilla hostages. Taking the hijacked planes to Jordan was a direct challenge to the authority of the government, and one which it could not ignore. As the fighting escalated, Iraq and Syria both threatened to intervene on the side of the guerrillas, and Libya switched its aid from the Jordanian government to the guerrillas.

On 16 September Hussein appointed a military government under Brigadier Muhammad Daoud, while the army Commander-in-Chief, who was sympathetic to the guerrillas, was replaced. On 17 September the government initiated a systematic attack on the guerrillas to liquidate their bases in the country and destroy their power. Fighting then became general in Amman and elsewhere in the country and lasted for the next 10 days. In the north of Jordan the guerrillas gained full control for a time; they were assisted by the Syrians as well as by three battalions of the PLA which Nasser had sent back from the Suez front. Later, however, the Jordanian army beat back the Syrian column which had intervened on the side of the guerrillas. Jordan now found itself virtually deserted: Libya threatened intervention and broke diplomatic relations, and Kuwait cut off its aid. On the other hand, the Iraqis, who might have turned the scales and still had 12,000 troops in Jordan from the time of the 1967 war, refused to intervene.

Jordan was bitterly criticized by the other Arab states, although they did not have militant PLO guerrillas on their territory. King Hussein made an approach to the USA for possible military assistance, but then under intense pressure from Arab leaders agreed to a ceasefire (albeit only when his army had gained the upper hand in the fighting). His commanders would have preferred to keep fighting until they had completed the destruction of the Palestinian forces. Following intense efforts at mediation by Arab leaders, and especially by Nasser, Hussein and Arafat signed an agreement in Cairo to end the war; this took place on 27 September, the day before Nasser died of a heart attack. On 13 October a further agreement was signed between Hussein and Arafat in Amman. Over the next months, however, a form of on–off war between the guerrillas and government forces was to continue. Gradually the guerrillas were to be driven out of Amman and then northwards to the Syrian border. About 1500 people were killed in the fighting in Amman.

By the beginning of 1971 the Jordanian army was ready to move in and drive the guerrillas out of their remaining strongholds. Egypt, Syria and Algeria warned Jordan not to liquidate the liberation movements; Iraq withdrew some of its troops, though still leaving two brigades in Jordan. In April the Jordanian government felt strong enough to order the guerrillas to withdraw the balance of their forces from Amman. They did not do so, but it was not until 13 July 1971 that an attack was launched on the guerrillas in the Jerash-Aljoun area of Amman. The fighting lasted for four days, but at the end of it the last guerrilla bases had been destroyed and between 2300 and 2500 guerrillas had been taken prisoner. The majority of these prisoners were released a few days later and allowed either to resume normal lives in Jordan or to leave for other Arab lands.

King Hussein's tough action had rid Jordan of the state within a state, but it had also earned bitter opposition from most of the Arab world. Egypt, Libya, Sudan and the two Yemens each came out with public criticisms of Jordan; Syria and Iraq closed their borders with Jordan, whose relations with Syria were to be especially bad for the next year or so.

Aftermath

For the following three years Jordan was almost totally isolated in the Arab world, but in September 1973 King Hussein met Presidents Assad (Syria) and Sadat (Egypt) in a reconciliation summit, following which diplomatic relations were restored with Jordan. This reconciliation was condemned by the more hardline Arab states as well as Al Fatah, but slowly Jordan continued to return to favour, helped by the amnesty which Hussein now gave to all political prisoners.

Jordan stood aside from the Yom Kippur War of 1973, although units of the Jordanian army went to fight with the Syrians in the Golan Heights. Subsequently, the outstanding political question was that of who should speak for the Palestinian Arabs, a role which Jordan had considered its own ever since the annexation of the West Bank in 1949. In September 1974 Egypt and Syria agreed to support the claim advanced by the PLO that it should be the 'only legitimate representative of the Palestinian people'. Immediately after this Jordan refused to take part in further peace talks. At the Rabat Arab Summit of October 1974 20 Arab leaders recognized the PLO as sole legitimate representative of the Palestinians with the right to establish national authority over any liberated Palestinian territory. This decision Hussein was compelled reluctantly to accept; he therefore gave up Jordan's claims both to the West Bank (whenever it should be recaptured from the Israelis) and to speak for the Palestinians. At the same time Hussein said he would continue to work for the liberation of the West Bank and that, meanwhile, he would recognize the full citizenship rights of Palestinians in Jordan. In November 1974 the PLO leader, Yasser Arafat, was invited to address a plenary session of the United Nations General Assembly.

The events of 1987–1990: the *intifadeh*

In 1988 King Hussein announced that Jordan would cut its legal and administrative claims to the Israeli-occupied West Bank (which Jordan had occupied in 1950 and Israel had taken in 1967); by doing this King Hussein finally acknowledged that Jordan gave up its claims to the West Bank, recognized the Palestinian claim for a separate state and abandoned its role as spokesman for the Palestinians. In reaction to this move by Jordan the Palestine National Council (PNC) proclaimed a state of Palestine on 15 November 1988. Then, in April 1989, the PNC elected Arafat President of the newly proclaimed though non-existent state of Palestine.

Meanwhile Palestinian desperation in the occupied territories (the West Bank and the Gaza Strip) had reached new heights and an incident in December 1987 sparked off stone-throwing attacks on Israeli soldiers which were soon to escalate into an uprising or *intifadeh*. At first about a twelfth of the 600 towns and villages of the occupied territories were affected by the *intifadeh*, and by December 1988 (a year after the initial riots) about 300 Palestinians had been killed by Israeli security forces, while 6000 were in detention. The violence escalated during 1989 with an increasing number of weapons appearing and the growth of the Islamic Resistance Movement (Hamas). By 1990 Israel faced a new and formidable internal enemy and the *intifadeh* seemed set to continue indefinitely.

THE ISRAELI INVASION OF LEBANON 1982

Background

Israel's first consideration with regard to any of its neighbours has always been national security, and the years 1948 to 1970 were relatively free of confrontations between Lebanon and Israel. Their relations became far more difficult, however, following the expulsion of the Palestinians from Jordan after the failure of the 1970 uprising. A majority of the Palestinian activists then moved to Lebanon and from that time onwards were to use Lebanon as a base from which to launch attacks on Israel. Later, when the Lebanese government became ineffective during the civil war of 1975–6, the PLO found that it could operate with much greater freedom, launching attacks across the border into Israel from southern Lebanon with little or no restraint placed on its forces by the government. As a result Israel was drawn increasingly into the affairs of Lebanon, and during the course of the civil war it was to blockade Tyre and Sidon in order to prevent the delivery of arms to the PLO; train a Lebanese military contingent in Israel and supply it with tanks; and supply military equipment for use in the war by the Lebanese Christian militias. Then, in the summer of 1976, Israeli forces briefly occupied considerable areas of southern Lebanon. Israel's justification for these interventions was to safeguard its northern border with Lebanon and strike at the PLO camps so as to lessen their ability to carry out cross-border raids. From this time onwards, indeed, Israel was to make frequent cross-border raids against PLO targets in southern Lebanon.

The events of 1978

In March 1978 the Palestinians carried out a major incursion into northern Israel from Lebanon. The Israeli response was a large-scale invasion of southern Lebanon. On 14–15 March some 20,000 Israeli troops moved into southern Lebanon in order to destroy PLO bases. The Israelis also hoped that their move would force the Lebanese government to control the PLO in the future. Towards the end of the month a United Nations peace-keeping force (UNIFIL) was deployed in southern Lebanon, enabling the Israelis to withdraw during June. But Israel continued to supply arms to the Christians in the south, whom it came to regard as necessary allies against the PLO. Despite the fact that PLO bases had been destroyed and the Palestinians had fled the area of southern Lebanon, they were soon to return. None the less, for a time at least, Israel appeared to have strengthened its position.

Other developments, however, ensured an escalation of PLO activities based on Lebanon and acted as a prelude to the Israeli invasion of 1982. When the Camp David Accords of 1978 between President Sadat of Egypt and Prime Minister Begin of Israel appeared likely to lead to a more permanent settlement in the region the PLO became increasingly determined to frustrate the peace initiatives. None the less they went ahead, and on 26 March 1979 the Egypt–Israel Peace Treaty was signed in Washington by Begin and Sadat. It was the first ever treaty between Israel and an Arab state. The immediate result was to produce an almost total Arab economic and political boycott of Egypt.

By 1980 Israel had become more beleaguered than at any time since its emergence as a state in 1948. It was condemned at the United Nations for its refusal to withdraw from the occupied territories, opposed through most of the Third World and by the Communist bloc, and no longer even sure of the American support which it had come to take for granted. During the year Lebanon appeared to be sliding into anarchy, breaking down into zones controlled by Muslim, Christian or Palestinian commandos or militias, and Israel carried out armed incursions against

PLO positions more or less with impunity. The Lebanese army seemed incapable of withstanding these Israeli incursions and therefore turned to the Syrians, who then made up part of the Arab Deterrent Force in Lebanon (see Part V, pp. 439–445). The United Nations Interim Force in Lebanon (UNIFIL) monitored Israeli attacks in the south, but was unable to deter them. In August 1980 Israel launched a major cross-border attack in which it deployed 600 soldiers and struck at PLO camps to the north of the Litani river. This was its heaviest incursion since 1978 and led to the deaths of 25 Palestinians and Lebanese. In October 1980 the Lebanese government complained to the United Nations that its observers in southern Lebanon were subject to constant harassment by the Israelis.

Lebanon in 1981 was in a highly volatile state: Syria had substantial forces stationed in the country and these became involved in battles between Muslims and Christians, while the PLO remained as an unpredictable and dangerous factor in the middle of everybody. During the year the American Special Envoy, Philip Habib, negotiated a ceasefire between Israel and Lebanon. However, Israel regarded the Syrian missile batteries in the Bekaa valley as a provocation which had to be removed. In March 1981 Israel turned down a UNIFIL request to withdraw its forces from southern Lebanon and its Army Chief of Staff, General Rafael Eitan, said that a war of attrition between Israel and the PLO in southern Lebanon was likely to occur unless the PLO gave up its attempts to infiltrate the southern buffer zone of Lebanon, which was controlled by the Christians. During both March and April Israel became more and more involved in cross-border raids against PLO bases.

On 30 June elections in Israel narrowly returned Menachem Begin to power, and shortly afterwards Israel launched a series of attacks on PLO bases in Lebanon, which included air strikes against bridges over the Litani and Zahrani rivers. These raids culminated in a major attack – 17 July – on the PLO headquarters in the centre of Beirut, in which an estimated 300 were killed and 500 injured. Then, on 24 July, under the auspices of the US envoy, Habib, Israel and the PLO agreed a ceasefire.

These Israeli attacks were widely condemned abroad (they led the US administration to suspend the delivery of a number of F-16s) and also met growing opposition inside Israel. Shortly after the ceasefire Palestinian guerrillas attacked a bus in Israel, wounding four; this produced in its turn a retaliation on 1 October when a car full of explosives was detonated outside the PLO office in Beirut, killing 80 people. Another 20 people were killed on 15 December when a bomb destroyed the Iraqi Embassy in Beirut.

Such violence allowed the PLO and its leader, Yasser Arafat, to make the point that no settlement was possible that did not take the PLO into account. Two other events of 1981 heightened general Israeli–Arab tensions and made another explosion seem increasingly likely: these were the Israeli bombing of the French-constructed Osirak nuclear reactor near Baghdad on 7 June; and the assassination of President Sadat of Egypt on 6 October.

The build-up to war 1982

The constant confrontation across the border, coupled with growing anarchy inside Lebanon, had a momentum of its own; it ended in the June 1982 Israeli invasion of southern Lebanon, code-named 'Peace for Galilee', whose aim was the elimination of the PLO. On 19 January 1982 Israel's Prime Minister, Menachem Begin, told President Reagan that Israel would not attack Lebanon despite PLO and Syrian provocations. In any case, during the first four months of the year Israel's main concern was with its final evacuation of Sinai; while this was in progress the PLO continued to build up its bases in southern Lebanon where it began to deploy guns and rockets against the north of Israel. Israel subsequently was to exaggerate this build-up (at least on the basis of US intelligence). In the course of the first half of the year Israel repeated, more than once, its assurance to President Reagan that it would not attack Lebanon even after PLO attacks inside Israel. At the same time Israel and Lebanon continued to hold negotiations about peace and the position of the PLO, although these produced no agreements. For their part the Lebanese Christian leaders were more interested in action against the PLO, which they regarded as a source of danger in their own midst.

At the end of May Israel's Foreign Minister, Itzhak Shamir, said that Israel needed to destroy the PLO as a fighting force. Then, on 3 June, the Israeli Ambassador to Britain, Shlomo Argov, was shot and badly wounded by a Palestinian. This was the signal for the war that by then everyone expected, and on 6 June 1982 60,000 Israeli troops crossed the border into Lebanon. The Israeli objectives can be summarized as follows: to secure control of a band of territory in southern Lebanon as a buffer zone; to destroy the PLO bases; to destroy the PLO altogether if this could also be managed; and to help bring to power in Lebanon a government which would be prepared to make peace with Israel.

The invasion of June 1982

On 5 June Israeli jet aircraft attacked PLO targets in Beirut; on 6 June the invasion of Lebanon began; on 7 June Tyre was occupied; on 8 June, Sidon; on 9 June, Damur. Also on 9 June Israeli jets attacked Syrian missile bases in the Bekaa valley. Although at first Israel claimed that its objective was only to push the PLO back from Israel's borders, its aims soon became far more ambitious and included cutting off the Syrian force of 4000 then in Beirut from its support in the Bekaa valley. As it happened the Syrians wished to avoid a direct confrontation with Israel at that time and agreed a truce on 12 June, which was accepted by Israel on 22 June.

Under extreme pressures from the USA the Israelis, who had advanced to the outskirts of Beirut, agreed to halt while the American envoy, Philip Habib, and the Lebanese government negotiated with the PLO. By 4 July Habib had secured a PLO promise to agree to an undertaking to evacuate Beirut, although the PLO then strung out negotiations for the better part of two months. By 14 July the Israeli forces had completed their encirclement of Beirut, and although they did not enter the city, they carried out massive bombardments of West Beirut as a means of maintaining pressure during the negotiations with the PLO.

Finally the PLO agreed (or perhaps were persuaded) to evacuate Beirut, and on 21 August under the supervision of a joint US–French–Italian force finally did so. Meanwhile, the Lebanese elections had been held and returned Bashir Gemayel as the new President-elect, but on 14 September he was assassinated, precipitating another crisis. Following his death, Israel changed its tactics and ordered its troops into West Beirut with the apparent task of ensuring that no large-scale massacre of Palestinians or Muslims followed his death. But on 16 September Lebanese Christian forces entered the Sabra and Chatila refugee camps, and hundreds of men, women and children were massacred. In the meantime the Israeli Defence Force (IDF) took large quantities of equipment from the deserted PLO positions in southern Lebanon, including some 500 pieces of artillery.

The course of the struggle

The Israeli invasion of Lebanon turned into a full-scale pursuit of the PLO by the IDF wherever they could be found. At the same time the Israelis achieved a secondary objective, which was to drive the Syrians out of at least some of their bases in Lebanon. From mid-June onwards Beirut was surrounded and cut off by the Israelis in order to force out the 6000 PLO thought to be stationed there, with the result that law and order in the city broke down.

Mid-September witnessed a climax to the war, though not what Israel had expected or planned: on 14 September Gemayel was assassinated; on 16 September the Sabra and Chatila massacres took place; on 20 September President Reagan agreed to send US troops to act as part of a peace-keeping force to supervise the Israeli withdrawal, and the first US Marines were back in Lebanon on 25 September. Thereafter everyone quarrelled about the pace and conditions that should govern the Israeli withdrawal: Arafat said the PLO would leave at the same time the Israelis did; the Israelis and the Lebanese only began talks at the very end of the year (28 December).

During 1983 Syria was to play a crucial role: it supported the PLO radical rebels who attacked Arafat's Tripoli base; and it refused to agree to any peace in Lebanon until the Israelis had withdrawn. At the same time Syria called on the USA for a new initiative over the Golan Heights, which were still held by Israel. In fact, as it was to become increasingly apparent, the war had resolved very little and Lebanon itself continued in a high state of anarchy.

Estimated costs and casualties

Casualty figures for this war are almost impossible to estimate accurately, although casualties for specific actions – such as that of 17 July 1981 (see above) – were given at the time. Israeli forces did massive damage to southern Lebanon and the city of Beirut by their air strikes and bombardments, and caused heavy civilian casualties. Their degree of responsibility for the Sabra and Chatila massacres will probably never be precisely established (328 were found dead but a further 991 were reported missing). Israel was unwilling to produce estimates for the civilian casualties which resulted from its actions, although thousands were reported to have died during the siege of Beirut. The costs to the Israelis were high in both material and international reputation, but the credibility of the PLO suffered what at the time appeared to be an irreversible defeat, and Yasser Arafat's prestige took a nosedive. By 20 December 1983 the PLO had been forced to leave their last Lebanese base in Tripoli and retire to Tunisia. The costs to Syria of its confrontation with Israel in 1982 was an estimated $1 billion, and by 1984 its military commitments in Lebanon were costing $250,000 a day, although as much in relation to the Christian–Muslim rivalries as in relation to the Israelis.

The immediate results of the 1982 invasion

The Israelis achieved their primary aim when in August 1982 the PLO were forced to leave Beirut, although the subsequent assassination of President-elect Bashir Gemayel and then the Sabra and Chatila massacres created a new, unlooked-for situation. None the less, Israel so far succeeded in its objectives as to force the PLO out of southern Lebanon and Beirut and – for a time – from the country altogether, while also inflicting a defeat on the Syrians. Moreover, it achieved these objectives without any interference – apart from protests – by other Arab states.

In response to widespread criticisms that it had colluded with the Sabra and Chatila massacres the Israeli government appointed its own commission of inquiry (the Kahan Commission), which reported in February 1983. It found that both military and political leaders had some degree of responsibility: the Defence Minister, Ariel Sharon, by negligence; as well as the Chief of Staff, Raphael Eitan, and other military leaders. Sharon resigned as Defence Minister, but remained in the cabinet. In Israel itself there were major demonstrations during 1983 against the interventions in Lebanon; meanwhile, negotiations about withdrawal were to drag on throughout the year. On 17 May 1983 Israel and Lebanon did reach an agreement under which normalization of relations would follow six months after the implementation of its main heads. These were the legalization of the international boundary between the two countries; the end of the state of war between them; and the stipulation that all foreign troops should be withdrawn. This last cause was the sticking point since Israel said it would only withdraw when the PLO and Syrian forces had also left the country. In addition the 17 May agreement stipulated a security zone in southern Lebanon. Syria was bitterly opposed to this agreement and tried to prevent its acceptance, but the Lebanese Parliament approved the agreement on 14 June 1983. Pressures on Israel, both external and at home, meant that by mid-1983 it had reduced its troop levels in Lebanon to 20,000 men.

Before they withdrew from the Shuf mountains and the outskirts of Beirut the Israelis warned President Gemayel – 3 September 1983 – but this did not prevent fighting from breaking out in their wake between Christians and Druze on the one hand and Muslims on the other, who moved in as the Israelis went. Back in Israel the manner of the withdrawal which had resulted in Christian and Druze deaths was questioned, especially as it put the Israeli–Maronite Christian alliance at risk.

On 14 January 1984 Major Saad Haddad, commander of the independent militia which had controlled southern Lebanon, died, depriving Israel of an important ally. Then another setback for Israel came when President Mubarek of Egypt met with Arafat, an encounter which was welcomed by Washington. Israel opposed the deployment of the UN forces in southern Lebanon in order to prevent a return of the PLO, although later it was to support such UN deployment. For most of the year Israel and Lebanon negotiated about the security of Israel's northern border before Israel was prepared to withdraw completely from Lebanon. On 5 March, as conditions in Lebanon deteriorated (see Part V, pp. 439–446), the Lebanese government abrogated the 1983 agreement with Israel. For the rest of the year the Lebanese talked of taking over areas still occupied by the Israelis, and Israel in turn talked of an early withdrawal; in the event, neither happened.

The Israeli withdrawal 1985

On 14 January 1985 Israel announced that it would begin to withdraw from Lebanon in five weeks' time and that the withdrawal would be divided into three phases. By April it had completed the first two stages of its withdrawal; by 6 June (the third anniversary of the invasion) the last Israeli troops had quit Lebanon. However, the last part of the withdrawal was marked by further bloodshed. Shia militants made constant hit-and-run attacks on the withdrawing Israelis and claimed that they were chasing them from the country; in fact the militants only received help on the ground from between 20 and 30 villages out of 200 in the southern region.

Following the deaths of two Israeli officers on 19 February, Israel launched its 'Iron Fist' policy against those villages that it suspected of harbouring the guerrillas who struck at Israeli forces. Under this policy Israeli troops stormed these villages, killed or wounded the inhabitants and took the men off to prison camps. A week after launching the policy Israel imposed dusk-to-dawn curfews in the areas it controlled and banned single-occupant vehicles for fear of bomb fanatics. During March a number of bomb outrages occurred, including one at a mosque in Maarake leading to 15 deaths, for which the Lebanese government blamed Israel. The Israelis also clashed with UNIFIL forces and (7 March) had a two-hour tank battle with the Lebanese. In Beirut (7 March) a car bomb killed 85 and wounded 250; then, on 10 March, a suicide car bomber killed 12 Israeli soldiers near the Israel–Lebanon border. In retaliation the Israelis attacked the Shiite village of Zvapiye, killing 35, wounding others and taking away the men as prisoners.

Bitter opposition at the United Nations produced a resolution condemning Israel's conduct in southern Lebanon; the USA was obliged to veto it since 11 members of the Security Council supported it, while Britain, Australia and Denmark abstained. According to the United Nations observers, the result of the Iron Fist policy was to escalate attacks on the Israeli forces. At the same time, fighting in the south degenerated into Christian versus Muslim battles, while the Israelis attacked Shiite villages.

The Israelis also violated the terms of the Geneva Convention at this time by transferring 1000 Shiite Lebanese prisoners to Israel to be held there until the security position had improved. As the Israelis withdrew, Muslim militias fell on Christian villages, but the Israelis said they would not intervene to help the Christians even though these had been their allies. During May, towards the end of their withdrawal, the Israelis fortified their border with Lebanon with a series of defensive ditches. When the withdrawal had been completed it was less than clear what fate awaited the Christians who had supported them.

Later in the year, following a PLO attack on Israelis in Larnaca, Cyprus, in which three were killed, Israel (1 October) carried out a reprisal raid against PLO headquarters in Tunisia. Yet slowly in the second half of the year Israel recovered a little of its international standing, which the manner of its withdrawal had done so much to damage. In southern Lebanon sectional fighting continued in the wake of the Israeli withdrawal. Israel had left a number of military advisers behind to assist the South Lebanon Army (SLA), consisting of some 2000 Maronite Christians whom they wished to keep as a buffer. The Israelis made it plain that they reserved the right to re-enter the Lebanon security zone along the border up to a distance of 10 km (6 miles), and this was the area which the SLA was to patrol and control.

During the second half of 1985 the PLO, which was still recovering from its expulsion from Lebanon as a whole, made little impact. The Shia guerrillas in the south, however, demanded a more prominent say in Lebanese developments as a result of their campaign against the withdrawing Israelis. And despite its with-drawal, Israel – through its advisers – in fact maintained a presence in southern Lebanon; in September 1986 it even reinforced its troops there. From 1985 to the end of the decade the Israelis were often to intervene in Lebanon.

Although the Israeli position was that it would not deal with the PLO, in fact it was prepared to do so for particular purposes. Thus, on 20 May 1985, Israel negotiated with the PLO for an exchange: three Israeli soldiers for 1150 Palestin-ians then held in Israel. During 1986 the PLO gradually came back into Lebanon: in April, for example, they re-established themselves in Sidon, which led to an Israeli air attack on the city. In September 1987 three Israeli soldiers were killed in a clash with pro-Syrian guerrillas in Lebanon. This produced an Israeli reprisal on 15 December with an air attack on guerrilla bases in southern Lebanon. The PLO gradually set up a new generation of bases in southern Lebanon. During 1989 Israel staged a total of 18 raids on Lebanese and Palestinian targets, killing 40 people. Their first raids of 1990, on 19 January, were directed at a pro-Iranian Hizbollah (Party of God) target and a PLO radio station; four people were killed and 13 injured. Little in fact seemed to have changed.

SYRIA AND LEBANON: THE 1976 INVASION AND ITS AFTERMATH

Background

Lebanon's geographic position, sandwiched between Israel and Syria, its small size and its peculiarly mixed terrain – a flat coastal region overlooked by mountains – make it the natural confrontation point for the opposed states of Israel and Syria, as it has been the fighting ground for contending empires throughout its history. In the troubled politics of the Middle East Syria's principal concern with regard to Lebanon has always been to prevent it falling under Israeli domination; only this can explain Syria's apparently paradoxical shifts from supporting the PLO and the Muslims to supporting the Christians. Thus, when it appeared that PLO militancy was bound to lead to an Israeli invasion of Lebanon it became a Syrian interest to break the power of Arafat's section of the PLO, so Syria found itself in the unenviable role from the point of view of a radical Arab state of supplying the Christian militias with arms so that they could prevent the PLO taking strategic strongholds.

Following the destruction of the 1973 Yom Kippur War, Syria received huge arms replacements from the USSR which enabled it completely to re-equip its army. Then, in 1974, Syria's hard line in support of the PLO helped persuade the Arab Summit at Rabat to recognize the PLO claim to the West Bank in place of Jordan's claim. Thereafter, Syrian relations with Jordan were to improve; in April 1975 King Hussein visited Damascus, while in June President Assad visited Amman. Syria bitterly opposed the second agreement on disengagement in Sinai between Egypt and Israel (September 1975) on the grounds that it both weakened united Arab opposition to Israel and was a betrayal of the PLO.

Civil war in Lebanon and Syrian intervention

The civil war in Lebanon of 1975–6 between Christians and Muslims became so violent that it threatened the balance of the whole region. President Sadat of Egypt supported the Christians, or at least gave them encouragement. President Assad of Syria aided the left: that is, the Shiite Muslims and the Palestinians. To begin with Syria's principal concern was to protect the position of the Palestinians in Lebanon. In consequence, in January 1976, Syria despatched about 2000 troops to Lebanon, an act which at once raised fears of Syrian ambitions to control Lebanon. At first Assad was able to obtain a ceasefire, in return for which he said he would control the Palestinians in Lebanon. That promise led Arafat and that part of the PLO which he controlled to fear Syrian domination.

It seemed increasingly likely during the first half of 1976 that the 'left' in Lebanon – the Shiites and the Palestinians – would emerge on top in the civil war. Such an outcome would be likely, in its turn, to produce a PLO-dominated state or lead to partition, and either development would act as an open invitation to Israel to intervene. That was what Syria most feared, and it led to the supreme irony of Syria invading Lebanon in June 1976 in order to break the power of the PLO.

An Arab League meeting of 8–9 June authorized Syria and Libya to send troops into Lebanon as a peace-keeping force, although in the event only Syria sent a force. That June, 20,000 Syrian troops with 450 tanks moved into Lebanon; their arrival sparked off a series of new alignments. Both Iraq and Libya, which had written off the PLO as ineffectual, now decided to support it again. By the end of June the Christians, now receiving Syrian help, reversed the fortunes of the war and captured two PLO refugee camps. Lebanon became 'partitioned', in fact if not in law, by a line through the centre of Beirut and on towards Damascus; this left the Christian government in control of the northern half of the country and the Druze, Muslim and PLO factions in control of the southern part of the country.

Immediate results of the Syrian intervention

Fighting continued from June to October when, under intense Arab pressures from two summits (in Riyadh and then Cairo), a ceasefire was agreed. Syria, as the instrument of the Arab League, was to maintain a peace-keeping force of 30,000 men in Lebanon. The civil war (or that major phase of it) came to an end in November. But in the period 1976 to 1978 frequent Israeli interventions in southern Lebanon prevented Syria from imposing its own peace on the area, so

Syria found itself in the half-way position of preventing a full-scale war but being unable to bring about a full-scale peace. And as other powers which intervene have discovered, Syria found it was far more difficult to extricate itself from Lebanon than it had been to intervene. Moreover, maintaining the 30,000 troops which made up the Arab deterrent force in Lebanon became a major drain on the Syrian economy.

A permanent presence

Although from 1977 onwards the Syrian army was the dominant force in northern Lebanon, the constant faction fights weakened its influence and power. In the summer of 1980, for example, the Phalangist militia occupied Zahle in the Bekaa valley. Syria regarded this as vital to its security against Israel, and the result was an increase of Syrian clashes with the Christian militias. The Israeli air force made a series of sorties against Syrian positions in the Bekaa valley, and, following the shooting down of two of its helicopters by the Israelis in April 1980, Syria moved SAM missiles into the valley. The growing Israeli–Syrian confrontation of 1980 looked as though it would lead to full-scale war. At the end of June Syria lifted its siege of Zahle (which the Israelis had opposed) following mediation by Saudi Arabia and Kuwait. Syria, however, kept its SAM missiles in the Bekaa valley.

Israeli invasion of southern Lebanon 1982

In June 1982 Israel invaded Lebanon (see above, pp. 313–317), with 60,000 troops inflicting defeat on Syrian forces in the south of the country and destroying their missiles in the Bekaa valley. But Syrian forces remained in strength in the north of the country and in the Bekaa valley, although the Israeli investment of Beirut meant that they were isolated from Syria. Some Syrian forces were trapped in Beirut by the Israelis; these were evacuated between 21 August and 1 September 1982 under the auspices of the American-led international peace-keeping force.

The principal Israeli objective in invading Lebanon was to destroy the PLO. It succeeded – for the time being – and forced them to retreat from southern Lebanon and Beirut. It also helped to create the situation which was to erupt in 1983 when the PLO divided into two factions, Syria siding with the more radical anti-Arafat group and helping to force him and his followers out of Lebanon.

Growing Syrian influence 1983–1985

On 17 May 1983 Israel and Lebanon concluded a peace agreement which laid down a time limit of three months for the withdrawal of all foreign troops from Lebanon. Syria, however, would not withdraw its forces from northern Lebanon, thus providing Israel with an excuse to delay its own evacuation. President Assad argued that Syrian forces, unlike the Israelis, were in Lebanon by invitation and that the Israelis should not make their withdrawal conditional on Syrian withdrawal. He further maintained that the continuing Israeli presence in Lebanon was a threat to Syria. By July 1983 Syria had increased its forces in Lebanon to 40,000: half in the Bekaa valley and half in the north. Now Syria's hope was to unite Druze and Shiite factions in a common front favourable to Syria against the Christian government of Gemayel.

The battle for control of the PLO now erupted. In May 1983 radical members of the PLO, who were opposed to Arafat's leadership on the grounds that he had surrendered at Beirut, began fighting his supporters, who had retreated to the Bekaa valley. Arafat accused both Syria and Libya of fomenting this revolt, and stated his belief that Syria hoped to gain control of the PLO. The fighting became very bitter. By November 1983 the Syrian forces were supporting the rebel PLO faction under the leadership of Abu Musa, which had trapped Arafat in Tripoli. After further fighting Saudi Arabia mediated to secure a truce, which allowed Arafat and 4000 followers to be evacuated from Tripoli in December 1983. They went to Tunisia where they were allowed to set up a new base. It soon became plain, however, that in supporting the radical faction of the PLO Syria had not in fact gained control of the movement.

When the Israelis withdrew from Beirut to deploy their forces south of the Awali river the Syrians remained in the capital (September 1983) and this ensured their continuing influence. They occasionally exchanged fire with the US fleet off Beirut, which remained to support the international peace-keeping force. By March 1984 Syria was in a position to force President Gemayel to abrogate the 17 May 1983 peace agreement with Israel and to reconvene the National Reconciliation Conference of Lebanon's rival factions.

Syrian policy now was to press for greater Muslim representation in the government, while at the same time offering guarantees to Gemayel. By the end of 1984, however, both the Syrian attempt to obtain Christian concessions to the Muslims and its efforts to build up a united front of Gemayel's opponents had broken down.

By mid-1984 major home and international pressures were forcing Israel to withdraw from Lebanon; Syria had always rejected the Israeli claim that both powers should withdraw simultaneously, and now Syria found it would remain in Lebanon after the Israelis had finally withdrawn unilaterally. Paradoxically, once Syria found itself alone in Lebanon, its influence declined since it could no longer be seen as a counter-balance to Israel.

The later 1980s

Syria's position in Lebanon became increasingly uneasy during the second half of the 1980s: it was expected to keep order and in fact wished to get out. The Israeli withdrawal, which was carried out between January and June 1985, left Syria as the only external power in Lebanon. Syria used the occasion to reduce its commitment by evacuating about 10,000 troops, but it still retained a force of 25,000 in Lebanon. After the Israeli departure the Gemayel government found itself mainly dependent for its survival on the Syrians. The various factions became divided over the Syrian question – whether they should accept or reject Syrian leadership – while there was pressure on Syria to take on the impossible task of disarming the various rival militias.

During 1985 the Christians split into further factions: Samir Geagea, a Christian regional commander, revolted against Gemayel because of his readiness to accept the Syrian line that there should be equal Christian–Muslim representation in government. Geagea obtained strong support from Christians with the result that faction fighting increased and Syria was unable to control the situation. None the less, Syria made its most determined effort yet to produce a Christian–Muslim agreement, and by December 1985, under the chairmanship of Syria's Vice-President, Abd al-Halim Khaddem, leaders of Christian, Druze and Shia militia actually signed an agreement that would have led to the phasing out of the built-in Christian majority in the Assembly.

At the same time Syria opposed efforts by Arafat and King Hussein of Jordan to begin new peace negotiations with Israel. By 1986, however, it had become clear that the Syrian presence in Lebanon did not give it much influence over events, while anti-government violence, including bomb outrages in Damascus, appeared to be encouraged from Lebanon. Syrian influence in Lebanon did increase somewhat during 1987, but in 1988, when President Gemayel's term of office came to an end and Lebanese leaders failed to agree on a successor, the country appeared to move closer to partition and Syria found its peace-keeping role even more difficult. Its position was made still more unstable by the growing influence in Lebanon of Iran, which was supporting extremist Islamic groups and apparently trying to create its own outposts of influence in the country. With Gemayel's departure the various Christian factions – the Maronites, Samir Geagea's militia (the Christian Lebanese Forces Militia) and General Michel Aoun, who was then head of the military government in east Beirut – between them argued, correctly as it appeared, that Syria's ability to impose solutions had all but disappeared. As the 1990s began Lebanon seemed set for ever-increasing violence; Israel was launching air attacks on pro-Iranian Hizbollah (Party of God) and PLO targets in southern Lebanon; and Syria was sitting uneasily in place with little influence and less policy.

PART V

Civil Wars: Ideological

Civil wars: ideological

THE AMERICAS

INTRODUCTION

The following 47 entries cover a range of extremes from a local mini-uprising (the revolt of the ranchers in Guyana) through a major civil war (Nigeria) to a state of apparently permanent civil strife (Colombia). There is a real problem of definition: at just what point does civil strife, violent eruptions against a repressive regime, turn into a civil war; when does a street confrontation between, for example, strikers and strike breakers become something more; how many people must die before violence qualifies for civil war status? There are no easy answers to these questions, and some of the examples included here might have been left out. Thus, under the Americas I have included 'Bolivia: ripe for revolution'. It is an account of the abortive attempt by Che Guevara and a handful of followers to stir up a revolution in a country which in terms of oppression and economic conditions was – and is – ripe for it. Had the revolt been led by an unknown instead of Che Guevara, we should probably not have heard of it at all, but such was Guevara's charisma and reputation that the Bolivian government deployed 3000 troops against him and his tiny, ill-fated band of followers, and the event made world headlines.

A number of elements occur repeatedly, although the emphasis changes from region to region: in Africa ethnic rivalries play an especially important part in the civil wars; in the Middle East it is the element of religion; in Latin America the divide between 'haves' and 'have-nots'; and in almost every case – sooner or later – an ideological element becomes an essential part of the violence. It may be a simplistic Communism versus capitalism divide, but it is usually more complex. Sometimes ideology lies at the root of the conflict; more often there are wider causes, and the different sides then turn to ideology to boost their claims

Finally, few conflicts escape interference from outside; it is almost impossible for a civil war to take place without the Americans, the Soviets, the British, the French, the Cubans, Libya or some other regional power poking a finger into the mess in pursuit of an advantage that is outside the original cause of the quarrel.

Africa

The civil wars in Angola and Mozambique have been given greater in-depth treatment than most of the others because of their impact beyond their borders. After 15 years of liberation warfare against the colonial power, Portugal (see Part I), Angola continued without a break from 1975 to 1990 in a civil war, which outside intervention turned into an ideological war as well. The war must be rated one of the most important anywhere in the Third World: it involved the USA, Zaire and South Africa on the one side, and the USSR and Cuba on the other; the

Map 15   Civil wars – ideological

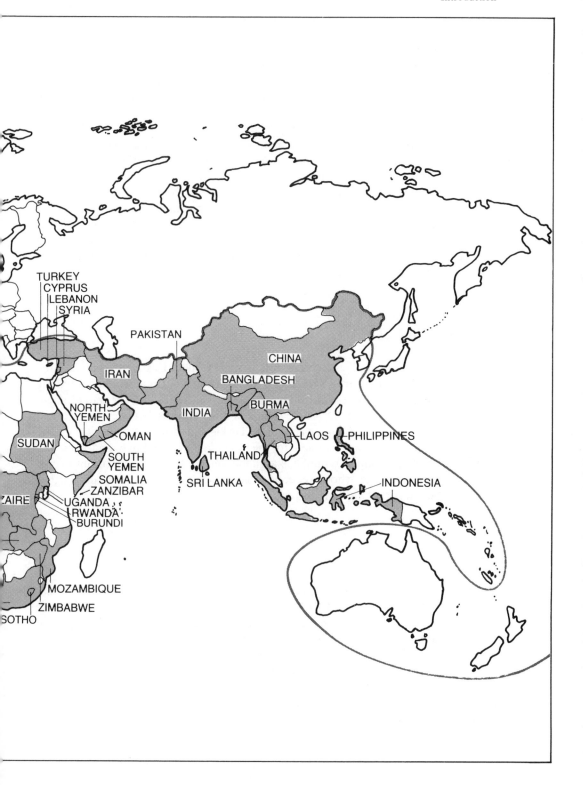

battle of Cuito Cuanavale was the largest battle fought on the continent since the Second World War and the desert campaign; as a direct result of developments in Angola, Namibia achieved its independence; and as an indirect result, the changes in South Africa that were initiated under its new President, F. W. de Klerk, at the beginning of the 1990s were undoubtedly brought closer. What began as a factional fight for power in the post-independence era turned into a pivotal cause of change in the region.

A number of these wars, at least in part, have their roots in the colonial era and represent attempts to sort out the political–social legacy left behind by the departing colonial authorities: this is the case in Burundi, Nigeria, Rwanda, Uganda, Zaire and Zanzibar. It is, however, difficult to apportion responsibility. The colonial powers have much to answer for in Africa, yet age-old ethnic feuds, such as that between the Hutu and Tutsi in Burundi and Rwanda, predated the colonial era by centuries. Some wars, such as the Nigerian civil war of 1967–70, are easy to chronicle with (relatively) obvious causes, a beginning, middle and end; others, such as Uganda, which really consists of a series of civil wars that run into each other, are far more complex.

The Middle East

The element of religion plays a crucial role in most Middle East conflicts, yet three of these wars – Oman, North Yemen and South Yemen – are more than anything else about the painful process of bringing backward societies into the modern age. The Cyprus war concerns the bitter long-standing hatreds between Greek and Turk, and has the added dimension of a Turkish invasion and partition. The double revolution in Iran that led to the downfall of the Shah and then the establishment of an Islamic republic is arguably one of the most important events of the century, and one whose repercussions throughout the region and farther afield will be felt for a long time to come.

Asia

Since 1945 the world has seen a major shift of power away from Europe to Asia, and two of the countries dealt with here – China and India – are potential future superpowers. In five of the nine cases studied, Communism is a major factor in the civil wars, and in the case of China the civil war was as important in its way as the Russian Revolution of 1917. It could be argued that China should not be included in the Third World at all, for in many respects it is a major power – and is treated as such. At the same time, if obvious indicators of development or poverty are taken into account, such as a per capita GNP of only $300, then if qualifies still as a Third World country.

The Americas

The wars in Central and South America, more than those anywhere else in the Third World, concern the divide between the 'haves' and 'have-nots'. The Maoist Sendero Luminoso (Shining Path) guerrillas in Peru are a product of this divide, as are the Sandinistas in Nicaragua, who came to power in one of the most popular revolutions on the continent and then were defeated primarily because of persistent US backing for the right. And that is the other element in the Americas: again and again US involvement, designed primarily to maintain the status quo, becomes a crucial factor in almost all Latin American struggles. Washington may claim to be fighting the spread of Communism, helping to break the power of the drug traffickers or preventing Castro from spreading subversion, but the end result is the same: the right rather than the left wins the war more often than not.

In no other part of the world has endemic civil war between rich and poor been so permanent an aspect of regional politics as it is in Central and South America, and in a number of those countries – Colombia, El Salvador, Guatemala, Peru – there seems little prospect of any end to the fighting.

AFRICA

THE ANGOLAN CIVIL WAR 1975–1990 (ONGOING)

Introduction

Angola has been in a state of war since 1961 when the first major insurrections against Portuguese rule took place. Following the coup of April 1974 which brought an end to the authoritarian government of Marcello Caetano in Lisbon, and once it became clear that Portugal intended to give up its attempt to hold on to its largest African colony (by then it was in any case fighting a losing war), the liberation movements turned their attention to the independence succession. During the second half of 1974 and still more through 1975 a power struggle to seize control at independence developed between the three liberation movements. The majority of the Portuguese settlers, who saw little future for themselves in Angola, began to leave, crippling the country's infrastructure and administration in the process, while the military and colonial authorities, who began by trying to hold the ring between the African contenders for power, in the end simply wanted to escape from a situation that was rapidly getting beyond their control.

The background 1974–1975

There were three liberation movements which, with varying success, had fought against the Portuguese: the Popular Liberation Movement of Angola (Movimento Popular de Libertação de Angola – MPLA), the National Front for the Liberation of Angola (Frente Nacional de Libertação de Angola – FNLA) and the National Union for the Total Independence of Angola (União Nacional para a Independência Total de Angola – UNITA). In 1974, once Portugal had recognized Angola's right to independence, the three movements did make several attempts – more or less willingly – to form a coalition and work together, but each attempt ended in failure. The Portuguese set 11 November 1975, as the date for Angolan independence, and by the time of their departure the liberation movements had split apart irrevocably: the MPLA proclaimed one government (the People's Republic of Angola, PRA), while the FNLA and UNITA, in what proved to be a very temporary alliance, proclaimed a second government, the People's Democratic Republic of Angola.

At the beginning of 1975 the military strengths of the three groups were approximately as follows: MPLA 6000, FNLA 15,000, UNITA 1000. During 1974 the FNLA had received about 450 tons of Chinese military equipment and, at least on paper, was the strongest of the three.

On 15 January 1975, the Portuguese government signed an independence agreement with the three nationalist groups; it was a bid to get the three to work together in a transitional government in which each movement would have equal representation. A National Defence Commission was to integrate 8000 troops from each organization with 24,000 Portuguese troops to form a single army. Later the Portuguese troops would be withdrawn. In fact the three groups could not – or would not – work together, and the Alvor agreement began to fall apart almost at once. At this stage it was clear that the differences between the nationalist movements were not primarily ethnic (for example, both the MPLA and UNITA drew their support from the large Mbundu group); nor were they differences about the problems which an independent Angola would face. They were factional: about power and who was to wield it.

In the tiny oil-rich enclave of Cabinda on the north bank of the Zaire river a small fourth liberation movement of dubious nationalist credentials demanded a separate independent state of Cabinda. This movement – the Front for the Liberation of the Enclave of Cabinda (FLEC), which enjoyed covert French support – was opposed by all three of the main movements, each of which insisted that Cabinda was an integral part of Angola.

The FNLA had had the support of President Mobutu of Zaire since its early days, and from 1973 it also obtained substantial support from China. The USSR had provided some support for the MPLA (as did China for a time), while the USA and South Africa supported the FNLA and later UNITA. When the FNLA disintegrated Zaire transferred its support to UNITA. At first UNITA had no external support so it turned to South Africa, which had its own reasons for interfering in Angola. Early in the run-up to independence the MPLA took control of the capital, Luanda, but in the country at large factionalism rapidly increased. The result was a growing civil war, which was to last from 1975 to 1990 and continue after a settlement had been achieved in Namibia.

The external factor

During the course of the independence struggle the liberation movements had been obliged to turn to outside powers for military and financial support, and since Portugal was part of the Western camp (in the Cold War) and a member of NATO, using its NATO arms illegally to prosecute its colonial wars in Africa, it was inevitable that the liberation movements would look for help to the Communist bloc. As a result, both the USSR and China were already providing arms to the liberation movements long before independence was on the agenda. But once a timetable for Portuguese withdrawal had been fixed and the power struggle between the factions escalated, each of them looked urgently for support outside Africa. The three liberation movements thus turned what was essentially a civil war into a much wider Cold War struggle. The MPLA had received moderate Soviet support for years; during the confrontations of 1975, however, this was to be vastly increased. At the same time Cuba entered the equation on the side of the new MPLA government, supplying thousands of troops.

The FNLA and UNITA turned to the West – principally the USA – which supplied them with military equipment and money through Zaire. During the summer of 1975, for example the Ford administration lobbied Congress to provide

$81 million for Zaire, part of which was to be used to recruit mercenaries to fight the MPLA. The departing Portuguese also provided considerable support to the anti-MPLA factions – $60 million of covert aid in July 1975.

The third important external factor was supplied by South Africa, then the colonial power in Angola's southern neighbour, South West Africa (subsequently Namibia). The South Africans supported both the FNLA and then UNITA, and were to continue funding and arming the latter through to 1989. South Africa's motives were to destabilize what was potentially a powerful socialist state to its north, and to destroy SWAPO (South West Africa People's Organisation) bases in Angola. Pretoria also wished to demonstrate to the West that it was a firm ally against Communism.

In December 1975 the US State Department exerted sufficient pressure on Gulf Oil, which operated the oilfields in Cabinda, to persuade it to suspend royalty and tax payments to the new MPLA government in Luanda. Thus, what might have remained a post-independence power struggle between factions was rapidly drawn into the Cold War, with the two superpowers supporting opposing sides in escalating civil strife. The MPLA government, which immediately took control of most of Angola at independence, was to be reinforced during subsequent years by the presence of Cuban troops, some East German troops and Soviet advisers and technicians, but although it was the *de facto* government of Angola, it was unable to defeat its rivals, both of whom received continuing military aid from the USA and other African countries, including South Africa. As a cartoon in the *Boston Globe* of 1988 showed, President Reagan wished to give aid to a Chinese-trained guerrilla movement bankrolled by South Africa to make attacks on US-owned oil refineries guarded by Cuban troops at the request of a Marxist Angolan government.

The growth of faction fighting 1975

During the first half of 1975 Portugal's policy in Angola was one of 'active' neutrality as between the three liberation movements. Its principal objective was to maintain a semblance of law and order, and to this end it increased its military presence from 24,000 to 27,000 troops. It rapidly became clear, however, that Portuguese troops had lost any desire to fight in Angola; they simply wanted to leave and return to Portugal. There was, in fact, no role left for Portugal except withdrawal, which was the only thing that the three liberation movements wanted it to do.

The first real faction fighting broke out in February 1975 between the MPLA and a group of its own dissidents (followers of Daniel Chipenda) who had been expelled from the party. Chipenda took his considerable forces to join the FNLA and fighting then broke out between the MPLA and the FNLA. Although the FNLA had quite substantial military forces, it was politically weak in the countryside since much of its support was derived from the million-strong Bakongo of the north, many of whom at that time had crossed into Zaire as refugees. Nor had it any base in the capital, Luanda. But with funds from the USA and Zaire the FNLA was able to buy up a television station and a newspaper with which to mount a political campaign against the MPLA. At the same time it moved troops across the border from Zaire south to Luanda, ready for a direct confrontation with the MPLA. This took place during March and April 1975, and disruptions in the capital were sufficiently severe that the May Day parades by the National Union of Angolan Workers (UNTA) had to be cancelled. Casualties from the fighting included 700 dead and 1000 wounded. Further MPLA–FNLA fighting occurred in the north and south of the country. A ceasefire was negotiated on 12 May, but this had broken down by the end of the month. June saw fighting in Cabinda and in Luanda; this involved UNITA for the first time when MPLA forces attacked the UNITA offices. Up to that point UNITA, the weakest of the three groups, had called itself the peace party.

As chaos mounted in Angola, Kenya attempted mediation. From 16 to 21 June the three leaders – Agostinho Neto (MPLA), Holden Roberto (FNLA) and Jonas Savimbi (UNITA) – met at Nakuru, with President Jomo Kenyatta of Kenya acting as chairman. A brief accord was achieved, but it broke down within days. On 9 July renewed fighting erupted in Luanda during which the MPLA drove the FNLA out of all its newly established Luanda footholds. Then, on 21 August, UNITA formally declared war on the MPLA, whose forces meanwhile had been attacking UNITA wherever they came in contact. In a series of battles in southern cities – Luso (now Lwena), Benguela, Lobito, Moçâmedes (now Namibe), Sa da Banderia (now Lubango) – UNITA forces were defeated and expelled. By August the MPLA was already receiving sufficient arms from its external allies that it felt strong enough to take on both the FNLA and UNITA.

At the end of August 1975 Portugal made a final effort to reconcile the three groups, but it was a doomed attempt from the start. In Cabinda the MPLA had established its control, although in Paris FLEC still talked of secession. Despite his claim to support the FNLA (which opposed Cabindan secession), Mobutu also provided FLEC's leader, Luis Ranque Franque, with aid ready to take advantage of any breakaway that might occur. After considering providing FLEC with support, the Congo (Brazzaville) decided to support the MPLA. By September the MPLA appeared to be emerging as the dominant force in Angola: it controlled the capital and 11 of 16 districts, as well as the seaboard and all the country's major ports.

Independence

In the end the Portuguese simply went with hardly any pretence at an orderly transfer of power, and on 11 November, Independence Day, two rival groups proclaimed separate governments. In Luanda Agostinho Neto's MPLA proclaimed the People's Republic of Angola and Neto was sworn in as the country's new President. In Ambriz (north of Luanda) Holden Roberto announced the Popular Democratic Republic of Angola, while in Lisbon UNITA announced the formation of a coalition between the FNLA and UNITA, having its headquarters at Huambo in the south of the country.

While no foreign governments were prepared to recognize the Huambo government, there was also no rush to recognize the MPLA government in Luanda. At first it was mainly the Communist bloc countries which did so. But although they did not formally recognize the Huambo government, the USA, South Africa, Zaire and Zambia did continue to provide its two parties with assistance. In fact the FNLA and UNITA fell out with one another in December 1975 (only mutual hatred of the MPLA had temporarily united them); there was heavy fighting between their forces in Huambo and Lubango, and the FNLA were driven out by UNITA.

The South African invasion of 1975

South Africa had sent its forces into Angola in 'hot pursuit' of SWAPO for some years before the end of Portuguese rule in Angola, so the South African Defence Force (SADF) was already used to mounting cross-border operations into Angola from South West Africa. In August 1975 South African forces occupied the area of the Cunene where the Ruacana Falls hydro-electric scheme, in which South Africa had a major financial stake, was under construction. On 23 October, as civil strife in Angola escalated, South Africa invaded southern Angola in support of the FNLA and UNITA. The South African objective was to produce a stalemate between the two sides to enable Pretoria to exercise some kind of balance. Between 1500 and 2000 regular troops equipped with armoured cars invaded Angola. By 26 October the South African column had driven the MPLA from Lubango; this was followed by Namibe and then in the first week of November by Benguela and Lobito. On 12 November, the day after independence, the South Africans took the town of Novo Redondo (now N'gunza Kabolo), which was 160 km (100 miles) north of Lobito.

There was an immediate Soviet response to the South African threat: it supplied massive quantities of arms and flew in the first 1000 Cuban troops to reinforce the MPLA. By mid-December 1975 some 27 shiploads of military supplies for the MPLA had offloaded at Luanda, as had between 30 and 40 cargo planes. Soviet arms included T54 and T34 tanks and 12 MiG-21s. By January 1976 the US Secretary of State, Henry Kissinger, could claim that the USSR had supplied the MPLA with about $200 million worth of armaments. The rapid arrival of Soviet arms and Cuban troops meant that by 20 November the South African advance could be halted, as it was, on the river Keve.

At the beginning of the internal struggle in Angola other African states held back: some waited to see what would happen; others were reluctant to recognize an avowedly Marxist regime. But the South African intervention on the side of the FNLA and UNITA tipped the balance in favour of the MPLA. On 27 November Nigeria (then at the height of its oil wealth influence in Africa) recognized the MPLA government. Nigeria was followed by Tanzania, also highly influential as a 'lead' country, under Julius Nyerere. In each case they gave South African intervention as the reason for their recognition.

A special Organization of African Unity (OAU) Summit called for 12–14 January 1976 found its membership exactly split over the issue of recognition, with 22 states having recognized the MPLA, 22 in favour of a government of national unity and two (Ethiopia as OAU host country and Uganda providing the OAU chairman for the year) abstaining. By that time there were an estimated 9000 Cuban troops in Angola to support the MPLA as well as 6500 former Katangese gendarmes and possibly 400 Soviet advisers.

South Africa, which had thought to obtain Western (US) endorsement of its invasion as a blow against Communism, soon found itself to be isolated. Kissinger warned Pretoria not to expect Western support, and on 4 February 1976 the

Pretoria government announced that its forces had been pulled back to a cordon 80 km (50 miles) deep on the Angolan side of the Angola–Namibia border. Meanwhile, the success of the MPLA led to further African recognitions. By 2 February 25 African states had recognized the MPLA government, providing a simple OAU majority that entitled Neto's MPLA to take its seat in the OAU, which it did on 10 February. In mid-February (17–18) the EEC, followed by Portugal, recognized the MPLA government, and by 22 February the new state of Angola had been recognized by 70 countries world-wide.

In the south of Angola the MPLA had captured all the UNITA-held cities by the end of February. Then, on 27 March, South Africa withdrew from its cordon after reaching an agreement with the MPLA. A key factor in bringing about the South African withdrawal was the post-Vietnam mood prevalent in the USA. Washington at that time simply did not want the USA to become too involved with UNITA and what looked like a long-term civil war in Angola, hence its uneasiness at South Africa's invasion and Kissinger's warning to Pretoria that it would find itself operating on its own.

The new government takes control 1976–1980

Fighting on the eastern front between the MPLA and the FNLA (November 1975 to January 1976) was fluid: for example, although the MPLA captured the cities of Lwena and Cangombe in November, UNITA retook them the following month. It was a foretaste of what was to come in a vast, sparsely populated region. In December 1975 the MPLA launched a major offensive against FNLA positions to the north of Luanda, capturing Ambriz on 12 January. The FNLA collapsed fairly rapidly in the face of the MPLA attack, and by mid-February most of its positions in the north of the country had been overrun. A number of British and other international mercenaries attempted to defend the FNLA positions but were unable to do so.

At the end of January 1976 the MPLA launched another offensive in the south of the country against UNITA, and by the middle of February it had also overrun most of UNITA's strongholds. As a result of these defeats both the FNLA and UNITA changed their tactics and began to wage guerrilla campaigns, but while the FNLA never became formidable guerrilla fighters UNITA certainly did, although in 1976 its successes still lay in the future. Having apparently defeated its two rivals, the MPLA turned its attention in early 1976 to dissidents in its own ranks, and then established the framework of a Marxist-oriented one-party state. Yet despite the fact that Neto was obliged to continue relying on a Cuban military presence as well as Soviet aid, he also insisted that Angola should be non-aligned. He attempted to create ties with Western countries and said that foreign investment would be welcome.

In June 1976 a show trial of captured white mercenaries was mounted in Luanda; there were nine Britons, one Irishman and three Americans. The main objects of the trial were to publicize the sordid nature of mercenary activity in Africa and to deter others. Four of the mercenaries were subsequently executed by firing squad, while the remainder received long prison sentences.

By mid-1976 the MPLA government had reached an agreement with Gulf Oil, which resumed production in Cabinda so that by August oil output was up to 75 per cent of pre-independence levels. When, following mediation by Andrei Gromyko for the USSR and James Callaghan for Britain, the MPLA had guaranteed the safety of the Calueque dam (part of the Ruacana Falls hydro-electric project), the South Africans withdrew fully from Angola (March 1976). It then began to appear that the government in Luanda had both won the internal power struggle and reasserted the territorial integrity of Angola as a whole. But these immediate successes did not prevent the long years of guerrilla warfare which followed.

Guerrilla warfare

UNITA was able quite quickly to transform its regular troops into guerrilla units, while the leadership including Savimbi remained in the country to lead the opposition to the MPLA government. Already during 1976 UNITA began to mount attacks on the Benguela railway and effectively prevented its use. The guerrilla war became wide-ranging not least because Angola as a country lends itself to guerrilla activities. In August the government launched another campaign against UNITA in the south and some 8000 people fled as refugees into Namibia, while others crossed into Zambia and Botswana. By the end of 1976 the campaigns were savage: in the village of Canhara Calomalanga in Huambo, for example, UNITA supporters massacred 287 people, while Luso was reported to have become a ghost town.

On the political front Angola's neighbours were adopting positions which they were to maintain for years to come. Despite having come to terms with the MPLA government, Zaire continued to provide support for UNITA, as for a while, did Zambia, while the South African government was only too ready to take advantage of the situation in Angola to raid across the border and strike at SWAPO bases.

Zambia was the first of Angola's neighbours to make terms with the Neto government. An MPLA delegation visited Lusaka in March 1976 and an agreement was reached; Zambia then impounded a UNITA plane in Zambia, closed its airspace to both UNITA and the FNLA and prohibited them from establishing bases on its soil. By the end of 1976 there were an estimated 19,000 Angolan refugees in Zambia, and in December Zambia expelled all UNITA officials. By March 1977 relations between the two countries were sufficiently amicable for President Kaunda to announce that he would visit Neto in Luanda.

South Africa was to provide UNITA with backing from 1976 onwards, and although the extent of its support would vary depending upon circumstances, it was to be a relatively fixed factor in the civil war for the next 15 years. South African support included training for UNITA forces at Grootfontein in Namibia. Following the capture of a South African soldier fighting with UNITA in Angola, the PRA government halted work on the Calueque dam. On 16 November 1976 Neto accused South Africa of turning Namibia into a 'base for aggression against Angola', while the following month the UN High Commissioner for Namibia, Seán MacBride, said that South Africa was preparing a 'destabilization pro-gramme' against Angola.

The Cuban factor, meanwhile, had become of major importance. By mid-1976 there were approximately 18,000 Cuban troops in Angola as well as a substantial number of technical, economic and health personnel such as doctors (perhaps 500 in all at this stage). The civil war continued through 1977 with UNITA both obtaining South African support and fighting against SWAPO, while the FNLA and FLEC obtained support from Mobutu. Neto found that he had come to rely on the relatively massive Cuban support which Castro seemed willing to provide more or less indefinitely. At the same time Neto increased the size of the MPLA armed forces to 50,000. During 1977 UNITA, rather than the FNLA emerged as the main rival to the government. Both sides took reprisals against peasants who refused to join them. UNITA also declared that it was at war with SWAPO; its Foreign Minister, Jorge Sangumba, said in Kinshasa (Zaire), 'One of the decisions we in UNITA have taken is that we will drive SWAPO out of its bases in Angola.'

While UNITA was developing into a formidable opponent to government, the FNLA failed to meet the challenges of the new situation, and although it mounted a number of cross-border raids into Angola from Zaire during 1977, it had not reorganized its forces into effective guerrilla units. A certain amount of fighting also occurred in Cabinda at this time, but FLEC by then was weakened by internecine power struggles. By 1979 the MPLA army had considerably improved its efficiency; it was equipped with quantities of modern arms supplied by the USSR and aided by the powerful Cuban military presence in the country.

The period 1980–1985

At the end of 1979 the government launched another major offensive against UNITA, and by April 1980 it had inflicted severe casualties on it. At the same time, as part of a policy of reconciliation with Angola, Mobutu refused to allow UNITA bases in Zaire. One problem added to another and Savimbi's poor performance in 1980 led to a reduction in South African support, although in June the SADF attacked SWAPO bases in southern Angola. In August 1980, however, UNITA saboteurs managed to do serious damage to oil storage tanks in Lobito.

During 1981 South Africa considerably increased its incursions into southern Angola, ostensibly against SWAPO bases. In August (while it was negotiating the future of Namibia with the UN) South Africa launched a major attack with ground and air forces that led the government in Luanda to call for general mobilization. Four out of five members of the Western 'Contact Group' – France, West Germany, Britain and Canada – condemned the South African attack, in which Pretoria claimed to have eliminated a number of SWAPO bases as far as 145 km (90 miles) into Angola. South Africa also claimed to have killed a number of Soviet soldiers in Angola and to have captured a Soviet sergeant-major, and its forces inflicted considerable damage on Angolan air defences and missile sites.

The USA adopted a tougher line towards Angola in 1981. In the first place the administration argued that it would not recognize the MPLA government as long as 20,000 Cuban troops were in the country. Then the Senate voted to repeal the ban on aid to Savimbi's UNITA (this was the beginning of a regular flow of aid to UNITA through Zaire). Savimbi claimed that UNITA was obtaining aid from Saudi Arabia, Qatar, Morocco, Senegal and Côte d'Ivoire. Late in the year he visited Washington. The government in Luanda justified the continuing presence of Cuban and East German forces in the country on the grounds that South Africa was assisting UNITA.

By 1982 the government was spending half its revenue in the war against UNITA and in responding to South African incursions. UNITA maintained its attacks on the Benguela railway, and Savimbi was having considerable success in his overseas tours to seek support. His greatest achievement was to tie the possibility of any agreement with the MPLA government to the question of the withdrawal of Cuban troops from Angola, a condition that suited both Washington and Pretoria. In July 1982, however, Fidel Castro said that Cuban forces would not be withdrawn from Angola until the South Africans had withdrawn from Namibia and had ceased their attacks on Angola. And so a kind of circular diplomacy developed with each participant in subsequent negotiations or manoeuvres tying his agreement to the Cuban–Namibian factor. The USA exerted pressure on Angola to remove the Cubans in order to persuade South Africa to reach an agreement over Namibia. Angola insisted that the Cuban presence was not to be linked to a Namibian settlement.

In March of 1982 the Angolan Defence Staff claimed that the South Africans then occupied 129,500 square kilometres (50,000 square miles) of Angolan territory. While denying this assertion, South Africa admitted that its forces had killed 201 SWAPO guerrillas inside Angola. In May and September the South African air force operated over Angolan air space and claimed to have shot down a Soviet MiG. In August the SADF carried out a major operation in southern Angola in which it claimed to have killed 300 SWAPO and destroyed caches of arms. At the end of the year Angolan and South African ministers met to discuss a ceasefire.

The guerrilla war intensified in 1983 with increasing South African involvement. On 31 January South African troops did major damage to the Lomaum dam in Benguela province, causing flooding and loss of power supplies to three provinces. The renewed fighting had the effect of disrupting peace talks held that February between Angolan and South African representatives in Cape Verde. In May Angola's President, José Eduardo dos Santos, visited Moscow where President Yuri Andropov reaffirmed Soviet support for Angola in the struggle against white South Africa. In July the government announced an amnesty for FNLA and UNITA rebels both inside and outside Angola. But in August the Foreign Minister, Paulo Jorge, insisted that the government would not deal with rebels who were agents of South Africa. South of Angola, meanwhile, no progress was achieved in the UN Namibia negotiations with South Africa, where the insistence by both South Africa and the USA on tying the Namibia issue to the Cuban troops issue produced a predictable stalemate.

In December 1983 South Africa launched another major offensive from Namibia into Angola, which it justified on the grounds that SWAPO was about to launch attacks into Namibia from its Angolan bases. Once into Angola the South Africans wished to remain, again insisting on the removal of the Cubans. But following a UN resolution condemning their action, the South Africans began to withdraw in mid-January 1984, and by the end of the first week of February a ceasefire was agreed between the two sides. In mid-February Angolan officials met with South African and US representatives in Lusaka (Zambia); the South Africans agreed to withdraw from Angola, and in return Angola promised that it would not permit any Cuban or SWAPO forces to occupy the vacated areas.

At Lusaka there was a suggestion on the South African side that all Cubans need not leave Angola before a Namibia settlement had been achieved because of the UNITA threat to the Luanda government. A shift of emphasis was apparent. In March President dos Santos visited Cuba where he and Castro agreed that there could be a slow withdrawal of Cuban troops provided South Africa implemented Namibian independence. By November 1984 the Luanda government had conceded that there was a linkage between Cuban withdrawal and Namibian independence. Both sides made an effort during 1984 to maintain the ceasefire, and at one point Angolan troops clashed with SWAPO forces in order to prevent them moving into the areas vacated by the South Africans earlier in the year.

In the course of the year Savimbi called for a government of national unity in which he could play a part, and he threatened to begin attacks on cities if his call for such an approach was ignored. Following his demand with action, UNITA forces attacked the town of Sumbe 260 km (160 miles) to the south of Luanda in March, and other attacks on towns were mounted by UNITA during the year. In July UNITA cut an oil pipeline in Cabinda, and 16 Britons and one Portuguese were taken prisoner and held as hostages for 11 weeks in an effort to force the British government to deal directly with UNITA. Generally, UNITA managed to mount attacks over a wide area even if many were only small scale. The results were constant shortages of fuel and food, and disruption of communications. Moreover, an estimated 100,000 people became displaced. In December 1984 UNITA forces attacked the diamond town of Cafunfo and killed about 100 government troops; they also captured European technicians and again managed to focus world attention on UNITA.

None the less, in 1985 President dos Santos repeated his determination not to deal with UNITA, and despite the promises of the previous year, South African troops remained in parts of southern Angola, supposedly as a precaution against SWAPO attacks. In April, following US mediation, Angola agreed to send home 10,000 Cuban troops as a gesture, while South Africa promised an immediate withdrawal from Angolan territory. But in May a South African seaborne group was intercepted when it landed in Cabinda intent on sabotage. Then in June, at a meeting of Non-Aligned Movement, President dos Santos called for mandatory sanctions against both South Africa and the USA to stop their aid to UNITA. Further South African attacks against SWAPO positions in Angola were mounted in June and September. However, it was becoming clear that the long years of war and modern Soviet equipment were working to Angola's advantage. Its better equipped and trained forces were achieving more successes against UNITA, and its air force was doing considerable damage to UNITA ground forces. During a major Angolan offensive of September–October 1985 the SADF admitted that it was assisting UNITA.

Changing patterns

Changes of mood in South Africa during 1985 signalled the beginning of a new period for the whole region, though this may not at once have been apparent. None the less, the second half of the decade was to witness major shifts in international attitudes towards South Africa and a growing realization among whites in the Republic that the apartheid stalemate could not continue indefinitely; repercussions from these new attitudes were to have their effects in the Angolan war. This, in any case, had two distinct aspects. The first was the straight fight between the MPLA government and UNITA; the second was the fight between SWAPO with its bases in southern Angola and the South African forces in

Namibia. Although the two 'wars' had apparently become inextricably intertwined, the period 1986–9 was to see the SWAPO aspect of the confrontation disengaged from that between the Angolan government and UNITA as the peace process for Namibia was finally brought to a successful conclusion.

None of this was obvious at the beginning of 1986. The war with UNITA continued unabated. In January Savimbi visited Washington where he was well received by the State Department. In May combined government and Cuban forces launched a major offensive against UNITA positions, and although UNITA, well armed by its US ally, was able to offer tough resistance, thousands of peasants fled from the fighting into Zambia. By this time central Angola had been so devastated by war that the UN had to appeal for financial help to mount an airlift of food into a region that was no longer capable of feeding itself. Many South African attacks, supposedly against SWAPO targets, were in fact against Angolans; in one such attack in May, South African troops killed 56 Angolan soldiers. At the same time Angola–Zaire relations deteriorated with Luanda accusing Mobutu of providing both sanctuary and support for UNITA forces.

In August UNITA claimed that Soviet chemical weapons had been used to kill or blind some of its forces, and there were then thought to be several hundred Soviet military advisers in the field with Angolan and Cuban troops. Savimbi warned Kaunda of Zambia not to support the Luanda government, and claimed that his well-trained army (of 28,000) then controlled one-third of Angola. At that time the USA was supposedly supplying UNITA with Stinger surface-to-air missiles.

1986–1988

In September 1986 the US House of Representatives voted 229–189 to provide UNITA with financial aid worth $15 million which President Reagan had approved earlier in the year. It was seen by the President and his supporters as crucial to stemming Soviet expansionism in southern Africa. At the same time, however, the Reagan administration was considering additional limited sanctions against South Africa.

During April 1987 UNITA mounted some daring and successful attacks on the Benguela railway at a time when the Luanda government, backed by several other African governments, was attempting to raise financial support from the West to rebuild the line. A fully rehabilitated Benguela railway would have major strategic value in reducing the dependence of the frontline states on routes through South Africa. Savimbi offered to reopen the line 'unconditionally' provided it was not used to ship government military supplies. He then at once attached a condition: that a demilitarized zone should be established 48 km (30 miles) deep on either side of the railway, thus effectively neutralizing a number of government garrisons. The government refused to treat with Savimbi, which may have been the real purpose of his offer.

US Assistant Secretary of State for African Affairs, Chester Crocker, visited Luanda in July, but neither side was prepared to alter its fundamental position despite earlier hints of movement: Crocker insisted that the Cubans had to leave as a prelude to a Namibia settlement; Angola that their presence in the country was an internal affair. By 1987 South Africa had ceased any pretence about its forces inside Angola: they were there permanently and fought alongside UNITA.

The changing nature of the war from South Africa's viewpoint became apparent at the beginning of November 1987 when an engagement against SWAPO inside Angola resulted in 10 white and two black South African soldiers being killed. Despite the South African claim that the action had been against SWAPO, opposition circles in South Africa believed that the action had been against Angolan and Cuban forces, and that the SADF wished to disguise the circumstances in which white casualties – always a sensitive political issue – had been incurred. The SADF claimed to have killed 150 SWAPO guerrillas.

In mid-November the SADF head, General Jannie Geldenhuys, admitted that his forces had intervened on the side of UNITA in a battle near Cuito Cuanavale, after Cuban and Soviet forces had joined the Angolan government troops in what appeared to be shaping up into a large-scale conventional battle rather than guerrilla warfare. It was in fact the beginning of the most crucial engagement of the 12-year war. Some of the heaviest fighting of the war had centred on Mavinga, held by UNITA, where both sides were said to have suffered very heavy casualties. At its Jamba headquarters UNITA said it would put on show two Cuban pilots whose MiG-23s had been shot down. The South Africans also lost two aircraft and were beginning to be concerned at the development of Angolan airpower.

The South African propaganda machine then tried to minimize the extent of its casualties and of its involvement with UNITA. The Angolan news agency, Angop, had claimed that 230 South African troops had been killed over the past few months, while Savimbi denied categorically that South African forces had fought alongside his own UNITA forces. The reason for Savimbi's denial, however, was his claim that UNITA had just won its biggest victory of the entire war – and he did not wish to share the victory with the South Africans.

In South Africa itself there was growing criticism of government policy in Angola, and there were demands from whites for accurate explanations of casualties. Following a call by Savimbi for the removal of all non-African troops from Angola and power-sharing talks between the government and UNITA, Nigeria's President, Major-General Ibrahim Babangida, offered to contribute a Nigerian peace-keeping force of between 10,000 and 15,000 troops. Other African states, including Kenya, Côte d'Ivoire, Zaire, Senegal, Togo and Gabon, offered to help in finding a solution, while the frontline states held a special meeting in Botswana to consider what appeared to be a major setback for the Luanda government. Savimbi claimed that his forces had killed 2000 MPLA troops including Soviet and Cuban soldiers, although Moscow denied that any Soviets had been killed. On 15 November President dos Santos claimed that South Africa had more than 3000 troops and 70 armoured vehicles in Angola with another 30,000 troops along the Namibian border.

Although it appeared that UNITA had halted the government offensive against its positions (by incurring heavy casualties), the claims that it had achieved a major victory were belied by the fairly massive South African intervention (denied unconvincingly by Savimbi) and the admission of substantial South African casualties. Early in December South Africa announced that it was withdrawing its forces from the Angolan war, although this seemed a move more to quieten white civilian fears at home than to end its Angolan interventions. By December, in any case, the year's campaigning was normally over. The South African intervention, despite denials by Savimbi, had clearly played a crucial part in halting the government advance against UNITA – at least for 1987.

The battle of Cuito Cuanavale: a turning point

In mid-January 1988 Angola said that its troops were fighting a South African force of 6000 backed by artillery and armoured vehicles round the strategic garrison town of Cuito Cuanavale in the south-east of the country. Cuito Cuanavale was the Angolan army's main forward position in Cuanda Cubango province, and was vital to its campaign against UNITA. It was clear that Pretoria's claim of the previous December that it was – yet again – withdrawing from Angola had been untrue. By the end of January the South Africans had been bombarding the town for three weeks (using long-range G5 howitzers), the fighting had been severe, the town's 6500 inhabitants had been evacuated and the Angolan air force had made daily sorties against the forces of UNITA that were investing the town.

The significance of Cuito Cuanavale to both sides became increasingly apparent as the battle continued. Its loss would be a major setback for the government since it was one of a line of forts, from Namibe on the coast through Lubango and Menongue to Lumbala near the Zambian border, which controlled a sophisticated system of Soviet radar that monitored South African air activity deep inside Angola. The town was also the most southerly government base and put the Angolan air force within striking distance of the UNITA headquarters at Jamba. By the time the battle got under way there was a new confidence apparent in the Angolan and Cuban pilots flying their MiG-21 and MiG-23 planes, while new anti-aircraft missile batteries round the towns were restricting South Africa's air support for UNITA. In addition Cuito Cuanavale was a strategic crossroads for two rivers and the point from which the whole south-eastern corner of the country could best be controlled.

Although by the end of January UNITA claimed that Cuito Cuanavale was about to fall and the South Africans claimed to have put its airfield out of action, the battle continued fiercely. The South Africans acknowledged privately that the Angolan MiGs, operating from Menongue, were still strafing their positions. Part of the politics surrounding the battle concerned the American-led negotiations for a Namibian settlement. A defeat for Angola would make it easier to force Luanda's hand over the question of the Cuban presence, by this time reckoned to be as many as 40,000 troops. The strength of the South African intervention came after it became clear that UNITA was unable on its own to halt the government advance on Jambe. But the South Africans were deploying part of the South West Africa Territorial Force (SWATF) from Namibia and, after the white casualties of 1987, appeared reluctant to deploy more white soldiers in Angola, a consideration that would become increasingly important as the battle continued. Casualties on both sides were heavy, though neither was ready to publish figures.

Although talks in Luanda between the Angolans and the Americans at the end of January ended acrimoniously, a State Department spokesman, Charles Redman, claimed in Washington: 'The Angolan delegation has for the first time affirmed its acceptance of the necessity of the withdrawal of Cuban troops from Angola in the context of a settlement.' And it became clear that Angola would agree to the withdrawal of the 40,000 Cubans provided the USA and South Africa ended their support for UNITA, that South African forces were withdrawn from Angola and that UN Resolution 435 bringing Namibia to independence was implemented.

By mid-February the battle was still raging and the South Africans were reported to have increased their forces to 7000, while both sides were registering heavy losses. UNITA claimed to have killed 92 government troops and 17 Cubans, while South Africa admitted the loss of five white soldiers. Then South Africa admitted that one of its pilots, Major Edward Every, was missing after his plane (one of two Mirage fighters attacking Cuban and Angolan positions) had been shot down. The admission was important because it highlighted the growing intensity of the air war; it was becoming increasingly obvious that South Africa had lost air superiority, something it had always enjoyed until the mid-1980s. What had altered the balance was the installation of a Soviet air defence network that employed SA-8 missiles and ground-based radar. On the other hand, from late 1986 onwards the USA had been supplying UNITA with Stinger missiles.

By the end of February, with the Angolans dug into bunkers in and around Cuito Cuanavale and the South Africans and UNITA having failed to take the town after repeated attempts, the battle had developed into one of the largest conventional military clashes in Africa. By then the South African force had possibly grown to as many as 8000; UNITA was playing a secondary role, its guerrillas harassing the government forces. FAPLA (the government army) was holding Cuito Cuanavale with about 10,000 troops using Soviet tanks, armoured personnel carriers and anti-aircraft missiles, manned in part by the 50th Division of the Cuban army. The battle had become one of major scale.

A further factor of enormous significance was the realization on both sides that the South Africans were losing their military superiority. Until Cuito Cuanavale the South Africans, more or less with impunity, had raided the territories of their neighbours – not just Angola – in pursuit of their destabilization policies. Now they found that years of tough warfare, massive supplies of sophisticated Soviet hardware, intensive training and support from the Cubans had between them created a formidable enemy. Not only were the estimated 10,000 Angolan troops in Cuito Cuanavale able to hold at bay the 8000 South African troops as well as their UNITA allies, but Soviet radar and SA-8 missile batteries were destroying South African air superiority. In March Angola claimed to have downed 40 South African planes since September 1987, and although this figure may have been too high, the South African losses were certainly serious. These new military conditions were made yet more formidable for South Africa by growing internal unrest and the effect of international military sanctions, which prevented the SADF from obtaining the most up-to-date equipment, most especially for its air force.

By mid-March the South African forces, whose numbers were estimated to have increased to 9000, began to fan out in southern Angola in the hope of assisting UNITA to gain a foothold in the western provinces. Then Pretoria launched a new peace initiative and began direct negotiations with the Luanda government. The Angolans put fresh proposals to US Assistant Secretary, Chester Crocker, but the stumbling block remained the timetable for a Cuban withdrawal. Despite claims by Savimbi that the Angolan government was exhausted, there was no sign of a let-up in the fighting. A 500-vehicle convoy of South African reinforcements and supplies was sent (mid-March) to reinforce the 8000 SADF troops investing Cuito Cuanavale. Meanwhile, reports suggested that there had been thousands of casualties in the biggest – and longest lasting – battle that had ever taken place in southern Africa. At the same time talks in Geneva continued between the US delegation led by Chester Crocker (who by then had been at it for eight years), the South Africans and the Angolans, still searching for a formula that would bring Namibia to independence and get the Cubans and South Africans out of Angola.

In late March the South Africans attempted a major flanking operation to the west of Cuito Cuanavale to cut off its supply lines to the north, aiming at the town of Punto Verde. The South African convoys only travelled at night, however, so as to avoid Angolan and Cuban air attacks, and the frontline troops engaged at Punto Verde were mainly the special 32 Battalion of Angolan refugees under white command, or black Namibian soldiers of 101 Battalion from Ovamboland. Although white specialist troops were attached, Pretoria was not using white combat troops for fear that casualties would produce unwelcome political repercussions at home. In Lusaka a one-day summit of the six frontline states unanimously endorsed Angolan proposals for a timed withdrawal of the Cubans in return for Namibian independence, the withdrawal of South African forces from Angola and an end to US and South African support to UNITA (the same formula Angola had proposed earlier). At the end of March President dos Santos indicated that he would be prepared to talk with Savimbi to end the civil war.

Negotiations

By April it had become clear that the USSR and Cuba had accepted linkage – the withdrawal of Cuban troops being tied to a Namibian settlement – and following a meeting between US Secretary of State George Shultz and Soviet Foreign Minister Eduard Shevardnadze, the two superpowers began to work together to reach a solution. After a series of diplomatic manoeuvres during April a meeting was arranged for the first week in May to be held in London; it would be between Angola, Cuba and South Africa, chaired by the United States. The meeting represented the culmination of efforts based on a combination of war-weariness, the growing South African realization that it was not winning the long battle of Cuito Cuanavale, the Soviet desire to work with instead of against the USA and bring peace to the area, and the long and patient diplomacy of Chester Crocker. Neither SWAPO nor UNITA was invited to take part in the talks. These, in fact, turned out to be the first in a series which lasted to the end of the year. In London it was agreed that the participants should meet again within weeks; this second meeting took place in Brazzaville, Congo.

In Lisbon at the end of May the Deputy Soviet Foreign Minister, Anatoly Adamishin, held talks with Chester Crocker and subsequently said, 'The United States and the Soviet Union are trying to reach an agreement that will provide a political framework for the countries in conflict to resolve their own problems, something along the lines of the agreement reached on Afghanistan.' At the same time the South African Foreign Minister, Pik Botha, said in Cape Town that his government was preparing plans for Namibian independence provided Cuban forces left Angola. The USA, however, was establishing bases in Zaire for UNITA to work from once a settlement with South Africa had been achieved.

At the beginning of June, after lengthy talks in Moscow between Chester Crocker and Anatoly Adamishin, the USA and the USSR set a target date of 29 September (the tenth anniversary of UN Security Council Resolution 435 calling on South Africa to give independence to Namibia) for reaching agreement on the war in Angola. But the South African Defence Minister, Magnus Malan, threatened that South Africa might reconsider the peace efforts; he was referring to the Cuban troop build-up in southern Angola – south of Cuito Cuanavale – and the claim advanced by Castro that Pretoria had been forced to negotiate because of defeat at the hands of the Cubans. The SADF reported strange troops – Cubans, Soviets and possibly East Germans – in southern Angola only a few miles from the Namibian border. According to the defence magazine *Jane's Defence Weekly* (quoting South African intelligence sources) 10,000 Cubans with 400 tanks moved to within four miles of the Namibian border; other Western reports, however, put the figure at 3000 to 5000 Cubans with radar units and MiG-23s. What had become evident by early June was the fact that South Africa's major military effort to take Cuito Cuanavale had failed: it had cost the Republic substantial losses of aircraft, tanks and troops, including about 60 white deaths. The Cuban manoeuvres were in the context of the ongoing peace talks and to make it more difficult for South Africa to renew large-scale hostilities.

The third series of talks were held in Cairo at the end of June. They were described as fiery, the most important question relating to the deployment of Cuban troops near the Namibian border. Immediately after the talks the South Africans suffered a severe military setback near the Namibian border when 12 white soldiers were killed in two clashes with Cubans near the Calueque dam development. The Cuban air attack also demonstrated how South Africa had lost its former air superiority. The fairly massive Cuban build-up along the Namibian border was clearly designed as a bargaining counter to be used in the forthcoming negotiations. It was also a signal that South African military superiority in the region was not as invincible as once had been the case. And, perhaps, the Cubans wished to have one final encounter with the South Africans before leaving Angola. In Washington, at the end of June, Savimbi met with President Reagan, reinforcing American backing for UNITA. Later, in London, Savimbi said, 'If the Cubans leave Angola there is no way the MPLA can remain in power without making a reconciliation with UNITA.'

The next set of talks were held in New York in mid-July, where agreement was finally reached linking a Cuban withdrawal to Namibian independence, although no timetable was set. At the same time South Africa made a major concession when it agreed to withdraw its forces from Angola before the beginning of any Cuban disengagement. Then, early in August, a new set of talks began in Geneva at which a ceasefire was agreed, although much remained to be settled. It was a slow process representing the distrust of 13 years of bitter fighting, yet gradually the details of an agreement were hammered out.

Prior to the next round of talks in Brazzaville at the end of September renewed fighting occurred in central Angola between government forces and UNITA. The Brazzaville talks did not produce a solution by the deadline of 29 September, nor was the next deadline of 1 November met. As it became clear that the talks were heading towards success, UNITA, which had the most to lose, increased its military activity. Yet by the beginning of December, apparently confident that an agreement would go through, the Cubans had begun to pull their forces back from the Namibian border area to bases north of the 13th parallel south.

Finally, after the year-long negotiations the participants met once more in Brazzaville (early December), this time with the Soviet Deputy Foreign Minister for African Affairs, Anatoly Adamishin, in attendance. Under the Brazzaville protocols Cuba agreed to withdraw its 50,000 troops from Angola over 27 months (three-quarters in the first 12 months of the withdrawal period); South Africa agreed to the implementation of UN Resolution 435 in Namibia during 1989, leading to independence in 1990; and a joint commission consisting of the USA, the USSR, Cuba, Angola and South Africa would arbitrate any complaints over the implementation period. Another clause in the agreement also required the withdrawal of the African National Congress (ANC) presence from Angola – an estimated 8000 to 10,000 members of its army. But last-moment hitches delayed the signing to yet another meeting.

This took place on 22 December 1988 in New York. South Africa, Angola and Cuba formally signed agreements whereby the Namibian independence process would begin on 1 April 1989 and all Cuban troops would be out of Angola by July 1991. But the agreement did not cover the war between the Angolan government and UNITA. The USA maintained that its aid to UNITA was a separate issue, and the agreements left open the question of whether or not South Africa would continue its aid to UNITA. Before the end of the year the South African ANC leader, Oliver Tambo, announced from Lusaka that the ANC was closing its Angola bases and moving its forces elsewhere.

1989

As the first Cuban troops departed from Angola in January 1989 the government issued a one-year amnesty to persuade UNITA rebels to surrender, although few availed themselves of the opportunity to do so. President dos Santos then suggested that the USA should finally recognize his government, but Washington did not respond positively; rather it now appeared to link recognition with a settlement between the MPLA government and UNITA. Moreover, the new American President wrote to Savimbi (6 January 1989) to promise continued American support.

Although there were the beginnings of contact between the government and UNITA, the bush war continued. UNITA had about 40,000 trained guerrillas as well as a further 30,000 irregular fighters and held larger areas of the country than the government, but it held no towns. The government forces included about 160 MiGs, helicopter gunships, an army of 50,000 and a further 50,000 reservists. The government, moreover, was in firm control of the Cabinda enclave and the oilfields, which yield an annual income of approximately $2 billion. In mid-February, however, the USA appointed a new airline (Tepper Aviation) to ferry weaponry to UNITA, and seemed as determined as ever to continue its support for the dissidents.

A new peace process

Contacts between the MPLA and UNITA and pressures from African governments led to the Gbadolite meeting of June 1989. Leaders of 11 African countries met at Gbadolite in Zaire to search for a political settlement in Angola. On 22 June President dos Santos of Angola and Jonas Savimbi of UNITA shook hands and agreed a ceasefire, while Savimbi – apparently – also agreed to go into exile for two years. It looked like the beginning of peace in Angola, yet almost at once the ceasefire was violated and Savimbi denied that he had agreed to self-exile; Washington said it would not end support to Savimbi and, indeed, increased this to $45 million for the year.

In September eight African heads of state meeting in Harare (Zimbabwe) produced another agreement in an attempt to end the war, but this too was ignored by Savimbi and if anything the fighting became more severe. The key to a peace settlement lay with the US government: President dos Santos argued that as long as the USA supplied Savimbi with weapons the war would continue. By the end of September Savimbi claimed that since Gbadolite his forces had killed 1000 government troops, while UNITA had lost 300. In October Savimbi visited Britain where, after a change of policy, he was met by the Foreign Secretary, John Major. Later, in France, he met President Mobutu of Zaire, the new US Assistant Secretary for African Affairs, Herman Cohen, and the Angolan Foreign Minister, Pedro Van-Dúnem, in yet another attempt to patch up the peace process.

In January 1990 another African summit – the fourth since Gbadolite – due to be held in Luanda was cancelled. By the end of the month a fierce battle was being waged by government forces against UNITA in an attempt to capture the UNITA-held town of Mavinga in the south-east of the country. Heavy casualties were reported on both sides and another military stalemate appeared likely. The most obvious prospects for 1990 appeared to be a continuation of the struggle, especially as the USA was reported to have doubled its aid from the figure of $45 million it provided for UNITA in 1989 to about $80 million for 1990.

Estimated costs and casualties

It is impossible to estimate precisely the damage done by this 15-year war, but it has been a disaster for Angola in terms of loss of life, destruction of towns and infrastructure, loss of revenue and a virtual standstill to any kind of economic development. In September 1986 the government claimed that 600,000 people out of the total population of 8.5 million had been displaced by the war, although independent aid agencies suggested the figure was much higher. In February 1987 the United Nations named Angola as one of five countries in need of food aid. By then, in what ought to be one of the richest countries in Africa, 50 per cent of food requirements had to be imported. Another government estimate suggests that there are 20,000 or more Angolans without limbs as a result of the war.

External interventions have undoubtedly increased the suffering in Angola. It is inconceivable that UNITA could have continued for 15 years and proved so formidable an adversary to the Luanda government without US and South African aid as well as the backing of Zaire and, sometimes, of Zambia. Similarly, the MPLA government has relied on massive Soviet military assistance, the presence of perhaps 1000 Soviet advisers and a Cuban military presence that at its greatest reached 50,000 men. During the 1980s US assistance to Savimbi was at the rate of $15 million a year, increased to $45 million in 1989 and possibly up to $80 million in 1990. More assistance came from South Africa, possibly worth $160 million altogether. There are no reliable figures to indicate the costs borne by the USSR in supporting the MPLA government, but they have been enormous. In 1988 the

USA estimated that the USSR had supplied about $1 billion worth of arms to Angola in the previous two years. It also estimated that each Cuban in Angola cost the Luanda government about $10,000 a year, although neither Cuba nor the USSR was ever paid in full for what it supplied, whether in men or materials. Even so, the bulk of Angola's oil earnings – as much as $2 billion in a good year – have gone to pay for the war. As a result, just about everything else for which a government is normally responsible – services and infrastructure – have simply been neglected and have run down.

The Cubans have never provided casualty figures, but Western estimates suggest these may have been as high as 10,000 dead since they first went to Angola in 1975. Nor have they ever said how many troops they had in Angola, although generally agreed Western estimates suggest 18,000 in the early years, gradually increasing to about 50,000 in the last two or three years before they began to withdraw.

In 1989 there were about 600,000 Angolans displaced within Angola and a further 400,000 refugees outside the country. In September 1989, in the fourteenth year of the civil war, it was estimated that 100,000 had been killed and that £7 billion worth of economic destruction had been inflicted on the country. And in February 1990 reports from the government agency UTAE and FAO claimed that 900,000 people in the four southern provinces of Huila, Namibe, Cunene and Cuanda were in 'acute danger of starvation'.

Results 1990

The agreement of December 1988 which led to the peace process in Namibia and the withdrawal of the Cubans clearly marked the end of one phase of the war, even if the civil war between the government and UNITA continues for many more years. The terrible devastation through most of Angola since 1975 has set back development, so it will be years before the country even begins to realize its economic potential. The involvement of the USA, the USSR, Cuba, South Africa and Zaire meant that a war which might have been contained instead became one of major proportions. The most startling military result of the war was the battle of Cuito Cuanavale, which must go down as a turning point in the history of southern Africa. That battle saw an end to the myth of South African military superiority in the region; the military events surrounding it demonstrated the importance of sanctions against military equipment, for these had ensured that South Africa lost air superiority; and it helped persuade South Africa to abandon a policy which assumed that Pretoria could always intervene successfully with military might. Above all, it can be seen as the starting point of the Namibian peace process, for although pressures had been mounting on South Africa for a long period, it was its defeat at Cuito Cuanavale that finally brought South Africa to the negotiating table with the intention of coming to a settlement.

Conclusions

In mid-1990 it is not possible to predict how long the civil war will continue, but as long as the USA insists on supporting Savimbi and UNITA with finances and weapons the prospects for peace are not good. On the other hand, developments in South Africa and, more generally, pressures throughout the region for peace could bring an end to the war in the early 1990s.

BURUNDI: CIVIL WAR BY MASSACRE

Introduction

Deep suspicions between the Bantu-speaking Hutu and the Nilotic Tutsi peoples of Burundi go back centuries. The main ethnic group to inhabit Burundi, the Hutu, were probably fully settled in the region as early as the eleventh century. Three or four centuries later the Tutsi arrived as warrior invaders; they subjugated the Hutu and the original Twa people, whom they treated as inferiors. They established a complicated set of land laws which ensured their own continuing predominance, although the Tutsi only represent 15 per cent of the total population. By the middle of the nineteenth century the Tutsi had extended their control to southern Rwanda and western Tanzania.

In 1885, during the Scramble for Africa, Burundi came under Germany's sphere of influence, being incorporated into German East Africa in 1906. The Belgians moved in from the Congo to take control in 1916 (during the First World War), and in 1923 the area became part of the Belgian mandate of Ruanda–Urundi. Under the Belgians tribal differences were emphasized, so major ethnic tensions existed at independence. As a matter of policy the Belgians had entrenched power in the hands of the minority ruling Tutsi, and from independence onwards ethnic divisions between Tutsi and Hutu moved towards a climax. The Tutsi in Burundi were made even more conscious of their minority standing shortly before independence by the violent and successful Hutu uprising against Tutsi in neighbouring Ruanda at the end of the 1950s. In any case, groups related to the Tutsi and Hutu across the borders in neighbouring Tanzania and Uganda make the entire region sensitive to Hutu–Tutsi antagonisms.

When independence came in 1962 Burundi emerged from Belgian control as a kingdom under the Tutsi ruler, Mwami Mwambutsa IV. Growing Hutu unrest came to a head in 1965 but was brutally repressed, although the abortive coup did force the king to flee to Europe. On 6 July 1966 he was deposed by his 19-year-old son, who assumed the title of King Mwami Ntare V. King Ntare appointed Michel Micombero, a former Defence Minister and Chief Secretary of State, as his Prime Minister. Five months later, on 28 November 1966, Micombero overthrew the monarchy, exiled the King and established a republic with himself as President. This action, while bringing Burundi more into line with what was happening elsewhere in Africa, destroyed the only stabilizing force which had been accepted as such by the Hutu.

From 1966 to 1972 a series of purges eliminated the Hutu from high office and the army. By 1971, for example, the Conseil suprême de la République (CSR) or cabinet had 23 Tutsi, but only two Hutu and two Twa. Some Tutsi moderates were also purged from their positions in 1970 and 1971. Several reasons combined to encourage the 1972 uprising by the Hutu: differences of wealth between the ruling Tutsi and the peasant Hutu, which growing tensions emphasized; a division in the ranks of the Tutsi between conservatives and extremists, which encouraged the Hutu to believe they could exploit the situation; and the return from exile of Ntare V, who had a personal motive to overthrow the Micombero regime.

Ex-King Ntare returned to Burundi at the end of March, and although his safety had apparently been guaranteed by Micombero in correspondence with Uganda's President, Idi Amin, he was at once placed under house arrest and accused of plotting to overthrow the government. There followed a Hutu-inspired coup attempt which failed. This, in turn, sparked off massive and brutal Tutsi reprisals, which were aimed particularly at the educated Hutu.

Massacre and counter-massacre 1972

The Hutu uprising was launched on 29 April in an attempt to overthrow the Tutsi government and, still more, Tutsi domination. In southern Burundi armed Hutu attacked and killed Tutsi indiscriminately. Supporters of the ex-King attempted to free him but were unsuccessful, and Ntare was executed. It seems clear that the uprising was backed by the ex-King and aimed to overthrow Micombero and the Tutsi who supported him. Tracts found on dead Hutu during the massacres which followed showed they intended to massacre the Tutsi.

The uprising did not succeed. The government had been expecting trouble and a systematic Tutsi campaign to massacre the Hutu followed. Any Hutu still in the armed forces were eliminated, but in particular the anti-Hutu massacres were aimed at the educated, over a third of whom are thought to have been killed. Estimates of the dead vary widely (see below), but it is possible that 200,000 Hutu were killed in the six weeks that followed the 29 April uprising.

Although Micombero had officially proscribed ethnic distinctions, this was not apparent in the higher echelons of government, where the Tutsi predominated. When the uprising began Micombero claimed that he faced an external invasion and that Ntare had brought foreign mercenaries with him, though there was little evidence of this. Immediately he turned to his two neighbours for support, and both Tanzania and Zaire provided some military assistance: Zaire sent about 100 troops and several jet aircraft to assist the Micombero government restore law and order; Tanzania provided 17 tons of arms. Later, however, as the extent of the repression became apparent, both countries withdrew or curtailed their assistance.

The Hutu launched their attacks simultaneously throughout the south. Bands of Hutu came into towns and set about slaughtering the Tutsi; men, women and children were killed indiscriminately, homes were burned, border posts were attacked and (according to government sources) 25,000 Tutsi were forced to flee. Micombero claimed that the rebellion was led by dissidents from Zaire, but this was never proven. In the capital, Bujumbura, the uprising appears to have taken the government and officials by surprise; many were attending a dance when the alarm was sounded. At least some of the initial reprisal slaughtering could be put down to panic; later, however, reprisals developed into a systematic massacre with the educated Hutu singled out as particular targets so as to deprive the Hutu of their future leadership.

Estimated casualties

It was impossible at the time or later to obtain more than general estimates of the total numbers killed, but they were very high. Estimates vary from a low of 80,000 dead through 100,000 to a high of 250,000, and the probability is that 100,000 Hutu lost their lives. In addition about 500,000 people were rendered homeless and perhaps 40,000 became refugees in the neighbouring territories of Zaire and Tanzania. Although many thousands of Hutu peasants were slaughtered, the main targets of the Tutsi were priests, teachers, university students, those in commerce and the army (which was completely purged of Hutu) and secondary school children. One-fifth of all secondary school children were killed or disappeared (all were Hutu), and in some cases, according to eye witnesses, children were dragged from their classes and killed. One witness, a Roman Catholic priest, estimated that as many as 15,000 bodies were buried in one huge mass grave.

The aftermath

On 21 June 1972 the head of Burundi's armed forces announced that peace had been restored and that military operations had ceased. In July President Micombero ended what had been a 12-week state of emergency. Throughout the massacres foreign powers had been unable to do anything to lessen the slaughter, and African states took the line that what was happening was an internal matter for Burundi. Only President Gregoire Kayibanda of Rwanda publicly condemned what was happening and urged moderation. Micombero either ignored pleas for moderation or made what had been said appear as though he was receiving support. By June, according to UN estimates, there were 40,000 refugees in Tanzania and Zaire. At the same time about 50,000 Tutsi from Rwanda crossed the border into Burundi to join the ruling élite of fellow tribesmen. Six weeks after the uprising bodies could still be seen along the shores of Lake Tanganyika; the roads to Rwanda, Tanzania and Zaire were closed; Bujumbura was sealed and no one was allowed in or out.

Subsequently, Micombero was to claim that 25,000 Hutu had been in training for the uprising and that captured lists showed the names of thousands of Tutsi to be killed. He also suggested that those who had taken part in the uprising had been drugged and so had killed indiscriminately. He claimed that between 50,000 and 100,000 people had been killed in a relatively small area of 800 square kilometres of the south and that most of these were Tutsi. Possibly 15,000 had been killed in the Martyazo district on the first day of the uprising. The rebels had been especially effective at the town of Nyanza Lac, where they had also stolen 4 million Burundi francs from the bank and announced the creation of an independent republic. The President asserted that the Hutu intention had been genocide and that they had planned a victory parade in Bujumbura at which he was to be displayed as the last surviving Tutsi.

But missionaries objected to Micombero's figure of 50,000 Tutsi dead. They estimated that only about 2000 Tutsi had been killed and possibly as few as 500. On the other hand, they estimated that a minimum of 80,000 Hutu had been slaughtered and perhaps very many more.

In June, despite continuing repression, Micombero announced that peace had been restored. The new cabinet (by an apparent coincidence Micombero had sacked his cabinet on 29 April only hours before the uprising occurred) consisted of pro-Micombero Tutsi; as a result, the Tutsi minority emerged after the uprising with an absolute monopoly of power.

International reaction was one of shock. From exile in Switzerland the old King, Mwambutsa IV, said that Micombero's government was trying to exterminate the Hutu. Relations with neighbouring Rwanda became seriously strained following the only public criticisms of the massacres to be voiced by any government. All other African governments kept quite, a line what could be explained in part by continuing African fears of external interference with their newly achieved independence, and in part by the general fragility of many African states which faced complex ethnic rivalries of their own.

A flow of Hutu refugees into Tanzania continued into 1973. In March, for example, a Burundi military aircraft bombed border villages in Tanzania where refugees had settled. There was another similar air attack in June with the result that Tanzania refused landlocked Burundi access to the port of Dar es Salaam until Micombero's government had paid compensation.

Following the coup of 1976 which toppled Micombero and brought Jean-Baptiste Bagaza to power, the government made some genuine efforts at Tutsi–Hutu reconciliation, principally by means of land reform in favour of the Hutu peasants and at the expense of the Tutsi landlords. During Bagaza's presidency, which lasted until 1987, ethnic antagonisms were kept in check, but the legacy of hatreds went very deep and in 1987 the great majority of all important posts still remained in Tutsi hands.

The massacres of 1988

In mid-August 1988 another upheaval occurred in Burundi, costing a minimum of 5000 lives but more likely double that figure. On 17 August, just before the violence, the Minister of the Interior, Lt.-Col. Aloys Kadoyi (a Tutsi), said the government was determined to punish harshly those who hatched 'diabolical plots' against the country. He also claimed that criminals from neighbouring countries had been unmasked. The killings took place mainly in the commune of Marangara in Ngozi province and at Ntegi in Kimundo province. About 10,000 lives (3000 families in Bujumbura and the rural areas) are estimated to have been lost. A few were Tutsi, but the great majority, once more, were Hutu. It was a repeat of 1972, though on a much-reduced scale. The Hutu did not have arms and were easily dealt with by the Tutsi; the latter controlled the army as well as holding almost all positions of any influence or importance. No casualty figures were released by the government, but the new flood of Hutu refugees, mainly into Rwanda (65,000 according to the UN), were testimony to Hutu fears.

The fact that this uprising and the counter-massacre were on a far smaller scale than that of 1972 is indicative of the dominance which the Tutsi had ensured for themselves in the intervening years and, perhaps, of the fact that so many educated Hutu who might have provided the leaders for a more successful uprising had been exterminated on the earlier occasion. The deposed former head of state, ex-President Bagaza, was living in neighbouring Uganda at Masaka near the Burundi border. This added to the fears of the Buyoya government, for he still had an important following in Burundi.

The future

President Pierre Buyoya, who had ousted Bagaza in 1987, tried to heal the wounds of August 1988 when on 19 October he appointed a new cabinet in which for the first time ever the Hutu had a majority (12 out of 23), including the Prime Minister, Adrien Sibomana. This represented a real effort to reassure the Hutu as well as a recogniton of political realities in terms of ethnic numbers. Other posts which went to Hutu ministers included finances, territorial management, tourism, environment, higher education, research, social affairs, public administration and public health. The ministries included some of the most important and sensitive. Whether Burundi can rise above its terrible ethnic hatreds and suspicions remains to be seen.

THE GAMBIA: COUP ATTEMPT, SENEGAL TO THE RESCUE

Background

One of Africa's smallest and apparently most stable countries, The Gambia, became independent in 1965 and maintained a multi-party democratic system under its first President, Sir Dawda Jawara. By the beginning of the 1980s, however, the country faced mounting economic problems: these were the result of drought and an extremely narrow economic base. A fall in the harvest of the main export crop, groundnuts, from 132,000 tonnes in 1973/74 to 78,000 in 1980/81 sent repercussions throughout the minuscule economy. Economic and political unrest came to a first climax in October 1980.

The country had a small paramilitary Field Force of about 500 men but no army, so any threat beyond the capacity of the Field Force – or a mutiny by it – meant that the government had to invoke outside aid if it was to survive. This was the case in October 1980 when, following economic ills and a drought, the deputy head of the Field Force was murdered; the President invoked the 1965 defence agreement with neighbouring Senegal, which sent 150 troops to assist the Gambia government in maintaining law and order. Two opposition groups – the Gambia Socialist Revolutionary Party (GSRP) and the Movement for Justice in Africa – Gambia (MOJA–G) – were proscribed, while the leaders of MOJA were also put on trial for sedition. In November, when the crisis had passed, Jawara accused Libya of destabilization tactics and expelled its diplomats from Banjul.

Although in 1980 the troops sent by Senegal turned out to be of only precautionary value, it was to be a different story in 1981.

Attempted coup: July 1981

President Jawara was in London at the end of July 1981, attending the wedding of Prince Charles and Lady Diana Spencer, when the coup was attempted. It was led by Kukoi Samba Sanyang, who had been an unsuccessful candidate in the country's elections the previous year. Sanyang, with a small band of civilian followers and disaffected members of the Field Force, seized a number of strategic places in the capital, including the broadcasting station. He announced the formation of a National Revolutionary Council and claimed to have dissolved the National Assembly. Jawara heard the news in London and stated his determination to return and defeat the coup. Part of the 500-strong Field Force had joined the coup makers in their attempt to overthrow the government, although the balance of the troops and the police remained loyal to the government and resisted the coup.

While still in London President Jawara managed to telephone his cabinet and Vice-President, whom he instructed to liaise with President Abdou Diouf of Senegal to invoke once more the provisions of the mutual defence pact between the two countries. The rebels took a number of hostages, including one of Jawara's wives and eight of his children, her father and several government ministers, whom they later threatened to kill if the Senegalese troops were not withdrawn. Meanwhile, arms belonging to the Field Force had been handed out to anyone ready to support the coup, with the result that Banjul was subjected to much violence and looting. Initial support for the coup, where it had existed, soon evaporated in a welter of unjustified and lawless violence.

At the beginning the coup appealed to youth, the unemployed and other disgruntled elements in a society whose economic fragility had become apparent the previous year. But the indiscriminate way in which the coup makers armed youths and released prisoners or anyone else who claimed to support them, and the looting and revenge killings which followed, soon turned the majority against the coup. Possibly half the eventual total of casualties resulted from looting and personal vendettas. Further, Sanyang's incoherent broadcasts as well as the broadcast pleas of his hostages turned people against him.

As the President was to claim later, the coup makers belonged to no political party and were nonentities. The dozen men who made up the National Revolutionary Council had no experience. Apart from Sanyang they included Dembeh Janneh, Kartong Farti, Jankun Sahor, Simang Sunneh, Cambeng Barji, Husenu Jawwor, Momodu Sannenj, Demba Camara and Abai Songor. A major factor in quelling the coup was the firm determination shown by Jawara, who returned to The Gambia via Dakar where he co-ordinated the help from Senegal.

Senegal's intervention

On 31 July Senegalese paratroopers captured Yundum airport outside Banjul, while other troops crossed the Gambian borders at several points. By 1 August President Jawara could claim from Dakar that the rebellion had been crushed, and he called on the rebels to surrender. But at that stage they still controlled Gambia Radio. On 2 August Jawara arrived back in Banjul. All the hostages taken by the rebels were freed after Senegalese troops closed in on the last rebel stronghold at the Field Force barracks at Bakau. The rebels had been isolated at the barracks and most of them were captured, although a few, including Kukoi Samba Sanyang, escaped. Altogether 3000 Senegalese troops had been employed, and the rebellion was crushed in a week. The British SAS are also reported to have played a part in rescuing the hostages.

In Senegal President Diouf said that Senegal's troops had intervened 'at the request of The Gambia's legitimate authorities and by virtue of agreements duly negotiated'. Subsequently, the Senegalese troops remained in The Gambia; they were efficient and well behaved but, inevitably, their presence came to be resented.

Estimated costs and casualties

The first casualty figures gave nine Senegalese dead and 32 wounded in the fighting against the rebels. On 4 August it was reported that about 300 people had been killed, but later estimates increased the number to 800 and then 1000. In addition 1000 people were rounded up afterwards and detained under the state of emergency which was enforced when Jawara returned. Extensive damage was done to property in Banjul, estimated at about £10 million. Sanyang and a handful of other coup makers escaped first to Guinea-Bissau and then on to Cuba. At the end of August UN relief officials came to the country to assess the damage and what the UN might do.

The aftermath

On 3 August, after his return, President Jawara promised the rebels that their lives would be spared if they laid down their weapons and released their hostages. Rumours to the effect that the rebels had been supplied with arms by the USSR were unfounded; the arms in fact had been looted from the Field Force armoury. On 4 August the cabinet met for the first time since the coup, issuing a statement that the violence was the fault of 'a band of rebels assisted and supported by external forces'. The idea that the coup had been assisted from outside was to persist for a while. Sanyang, for example, was known to have attempted to telephone Libya, but his rebels had already damaged the telecommunications equipment that would have made such a call possible. Both the USSR and Libya denied any involvement. Subsequent evidence suggested that there had been no external involvement in or support for the coup.

Results: immediate and longer term

As President Jawara said at the time of the coup, it gave The Gambia a bad name. It certainly damaged the reputation of a country which until that time had seemed a model of stability. President Nyerere of Tanzania praised Senegal for its intervention, but for The Gambia such intervention was a mixed blessing since it emphasized the inability of the country to look after itself. At the conclusion of the coup violence only about 60 of the Field Force remained loyal, and it was plain that the government would be forced to rely on Senegalese troops to maintain law and order for some considerable time to come. Hundreds had died for no obvious reason, and there was no indication of any thought-out policy on the part of the coup makers. On the brighter side, The Gambia received extensive assistance to rebuild the damage that had been done, although there followed an initial worsening of the economy. When the final plotters were put on trial in 1984 neither they nor any of those tried earlier and condemned to death were executed. In February 1985 the state of emergency was finally lifted.

Senegambia

The concept of Senegambia – the merger of Senegal and Gambia – had been discussed for many years (from before independence in 1965), and the events of July and August 1981 helped to hasten a process that was slowly coming into reluctant operation. The fact that the Gambian government had been forced to call on Senegal to save it from the coup merely emphasized the limited extent to which the country could realistically claim to be independent. There were, however, immediate fears after the aborted coup that the ready and fairly massive military intervention provided by Senegal was merely the prelude to annexation. Whatever validity such fears had, the fact was that the Confederation of Senegambia was almost certainly hastened by the events of 1981 and came into being on 1 February 1982. (Its subsequent history was to be less than happy, for The Gambia steadily resisted real integration and by the end of the decade the concept had virtually collapsed.)

The events of July–August 1981 in The Gambia served to emphasize the problems of small states when threatened (see also, for example, Part II, pp. 159–161).

LESOTHO: FROM COUP TO CIVIL STRIFE

Background

Lesotho (formerly Basutoland) is entirely surrounded by the territory of South Africa and is at the economic mercy of its giant neighbour. The South African factor must therefore always be taken into account when any development in Lesotho is assessed; the Republic is always there as a backdrop, acting as a spur or inducing caution. In 1965, the year before independence, the Basutoland National Party (BNP) which had been formed by Chief Leabua Jonathan in 1958 won pre-independence elections. The BNP was then regarded as the most conservative party and, therefore, the party most acceptable to both the British and the South Africans. Jonathan is reported to have received organizational and financial support from South Africa. He adopted a political line which he was to use throughout his period of power, though with different variations: that while he was opposed to apartheid, he was also the person most able to deal with the South Africans.

During the period 1966 (from independence) to 1970 (when a new election was due) Jonathan strengthened his position with a number of measures. These included limiting the King's powers, deporting four of his ministers and arresting members of the opposition on charges that subsequently could not be sustained and had to be withdrawn. Jonathan also used South African officials in sensitive positions. He increased the armaments of the paramilitary police and purged their ranks of personnel not considered to be loyal to him.

The 1970 elections

Elections as provided for under the constitution were held in 1970. By noon of 30 January 1970, as the election count was made, it became clear that the ruling BNP and the Basutoland Congress Party (BCP) were running neck and neck, and when the BCP had 32 out of 60 seats Jonathan acted. At 3 p.m. that day he went on the radio to declare a state of emergency, claiming that the opposition had used threats and spread an atmosphere of violence. He suspended the constitution and had Ntsu Mokhehle, leader of the BCP, arrested.

The next day, 31 January, Jonathan said he would hold another election as soon as it was possible to do so in peaceful conditions. At a press conference he said, 'I have seized power. I am not ashamed of it.' He detailed incidents of violence and intimidation as his excuse. Opposition publications were banned and the courts temporarily suspended from operation. The King, Moshoeshoe II, was placed under house arrest on the grounds that he had supported the opposition; later he was to leave the country and go into exile in the Netherlands. A British reaction to the coup was to suspend the aid on which Lesotho relied; from prison Mokhehle insisted later that a resumption of British aid would ensure an end to serious opposition to the government.

In the *Government Gazette* of 16 February the suspension of the constitution was confirmed, the election results were declared invalid and the emergency powers that Jonathan had assumed were also confirmed. It was reported that from prison, where he had been visited by Jonathan, Mokhehle had agreed that the state of emergency was lawful, but his willing acquiescence in this was denied by his followers.

The country's small paramilitary police force, on which Jonathan depended for the maintenance of law and order, was officered by British expatriates and these were not withdrawn by Britain. It was also reported that South Africa had made available Sotho-speaking police and lent Jonathan helicopters and light aircraft, as well as providing supplies of arms and ammunition.

The outbreak of violence

During February and March the opposition took to the hills and Clement Leepa, a former Assistant Commissioner of Police, became their military commander. Immediately, however, the government launched a campaign to intimidate members of the opposition. About 1000 men opposed to the Jonathan takeover took up arms against the government, and an estimated 500 of them were to be killed by the mobile police. During initial fighting in February about 30 people were killed. Then, on 3 March, Leepa and his followers were attacked in a full-scale operation by government forces in their headquarters and training centre in caves about 50 km (30 miles) north of the capital, Maseru. The government used helicopters and light aircraft, and between 150 and 300 of the opposition forces were killed. The remainder took to the hills and for a time came to control a number of villages, including Buthe Buthe, Leribe and the Oxbow settlements. They attacked police stations and were met by increasingly tough retribution. The 500-strong police force was accused of using terrorist tactics – killing, burning, torturing and beating – against villages or districts known to be sympathetic to the guerrillas. In April the police trapped and killed a gang of about 20; others were killed at Kao in the eastern mountains. The security forces also dropped grenades from the air, sometimes against people who were not involved in the rebellion.

Aftermath 1970

By the end of April 1970 the government appeared to have crushed the opposition and to have full control of the situation. On 12 August Jonathan claimed that the opposition parties had refused his invitation to round-table talks and had declined to join in a coalition government. Then in October Jonathan announced a five-year 'holiday' from politics. On 4 December the King returned from the Netherlands, having agreed not to become involved in politics.

Following the coup, the British High Commission expressed disapproval by confining its activities to 'working relations' and suspending aid. On 12 June, however, Britain resumed aid and in addition supplied emergency aid on the grounds that the country would break down if it did not do so. The South African government claimed to agree with Jonathan's plea that his actions had been in order to forestall Communism. Most of Africa demonstrated disapproval of Jonathan's behaviour.

Later unrest

Fresh violence erupted in January 1974 when five police stations were attacked by armed bands who were followers of Mokhehle. Jonathan reacted with severity, and Mokhehle and six other leading members of the BCP fled to South Africa. The paramilitary security forces and the police hunted down the dissidents in the mountains on the border with the Orange Free State. A number were killed and about 200 people were detained, of whom 14 were charged with treason. By this time, however, Jonathan was to claim that South Africa was assisting and harbouring the rebels. In February 1974 a law was passed making it an offence to harbour or conceal conspirators against state security and giving the government powers to detain suspects for 60 days without trial. Later, in two trials, some 35 BCP supporters were given jail sentences.

In 1978 Jonathan warned of new threats to national security and claimed that certain opposition groups had left the country to obtain military training. There were a number of bomb incidents in 1979. Basically these incidents represented continuing opposition to government repression and refusal to allow democratic elections.

The Lesotho Liberation Army (LLA), which was the military wing of the BCP and had been formed by the dissidents, was responsible for increased acts of violence against the government at the beginning of the 1980s. Jonathan accused South Africa of harbouring the LLA and allowing it to operate across the border. In the period May–August 1982 Jonathan blamed the·LLA for the assassination of the Minister of Works, Jobo Rampetsa, and of the Secretary-General of the BCP, who had condemned the use of violence. Although Jonathan promised to hold elections in 1983, he went back on his word and none were held. Opposition to his government increased until, in January 1986, assisted by a three-week blockade of the country mounted by South Africa, Major-General Justin Lekhanya mounted a successful military coup and overthrew Chief Jonathan. Since then King Moshoe-shoe II has ruled through a Military Council, although real power has been in the hands of Lekhanya.

LIBERIA: TRIBAL CIVIL WAR 1990

Introduction

President Samuel Doe of Liberia seized power during a bloody coup in April 1980; in the subsequent decade his government became a byword for corruption and brutality towards its opponents. By the end of the 1980s there were plenty of Liberians anxious to see a change of rule, yet when the rebellion began there were no obvious indications that it was anything more than a bloody uprising against government authority in one particular part of the country.

Over Christmas 1989 fighting erupted in Nimba county on the border with Côte d'Ivoire, and within 10 days an estimated 10,000 people had fled across the border as refugees to escape the violence. They reported that rebels had destroyed a number of villages and killed dozens of civilians. Large areas of Nimba county appeared to have fallen to rebel control; the government in Monrovia placed the capital under curfew. Most of the rebels came from the Gio tribe, which is the principal ethnic group in Nimba; they made a point of attacking members of the Krahn tribe from which Doe comes. The rebels called themselves the National Patriotic Front. Their leader at this time appeared to be Charles Taylor, a former junior minister under Doe, who had fled the country on corruption charges in 1984, taking an estimated $900,000 to the USA. There he had escaped from a Boston jail after having been arrested for extradition to Liberia. Liberians, therefore, did not quite see him as a liberating hero.

In the middle of January Côte d'Ivoire claimed that 30,000 refugees had crossed into the country to escape 'genocide'. Charles Taylor claimed that his National Patriotic Front had 5000 men, who were fighting supporters of Doe in the President's home county of Grand Gedah. Diplomats in Monrovia estimated that no more than 50 troops on each side had actually been killed, although figures for civilians were far higher. What had become clear was the fact that the rebels, who were mainly Gio, were attacking members of the Krahn group, while government forces were retaliating by attacking the Gio. The government sent two army battalions to deal with the rebellion. By the end of January 1990 as many as 50,000 people were thought to be hiding in the bush in Nimba county to escape retribution from government forces. Then, as so often with rebellions, a lull in activity followed.

Renewed fighting: April 1990

In mid-April President Doe claimed, 'There is no inch of this nation not under the control of the government.' The claim was belied by conditions in Nimba county, the sudden eruption of new fighting and a subsequent advance on Monrovia by the rebels. At the end of April the USA advised its 5000 citizens in Liberia to leave, and British Airways laid on special flights from Monrovia for British and Commonwealth citizens. The rebels were then within 110 km (70 miles) of Monrovia and what had started as a small rebel force of 150 had grown to 3000 with reputed support from Libya. They faced a Liberian army of 7000. The President now established himself in the Executive Mansion with a special bodyguard of 1000 Krahn troops. The US-based human rights group, Africa Watch, claimed early in May that there were then 300,000 refugees from the savage inter-tribal fighting and that most of the casualties had been Gio or Mano people. Its report suggested that Doe's 10-year period of office had been a reign of terror.

By mid-May Charles Taylor claimed to have a force of 10,000 and his troops had captured Buchanan, the country's second port. A week later his forces captured the town of Kakata, only 65 km (40 miles) from Monrovia. Then, at the very end of the month, they attacked Robertsfield, the capital's airport. By early June government troops were turning on members of their own side who belonged to the wrong ethnic groups. Charles Taylor refused to talk to other exile groups, and most observers believed he was more interested in power for himself than in any moves to restore democracy. By this time the USA and Britain had sent warships to lie off Monrovia ready to evacuate their citizens and the US flotilla was reported to be carrying 2100 Marines, presumably for possible intervention.

By the first week of June government officials in Monrovia estimated that half the capital's population of 750,000 had fled as the Patriotic Front forces closed in. President Doe claimed that he had authorized the US Marines to come ashore to assist in ending the fighting and that he would welcome an international peace-keeping force if this could be agreed in the peace talks then being held in Sierra Leone between representatives of his government and the rebels. Meanwhile, discipline in the army began to break down. President Doe had placed members of the Krahn group in all top positions in the army, but many senior officers could neither read nor write and the troops were becoming increasingly demoralized as the rebels continued to advance on the capital. Reports of summary executions being carried out in Monrovia became increasingly frequent. At the peace talks in Sierra Leone the sticking point was Doe's refusal to stand down at once. Reports from Buchanan, which the rebels had overrun in mid-May, also told of indiscriminate killings.

By the end of June the rebels were closing in on the outskirts of Monrovia and independent estimates suggested that only about 1000 government troops still remained in the city. However, a demonstration of 5000 people calling on Doe to resign was broken up by government troops, while 4000 Gio and Mano took refuge in churches throughout the capital in fear of government reprisals against them.

July 1990

By the beginning of July Monrovia resembled a ghost city as the long-awaited invasion of the capital finally materialized. Wherever the army had faced the rebels it had been routed, and no one had any confidence it could keep them at bay. The rebels had destroyed the terminal building at Robertsfield airport, while ships were bypassing the port. The President was guarded by crack troops in the official presidential mansion, although the USA had offered to help him leave the country to save further bloodshed. The city clearly had no defences against the rebel advance.

The month was to prove one of constant rumours. The rebels rejected President Doe's conditions for his resignation. The tribal nature of much of the fighting was becoming increasingly apparent with government forces seeking Gio and Mano people and the rebels seeking out the Krahn. By early July an estimated 6000 Gio and Mano had taken refuge in Monrovia, in churches and at the Japanese Ambassador's residence. At the end of the first week of July the rebels were attacking the port of Monrovia with heavy artillery, while the army, or the remnants of it, for many soldiers had discarded their uniforms and fled, were seeking out Gio to take reprisals upon them.

The reputation of the rebel leader, Charles Taylor, did not inspire confidence. Formerly referred to as 'Superglue' for his alleged corruption, he was seen by many as little better than the man he was attempting to oust. The fighting continued in desultory on–off fashion throughout the month as gradually Monrovia fell, street by street, to the rebels. Many Liberians found it difficult to understand why the USA did not intervene with its offshore Marines.

By the end of the month, as thousands of people streamed out of Monrovia, the rebels were reported to have split. Charles Taylor, now apparently in command of 15,000 followers, declared that Doe would not be permitted to leave the country. At the same time, however, it was reported that he only controlled the eastern half of the capital and that other forces fighting the government troops in the centre of Monrovia were led by Prince Yormie Johnson. He claimed to have telephoned the US Embassy to ask for direct US intervention, but to have been told that the civil war was an internal matter for Liberia. Johnson also claimed to lead 7000 men. He described Taylor as 'a criminal and rogue' who had received $80 million from Gaddafi to stage a revolution in Liberia. Johnson, who had been an officer in Doe's army, had joined Taylor in 1987. They had split in February 1990 when the insurrection was already in progress.

At the very end of July, to complicate an already brutal and disintegrating picture, government forces massacred 600 men, women and children in a Lutheran church where they had taken refuge. By then an estimated 375,000 Liberians had fled into neighbouring countries. The ambassadors of the EEC countries called for an emergency session of the Security Council. In the centre of Monrovia government forces launched a counter-attack.

During the first week of August 1990 the USA sent in 200 Marines to evacuate 59 US citizens, while a number of West African governments belonging to the

Economic Community of West Africa (ECOWAS) under Nigerian leadership co-ordinated plans for intervention in Liberia to end the civil war. The West African group consisted of The Gambia, Ghana, Guinea, Nigeria and Sierra Leone. It prepared a military force under the command of Lt.-Gen. Arnold Quainoo of Ghana, but requested US aid to help fund the operation. In Monrovia, meanwhile, the civil war had become bogged down between a beleaguered President Doe in his presidential palace on the one hand, and the two rival factions of Taylor and Johnson, each holding part of the city, on the other. The West African multinational force then made it plain that it would not intervene until the three sides had agreed to a ceasefire. President Doe was killed in September, but it was not until February 1991 that the three rival factions signed a ceasefire under ECOWAS auspices. A national conference was to pave the way for elections.

MOZAMBIQUE: THE WAR AGAINST RENAMO

Introduction

By the early 1970s the Portuguese were fighting a full-scale war against Frelimo (Frente de Libertação de Moçambique) in the northern third of Mozambique, while the Zimbabwe nationalists (Zimbabwe African National Union, ZANU) were becoming increasingly effective in neighbouring Rhodesia, so the two colonial regimes faced mounting pressures. In Rhodesia Ian Smith's Head of Security, Ken Flower, who ran the Central Intelligence Organization (CIO), floated the idea of creating a black terrorist group during joint Rhodesian–Portuguese–South African security talks in 1971 and 1972, although nothing then came of the suggestion. But in March 1974 Flower visited Lourenço Marques (Maputo) where his opposite number, the Director-General of Security, Major Silva Pais, agreed to Flechas on a basis of 'unconventional, clandestine operations by local Africans'. (The idea of Flechas (arrows) or pseudo-terrorists had originated with the Portuguese in Angola during the 1960s.) It was also agreed that the Rhodesian security forces would continue their 'hot pursuit' of freedom fighters across the border into Mozambique.

Beginning that April, before the coup which toppled the government of Marcello Caetano in Lisbon and continuing after that event, the Rhodesian CIO recruited Mozambicans to form a terrorist organization to operate inside Mozambique without relying on Rhodesia for support, although the need for external back-up became a permanent aspect of the group's later existence. Variously known as Resistência National Moçambicana (Renamo) or Movimento Nacional da Resistência de Moçambique (MNR), the movement was to become a formidable destructive force during the 1980s. The ease with which Africans could be recruited for Renamo during 1974–5 convinced Flower and the CIO in Salisbury (now Harare) that this approach would pay dividends. At first the intention was to keep the terrorist group small and use it as the 'eyes and ears' of Rhodesian intelligence. This objective became especially important once Mozambique became independent (June 1975) and allowed the ZANU guerrillas to operate freely from its territory. Later, however, Renamo developed into a different kind of organization.

The bitter liberation struggle which preceded independence in Mozambique created the conditions for continuing violence after 1975. At or shortly before independence there were an estimated 250,000 Portuguese in Mozambique, yet by

1978, following a mass exodus, only about 15,000 remained. Not only did the Portuguese take with them most of the skills necessary to a modern economy, but on departure they also carried out much wilful destruction, with the result that the economy was thrown into chaos and the new government faced an extra dimension of reconstruction quite apart from the post-war problems which it inherited. Further, once the Frelimo government had decided to obey the UN call to apply sanctions to neighbouring Rhodesia and had made plain its support for the African National Congress (ANC) in South Africa, it laid itself open to constant harassment by the military of both Rhodesia and South Africa, which from that time onwards mounted periodic raids into Mozambique.

In the first years after independence Mozambique faced four major problems: the loss of skills represented by the exodus of the Portuguese; the chaotic state of the economy; the presence of Zimbabwean freedom fighters on its soil, which attracted Rhodesian cross-border raids; and discontent among sections of its own (Frelimo) freedom fighters, who expected greater rewards for their long fight in the bush than were then forthcoming. Such conditions provided fertile ground for the creation and development of a dissident terrorist group.

Outbreak and response

It is particularly difficult to pinpoint the beginnings of the Renamo dissidence in Mozambique because the early activities of the movement are lost in the wider confusion of the final fighting between the Portuguese and Frelimo before independence, and in the growing cross-border violence as ZANU forces moved back and forth into Rhodesia and the Rhodesian security forces made their periodic raids on ZANU bases in Mozambique. At that time Renamo acted as a fifth column or spy unit for the Rhodesians. In January 1976, at Quelimane about 320 km (200 miles) north of Beira, the new Mozambican President, Samora Machel, met with Presidents Kenneth Kaunda and Julius Nyerere of Zambia and Tanzania and committed himself to support the liberation struggle in Rhodesia. Already by February there were about 10,000 ZANU guerrillas in camps along the Mozambique–Rhodesia border area (an open invitation to cross-border reprisals). In March 1976 Mozambique formally closed its border with Rhodesia and applied UN sanctions. Later, in August of that year, after Renamo spies had provided background information, the Rhodesian security forces (the Selous Scouts) attacked the ZANU base camp at Nyadzonia (Pungwe), killing over 1000 ZANU (many of them women and children). Thus, to all intents and purposes, newly independent Mozambique found itself at war along its western border with the increasingly embattled Rhodesians from 1976 until 1980 when Rhodesia became independent as Zimbabwe (see Part I, pp. 62–68).

Over this same period the new government was trying with only limited success to deal with crippling problems of near economic collapse, while also attempting to integrate its largely peasant-recruited Frelimo forces into urban or newly settled life. Under these conditions it was easy enough for the Rhodesian CIO to establish Renamo and for the movement subsequently to grow in the general confusion which then existed.

Course of the struggle

Although it had won the war, Frelimo was to discover that it was far from securely based: its members were rural peasants, unaccustomed to life in the towns which they now occupied, often difficult to control and ready to enact reprisals against those they regarded as enemies or collaborators with the Portuguese. Such behaviour played into the hands of would-be dissidents seeking a justification for their new role. Although the government had committed itself to supporting the struggle in Rhodesia, it tried to keep tight control over the Zimbabwean freedom fighters. Frelimo's support for the liberation struggles in general and the African National Congress in particular also provoked South Africa into military and other reprisals, not least upon Mozambique's fragile economy, and these represented the beginning of years of destabilization tactics from Pretoria.

During 1977 Zimbabwean guerrillas infiltrated across the border from Mozambique into Rhodesia and the Rhodesian security forces increased the number of their cross-border operations, not least because camps in Mozambique made easier targets than guerrillas in the bush. According to President Machel, between March 1976 and April 1977 there were 143 Rhodesian acts of aggression across the 1100 km (700 mile) border, in which 1432 civilians, including 875 Zimbabwean refugees, were murdered. The Rhodesian forces made a point of striking at economic targets and disrupting communications. None the less, Machel gave total support to ZANU. At this time there was little overt evidence of opposition movements against Frelimo, and claims that guerrillas were operating against the government appeared to have small foundation. The United Democratic Front of Mozambique (FUMO) attempted to obtain arms in Europe for a struggle in Mozambique but with little success, while the Renamo army claimed that its guerrillas were fighting under six former Frelimo commanders. At that time the Mozambican armed forces (Frelimo) numbered 19,000.

In 1978 the importance of Mozambique's economic links with South Africa became increasingly apparent. Three of these were vital sources of revenue: transit dues for South African imports and exports through Maputo; remittances on behalf of Mozambican labourers working in the South African mines; and power supplied to the Republic from the giant Cabora Bassa dam in Tete province.

By 1979 ZANU was clearly winning the war in Rhodesia. In Mozambique, however, the disruptions caused by Renamo had become sufficiently serious to persuade Machel that the safety of his own regime depended on an end to the war in Rhodesia. Thus, in December 1979, when the ZANU leader Robert Mugabe wished to abandon the Lancaster House talks in London and renew the struggle, Machel exerted major pressure on him to settle with Britain's Foreign Secretary, Lord Carrington. Mugabe reluctantly agreed. In the four-month period January to April 1980, when Lord Soames became Governor of Rhodesia and, precariously, the guerrilla forces of ZANU and ZAPU were integrated, the Rhodesian security chief, Ken Flower, advised Renamo that its members could do one of three things: revert to civilian life; fight on but without further support from Rhodesia; or be 'transferred' to South African control. Most of the Renamo personnel apparently chose the third option, and the South Africans were enthusiastic to take over control of the movement. Robert Mugabe became Prime Minister of an independent Zimbabwe on 18 April 1980. Flower told him that he had been responsible for the creation of Renamo and that he had handed it over to South Africans; he was retained by Mugabe as security adviser. The stage was set for a new phase in the civil struggle inside Mozambique; during the 1980s this was to escalate to horrific proportions.

The immediate prospects for Mozambique, however, appeared somewhat brighter. The frontier with Rhodesia was officially reopened on 12 January 1980, and with Zimbabwean independence (18 April) the problem of cross-border raids and the consequent confusion which had played into the hands of Renamo appeared to have been resolved. Mozambique became a founder member of the Southern Africa Development Co-ordinating Conference (SADCC) in 1980, and the organization's first funding conference was held in Maputo. This opened up prospects of increased development assistance, while the part Machel had played in exerting pressure on Mugabe to settle appeared to have earned a degree of British 'gratitude', also in the form of increased aid.

None the less, the security situation was deteriorating. In May Mozambique and Zimbabwe held discussions on security at a time when Renamo guerrillas were operating in Manica, Sofala and Tete provinces. Substantial Frelimo forces had to be deployed against them, and it seemed possible that Renamo had a base somewhere in Zimbabwe.

1981

At the beginning of 1981 the future for Renamo looked doubtful: its original mentor, the Rhodesian government, had disappeared with Zimbabwean independence, and as yet South Africa had not fully formulated its approach towards Mozambique. But this was soon to change as Pretoria adopted a policy of economic disruption and urged Renamo to destroy lines of communication – the railways which served Mozambique's landlocked neighbours, Malawi, Zambia and Zimbabwe. In particular, the guerrillas were to harass the Beira Corridor route.

In January South African troops raided houses on the outskirts of Maputo, which they claimed were headquarters of ANC guerrillas. The raid was a double embarrassment to the government because eight Frelimo officers ordered their men not to resist the South Africans. They were later put on trial, but two of them, Lt.-Col. Fernandes Baptista and Lt.-Col. Jossias Dlakhama, escaped custody. It transpired that Baptista had spied for the CIA. In April the Renamo guerrillas attacked the Cabora Bassa hydro-electric power station on the Zambezi and cut the power lines (it then supplied 10 per cent of South African requirements), indicating that South African control was far from certain or clear cut. In June major fighting occurred in the north of the country between Frelimo and Renamo; hundreds of refugees who fled into Zimbabwe complained of ill-treatment received from both sides. Frelimo then began to establish fortified villages as a defence against Renamo (similar to the fortified villages or *aldeamentos* that the Portuguese had created a decade earlier). In July Machel and Mugabe met to discuss the problems of the refugees and joint security. By the end of the year Renamo was enjoying something of a comeback, and its guerrillas were active in Manica and Sofala provinces. This resurgence of Renamo was sufficiently serious to persuade the government to recall Frelimo commanders who had been released from military service, to set up 'people's militias' and to distribute arms.

During the liberation struggle Frelimo had been largely dependent on the

USSR, the DDR and other Communist countries for its external support, but in the early 1980s it began to realize the necessity of mobilizing Western support in order to exert pressures on South Africa and so contain its destabilization policies.

1982

Renamo began to operate on a wider front during the year; it received military equipment from South Africa and concentrated on road and rail links which allowed Mozambique's landlocked neighbours to be less dependent on routes through South Africa. It was sometimes believed that South African troops were directly involved in the field with Renamo, although the evidence was uncertain. In May the Frelimo army embarked on an exercise to make the Beira Corridor, which was vital to Zimbabwe, safe from Renamo attacks. Machel announced that further arms were to be given to civilians. Another Renamo tactic (comparable to that used by UNITA on the other side of the continent in Angola) was to attack or abduct foreign workers in an effort to frighten them into leaving the country. Thus in May 40 Swedish workers fled to Zimbabwe after two of their number had been killed; a Portuguese worker was also killed, and six Bulgarians were taken hostage. Generally, and particularly with sabotage to the Beira pipeline, Renamo greatly increased the strains on an already faltering economy. In October Machel had a secret meeting with Nyerere of Tanzania to request that the number of Tanzanian troops in the country, then 2000, should be increased. In November he met with Mugabe to ask for increased Zimbabwean assistance to fight Renamo.

1983

Attempts to resuscitate the economy during 1983 were largely thwarted by Renamo activities, with the guerrillas active in all provinces apart from Cabo Delgado in the north where the Tanzanian troops were stationed. Even the presence along the Beira Corridor of several thousand Zimbabwean troops did not altogether protect the railway from sabotage. In August Machel appointed eight new Frelimo commanders to lead the fight against Renamo, and a major campaign was mounted in Zambezia, the country's richest, most populous province. An apparently successful government campaign was waged in Inhambane province in the south. Yet Machel publicly admitted that part of Renamo's success stemmed from the military inertia of Frelimo forces, which in many instances did not wish to take the field: they were ill-equipped and malnourished. He also accused South Africa of assisting Renamo; in any case the SADF raided Maputo twice during the year (May and October) to attack so-called ANC targets. In his developing campaign to woo Western support and financial aid Machel visited a number of Western countries, including Britain, France and Portugal. One result of that was to make the USSR cut off its aid to Mozambique.

1984: the Nkomati Accord

South African policy with regard to its neighbours at this time was to neutralize them as bases from which the ANC could operate and, by destabilization tactics against lines of communication, to force the landlocked countries to the north of it to use routes through the Republic for their imports and exports. South African support for Renamo appeared to pay off handsomely during 1984 when on 16 March the Mozambique and South African leaders met at Nkomati on their joint border and agreed to prevent the activities of opposition groups in one another's territories. In essence this meant that Mozambique had to withdraw its support from the ANC and that South Africa had to do the same in relation to Renamo. The ANC condemned the Nkomati Accord, as did President Nyerere, but at that time Mozambique had little choice. The government urgently needed a respite from the fighting and some economic co-operation from South Africa. In fact it got little of either. Not all the Frelimo leadership agreed with the Nkomati Accord and there was no noticeable decline in Renamo activity. In June South Africa's Foreign Minister, Pik Botha, visited Maputo to assure the Mozambique government that South Africa intended to keep its side of the Accord.

Frelimo did keep its side of the agreement: members of the ANC had to live in controlled refugee camps or leave the country, while the ANC mission in Maputo was reduced to 10 political representatives. About 800 ANC left Mozambique for other destinations. In July Machel visited China and North Korea, both of which endorsed the policy represented by the Nkomati Accord. It became clear in the second half of the year, however, that Pretoria had not kept its side of the agreement. Renamo activities increased with South African backing, and by August the guerrillas were active in all 10 of the country's provinces. Also in August South Africa agreed to provide financial assistance to redevelop the port of Maputo. Meetings between Frelimo, Renamo and the South Africans were held during August and September, leading to a joint Pretoria Declaration of 3 October to end the armed conflict. In fact no ceasefire took place, and in November Renamo announced a new offensive throughout Mozambique. In reaction the government launched a series of campaigns in which 100 Renamo bases were destroyed and 1000 guerrillas killed. Despite the success of this campaign early in 1985, large areas of the country remained subject to Renamo attacks.

1985

During 1985 Maputo several times demanded that South Africa should keep its side of the Nkomati Accord, but although Pretoria protested its innocence, there was little evidence that it was doing anything of the sort. Early in the year Pretoria did make a show of persuading Renamo to make peace, but nothing came of it. Meanwhile, the pattern of the war became increasingly clear: the rural areas were subject to Renamo raids, villagers were forcibly conscripted to act as porters or soldiers, and the towns found themselves increasingly in a state of siege. Support for Renamo continued to be provided by South Africa and Portugal, although after considerable pressure Portugal's Prime Minister, Mario Soares, placed restrictions on Renamo personnel resident in the capital. A joint South

Africa–Mozambique security mission operated through 1985, and the South Africans restricted air space along the border in a move ostensibly designed to control Renamo activities. But in April, after a joint operations centre had been established near the border, Renamo guerrillas destroyed a nearby railway bridge, severing rail links between the two countries.

During the June celebrations of 10 years' independence, Machel said that Mozambique had to adopt a war economy because of continuing Renamo activities. In July Machel met with Mugabe and Nyerere in Harare to discuss the security situation in Mozambique, and Zimbabwe agreed to increase the number of its troops in Mozambique to fight Renamo. In August Zimbabwean and Frelimo forces captured Casa Banana, the Renamo headquarters in Sofala province, although the guerrillas melted away; captured documents clearly demonstrated that the South Africans had continued their support for Renamo ever since the Nkomati Accord, leading Pik Botha (South Africa's Foreign Minister) to claim (19 September) that South Africa had only breached the Accord technically and that this had been done to induce Renamo to make peace. In its embarrassment Pretoria then made counter-claims that the Portuguese were helping Renamo (the government said it could not control the activities of the many Portuguese living in South Africa who had fled there from Mozambique after independence) and that there were Renamo bases in Malawi.

Meanwhile, Mozambique was suffering from the drought which affected the region, and both the USA and Britain offered relief aid. Britain also promised to run a military training programme for the Frelimo army (although in Zimbabwe rather than Mozambique), while in July, following the Harare meeting (see above) another 5000 Zimbabwean troops were committed to the 2000 already operating in Mozambique.

1986: the death of Machel

The security situation in Mozambique deteriorated rapidly in 1986; in February Renamo guerrillas recaptured Casa Banana from the Frelimo troops who had been left to guard it, forcing the Zimbabwean troops to mount another operation in April to retake it. By this time an estimated 42 per cent of government expenditure went on the war effort, either in operations against Renamo or in preparedness to meet South African incursions. Renamo attacks on the railways hit a vital source of revenue, transit dues from Mozambique's landlocked neighbours. Pretoria now added to Mozambique's economic troubles by announcing that it would no longer recruit there for workers for the South African mines, and that those Mozambicans then working in South Africa would not have their contracts renewed. This was equivalent to the loss to Maputo of about $90 million a year in hard currency. South Africa claimed in justification that Mozambique was still assisting the ANC.

The war situation deteriorated steadily through the year. Machel demanded that President Banda should hand over Renamo rebels in Malawi, but instead Banda simply expelled several hundred into Mozambique and they proceeded to ravage the border area and seize several small towns in the north of the country. Renamo then declared war on Zimbabwe. Following a meeting with Kaunda and Mugabe in Lusaka, Machel's plane crashed (19 October) on its return flight to Maputo.

The reasons for the crash have never been satisfactorily explained, but South Africa was immediately accused of responsibility and tension between the two countries mounted. The South African trade mission in Maputo was sacked. The South Africans then claimed that documents found at the crash site showed how Mozambique and Zambia were plotting to overthrow the Banda government of Malawi because of its continuing support for Renamo.

Mozambique's Foreign Minister, Joaquim Chissano, became President in Machel's place, and Maputo intensified its pressures on Malawi to cease its support for Renamo. These pressures bore fruit in December when the two countries entered into a joint security agreement. Subsequently, Malawi committed a small number of troops to Mozambique; these were used to guard part of the Nacala rail link which was about to be rehabilitated with international aid (there were 300 Malawi troops in Mozambique by April 1987). In December Chissano also said that he wanted to continue with the Nkomati Accord.

1987

The war situation deteriorated further during 1987. In January Chissano visited Mugabe, who agreed to increase Zimbabwe's military assistance until Renamo had been defeated. Government forces appeared to be more successful in some of their campaigns against Renamo, although this did not alter the overall situation. In February joint Frelimo–Zimbabwean forces captured five towns in northern Mozambique which had been seized by the rebels late in 1986. By that month international aid agencies estimated that about 4 million Mozambicans faced starvation and destitution unless aid could be brought to them; 1 million people were calculated to have left their homes in Zambezia province alone. March was an encouraging month for the government: military reorganization, coupled with the presence of Tanzanian and Zimbabwean troops, appeared to give it greater control of the affected areas, while Malawi seemed finally to have abandoned its support for Renamo. Then in May another South African raid on supposed ANC bases in Maputo brought the Nkomati Accord to an end.

In May Renamo attacked targets across the border in Zimbabwe as a retaliation for Zimbabwe's military support for the Frelimo government. By that time the Mozambican–Zimbabwean border had become an open area: there were an estimated 40,000 Mozambicans living in refugee camps inside Zimbabwe and another 40,000 roaming the countryside looking for work. The Zimbabwean authorities feared that Renamo guerrillas would infiltrate the country as refugees, so during April and May the Zimbabwean and Mozambican armies rounded up Mozambicans they found outside the refugee camps and sent them back to Mozambique. Also in May, following Renamo incursions across their border, Zambian troops in hot pursuit found and destroyed two Renamo bases.

In July Renamo forces took the southern town of Homoine, where they massacred 424 people, although Chissano was to accuse South Africa of responsibility. Pretoria denied this, but suggested a renewal of the Nkomati Accord. In August Renamo mounted major attacks in southern Gaza and Inhambane, and in October their forces ambushed a convoy on a road 80 km (50 miles) north of Maputo, killing 270 people and destroying 80 vehicles. Other attacks along the road earlier in the year suggested that Renamo was attempting to isolate Maputo.

These Renamo forces, operating along the coastal area of Calanga, were apparently supplied by sea from South Africa. The highway is the only link between the capital and the southern provinces of Gaza and Inhambane. It is the key to the government's effort to revive the country's sagging economy, and vital as an artery to transport food to the capital; it is also used by relief agencies sending food to victims of war and drought in the north. A similar ambush of a convoy, resulting in an estimated 63 deaths and 78 wounded, was mounted to the north of Maputo at the end of November. These ambushes demonstrated the ineffectiveness of the Frelimo escorts, who appeared to be either badly trained or lacking the will to fight back. Such attacks, close to the capital, had a demoralizing effect on the international community, including aid workers: the Frelimo forces gave the appearance of military incompetence and of lack of any concept of how to guard convoys, while there seemed to be a marked reluctance to pursue the Renamo guerrillas after an attack had been repulsed.

Although the government faced troubles throughout the year, Renamo was also rent by bitter divisions, with Paulo Oliveiro advocating peace and Afonso Dhlakama, Renamo's leader, insisting that the war should continue. In November two of Oliveiro's supporters were killed in a mysterious car crash. Possibly in response to these divisions Chissano announced a law of pardon in December and an amnesty for members of Renamo who surrendered; this had some effect, for about 200 Renamo came in during January 1988, while in March Paulo Oliveiro defected to the government. Two major Renamo bases were captured during December and three more were destroyed in March 1988, in both cases with the assistance of the Zimbabwean troops.

From 1987 onwards Mozambique moved politically sharply towards the West. Chissano visited Britain, which promised £15 million in aid and agreed to increase its military training. In June 1987 Mozambique reached agreement with the International Monetary Fund (IMF). In October it sent a delegation with observer status to the Commonwealth heads of government meeting (CHOGM) in Vancouver, Canada, at which a special Commonwealth fund to assist Mozambique was established. The year also saw major strides in the huge international aid effort to rehabilitate the Beira Corridor and port, which will eventually cost $600 million. Such developments were welcome in Mozambique, which had come to see the West rather than the Communist bloc as its economic lifeline.

1988

The guerrilla war continued unabated during 1988 with Renamo ambushing convoys and attacking villages and communications. In particular it sabotaged work on the Chicualacuala railway line from Zimbabwe to Maputo, which was being rehabilitated with British and other international aid. Renamo now had an estimated fighting force of 20,000, operating in every province and sometimes across the border in Zimbabwe. The Renamo forces might appear as major units, up to 600 strong, hitting at strategic targets; more often they appeared as small bands armed with machetes who simply killed, raped and robbed. By this time government control was notional in large parts of the country outside Maputo and a handful of towns. The Frelimo army appeared to have disintegrated except for a few of the better units, and the government relied increasingly on the Zimbabwean troops (about 10,000) and Tanzanian troops in the north (about 3000). Mass starvation in the countryside was made worse by the constant movement of refugees fleeing from brutal atrocities; sometimes the population of an entire village would be murdered or mutilated. It was not always clear whether the endless disruptions in the rural areas were only the work of Renamo; many 'bandits' in the bush simply had arms and sought the next meal where it could be found.

The 'President' of Renamo, Afonso Dhlakama', probably controlled about half the Renamo forces. His group had worked closely with South African military intelligence since 1980 and had received training at the South African base of Voortrekkerhoogte, where the Republic's Special Forces are trained. After the Nkomati Accord South Africa scaled down its support for Renamo, although this remained substantial and included the 'maintenance of the communication system and periodic air and sea drops'. Some of these drops were officially authorized; others were carried out by Renamo sympathizers within the South African security system. South Africa's principal concern has always been to disrupt communications so that the landlocked frontline states, such as Zimbabwe and Malawi, are forced to trade through the Republic. Other Renamo backers include the Portuguese, those who fled in 1975 and right-wing American groups, each intent on forcing Mozambique to abandon Marxism-Leninism and return to capitalism. What appeared clear by 1988, after years of war, was the fact that Renamo had no ideology: it is 'anti-Communist', but that is all. Its principal contribution to post-independence Mozambique has been to create widespread devastation and misery. Yet despite a divided leadership and no obvious creed, Renamo has proved remarkably successful at maintaining itself in the field and bringing an originally populist and apparently triumphant liberation government to its knees. On one of the rare occasions when Dhlakama did give an interivew, he said that Renamo's strategy was 'to make problems for the enemy'.

During 1988 Western countries provided substantial aid to Mozambique, mainly in the form of food aid for its semi-starving population; in order to ensure the supplies were delivered the donors were also obliged to provide protection. Britain, for example, provided armoured trains. Rehabilitation work on the Chicualacuala line was constantly sabotaged by Renamo, whose guerrillas killed railway workers and troops guarding them. In April Mozambique's Minister of International Co-operation, Jacinto Veloso, met South Africa's Foreign Minister, Pik Botha, at Cape Town where they agreed to reactivate the Joint Security Commission (set up under the Nkomati Accord) which had lapsed in 1986. In Lisbon Evo Fernandes, a rival of Oliveiro who wanted Renamo to maintain strong links with South Africa, was shot.

The government found itself obliged to rely increasingly on the Zimbabwean and Tanzanian troops in the areas where these operated since its own forces remained ill-equipped and under-nourished and suffered from low morale. One major breakthrough for the government came when a senior US State Department official, Roy Stacey, Deputy Assistant Secretary of State for Africa, denounced Renamo as a brutal terrorist organization, thereby forestalling attempts by right-wing Senators to provide the movement with aid. He described Renamo as 'waging a systematic and brutal war of terror against innocent Mozambican civilians through forced labour, starvation, physical abuse and wanton killing'.

The twists in the war appeared endless and unpredictable. In May 1988 South Africa offered Mozambique about 82 million rands worth of military assistance to protect the Cabora Bassa hydro-electric scheme on the Zambezi against the Renamo guerrillas. In the previous three years these had destroyed 520 pylons over 160 km (100 miles) carrying the power to South Africa. The object was to restart the Cabora Bassa project, which had been designed originally to supply the Republic with power. Although Mozambique ruled out the stationing of South African troops in the country to safeguard the pylons, it was prepared to accept South African assistance in training 1500 Frelimo troops for the task. An agreement was later signed in Lisbon between Portugal (which 'owns' most of the dam), Mozambique and South Africa to reactivate the project by 1990.

During June the government launched a new offensive against Renamo, which resulted in another flood of refugees into Malawi and Zimbabwe. In July President Chissano visited Malawi and with President Banda reaffirmed their joint security agreement of December 1987. In August President Chissano gave his support to a plan by Church leaders to meet Renamo leaders in an effort to end the war. A Peace and Reconciliation Commission headed by the Anglican bishop Denis Sengulane of Maputo prepared to meet with Renamo leaders, although the meetings did not take place until 1989.

1989

In February 1989 South Africa's Foreign Minister, Pik Botha, suggested that the USA might undertake a mediating role in Mozambique and that South Africa could do what it had done in Namibia and bring about peace. The US State Department was then claiming that Renamo had killed 100,000 Mozambicans since 1984. Once more Pik Botha repeated that South Africa was not supporting Renamo. Meanwhile, an estimated one person in 12 in Malawi was a Mozambican refugee, and early in 1989 further refugees were arriving at the rate of 20,000 a month, bringing the total there to more than 650,000. In Lisbon representatives of Renamo rejected a South African peace plan, claiming that South Africa had become an ally of the Mozambique government. But US intelligence reports in March showed that South Africa was continuing its support for Renamo.

A possible 'peace' breakthrough occurred when Renamo said it would lay down its arms for a month in order to allow food to reach starving people: 'For humanitarian reasons . . . Renamo has decreed a unilateral ceasefire in all Mozambique from 1 April to 30 April' the statement said; it was issued in Lisbon. In June President Chissano offered peace talks with Renamo rebels if they renounced violence and agreed to adhere to constitutional rule. The pledge was contained in a 12-point Frelimo position paper on how to end the war. This was a major advance from the December 1987 offer of amnesty which by June 1989 had been accepted by some 3000 rebels. Meanwhile, Church officials had been meeting with representatives of Renamo. In June more formal meetings were held in Nairobi (Kenya) between the Church leaders and representatives of Renamo. The peace moves received added impetus from a speech by Dhlakama at Renamo's first ever congress, held in the central Gorongosa region that June, when he was reported to have said, 'Let us settle what differences remain with words, with dialogue and with noble intent.' He called on Frelimo to agree to a two-year transitional government. At Gorongosa Renamo made changes in its hierarchy, most notably by removing Artur Janeiro de Fonseca from external relations (he had close links with South Africa) and replacing him with Raúl Domingos, former chief of staff of the rebel army. But a scheduled meeting in Nairobi between the Church leaders and Dhlakama was called off after government troops launched an attack on the Renamo base at Gorongosa.

A meeting in July between Chissano and the South African President-in-waiting, F. W. de Klerk, saw considerable agreement between them and the possibility of closer co-operation. Then, despite the earlier setback, Dhlakama went to Nairobi at the end of July for talks with the Mozambican Church leaders. President Moi of Kenya visited Maputo and assured Chissano he would help in the peace nego-tiations. Although the Church–Renamo talks in Nairobi ended without any agreement, they represented the beginning of a process that, it was hoped, would lead to peace in the relatively near future. But by October the situation had worsened: efforts by the USA, Kenya and Zimbabwe to mediate between Renamo and the Mozambique government had failed to persuade Renamo to meet with Frelimo for face-to-face negotiations. Early in December, however, the two principal mediators, Presidents Moi and Mugabe, met in Nairobi and urged both Renamo and the Frelimo government to drop preconditions to talks.

1990

Early in 1990, faced with growing industrial unrest and an army that was often not paid for months, President Chissano announced a number of major constitutional changes, including direct elections for a fixed-term presidency, the abolition of the death penalty, a ban on torture, the right of all Mozambicans to due process of law including the presumption of innocence until proved guilty, and a guarantee of freedom of opinion, association and religion and the right to strike. The proposed new constitution represented the most radical changes in the political system since independence. At the end of January the US government formally declared that Mozambique was no longer regarded as a Communist state, opening the way for much wider American economic support. Such changes indicated a Mozambique that was far more politically acceptable to the West, and in the light of the fast-moving political changes in both eastern Europe and South Africa such acceptance was likely to prove crucial to Mozambique's survival. In February, however, Renamo managed to abduct a British scientist and a Zimbabwean businessman travelling in the Beira Corridor. The abduction served to emphasize both that the war continued and that the much-guarded Corridor was not safe.

Estimated costs and casualties

Reckoned to be one of Africa's most savage conflicts, the civil war in Mozambique has had results that can only be quantified in broad generalities. By 1988, for example, it was estimated that Renamo activities had forced at least 870,000 Mozambicans to flee the country as refugees, had displaced 1 million villagers inside the country and had put a further 2.5 million at risk from starvation. About 100,000 civilians had been killed and far larger numbers wounded or maimed. A further result of the general insecurity was to make worse the famine that in 1988 already threatened 4.5 million people. Commenting on Mozambican refugees early in 1988, the executive director of the World Food Programme (WFP), James Ingram, said that the pace of refugee exodus from Mozambique was increasing and that there were then 420,000 refugees in Malawi, 350,000 in South Africa, 22,500 in Swaziland, 30,000 in Zambia, 64,500 in Zimbabwe and 15,000 in Tanzania, making 902,000 altogether. Figures vary, and that for Malawi is lower than most other estimates, which suggest 650,000 or more. But whichever figure is accepted, there are not far short of 1 million Mozambican refugees outside their own country.

By mid-1988 the Mozambique government was requesting $380 million in emergency assistance to help feed 6 million people then estimated to be threatened by famine. Other aid to the government included $600 million from a consortium of donors to rehabilitate the Port of Beira and the Beira Corridor; these funds were pledged under SADCC following a meeting in 1983. The Corridor is essential to Zimbabwe as its shortest, most economical route to the sea. Only war conditions and South Africa's policy of destabilization ensured that such aid would be forthcoming. Britain became a top source of aid to Mozambique during the 1980s, providing financial assistance for the rehabilitation of the Chicualacuala link from Zimbabwe to Maputo and providing substantial amounts of non-lethal military aid as well as conducting a military training programme for Frelimo units on secondment to a training camp at Nyanga in Zimbabwe. British training at Nyanga (one company of 150 men every four months) was doubled in September 1989 to two companies.

In a fluid situation such as that in Mozambique the ongoing scale of the human disaster is hard to pinpoint. Thus in the early months of 1989, according to the Health Ministry, about 130 people a day were dying in two isolated districts of Zambezia province (Gilé and Ile), while 3800 people (mainly children) had died of a measles epidemic there in January and February. The war situation makes it impossible either to control such outbreaks or even to assist work to combat them effectively. Mozambique appealed to the United Nations for emergency aid for the third year running in 1989; it was estimated that 7.7 million people, almost half the country's total population, would require donated food to survive.

Results: immediate and longer term

Such suffering and devastation as well as the ongoing war have meant that large areas of the country have either been deserted or received no kind of development for years. A generation of children have received little or no education, so (as international aid donors discovered in Beira) it will take years before Mozambique is again able to produce people for industry even at quite low skill levels. The war, in other words, has set back economic development by two decades and reduced the country to an even greater state of aid dependence than at independence – assuming that conditions will allow the aid to be used effectively on the ground.

The war has also spilled over into neighbouring countries. It is a question not simply of refugees (see above), but of actual fighting. Renamo declared war on Zimbabwe in October 1986 in the hope of forcing that country to withdraw its troops from Mozambique. In the Zimbabwe border area next to Mozambique 375 Renamo raids were carried out in the 30 months after the Renamo declaration of war, resulting in 335 civilian deaths, 280 wounded, 667 kidnapped and over 400 missing. Over the same period the Zimbabwe security forces lost 22 dead and 44 wounded, with 29 rebels killed, five wounded and 45 captured.

At the end of 1989 there were about 10,500 Zimbabwean troops, 3000 Tanzanian troops and possibly 600 Malawi troops operating in Mozambique in support of Frelimo and mainly deployed to guard the railway links: the Nacala link from Malawi to the Indian Ocean Port; the Tete Corridor linking Malawi to Zimbabwe; the Beira Corridor from Zimbabwe to the Port of Beira; and the Limpopo (or Chicualacuala) railway to Maputo.

The war has drawn in all of Mozambique's African neighbours: from 1980 onwards South Africa has been Renamo's principal backer, and Pretoria's assistance has certainly prolonged the war and increased the suffering immeasurably, even though a total South African withdrawal would not have stopped it altogether. Zimbabwe and Tanzania have each supported the Maputo government, and the military help provided by Zimbabwe in particular has been crucial in ensuring the survival of the Frelimo government. Zambia has not committed itself to military assistance, but it has been a firm ally of the Frelimo government ever since independence and has faced periodic border problems with Renamo forces. Malawi has been equivocal, either supporting Renamo as Mozambique has accused it of doing or at least turning a blind eye to Renamo activities on its borders. But from 1987 Malawi has found itself obliged to commit troops to help guard the Nacala rail link, which is vital to its own economy, and to co-operate with Zimbabwe, whose forces have kept open the Tete Corridor for Malawi's imports and exports.

During the 1980s Britain and the Commonwealth became substantial sources of aid to Mozambique; in Britain's case it could be argued that its apparent readiness to assist the Frelimo government was motivated, at least in part, by a desire to demonstrate to the frontline states that London was on the progessive side as the confrontation with South Africa loomed – even while Britain's Prime Minister, Margaret Thatcher, argued forcibly against applying sanctions to the Republic. The US role was more ambivalent, opposition to Communism always taking priority in its dealings in the area, although from 1988 onwards Washington became unequivocal in its condemnation of Renamo. Following the Frelimo Fifth Congress of August 1989, at which Marxism-Leninism as a creed was abandoned, the USA became far readier to assist the Maputo government. The USSR, which had been a main source of aid ever since independence, began to change its southern Africa policy once Gorbachev came to power in 1985, and by 1989 its message in Mozambique as well as Angola was to negotiate while it phased out its military assistance.

As of March 1991 the war continued, but the prospects of Mozambique coming to a settlement seemed somewhat brighter. The political climate necessary to attract Western assistance had markedly improved following the changes under Chissano in 1989 and early 1990, and the hope was that Renamo would soon be persuaded to negotiate a peace.

THE NIGERIAN CIVIL WAR 1967–1970

Origins

As the colonial power, Britain brought together four major ethnic groups – the Hausa and Fulani of the north, the Yoruba of the west, and the Ibo of the east – to form a single nation, Nigeria. By 1960 each of these groups was larger in population than most other individual African states then just emerging to independence. The British colonial authorities created strong regional governments and then maintained an equilibrium from the centre. The result at independence was three powerful regions, which corresponded to the major ethnic groups, exerting constant centrifugal pulls against a weak centre. The Ibo, moreover, were by and large the most aggressive and best educated of the three main groups, and some 2 million of them were spread over the federation outside the Ibo heartland of the eastern region and, most particularly, in the more traditional and conservative north, where they held many important jobs and where their presence was often a cause of resentment.

After Nigeria became independent in 1960, the overriding political problem was to maintain a balancing act between strong regional governments, seeking greater autonomy, and a weak centre. But after six troubled years of multi-party democracy, the army took power in January 1966. There was a rapid descent into near chaos during the immediate post-independence years, with increasing instability, riots and widespread corruption, so it looked less and less as though the system could be sustained. Then, on 15 January 1966, a section of the army under Major Chukwuma Kaduna Nzeogwu from Kaduna attempted to overthrow the Federal Government. In the north the Premier, Alhaji Sir Ahmadu Bello, the Sardauna of Sokoto, was killed and the army took over the Kaduna radio station to proclaim martial law. Major Nzeogwu said the aim of the coup makers was to create 'a free country, devoid of corruption, nepotism, tribalism and regionalism'. In the west the Premier, Chief Akintola, was killed. In Lagos the Federal Prime Minister, Alhaji Sir Abubakar Tafawa Balewa, and his Finance Minister, Chief Festus Okotie-Eboh, were killed. Nine senior army officers loyal to the government were also killed.

But this first coup attempt was foiled by loyal troops led by Major-General Aguiyi-Ironsi, General Officer Commanding the Nigerian army. None the less, the shock to the political system was sufficiently great that on 16 January the acting President, Dr Orizu (President Azikiwe was then out of Nigeria receiving medical treatment), announced that the Council of Ministers had decided to hand over to the military; Major-General Ironsi accepted on behalf of the armed forces and was invested with authority as head of the Federal Military Government (FMG) and Supreme Commander of the Armed Forces. Although this coup of 'the majors' was defeated by loyalists, it meant an end to the first republic and swept away the old system represented by the politicians who were killed.

General Ironsi issued a series of decrees effectively suspending the constitution and banning political parties. Military governors were appointed to the regions. The mutineers surrendered and pledged loyalty to the FMG, which promised reforms and the maintenance of 'One Nigeria'. Then, on 24 May 1966, General Ironsi issued Decree 34, which abolished both the federal form of government and the regions (which were replaced by a series of provinces), unified the top five

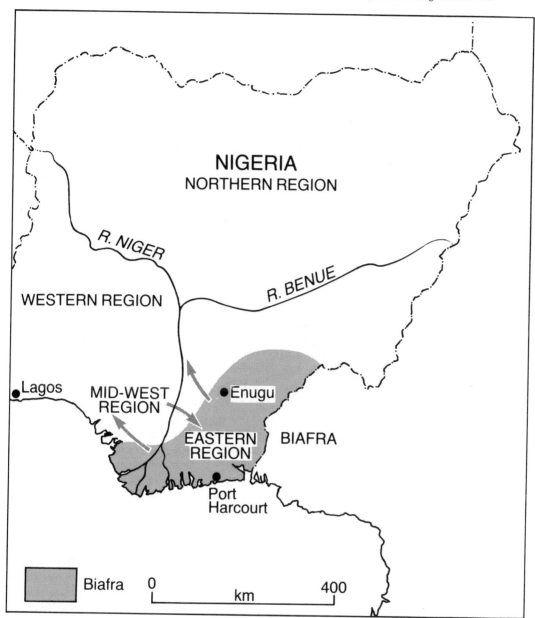

Map 16 Nigerian civil war

grades of the public services and introduced provincial administrations. The FMG then became the National Military Government (NMG). But five days after the publication of Decree 34 there were violent demonstrations in the north where many Ibo (often in the public services) were attacked and killed and their property destroyed. Then, on 29 July, when he was on a tour of reconciliation round the country, General Ironsi and his host, Lt.-Col. Fajuyi, the Military Governor of the western province, were kidnapped and killed at Ibadan by soldiers of the north. This action sparked off the second coup attempt in which some 200 officers of eastern Nigeria (Ibo) were killed. There was talk of secession by the north.

For three days Nigeria was without a head of state before Lt.-Col. Yakubu Gowon, the Chief of Staff, emerged as leader of the country on 1 August. He called for a review of the system since national unity at that point was near to disintegration. On 3 August he granted an amnesty to Chief Awolowo (arguably the most influential political figure in the country), Dr Okpara (a former Premier of the eastern region) and others who had been detained by the army in January. On 31 August Decree 34 was rescinded and the regions restored. A series of conferences were then held in the hope of reconciling differences, but those with the Ibo regional commander, Lt.-Col. Chukwuemeka Odumegwu Ojukwu, failed. There was a new outbreak of anti-Ibo demonstrations in the north during August and September, in which between 10,000 and 30,000 Ibo were killed. This prompted an exodus of Ibo from the north, and about 1 million fled back to the eastern region. In addition about 400,000 Ibo from the western region and a further 100,000 from Lagos also returned to the eastern region. The northern massacres occurred while an Ad Hoc Constitutional Conference with representatives from the four regions (the north, the west, the mid-west and the east, plus Lagos) was meeting in Lagos. It failed to come up with any solutions.

There was growing acrimony between the Federal Government and Ojukwu, who spoke for the eastern region, and, following the flood of refugees from the rest of the country into the eastern region, demands for secession became increasingly insistent. Another attempt to prevent collapse took place in January 1967 when a conference was held at Aburi in Ghana under the chairmanship of that country's head of state, General Ankrah, but the Federal Government and the representatives of the eastern region disagreed in their subsequent interpretations of what had been accepted.

Then, on 26 May, in a move designed to break the deadlock, Gowon announced the division of the country into 12 states; in fact this precipitated a civil war in which the overriding concern (akin to that of Americans in their civil war) was the determination in Lagos, supported by most of Africa, to maintain the integrity of Nigeria.

Outbreak and response

The creation of 12 states in place of the regions – the eastern region was divided into three states – produced an immediate crisis in the east, where Colonel Ojukwu called an emergency meeting of the Eastern Nigeria Consultative Assembly to review the situation. On 27 May Gowon gave a broadcast in which he proclaimed a state of emergency and announced the division of the country into 12 states: six northern states, three in the east, one in the west, one in the mid-west and Lagos.

The Eastern Nigeria Consultative Assembly reacted to Gowon's broadcast by empowering Ojukwu to declare an independent state, and on 30 May Colonel Ojukwu proclaimed the Independent Republic of Biafra. Gowon then announced that Ojukwu had been dismissed from the army and relieved of his post as Military Governor of the eastern region. The new 'state' of Biafra consisted of the former eastern region, the great majority of whose people where Ibo.

The first fighting between Federal and Biafran troops occurred on 6 July following a Federal Government announcement that it was taking 'clinical police action' to end the rebellion. In July 1966 (one year earlier) the Federal army had only been 9000 strong, but by July 1967 it had been increased to 40,000 in the reorganization which had followed the withdrawal of eastern troops, and Biafra was expected to collapse in a matter of weeks. The Biafran army, meanwhile, had been organized round a nucleus of 2000 officers and men who had withdrawn from the former federal army; by July 1967 this had been hastily increased to around 25,000 men. At the beginning of the war eight battalions of the Federal army advanced on Biafra from the north, but this had been expected: the Biafrans were dug in to meet them and offered much stiffer resistance than had been anticipated.

On 9 August the Biafrans went on to the offensive, crossed the Niger and occupied the city of Benin and the ports of Sapele and Ughelli. This offensive was a clear challenge to Federal authority and altered the nature of the war. Had the Biafrans merely attempted to hold their own region, the course of the war might have been very different.

International support and interventions

The size and economic potential of Nigeria meant a rapid lining up of international interests on one or other side in the struggle. Britain, the former colonial power and at that stage the most involved outside power as far as Nigeria was concerned, began by hedging its bets since both Shell and BP had large stakes in the oil, which was mainly located in the eastern region. But then Britain came down firmly on the side of the Federal Government and was to be a principal source of light arms throughout the war. France, on the other hand, supported Biafra (assuming that a break-up of the largest Anglophone state in West Africa would be to the advantage of French interests in the region) and was to provide arms principally through its proxies, Côte d'Ivoire and Gabon. The USSR, which for its own historic reasons always opposes the break-up of federations, supported the Federal Government, not least because it saw the opportunity of obtaining a footing in a region where at that time it had minimal influence. It was to supply the Federal Government with military aircraft – MiG fighters and Ilyushin bombers – (which Western countries, including Britain, were unwilling to supply) and became a major source of arms (about 30 per cent of the total). The Lagos government always insisted that such Soviet support was taken without any strings being attached to it. The US Secretary of State, Dean Rusk, in a famous press statement of 1967 made a monumental gaffe when he said, 'We regard Nigeria as part of Britain's sphere of influence', a remark that understandably went down ill in Nigeria. In essence the USA, like a good many other countries, simply did not wish to become entangled in the Nigerian question. Both Portugal, which was then fighting colonial wars to retain control of its African colonies (see Part I, pp. 10–14, 33–36, 40–45), and

South Africa, which was constantly on the look-out for failures in independent black Africa that would make it easier to justify white minority rule in the south, had a vested interest in supporting Biafra and encouraging a break-up of Africa's largest and most powerful black state.

The civil war which followed was to be bitter and bloody, and before its conclusion in January 1970 it had led to a minimum of 1 million and perhaps as many as 2 million deaths.

Course of the struggle

The Biafran offensive of 9 August plunged Nigeria into a full-scale civil war. On 17 August the Biafrans crossed the Ofusu river to reach Ore in the western region, and appeared to be set to advance on both Lagos and Ibadan. By 20 September the man whom the Biafrans had installed as Administrator in the mid-west, Major Albert Okonkwo, proclaimed the 'independent and sovereign Republic of Benin', a declaration which was a direct threat to the entire state structure of Nigeria. These Biafran advances prompted Gowon, now promoted to General, to say, 'From now on we shall wage a total war.' Federal superiority in numbers, arms and training was soon to be felt. A Federal counter-offensive led to the re-occupation of the mid-west by 22 September, and then, on 4 October, Federal troops occupied Enugu, the Biafran capital. At the end of 1967 Biafra's second port, Calabar, fell to Federal forces, to be followed by the river port and commercial centre of Onitsha and shortly afterwards by the big towns of Aba, Umuahia and Owerri. Thus, despite their early successes, the Biafrans found that they were hemmed in by superior Federal forces in the north, west and south, and after the loss of Port Harcourt in May 1968 they had no further access to the sea and could only be supplied by air.

Peace talks held in the spring of 1968 were abortive. Thereafter Federal tactics were to blockade Biafra; starvation became the main weapon of war and estimates for deaths from this cause range between a low of 500,000 and a high of 3 million. The fledgling state of Biafra was reduced to only a tenth of its size just a year after it had been proclaimed. The civilian suffering that now followed during the remaining 18 months of the war divided world opinion. In a counter-attack during 1969 the Biafrans retook Owerri for a while and recrossed the Niger, but this was a temporary military success that could not be sustained. The last 18 months of the war consisted largely of a process of slow military strangulation as an ever smaller Biafran enclave could only be supplied by air. During December 1969, as peace efforts were under way, Federal forces pushed deeper into Biafra, forcing the government to keep moving from one centre to another.

Four African states recognized Biafra during the course of the war – Tanzania (13 April 1968), Gabon (8 May 1968), Côte d'Ivoire (14 May 1968) and Zambia (20 May 1968) – claiming that their main reason for doing so was the failure of the Federal Government to seek a peaceable solution to the conflict. On 23 March 1969 Haiti recognized Biafra. These recognitions meant an increase in material support. French arms were supplied through Abidjan, Côte d'Ivoire, and Libreville, Gabon; Portuguese supplies came through Portugal's West African colony, later Guinea-Bissau. In addition a number of charitable organizations led by the International Red Cross (IRC), Joint Church Aid and Caritas insisted on sending relief supplies to Biafra by air, despite the objections of the Federal Government. But then, in June 1969, a Federal MiG shot down an IRC relief plane, killing its crew of four; thereafter the Red Cross stopped its flights, although the other charities continued.

Early in the war Biafra obtained a number of old DC aircraft from Rhodesia at a time when the Federal Government had no war planes. Lagos therefore approached a number of Western governments, including Britain and the USA, but they turned down its requests on the grounds that they did not wish to escalate the war. That was when Nigeria accepted the Soviet offer to supply military aircraft.

The war initially had a major adverse impact on Nigeria's new oil industry since most of the oil region was in the war zone, but by 6 September 1968 most of the oil was once more under the control of Federal forces, and shortly thereafter oil was being pumped from the Bonny terminal at the rate of 441,285 barrels per day as opposed to a low of 57,872 barrels per day in December 1967.

Despite the growing signs during 1967 and 1968 that Biafra was bound to lose the war, the Ibo none the less retained a quite remarkable faith in their leader, Ojukwu. Losses were explained away over Biafra Radio by accusations of treachery on the part of army officers or foreign mercenaries and by the extent of foreign support for the Federal Government (from Britain, the USSR, Egyptian air pilots flying for the Federal forces and so on). Biafra maintained a remarkable international propaganda campaign that created a great deal of sympathy for its cause, with heavy emphasis on the human sufferings endured by the civilian population. The reality through 1969, however, was of growing Federal superiority and a tightening grip by its forces on Biafra. The appeal of Biafra meant that special non-government groups became involved, such as the group of Swedish pilots under Count von Rosen who took nine specially modified MFI-9B aircraft to assist Biafra. Even as the general strangulation of Biafra took effect, the beleaguered 'state' launched several successful counter-offensives, including an attack (9 May 1969) on Federal-held oil installations. But the basic Federal strategy of strangulation by blockade and starvation worked. By the end of the year Biafra had been reduced to a small enclave served by one airstrip, while its economy was in ruins and its people starving. The Federal army, meanwhile, had been increased to about 200,000 men.

The Biafrans were finally routed in a series of battles at the end of 1969 and in the first 10 days of January 1970. In its final assault the Federal Government deployed an army of 120,000. Owerri, the last major town, fell on 9 January, followed by the airstrip at Ulli. The war was over. The Biafrans had shown an astonishing resilience right up to the end. This was reinforced in part by the belief (carefully fostered) that they faced genocide if they surrendered, a view that was strengthened by Federal atrocities. On 10 January 1970 Ojukwu handed over power to Major-General Philip Effiong, the Biafran Chief of Staff, and fled (11 January) to Côte d'Ivoire, where he was given political asylum.

Attempts at mediation

The OAU, the Papacy and the Commonwealth each made attempts to mediate, but without success. A majority of countries continued to recognize the FMG throughout the war. A series of mediation attempts were launched in 1967 by the OAU, which insisted that a settlement had to be 'within the context of one Nigeria'. At the September 1967 Kinshasa OAU Summit a Consultive Peace Committee was appointed under the chairmanship of Ethiopia's Emperor, Haile Selassie, but it made little headway. African leaders were afraid that secession by Biafra would trigger off secessionist movements elsewhere on the continent. In addition, Africa wanted its largest, most powerful all-black state to survive intact; this was especially important at a time when the continent as a whole was coming to realize just how weak it was collectively in the face of external pressures. Part of the problem in these and later negotiations was a difference of interpretation: while the FMG meant negotiations about the form a united Nigeria would take, Biafra meant negotiations about its secession.

In October 1967 the Secretary-General of the Commonwealth, Arnold Smith, launched a Commonwealth initiative. A preliminary meeting was held in London in April 1968, but Biafra objected to holding a full-scale meeting there because Britain was seen to be a main supporter of the FMG. Kampala, Uganda, was therefore selected as the venue for a meeting in May. The FMG delegation was headed by Chief Anthony Enaharo, the Federal Commissioner for Information, and the Biafrans were led by Sir Louis Mbanefo, their Chief Justice. But the talks broke down within a week. After that the OAU made a number of approaches to the Biafran leadership, and Ojukwu went to Niamey (Niger) to address the OAU Commission in July 1968. There was a further meeting in Addis Ababa (Ethiopia) that August which only Ojukwu attended; another in April 1969 in Monrovia (Liberia) to which no one came; and a final meeting of the Consultative Peace Committee in December 1969, although by then the war was all but over.

Estimated costs and casualties

During the war the FMG received military aid from Britain and the USSR; Biafra from France and Portugal. The USA, Netherlands, Czechoslovakia, Italy and Belgium vetoed supplying arms to either side. The FMG got the bulk of its small arms and ammunition from Britain; its MiG fighters and Ilyushin bombers from the USSR. British arms exports to Nigeria averaged no more than £70,000 worth a year prior to the war, but by 1969 Britain was supplying arms at an annual rate of £10 million, compared to the USSR's £3 million (i.e. 70 per cent of the total came from Britain). In 1969, for example, Britain supplied 40 million rounds of small arms ammunition and six ships for the Nigerian navy with a further two under construction. The British government maintained that it was only supplying Nigeria with the sort of quantities of arms it had made available before the war and had not escalated its support, a contention that did not bear examination.

The war was prolonged by two main factors: the Ibo belief that they were fighting for survival rather than simply for secession; and international involvement, especially of the non-government organizations. Charitable organizations provided relief despite objections from the FMG, and such relief undoubtedly prolonged the war not only by keeping the Biafrans going on the ground, but also by encouraging them in the belief that more help was on the way. When the IRC pulled out of the area (after one of its planes had been shot down) it had been feeding up to an estimated 850,000 people.

Military casualties on both sides came to approximately 100,000, although no absolute figures were ever produced. Between 500,000 and 2 million civilians died, mainly as the result of starvation. Already in June 1968 Biafra announced the existence of 4.6 million displaced persons, including those who had fled back to Biafra from the other regions of Nigeria. There were then about 750,000 Biafrans in refugee camps, although most of the displaced Biafrans managed to stay with relatives. About 20 in every 500 in the camps (mainly children and nursing mothers) were then dying each month. The FMG offered to allow a 'mercy corridor' for supplies for the starving, but Biafra refused this on the grounds that such food would be poisoned. As a result of this stand, Biafra was forced to depend solely on the air corridor. When the war finally came to an end the Ibo had fought staunchly for 900 days; by the autumn of 1969, however, ammunition had to take priority in all supply runs, with the result that diet fell below the subsistence level for the more than 3 million civilians who were crowded into the remaining Biafra enclave of 4000 square kilometres (1500 square miles).

Results: immediate and longer term

On 9 January 1970 Owerri, which had been Biafra's provisional capital since the fall of Umuahia, fell to Federal troops; the next day Ulli airport, Biafra's only link with the outside world, also fell. On 11 January Ojukwu flew into exile in Côte d'Ivoire, and then on 12 January General Effiong announced Biafra's surrender. Three days later (15 January) at Dodan barracks, the headquarters of the Supreme Military Council in Lagos, General Effiong signed the formal act of surrender and declared, 'We accept the existing administrative and political structure of the Federation of Nigeria. Biafra ceases to exist.'

The war, with its terrible suffering, had nevertheless kept Africa's largest black state intact. In the post-war period which followed, General Gowon's greatest achievement was probably the manner in which he presided over the reintegration of the defeated Ibo into the mainstream activities of Nigerian life. The country was helped economically by the huge oil price rises which came in 1973 as a result of pressure by the Organization of Petroleum Exporting Countries (OPEC) following the Yom Kippur War (see Part IV, pp. 301–306). As a result, Nigeria was able to launch its mammoth Third Development Plan in 1975.

As a result of the war and the oil price explosion, Nigeria was to enjoy a period of economic boom and unprecedented influence in Africa during the second half of the 1970s. During the course of the war Nigeria had, in any case, learnt a healthy disrespect for the motives of the major powers, and this undoubtedly contributed to the independent lines it was to take in the late 1970s over issues such as association with Europe under the Lomé Convention and an African approach to South Africa.

RWANDA: THE PEASANTS' REVOLT

Origins

Antagonisms between the Hutu and Tutsi in both Burundi and Rwanda have their roots far back in history when the incoming Nilotic Tutsi conquered the Bantu-speaking Hutu. For several centuries the Hutu were to be the subservient or peasant group to the ruling Tutsi, a situation that was to last almost to independence, despite the Tutsi accounting for only 15 per cent of the total population of Rwanda. When in 1899 the German colonizers joined Rwanda and Burundi to form Ruanda-Urundi they maintained the old order of Tutsi dominance. During the First World War (in 1916) the colony was occupied by Belgian troops; in 1923 it became a Belgian mandate under the auspices of the new League of Nations. At the end of the Second World War the mandate became a trusteeship under the new United Nations and remained under Belgian control. The Belgians maintained the form of indirect rule – which favoured the Tutsi – as they had inherited it from the Germans.

The peasants' revolt of 1959

The Tutsi still retained their position of dominance at the end of the 1950s as independence approached. On 25 July 1959 the King, Mutara III, died in suspicious circumstances; he was succeeded by his son, who was sworn in on 9 October as King Kigeri V. The event sparked off a Hutu uprising against the existing order. The troubles began with the swearing in of the King, but came to a climax during the first week of November. Hundreds of people died and many Tutsi fled to the neighbouring countries of Uganda, Tanzania and Zaire (then still called the Belgian Congo). The uprising came to be called the 'peasants' revolt' and marked the determination of the Hutu to throw off Tutsi domination.

The Belgians first restored order and then hastened the democratic reforms which were the prelude to independence and which, by their nature, were bound to favour the Hutu. Municipal elections were held in June–July 1960 and gave a massive victory to the main Hutu party – Parti de l'émancipation du peuple hutu (Parmehutu) – led by Grégoire Kayibanda. Although still not independent, Rwanda none the less declared itself a republic in January 1961 and the King went into exile. Then, on 25 September 1961, a referendum was held under the auspices of the UN (a form of face-saving for the Belgians, who were still nominally the mandatory power, and for the UN itself, which favoured a reunification of Ruanda and Urundi before they became independent); the people voted overwhelmingly for Parmehutu under Kayibanda and for the abolition of the monarchy. On 2 October 1961 Belgium formally recognized that Rwanda was a republic, although the country did not become independent until 1 July 1962, with the Hutu in control – a reversal of centuries of history. Gregoire Kayibanda, the Parmehutu leader, became Rwanda's first President. Following independence, leading Tutsi were deprived of political or civil service positions in a process that placed the Hutu in all the important jobs.

The events of 1963

On 29 November 1963, a group of Tutsi refugees from 1959 who had assembled in Burundi from the countries to which they had fled crossed into Rwanda, apparently determined to regain control and restore the monarchy. They seized a number of places including a border post and were within a few miles of the capital, Kigali, before they were beaten back by government forces. This first group were checked without much difficulty. But on 20 and 27 December larger raiding parties provoked much bigger clashes. Once they had been repulsed, anti-Tutsi reprisals followed and an estimated 20,000 Tutsi were massacred by the Hutu. Many more Tutsi were now forced to leave the country.

Results

This abortive attempt really marked the end of Tutsi power in modern Rwanda. The brutality of the massacres – though hardly on the scale of those that took place in neighbouring Burundi (see above, pp. 351–355) – represented a working-out of age-old tribal antagonisms between the two groups. There was a resurgence of Hutu–Tutsi violence 10 years later in 1973. One result of this new explosion was the military coup which overthrew President Kayibanda and brought Col. Juvenal Habyarimana to power. He was to prove far more conciliatory towards the Tutsi, and a policy of Hutu–Tutsi reconciliation followed.

SOMALIA: CIVIL WAR – NORTH VERSUS SOUTH

Origins

When the independent state of Somalia was formed in 1960 it was composed of two parts: the former British Somaliland in the north and the former Italian Somaliland in the south. At one level, given rival colonialisms prior to independence, it is astonishing that the new state worked as well as it did for its first 20 years. Somali irredentism in relation to its 'lost' territories, which culminated in the Ogaden war of 1977–8 (see Part III, pp. 190–198), no doubt helped to foster a sense of unity that would not otherwise have been so apparent. But following the Somali defeat in 1978 and the subsequent deep economic troubles which the country faced, it was unsurprising that other strains in the fabric of Somali life came to the forefront. Among these were substantial differences between the people of the north and the south.

Two dissident groups were formed at the beginning of the 1980s: the Somali National Movement (SNM) in the north, which was assisted by Ethiopia in the period 1978–82 following the end of the Ogaden war; and the Democratic Front for the Salvation of Somalia (DFSS). During the early 1980s these groups had little impact and were irritants to the government rather than posing a more serious threat. But on the other hand, following Somalia's defeat in 1978, President Siad Barre was to be more or less constantly on the defensive, so any dissident movement tended to become more important than perhaps its actions or claims merited simply because of the attention which the government gave to it.

The DFSS was created in 1981 by bringing together three separate dissident groups which were centred on the Mudugh region. The Front had some early successes in minor attacks on the government, but before long it fell prey to a series of internal dissensions. The SNM was also launched in 1981 (in London) and became the more serious of the two movements. Its appeal was to people in the north – former British Somaliland – and a mutiny there in 1982 was followed by rioting. There was sufficient unrest and opposition to the government for the movement to thrive, at least in the sense of attracting adherents.

In 1982 the SNM set up its headquarters in neighbouring Ethiopia, from where it was able to organize unrest in the northern towns of Somalia and also, periodically, to launch cross-border attacks on government targets. It was almost wholly Issaq (a Somali clan) in its membership, and it drew considerable support from businessmen and merchants, whose activities suffered as a result of Barre's economic policies, as well as from the large Somali community living and working in the Gulf. The DFSS and the SNM made a number of attempts to combine into a single, more effective movement, but without success.

Escalating dissent

During the first half of the 1980s the two movements had few real successes. In 1983 the SNM attacked the prison in Mandera to release hundreds of prisoners, including a number of political detainees; the action focused attention on general dissatisfaction with the Barre government. In an effort to recover lost ground and lessen northern hostility to his regime, Barre announced an amnesty for dissidents in 1983 and then stepped up aid to the north in 1985. In October 1985, however, the SNM claimed to have killed 160 government soldiers in Hargeisa district; a year later (December 1986) the SNM claimed to have killed 120 government troops in Burao district.

In 1985 the DFSS occupied a strip of land on the Ethiopian border which it had first taken with Ethiopian help in 1983. But the movement was now to be rent with internecine squabbling, and its leader, Colonel Abdullah Yusuf, was arrested by the Ethiopians. Then in 1986, following a conference between Ethiopia and Somalia in Djibouti, the Ethiopian government agreed to scale down its support for the DFSS. None the less, the DFSS continued to hold the strip of land along the Ethiopian border.

A principal complaint of northerners was simply that their region was neglected by the government in Mogadishu, which was more concerned with the south of the country; the SNM fed upon this complaint. Up to this time, however, the activities of the two movements did not represent a major threat to the government; this was to change in 1987.

Outbreak and response

During 1987 dissidence in the north increased dramatically. There were anti-government demonstrations at Hargeisa to which the government reacted with mass arrests and by imposing a curfew. At the beginning of the year the SNM launched a series of guerrilla attacks against government positions from its bases in Ethiopia; its forces isolated Hargeisa and cut road links with Djibouti. In February, with Ethiopian support, it engaged in a border clash. This was on quite a considerable scale in the region of Burao: the government claimed that its forces killed some 300 invading Ethiopians, destroyed a number of tanks (11 out of 22 used in the attack) and wounded or captured hundreds more. The Somalis admitted to 30 dead and 25 wounded.

In May 1987, for the second time in the year, the SNM claimed to have captured Hargeisa, Burao and Berbera, but this was denied by Mogadishu and not borne out by foreign observers. The chances of any *rapprochement* between the government and the dissidents were not helped by the drought which affected central Somalia during the year, leading the government to declare a state of emergency. The border dispute with Ethiopia continued, so the Mogadishu government was generally on the defensive.

Civil war

During the course of 1988 the SNM-led rebellion develolped into a full-scale civil war. Early claims of victories by the SNM turned out to be greatly exaggerated, so when truly heavy fighting took place there was considerable international scepticism as to which claims should be believed. On 3 April 1988 Somalia and Ethiopia finally came to an agreement over the Ogaden dispute, at least to the extent of accepting the status quo: Somalia agreed to withdraw support from anti-government forces in Ethiopia, and in return Ethiopia undertook to withdraw from the strip of land it had held since 1983 (where the DFSS had been involved) and to withdraw its support from the SNM. It was in response to this agreement – partly because they were obliged to give up their Ethiopian bases – that the SNM launched a full-scale offensive at the end of May, capturing Burao and several smaller towns. Then its forces attacked Hargeisa and besieged the port of Berbera. The government reacted with large-scale military operations, bombing and shelling the towns which the SNM held and causing much damage to both Burao and Hargeisa. In these engagements up to early June 1988 an estimated 10,000 people were killed and about 100,000 refugees fled to Ethiopia.

At the beginning of June, Western governments, backed by the United Nations, evacuated their personnel from northern Somalia; they left Hargeisa in the first week of June, although they claimed that the town remained in government hands. SNM claims to have taken Berbera were denied by the government. In Hargeisa rebel sympathizers were summarily shot; one foreign observer claimed that the bodies of sympathizers were left in the streets as an example to the population and that 'The army is carrying out a massacre among the civilian population.' About 1000 casualties were taken for treatment to the Hargeisa hospital.

In the welter of claims and counter-claims made during mid-1988 it became clear that the SNM had achieved a major breakthrough: it had widespread support among the northern Issaq people and enjoyed much sympathy over its demand for greater northern autonomy and a larger share of the country's resources.

On 5 June President Siad Barre claimed that normality had been restored after the SNM 'suicide attack', but this claim was not born out by subsequent developments. At the beginning of July the Somali air force was engaged in bombing rebels who were still holding out in Hargeisa, while government forces launched a full-scale operation to regain control of the northern towns. Both sides then claimed to control Hargeisa as well as Burao and other northern towns. Much of Hargeisa had been destroyed in the fighting, however, and more than 100,000 refugees had arrived in Ethiopia, which appealed for international relief to assist them. This began to arrive on 17 June. Later the number of refugees was estimated to have increased to between 110,000 and 120,000. Reports that the Somali troops had massacred large numbers of the civilian population of Hargeisa who were sympthetic to the SNM were confirmed by Amnesty International. By September the government claimed that it had restored its control in the north, although the SNM claimed to control the countryside and parts of Hargeisa and other towns.

Assessments

The fighting in mid-1988 reduced the towns to rubble and killed an estimated 50,000 people in June, July and August. More than 400,000 refugees were reported to have fled to Ethiopia. Hargeisa, which had once housed a population of 500,000, had been reduced to a ghost town with whole sections flattened in the artillery duels between the two sides. According to Somali government sources, 14,000 buildings were destroyed and 12,000 heavily damaged before the army regained control of the town. When Burao was recaptured from the SNM in mid-July it too had been wrecked and subsequently deserted. After these devastating battles the SNM reverted to guerrilla tactics. By early October government forces claimed to control most of the main roads in the north, although ambushes still took place on side roads. This mid-1988 phase of the war was reckoned to have cost the government the equivalent of 40 per cent of its annual revenue.

The next phase

By November 1988, although government forces appeared to be generally in control (there was still fighting in Hargeisa) and the SNM were operating as guerrillas in the countryside, the government was far from secure and was reported to be importing nerve gas from Libya. The situation did not improve during 1989.

In January 1989 Mogadishu launched a major campaign in an effort to win foreign support for a major programme to bring peace to the war-torn north. A series of economic and political reforms were announced, including an amnesty for those who took part in the May, June and July uprising. The government sought a political solution to the northern claims of neglect. It was then believed that as many as 50,000 had died in the fighting. Mogadishu was particularly sensitive to widespread claims that its forces had abused civil rights in the war, and it made efforts to counter such claims. But although political prisoners (between 250 and 300) were released, the government was not prepared to offer the SNM either a ceasefire or talks. An uneasy year saw President Barre become more and more isolated. In September his wife left him, while an increasing number of influential Somalis were also leaving the country for Kenya, where they purchased passports and continued to Commonwealth countries which did not require a visa.

A report prepared by the US State Department, *Why Somalis Flee*, accused the Somali army of extreme brutality and the murder of 5000 civilians (members of the Issaq clan who supported the SNM) over the period May 1988 to May 1989. In renewed fighting in the north the SNM wrecked more towns. Between 30,000 and 50,000 SNM were in Djibouti – not recognized as refugees – and crossed into Somalia at night to engage in guerrilla activities. Although Djibouti avoided any involvement in the war, its sympathies were with the SNM, whose supporters are Issaqs like many of the people of Djibouti. By the end of the year the SNM was laying siege to a number of northern towns, Siad Barre had been deserted by the USA, which had been his most important ally since the Soviets had left in 1976, and there was no sign that the brutal spasmodic warfare would come to an end.

The main problem facing Somalia at the end of 1989 was simply that of what would happen when the Barre regime finally toppled, as everyone assumed would be the case. The SNM, apart from its hatred for Barre, did not appear to have any coherent policy. The government had meanwhile concluded a secret deal with South Africa for military assistance. In the northern two-thirds of the country economic activity had come to a standstill and most of the population had either fled or taken up arms.

In January 1990 the American human rights group, Africa Watch, claimed that Somalia had killed between 50,000 and 60,000 civilians over the previous 19 months and driven about 500,000 into exile. The majority of the victims were members of the Issaq clan. The claims were denied by the government.

In August 1990 the SNM joined forces with other dissident groups including the United Somalia Congress and the Somali Patriotic Movement; during the second half of 1990 government control throughout the country began to collapse. Fighting erupted in Mogadishu at the end of the year, foreign embassies were evacuated and by mid-January 1991 President Siad Barre had fled the country. It was far from clear which faction would emerge in control and by mid-February the country was on the verge of disintegration.

SOUTH AFRICA: ESCALATING CIVIL STRIFE – SOWETO TO MANDELA'S RELEASE

Origins

The history of South Africa from the arrival of the first Dutch settlers at the Cape has been one of race tensions and a struggle for control by the whites over the Africans. Until the creation of the Union of South Africa in 1910 the settlers assumed – in an imperial age – that white superiority was automatic. Two years after the Union came into being the African National Congress (ANC) was formed, and so began the long struggle for equality between the races. Racialism and then the formal separation of the races have long been seen as a smouldering powder keg that must eventually plunge the country into violence. From 1946 the subject of South Africa's racial policies has been raised every year in the General Assembly of the United Nations.

In 1948 the National Party won the elections under Dr Daniel Malan, who became Prime Minister. Thereafter laws of racial separation were systematically applied to every aspect of South African life and the word 'apartheid' entered international politics. During the 1950s the main structure of apartheid was put in place by Dr Hendrik Verwoerd, who became Prime Minister in 1958 and is generally regarded as the intellectual high priest of the apartheid state. In 1960 countrywide peaceful demonstrations against the pass system were mounted, but at the township of Sharpeville the police lost their nerve and fired on the crowd, killing 87. The Sharpeville massacre became a symbol of the race problems of South Africa. The ANC and the Pan-Africanist Congress (PAC) were banned, and shortly thereafter the ANC turned to the armed struggle.

In 1962 The General Assembly of the UN called on its members to break diplomatic relations with South Africa, boycott its goods and refrain from exports (including arms) to the Republic; the UN Special Committee on Apartheid was established. In 1972 the Security Council meeting in Addis Ababa (Ethiopia) recognized the legitimacy of the anti-apartheid struggle and requested all nations to adhere strictly to the UN arms embargo. In 1975 the UN General Assembly proclaimed that the UN and the international community had a special responsibility towards the oppressed people of South Africa.

From 1960 (the year of Sharpeville) onwards tensions mounted in South Africa as more and more African colonies to the north became independent. The Rivonia treason trial of 1963–4 acted as the climax of mounting black opposition to the government, resulting in Nelson Mandela and other leaders of the ANC being sentenced to life terms in prison. Then, during the 1970s, the Portuguese African empire collapsed and Angola and Mozambique became independent (with Moscow-oriented governments in control), while the war in Rhodesia also moved increasingly in favour of the black majority (see Part I for the independence struggles in these three territories). These events, and most particularly the collapse of Portuguese power in neighbouring Angola and Mozambique during 1975, had repercussions inside South Africa and formed the backdrop to the events of 1976.

The Soweto uprising 1976

The Soweto riots of June 1976 were the most violent in South Africa's history since the creation of the Union in 1910. They began as a protest by schoolchildren at the proposed introduction of Afrikaans as one of the two languages of instruction in the schools; it was felt that if Africans were to be taught in Afrikaans – a minority language in world terms – they would be further isolated from mainstream education.

The main riots erupted on 16 June and were to last for three weeks, with each day bringing its own casualties and arrests as well as massive destruction of property. Soweto, whose name is an abbreviation of 'south-western township', had become a sprawling city of 4 million. Lying on the south side of Johannesburg, it is difficult to control at the best of times, and in 1976 it became a battleground between rioters and police. The riots spread to other townships on the Rand east and west of Johannesburg, to Pretoria, Natal and the Cape, and involved Indian and coloured youths as well as blacks. The riots were basically spontaneous, an expression of deep anger at a system which dehumanized the black majority. Although the authorities believed they had suppressed the rioting at the end of three weeks, outbreaks continued to occur to the end of the year. One result was that large numbers of black youths fled from Soweto and other townships, crossing the borders into neighbouring countries in order to join the exiled ANC or PAC.

The year was a turning point in South African history and even conservative whites admitted as much. From that time onwards South Africa became increasingly politically volatile, likely to explode at any time. During 1977, in the aftermath of Soweto, the security forces imposed major restrictions on black organizations, and in October 18 black movements including the Black Consciousness Movement were suppressed and 50 of their leaders arrested. Eventually the government was obliged to make certain concessions: electricity was extended to the townships, and the insistence on teaching in Afrikaans was dropped.

The Soweto uprising marked the emergence of a black generation which had become deeply radicalized and was prepared to resort to violence rather than quietly accept the dictation of the white minority. The black youths were to remain radicalized and provided the main force behind the next series of eruptions, which began in 1984.

Casualties

Ten thousand schoolchildren demonstrated in Soweto on 16 June 1976; 10 days later official figures gave 175 Africans dead, 1140 injured and 1300 arrested. By the end of 1976 the official death toll had risen to 360, although unofficial figures placed it above 500. The unrest spread to many townships and altogether lasted for a year. The final (official) count for 1976 was 360 shot dead, 1381 convicted of offences (927 of those convicted were under 18), 528 given corporal punishment, 2915 taken to court (of whom 1632 were charged with acts of public violence), 19 trials under the Terrorism Act and 697 detained for security reasons.

The watershed years 1984–1988

The violence of 1976 was not a one-off explosion of resentment, but the beginning of a permanent smouldering antagonism that could erupt at any time. Moreover, no matter how slowly, world opinion especially in Western countries was at last veering round to the black cause.

The next great wave of violence was to begin in 1984, eight years after Soweto. This time the disturbances, which took the form of strikes and general unrest, were to be on a greater scale and were to last longer. They were sparked off by the introduction of constitutional reforms which created a tricameral legislature with assemblies for the 'coloureds' and Indians, but not for the blacks. At the same time that these reforms were being introduced and President P. W. Botha was talking of other reforms, South Africa was exerting maximum pressure (destabilization) on its neighbours: 1984 was the year of the Nkomati Accord with Mozambique (see above, pp. 364–377). The reforms met growing opposition in the black townships, where the people were deeply frustrated by economic conditions, high unemployment and the lack of any political say. In December 1984 34 trade unions came together to form a new Confederation of South African Trade Unions (COSATU), which became an increasingly vocal and influential organization for change: it demanded the release of the ANC Vice-President, Nelson Mandela, the abolition of the pass laws and an end to foreign investment.

During 1985 opposition took a number of forms: for example, 350,000 residents of Vaal townships mounted a rent strike and an estimated 90 per cent of students boycotted matriculation exams. The year was the twenty-fifth anniversary of Sharpeville, and during a peaceful demonstration at Uitenhage on 21 March the police fired on the crowd, killing 20 and wounding many more. The government claimed that the unrest originated with ANC–Communist agitators, but in fact most of it was spontaneous and from a variety of grassroots organizations which had one thing in common – defiance. Troops of the South Africa Defence Force (SADF) were used to reinforce the police in the townships. A much-publicized and successful part of the defiance campaign consisted of boycotts of white-run businesses and shops.

Much of the violence was by black against black: those who were seen as collaborators with the government became prime targets for attack, and the practice of necklace killings became an ugly part of the general violence – informers or black police having tyres soaked in petrol placed round their necks and set alight. In August 1985 there was a severe outbreak of violence in Natal, this time by blacks against Indians. Then, in December, attacks on whites were escalated. The year was one of general political ferment. The white politician Frederick van Zyl Slabbert and the Zulu Chief Buthelezi formed the National Convention Alliance; a group of top businessmen visited Oliver Tambo, President of the ANC, and the ANC hierarchy in Lusaka (Zambia); and COSATU achieved a membership of more than half a million. The black townships became increasingly ungovernable, and on 21 July 1985 a state of emergency was declared in 36 magisterial districts (black townships).

The state of emergency was lifted in March 1986, but was reimposed with even more draconian conditions on 12 June. It was estimated that, following the reimposition of the state of emergency, 23,000 people were held in detention under its terms and that more than half of these were under 25. Violence continued throughout the year; it took the form of continuing rent strikes, school boycotts, consumer boycotts and attacks on local government offices and personnel and security personnel. A new aspect of the revolt was the emergence of street-level organizations, a form of mini-local government at grassroots level.

In 1986 the United Democratic Front (UDF), which was seen increasingly to be a surrogate for the banned ANC, claimed 600 affiliates and more than 2 million members, while 13,000 detainees were believed to be UDF members. On May Day 1.5 million workers came out on a general strike; this was repeated on 16 June (the tenth anniversary of the Soweto uprising). There had been widespread expectations of government concessions during 1986, but these proved false and President Botha continued to maintain that government policy was one of group self-determination. In many townships government control all but vanished and the 'young comrades' – radical black youths – took effective control.

One breakthrough did occur in 1986: the government formally committed itself to unscrambling the apartheid system, which had been the main plank of National Party policy ever since 1948; even though little was actually done then or later, the commitment represented a major triumph for the opponents of the system. Parallel with its home repression during 1986 the government continued to employ destabilization tactics against its neighbours: in January it blockaded Lesotho, ensuring the collapse of the Jonathan government; in May raids on Botswana, Zambia and Zimbabwe were designed to bring an end to the negotiations inside South Africa by members of the Commonwealth Eminent Persons' Group (EPG).

The state of emergency was maintained through 1987, and police, military and black vigilante action combined to bring a certain order to the townships. Yet rent boycotts now involved an estimated 650,000 households and cost local authorities R720 million. On 5–6 May a national general strike brought out an estimated 3 million black workers and students; a similar strike was held on 16 June. Together these represented the biggest industrial actions in South African history.

The state of emergency was maintained throughout 1988. In February the government banned the UDF and 16 other organizations and placed restrictions on COSATU, which by then numbered 800,000 members. The year saw more restrictions placed on the press and a growing movement among young whites to refuse military service on conscientious grounds. There were a number of treason trials of black leaders, and the government claimed that 17 per cent of those arrested under the emergency were still in detention. Up to October 1988 the government claimed that there had been 262 terrorist attacks as opposed to 230 in 1986 and 235 in 1987.

Casualties

Over the four years 1984–8, despite the state of emergency and sweeping police powers, the situation steadily got worse. Estimates of killings rose from 1.7 a day prior to the emergency to 3.3 a day after its imposition (for the period July to December 1985). Between September 1984 and December 1985 1000 were officially estimated to have been killed in the unrest, the great majority of them black. When the emergency was lifted in March 1986 there had been 8000 arrests and an admitted 757 deaths during the actual time of the emergency.

The South African Institute of Race Relations claimed that 825 deaths had resulted from unrest between September 1984 and October 1985; at the same time official figures gave 504 deaths for this period from security force actions and 232 deaths from other actions. By November 1985 5253 people had been detained without trial, of whom 3063 were released. Thousands more blacks had been arrested and there were widespread reports of torture. Leading members of the UDF, including the Reverend Allan Boesak, were arrested on treason charges.

Other casualty reports are higher: in the two years to Setember 1986 a total of 1776 people, including 56 members of the security forces, are estimated to have been killed. In the violence at the Crossroads township outside Cape Town in May 1986 72 people were killed and 80,000 rendered homeless in the battles between the young comrades and the older vigilantes.

Chief Buthelezi and the Inkatha Movement

Increasingly from the mid-1980s there occurred an escalation of violence in Natal between the members of Chief Mangosothu Buthelezi's Zulu Inkatha Movement and members of the UDF; in essence this was a power struggle between Buthelezi (making a bid for recognition as one of the key black figures who would eventually negotiate with the white government) and the UDF, which represented nationwide black aspirations as opposed to tribally based (Zulu) aspirations. The seeds of the conflict were sown in 1983 when the UDF was formed. The UDF acted on behalf of the exiled ANC, and its support came from those who were determined to carry on an uncompromising battle against the government. The UDF obtained substantial support in Natal, especially from the better educated blacks. At that point Chief Buthelezi saw his Inkatha power base being eroded like that of the white government. The result was an unholy alliance between government forces of law and order and Inkatha, and when the Inkatha strong-arm groups attacked the UDF the police did little to restrain them. A civil war between the two groups was exactly what Pretoria was happy to see occur.

During 1987 an estimated 497 people died in clashes between the Inkatha and the UDF; it was the beginning of a new civil war separate from that being waged against the government. In September 1988 Inkatha and COSATU held meetings and worked out a peace accord, but this did not last. By the end of October 1988 an estimated 511 people had been killed in Inkatha–UDF clashes.

By March 1990, when Nelson Mandela had been released, more than 3000 people had been killed in the preceding three years in the Inkatha–UDF clashes, and Mandela clearly saw it as a main priority to bring an end to this killing. Late in March Mandela and Buthelezi agreed to meet in an effort to bring the faction fighting to an end. They did so after a major flare-up in fighting took place in the black townships outside Pietermaritzburg where at least 80 people were killed (bringing the death toll for March alone to 230), while hundreds were wounded; in addition some 200 houses were destroyed and about 12,500 people forced to flee to refugee centres. Yet almost at once the talks were cancelled as a result of ANC pressure on Mandela; it was felt that the meeting was untimely and that the ingrained Inkatha–ANC hatreds were too great. Buthelezi claimed to be a national leader who transcended the tribal divides of South Africa, although the evidence did not support this. He simply did not command the nationwide support accorded to Mandela, and that fact made his control of Inkatha all the more important since its ability to cause trouble represented a major lever for gaining a place at the negotiating table. Moreover, by March 1990 there was abundant evidence that Inkatha and the police had worked together, the government seeing the Inkatha–UDF conflict as a means of holding the ANC and its supporters in check.

Talks between Mandela and Buthelezi may bring peace, but the hatreds go deep. By April 1990, as other political developments in South Africa were moving at considerable speed, it appeared that Buthelezi's influence was on the wane.

Results: continuing

Two developments of crucial importance to the region took place in 1989: South Africa finally withdrew from Angola and agreed to the UN peace process in Namibia, which led to independence in March 1990 (see Part I, pp. 332–351); and F. W. de Klerk succeeded P. W. Botha as President, bringing an era to an end. Immediately, however, a sort of interregnum followed the 1989 elections while everyone waited to see what de Klerk would do. Then, on 2 February 1990, President de Klerk gave a speech in which he lifted the ban on the ANC and other political parties; a week later he released Nelson Mandela. It really did appear that a new era had opened in South Africa. The commitment to end apartheid and the achievement of Namibian independence also helped to create a new mood in South Africa. But these developments did not mean any quick solutions, and South Africa is likely to witness many crises and considerable violence during the first half of the 1990s before a permanent long-term political solution broadly acceptable to the population as a whole has been achieved.

SUDAN: NORTH–SOUTH, AN OLD PATTERN OF MISTRUST

Origins

The spread of Islam southwards from Egypt in the fifteenth and sixteenth centuries did not reach as far as the south of Sudan, the region that in the nineteenth century came to be known as Equatoria. In any case, the black southerners had long been regarded by the northerners as an inferior people and a source of slaves. The northern two-thirds of Sudan consists of Muslim Arabs or arabicized peoples, while the inhabitants of the south are members of the black Nilotic tribes who follow Christian or animist beliefs. The Egyptian conquest of Sudan in the early nineteenth century did not include Equatoria, and the influence of the Islamic religious leader called the Mahdi at the end of the century did not extend to the Dinka, Shilluk or Nuer people of the south.

Following the British conquest of Sudan at the end of the nineteenth century and the establishment of the Anglo-Egyptian Condominium (nominally controlled by the two powers, but in fact ruled by Britain), the British kept the administrations of the north and south sufficiently separate that the weaker group, the southerners, did not feel threatened by the dominant northerners until the rise of pre-independence nationalism. Indeed, during the 1920s, Britain inaugurated a Southern Policy which aimed to insulate the three southern provinces with their non-Muslim black populations from nationalist developments to the north, where events in Egypt were having a growing influence, and to assimilate them instead into an East African Federation based on Nairobi which would include Kenya, Uganda and Equatoria. That at least was the theory. This policy, which contained the seeds of southern separatism, was not popular with northern nationalists. During August 1955, when independence was only a few months distant, two companies of the Sudan Defence Force who formed part of the Equatoria army mutinied, and although the troubles were put down quickly, their action was a foretaste of developments to come and could be seen as the spark which ignited the first part of a civil war that is still going on.

This first civil war, whose causes were already surfacing in 1955, was to last to 1972. Its roots may be seen in growing southern resentment at the government of the north centred on Khartoum. Once the British had left, old resentments at northern domination came into the open. These were a mixture of Christian and animist rejection of Islam and fear of exploitation that had its roots in a not so distant slave trade. Such historic fears were fuelled after independence by the further legitimate complaint that the south did not receive its proper share of development, but was exploited for the benefit of the north.

Outbreak and response

Fears of northern exploitation led to disturbances in the south at the time of independence (1 January 1956), and from then onwards overt differences between north and south suggested that only the greatest political sensitivity allied to caution would prevent a rupture between the two disparate parts of the new state. Unfortunately, such sensitivity was not often forthcoming from Khartoum, and from 1956 onwards a steady build-up of resentment against the north took place in the south.

In November 1958 General Ibrahim Abboud, the Commander-in-Chief of the army, took power in a coup and instituted a series of reforms. His policies towards the south stirred up fresh antagonisms. The army, in the name of greater unity, introduced in the south measures whose main purpose was to spread Islam and the use of the Arab language, neither of which was welcome. Furthermore, civil service and police posts in the south were given to northerners in a pattern of classic 'colonial' exploitation, while education, which had been taught in English and handled by the Christian missionaries, was now to be shifted towards Islam and taught in Arabic. In October 1962 a strike in southern schools led to anti-government demonstrations, which prompted many students to flee across the borders into neighbouring countries.

About 500 former soldiers of Equatoria province now came together to form the Anya Nya movement. This guerrilla organization began without arms and without much obvious purpose except opposition to northern domination, and its members lived off the country. But in 1963 a former lieutenant in the army, Emilio Tafeng, became its leader; he organized the guerrillas and made them into an effective movement. It was Tafeng who first used the name Anya Nya (a snake poison) for the guerrillas.

Civil war 1963–1972

Between 1962 and 1964 foreign Christian missionaries were expelled from the south of Sudan in a move which was seen as a prelude to Islamicization. In September 1963 a rebellion broke out in eastern Nile province; it was led by Anya Nya, which by then had come to the conclusion that only by armed resistance could it bring enough pressure to bear on the Khartoum government to force it to listen to southern grievances. The immediate response from the north, however, was greater repression.

Yet, in the north, there was growing disillusion with the military government, especially among the intelligentsia, and as the demand for a return to democracy grew stronger, so the issue of the south came to be used as a weapon against the government. This northern concern helped to highlight southern grievances even if the reason for it had little to do with genuine northern sympathy for southern problems.

From 1963 onwards Anya Nya maintained training camps outside Sudan in Zaire and Uganda, while inside the country it waged a guerrilla war which consisted largely of ambushes of government forces. By the end of 1964, a year after Tafeng had reorganized it, Anya Nya had increased its membership to about 2000 and was now sufficiently important and effective that southern political groups made approaches to it seeking co-operation. Both the Azania Liberation Front and the Sudan African National Union (SANU) made contact with Anya Nya; however, the movement did not allow itself to be taken over by the politicians and continued to maintain its own identity.

In October 1964, when the greater part of the Sudan army had been moved to the south to deal with the rebellion, students at the University of Khartoum demonstrated against the government's southern policy. The demonstrations spread, the government lost control and General Abboud resigned. During the next five years (1964–9) a series of coalition governments ruled Sudan. Early in 1965 one of the first actions of the new civilian government was to offer a general amnesty and then to hold a north–south conference; although the conference did not come up with any solutions, it did increase awareness of the differences and problems that existed between the people of north and south Sudan. The difficulty lay in the fact that the civilian governments of this period were weak and riven by factions. As a result the war smouldered on; it was essentially a war of attrition whose principal victims were the peasant farmers in the south, many of whom were to suffer from famine and displacement as a result of the fighting.

In 1967 a political figure of southern Sudan, Aggrey Laden, set up a Southern Sudan Provisional Government and established administration in the areas which by then were controlled by Anya Nya. From this time onwards the guerrillas called themselves the Anya Nya Armed Forces (ANAF), and by 1968 they had an estimated 10,000 members. Yet Anya Nya still had no clear policy, even though it set up a revolutionary government in 1969 which Aggrey Laden joined. Its main strength was derived from tribal affiliations and though there were rival groups they made little impact. By 1969 the government took Anya Nya sufficiently seriously to use the air force to seek out and attack the rebel hideouts; at the same time the numbers of southern refugees were greatly increased as a result of the northern policy of razing villages that had sheltered the rebels. This did nothing to reconcile the government of the north to southerners who were not necessarily in sympathy with Anya Nya tactics.

Nimeiri takes power 1969

On 25 May 1969 a group of young army officers led by Colonel Gaafar Mohamed al-Nimeiri seized power in Khartoum. The new government faced Communist threats from the left and the Umma Party on the right. At first under Nimeiri the war in the south escalated. There was heavy fighting through 1970 with Anya Nya attacking convoys and strategic targets such as bridges; in October of that year the government launched a major military offensive in the south. A significant Anya Nya attack of 5 January 1971 at Pachola resulted in the deaths of more than 150 members of the government forces.

Nimeiri, meanwhile, was concerned to consolidate his position and destroy or nullify the opposition of the Communists and Umma Party. The worst crisis came in July 1971 when for three days (19–21 July) he lost control of the government during a major coup attempt that very nearly succeeded in toppling him. Thereafter, Nimeiri took to himself much greater power as President and made the Sudan Socialist Union (SSU) the sole legitimate party. In the south the rebel groups united under the leadership of Major-General Joseph Lagu, who took over from Tafeng to become both military and political leader of Anya Nya (or the Southern Sudan Liberation Movement as it was also called), and from its headquarters in the Immatong mountains he entered into secret negotiations for peace with Nimeiri. The big issue for the south was that of regional autonomy. At this time about 20,000 of the Sudan armed forces (two-thirds of the total) were committed to the war in the south, while part of the Sudan air force, using MiG-21s operated by Egyptian pilots out of Juba, was also employed against the rebels. Israel was accused at this time of providing military assistance to Anya Nya, although the movement rejected Soviet offers of aid because it feared to internationalize the conflict.

The peace of 1972

It was to be Nimeiri's greatest achievement to bring an end to the 17 years of civil war which had afflicted Sudan since independence. By then Anya Nya had come to represent the black south, whose people regarded the Arab north (which outnumbered the south by three to one) with deep suspicion. Negotiations between Nimeiri's government and the leader of Anya Nya, Joseph Lagu, led to the Addis Ababa Agreement of 27 March 1972. The Agreement gave regional autonomy to the Sudan's three southern provinces – Bahr al-Ghazal, Equatoria and Nile – and allowed a regional legislative assembly and executive headed by a President (who was a national Vice-President) to control most internal affairs of the region. In addition, special arrangements were made to integrate southerners into national jobs; this included members of Anya Nya, who were to be taken into the army and police. There was also the promise of economic development to be funded by the north. Despite religious and cultural differences between north and south, lack of development was at the heart of the problem. The subsequent failure of the north to keep its promise and allocate a fair share of development funds to the south was a root cause of the renewed hostilities a decade later.

At the time the ceasefire came into operation an estimated 12,000 Anya Nya came out of the bush; of these, half were to be absorbed into the armed forces and police, while Lagu became Officer Commanding in the south. Much goodwill was generated at the time, and it really did appear that one of Africa's apparently intractable problems had been solved. An important role in the peace negotiations was played by Canon Burgess Carr of the World Council of Churches (WCC), whose recent decision to give support to the liberation movements in southern Africa made the WCC an intermediary acceptable to both Nimeiri and Anya Nya. Nimeiri's major concession was that Sudan should not be an Islamic republic; the south gave up talk of secession.

Post-war reconstruction

The tasks following years of warfare and general disruption were formidable: there was need, above all, for agricultural projects to restore food production, and for the creation of jobs for an estimated 250,000 displaced people who had flocked to the towns during the war and had no means of support. Nimeiri demonstrated his sincerity by calling on the international community to take part in a major conference at Khartoum where the UN specialized agencies, the International Red Cross (IRC) and some 26 mainly Western humanitarian relief organizations met to discuss relief and rehabilitation measures for the south.

Costs and casualties

An estimated 500,000 people died over the 17-year period of the civil war, the majority of these from starvation and disease resulting from the dislocations of war rather than from actual fighting. In the year following the Addis Ababa Agreement 1,190,320 displaced people either emerged from the bush or returned from exile in neighbouring Ethiopia, Uganda or Zaire to take up normal lives again in the south. This huge exercise in refugee rehabilitation was described by the United Nations High Commissioner for Refugees (UNHCR), Prince Sadruddin Khan, as 'a milestone in the history of refugee problems in our time'. The exercise was carried out by the UN and its agencies, and voluntary organizations from more than 30 countries assisted with £10 million of international aid.

A year after the peace, which appeared to be holding remarkably well, large numbers of people who had been displaced by the war had returned to their villages, while 6000 members of Anya Nya had joined the army and another 9000 had returned to their villages. When Nimeiri visited the south on the anniversary of the peace he was given a hero's reception; the resolution of the conflict was pre-eminently his achievement.

The second round 1983–1990

When he came to power in 1969 Nimeiri said that the war in the south had to be ended by negotiation; he then claimed that successive governments had neglected, mistreated and cheated the south. He established a Ministry of Southern Affairs to work out a policy for the region, and put a southerner, John Garang, in charge of this ministry. It is both ironical and sad that, just as ending the war in the south was Nimeiri's greatest achievement at the beginning of his period of power, so his sacrifice of the south on the altar of Islamic fundamentalism – his hope of clinging to power – was his final failure.

By 1983 Nimeiri's popularity had all but disappeared, and as his power slipped, so he resorted to expedients to hold on. Primarily this meant making more and more concessions to the Islamic fundamentalists, who were demanding that Sudan should become an Islamic state and that Sharia law should be applied throughout the land, an idea that was anathema to the south. The war in the south resurfaced when, in a move that was seen as ending its autonomy, the south was divided into three separate regions each with its own governor and assembly and when, under pressure from the Muslim Brotherhood, Islamic (Sharia) law was introduced in September 1983. The result was predictable: a growth of unrest, a stream of refugees into Ethiopia and a return to the bush of old or new members of Anya Nya to resume the war. In any case the new regional arrangements went against the Addis Ababa Agreement of 1972.

This time round the southern rebels called themselves the Sudan People's Liberation Movement (SPLM) and their army the Sudan People's Liberation Army (SPLA). The SPLA in effect militarized the south: they kept to guerrilla tactics, threatening communications to the towns and the towns themselves, but either did not take the towns when they could or occupied them briefly and withdrew when confronted by the government forces. These tactics prevented the distribution of food and rapidly aggravated the situation until large parts of the south faced famine. Later the SPLA descended on villages, forcing these to provide food and conscripting the young men as fighters. As a result, more and more southerners were to flee their homes, crossing the borders into neighbouring countries as refugees or moving northwards as displaced people within Sudan.

Opposition to Nimeiri's rule increased throughout 1984; it spread from the south to the north. The severity of the application of Sharia law caused deep resentment in the north of Sudan as well as the south during 1984, and Egypt protested at the severity of Sharia punishments. As a result of growing international pressures as well as several abortive coup attempts, Nimeiri decided to soften his approach to the south in September 1984, just one year after the introduction of the changes which had led to a renewal of the war. He annulled the state of emergency, rescinded the division of the south into three regions and lifted the application of Sharia law to the south. But these moves came too late to bring an end to the unrest, while the famine, exacerbated by a return of refugees from neighbouring countries, continued. When, in March 1985, Nimeiri left on a visit to the USA the SPLA was in control of large areas of the south, and major famine once more was forcing thousands to flee to Ethiopia as refugees.

The coup of 1985 and return to civilian rule

On 6 April 1985 the Minister of Defence, General Abd ar-Rahman Siwan al-Dahab, replaced Nimeiri in a bloodless coup to become head of state. The new leader promised a return to civilian rule within 12 months. The south was offered three seats on the interim Council of Ministers and self-rule during the 12-month period before civilian rule was restored. However, nothing was done about the Sharia law, which was deeply resented by the south. The south saw little change in these proposals and its response was predictable: the SPLA claimed five seats on the interim Council of Ministers and an end to Sharia law. Meanwhile, the famine grew steadily worse and was only likely to be overcome by a huge international aid effort. In February 1986 the SPLA refused a UN request to allow a convoy to take relief supplies to the 900,000 then estimated to be facing starvation, although some supplies were airlifted to Juba. In the elections of April 1986 the Umma Party won 99 out of 264 seats and Sadiq al-Mahdi became Prime Minister of a coalition government. But the voting in 37 southern seats (out of 68) had been suspended because of rebel activities.

In a first tentative move to resolve the dispute Sadiq al-Mahdi met the SPLA leader, John Garang (formerly the head of Nimeiri's Ministry for Southern Affairs), in Ethiopia on 31 July 1985, but nothing came of it. Garang insisted that the state of emergency and Sharia law had to be lifted completely as a precondition for peace talks. But Sadiq was only prepared to limit the application of Sharia law to the north and insisted on a ceasefire as his precondition to the talks. On 16 August 1986 the SPLA shot down a Sudan Airways flight and the government suspended all negotiations.

Northern Sudan, certainly since the days of the Mahdi, has been subject to strong fundamental Islamic influences, and these now came to dominate government decisions under Sadiq al-Mahdi (the direct descendant of the nineteenth-century Mahdi who had fought the British). The northern political parties are rooted in Islamic sects, while Sadiq himself was the spiritual head of the Ansar movement, Sudan's largest Islamic sect.

At the same time international involvement in the war appeared to be increasing. Ethiopia supported Garang's SPLA as a counter-balance to Khartoum's support for the rebels in Eritrea, while the extent of Sudan's international debts at £9 billion made the government susceptible to Western pressures. By the end of 1986, both sides in the debilitating war were in urgent need of peace, with an estimated 5 million southerners facing possible famine. And yet 1987 saw an escalation of the war, with fighting more bitter and brutal and the economy steadily deteriorating. The Muslim Brotherhood became increasingly influential in the north, criticizing the government throughout 1987 for not ending the war, even as it insisted that Sharia law should be applied throughout the country. There was little indication that Sadiq, even if willing to do so, had the capacity to end the war. In April there occurred one of the worst incidents in deteriorating north–south relations when 1000 Dinka people were massacred near el-Dhaein in Darfur province. In August a similar massacre took place in Wau when 300 Dinka died. The Dinka make up the bulk of the SPLA army and are seen as the backbone of the rebellion.

The inclusion in the Sadiq government of members of the National Islamic Front (NIF) only served to frighten the south further as to the intentions of Khartoum. By the end of 1987 the war had been carried north by the SPLA into Blue Nile province, which until that time had been seen as part of the north. The huge floods of August 1987 exacerbated an already desperate situation, especially round Khartoum where an estimated 1 million displaced people from the south were living in wretched shanty town conditions – although the deaths among these people were the result of starvation and lack of aid rather than flooding.

1988: steady deterioration

The south slid closer to anarchy and starvation during 1988, with various international aid organizations attempting to come to agreement with the SPLA to allow airlifts of food into the country. Juba, with a normal population of 100,000 had swollen to twice that number with refugees, while only a handful of garrison towns in the south remained in government hands. In a number of southern towns supplies would be flown in by the government for the garrisons alone, while the people were left to starve; convoys of supplies coming up from Kenya and Uganda were constantly attacked by the SPLA. Yet while the south was starving, there was a surplus of food in the north. In April 1988 Sadiq was re-elected Prime Minister of a government of national reconciliation, although this only served to emphasize north–south divisions. There was little indication that the south trusted him, and in Khartoum it was proposed that Sharia punishments should be more severe.

Towards the end of the year, which was characterized by endless political manoeuvring in Khartoum rather than by any decisive moves towards ending the war, it was finally announced that Sadiq and Garang would meet in October. In the meantime the SPLA was successfully attacking food convoys and fighting near the outskirts of Juba, the southern capital. More than 1 million displaced people from the south had moved north to Khartoum, and their presence in the capital was used by international aid organizations to exert pressure on the government in the hope of bringing about a truce in the fighting. The signs were, however, that Sadiq and Garang were equally suspicious of one another and equally reluctant to talk peace. Large numbers of refugees fleeing into western Ethiopia were believed to have died on the way; a high proportion of them were boys and men attempting to escape from conscription into the SPLA.

In November 1988 the SPLA leader, John Garang, met with senior members of one party in the coalition government (the Democratic Unionist Party, DUP) in Addis Ababa (Ethiopia) in an effort to achieve a peace settlement. Once more the talks foundered on the determination of the fundamentalists in Khartoum to introduce Sharia law throughout the country. In the capital, supporters of the militant National Islamic Front took to the streets to attack black Sudanese from the south, chanting 'No peace without Islam!' The Prime Minister, Sadiq al-Mahdi, continued to sit on the fence, refusing to commit himself to the peace accord which the SPLA and the DUP had agreed in Addis Ababa. Through December, despite pressure from the international community, peace attempts all came to nothing. The war situation was complicated by the fact that the Ethiopians assisted the SPLA in the south, while the Sudanese assisted the Eritrean nationalists from the north-east of Sudan. A coup attempt against the government failed, but it served to emphasize the generally unstable nature of the coalition over which Sadiq presided. Then, at the end of December, the DUP left the coalition: partly because its peace plan for the south had been rejected by parliament; partly because of steep price rises introduced by the government.

At the end of a disastrous year it was estimated that at least a quarter of a million people had died as a result of famine, largely because neither the government nor the SPLA would allow food supplies to be taken to the people in the south. It was a war in which few military casualties occurred; the majority who died were civilians either killed by raiding parties or starved to death. The SPLA, variously estimated at between 20,000 and 40,000 strong and recruited mainly from the Dinka, had control of the greater part of the south, while government forces were confined to three major towns and a handful of small garrisons.

1989

In February 1989 senior officers of the army gave the government an ultimatum to reform itself and end the civil war. Western donors by then were hinting that further aid might be dependent on the government's ending the war in the south. Yet the government continued to procrastinate, and less than a week after the ultimatum the army group disintegrated. At the same time yet another southern garrison, Torit, fell to the SPLA. In March the Prime Minister formed a new government and said it was prepared to move towards peace talks with the SPLA. In fact, throughout the year, convoys of supplies were attacked, the UN and international aid agencies attempted with varying success to get supplies through to the south, and people continued to die of starvation while the government took no action. By June, when the SPLA leader, Garang, was offering to extend a temporary ceasefire agreed in May and allow food convoys through the war zone, the Prime Minister, Sadiq al-Mahdi, was appealing for more money to finance a continuation of the war. A constitutional conference was scheduled to be held in September. On a tour of the West to gain support for his cause, Garang denied that he wanted the south to secede from the rest of Sudan. Later in the month another coup attempt, apparently to restore the exiled Nimeiri to power, was foiled.

Then, at the very end of June, the 'National Movement for Correcting the Situation' under Brigadier Omar Hassan Ahmed el Beshir finally mounted a successful coup, suspended the constitution, and dissolved Parliament and all political institutions. El Beshir, now a general, assumed the posts of Prime Minister, Defence Minister and Chief of the Armed Forces. Sadiq al-Mahdi, despite many protests that he intended to do so, could not as head of the Ansar sect abolish Sharia law; it remained to be seen what the new group would do to resolve the war in the south. By the time this coup took place the war was costing an already crippled economy an estimated $1 million a day to fight. General el Beshir invited John Garang to peace talks, which were scheduled to start a week after his assumption of power. But negotiations dragged on and no solution to the war emerged, while it became increasingly plain that el Beshir was also a prisoner of the fundamentalists. By the end of 1989 the United Nations estimated that 500,000 people had died since 1983, mainly from disease and famine but also from fighting and a series of massacres.

Early in 1990 an estimated 600 people were massacred in central Sudan in clashes between Muslim Arab tribesmen and non-Muslim Shilluk of the south. Later in the month SPLA shelling of Juba led to about 20 fatal casualties and forced a relief plane to turn back from the southern capital. By then Juba had a population of 300,000, of whom two-thirds were refugees. By early April a major battle between the SPLA and government forces was taking place round the southern town of Yei. The government, at least for the time being, had stopped talking peace and was appealing to Arab countries for support so that it could 'destroy the SPLA by the 1990s'.

Forecast

The Khartoum government in 1990, led by General el Beshir, appeared to be dominated by Islamic fundamentalist interests which still insisted on Sharia law; the SPLA controlled most of the south, and the two sides retained their deep suspicions of each other. The international aid-relief community was trying – with great difficulty – to provide supplies for the population in the south, much of which faced starvation. The civilians were the principal sufferers from the war.

Sudan, meanwhile, had an economy in ruins, perhaps 2 million displaced persons within its borders and about half a million refugees in neighbouring countries, while a high proportion of its people in the south faced starvation in what had become one of the most brutal and debilitating wars on the continent. All the indications were that the war was set to continue indefinitely.

UGANDA: A TROUBLED INDEPENDENCE

Introduction

When the British moved into the area of Uganda from the coast in the last decade of the nineteenth century they established a number of protectorates over the kingdoms they found: over Buganda, the largest and most powerful, in 1894; and over the smaller kingdoms of Bunyoro, Toro, Ankole and Bugosa in 1896. During the 60-odd years of its colonial rule Britain attempted to persuade these kingdoms, and principally Buganda, that they should become part of a unitary state, yet it never used its power to force the issue. At independence in 1962, therefore, the relationship between the kingdoms (and this really meant Buganda) and the central government was unresolved. Many Bugandans wished to secede and keep their monarchy intact, while the new politicians wanted to centralize power in a unitary state. Uganda, in any case, represented a number of ethnic groups (of which the Buganda were simply the most important) competing for influence at the centre. Milton Obote, who became the Prime Minister at independence, tried to control the south by offsetting his northern Langi supporters against them, and in the process militarized the state.

The overthrow of the Buganda monarchy 1966

The crisis between the central government and the Kingdom of Buganda was brought to a head in 1966. From 1963 until that year the country had been a federal republic with the Kabaka (King of Buganda) as President. In February 1966 Obote suspended the constitution, gave himself full executive powers and arrested five ministers who were most critical of his actions. In April he published a new constitution with himself as President. In Buganda the Lukiko (Parliament) passed a resolution denouncing the new constitution. Later, in May, Buganda announced its secession from Uganda. Obote declared a state of emergency in Buganda and sent in the army under Colonel Idi Amin against the Kabaka, Mutesa

II, and his followers at Mengo. After some fierce fighting the Buganda were defeated, although the King escaped to England where he died in 1969.

The extinction of the Kingdom of Buganda (the other, smaller kingdoms then also lost their status as such) destroyed the old political fabric of Uganda. Obote found himself in an increasingly dictatorial situation in the centre, more and more dependent on the army to maintain political control.

The Amin Years 1971–1979

On 25 January 1971 Major-General Idi Amin mounted a successful coup while Obote was in Singapore attending the Commonwealth Conference. For the rest of the decade Obote was to be an exile in neighbouring Tanzania, where his friend President Nyerere was more than sympathetic to his determination to regain control of Uganda. On 7 July 1971 Amin closed Uganda's borders with Tanzania, claiming that 700 Ugandans had been killed while fighting against pro-Obote guerrillas who had entered the country from Tanzania. A year later, on 17 September 1972, about 1000 Obote supporters again invaded Uganda from Tanzania, but by 20 September they had been defeated. In retaliation for this attack the Uganda air force bombed the Tanzanian towns of Bukoba and Mwanza on Lake Victoria. The nature of what should have remained a civil quarrel was widened when Libya sent five transport planes with 399 military technicians and equipment to help Amin after he complained that Britain and Israel were behind the invasion. However, through the mediation of the Somali Foreign Minister, a ceasefire was agreed on 21 September and signed on 5 October. A state of tension between the two countries was to be a feature of the decade until 1979, when exiled Ugandans supported by 10,000 Tanzanian troops invaded Uganda to bring about the downfall of Amin (see Part III, pp. 218–221).

Under Amin Uganda became notorious in Africa for the disappearance, murder or massacre of individuals and groups seen as threats to the Amin regime; these included politicians, soldiers (including whole units), intellectuals and business-men, and they came from the Buganda, Acholi, Alur, Jonam, Lango and Ankole tribes. More than 250,000 Ugandans are believed to have been killed under Amin's rule, and many more fled the country.

The return of Obote

Following the overthrow of Amin in 1979, the 10,000 Tanzanian troops who had supported the rebels remained in the country. Their presence became a factor of crucial importance over the next two years, ensuring the downfall of the two Presidents who succeeded Amin: President Yusuf Lule in June 1979 and President Godfrey Binaisa in May 1980. Neither of these men was a supporter of Obote or wished to introduce socialism into Uganda, so both lost favour with President Nyerere. Binaisa was overthrown by a six-man Military Commission headed by Brigadier David Oyite-Ojok, who favoured Obote. Binaisa had attempted to dismiss Ojok, who was head of the army, claiming that the soldiers were out of control, looting and killing civilians. Ojok and Paulo Muwanga now brought a number of pro-Obote men into the government, and Obote himself returned to Uganda on 27 May 1980 to announce that he would lead the Uganda People's Congress (UPC) in elections to be held at the end of the year. It was significant for the future that the Baganda could not forgive him for the overthrow of the Kabaka in 1966. In the north of the country famine among the Karamoja led to fighting over relief supplies. Then in December Obote won the elections, the UPC taking 68 of 126 seats.

Obote's first full year as President (1981) was an uneasy and violent one for Uganda. Missionaries laid many complaints against the army for its indiscipline, and a series of bomb attacks on police stations and army bases were said to be the work of the Uganda Freedom Movement, which was opposed to Obote. In the north-west of the country fighting took place between the army and pro-Amin groups. During 1982 opposition to Obote grew steadily stronger and appeared to come from many quarters. The President appealed for exiles to return home. Acts of violence continued all year, many of them in or near the capital; in February a group of guerrillas launched a heavy attack on Malire barracks in Kampala.

During 1983 escalating violence in the north caused thousands of people to flee as refugees into southern Sudan. In the area to the north of Kampala 100,000 people who had come to refugee camps to escape guerrilla activities now found themselves under attack from both guerrillas and the army, whose soldiers were often clearly out of control. Guerrillas opposed to Obote became even more active in the area north of Kampala during 1984: they attacked the military barracks at Masindi in February and a power-station in August, plunging Kampala into darkness for five days. The army carried out a series of anti-guerrilla operations, but civilians more often than not were the victims and the army's reputation for brutality and cruelty increased. Although reports were contradictory, thousands of people in the centre of the country were believed to have been killed during these army operations. In the Karamoja region of the north, cattle raiders forced many people to flee from their villages. By the end of 1984 much of Uganda was in a condition of anarchy.

Anti-government rebels became increasingly active in 1985, and there was a commensurate rise in government reprisals. Britain agreed to increase army retraining, but expressed growing disquiet at the behaviour of Uganda's soldiers. The situation took a further sharp decline when the principal anti-government group, the National Resistance Army (NRA) led by Yoweri Museveni, began operations in the western province. This new offensive widened the struggle against Obote and demonstrated that the rebels considered themselves to embrace national interests rather than simply to be fighting on behalf of the Baganda.

The downfall of Obote: Museveni comes to power 1986

On 27 July 1985 the army mounted a coup against Obote, who fled first to Kenya and then to Zambia. The Acholi soldiers complained that those from the Lango (Obote's home area) were favoured at their expense. As a result, the brigade under Brigadier Tito Okello mutinied and seized Kampala. The NRA under Museveni expected a share in the new government, but instead the mutineers appointed a council under (the now promoted) General Tito Okello, while Paulo Muwanga, who had been Vice-President under Obote, was made Prime Minister.

His appointment on 1 August was seen by the NRA as making the new government no different from that of Obote. When, in addition, the government enlisted former Amin soldiers the NRA decided to remain in the bush and continue the war.

Muwanga was too heavily associated with the past and he was therefore dismissed from the government later in 1985, when the Military Council under Okello and the NRA met for talks in Kenya with President Moi acting as mediator. A peace treaty was signed between the Military Council and the NRA in Nairobi on 17 December: the NRA guerrillas were to be absorbed into the national army, and an observer force drawn from Kenya, Tanzania, Britain and Canada was formed to monitor the accord. Elections were scheduled for July 1986. General Okello, however, did not keep his side of the agreement, which included the withdrawal of all forces from Kampala and a seat on the new Military Council for the NRA. In mid-January 1986 Museveni and the NRA renewed the guerrilla war. There was heavy fighting with high casualties, including many civilians, before the NRA captured Kampala – the city having been sacked by Okello's forces before they withdrew to the east. On 29 January Yoweri Museveni was sworn in as President of Uganda; he formed a broad-based government drawing ministers from the Democratic Party, including its leader Paul Ssemogerere, and from Obote's UPC as well as from two smaller guerrilla groups.

Okello's forces retreated eastwards towards Kenya and then turned north. They devastated villages and towns through which they passed, but failed to raise support for their cause. As a result, the group began to disintegrate and the soldiers either discarded their weapons and merged into their villages or fled across the borders into Sudan and Zaire. The NRA in pursuit showed marked restraint, in contrast to the other soldiers that the country had become accustomed to, and this gained them growing support, especially as they were largely recruited from the south of the country. Museveni adopted a policy of national reconciliation and announced that he would rule by decree for a maximum of four years. He still faced threats to his power mainly from the north-west of the country and from former members of Okello's and Amin's armies.

In March 1986 Museveni claimed that the civil war had come to an end. The claim was premature, however, for there were to be frequent attacks on towns and other targets through 1986 and 1987. Many people were killed during 1987, and in June of that year the Federal Democratic Movement broke with the National Resistance Movement (NRM) to join forces with the Uganda People's Democratic Movement: they aimed to overthrow the Museveni government.

A new movement was formed in December 1986 and caused fresh problems during 1987: it consisted of 6000 followers of Alice Lakwena, a priestess from northern Uganda, who claimed that God had instructed her to overthrow Museveni. But her rebel forces (the Holy Spirit Movement), who were poorly armed and believed that magic would protect them from bullets, were defeated during October when 1490 were killed by the NRA. Before its defeat the movement turned on members of the Uganda People's Democratic Army, the rebel group which had launched Lakwena, and stole their guns. The campaign against her was directed by Museveni in person. Alice Lakwena was wounded and fled to Kenya with only a handful of followers; there, however, she was imprisoned by the authorities for crossing the border illegally.

Despite the reputation of the NRA for good behaviour in the field, the constant movement of troops to put down guerrilla activity during 1987 led to charges of brutality. In January 1988 the Uganda Federal Army, another rebel group, carried out a bomb outrage in Kampala in which a Libyan diplomat was killed. Despite appeals by Museveni, rebel activity continued: in February, for example, guerrillas ambushed a bus, killing 19 and wounding 47. In mid-1988 the Uganda People's Democratic Army finally came to terms with the government. In June there was an assassination attempt by mutinous NRA troops against Museveni. Although thereafter guerrilla action declined and Museveni appeared to have obtained a firm grip on the country as a whole, yet, after more than 20 years of civil strife, Uganda remained highly volatile.

Costs and casualties

Once described by Winston Churchill as the pearl of Africa, Uganda suffered appalling destruction and misery under its successive tyrants and civil wars. According to Amnesty International, 300,000 Ugandans were killed in the Amin years (1971–7), while many more fled the country. Amin wrought particular carnage among the Acholi and Lango tribes. On a visit to Britain in 1985 the leader of the opposition Democratic Party, Paul Ssemogerere, claimed that 500,000 people had died since Obote took office at the end of 1980 (more than all those slaughtered under Amin). Another Amnesty report of 1985 alleged many instances of torture of civilians by the soldiers. When Museveni took power at the beginning of 1986 he claimed that up to 800,000 Ugandans had been killed under Amin, Obote and Okello, a figure that bore out the Amnesty and Ssemogerere claims. Lawlessness and killings also continued for the first few years of Museveni's rule.

The population of Uganda was 6,500,000 in 1959, 9,550,000 in 1969 and 12,630,000 in 1980, so 800,000 deaths represent more than 10 per cent of the population on the eve of independence.

Apart from deaths and maiming there were at least 100,000 Ugandan refugees in Sudan at one stage; numbers of exiles in that country and in Zaire fluctuated over the years. The economy of what at independence had been one of the most promising countries on the continent had all but collapsed. Meanwhile, two generations of young people had grown up with violence as a way of life.

The future

Much depends on the ability of Museveni to restore confidence and prevent another round of violent change. What Uganda needed at the beginning of the 1990s was a long period of peace and economic development. Whether it will receive this remains to be seen.

ZAIRE: THE CONGO CRISIS 1960–1965

Background

The Congo Free State (now Zaire) was the creation of King Leopold II of Belgium (ably assisted by Henry Morton Stanley, the explorer), and the King's determination to get the great powers to recognize his rights in central Africa was a main reason for the Berlin Conference of 1884–5 which sparked off what came to be known as the Scramble for Africa. The revelation of brutal forced labour in the Congo finally persuaded the Belgian Parliament to take control of the King's 'possession' in 1908, when it became the Belgian Congo. It continued to have a troubled history and by the late 1950s very little had been done to prepare the huge territory for independence.

Congolese parties demanding a political say in events only appeared in 1956, and the first democratic local elections were held in 1957 when the Abako Party led by Joseph Kasavubu won a sweeping victory. Until that event no one – black or white – had any political voice in the Congo, which was controlled entirely from Brussels. By 1958, however, a number of political programmes for the future had been published. Riots in 1958 and 1959 in Elizabethville (now Lubumbashi) and Leopoldville (now Kinshasa) forced the Belgian authorities to make concessions and begin political modernization. At a meeting in Brussels during February 1960 it was agreed that the Congo should become independent on 30 June of that year. A new constitution established six provincial governments, each with similar powers to those assigned to the central (federal) government. It was a recipe for disaster. In pre-independence elections Patrice Lumumba, leader of the Congo National Movement, won the most seats (though not an absolute majority). He was elected Prime Minister on 30 May, while Joseph Kasavubu became head of state. This was just a month before the Congo became independent.

Outbreak of violence

Rioting broke out in several parts of the country within days of independence, and on 5 July the Force publique mutinied over pay and conditions. These immediate troubles were to continue for several months and caused a high proportion of Europeans to flee the country. Moise Tshombe, the leading politician from Katanga province (now Shaba, the centre of the country's rich mining industry), accused Lumumba of wanting to sell out to the Soviets. The crisis which followed was to witness major big power interventions (in part through the United Nations) and the involvement of the USSR for the first time in black Africa.

The unrest which exploded in riots after independence, and especially in the Force publique, was the result of false political expectations of what might follow independence, the fact that Belgian officers remained in control of the Force publique where, apparently, there was to be no change or promotion for Congolese, and the spectacle of certain groups – politicians and civil servants – acquiring rapid wealth in the run-up to independence as a result of their positions, while others did not see any comparable advantages for themselves.

On 11 July Tshombe announced the secession of Katanga province from the

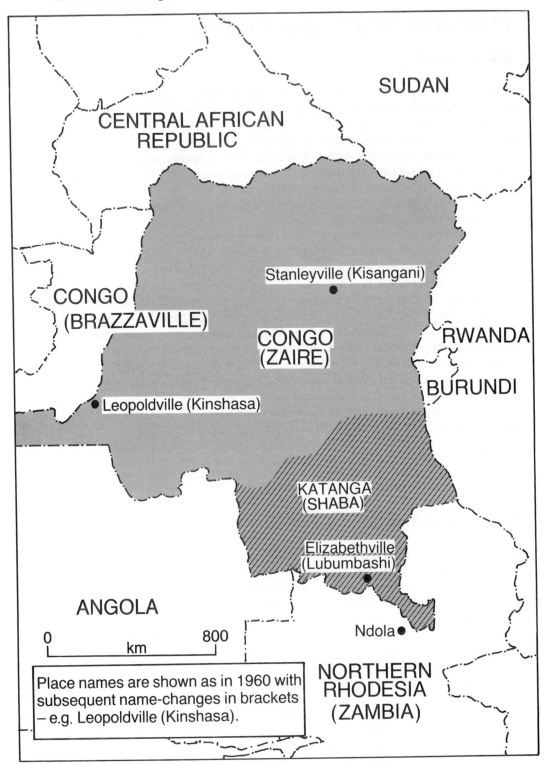

Map 17 Zaire crisis 1960–5

Congo, and the following day Prime Minister Lumumba appealed to the UN to help restore order and keep the country united. Reports of Belgian interventions in the troubles (Belgian troops had remained in the country after independence) exacerbated the situation and created greater unrest, with the result that there was an exodus of most Belgians as well as other Europeans working in the country. Other reports told of Europeans being killed. Lumumba hoped that a UN presence would ensure that Belgian troops were withdrawn as well as preventing the Congo becoming a pawn in the Cold War. His appeal to the UN was answered swiftly and a combined force of African and Swedish troops was sent to keep the peace.

The eruption of troubles led to several other secessionist attempts apart from Katanga, most notably in Kasai province. It was soon evident that to regain control of the entire territory presented a major task: Zaire (the Congo as it then was) is Africa's third largest country, covering 2,345,409 square kilometres (905,568 square miles), with more than 200 ethnic groups and poor communications between regions. Central government troops were able to crush the attempted secession by Kasai province, but they were not strong enough to penetrate Katanga, although Brussels was not prepared to recognize Katangan independence. Following the arrival of the UN force, a power struggle developed between the Prime Minister, Patrice Lumumba, and the President, Joseph Kasavubu, which ended in Lumumba's arrest and imprisonment and later his murder in Katanga on 17 January 1961.

Secession and the role of the United Nations

Katangan secession on 11 July 1960 was aided by Belgian officers and the international mining companies. Tshombe was seen as little more than a puppet of the Belgians and the mining companies, but this was only partly true. He turned out to be a relatively adroit politician as well as power-monger in his own right. Central government forces were unable to penetrate and retake control in Katanga, where Tshombe was supported by powerful Western interests, particularly the Union minière du Haut-Katanga, while Belgium supplied military, technical and financial assistance. Katanga at that time – and later – was a source of major wealth to Belgium, and the Belgians now sent mercenaries to Katanga to reinforce and safeguard Tshombe and to guard their own mining interests. A Katanga Gendarmerie of 10,000 men was created.

In September Kasavubu dismissed Lumumba. The military commander, Colonel Joseph-Désiré Mobutu, now carried out his first coup. He kept Kasavubu in place, but established a College of Commissioners who were to rule the country for the next five months. Lumumba, meanwhile, fell into the hands of members of Mobutu's College of Commissioners; later he was taken to Katanga where he was reportedly tortured and then murdered. After his death Lumumba was raised to the status of African nationalist martyr, and his followers, led by Antoine Gizenga, set up an alternative government in Elizabethville. The UN did not intervene to prevent Lumumba's death, and this apparent inability to act or lack of urgency to do so was long regarded in Africa as something worse than a straightforward failure. The UN was to maintain a presence in the Congo for four years; inevitably this became increasingly controversial because Cold War as well as vested interest arguments about what it should do made it increasingly difficult for the UN to maintain impartiality.

On 2 August 1961 a new national government was established by Kasavubu in Leopoldville, where he appointed Cyrille Adoula as Prime Minister and brought in Antoine Gizenga (Lumumba's supporter) as Deputy. Adoula was to be Prime Minister for the next three years. Then, in September 1961, the UN Secretary-General, Dag Hammarskjöld, was killed in mysterious circumstances when the plane in which he was travelling on a flight from Ndola in Northern Rhodesia (now Zambia) to negotiations with Tshombe in Katanga crashed. It was not until the end of 1962 that UN forces finally took the offensive against breakaway Katanga, and on 15 January 1963 Katangan secession was formally ended. Tshombe went into exile in Europe.

The climax of 1964

Despite the continuing UN presence and the collapse of Katangan secession, the overall situation in the Congo continued to deteriorate throughout 1963 and into 1964 with no effective central government and a general growth of lawlessness. A revolt in Kwilu, one of the Congo's richest provinces, took place early in 1964 under the leadership of Pierre Mulele, who had been Minister of Education briefly under Lumumba. His followers, or Mulelists as they came to be called, were mainly youths aged 13 to 18. By the end of January 150 officials had been killed and there had been many attacks on missionaries. Mulele had been on a visit to China and was believed by his opponents to have been 'indoctrinated'. In theory the Congolese army of 30,000 should have had little difficulty in dealing with the Mulelists, who were ill-armed and at most numbered 4000. In practice threats to central government elsewhere in the huge country, as well as the increasing unreliability of most of the army, allowed the Mulelist revolt to grow into a major threat to the Congo's stability. The Mulelist youths were taught that they were immune to bullets.

In March 1964 some 400 members of the Katanga Gendarmerie crossed into Angola where they underwent training under Tshombe's white mercenaries (others were believed to be in training in northern Rhodesia); later the Gendarmerie (or those who did not disperse) became an important factor in Angola where some became involved in fighting that country's civil war, while others in 1978–9 were to take part in the two Shaba invasions of those years (see Part III, pp. 000–000).

The last UN troops left the Congo on 30 June 1964, and at once the country erupted into another round of violence. This was especially the case in Kwilu and the most easterly and northerly regions. During July, in circumstances that have always been difficult to explain, Tshombe was invited back to become Prime Minister (Adoula resigned) and at once raised a force of European mercenaries to combat the growing rebellion. These first mercenaries were of little use and fled before the rebels to the Uganda border. For a time the rebels appeared to be carrying all before them, and by the end of July, at a time of intense fighting, they held about 500,000 square kilometres (200,000 square miles) of territory. Meanwhile, the Congolese army of 30,000 had virtually disintegrated and had been reduced to an effective 5000 men. However, a US–Belgian paratroop 'rescue' operation was mounted in November 1964 (see below), the effect of which was to save the original mercenaries whom Tshombe had engaged and to reverse the successes of the rebellion.

On 5 August the rebels, calling themselves the Popular Army of Liberation, took Stanleyville (now Kisangani), the third largest town in the Congo. They were linked to the National Liberation Committee, made up of left-wing exiles, so the rebellion had all the features of a potential Communist takeover. This was one (though not the principal) factor in persuading the USA to intervene. On 19 August heavy fighting took place in the town of Bukavu: the Congolese army managed to hold out and an estimated 300 rebels were killed; some were found to have been drugged prior to the attack. The next day Tshombe claimed that the body of the rebel leader Mulele had been found, and the news was thought to signal the end of the Mulelist rebellion.

By early August it had become clear that the USA had committed itself to full support of the Tshombe government. On 6 August Tshombe asked for US military assistance, but at that stage both the USA and Belgium said they would not send troops, although they were prepared to provide technical assistance. Late in August the USA sent four air force transport planes and 50 paratroop guards to the Congo, the latter to be placed at the disposal of the US Ambassador. This was the beginning of a long US involvement with the Congo and later with Mobutu. On 18 August Tshombe appealed for African troops to help him fight the rebels, claiming that the rebellion was fomented by the Chinese. At this time it seemed likely that China saw the Congo as an area for increased intervention; the Chinese were operating from their embassy in Burundi, and a Chinese general was said to have been responsible for the tactics which had produced the rebel gains in eastern Congo. The USSR, meanwhile, had condemned US and Belgian military assistance to the Tshombe government.

On 7 September the rebels holding Stanleyville announced a government under the leadership of Christophe Gbeny, who had served as a minister under Lumumba. Tshombe's recruiting agents, meanwhile, were offering white South African and Rhodesian mercenaries pay of £100 a month. At the Organization of African Unity (OAU) meeting of Foreign Ministers in Addis Ababa (Ethiopia) that September a majority supported Tshombe, and for a brief spell it seemed that he was about to gain African credibility, although he was refused admission to the full OAU heads of state meeting in Cairo the next month. In fact his survival depended on his acceptance of Belgian military aid and his use of mercenaries recruited from southern Africa (led by Michael Hoare, who was to appear elsewhere on the continent in his mercenary role). By early October there were between 400 and 500 mainly South African and Rhodesian mercenaries in the Congo; some were employed in training Congolese forces in Kanina preparatory to retaking Stanleyville.

Finally, in what was the climax to the Congo troubles, the USA used its transport planes, flying by way of Britain's Ascension Island, to carry 600 Belgian paratroopers to the Congo. On 24 November the paratroopers were sent as the vanguard into Stanleyville, where the rebels then held some 1200 European hostages. The Congolese National Army, led by mercenaries, followed. About 250 of the hostages were killed; subsequently, most of the remaining hostages were traced. The USA defended its intervention on humanitarian grounds – to save the hostages – rather than as an exercise to assist the Congo military, but many doubts about the operation were voiced then and later. For example, under American pressure Kenya's President, Jomo Kenyatta, had called the OAU Congo Committee in Nairobi to discuss the crisis; while it was sitting news came through of the US–Belgian intervention and Kenyatta felt he had been used by the

Americans to provide a smokescreen while they prepared and carried out their airlift.

Half-way through November – before the US rescue operation – Kasavubu dismissed Tshombe just when his Council of National Alliance of the Congo (CONACO) appeared to be winning the elections which were then being held. By the end of November, however, the rebellion began to fall apart. Those taking part divided into two groups: the Simbas, who were quite well led and included at least some soldiers who had had military training; and the Jeunesse, a group of young, uneducated and untrained rebels (the Mulelists).

Mobutu establishes military rule 1965

The rebellion continued into 1965, although early in the year government forces held all the main towns: Katanga had its Gendarmes back from the bush and Kasai was again under full central control. The going rate for mercenaries with danger money had risen to £200 a month. By March 1965 the Congo National Army with its mercenary leaders was winning the war. A great deal of slaughter took place as the Congo National Army terrorized the population while relying on the mercenaries to lead any military actions. By July it was clear that the rebellion was coming to an end. The mercenaries were responsible for a growing list of brutalities, carrying out horrific tortures on prisoners before killing them. By November the rebellion was over.

On 24 November General Mobutu took power: he suspended President Kasavubu and his Prime Minister, Kimba, who had replaced Tshombe, and took all executive power into his own hands. This marked the beginning of the Second Republic and the re-establishment of a minimum of law and order. It also marked the beginning of Mobutu's long rule.

Estimated costs and casualties

By December 1964 the rebels were believed to have killed about 20,000 Congolese, 5000 of them in Stanleyville. The Congo National Army killed many in reprisals, especially in Stanleyville, though no accurate figures are available. The mercenaries were responsible for indiscriminate killing in the villages through which they passed. Also by that date 175 Europeans (a reduction on earlier estimates) were known to have been killed and many more wounded. Given the chaotic conditions of the Congo over the years from independence until the end of the rebellion in 1965, no accurate figures for casualties have ever been compiled. An estimate of 30,000 is often quoted, but the chances are that deaths were very much higher. Possibly 300 Europeans died altogether in the Congo troubles (their deaths attracted most of the media attention in the West).

Damage to property and the disruption of mining activity was enormous, and the readiness of the Belgians and Americans to intervene was heavily influenced by Western investment in the Congo's mineral wealth. Other costs are more difficult to quantify. The generally savage conduct of the mercenaries from southern Africa became notorious and did no good to their (white) cause. The Congolese army, except for one or two units, showed itself to be almost useless.

Results

The five years of disruption, bloodshed and civil war which followed independence made the name Congo synonymous with chaos in black Africa, and coloured Western perceptions of Africa for a generation. No one came well out of the affair. The Congolese leaders showed themselves unable to control their country-men; the Belgians, whose efforts to prepare the country for independence had been minimalist (only an estimated 17 Congolese out of a population of 14 million had university degrees), appeared only too ready to return in the ensuing chaos in order to safeguard their own interests. Apart from the Suez crisis of 1956 in Egypt, the Congo crisis provided the first major occasion when the two superpowers became involved in black Africa, and each appeared far more concerned with Cold War considerations and countering the other's moves than with helping the Congo overcome its problems. The Chinese opportunistically stirred up trouble, seeing in the Congo a possibly profitable entry to the Third World. In Katanga capitalist interests from Britain and Belgium in particular were ready to support Tshombe's secession to the detriment of the Congo's future, but to their own advantage. In a felicitous phrase Tshombe himself was described as the 'darling of imperialism of all kinds'. The white mercenaries from both Rhodesia and South Africa gave white racism an even worse name than it had earned already. The United Nations, pulled in many directions by powerful conflicting interests, did its best, but inevitably became tainted with the Western interests that were able to exert greater influence; its non-intervention to rescue Lumumba, considered in the West a dangerous Marxist political figure, will long be seen as a failure on the part of the world body. Even so, the peace-keeping operation in the Congo was a landmark for the United Nations. In the end the Congolese themselves sorted out the political breakdown in the person of Mobutu, a strongman who was to rule the country for the next quarter of a century.

ZAMBIA: THE LUMPA UPRISING 1964

The Lumpa Church

One of the militant sects which periodically arise in Africa (and elsewhere), the Lumpa Church came into being at the end of the 1950s in north-eastern Zambia. It was led by Alice Lenshina from Chinsali, a former member of the Church of Scotland who claimed that she had died and then risen from the dead to root out witchcraft. Although confined to a small number of people in a corner of Zambia (its appeal was a simple fundamentalist one reinforced by fear), the Lumpa Church became important because Lenshina told her followers that they could not belong to it if they also joined a political party. This was during the time immediately prior to the break-up of the Central African Federation (and shortly before Zambian independence in 1964) when the whole of Northern Rhodesia (as it then was) had become intensely political. As a result, members of the Lumpa Church became militant opponents of the United National Independence Party (UNIP) led by Dr Kenneth Kaunda, which was then establishing its political dominance throughout the country.

At the end of 1963 violence erupted between members of the Lumpa sect and UNIP: two UNIP supporters were hacked to death and seven other people died in fighting with spears, axes and muzzle-loading guns, while a further six people were reported missing. The police made 40 arrests. On 29 December 1963 Dr Kaunda went to the region in an attempt to halt the vendetta between his followers and the Church, but to no avail. By 2 January 1964 the death toll had risen to 10 and a further 35 people had been arrested by the police.

The Lumpa war

The troubles between the Lumpas and the ruling party, UNIP, that had been smouldering for two years broke out into major violence during July and August 1964. The principal grievance which ensured a head-on collision was the refusal of the Lumpas to belong to a political party: this came to be interpreted by UNIP as positive opposition to the party and government. The Lumpas set themselves up in stockaded villages; when the police attempted to make them leave these villages fighting erupted. In July an Assistant Inspector of Police and a policeman were stabbed to death when they entered an apparently deserted Lumpa village; police then stormed the village and 19 villagers were killed. Subsequently, the police took 36 prisoners (of whom 33 were women) and 55 children. After further clashes between police and the villagers the Governor assumed emergency powers.

On 31 July (after half the Northern Rhodesian army of three battalions had been moved into the district to support the police) police and troops stormed the stronghold of Alice Lenshina; an estimated 100 villagers were killed in the attack. Police and troops then had to be flown to Lundazi where a fresh outbreak of violence occurred four days later; deaths in this violence raised the total to nearly 300. The Prime Minister, Dr Kaunda, then outlawed the Lumpa sect and ordered the capture of Alice Lenshina. Fighting continued for about a week. On 11 August official casualties (deaths) were given as 491. Alice Lenshina surrendered to government forces shortly afterwards and was imprisoned.

Aftermath

The Lumpa Church died away after the imprisonment of Lenshina, although there were occasional manifestations of the Church in the following years. Northern Rhodesia became independent as Zambia on 24 October 1964.

ZANZIBAR: AFRICAN–ARAB REVOLUTION 1964

Background

Zanzibar had been the centre of Arab slave-trading activities in eastern Africa for several centuries until the trade was finally brought to an end in the nineteenth century. Following the Anglo-German Treaty of 1890, in which the two powers agreed their various spheres of influence in those regions where they were then in contact on the African continent, Britain established a protectorate over Zanzibar. During the 70 years of its rule Britain worked through the Arab minority on the island rather than the African majority. By 1963, the year of independence, there were 50,000 Arabs on Zanzibar out of a population of 300,000. During the 1950s, in an effort to forestall growing African nationalism, the Arabs manoeuvred to keep political power in their hands, and this, in large measure, was the situation when Zanzibar obtained independence from Britain on 10 December 1963. Even so, the underlying current of African–Arab ethnic suspicion had become increasingly apparent: for example, the elections of 1961 were followed by anti-Arab demonstrations leading to riots in which more than 70 Arabs were killed. At the time of independence the economy was in a depression with the world price for cloves (Zanzibar's main export) declining.

The revolution

Early in 1964 the government weakened its position by dismissing a number of the police who were from the mainland because it doubted their loyalty. On 12 January self-styled 'Field Marshal' John Okello (a Ugandan by origin) led a number of ex-policemen in a revolt that toppled the government and sent Sultan Seyyid Jamshid bin Abdulla into exile. The 700 armed insurgents captured the police armoury, the radio station and other strategic points in Zanzibar, and within a short time the whole island was under rebel control. A new government was announced: it was led by Abeid Karume, who became President; his two principal associates were Othman Sharif (Minister of Education) and Abdulla Kassim Hanga (Vice-President). The government was drawn initially from members of both the Afro-Shirazi (African and strongly anti-Arab) and the Umma (Arab) parties. It was swiftly recognized by the USSR, China and the GDR, and was regarded in the West as strongly influenced by Marxism and contacts with China and Cuba.

On 13 January John Okello announced that he had been the strongman of the revolution. The new government was recognized by Kenya and Uganda. Martial law was declared and it appeared that the government had majority support in the island. On 14 January Okello announced the death sentence on a number of former ministers; the island of Pemba declared its support for Zanzibar. On 15 January the proposed executions were cancelled and Zanzibar was reported to be quiet. On 16 January Okello announced in an interview that a 14-man Revolutionary Council had been set up, but claimed that he had powers equal to those of the whole government. On 17 January the deposed Sultan arrived in Britain. At the request of the new government Tanganyika sent an estimated 200 police to

Zanzibar to help maintain law and order until the Zanzibar force had been reorganized.

Costs and casualties

Immediate estimates of casualties were in the region of 500, mainly Arabs killed in the resistance to the revolution. Three weeks after the revolution, however, the Zanzibar government had still not produced any final list of casualties. At that time some 2500 people were in prison, detention or refugee camps, although only about 400 were thought to be political prisoners. Other, later estimates suggested that some 5000 Arabs were killed altogether and that another 5000 fled into exile.

Results: immediate and longer term

The Zanzibar revolution must have influenced events on the mainland later that January when army mutinies occurred in Tanganyika, Kenya and then Uganda (see Part II, pp. 122–125), although to what extent is uncertain.

The revolution itself was clearly an African one – a revolt against Arab domination no doubt fuelled by memories of the slave trade and the particular role in that trade which had been played historically by Zanzibar. Further, the political system had appeared to be rigged, so the Afro-Shirazi Party, which had polled 54 per cent of the votes in the pre-independence elections, had none the less lost to the Arab minority party. Now the Afro-Shirazi Party was proclaimed the sole party, although the Revolutionary Council continued to rule by decree. The new government was clearly left wing in its orientation and this was confirmed in the months after the revolution; the Foreign Minister, Abdul Rahman Muhammad Babu (who subsequently played a leading political role in the United Republic of Tanzania), said that he wanted to create a people's republic in Zanzibar.

Okello, the curiously naïve man who led the revolution, left Zanzibar in February 1964, saying that his mission was accomplished and that he was going to devote himself to liberating South Africa and Mozambique. He had proved an embarrassment to Zanzibar from the time the Sultan went into exile and was not now permitted to return to the island. He was also seen as an embarrassment in both Kenya and Uganda where he was regarded as a potential magnet for dissidents.

Britain recognized the new Zanzibar government on 23 February and was followed by the USA and the Commonwealth countries. But the government continued to be regarded warily in the West because of its contacts with Communist countries.

Fear of an unknown quantity offshore (a left-wing regime that might be a source of destabilization to mainland Tanganyika) was undoubtedly a factor leading President Nyerere to propose the union of Tanganyika and Zanzibar which was announced on 23 April 1964; on 27 April the two countries formally became one at ceremonies in Dar es Salaam, and President Karume became First Vice-President of the new state. Tanganyika was disturbed that Zanzibar was moving away from non-alignment towards the Communist bloc, and it was hoped that the union would arrest that process.

In October 1964 the United Republic of Tanganyika and Zanzibar changed its name to the United Republic of Tanzania. Over subsequent years, although there were periodic strains between the mainland and Zanzibar, which often followed courses that were not approved in Dar es Salaam, the union held and appeared to work moderately well.

ZIMBABWE: WAR AGAINST THE DISSIDENTS

Introduction

The white-settler-controlled colony of Rhodesia became independent as Zimbabwe on 18 April 1980 after 15 years of unilateral independence (UDI) and guerrilla warfare (see Part I, pp. 62–68). During the early 1960s a split had occurred in the nationalist movement, and the two main groups to emerge were the Zimbabwe African National Union (ZANU) and the Zimbabwe African People's Union (ZAPU): the former (ZANU) became identified with the Mashona people of eastern Zimbabwe; the latter (ZAPU) with the Ndebele of the west and south (though neither movement was exclusive). During the second half of the 1970s, as the war against the white regime of Ian Smith moved to its climax, ZANU operated out of Mozambique, ZAPU from Zambia. Various efforts were made to bring the two groups together, but deep suspicions separated them and their leaders, the ascetic Marxist Robert Mugabe of ZANU and the more emotional Joshua Nkomo of ZAPU, who had little in common. None the less, under intense pressure from the frontline states they combined (uneasily) in the Patriotic Front and worked together during the Lancaster House meetings in London at the end of 1979. These eventually produced a formula for a return to legality and the end of UDI in Rhodesia, where the Smith government in any case by then was losing the guerrilla war.

A ceasefire was finally agreed on 28 December 1979 and marked the end of the civil war. The guerrilla forces of the Patriotic Front – that is, both ZANU and ZAPU – were then given a week in which to report to assembly points under the supervision of a Commonwealth monitoring force preparatory to integration in a new Zimbabwe army. ZAPU's Nkomo returned to Rhodesia on 13 January 1980; he was followed two weeks later by Robert Mugabe (ZANU), and the stage was set for an election campaign that would determine the first government of an independent Zimbabwe.

Considerable violence between ZANU and ZAPU supporters occurred during the campaign, foreshadowing events to come. ZANU (PF) won a convincing victory, taking 57 of the 80 African seats (20 were reserved on a special roll for white voters, who returned members of the former Rhodesia Front – renamed the Republican Front, RF), while Nkomo's ZAPU took 20 seats and Bishop Muzorewa's United African National Congress (UANC) took only three seats. The results were undoubtedly a shock for ZAPU: both Nkomo himself and many of his international backers appear to have believed that he would become independent Zimbabwe's first political leader, even if he had to form a coalition with Bishop Muzorewa or the RF. Instead, Mugabe had an absolute majority. In a spirit of conciliation he formed a coalition government; Nkomo was appointed Minister of Home Affairs and three other ministries also went to ZAPU.

A feature of the Mugabe government throughout the 1980s was its deep sense of insecurity and suspicion at any manifestation of opposition. Given the political situation in the region as a whole – civil wars in Angola and Mozambique, South Africa using destabilization tactics against its neighbours, and a white minority inside Zimbabwe, most of whom had been solidly behind the Smith government and had yet to prove their loyalty to a black government – such suspicion was perhaps not surprising. Thus, dissidence by the second most powerful ethnic group in the country – the Ndebele – whose leader, Joshua Nkomo, had a continent-wide reputation and a wide following outside Matabeleland, simply was not going to be tolerated by Mugabe.

Independence 1980: an uneasy alliance

Following independence Mugabe's generally pragmatic approach to political and economic problems reassured both the West and the white minority of its future place in Zimbabwe. But relations between Mugabe and Nkomo were uneasy from the start; problems arose at once during the integration of the ZANU and ZAPU guerrillas in the new Zimbabwe army when a number of violent incidents took place. In July such ZANU–ZAPU violence was used as the reason for extending the state of emergency for another six months; this was to happen throughout the 1980s. In September 1980 Mugabe, who had become the first independent Prime Minister, ordered the army and the police to take action against 'dissidents', and this resulted in army units moving into Ndebele areas that were overwhelmingly pro-ZAPU. In November fighting broke out in Bulawayo (Zimbabwe's second city and the heartland of the Ndebele) between members of ZAPU and ZANU, and some 50 people, including a number of civilians, were killed. It was not an auspicious start to either independence or reconciliation.

Relations between Mugabe and Nkomo deteriorated during 1981. At the beginning of the year Nkomo attacked the decision to transfer control of the press to the Zimbabwe Mass Media Trust on the grounds that it would be a ZANU mouthpiece. On 10 January he was demoted in a cabinet reshuffle to be minister without portfolio responsible for security matters (an adroit move by Mugabe since it made Nkomo responsible for disciplining dissidents). Clashes between ZANU and ZAPU supporters took place in February in both Bulawayo and Gwelo; fighting spread and involved a number of guerrillas who had not disbanded at independence but remained in the bush. Nkomo was unable to persuade the dissidents to lay down their arms for several days, by which time more than 200 people had been killed. The fighting reflected the continuing suspicions of the two main ethnic groups and their former guerrilla armies – ZANLA and ZIPRA. The government prepared to disarm the remaining guerrillas, although Nkomo's supporters feared this would weaken Nkomo's position in relation to Mugabe. None the less, the disarming was reportedly completed by May 1981. Thereafter, the government decided to reduce the size of the army by half since by then it was consuming 20 per cent of the annual budget.

1982: a year of violence

At the beginning of 1982 Nkomo denounced Mugabe's political moves towards more socialism and his claim that in future policies would only be those approved by ZANU. In February Nkomo turned down a proposal to merge ZANU and ZAPU. Then large caches of arms were found on farms belonging to known Nkomo supporters, and on 17 February Mugabe dismissed Nkomo and three ZAPU ministers from the government on the grounds that they were planning a coup. Later in the year the government linked members of Smith's RF with ZAPU and the arms caches when four whites were found guilty of a plot to overthrow the government and assist Matabeleland to secede. In April the government claimed it had discovered a number of ZAPU camps where men were being trained to overthrow the government. Nkomo himself was put under investigation, although he condemned dissidents who had formerly served in ZIPRA.

Violence erupted in Matabeleland during May, and Nkomo laid the blame on the government because of its announced intention of creating a one-party state. In June the government launched a major campaign against dissidents, and despite further denunciations of dissidence by Nkomo, the violence escalated. The houses of the Prime Minister and Enos Nkala, an Ndebele minister who was a member of ZANU, were attacked by dissidents. In Bulawayo government forces arrested hundreds in a search for dissidents, and Mugabe openly accused Nkomo of links with the dissidents. A meeting between Mugabe and Nkomo in August failed to resolve their differences. On 14 September Nkomo called for a political solution and condemned violence by the security forces. He accused the 5th Brigade, recruited specially from ZANU members and trained by North Koreans, of atrocities and brutality among the Ndebele. The government made the situation worse by announcing that a 6th Brigade was also to be formed from ZANU supporters because the government doubted army loyalty (a clear reference to ZIPRA members, a number of whom, loyal to Nkomo, had defected). Violence continued throughout the year, and on 24 December a major series of incidents took place in which cars, buses and a train were attacked, leading to three deaths and 21 injured.

Nkomo's flight: March 1983

In March 1983, following an army search through Bulawayo for dissidents, Nkomo fled the country to Botswana and then to Britain, claiming that his life was in danger. A growing number of accusations were levelled at the 5th Brigade for brutality in the war against dissidents; in the Senate the former white Prime Minister, Garfield Todd, accused the government of conducting what he called a 'conflict of terror', while bishops of the Roman Catholic Church censured army brutality. In response Mugabe claimed that the dissidents were trying to hold back development and were operating from bases in Botswana; he promised that if evidence of army brutality was produced it would be investigated, but he rejected the complaint of the Roman Catholic bishops as one-sided. When six former members of the ZAPU military were acquitted of plotting to overthrow the government they were none the less rearrested and held under indefinite detention.

In August, after a six-month absence, Nkomo returned to Zimbabwe to reclaim his seat in Parliament; efforts were made, unsuccessfully, to deprive him of it on the grounds of prolonged absence, but when he did resume his seat he was met by hostility from ZANU members. The troubles in Matabeleland did not die down, and in February 1984 the Minister for Home Affairs, Simbi Mubako, imposed a dusk-to-dawn curfew over about 6500 square kilometres (2500 square miles) of southern Matabeleland and ordered large numbers of troops into the area to seek out dissidents. Nkomo and the Roman Catholic Church continued to accuse the army of atrocities against civilians suspected of supporting the guerrillas; according to Church sources, the government prevented food from reaching drought-stricken districts if these were also affected by dissident activities.

Opposition parties were now banned from holding meetings in the centre of the country, and it appeared that the dissidents were becoming effective outside Matabeleland. Tensions increased dramatically in November 1984 when a ZANU Senator, Moven Ndhlovu, was assassinated in Beitbridge; his death was followed by riots. Mugabe then sacked the last two members of ZAPU from his government and said that ZAPU had to be declared an enemy of the people. Other ZAPU officials were detained and at the end of November a leading ZAPU supporter of Nkomo was shot dead.

The 1985 elections

The first general elections since independence were due in 1985; they were accompanied by a good deal of violence and strong-arm tactics. Nkomo found he had great difficulty in addressing meetings because he faced organized interruptions and violent opposition. In February five supporters of Bishop Muzorewa were shot dead at Hwange. In Bulawayo ZANU and ZAPU supporters fought battles in the streets. On 2 March 1985 troops sealed off Bulawayo to search it for dissidents, although Nkomo described this as an exercise in intimidation. The Roman Catholic Commission for Justice and Peace presented the government with its report on violence by members of ZANU against their critics. Despite all this, the ruling party, ZANU, increased the number of its seats from 57 to 63, while ZAPU dropped from 20 to 15. Subsequently, Mugabe appointed Enos Nkala (who was regarded as a turncoat by ZAPU) as Minister of Home Affairs. He took an especially strong line on dissidents and threatened to destroy ZAPU. During the remainder of the year pressures on ZAPU were greatly increased: tactics against the party included the arrest of senior officials, the eviction of ZAPU from its headquarters in Harare and the confiscation of Nkomo's passport. Then at the end of the year Mugabe and Nkomo held the first of a series of talks about possible unity.

During 1986 and 1987 unity talks between the two leaders became an on–off feature of Zimbabwe politics, and it became clear that tactically Mugabe held the whip hand: he was prepared for unity (on his terms), while Nkomo and his followers realized that they had no chance of office, as opposed to rebellion, unless they came to terms with the ruling ZANU. In March 1986 Nkomo made a joint appeal with Nkala for peace in Matabeleland, and the following month Nkomo criticized members of ZAPU who endangered the unity talks by fomenting tribalism. Matters took a turn for the worse in July when 100 people were arrested in Beitbridge under the state of emergency, but in October Nkala announced that all ZAPU detainees were to be released. In part a 'cat and mouse' game had opened up, with the government periodically demonstrating its strength against ZAPU and then making more conciliatory gestures.

The achievement of unity

Insurgency by the dissidents continued in Matabeleland through much of 1987 and the government maintained the state of emergency. In August it appeared that ZANU and ZAPU were close to announcing a merger, but then the two parties drew back. On 22 September the Minister of Home Affairs, Nkala, announced that he had ordered the shut-down of the ZAPU offices, giving as his reason the continuing violence in Matabeleland. Mugabe came out in support of Nkala and said the evidence showed that ZAPU was linked to the dissidence. Yet, despite such moves and continuing tension, unity between ZANU (PF) and ZAPU was announced on 22 December 1987; suddenly, it seemed, an end to the long years of dissidence was in sight. At the end of the year, following a change in the constitution, Mugabe became the Executive President of Zimbabwe rather than Prime Minister. He increased his cabinet to 27 in order to include in it a proportionate number of ZAPU ministers without excluding ZANU members.

The two parties sought the ratification of their members in 1988: on 2 April the last ZAPU congress agreed to unity and was followed by ZANU a week later. The troubles were not entirely over. On 19 April a Roman Catholic missionary was killed in Matabeleland and there was a question mark over whether dissidents in the bush would end the conflict. Mugabe then announced an amnesty for political offenders and many of the guerrillas in the Matabeleland bush came in to surrender by the 3 May deadline. By the middle of 1988 it did seem that the war of the dissidents had at last come to an end.

Estimated costs and casualties

The war of the dissidents in the decade following independence added burdens of security and fears of additional subversion at a time when Zimbabwe already faced the prospect of destabilization from South Africa; it also increased tribal bitterness after 15 years of war against the white minority regime of Smith, and held back development, especially in Matabeleland where the fighting took place. Deaths for the whole period have been estimated at about 3000, though they may have been higher (they included a small number of white deaths, such as those of a group of young white tourists who were kidnapped and subsequently murdered). Many more people were injured, others were imprisoned and Zimbabwe's reputation suffered from the evidence of brutality and atrocities carried out by the army.

Results: immediate and longer term

At one level the war was one of 'winners and losers': ZANU convincingly won the elections before independence and emerged as the ruling party, while ZAPU, whose members had also fought the long war against white minority control, saw itself excluded from power. The government was deeply worried by the security situation and was afraid that Zimbabwe would go the same way as Angola and Mozambique, where civil wars were showing what happened when one group refused to accept the results of independence, hence its tough reactions to the dissidents. There was also a strong tribal element to the war as between Mashona and Ndebele, and a further fear that Ndebele connections with their Zulu cousins in South Africa would provide a conduit for South African subversives to enter the country. The acceptance of unity by Nkomo and ZAPU opened the way for them to partake in the political rewards of office in a country the leader (Mugabe) and ruling party (ZANU) of which had repeatedly stated their intention of establishing a one-party state. The struggle, in essence, was about a share of political power. By the end of the decade unity appeared to be working well, while Nkomo had consolidated his own position as the trouble-shooter for his one-time rival for power, Mugabe.

THE MIDDLE EAST

CYPRUS: EOKA–B AND THE TURKISH INVASION OF 1974

Background

The island of Cyprus had been Greek from ancient times; in the 1570s, however, it was taken by the Ottoman Turks, who built up a Turkish–Muslim population; then in 1878, following the Congress of Berlin which ended the Russo-Turkish War (1876–8), Britain occupied Cyprus and was to hold it until 1960. Following a long and bitter independence struggle against Britain, intertwined with demands for *enosis* (union with Greece), Cyprus became independent in 1960 (see Part I, pp. 69–73).

The constitution of 1960 attempted to achieve a balance between Greek and Turkish claims, but from independence onwards distrust between the two communities steadily escalated: they disputed the intergration of the armed forces, the composition of the civil service, the fairness of taxes, in fact everything that would make the state work on a reasonable unitary basis. Polarization rapidly increased between the two communities, 80 per cent Greeks and 20 per cent Turks – the one group still pulled by the attraction of *enosis*, the other by close affinities with Turkey – and both Greece and Turkey provided covert support for their respective sides, so a collision seemed inevitable.

Communal strife and UN intervention 1963–1964

Communal strife between Greek and Turk escalated through 1963, and the two racial groups increasingly divided into separate geographic communities. By late 1963 there was street fighting between Greeks and Turks which was escalating towards civil war. The situation was made worse by the Greek and Turkish governments which each provided clandestine arms to their respective ethnic groups, which began to form irregular fighting forces. At first British troops who were stationed on the island in two sovereign bases helped keep the peace between the two sides, but their intervention was too reminiscent of the independence struggle of the 1950s and merely produced growing anti-British violence. This was to continue until, in response to the plea of the Cyprus government, the UN sent a peace-keeping force of 7000 men in May 1964.

In July 1964 General Grivas, who played a major part in the independence struggle against the British, returned to Cyprus from Greece; he hoped to impose order and was given control of the National Guard. He brought with him a number

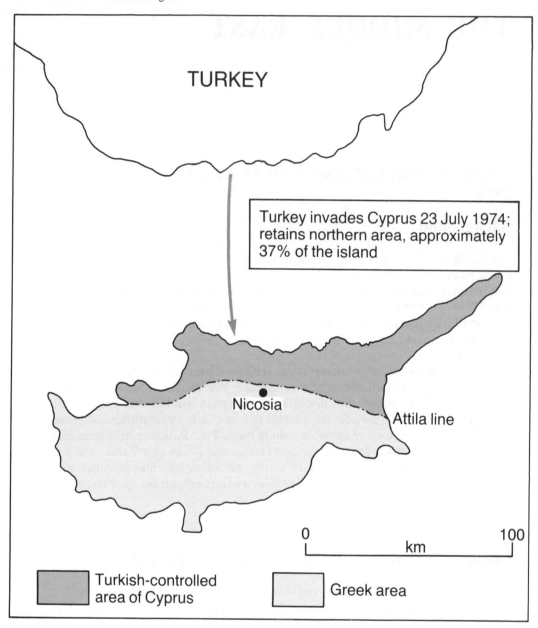

Map 18 Cyprus

of Greek volunteers from the mainland. In August Turkish war planes attacked Greek Cypriots, while Archbishop Makarios – the Cypriot leader – sought help from Egypt and the USSR. The Turks threatened to invade Cyprus but were warned off by US President L. B. Johnson. Fighting between Greek and Turk continued through 1964 until the UN managed to arrange a ceasefire. During 1965 the government made an effort to defuse the situation by reforming laws to which the Turkish community most strongly objected, and an uneasy peace prevailed. Yet no real progress was made in the years 1964–70, though a series of bilateral communal talks were held between Greek and Turk in an effort to find a more lasting solution to communal differences.

The year 1967 saw a dangerous escalation of Greek–Turkish antagonisms. In November a number of Turks were massacred by Greeks; Grivas was held responsible and disgraced. He was recalled to Greece. Then in December the Turkish community in Cyprus set up its own *de facto* government, and although the UN peace-keeping force remained in the island, it did little more than maintain an uneasy calm. From this year Greek nationalists formed terrorist bands in a National Front; in 1969 they began new terrorist tactics aimed at achieving union with Greece. They had little appeal, however, and in the 1970 elections only one candidate favoured union with Greece.

General Grivas returned secretly to Cyprus from Greece in 1971 to make contact with the National Front, which he now reorganized as EOKA–B, the successor to the EOKA terrorist movement that had fought the British in the 1950s. Grivas' followers, possibly numbering 3000 altogether, were fanatically loyal to him. They infiltrated the National Guard and proceeded to attack government targets, increasingly challenging the authority of Archbishop Makarios, who opposed the use of violence to achieve *enosis*. They obtained weapons by raiding police stations or gunsmiths.

Prelude to the Turkish invasion 1973–1974

Makarios won the presidential elections of February 1973 unopposed; he explained his non-violent stance, which was far more conciliatory to the Turkish minority than the line taken by Grivas and EOKA–B. Despite this victory, EOKA–B staged a series of bomb outrages which were to continue for the rest of the year. Grivas tried to prevent deaths and made government buildings the main targets for his bombing campaign. Plans to assassinate Makarios were unsuccessful. Then in January 1974 Grivas died. Makarios, in a gesture of conciliation, released 100 EOKA–B prisoners in an amnesty.

On 15 July 1974 a coup was mounted against Makarios by the National Guard led by Greek officers from Greece. It was temporarily successful (EOKA–B was heavily involved) and Nicos Sampson, who had been in the original EOKA movement and was associated with Grivas and EOKA–B, now became President. He lasted eight days. Makarios fled to Malta and then to London. The coup attempt, which appeared to bring Cyprus far closer to joining Greece, led to the Turkish military intervention on 24 July. Thereafter, EOKA–B declined in importance; Makarios returned as President until his death in 1977; and Sampson was sentenced to 20 years in prison.

The Turkish invasion of Cyprus: July 1974

On 23 July 1974 the military junta in Athens fell from power and Konstantinos Karamanlis became Prime Minister. Sampson resigned as President of Cyprus to be replaced on a temporary basis by the President of the Assembly, Glafkos Clerides, until Makarios returned. On the following day 24 July, between 30,000 and 40,000 Turkish troops invaded northern Cyprus. There was strong resistance and were substantial casualties, but the Turks established a bridgehead at Kyrenia and then advanced to Nicosia, creating a corridor between the two towns. The UN then managed to arrange a ceasefire on 30 July and established a buffer zone between Greeks and Turks. The Turks halted further activity while talks were held in Geneva between Britain, Greece and Turkey (the three original guarantor powers of Cyprus's independence), but these resolved nothing and ended 13 August. The next day the Turks resumed hostilities until they had taken all of northern Cyprus, from Morphou in the west to Famagusta in the east, along what came to be called the Attila Line. By 16 August the Turks had control of approximately 37 per cent of the island. The Turkish Cypriots were overwhelmingly in support of the invasion and the subsequent *de facto* partition of Cyprus. On his return to resume the presidency Makarios was prepared – he had no option – to accept Turkish autonomy in the Turkish-occupied part of Cyprus, but he would not agree to formal partition.

It was a short but brutal war; the Turks brought overwhelming military power to bear, while Greece was not in a position to do anything and neither Britain nor any other country was prepared to intervene against the Turks. As a result of the war, about a third of the population was displaced, Turkish Cypriots moving from the Greek-held part of the island to the Turkish area and Greek Cypriots moving in the other direction; subsequently, refugee camps became recruiting centres for terrorists. Only the government of the Greek Cypriot-controlled part of Cyprus was recognized internationally. In February 1975 the Turks proclaimed the Turkish Federated State of Cyprus, and Denktash, the Turkish Cypriot leader, announced that the Turks wanted a federation and not secession. Talks between the governments of the two Cypruses were to be held on and off until 1983 when Turkish Cyprus declared independence. As a result of this invasion, Cyprus remained divided into two *de facto* autonomous areas: the Greek area, comprising 60 per cent of the island, and the Turkish area, comprising 35 per cent; Britain still controls 5 per cent in the form of two 'sovereign' military bases.

The Turkish Republic of Northern Cyprus 1983

On 15 November 1983 the Turkish Cypriot President, Rauf Denktash, declared independence and the formation of a Turkish Republic of Northern Cyprus. Only Turkey recognized the new 'republic'. This UDI plunged Cyprus into a major crisis, although admittedly ending what had at best been a very tenuous connection between the two parts of the island. Denktash had threatened a UDI earlier in the year following a resolution at the UN in May which had called for the immediate withdrawal of Turkish troops from Cyprus. Denktash then abandoned the communal talks about the creation of a federal republic which had been dragging on since 1974. The UN Secretary-General, Javier Pérez de Cuéllar, then attempted to define new negotiating positions, but his initiative failed, However, moves towards calling a Greek–Turkish summit were under way when Denktash declared independence, and that did nothing to help relations between the two sides. Following the declaration, Denktash was unable to secure the hoped-for support of Islamic nations for his move, while Spyros Kyprianou, the President of Greek Cyprus, obtained immediate Security Council condemnation of the Denktash move. Denktash then found that most produce from the Turkish part of Cyprus was banned in Europe.

After 1983 the two sides continued to call for a resolution of their inter-communal differences and the creation of a new federal system of government. A summit meeting in January 1985 between Kyprianou and Denktash did not achieve anything. Two years later (1987) the Turks were reported to have increased their troops on the island from 20,000 to 36,000, although Turkey denied this. Reunification talks held in 1989 were again deadlocked.

Estimated costs and casualties

Communal strife and violence has been a feature of Cyprus ever since the first post-independence outbreak in 1963. The Turkish invasion of 1974 disrupted the island's lucrative tourist trade, since about 65 per cent of the tourist attractions were situated in the Turkish part of the island. Moreover, the north is the economically more valuable part of Cyprus and, according to Greek claims, accounts for 70 per cent of the gross output of Cyprus.

The war of 1974, brief though it was, displaced 225,600 Cypriots out of a total population of 650,000: of these 183,300 were Greek Cypriots. During adjustments in 1975 some 9000 Turkish Cypriots were allowed to move north and 800 Greek Cypriots were allowed to move south into their respective ethnic areas. In January 1977 the report of the European Commission of Human Rights found Turkey guilty of committing atrocities in Cyprus.

Results: ongoing

According to Greek Cypriots, there has been Turkish migration into northern Cyprus ever since 1974 and the people there are beginning to think of themselves as Turks rather than as Cypriots. As many as 60,000 were thought to have immigrated into northern Cyprus by 1987. However, there has been no inter-communal strife in Cyprus since the partition which followed the Turkish invasion of 1974, and the Turks claim that their 20,000 troops ensure that the peace is kept. The National Guard of Greek Cyprus numbers 12,000 and is not strong enough to take on the Turks, who could reinforce their troops in 24 hours through two northern ports. The UN peace-keeping force of 2500 men is another factor making for stability. The Cyprus problem (in 1990) appeared no nearer a solution. The Greek and Turkish Cypriots are separated by language, culture, history and religion, and the suspicions between the two sides continue to be supported respectively by Greece and Turkey.

IRAN: THE 1979 REVOLUTION AND THE FALL OF THE SHAH

Background

Shah Mohammed Reza Pahlavi succeeded his father in September 1941 when the latter was forced to abdicate by Allied – British and Russian – pressure because of his pro-German sympathies. His early years were to be troubled, and at first he was little more than a puppet of the Allies. At the end of the war a Communist 'popular' government was briefly established in Azerbaijan, but this was removed in 1946. In 1951 Prime Minister Mossadeq nationalized Iran's oil (then controlled by the Anglo-Iranian Oil Company) and sparked off an international crisis. An abortive coup attemp in August 1953 persuaded the Shah to flee the country for a few days until General Zahedi had forced Mossadeq to resign. A period of instability followed, however, and it was not until 1961 that the Shah felt strong enough to assert himself and embark on a period of direct and increasingly autocratic rule.

In May 1961 he dissolved the Majlis (Parliament), and the following year he introduced the first of his Land Reform Acts. The minority of landholders had to surrender their land to the state for redistribution; these landholders included the Shia Muslim hierarchy. The Shah's reforms of the early 1960s came to be known as the White Revolution. They included profit sharing in industry, compensation (in the form of shares in industry) to the landholders who had lost their land, and a greater say in national affairs for both cultivators (small farmers) and workers. Co-operatives were established in the rural areas, and these provided capital for rural development. There were government campaigns to reduce adult illiteracy, and education was taken out of the hands of the clergy.

The Shah's White Revolution changed the country's power structure. Apart from depriving the landlords of their land, it made a major enemy of the Shia clergy since it deprived the clerical establishment of its land and lessened its grip on education, the greatest source of its power. In the early days the White Revolution was popular and was voted massive approval in January 1963. By 1971, when the process of land redistribution had been completed, about 2,500,000 families representing a farming population of more than 12 million had become direct beneficiaries of the reforms; over the years 1960–72 owner-occupied farmland in Iran had increased from 26 to 78 per cent. Between 1960 and 1978 per capita income rose from an average of $176 a year to $2500 a year. This was an impressive achievement, helped by the massive increase in oil prices during the 1970s which, for example, allowed the government to allocate $68 billion to the 1973–8 Fifth Development Plan. But there was a heavy price to pay for these reforms. The Shah underestimated the enmity and bitterness which his revolution caused among the Shia clergy; he also underestimated the deeply conservative nature of his people in his rush to modernize.

The growing crisis

The Shah's mistake was to attempt too much too quickly in a society that was conservative, semi-illiterate and heavily influenced by a powerful Muslim clergy. In both agriculture and industry too great a burden of change was imposed on people not sufficiently educated to absorb it, and this resulted in growing disquiet among increasing numbers of people at changes in the nature of Iranian society. But as the years went by and the Shah became more confident that he was right, opposition was ruthlessly suppressed by the secret police (SAVAK).

During the 1970s two opposition groups – the Fedayeen and Mujaheddin – each with several hundred followers, waged anti-government terrorist campaigns in the cities. The Mujaheddin were especially opposed to the huge influx of foreigners that the Shah's modernizing developments had brought into the country; they singled out the Americans as the most blameworthy. They also attacked modernization for undermining traditional Islamic values. Though left-wing opposition as well as calls for greater openness and democracy played their part in bringing about the Shah's downfall, it was the resurgence of Islam led by the hardline clergy which was to prove crucial to the events of 1978 and 1979.

The religious classes had been opposed to the Shah's reforms from the beginning; they saw their own power being eroded in direct proportion as westernization and modernization took place. By 1976 the divisions in Iranian society rapidly becoming acute. It is the nature of absolute rule that only the ruler in the end can take the blame for what goes wrong. The Shah was opposed by the mass of students and the religious classes, although he was still supported by the new rich and the rising middle class. But a real indication of the insecurity of the regime was the fact that mid-1976 private capital was being transferred abroad at the rate of $1 billion a month. During the years 1976–7, partly as a result of US pressures, the Shah attempted to liberalize his regime. What he succeeded in doing was to open the floodgates for opposition of every kind. It was a classic example of 'too little too late': as controls were relaxed, so extremist groups became increasingly active, including the 'Dedicated Fighter' groups of the Mujaheddin. Then following liberalization, the new political groups which had emerged were attacked and their demonstrations disrupted by mobs. On the university campuses there was a growth of religious fervour, with many new students from traditional backgrounds being first shocked by big city life and then falling back on religious fundamentalism for security. Opponents of the Shah began to rally round the religious leader Ayatollah Ruholla Khomeini, who was living in exile in Iraq. One of Khomeini's sons died during 1977 and religious followers of the Ayatollah went to pay their respects to him. He took the opportunity of these visits to hold anti-Shah seminars: these were taped, and cassettes of them were later distributed in Iran to fan religious disaffection with the regime.

A key factor in the growing opposition to the Shah was the blatant materialism which had followed the White Revolution and the oil wealth of the 1970s; there was a growing gap between the conspicuously rich at the top and the majority, perhaps especially the urban poor who consisted of artisans and construction workers. The Shah's 15 years of modernization (1963–78) – the implementation of his dream to make Iran a Western-style society – had only been possible because of a state apparatus of oppression. The Shah and his reformers had ridden roughshod over traditional values and had produced glaring distortions between the rich and the poor. By 1978 the modernizing bubble was about to burst.

The events of 1978

There were perhaps three forces at work helping to bring an end to the Shah's rule. The first consisted of opposition from the educated middle classes who revolted at the oppression of his regime, as well as the guerrilla groups – the Fedayeen and Mujaheddin – who had conducted underground struggles against him since 1971. From 1977 these opponents of the regime were joined by remnants of the old National Front (of Mossadeq), who then emerged to protest at the denial of civil liberties. The second force was derived from the large urban populations, which divided between the urban poor, who were often migrants from the countryside lured by hopes of wealth that were not fulfilled; the 'merchants of the bazaar', who represented an old source of opposition and were allied to the clergy; and the artisan class. The last two of these three groups felt that they had been bypassed by the boom that had come with oil, which had gone instead to the so-called petro-bourgeoisie. The third force, which ultimately became heir to the revolution, consisted of the underground Muslim organizations that looked to the Ayatollahs and especially to the exiled Khomeini, and that were supported by religious acolytes, theology students and shrine officials. The religious establishment was able to mobilize large numbers of followers through various neighbourhood associations which it controlled.

Ruholla Khomeini (the Ayatollah) had gone into exile in 1964 (in Iraq), but in 1978 he moved to Paris from where he demanded the abdication of the Shah. A combination of pressures came to a head in 1978: the accumulating conservative backlash to the Shah's progressive measures; disappointed expectations; the increasing autocracy of the Shah, which was supported by the oppression most obviously represented by SAVAK, the ubiquitous secret police; and the glaring divisions which by then were all too obvious a part of Iranian society. In January 1978, in what turned out to be a disastrous government effort to undermine Khomeini, a government paper carried an article denigrating the Ayatollah in an attempt to discredit his life. As a result, theology students in Qom rioted on 9 January and a number were killed (about 10 according to the government, about 100 according to the opposition). Bigger riots followed at Tabriz on 18–19 February; the police lost control and the military had to be used to restore order for the first time since 1963. Demonstrations against the government continued through the spring and early summer, and by the middle of 1978 the Shah faced two powerful enemies: Khomeini and the hardline Imams; and the National Front, which wanted an end to autocratic rule.

August was crisis month. On 7 August the Shah declared that elections scheduled for June 1979 would be completely free. Immediately a dozen new political groups emerged, further demonstrations followed and then, in a terrible incident, the Cinema Rex at Abadan was destroyed in a fire in which 377 people were killed; the fire was widely considered to be the work of SAVAK. On 27 August the Shah replaced his Prime Minister, Jamshid Amuzegar, with Sherif Emami in the hope that Emami (a former Premier) would be able to establish a dialogue with the religious leaders. On 4 September, following the end of Ramadan, the largest anti-Shah demonstration yet took place when more than 1 million people marched through the streets of Tehran. A similar large demonstration took place three days later. During these demonstrations direct appeals were made to the army to join in the opposition to the Shah. The Shah reacted by declaring martial law (8 September): hundreds were killed in clashes with the army, press censorship was reimposed and opposition groups once more went underground.

The opposition was now carried into the workplace in the form of nation-wide strikes, and for two months (September–October) Iran was crippled by stoppages which affected the civil service, the airlines, telecommunications and finally the oilfields, which were the key to the country's wealth. And so on 5 November the Shah dismissed the Emami government, which had shown itself unable to control the situation, and in its place appointed a military cabinet under General Gholan Reza Azhari. But the new government was no more able to stop the strikes than its predecessor, and by December almost all non-agricultural activity had come to a halt.

On 10 and 11 December (the traditional days of mourning, 9 and 10 of the month of Moharram) huge demonstrations of as many as 2 million people took place in Tehran. The government and the military were powerless to stop them, and the Shah was reduced to a state of desperation. By this time any hope of compromise between the Shah and his many opponents had passed. Opposition to the monarchy was growing by the day. The initiative appeared to have passed to Khomeini in Paris. In Iran the less fundamentalist religious leaders called for a return to the constitution of 1906, which accepted a constitutional monarch, but from Paris Ayatollah Khomeini called for the creation of an Islamic republic. On 13 December, in the wake of the huge pro-Khomeini demonstrations, there were a rash of pro-Shah demonstrations organized by local military commanders; these inevitably produced violence between the two opposed sides and resulted in many deaths.

At the very end of the year, in a final bid to hold on to power, the Shah dismissed the Azhari government and appointed Dr Shahpur Bakhtiar as Prime Minister. Bakhtiar was a long-term opponent of the monarchy, and the Shah's hope, presumably, was that he could rally waverers to some form of radical programme. But by the end of 1978 the crisis had resolved itself into a confrontation between the Shah and the army on one side and Khomeini and the masses on the other, while middle voices were lost in extremist clamour. By this time and into January 1979 the nation-wide strikes were almost total, and there was no sign that they would be called off until the Shah went. On 1 January, a foretaste of what the year held in store, riots erupted in Dezful and Andimeshk (in the south of the country) and the army lost control of the situation.

The fall of the Shah

The Shah had been weak and vacillating as a young man; later his Western allies, busy reaping a rich harvest from Iran's oil wealth, helped build up the myth of the Shah as he wished to see himself: a masterful, formidable leader bringing a backward Iran into the modern world. Unfortunately, when it came to the test, the Shah was unable to sustain the myth. The first two weeks of January 1979 witnessed a total breakdown everywhere, with riots, a witchhunt against SAVAK and the army losing both control and the will to restore order. It was a classic revolutionary situation: a king being dethroned by the will of the people. On 15 January the Shah bowed to the inevitable and left Iran for a rest – in fact he was abdicating and going into permanent exile. The Prime Minister, Shahpur Bakhtiar, announced that SAVAK was to be disbanded and said that Iran would abandon its role as the 'policeman' of the Gulf. The Regency and Supreme Army Council which had been established to run the country in the Shah's absence was quite unable to do so, while Bakhtiar was suspect in the eyes of the Islamic and left-wing opposition, who thought he would try to protect what was left of the former regime. He was expelled from the National Front.

While almost everyone and every faction was unanimous in wanting an end to the Shah's regime, this unanimity did not extend to the succession. Once the Shah had left the country, the coalition of forces which had formed to force him out simply disintegrated. The parameters of this first revolution – the one which ousted the Shah – may be taken as the period from 9 January 1978 (when the theology students rioted in Qom) to 11 February 1979 (when Bakhtiar fell and fled the country). There now followed the second, or Khomeini, revolution.

The establishment of an Islamic republic

The revolution which led to the overthrow of the Shah was as much a reaction to over-penetration of Iranian society by the West as it was purely religious, although in the end Islam came to embody all the resentments against the westernization and modernization that had been carried out by the Shah. Following the Shah's departure, Prime Minister Bakhtiar was unable to come to terms with either the National Front or Khomeini. Huge, million-strong crowds demonstrated for Khomeini, and he arrived in Tehran on 1 February 1979 to wild rejoicing. He nominated a government to be led by Mehdi Bazargan, who had been in charge of oil under Mossadeq and was now the leader of the Iran Liberation Movement (an Islamic underground organization) from which Khomeini's advisers were largely drawn. Ten days after Khomeini's return Bakhtiar was forced to go into hiding (later he went into exile in France). His fall came after a meeting at the Tehran air force base when the army chiefs of staff withdrew their support.

The new Khomeini–Bazargan government quickly established its control throughout the country. On 30 March 1979 it held a referendum on the question of whether Iran should become an Islamic republic, and according to the government 99 per cent of those who voted said yes. On 1 April, therefore, Khomeini declared an Islamic republic. Fundamentalist measures were enacted, including the veiling of women and the repeal of the modern divorce laws. At the same time attacks were launched against Western influences and many of the Western-educated élite fled the country. Young revolutionaries occupied military bases and attacked opponents of the Islamic movement. Between them Revolutionary Guards and Islamic Committees recruited large numbers of young men to their ranks to form a rough militia to guard the revolution. Mock trials and executions of enemies of the revolution were carried out, and on 6 May the Army of the Guardians of the Islamic Revolution was formed. This carried out a reign of terror.

An Islamic constitution published in June gave the *ulema* (religious clergy) a major role in determining legislation, and also gave the President wide powers. But the constitution made no provisions for the non-Persian minorities, such as the Kurds, and so sparked off a series of minority revolts. In addition to the religion-oriented constitution, new laws imposed stringent controls on the press and restricted strike action. And so, quite suddenly, revolutionaries who had assumed that the passing of the Shah would mean greater liberty and more democracy found instead that another form of tyranny was to replace that of the Shah.

On 3 August a Council of Experts was elected to discuss the new constitution. The election produced a crisis between Khomeini and his opponents, who argued that the 73 experts did not represent a proper consensus of views and that there had been irregularities in the voting procedures. But once the elections were over, the Khomeini government closed down opposition papers and (after they had protested this censorship) banned those political groups which were critical of Khomeini. Those banned included the Fedayeen, the Mujaheddin, the National Democratic Front and the Tudeh Party. Although several hundred officials of the Shah's regime were executed, much of its apparatus remained in place at the end of 1979.

By the beginning of 1980 Khomeini had become the arbiter and centre of political power in Iran. On 25 January 1980 presidential elections returned Abdolhassan Bani-Sadr with 75 per cent of the votes, although there was only a 50 per cent turnout. Muslim fundamentalists now attempted to undermine the position of any prominent secular group. The ethnic minorities – the Kurds in the north-west, the Arabs in the south-west and the Baluchis in the south-east – made bids for greater autonomy, although only the revolt of the Kurds was important. The government had to mount a substantial campaign in Kurdistan to bring them to heel, and after six weeks of fighting the Kurdish-held town of Sanandaj fell to government forces in mid-May with an estimated 1500 deaths. Thereafter, the Kurds held the countryside (see Part I, pp. 73–81).

Khomeini broke relations with the West and with the rest of the Islamic world. On 4 November 1979 supporters of the revolution seized the US Embassy in Tehran and took 66 American citizens hostage; 14 of these were released almost at once, but 52 were to remain captive until 20 January 1981 and sour US–Iranian relations for a long time to come.

The period 1979–81 was one of constant and sometimes bewildering changes as the revolutionary factions and counter-factions vied for power. There was a great deal of violence. In November 1979 the revolution's first Prime Minister, Mehdi Bazargan, resigned and then the first President, Abdolhassan Bani-Sadr (who had opposed the taking of the American hostages) fled the country. The leader of the Mujaheddin-e-Khalq (Fighters for the People), Massoud Rajavi, was also forced to flee. The Mujaheddin, however, stepped up their terror campaign, and on 28 June 1981 bombed the headquarters of the Islamic Republic Party, causing many casualties. In the end, however, Khomeini triumphed. He re-established the twin pillars of an older Iranian society: the Shia Muslim hierarchy and the bazaar merchants.

Estimated costs and casualties

During 1978 many thousands are believed to have died, and many more died during the years 1979–81 as Khomeini and the fundamentalists established their control. Some died in fighting, some were hunted down and killed, and others were executed after summary or mock trials. The costs are impossible to measure. It is a question not so much of disruption to industry and the economy generally, although this was very great, but – far more important – of a complete change in a nation's way of life. It is doubtful whether the effects of this will ever be gauged with certainty.

Results: immediate and longer term

The most immediate result of the revolution was to replace the autocracy of the Shah with another autocracy of religious fundamentalists. In the longer term this was to have repercussions throughout the Islamic world as revolution was exported (if possible) to other Shia groups in the Gulf and as far afield as Sudan. Fear of Iranian influence was to dominate the politics of the Gulf states throughout the 1980s.

A second effect was to capitalize on the growing sense of disillusionment with the West and Western values. The Iranian message was that the Islamic world did not need the West, and although this was not to prove the case, as far as export markets and technology were concerned, Iran did demonstrate a remarkable capacity to manage with only a minimum of Western involvement.

Third, the Gulf War emerged directly from the turmoil of the second or Khomeini revolution. The attempted assassination of the Deputy Prime Minister of Iraq, Tariq Aziz, in April 1980 by a group claiming allegiance to Khomeini set in motion the crisis between the two countries which led Iraq to abrogate the 1975 Algiers agreement (17 September) and claim the whole Shatt al-Arab waterway. Iraq then invaded the south-west of Iran (the oil region), sparking off the bloody Gulf War (see Part III, pp. 227–241). Iraq, however, made the classic mistake of assuming that it could take advantage of the revolutionary situation inside Iran; in fact it achieved the opposite by providing an external enemy and enabling Khomeini to unite the people behind his government in their war effort. The revolution created large numbers of exiles: those who had done well under the Shah or who could not accept the Islamic revolution with its harsh dogmas. These exiles included such groups as the Guards of the Monarchical Regime, the Free Iran Movement, the Iranian Liberation Army, and the National Resistance Front.

The Iranian revolution saw the total collapse of a powerful monarchy and the emergence from its ruins of a very different Iran. The impact of the revolution outside Iran (in the Gulf, among hostage-taking groups in Lebanon, in Sudan, in terms of relations with the West) demonstrated that the change was of a fundamental nature – possibly one of the dozen most important events of the century.

LEBANON: PERMANENT CIVIL WAR

Background

From ancient times Lebanon has provided a refuge for racial and religious minorities; owing to its mountainous nature it has always been exceptionally difficult to control. Warring empires have halted on its fringes and, as both Israel and Syria have discovered in the present era, it is easier to become involved in Lebanon than subsequently to disengage. A period of direct Ottoman rule was inaugurated in 1840, and the following years saw a rising distrust between the Druze and the Maronite Christians. The Turks were happy to encourage this distrust as a means of dividing and continuing to rule. None the less, from about 1864 to 1914 there was a general increase in prosperity.

During the First World War the coastal regions were occupied by the British and French; subsequently, under the League of Nations system of mandates, France created Greater Lebanon in 1920. In 1941, during the early stages of the Second World War, General Catroux, the Free French Commander, proclaimed Lebanon an independent sovereign state. In 1946 France agreed to withdraw its troops. In 1948 Lebanon joined other Arab states in declaring war on the new state of Israel (see Part IV, pp. 283–291). During the Suez crisis of 1956 a state of emergency was declared in Lebanon, which, whatever the inclinations of its people and rulers, was inexorably drawn into the confrontations of the Middle East that focused on Israel, its neighbour to the south. In 1957, during the aftermath of Suez, Lebanon responded warmly to the American Eisenhower Doctrine, which offered economic and military aid to countries in the region willing to accept it.

Civil war and American intervention 1958

In March 1958 Lebanon refused to become a member of the United Arab Republic (UAR), formed in the wake of the Suez War by Egypt and Syria, or the Arab Federation of Iraq and Jordan, insisting instead that it would maintain its full sovereignty. In fact large segments of the Muslim population were probably more favourable to these new Arab alignments than to an independent Lebanon dominated by the Christian majority. Syria now advanced demands that the predominantly Muslim areas of Lebanon which had been incorporated into the French mandate in 1920 should be returned to Syria. There was strong opposition to the pro-Western stance that had been adopted under President Camille Chamoun; in March members of the government critical of its pro-Western policies were sacked. Anti-government disturbances began in the city of Tripoli in the north, but soon spread through the country: the Druze divided between pro- and anti-government factions. At this stage the USA promised to support the government by providing arms and police equipment.

The Cold War was at its height in 1958, so any major power activity has to be seen in that light. The USSR responded to the US offer of help by accusing Washington of interference in Lebanon's affairs. The Lebanese government accused the UAR of interfering and appealed to the Arab League to mediate and protect it, but the League was powerless to help and Lebanon then turned to the

United Nations. Opponents of the Chamoun government now seized parts of Beirut, Tripoli and Sidon as well as considerable areas of the countryside in both the north and south of the country, in what threatened to be a full-scale insurrection of Muslim versus Christian. The leaders of the insurrection demanded the immediate resignation of Chamoun; on 14 July (the same day that the monarchy in Iraq was overthrown by a *coup d'état*) Chamoun requested American intervention. The USA sent about 10,000 troops and warned the UAR not to interfere. The USSR and China protested, while the USA gave an undertaking that it would withdraw if requested to do so by the Lebanese government, or if it were replaced by a UN peace-keeping force.

On 31 July the Lebanese Chamber of Deputies elected a new President, General Fuad Chehab, who was then Commander-in-Chief of the army. He was to prove acceptable to both sides. Chehab was installed as President on 23 September; he then invited the leader of the insurgents, Rashid Karami, to become his Prime Minister. For a while Chehab was able, if not to unite them, at least to get Christians and Muslims to work together (he was the last person to do so). In his new cabinet he had four Christians, three Muslims and one Druze. On 27 September the USA agreed to withdraw its troops, and this was done by the end of October.

This first civil war was short, external intervention by the USA was effective (and it managed to withdraw quickly) and Chehab was strong enough to inaugurate a period of calm and prosperity with relative trust between the two major religious groups that make up the bulk of the Lebanese population.

Uneasy prosperity 1958–1975

During the 10 years from 1958 to 1969 Lebanon prospered and Christians and Muslims appeared able to compromise with each other. Yet it was very much a surface achievement, for the two sides never really trusted one another. The army and the security police were used to control the rivalries which existed but nothing was solved. Meanwhile, prosperity led to massive urbanization, so that 40 per cent of the population came to live in Beirut. However, if anything, prosperity increased the polarization that already existed since the prosperous urban population was mainly Christian and the poorer rural population Muslim. In the background lurked the Syrian factor: Syria continued to see Lebanon as part of a Greater Syria, while its leaders had never accepted the 1920 French decision to create a separate Lebanese state. Lebanon managed to keep clear of both the 1967 and 1973 Arab–Israeli wars, but was not helped by rumours that it had entered into secret agreements with Israel.

The real balance in Lebanon was tipped by the growing influx of Palestinians. Their numbers had been increasing steadily during the latter half of the 1960s; then, following the 1970 war against the Palestinians in Jordan (see Part IV, pp. 307–310), large numbers of Palestinians moved from Jordan to Lebanon, so by 1973 one in 10 of the population was Palestinian. Most of the Palestinians were poor and landless, which emphasized their inferior 'refugee' status. They were mainly employed as cheap labour. It was an explosive situation. The Palestinians became increasingly radicalized and began to join forces with the Lebanese rural poor who, like the Palestinians, were Muslims.

Ever since the formation of Lebanon in 1920, the constitution and then an unwritten agreement of 1943 (under which the President was always a Maronite Christian, the Premier a Sunni Muslim and the Speaker of the Chamber of Deputies a Shiite) had recognized the primacy of the Christians, who formed a majority of the population. By the 1960s, however, they no longer did so: once the influx of Palestinians had taken place, the Christians were in a minority, forming roughly 40–45 per cent of the population, although they insisted on retaining power commensurate with being the majority. By 1975, therefore, the Shiite and Druze sects were increasingly discontented, while the Phalange Party (Christians) and especially the Maronites held the dominant political positions.

In the latter part of the 1960s the Palestinians began to clash with the security forces, while the leadership of the Palestinian Liberation Organization (PLO) found itself less and less able to control its more radical factions. An agreement of 3 November 1969, reached in Cairo between the Lebanese government and the PLO, gave the latter a free hand in the refugee camps and on the Israeli border, while in return the PLO promised not to interfere in Lebanese politics. In fact the PLO was unable to deliver its side of the agreement, and from 1970 onwards the Palestinians became more and more involved in Lebanese politics, working with the Shiite left who represented the poorer sections of the Muslim population.

A vicious circle developed: PLO units raided across the border into Israel, the Israelis counter-attacked, the Christian right then attacked the PLO, while in the centre the government was unable to control these different factions. In 1970 Suleiman Franjieh became President by one vote; he was a right-wing hardliner. The economy was now in trouble, while an increasing gulf had developed between the rich and poor. The radical guerrilla groups became increasingly hostile to a government which was quite unable to prevent Israeli cross-border attacks, and in May 1973, prevented from making attacks on Israel, they abducted Lebanese soldiers instead, which led to heavy fighting between the army and Palestinians in their refugee camps. From this time onwards, despite a series of truces, the situation deteriorated steadily towards civil war. By 1974 the Palestinians were providing the forces which made up Kamal Jumblatt's Lebanese National Movement; the Shiite Muslims, representing the poor of the Bekaa valley region and the south, formed another group under Imam Musa as-Sadr, demanding political rights, economic justice and proper defence against Israeli incursions into the south. All the ingredients existed for a far greater civil explosion than that of 1958.

Civil war 1975–1976

Both Muslims and Christians were divided into a variety of groups and organizations, and a number of the Muslim groups were more or less aligned with the Palestinians and the PLO. In the beginning the civil war was confined to the north of Lebanon and Beirut. It was sparked off by an incident of 13 April 1975 when a busload of Palestinians was attacked by Phalangists and the passengers killed. A Muslim coalition was formed to fight the Christians. Once the fighting began in April 1975, violence became a daily occurrence and the country was all but torn apart by its rival factions; the central government barely functioned. The various factions had no difficulty in getting arms from their external backers, the army was unable and in many cases unwilling to keep the peace, and the fighting was brutal, fierce and apparently endless.

In the first stage of the war Egypt (President Sadat) supported the Christians, while Syria (President Assad) supported the Shiites and the PLO. Early in 1976 the Palestinians joined in the war on the side of the Shiites following a Christain attack on a PLO camp. It was soon apparent that the Palestinians and the Shiites were winning the war, and this brought about a shift of alignment by Syria, which believed that a Christian defeat would result in the emergence of a left-wing pro-Palestinian state or in partition, and that in either case this was likely to ensure Israeli intervention. Syria was more concerned to prevent Israeli intervention than to ensure a Muslim–Palestinian victory, and so it switched its support to the Christians and began to restrain the left. The ironical situation then arose in which both Syria and Israel supported the Christians since neither wanted to see the alternative of a left-wing Muslim–Palestinian state. Syria, therefore, supplied the Christians with arms, while at the same time preventing the Palestinians from taking strategic positions which would threaten Israel; the Israelis blockaded Tyre and Sidon, through which arms were delivered to the Shiites and Palestinians.

Against this rapidly deteriorating background Syria sent in 20,000 troops and 450 tanks to restore order; in fact they now became central to the conflict. By June 1976 the PLO had turned to Iraq and Libya for support, while Eygypt was also making contacts with the PLO leader Yasser Arafat in a move to ensure that Cairo sustained its claim to Arab leadership. The Christians, now backed by the Syrians, had reversed the situation and were winning the war. In late June, for example, they attacked and captured the Palestinian refugee camp of Jisr al-Basha after a week of bloody fighting. A second Palestinian camp, Tall al-Zaata, was besieged until August.

A new President, Elias Sarkis, who was a Maronite Christian and had the backing of Syria, the USA, Israel and Saudi Arabia, was elected on 8 May 1976 and installed on 23 September (he was to remain President until the elections of 1981). By that time Lebanon was effectively partitioned along the Green Line, which ran through the centre of Beirut eastwards along the main road to Damascus: north of the Green Line a Christian government operated; south of it Shiite, Druze and Palestinian forces were in control, more or less under the leadership of Kamal Jumblatt. A number of attempts to secure a peace resulted (25–26 October) in the Arab League Summit which established the Arab Deterrent Force made up essentially of the Syrian troops, which by then had been increased to 30,000.

By the time this (temporary) peace had been achieved most of the players were in position for the next stage in Lebanon's bloody history. Ironically, the Syrian intervention of 1976 had in the end been made as much to prevent the growth of Palestinian influence as to end the civil war. A kind of fiction grew up that the civil war only lasted for the 18 months from April 1975 to October 1976. In fact it was to continue more or less non-stop throughout the 1980s, although vastly complicated by Israeli invasions, the Syrian presence and interventions, and the bloody internecine fighting among the Palestinians (see Part IV, pp. 310–321).

The conflict widens: Israel and Syria

From 1977 onwards what had begun as a Lebanese civil war between factions that had long mistrusted one another now merged into a wider conflict which included Syrian manoeuvres to dominate Lebanon (which Damascus regarded as part of Greater Syria anyway), Israeli interventions to destroy the PLO, and a PLO factional fight which developed into a struggle for survival. As a result, purely civil war struggles which continued with their abiding ferocity were none the less sometimes lost sight of amid these wider conflicts. By 1977 Lebanon was effectively divided between the north controlled by Syria, a coastal section controlled by the Christians, and a south which was partly under Shiite Muslim or PLO control and partly under the control of Major Haddad and his Free Christian Army. Moreover, from this time onwards Israeli interventions in the south became more frequent and, with other objectives, prevented Syria from imposing a peace on the whole country. By 1978 the Syrians had again altered their stand in relation to the Christians, who were becoming too strong as well as too overtly pro-Israel; once more, Syria supported the Muslim left.

Between 1975 and 1982 the Palestinians underwent a fundamental change: they ceased to be refugees who embraced guerrilla groups and instead turned themselves into a conventional armed force able to intimidate their hosts, the Lebanese, as well as the various Christian factions, and by 1982 they had become sufficiently formidable to provoke the second, and major, Israeli invasion (see Part IV, pp. 310–317).

The 1980s

By 1980 there was no effective government control in the south, which was subject to Israeli interventions and a growing polarization between the Christian groups and the Palestinians. In the first nine months of 1980 some 1800 people were killed and another 1700 wounded. The Lebanese army was unable to withstand Israeli attacks unless it had Syrian support. At that time the Arab Deterrent Force and the UN Interim Force in Lebanon (UNIFIL) tended to sit back and watch events.

During 1981 some of the worst fighting since 1976 occurred, and an estimated 2100 people were killed in the course of the year. Israel increased its activity in the south and had a number of confrontations with UNIFIL, which it defied or ignored. The two wars – the civil and the Israeli–Palestinian – became hopelessly intertwined during the year, and Beirut suffered from heavy bombing.

The year 1982 saw the massive Israeli invasion which had the effect of putting other civil fighting into the shade. By mid-June Beirut was besieged by the Israelis, and thousands died in the months long bombardment of the city.

President Amin Gemayel (he had succeeded his brother Bashir, who was assassinated three weeks after being elected and before taking office) made a major attempt to bring about national reconciliation during 1983 when he invited 10 political leaders to talks in Geneva in October. But this was a doomed effort in a year of continuing and devastating violence, with the south occupied by the Israelis, the north by the Syrians, Beirut in ruins and subject to suicide bombings, and Arafat's section of the PLO under siege in Tripoli. The Israelis withdrew to the Awali river (in July) and then from the Shuf mountains in September to be replaced by the Lebanese army, but the hopelessness of the situation might be gauged from the fact that a ceasefire arranged on 26 September was the (estimated) 179th since 1975. The Prime Minister, Shafiq al-Wazzan resigned in readiness for a national reconciliation government. On 23 October 239 US servicemen and 58 French soldiers (part of the international peace-keeping force) were killed in suicide bomb attacks.

On 30 April 1984 the new government of Rashid Kamal included representatives of all the main political groups, although they clearly distrusted one another and its formation did not bring about an end to the violence. In August there was bitter fighting in Beirut between rival militias and the army and sectarian fighting in Tripoli which resulted in 100 deaths. On 28 August the Israelis attacked a Palestinian refugee centre killing or wounding 100 people. During the year the USA, Britain, France and Italy withdrew from the multinational peace-keeping force, and by the end of the year Lebanon appeared to be more divided and more violent than ever.

During 1985 the Israelis withdrew from the south of the country and President Gemayel and the Syrians managed to work reasonably closely with each other. Yet fighting continued throughout the year. (President Gemayel continued in office until 1989 when Rene Muawan became President (5 November) only to be assassinated (22 November). Elias Hrawi then became President.) The Israelis did not cease activities in the south, despite their withdrawal, while the Syrians embarked on a major attempt to end the civil war by bringing Christians and Muslims together. At first the initiative appeared to be having some success, but renewed violence in August in Beirut and Tripoli, where an estimated 200 were killed, destroyed its chances.

A peace initiative signed in Damascus (Syria) in December 1985 between three militia groups collapsed in January 1986, and by July the Syrians were using their troops in Beirut in an attempt to reduce the influence of the various militias in the city. In fact violence escalated. By the eleventh anniversary of the outbreak of the civil war (April 1986) violence had become endemic to Lebanon, economic recovery was impossible and, in a new development, Lebanon had become a centre for extremist groups prepared to take Western hostages.

The same failure to end the violence continued through 1987 into 1990. On 1 July 1987 the Prime Minister, Rashid Karami, was assassinated, once more putting back any possibility of an end to civil strife, although Syria attempted throughout the year to achieve a peace. The crisis deepened in 1988, and Lebanon appeared to have settled down to a permanent civil war of attrition between the various militias, with Christians fighting Christians and Muslims fighting Muslims as well as each other and periodic massive Israeli raids in the south.

The first months of 1990 witnessed brutal fighting in the south between the PLO and its allies and the Hizbollah, and even worse fighting in Beirut between rival Christian groups, with casualties running into many hundreds. Most observers of Lebanon saw no indication whatever that any form of compromise between the rival groups could be worked out, and the civil war with its attendant interventions from Syria and Israel seemed set to continue indefinitely.

Estimated costs and casualties

An accurate death toll is an impossibility, but perhaps 100,000 have died in Lebanon since the outbreak of the civil war in 1975. At least 20,000 Palestinians (perhaps twice that number) have been killed and 40,000 wounded. Casualties have extended to the Syrians (not published) and the international peace-keeping forces. By 1980 an estimated 500,000 Lebanese had left the country to seek work abroad, and thousands more have left since then. Several hundred thousand people have left their homes, especially in the south. The damage to property has been on a vast scale, with large areas of Beirut reduced to rubble and the same devastation affecting Tripoli, Tyre and Sidon, while many villages have been wholly or partly destroyed. The economy, which was once the envy of the Middle East, has been reduced to a holding operation when fighting is not taking place, and Beirut, which was once the banking and commercial centre of the Middle East, has now been replaced by Amman or other centres.

Results: continuing

The war – or wars – have been a catastrophe for Lebanon, which has become a shambles at the mercy of warring militias and external pressures, including the Syrians and the Israelis. One result of the ongoing troubles has been to turn Lebanon into a centre of the heroin trade. In political terms it is doubtful whether Lebanon will ever be able to return to the single state system that existed prior to 1975. In human terms the suffering has been so widespread and the hatreds have become so deep that generations will be needed to heal the situation – and the process cannot begin until the civil war is ended and Lebanon faces a real prospect of no further interventions by its neighbours. The prospects are bleak.

OMAN: THE DHOFAR REBELLION

Background

By the 1960s the Sultanate of Muscat and Oman (now called the Sultanate of Oman) had become an anachronism backed by the British at a time of rising nationalism throughout the Arab world (see Part I, pp. 81–83). The Sultan, Said ibn Taymur, was by then possibly the most reactionary ruler in the world – he maintained large numbers of slaves and insisted on laws that were medieval. He opposed any kind of development and when oil was found and exploited would only allow its revenues to be used for his armed forces. It was the arbitrary behaviour of the Sultan which provided the reason for rebellion, especially as an increasing number of Omanis had been to work in the Gulf and so had been brought in contact with both political and economic developments taking place through most of the rest of the Arab world. Local chiefs in Dhofar rebelled at the petty restrictions imposed on them by the Sultan, while dissident Dhofaris (those who had been to the Gulf) formed the Dhofar Liberation Front (DLF) in 1962, which in reality represented an attempt to modernize Oman.

The rebellion was to become increasingly ideological in its nature: the rebels were fighting a reactionary regime backed by the colonialist British, who elsewhere in the Arab world were being forced to retreat; and once neighbouring Aden (South Yemen) became independent as the People's Democratic Republic of Yemen (PDRY) in 1967, it provided a base and Marxist inspiration for the rebels. A great deal of politicization inevitably occurred with the rebels proclaiming their belief in democracy and socialism. It was also a war of modernization against the older institution of tribalism, which was backed by the British.

Outbreak and response

In 1963 tribesmen in the western Dhofar mountains revolted, triggering off a war that was to last until 1975; the original DLF consisted mainly of tribal dissidents, but they soon became radicalized and already by 1965 the movement was receiving Chinese support. In 1966 Dhofari soldiers made an unsuccessful attempt to assassinate the Sultan, but his rule seemed guaranteed as long as the British supported him with military aid, which included officers to run his Sultan's Armed Forces (SAF). However, the terrain of Dhofar – mountains, valleys and tropical forests – lends itself to guerrilla warfare, so a small force could easily sustain a war against larger conventional forces. In political terms the Sultan was handicapped: he was an embarrassment to more radical Arab leaders, who were unwilling to go to his aid when he was sending his forces (officered by the British) against his own people. At this time Oman was not a member of the UN and the other Arab states constantly raised the question of British involvement in the Sultanate.

Primarily, however, the insurrection was about bringing Oman into the modern world, and once oil had been discovered in 1967 this was inevitable: with a population of 750,000 in a country which had only three small primary schools it was impossible to deny development for long, especially in the light of what was happening elsewhere in the Middle East. Moreover, international companies wanted the lucrative contracts that development brings, but they were unable to manage the oil wealth unless the Sultan was either persuaded to change his policies or eliminated in a coup. The latter in fact was what took place in 1970.

Course of the struggle

The war went through three stages: the first covered the period from its opening in 1964 to 1967, when fighting was confined to the central region of Dhofar around Salalah (where the Sultan had taken up permanent residence) and Thamrit; the second phase ran from 1967, when Aden (South Yemen) became independent as the People's Democratic Republic of Yemen and at once became the principal supporter of the rebellion, to 1970, during which period the guerrillas 'liberated' western and eastern Dhofar and the Sultan's supporters were driven back into the Salalah bridgehead; the third and final phase of the war followed the coup of 1970, which brought the reforming Sultan Qabus ibn Said to power and saw him win the war although only with major international assistance.

During the late 1960s, as the full extent of the insurrection became apparent, the Sultan increased the size of his forces (SAF) with a commensurate increase in British involvement. Yet up to 1967 search and destroy missions had very little success. The SAF depended entirely on British officers, advisers and back-up personnel, as did the Sultan's air force on the RAF. By 1970 the strength of the Sultan's forces had been increased to 2500; but by 1973 these had been quintupled to 12,500. At the same time there was a steady build-up of British personnel, so by 1972 there were 250 British army officers (with a back-up of Pakistani–Baluchi NCOs) and RAF pilots serving in the Sultan's Air Force, with hundreds more ground personnel (RAF) as well as about 100 British Military Advisory Training Teams (BMATT). In the early stage of the rebellion the SAF was only able to free the plains round Salalah of attacks and threats. In the towns militant supporters of the DLF were rounded up, but both the UAR and Iraq were providing support for the DLF.

The year 1967 was momentous for the Arab world: it saw the spectacular defeat of the frontline Arab states by Israel in the Six Day War of June, a cataclysmic event which led to a number of realignments; and next door to Oman, after a long and bitter colonial war, Aden became independent (in November) as the PDRY, ready at once to provide the Dhofar rebels with an external base from which to operate. One immediate result of these events was that Saudi Arabia, which up to this time had hesitated to support the Sultan of Oman, now decided to do so in an effort to reverse the apparent march of left-wing progressive forces in the Arab world. From this time onwards the revolt was to be increasingly politicized: the rebels were backed by the radical Arab states as well as the Communist powers; Oman, increasingly, could depend on support from conservative forces in the region. Meanwhile, a new movement – the Popular Front for the Liberation of the Occupied Arab Gulf (PFLOAG) – appeared on the scene; it was Marxist and operated from South Yemen. By 1968 it had taken control of the rebellion. Broadly, as long as PFLOAG confined its operations to Dhofar it achieved substantial success, for its guerrillas were fighting on home ground and had short lines of communication into South Yemen, which was the source of their supplies. They were – for a time – more than able to match the Sultan's forces.

The coup of 1970

The rebellion increased pressures for change in Oman and was a contributory cause of the coup of 1970 since it was apparent that no kind of modernization would be carried out as long as Sultan Said continued to rule. A palace coup of 23 July 1970 deposed the Sultan in favour of his Sandhurst-trained son, Qabus. Britain was undoubtedly aware of the coming coup since all the Sultan's officers were British; at the very least it had foreknowledge and did nothing to stop it.

The new Sultan at once inaugurated a programme of economic and social reforms and began to bring Oman out of its isolation (Muscat was dropped from the title of the country, which now became the Sultanate of Oman). Qabus lifted most of the restrictions whereby his father had controlled the country, and about 10,000 Omanis working in the Gulf returned home. Despite opposition from the

PDRY, the Sultan obtained membership of the UN for Oman in 1971. However, these immediate liberalizing actions of the new Sultan did not end the rebellion, and although some of the original DLF rebels were prepared to come to terms with the new Sultan, PFLOAG was not. By then many of the rebels had moved leftwards to become radicalized and Marxist rather than simply nationalist, and they claimed that the reforms were only window-dressing for a regime that would remain much the same in real terms; PFLOAG was receiving both Soviet and Chinese money through South Yemen and at the time controlled the greater part of Dhofar.

1970–1975

Despite his reforms, the new Sultan had difficulty in establishing credibility with other Arab states because of his continuing reliance on the British. In the early 1970s military sweeps against the rebels bore little fruit. The DLF submerged itself in PFLOAG in 1971, although PFLOAG's claims (in relation to the Arabian Gulf) were too wide and did not attract support. Some of the most severe fighting of the entire war took place during the last three months of 1971 when there were a total of 290 engagements, in which the SAF lost 136 dead and the guerrillas 31. In May 1972 the Omani forces were at last able to mount a campaign against the area bordering the PDRY in an effort to cut rebel communications with their external base. This year (1972) saw the peak of PFLOAG activity. The guerrillas numbered no more than 800, backed by perhaps 1000 militia, but they were well-armed and had Soviet and Cuban advisers. However, when PFLOAG attempted to widen the war to north Oman (1970, 1972 and 1974) it was unsuccessful.

Unable to raise the support he needed from Arab states, the Sultan turned to the Shah of Iran, who sent a force of several thousand men to Oman in December 1973; they first went into action on 20 December in a substantial campaign in which they suffered 200 dead and achieved little. Both the Iranians and the SAF were pinned down by the rebels at the end of the year. This Iranian intervention spurred the Arab League to attempt mediation between Oman and South Yemen, partly in order to have the Iranians withdrawn from Oman. The rebels dropped the more pretentious title of PFLOAG and called themselves instead the Popular Front for the Liberation of Oman (PFLO); none the less, it was controlled by the People's Revolutionary Movement (PRM) from South Yemen and its Marxist-Leninist ideology made it anathema to the more conservative half of the Arab world, especially Saudi Arabia.

The war continued into 1975, by which time the rebels had acquired sophisticated weaponry including Soviet Sam-7 missiles, but a major government offensive at the end of that year largely destroyed the power of the insurgents, who were driven out of Dhofar into the PDRY. The eventual success of the Sultan's forces owed much to the British training in counter-insurgency as well as the presence of the Iranians. From 1976 onwards the insurgency was largely at an end, although rebel activity flared up from time to time.

The external factor

For a small-scale rebellion in an undeveloped country that by any standards was a political backwater, Oman received astonishing international attention. The British provided the core backbone to the SAF and throughout acted towards Oman as though it were a client state, if not a colony, becoming all the more tenacious in this regard once oil had been discovered. It was British counter-insurgency training for the army that in the end assured the Sultan of success. Jordan offered the Sultan some aid, but it was hard-pressed with its own problems at the time and the extent of its assistance was strictly limited. Much more significant was the intervention of the Shah of Iran, then at the height of his power and petro-dollar influence; his intervention was regarded with misgivings even by the most conservative Arab states, which deeply resented Iranian involvement in Arab affairs. The Shah at that time was pursuing a policy designed to make Iran the dominant power in the Gulf. The conservative Arab states, however, were deeply fearful of a Marxist regime coming to power in Oman and so were prepared to tolerate Iranian intervention.

The rebels obtained their support from the radical Arab states such as Iraq and Libya (apart from the PDRY after 1967), and also received arms and money from the USSR, China and Cuba. From 1973 the PFLOAG/PFLO maintained offices in Libya.

Estimated costs and casualties

In 1969 the Sultan of Oman's Air Force (SOAF) had 12 BAC-167 Strikemasters for use against the liberated areas; later in the 1970s, SOAF obtained 12 British Hawker Hunters, 9 Skyvan short-take-off transports and 12 helicopters, and spent a considerable proportion of its total oil revenues on military hardware. Both Australian and Rhodesian pilots flew for SOAF; Pakistan sent officers and NCOs for the army; India trained the Omani navy; Iran sent substantial military forces (several thousand troops) and worked closely with the British in a kind of dual imperial partnership; and Saudi Arabia – after initial hesitations – provided financial aid. The guerrillas relied on Soviet weapons and were largely trained by Soviet and Cuban advisers. The costs of the war for Oman were met from its considerable oil revenues, which had reached £400 million per annum by the early 1970s. Casualties on both sides ran into several thousands. The British were reluctant to give any figures with regard to British personnel serving in Oman.

Results: immediate and longer term

The main Dhofar rebellion came to an end with the campaign of 1975. In any case, by then the less doctrinaire of the rebels were beginning to defect after the reforms of the new Sultan, since these removed the original cause of their rebellion. The coup of 1970 was certainly regarded with favour by international (British) capital since only with the removal of the ultra-conservative Sultan Said, who was opposed to any development, could it reap the new and rich development contracts flowing from oil wealth. Following its defeat, the PFLO was afflicted by internal disputes and began to fall apart, although it continued to exist into the early 1980s

On a wider front Oman was supported by the 'status quo' states of the region, which included Pakistan, Iran, Saudi Arabia, India, the UAE and Jordan as well as Britain as the major outside power with long-standing historical interests in Oman. .

Saudi Arabia was responsible for arranging a ceasefire between Oman and the PDRY in 1976, and the Sultan then announced an amnesty for Omanis who had been fighting for the PFLO. Thereafter, periodic flare-ups occurred but many of the former rebels returned to their homes. In January 1977 Iran withdrew the bulk of its forces from Oman, although a small contingent was to remain until the Iranian revolution of 1979 when these were also withdrawn. There was some renewed fighting in June 1978 when a number of British engineers were attacked in the Salalah region, but by 1978–9 the PFLO had become an external force based in the PDRY, and although it still claimed to receive support from Cuba, it failed to recruit new members inside Oman.

In January 1981 a renewed PFLO threat caused Oman to close the border with the PDRY and request increased British military assistance. By October of that year, following mediation by Kuwait and the UAE, relations between Oman and the PDRY were normalized once more. In 1981 Oman became a founder member of the Gulf Co-operation Council (GCC), whose *raison d'être* was collective defence of the smaller Gulf states; it also continued its close relations – military and economic – with Britain.

Given the relative unimportance of Oman, its rebellion had attracted massive international attention and participation.

SYRIA: CONTROLLING THE MUSLIM BROTHERHOOD

Introduction

Although there is nothing new about violent opposition to governments, it is not always easy to decide just when such opposition becomes more than a civil disturbance and develops into a civil war. The uprising at Hama in 1982 is a case in point. A growing quarrel between the fundamentalist Muslim Brotherhood and the government of President Hafez al-Assad developed through the 1970s. President Assad of the left-wing Baath Party came to power in 1970, and both the President himself and other leading members of his government were drawn from the minority Alawite sect, once regarded as heretic but relatively strong in Syria (they come second in numbers to the Sunni Muslims, who make up 75 per cent of the Muslim population). Apart from being an Alawite, Assad pursued a number of left-wing policies, which included developing and maintaining close relations with the USSR, that were anathema to the Muslim Brotherhood. Assad was re-elected by plebiscite in 1978.

During the 1970s the main opposition to Assad came from two groups: Islamic fundamentalists, of whom the members of the Muslim Brotherhood were the most important and dangerous; and excluded factions of the Baath Party, some of whom received support from Iraq (with whom Syria was carrying on a bitter feud, mainly a question of rivalry for leadership in the Arab world). President Saddam Hussein of Iraq provided support for the National Front for the Liberation of Arab Syria.

The Muslim Brotherhood became increasingly important as an opposition group through the 1970s and was prepared to resort to terrorist tactics to make its influence felt. Although the same as the Brotherhood in Egypt, the Syrian branch was autonomous and had its main centres of activity in Hama and Aleppo. It had no official leadership – or membership – so the government has always had difficulty in pinning it down. During the 1970s and especially towards the end of the decade the Muslim Brotherhood conducted terrorist campaigns – bombings and assassinations – which were primarily directed against members of the Alawite sect. Since the sect was closely connected with the Assad leadership, such activities tended to undermine confidence in the government. In June 1979 a major attack was launched against the Aleppo artillery school and some 60 cadets were massacred, of whom 32 were Alawites. The Muslim Brotherhood was blamed for the attack and widespread arrests followed. The Brotherhood was also blamed for later killings. The Baath government now felt obliged to increase security measures against Sunni extremists. When the Gulf War began in September 1980 Syria supported Iran against its long-standing rival Iraq, but by doing so emphasized the extent of its isolation in the Arab world, which rallied to the support of a fellow Arab state.

The early 1980s

Syria was subject to many tensions during the first part of the 1980s: internal opposition to the government was reinforced by the high costs of intervention in Lebanon (see Part IV, pp. 317–321). During 1980 Syria's relations with most of its neighbours deteriorated, while there was continuing violence at home. In March violent incidents took place at both Aleppo and Hama (the centres of the Muslim Brotherhood), and a number of people known to be friendly to the government were assassinated. It was assumed that the Brotherhood was responsible. President Assad attempted to contain the growing threat of the Muslim Brotherhood when on 9 July he made it a capital offence to belong to it.

During the second half of the year the security forces tried to find and arrest members of the Brotherhood, but it is not clear how many activists were apprehended and how many went underground. At the same time the government accused outside powers – the USA, Iraq and Jordan – of plotting violence against it. Indeed the accusation that Jordan was harbouring Muslim Brotherhood plotters against Syria brought the two countries to the brink of war; in December Syria moved three divisions (approximately 30,000 men) to the Jordanian border, and the crisis was only defused following mediation by Saudi Arabia.

Civil violence directed against the government continued through 1980 and into 1981, and although the government organized militias of workers, peasants and students in its support, this had no noticeable effect. Acts of terrorism included an explosion in the office of the Prime Minister (17 August) which killed three people, and a huge car bomb explosion in Damascus (29 November) which killed 90 people; these were blamed on the Muslim Brotherhood. At the same time Syria was being drawn more deeply into the civil war in Lebanon (see above, pp. 439–445) as well as facing the possibility of an Israeli intervention in Lebanon, which duly took place during 1982. One way and another the possibility of a civil war was not far beneath the surface.

The 1982 uprising in Hama

The climax to this developing quarrel between the government and the right-wing fundamentalists of the Muslim Brotherhood came in February 1982. On 11 February government forces began a determined drive against militant members of the Brotherhood in Hama. Heavy fighting lasted for nearly three weeks, during which time the centre of the city was destroyed. Estimates of casualties place the dead between 3000 and 10,000. On 24 February President Assad claimed that the uprising had been defeated; the government also accused Iraq of having supplied the insurgents with arms. Although the Brotherhood was clearly at the centre of the uprising, other groups were also believed to have been involved.

On 20 February an opposition group which called itself the National Alliance of the Syrian People was formed: it included Baathists, Nasserites, Christians and Alawites as well as members of the Muslim Brotherhood. The government position remained difficult for the rest of the year; it was not made any easier in April when Syria closed its border with Iraq, including the oil pipeline, and entered into an oil agreement with Iran.

Conclusion

Although the government had dealt the Muslim Brotherhood a major blow when it put down the Hama uprising, it did not destroy the opposition. None the less, 1983 was a relatively quiet year. In December it became known that President Assad, the country's strongman, was suffering from a heart condition, and he continued a sick man into 1984. His partial absence from affairs of government produced a crisis at the end of February 1984 when tanks and troops appeared on the streets of Damascus as rival military commanders stood by (in case Assad died), but the crisis was defused when the President reasserted his personal authority.

Under Assad, at least for the time being, the Brotherhood's ambitions appeared to have been brought under control.

TURKEY: POLITICAL TERRORISM

Background

The military intervened in Turkish politics twice during the 1970s and 1980s: first in 1971–3 and again in 1980. On each occasion the civil government appeared unable to control radical political groups of both right and left.

The father-figure of modern Turkey, Kemal Atatürk, died in 1938 on the eve of the Second World War; his great achievement had been to bring Turkey into the modern world and make it a secular state, but it was not a democratic state. Turkey stayed out of the war until 1945, when it joined the Allies. There followed a general liberalization of political life, and the principal party to emerge was the Democratic Party, which won a massive election victory in 1950. The Democrats stayed in power from 1950 to 1960, but over the decade the economic situation became steadily worse and the government progressively more authoritarian and repressive. In 1960, when the Democratic Party was about to deprive the Republic People's Party (the main opposition) of its political rights, the army mounted a coup. However, the army did not stay in power for long, but produced a new constitution in 1961 and then returned the country to civilian rule. This lasted through the 1960s, but by the end of the decade there was mounting and increasingly violent opposition from the radical left. In 1971 the army called on the government to resign.

The crisis of 1971–1973

The Turkish People's Liberation Army (TPLA) was a left-wing group with revolutionary objectives; its leader was a young student activist, Deniz Gezmis. In 1971 the TPLA abducted four US servicemen from NATO bases, and it was this incident which led the military to intervene. The army imposed martial law and arrested Gezmis and 17 other TPLA leaders; Gezmis was executed in 1972. The military did not actually dismiss the civil government, but allowed it to function under military tutelage until 1973 when martial law was withdrawn and the military returned to barracks. The troubles soon erupted again, however, and during 1974 there were an increasing number of violent incidents between left-wing and right-wing groups at the universities, as well as clashes in eastern Turkey between the military and guerrilla groups.

The later 1970s: developing violence

At the end of the 1970s extremists from both left and right were killing each other at the rate of 1000 a year. On the political left were the Turkish Workers' Party, which had been represented in the Assembly since 1965, and the Revolutionary Youth Federation, which provided a basis for recruitment to the TPLA. Another left-wing group was the Turkish People's Liberation Front (TPLF), which appealed to its mainly young members to overthrow democracy in favour of a Marxist-Leninist state. This was active through the 1970s but came to an end with the military coup of 1980. On the right, Islamic fundamentalists and anti-Marxist groups were represented by the National Salvation Party and the Nationalist Action Party. The 1979 revolution in Iran brought greater immediate, if temporary, freedom to that country's Kurds, and this had an impact on the 8 million Kurds in eastern Turkey (see Part I, pp. 73–81).

Following a political amnesty in 1974, the TPLA re-emerged to become active once more in far-left circles, especially among students in Ankara and Istanbul; by 1976 its militants were clashing with the military. It now became apparent that

TPLA members had received training abroad in Communist countries from which they were also obtaining arms, and from 1976 onwards the TPLA attacked police stations, banks, right-wing newspaper offices and the offices of right-wing political parties. During 1977 260 people were killed in political incidents and the police arrested 50 members of the TPLA.

Major communal clashes between rival Muslim groups took place in Kahraman-maras in December 1978 when Sunni fundamentalists attacked Alevi (Shia) Muslims: 100 were killed and many more injured, leading the government to impose martial law in the region. These disturbances were one more element that helped persuade the military to take control in 1980. In 1978 and 1979 the TPLA provoked an increasing number of violent incidents in which some 2000 people were killed; they carried out political assassinations and attacks on US military (NATO) personnel. In the main the TPLA were middle-class intellectuals who were anti-American and pro-Marxist; women played an equal part with men in their organization.

By April 1979 the coalition government of Bulent Ecevit began to fall apart on the issue of how to tackle the escalating terrorism. The threat of violence led the government to impose daytime curfews on May Day to prevent parades or demonstrations in Ankara and Istanbul getting out of hand. In October 1979 Suleyman Demirel formed a rightist government and promised to take action against the terrorists. But no improvement in the situation followed, and on 2 January 1980 army generals issued a warning to all political parties to achieve a consensus.

The military crackdown 1980–1982

By 1980 the steady rate of political killings had become sufficiently high to justify fears that Turkey was on the verge of civil war and that national unity was threatened. By August 2000 people had been killed and there was no sign that the government was able to control the situation. On 11 September 1980 the army intervened in a bloodless coup and General Kenan Evren became head of state. The army argued in justification that there was political chaos, an ineffective police force and a resurgence of sectarian (religious) violence. The country was placed under martial law, the Assembly was dissolved, political parties and trade unions were banned and the constitution was suspended. Thousands of dissidents were then rounded up and detained.

The military none the less appointed a largely civilian government whose first tasks were to eradicate terrorism, reduce the power of political extremists and then return the country to civilian rule. By February 1981 the military claimed to have eliminated the main left-wing terrorist groups; certainly their effectiveness had been greatly reduced – at least for the time being. During the year following the military takeover (1980–1) only 282 political killings took place; at the same time the army seized large quantities of arms. By May 1982 the army had officially detained 43,000 people suspected of extremist political activism, although unofficial figures suggested that as many as 100,000 had been detained. It was plain in 1982 that the government and the military had control of the situation and were close to eliminating the violence, but there was a high price to pay in mass arrests and trials and the loss of civil liberties. By 1 September 1982 18,000 of those originally detained were still in prison awaiting trial, while 6500 had already been sentenced to prison terms. However, the suppression of terrorism at home did not apply to Turks overseas, where 1982 saw a growth of terrorist acts by Armenian dissidents against Turkish government people working abroad, principally diplomats.

A draft constitution published by the military government in 1982 received wide national support, and the following year the military National Security Council transferred its powers back to an elected Parliament.

Estimated costs and casualties

By the time the military had stamped out terrorist activity about 6000 people are thought to have been killed over the period 1977–80.

Results

A return to democracy, at first under military guidance, took place in the years 1982–5. In the elections of November 1983 which restored parliamentary rule Turgut Özal's Motherland Party won 211 of 400 seats, beating the right- and left-wing parties approved by the military. His victory was seen by most of Turkey as a conscious rejection of military rule. By July 1985 martial law had been reduced and was then only operating in 17 of Turkey's 67 provinces and those mainly affected by Kurdish dissidence.

Apart from the 6000 deaths and the general disruption to public life, this near- or pre-civil war situation cost Turkey a great deal in credibility, and its image suffered in the West because of the mass arrests and detentions and the widespread use of torture against prisoners. This bad image came, moreover, at a time when Turkey was campaigning for membership of the European Economic Community. On the credit side, the military intervention of 1980–2 helped to strengthen democratic trends in Turkey, for, as the people demonstrated in their support for Özal's Motherland Party in 1983, they decisively rejected the idea of military government.

NORTH YEMEN: CIVIL WAR 1962–1970

Background

Until the beginning of the 1960s North Yemen had remained one of the least visited or known countries in the world. Like Oman on the other southern extremity of the Arabian peninsula, it remained entirely backward in any sense of modern or progressive development. The Imam Ahmad had succeeded the Imam Yahya in 1948 and, like his predecessor, continued to rule North Yemen autocratically. During the 1950s he quarrelled with Britain over the future of his neighbour to the south, Aden colony and protectorate, to which he laid claim (see Part I, pp. 84–89), and he aligned himself with Egypt and Saudi Arabia in opposing the Baghdad Pact, although for nationalist rather than left-wing political reasons.

Yemeni opposition to the Imam came from two sources: progressive reformers who wished to move the country into the twentieth century; and conservative traditionalists from the different tribes who objected to the concentration of power in the hands of the one Hamideddin family. In 1961, when Syria quarrelled with Egypt and abandoned the Nasser-dominated United Arab Republic (UAR) which North Yemen had also joined, the Imam showed his pleasure by publicly attacking Nasser's policies over the radio. As a result, in December 1961 Cairo Radio opened a strong campaign against the Imam. Opposition to the Imam became increasingly open and violent in 1962, but he died on 18 September of that year while still in power. His son, the Crown Prince Mohammed al-Badr, succeeded to the Imamate and at once pronounced a general amnesty. At that time the progressive elements who wanted to bring about social change were to be found in the towns.

Outbreak and response

On 26 September, only eight days after al-Badr had come to power, Brigadier Abdullah al-Sallal, whom the Imam had trusted and appointed to command the Royal Guards, seized control of Sana and declared a republic. But though Sallal obtained immediate control over Sana and the other main towns and principal roads, he failed to capture the Imam, who escaped to the northern mountains where he rallied the tribes to his cause to launch a counter-revolution. Sallal formed a Revolutionary Command Council and announced the creation of a Yemeni Arab Republic which was immediately recognized by Egypt, Syria, Iraq and the Soviet bloc countries. Further, once it was clear that the deposed Imam would fight to regain his throne, Egypt was quick to send military aid in support of the new government. Saudi Arabia and Jordan, on the other hand, supported the deposed Imam, and a costly and bloody conflict soon got under way. Prince Hassan, the deposed Imam's uncle who had represented Yemen in New York City at the UN, now returned to assist the royalist cause. Sallal found that he was ill-equipped to fight the hill peoples and so appealed to Egypt for aid. Within three days of the coup Egyptian troops and equipment were being despatched to Yemen down the Red Sea.

Saudi Arabia and Egypt were to prove crucial to the developing civil war. The Saudis believed that the new republic would collapse without Egyptian aid; they also saw a progressive Yemeni republic as a threat to the interests of the Saudi royal family, and this fear was to be increased when Sallal spoke of his desire to create a Republic of the Arabian Peninsula.

During October 1962 the royalists launched their first offensive, capturing the towns of Marib, Harib, Sarwah and some others. In December 1962 the USA recognized the new republic and, following Washington's lead, some 50 other countries also recognized the North Yemen Republic, which then took its seat at the UN. Britain did not recognize the new regime. In March 1963 the republicans with their Egyptian allies counter-attacked, recapturing Marib and Harib.

It was apparent from the beginning of Sallal's coup, however, that he was dependent on the army and, still more, on the Egyptians if he was to stay in power. The civil war was to last for nearly eight years and had its greatest impact (in fighting) on the northern and eastern parts of the country.

Course of the struggle

Depending on how successful the royalists were, so the Egyptians – then determined to keep for themselves the radical leadership of the Arab world – increased their commitment to maintain the new republic. By 1964 Egypt had about 40,000 troops in Yemen. Their presence worked in two quite different ways: on the one hand, they ensured that the republicans held on to the towns and main lines of communications; but on the other, they fuelled anti-Egyptian nationalism among the Zaidi tribes, causing waverers to join the royalist cause. During 1963 both the UN and the USA attempted to mediate between Egypt and Saudi Arabia (the two principal backers of the war), but to no avail. On 30 April 1963 the UN did manage to persuade Saudi Arabia to cut off all aid to the royalists and Egypt to promise to withdraw its troops, and a 200-man UN observer team was sent to the country in June to see that these agreements were kept. Its task proved impossible, however – neither side abided by the agreement – and the observers were withdrawn in September. Other attempts at mediation fared no better. Meanwhile, a major rebellion against the British began in neighbouring Aden colony in 1963 (see Part I, pp. 84–89), and this further complicated the regional prospects for an early settlement.

In the spring of 1964 the royalists launched another offensive, regaining most of the towns they had lost in 1963; this, however, was answered by a fresh republican–Egyptian offensive in the summer, which led to the capture of a number of royalist strongholds, but not the headquarters of al-Badr. The war was to swing back and forth for several years, and although the Egyptians enjoyed superiority of numbers and modern equipment, they had little experience of fighting a guerrilla-style war in mountainous country, while lack of roads made it difficult to supply their forward troops. The royalists were helped by foreign mercenary officers from Britain and France as well as assistance (with British connivance) across the border from Beihan state in the Aden protectorate. The Egyptians, moreover, faced great difficulty in creating or trying to create an efficient army from the urban Yemenis with whom they had to work. Nor was Egypt able to buy over the opposing tribes, for in the matter of money Egypt could always be outbid by Saudi Arabia.

The self-esteem of the new Yemeni Republic was not helped by its overt dependence on Egypt. In April 1964, none the less, President Nasser visited Yemen. Then, on 28 April, the republicans published a new constitution: Sallal was President, but two other posts of Prime Minister and President of a Consultative Council were also created. A new peace attempt was made in October 1964 when representatives of the two warring sides met at Erkowit in Sudan with Egyptian and Saudi observers present; a ceasefire was agreed for 8 November and proclaimed throughout Yemen. A National Congress had been proposed and was to meet on 23 November, but neither side could agree on its composition and in the meantime the ceasefire broke down.

In December 1964 Sallal faced a political crisis in his own ranks when the President of the Consultative Council (Ahmad Naaman) and two Deputy Prime

Ministers resigned. They did so for two basic reasons: they resented Zaidi domination of government when the Shafis represented 60 per cent of the population; and they regarded Sallal as an Egyptian puppet. Naaman and his supporters wanted to find a compromise between the two sides and to do so without the interference of the Egyptians. Those willing to compromise in this way became known as the Third Force.

On 1 April 1965 the leader of the Third Force, Mohammed Zubairi, was assassinated, though it was not clear by whom. The result, however, was to boost the Third Force, and in order to contain it Sallal appointed Naaman his Prime Minister on 18 April. Naaman's subsequent attempts to come to terms with the royalists were not supported by Sallal or the other republican hardliners, and he resigned at the end of June 1965. Sallal then took over the premiership himself and became more hardline in his policies, until pressure from Egypt forced him to take more moderate elements into his government. During these changes a number of republican supporters defected to the royalists, who were able to mount a successful military campaign that summer.

Indeed in 1965 the royalists appeared to be winning the war, so Sallal and the Egyptians agreed to meet with the Saudis at Jeddah for the so-called Jeddah Agreement, whereby there would be a ceasefire followed by the formation of a provisional government drawn from both republicans and royalists and, a year later, by a national plebiscite. By that time all Egyptian troops would have been withdrawn from the country. In fact the Jeddah Agreement was a charade used by Nasser to obtain a breathing space while he reorganized, for he wanted to withdraw his troops from the north of the country, where they were suffering very high casualties, and regroup them in the towns. Neither side trusted the other at Jeddah.

During a visit to Iran in 1966 King Faisal of Saudi Arabia proposed a grouping of Islamic nations, which was regarded in Cairo as an attempt to undermine Nasser. In February 1966 Britain announced that it was to withdraw all its forces from southern Arabia (Aden) by independence, an announcement that appeared to play into Egypt's hands. Yet no accommodation between royalists and republicans was achieved, and renewed royalist military campaigns persuaded the Egyptians to withdraw their forces to the towns. Sallal had become extremely unpopular by this time, and the Egyptians detained him in Egypt for the best part of a year. In the summer of 1966, however, when an anti-Egyptian coup appeared likely in Sana, the Egyptians allowed Sallal to return and regain control. At this time Yemen was effectively divided between a republic based on the towns, which were controlled by the army and the Egyptians, and the other two-thirds of the country controlled by the royalists. The turning point came in 1967 with the June war between Israel and its Arab neighbours.

The search for peace 1967–1970

By 1967 it had become clear that the divisions in the country were not so much those between royalists and republicans as between those who wanted a country free of foreign influence (the conservative nationalists) and the more progressive ones. The Six Day War between Israel and its neighbours (see Part IV, pp. 296–301) transformed the situation throughout the Middle East, not least by undermining Nasser's dominant position. He was so weakened, in fact, that he felt obliged to cut his losses and withdraw from Yemen altogether. He agreed to do so at the Arab Khartoum Summit (29 August–1 September) in return for major financial aid from Saudi Arabia.

On 5 November 1967 the military in Sana carried out a coup and overthrew the republican government of Sallal. His more conservative successors under Qadi Irani hoped to work out a compromise with the royalists, but their initiative was destroyed when the royalists mounted a new military offensive and almost succeeded in taking Sana. The republicans then rallied, with the result that the war continued. Egyptian aid to the republicans was now replaced by aid from the USSR and Syria as well as from the newly independent South Yemen; Saudi Arabia, therefore, renewed its aid to the royalists to balance the flow from Communist and left-wing sources.

By the end of the year all the Egyptian troops had been withdrawn, as also had the British troops from neighbouring Aden, which became independent as the People's Democratic Republic of Yemen at the end of November 1967. Thus the military situation in the two Yemens had been transformed. By May 1968 there were divisions in the ranks of both the republicans and the royalists, and by August fighting had broken out between rival republican factions, although this was successfully brought to an end during September by the Commander-in-Chief, General Amri, when he formed a new government containing seven Shafis and nine Zaidis.

During 1969–70 the Saudis cut off further aid to the royalists in order to make them come to terms with the republicans; however, King Faisal would not recognize the government of North Yemen until it was more representative of all the people. In March 1969 the Republican Council resigned to make way for a new National Council that was to select a President and Premier. A National Assembly was formed with 57 seats, of which 12 were left vacant to accommodate the government of Democratic Yemen, and from this point onwards the idea of unity between the two Yemens became an increasingly important political factor for both. Although there was a renewal of fighting in January 1970 and the town of Sadaa fell to the royalists in February, the royalists finally came to terms with the republicans in May: North Yemen was to remain a republic, but royalists were admitted to the government.

Estimated costs and casualties

The war was immensely costly to Egypt, which in any case faced major problems elsewhere. Egyptian casualties came to 15,195 dead between October 1962 when it first became involved and June 1964. It suffered several thousand further casualties in the period from 1964 until its withdrawal in 1967. During the years 1962 to 1965 the war cost between $500,000 and $1 million a day, and most of that was also borne by Egypt. Altogether casualties on both sides came to perhaps 25,000 or 30,000. Saudi Arabia subsidized the royalists for most of the war.

Results: immediate and longer term

The war came to an end in 1970 when moderates on both sides were reconciled and the royalists agreed to join a republican government; thus the war brought an end to the Imamate. On 23 May 1970 a group of royalists led by the former minister, Ahmad al-Shami, arrived in Sana to negotiate a peace, and al-Shami was made the fourth member of the four-man Republican Council. In July North Yemen was recognized by Saudi Arabia, to be followed by Britain, France and Iran. The result, after nearly a decade of fighting, was the emergence of a moderate pro-Western republic.

In March 1971 elections were held for the Consultative Council as provided for in the 1970 constitution. There was fighting in 1972 with South Yemen until a ceasefire in October. This led on to an agreement that the two states would work towards unity, but although the sentiment for unity existed, huge political differences made an early agreement unlikely. In February 1977 the heads of state of the two Yemens met at Qaataba near their joint borders and agreed to establish a joint council which would meet every six months, alternately in Sana and Aden. Later in 1977 the northern tribes rebelled, and on 11 October Colonel al-Hamdi (head of state) was assassinated; his successor, Major Ahmed ibn Husayn al-Ghashmi, survived a rebellion in May 1978 but was later assassinated. Colonel Ali Abd Allah Salih became President on 17 July and set about conciliating the various internal factions, while also trying to balance the influence of the USA, the USSR and Saudi Arabia. There was another border war with South Yemen in 1979–80 (see Part III, pp. 241–245), which once more set back the possibility of union. Yet the idea did not die and indeed became a reality in 1990.

SOUTH YEMEN: THE PDRY – LEFT AGAINST LEFT

Background

After the bitter war of liberation against Britain (see Part I, pp. 84–89) a highly radicalized South Yemen simply contained too many political factions to be able to enjoy a post-independence period of constructive development. South Yemen became independent in 1967 when anti-Western nationalism was sweeping the Arab world, to be reinforced that year by the spectacular victory of Israel over its Arab neighbours in the Six Day War; when two of South Yemen's three neighbours (North Yemen and Oman) were engaged in civil wars in which South Yemen found it difficult not to engage; and when its left-wing Marxist leanings attracted enthusiastic backing from the USSR, which was only too anxious to find an ideological ally in the Arab world. In such circumstances it is not surprising that South Yemen faced a number of civil upheavals in the years following independence, either as a result of entanglements with North Yemen or arising out of the ideological differences and divisions that were already present in the ranks of the ideologues in its left-wing National Liberation Front (NLF).

1968: a year of two rebellions

Conflict broke out within months of independence between the Aden-based leadership of President Qahtan al-Shaabi (moderate left wing, but also becoming increasingly pragmatic) and the ranks of the National Liberation Front (NLF) based on the eastern interior of the country (the Hadramaut). Qahtan had established close ties with the colonial-trained army on which his power now rested and was opposed to the grassroots socialism which hard-left cadres of the NLF wished to implement in the Hadramaut: they, for example, wanted to establish popular committees in all the villages. A clash seemed inevitable, especially as Qahtan was becoming increasingly autocratic. It came in March 1968 when the NLF held its Fourth Congress, at which members came out in overwhelming support for the hard left and instructed the government to put through radical measures. On 19 March, following the Congress, a mass meeting of NLF cadres was held in Aden; the army – or sections of it loyal to Qahtan, whose more pragmatic policies were seen to have been pushed aside – now played a part by first breaking up the mass meeting and then (20 March) arresting a number of the leading NLF cadres, while also bringing about the dismissal of several of the more left-wing ministers. It was a straight conflict between hard left and centre left.

President Qahtan soon discovered that he was unable to allow the army to have its way, for demonstrations on behalf of the arrested NLF leaders broke out in Aden, Jaar, Yafra and the Hadramaut. Qahtan felt obliged to order the release of the imprisoned cadres and instead ordered the arrest of the army conspirators. In an attempt to pacify the opposition he also rushed through a land reform act. The arrests had caused disarray in the ranks of the left, but one left-wing group decided to launch a second guerrilla war in order to weaken the government's hold on the lower ranks of the army before it could become an instrument of oppression. It also aimed to stage a series of simultaneous uprisings.

In the eastern interior (the Hadramaut) the radicals set up popular councils, which operated separately from government-appointed officials and ousted members of the police and armed forces. In Mukalla they seized petroleum installations. On 14–15 May rebellions erupted in the towns of Jaar, Abyan and Shuqra, although a planned uprising in Aden did not materialize. The army, remained loyal to the government, and in June it counter-attacked and re-occupied Jaar and Abyan as well as making its presence effective in the Hadramaut once more. Many of the rebels were killed and others fled into North Yemen.

Having dealt with a revolt from the left, Qahtan now found that he faced another from the right: former leaders of the Federal Party who had fled to North Yemen before independence (some had been sentenced to death in their absence) returned in mid-1968 with backing from Saudi Arabia and North Yemen, where they had bases from which they could launch attacks on South Yemen. One clash had already taken place in February when the former ruler of Beihan had raided across the border from Saudi Arabia. In June these attacks from the right were stepped up, with further revolts encouraged in the Hadramaut. The town of Said was occupied by the rebels, while another revolt took pace in Radfan with backing from North Yemen.

These ex-nationalists who had lost to the left in the independence struggle had formed two organizations in exile: the Front for the Liberation of South Yemen (FLOSY) and the South Arabian League (SAL). At the end of July members of both movements invaded South Yemen from across the northern borders, cutting the road in Radfan and Aulaqi. On 2 August the commander of the PDRY security forces, Colonel Abdullah Salih Sabah al-Aulaqi, defected to North Yemen with 200 of his men and armoured cars. However, these dual uprisings (by FLOSY and SAL) were quickly put down by NLF forces, which (ironically, in the light of the earlier uprising) were joined by hard-left NLF partisans. By mid-August government forces had recaptured Said and the revolt was over. The government claimed that 109 rebels had been killed and 68 captured. There were to be further small revolts in October and November, but the government emerged stronger as a result of its successful reaction to the rebellion. In June of the following year, however, Qahtan was forced to resign in favour of a five-man Presidential Council.

Civil war and border war 1979

South Yemen helped to form North Yemen's National Democratic Front of dissidents, who had opposed its various governments during the 1970s. On 24 June 1978 the President of North Yemen, Major al-Ghashmi, was assassinated on the orders of or, by implication, with the knowledge of the President of South Yemen. Whatever the true explanation, it was enough to produce an explosion in South Yemen two days after Ghashmi's death, when forces of the far left overthrew the government of President Salim Ali Rubayyi, who was then executed. Rubayyi was a moderate Marxist and at the time of his death had been working on plans for a merger of the two Yemens. Heavy fighting now took place between troops loyal to the toppled President and ruling party militias. By this time the PDRY had moved further to the left and was very much part of the Soviet camp (it had been used as a staging post for the massive shipment of military equipment to Ethiopia in 1977 and 1978 during the Ogaden war (see Part III, pp. 190–198).

South Yemen became even more isolated in the Arab world as a result of the death of Rubayyi. There was an escalation of hostilities between the two Yemens, and on 24 February 1979 troops on both sides of their joint border fired on one another. Troops from North Yemen crossed the border to attack a number of South Yemini villages; South Yemen (now enjoying Soviet, Cuban and East German support) retaliated by invading North Yemen. This invasion led Saudi Arabia to call on the League of Arab States to take action; meanwhile, both Saudi Arabia and the USA rushed arms to North Yemen and a US task force was despatched to the Red Sea. At the same time fierce fighting took place in South Yemen between government forces and rebels of the United Front for Southern Yemen. There were also clashes between followers of the Prime Minister, Muhammed, and the President, Ismail. Rebels seized the airport at Beihan.

A ceasefire between North and South Yemen was finally achieved on 19 March 1979 (after several false starts), and both sides withdrew their forces from the border while a multinational Arab League patrol was established to keep the peace. Once more the two Yemens discussed the possibility of a merger. In October 1979, however, South Yemen entered into a 20-year treaty of friendship with the USSR under the terms of which Soviets would be able to station up to 18,000 troops in South Yemen; the treaty had the effect of maintaining and increasing the PDRY's isolation in the Arab world.

A bloody coup 1986

In 1985 President Ali Nasir Mohammed Husain was re-elected for another five-year term as Secretary-General of the ruling Yemeni Socialist Party (YSP). However, his position was not as strong as it appeared, for the new politburo also contained a number of his critics including Ismail, whom he had replaced as President in 1980. On 13 January 1986 there took place one of the most brutal and bloody coups that had ever been seen in the Arab world, and President Mohammed Husain was overthrown (although he escaped abroad). The coup rapidly turned into a civil war, fighting was so intense that casualties (dead) reached 10,000, while a further 12,000 became refugees, ending up in camps across the border in North Yemen. Damage to property during the fighting came to an estimated $140 million. The fighting was basically between Ali Nasir Mohammed's majority section of the party and opposing tribal elements; the latter won once they had gained the backing of the army. It was, in part, yet another bout of the fierce rivalry between members of the party in Aden and the more doctrinaire socialists of the Hadramaut. On 24 January the former Prime Minister, Haidar Aba Bakr al-Attas, was appointed interim President; the following October he was elected President for five years.

By August 1986 the new government, although it was as socialist as that which it had ousted, was fearful of the growing popularity of Mohammed in exile and had embarked on a series of arrests and executions, while demanding the return of Mohammed (then in exile in Ethiopia) and 47 of his supporters for 'crimes against the country'. In an effort to seize Mohammed's supporters its planes forced a Djibouti Boeing 720 to divert course and land in Aden, causing an awkward incident between the two countries. In the meantime Moscow (which had disavowed Mohammed after the coup) tried to heal the breach between the two sides, calling on the 'comrades in the Yemeni Socialist Party' to come together. At the same time Saudi Arabia extended massive aid to South Yemen and the Presidents of the two Yemens met once more to discuss unity. The al-Attas government released 2900 political prisoners and called on former supporters of Mohammed to return home from North Yemen.

By January 1987 the enormous damage done to Aden had been repaired, much of it with assistance from the USSR, which had been deeply embarrassed that the only Arab country with a Marxist government had erupted into violence. Once the army's only tank regiment (equipped with Soviet tanks) had joined the opposition to Mohammed, he had been doomed and the Soviets had felt obliged to switch sides. In the year following the coup the number of Soviet aid personnel, technicians and military advisers in South Yemen had markedly increased. While the new regime insisted on collective leadership, major rivalries between party factions raised the probability of further violence. Yet, remarkably, the new regime held on to power for the rest of the decade without another eruption taking place.

The question of unity

During the 1970s leading personalities from both Yemens moved back and forth between the two states and there was a genuine desire for union, even if the political obstacles to it remained formidable. The periodic border disputes and the violent nature of the internal rivalries in South Yemen did not alter the aspiration for unity. By early 1990, surprisingly, it appeared that unity really had come a step closer. Like other Marxist countries round the world, South Yemen suddenly found itself isolated among Arab nations following the collapse of Communist regimes in eastern Europe. Moreover, the state of the economy had deteriorated so that South Yemen was desperate to find an economic lifeline. It has discovered substantial oil reserves and these are larger than those in North Yemen, yielding 200,000 barrels per day in the late 1980s. Because the oilfields straddle the border between the two countries, they provide another pragmatic reason for a union.

The closer the possibility of union, the bigger the question mark posed by Saudi Arabia, for although Riyadh had given its blessing to a union, the Saudis were known to have reservations about its actually taking place. Unity means a state of more than 11 million Yemenis (9 million from the north and 2.2 million from the south, with another 2 million living abroad), an elected Parliament and reasonable economic prospects based on moderate oil reserves, whereas Saudi Arabia (although immensely wealthy) probably has only 8 million people – to whom it has refused even minimal democratic advances – while its army is mainly officered by Pakistanis. This represents a dangerous mix.

Saudi fears of a potential power rival in the Arabian peninsula were visible in May 1990 when tribesmen from the north of North Yemen, supported and armed by the Saudis, began disruptive tactics even as union was due to be proclaimed at the end of the month. The Saudis were exploiting the fears of the traditionalist tribal leaders at a union with the Marxist (godless) South Yemen where 22 years of 'scientific socialism' are seen to have weakened Islam. None the less, despite Saudi fears, the Yemen Arab Republic (North) and the Democratic Republic of Yemen (South) formally became one (21 May 1990) as the Republic of Yemen, with the North Yemen President, Ali Abdallah Saleh, becoming head of the new state, with Sana as the capital and with Aden as the main commercial centre.

ASIA

THE CREATION OF BANGLADESH
Origins

For two centuries India was the most important possession of the British Empire. From 1900 onwards agitation for independence, led by the Congress Party, became increasingly vociferous. Following the Amritsar Massacre of 1919 (see below, pp. 485–491), demands for independence became more strident and were accompanied by increasing violence, while at the same time growing communal distrust between the Hindus and Muslims of British India led to a further demand by Muslim nationalists for a separate state of Pakistan.

The British division of Bengal into western and eastern parts in 1905 had already established a principal of divison, even though that particular experiment, which the Indians bitterly opposed, was brought to an end in 1912. British imperial policies, especially its economic approach, had long caused trouble and misery in Bengal, and this resentment against the British was later to become an instrument of nationalism to be used by the Muslim League against the idea of a united India.

In 1947, at the partition of India, Bengal was again divided: West Bengal became part of India and East Bengal became the eastern half of the new Muslim state of Pakistan. East Pakistan was to be the 'poor relation' to West Pakistan, where the power lay. The people of East Pakistan soon came to distrust West Pakistan, whose officials flooded into East Pakistan to take up many controlling occupations; Urdu, the language of West Pakistan, was also made the official language. A further purely practical drawback lay in the 1000 miles of Indian territory which separated east from west.

During the 1950s East Pakistan became poorer while West Pakistan did reasonably well in terms of development growth. East Pakistan earned considerable foreign exchange from its tea and jute, yet complained that most of the value was taken by West Pakistan. Further, most foreign aid, negotiated in Karachi, was channelled into West Pakistan. By the 1960s, therefore, growing discontent in the eastern half of Pakistan had become focused on these grievances: half a country separated from the dominant half by 1000 miles of India, with a different culture and language. It was a situation that could not last. Perhaps most important for the coming clash was the fact that East Pakistanis were under-represented (and underestimated) in the army. But middle-class agitation did not obtain any adequate response.

The President of the East Pakistan Awami League, Sheik Mujibur Rahman, became the focus of this discontent. A state of emergency had been declared in 1965, but early in 1969 President Ayub Khan tried to reduce the level of protest by calling a round-table conference, which included opposition groups, and ending the state of emergency. His concessions came too late, however, and on 21 February 1969 Ayub Khan announced that he would not stand in the forthcoming presidential elections.

Outbreak and response

Protests and strikes increased throughout 1969 and gradually became more militant. On 25 March Ayub Khan resigned power to General Yahya Khan, who reimposed martial law. By now the Awami League was campaigning for East Pakistan autonomy: it argued for the limitation of central authority to foreign affairs and defence, and insisted that each wing of Pakistan should retain the use of its own resources, which, for East Pakistan, meant the full use of its earnings from tea and jute. The discontent was exacerbated by the cyclone and devastating floods of November 1970, which did massive damage in East Pakistan and caused an estimated 200,000 deaths; it was claimed that West Pakistan had been tardy in sending relief.

Elections were held in December 1970, and the Awami League won all but two of the seats in East Pakistan and gained an absolute majority in the new assembly with 167 out of 300 seats. In West Pakistan Zulfikar Ali Bhutto won 83 seats for the Awami League, but only gave partial support to Mujibur when the confrontation came to a head. Yahya Khan refused to accept Mujibur as Prime Minister, and in return Mujibur demanded full autonomy for East Pakistan except for foreign policy. In West Pakistan Bhutto rejected this demand and refused to bring his wing of the Awami League to Dacca to take part in the meeting of the new assembly. On 1 March 1971 President Yahya suspended the Constituent Assembly indefinitely, and Mujibur reacted by ordering a boycott and a general strike throughout East Pakistan. These followed and he had almost total support, in effect seizing power in East Pakistan on 10 March. President Yahya went to Dacca (now Dhaka) in mid-March in an attempt to find a compromise, but this proved impossible so he denounced Mujibur and his followers as traitors and decided to re-occupy East Pakistan with the army from West Pakistan. Mujibur and some of his colleagues were arrested, while others fled to India and proclaimed East Pakistan as the independent state of Bangladesh on 25 March 1971. Increasing repression by units of the army already in East Pakistan ensured a national uprising. The Mukti Bahini (freedom fighters) of East Pakistan now fought in both conventional and guerrilla fashion.

Course of the struggle

The army now instituted a regime of severe repression, which led to millions of East Pakistanis crossing the borders into India as refugees. Armed resistance to the army was provided by the Mukti Bahini in three forms: first, conventional warfare was waged by General M. A. G. Osmany, who created two brigades and conducted resistance along conventional military lines in the border territories of Assam and Tripura; second, guerrilla resistance was led by the radical leaders, Taher and Ziaddin, who were to oppose the subsequent intervention of India; and third, there was more general guerrilla resistance assisted by thousands of civilians and without formal command structure. Everywhere, however, the army came under attack.

As fighting grew in intensity and the country was reduced to chaos, the tide of East Pakistani refugees flooding into India increased. In December 1971, after nine months of fighting, India, which had its own political reasons for encouraging the break-up of Pakistan into two states, invaded East Pakistan on the side of the Mukti Bahini and other irregular groups fighting for independence (4 December). After only two weeks' fighting the Pakistani army was forced to surrender (16 December). In any case West Pakistan was encountering increasing problems, mainly of communications, in fighting the war: India had refused air passage, so all reinforcements had to circumvent the subcontinent. At the same time West Pakistan had to fight a second Indian army, although the fighting in the west was more even than in the east. The intervention of India was decisive, therefore, and ensured the emergence of an independent Bangladesh.

Estimated costs and casualties

According to UN estimates, war damage came to US$1.2 billion. There were widely varying estimates as to the total number of casualties. One estimate (Minority Rights Group) suggests 3 million dead as a result of the repression, the guerrilla action and the final full-scale fighting. This figure also includes the refugees who died on the mass exodus to India. About 10 million Bengalis are reckoned to have crossed the borders into India as refugees, and although again no reliable figures exist, many thousands of these died.

The casualties of the Pakistani army came to several thousands – a probable figure puts deaths between 5000 and 10,000. The army which surrendered to the Indians (16 December 1971) numbered 92,000. India mobilized and moved to East Pakistan between 130,000 and 140,000 troops; these advanced into the country in columns and the total number almost certainly did not enter East Pakistan. Larger numbers of Indian troops were mobilized on the other side of the continent to face West Pakistan.

There may have been as many as 200,000 guerrillas fighting at the peak of the war, although 50,000 is a more probable figure. One estimate suggests that while 100,000 guerrillas were in the field a further 100,000 were in training in India. India certainly provided training for some of the guerrillas. When the climax of the war arrived Bengali troops in various formations of the Pakistan army in East Pakistan killed their officers and deserted to join the guerrillas.

Results: immediate and longer term

With the surrender of the Pakistani army on 16 December 1971 the new state of Bangladesh came into being with Dacca (renamed Dhaka) as its capital, and the anomaly of a two-part Pakistan, separated by 1000 miles of Indian territory, came to an end. Bangladesh was rapidly accorded international recognition as a state and was already one of the most populous in the world. It faced many problems:

armed bands who had fought for independence did not disband; the country had suffered immense physical destruction, which had come immediately after the devastation of the 1970 cyclone; and, in any case, it was one of the poorest, most overpopulated regions anywhere in the world. As a result, the new state embarked on a period of instability, and its first President, Sheik Mujibur Rahman, was assassinated in 1975.

India had played a crucial role in bringing the new state into existence. It had a number of motives: it faced the huge influx of refugees which it wanted to return to Bangladesh; it wished to reduce Pakistan's power, which was effected by the break-up of that state into its two parts; and it was happy to see a weak new state on its eastern flank, which it could certainly influence if not control. Indeed, the newly independent Bangladesh began life fearing the possibility of a new form of Indian colonialism.

The emergence of Bangladesh altered permanently the geopolitics of the Indian subcontinent. Bangladesh became a member of the Commonwealth a fact which led Pakistan to leave the association (although it was to rejoin in 1989), and emerged on the world scene as another very poor suppliant for international economic assistance.

BURMA: ENDLESS INSURGENCY

Background

Burma was colonized by Britain in three stages during the nineteenth century; the process was completed – more or less – in 1885 after the third nearly bloodless war. In 1937 Britain separated Burma from India, but instead of pacifying Burmese nationalists the move raised fears that Britain intended to deny Burma the constitutional advances which were then being considered for India.

The main opposition to the British during the 1930s came from the Thakin movement, two of the principal leaders of which were Aung San and U Nu. When the Second World War began the British attempted to arrest Aung San, but he escaped to China and thence to Japan where with others he received military training. When the Japanese swept through the countries of the Far East they promised independence for Burma, but once there they reneged on their promise, which prompted Aung San who had supported them to plot against them instead. Only in 1943, when the tide of war turned against the Japanese, did they declare Burma independent. In 1945 Aung San offered to co-operate with Lord Mountbatten, the Allied commander in south-east Asia, and in March 1945 he and his army joined the British to fight the Japanese. The Japanese general surrender took place on 14 August 1945, but some of the Japanese forces were cut off in the Karen hills and continued fighting until mid-September. These eastern border regions with Thailand and China are geographically remote, peopled by distinctive ethnic groups and hard to control. They witnessed severe fighting against the Japanese at the end of the war, so a tradition of resistance had already been built up by the time Burma became independent.

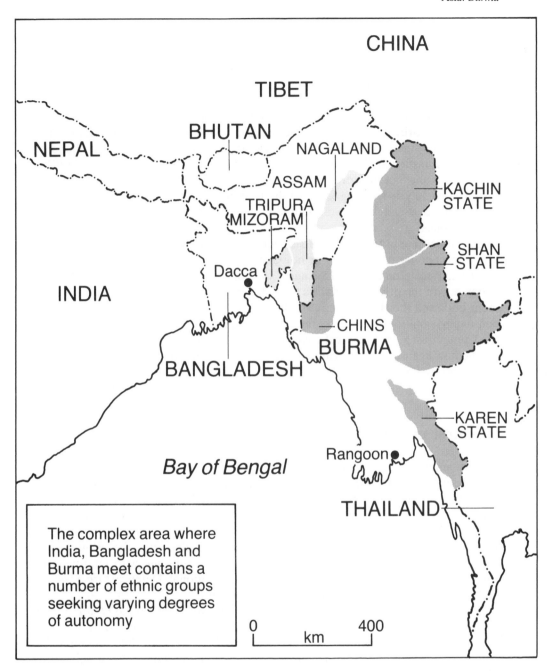

The complex area where India, Bangladesh and Burma meet contains a number of ethnic groups seeking varying degrees of autonomy

Map 19   A tangle of monorities

Independence

Under Burma's independence constitution of 1947 these frontier states (the Karen, Shan) were brought within the federal framework of the Burma Union. During the Japanese war a coalition – the Anti-Fascist People's Freedom League (AFPFL) – had been formed. When the war ended it was not prepared to co-operate with the returning British. The AFPFL had created its own guerrilla groups to fight the Japanese, and these remained after the end of the war to strengthen the hand of the League in demanding immediate independence. After a while the AFPFL, under the Aung San, was drawn into negotiations with the British. Unfortunately, however, in July 1947 Aung San and the leading members of his ruling Executive Council were assassinated. None the less, the AFPFL inherited political power at independence.

Burma became independent outside the Commonwealth on 4 January 1948 and opted for a policy of neutrality or non-alignment. The Burmese Communist Party (BCP) had been founded on 15 August 1939 and following the end of the war had agitated with the other nationalists for independence. However, when the government outlawed the BCP in March 1948, it split from the other nationalists, whose continuing agitations were concerned with regional or ethnic autonomy rather than the Communist aim of political control. The BCP then became the prime mover in a rebellion against the government the first phase of which lasted from 1948 to 1951. The BCP was joined by the Karens.

The first period of insurgency 1947–1954

Unrest among ethnic minorities was already causing problems before Burma became independent; once independence was achieved, the new government faced immediate Communist and Karen revolts. The main body of the AFPFL formed the successor government to the British, although a breakaway group – the People's Volunteer Organization (PVO) – split, with one part following the Communists into revolt. The BCP with their guerrilla arm, the White Flag, launched a full-scale rebellion in 1948 which was to continue with intermissions through to 1990. Also during 1948 the Karen National Defence Organization (KNDO) joined the BCP in fighting the government.

At independence the various minority groups were not prepared for a new relationship with the Burmese (historically they had regarded the Burmese as a colonial power long before the advent of the British); they felt pressured by Rangoon and responded with demands for greater autonomy if not secession. These minority groups included the Karens, Kachins, Shans, Mons, Chins and Arakanese. The most important of them – the Karens and Shans – revolted against the central government in an effort to establish autonomous regions or states. During 1948 the Communists and Karens in south and central Burma had major initial successes: they captured Mandalay and besieged the government in Rangoon. In 1949 the Karens declared an independent state at Toungoo, but this was attacked and captured by government forces in 1950. At the same time government forces captured the Communist headquarters at Prome, although both the Karens and the Communists continued the war.

An already confused scene was further complicated when the civil war in China came to an end and Nationalist troops of the defeated armies of Chiang Kai-shek took refuge across the border in eastern Burma. They resisted Burmese attempts to dislodge them and remained there until 1953–4 when, under UN pressure, they agreed to be evacuated to Formosa (Taiwan). Other ethnic groups now rebelled, and fighting also broke out between the different groups. None the less, by 1951 the government of Thakin Nu had managed to reassert central authority over most of the country.

The variety of insurgents

During what came to be called the constitutional period, from independence in 1948 to the coup which brought Ne Win to power in 1962, the main problem for the government was to secure the loyalty of the various non-Burmese peoples, but the government generally failed in this objective. The dissident minorities were a constant threat to national unity, and at one time or another almost every ethnic minority resorted to armed struggle, most of them having their own distinctive liberation armies or fronts. Increasingly over the years they came to engage in drug trafficking and smuggling as a means of providing income for their struggles, and to maintain the regions where they operated more or less independently of government controls.

The Communists have always been the most formidable opponents of the government, and wherever possible the BCP has maintained links with the ethnic opposition groups. The BCP with its 10,000-strong White Flag guerrillas has received the backing of China. The White Flag insurgents, who have on occasion tied down as many as 120,000 government troops, have their bases along the border with China and are usually in control of Wa province. They have, at various times, entered into alliances with the Kachin Independence Army (KIA) and the Shan State Army (SSA), and with their bases close to the Chinese border, from whence come their supplies, the Communists have always been difficult to control.

The Karens, who live in the strategically vital strip of land along the Thai border, are the most formidable of the ethnic minorities. Sino-Tibetan by origin, the Karens are Burma's second largest minority group and are more widely dispersed through the population as a whole than are other minorities, a fact that makes their claims to a separate state more complex, while also permitting a degree of infiltration denied to some of the other groups. The majority of the Karens live in the Lower Burma delta area, and many have mixed with Burmans and Mons.

Under the 1947 constitution it was proposed that the Salween district as well as various other areas should be united to form a Karen state. But the Karens demanded complete autonomy, and when this was denied they rebelled under the leadership of Saw Ba U Gyi. A Karen National Defence Organization was formed at independence, and its members occupied areas to the east of the Sittang river and in the Irrawaddy delta. They named their state Kawthule (the flowery land).

In 1954, in an attempt to bring Karen secession to an end, the government established a Karen state, which was inaugurated on 1 June of that year with its capital at Pa-an. Ten years later the state was renamed Kawthule. Then, under the

1974 constitution, which limited state autonomy, Kawthule was renamed Karen state once more. Only about a third of all Karens live in the area of the state.

The Karen National Liberation Army (KNLA), with about 4000 regular members, controls much of the border with Thailand and operates a border tax system. During the 1980s the KNLA administered substantial areas of Burma, in which it claimed to have eradicated a number of problems, such as gambling, prostitution, corruption and petty crime. Normally the KNLA uses guerrilla tactics, but sometimes its forces have engaged in more conventional warfare against government forces.

To the north of the Karens are the Shan people, and they too have been in rebellion against the central government. There are rival Shan groups and some of these are more concerned to operate as semi-independent organizations for business (drugs or smuggling) than to achieve genuine independence as a state. They are opposed to the Communists.

The Shan State Army (SSA) is one of the most significant of the rebel forces with which the government has to contend: in the early 1980s it could deploy up to 8000 men, half of whom would be well-armed and trained. The SSA was created in 1957 and began its life as the Shan State Independence Army, but changed its name in 1964. It operates along part of the Thai border east of the Salween. It possesses a range of weapons: many have been obtained from the BCP and include weapons originally used in the Vietnam War. By the mid-1970s the BCP had gained substantial influence in the SSA-controlled regions. However, in 1977 the SSA decided to break its connection with the BCP, although later it was obliged to compromise since the BCP had the most readily available supply of weapons.

Much of the dissidence has been possible because of the relaxed attitude to cross-border operations maintained by Thailand, along whose border many of the minorities are to be found. Although the Thais have steadily opposed the Communists, they have been more than friendly to the Karens, Shans and Mons, whose people, when necessary, have been able to find refuge in Thailand.

The basic problem, for which as yet no solution has been found, is the fear of these groups at the prospect of absorption by the dominant Burman culture with an accompanying loss or collapse of their own.

The smaller ethnic groups revolt periodically, although they do not individually amount to more than irritants to government. Thus the Arakan Liberation Front revolts against Rangoon from time to time. It was formed in 1974 to act for the Muslim Arakanese, but was badly mauled in the mid-1970s shortly after its formation; its leader, Khaing Mo, was killed in 1977, and it no longer appears to be significant. Other small groups include the Karen National Union, the Karennie National Progressive Party, the New Mon State Party and the Parliamentary Democratic Party, each of which has experienced varying fortunes over the years.

Course of the struggle

1954–1975

It is not easy to chart a struggle the essence of which is a state of perpetual warfare between the government made up of the majority people, the Burmans, on the one hand, and some 10 dissident groups representing ethnic minorities (plus the

Communists) on the other. The struggle has been on–off by nature: in some years there has been something like full-scale war; in others, desultory guerrilla action. Sometimes the government has attempted political concessions; at other times it has launched major military campaigns against the insurgents. These, moreover, have been able to obtain support from two of Burma's neighbours – the BCP has relied on China for support, and the ethnic minorities have received substantial aid from Thailand – yet these sources of aid have varied depending on Burma's diplomatic efforts at any given time.

By 1954, at the end of the first phase of civil dissidence, General U Ne Win, had managed to bring most of the country under central government control. Later, in 1958 briefly and in 1962 permanently, General Ne Win toppled the civilian government when it appeared unable to deal with the insurgents. During the 1950s government tactics alternated between the use of force and offering amnesties in order to induce the rebels to surrender; some were prepared to do so. Yet over this decade the amount of territory under the control of the dissidents expanded, and although for a time in 1958 it appeared possible that Burma might achieve peace with its dissidents, this did not happen and in 1959 the Shans and Kachins took to arms to demand autonomy. The Prime Minister, U Nu, called on General Ne Win to form a caretaker administration. Two years later, however, General Ne Win seized power in a coup, overthrew parliamentary institutions and arrested U Nu and others of his cabinet, including the minority leaders. The military then established its own Burma Socialist Programme Party (BSPP) which was to rule the country for the next three decades.

For a period (1962–7) the military government of Ne Win attempted to come to terms with the minorities, but it had no more success than its civilian predecessors. Then in 1967 the government launched a major military offensive. This was encouraged by the fact that the BCP experienced a split at this time. In 1962 it had switched its allegiance from Moscow to Beijing (by 1982 the BCP leader, Thakin Ba Thein Tin, actually lived in Beijing). The BCP was organized into military-administrative districts with the northern Shan state as its most important centre. It was relatively successful when it confined its operations to the area east of the Salween or the area bordering China's Yunnan province. Wherever it was able to do so, the BCP concluded alliances with the other insurgent groups, including the Shan States National Liberation Organization (SSNLO), the Shan State Army (SSA) and the Kachin Independence Organization (KIO). From 1970 to 1972 U Nu, now an exile in Thailand, organized a revolt against the government through the Shans and Karens, although it did not have much success. In 1975 government forces successfully ejected the BCP from areas to the west of the Salween river. In 1977 President Ne Win made two visits to China in an effort to persuade Beijing to withhold its support from the BCP, but without much success.

1975–1980

In 1975 nine of the insurgent groups formed the National Democratic Front (NDF); it included the Karens, Arakanese, Mons, Karennis, Shans, Kachins, Palaungs, Pa-Os and Was, and had a Karen president, General Bo Mya. But alliances were constantly changing. The KIO, for example, allied itself with the

BCP in 1976 and by 1980, as a result, had abandoned separatism in favour of left-wing ideals comparable to those of the BCP. It had 1500 guerrillas.

During the second half of the 1970s BCP activities were at their most aggressive, and there were high casualties on both sides when full-scale battles took place, as they did from time to time. But after attempting conventional warfare for a time, the BCP reverted to the guerrilla tactics at which it was most successful. When BCP forces attempted to infiltrate the lowlands they were usually rebuffed. In 1978 the government launched a major military campaign against the BCP near the northern border with China, and a year later it launched a similar campaign; in each of these campaigns heavy casualties were suffered by both sides. The Chinese, despite requests from Burma, continued to support the BCP mainly because Beijing feared that if it did not do so the BCP would turn to Vietnam and become part of the Communist encircling movement that was then directed from Moscow (see Part III, pp. 246–254). Burma was not strong enough to mount a direct challenge to China.

In May 1980 Ne Win offered an amnesty to all insurgents if they reported to the authorities within 90 days. One of the insurgents to accept the offer was the former Prime Minister, U Nu, who returned to Burma to become a Buddhist monk. The campaign against the insurgents was helped by the fact that both China and India tightened their border security and denied sanctuary to Burmese rebels. Between 3000 and 4000 individuals, including politicians and intellectuals as well as rebels, took advantage of the May 1980 amnesty; for example, about 1400 rebels and one rebel leader, Yan Naing, returned from exile in Thailand. But the Communist insurgency continued into the 1980s, although Chinese support was reduced; the Karens also kept up a low level of insurgency.

The 1980s

In 1981 talks were held between the government and the BCP, but nothing resulted from them, although for two years there was something of a lull in the fighting. Then in 1982 fighting on a substantial scale broke out once more. On 15 June 1982 the government announced that 67 Communists had surrendered with their weapons in the previous months. The following month Burma's Foreign Minister visited China in an attempt to persuade its government to cut off aid to the BCP, and although the Chinese made no overt concessions, their aid was reduced later in the year, forcing the BCP to turn to the opium trade as its principal means of earning revenue and so maintaining its supplies. Burma also managed to secure an agreement with Thailand to increase co-operation between their two armies in combating the activities of the BCP, Karens and other insurgents along their joint border. On the whole 1983 turned out to be a year of little action; the Burmese army shelled a Karen stronghold near the Thai border in July and then attacked it in November.

But in 1984 the government mounted a major campaign against all the insurgent groups; it was the largest of its kind since independence and was launched during the first three months of the year. The government's main objective was to smash the smuggling operations (opium and general goods) which had become the principal source of income for the different insurgents; apart from the BCP, the Kachins, Shans, Lahus, Karennis and Karens were also involved in the opium trade. On 15 April the government claimed that its forces had killed 2500 rebels and captured 650 in clashes that included some 16 battles in the border areas. The army suffered 528 dead and 1370 wounded. As a result of this campaign, more than 10,000 civilians became refugees and fled into Thailand.

The government launched a further major security operation in 1985, involving 3000 troops along the eastern border region of the country in another attempt to control the opium trade as well as the smuggling of gold, teak, gems, tin ore and cattle into Thailand in exchange for manufactured goods and guns. Later in the year the rebels changed tactics: in May they blew up a troop train near Port Moulmein; on 24 July they blew up a passenger train on the line from Rangoon to Mandalay, killing 67 and wounding 100. The Karens were thought to be responsible.

By 1986 the National Democratic Front had an estimated 12,000 guerrillas in action, as did the BCP, and it was rumoured that the two had united against the government. The merger was denied, and the Karens made it plain that they wanted nothing to do with the BCP. Later in the year (September) Thailand put its border forces on full alert when fighting broke out between the BCP and one of the guerrilla leaders, Khun Sa, who in effect was an opium warlord, for control of the local trade. Khun Sa lost two of his opium camps to the BCP.

Guerrilla insurgency throughout 1987 drained the resources of the government and diverted much of the country's wealth. A bloody offensive against the BCP along the Chinese border left 650 Communists and 175 government troops dead. A recognition of just how much damage years of insurgency had inflicted on a once rich country came when the government was humiliatingly forced to ask the UN to downgrade its status to that of a least developed nation. After 25 years of Ne Win and his inflexible socialist ideas Burma was worse off than at any time since independence. What was also apparent was the generally run-down state of the army – unusual under a military regime – with poorly trained and equipped troops; losses in engagements against the insurgents were therefore consistently higher than they need have been.

In 1988 Ne Win finally resigned after ruling Burma for 26 years. He was replaced by Sein Lwin, who was also forced to resign in August after violent protests. The country appeared on the verge of political chaos. Although over the years the figures have varied, by 1988 the total guerrilla strength of the National Democratic Front (now covering 10 minority groups) stood at about 20,000, of which the Kachin had 8000 troops and the Karens 4000. The Burmese army stood at 186,000. Tactics have changed: while the Burmese army attempts to force the guerrillas into full-scale confrontations, the guerrillas work out co-ordinated defence tactics, going to the defence of any one group that is the object of attack. Leaders of the NDF, however, find it difficult to obtain much outside support or sympathy, mainly perhaps because they are so deeply involved in the opium trade. The opium Golden Triangle is situated in Shan state, and the Shan, especially the rebels, cultivate opium. On the other hand, opium trafficking is punishable by death among the Kachin and Karen resistance groups. Such distinctions do not make much impression outside Burma.

In September 1988, when Saw Maung, a former soldier, toppled the new civilian government, violence and riots in Rangoon resulted in an estimated 1000 deaths. At the same time the Karens claimed that 2000 students and others had fled the Rangoon violence to areas under Karen control along the Thai border. And in the north-east, BCP rebels attacked three army outposts, which they captured at a cost of about 130 rebels and 48 government troops killed. Then in October another major engagement took place between Karen rebels and government forces when 1000 Karens attempted to seize a government post on the Thai border. What seemed clear at the end of the Ne Win era was the continuing nature of the anti-government insurgency after more than 40 years.

At the beginning of 1989 five armies were engaged in fighting to control the largest opium crop ever harvested in Burma's section of the Gold Triangle: these were the Burmese and Thai armies engaged with the BCP, the Shan army of Khun Sa (the opium baron) and remnants of the Chinese Kuomintang who were still to be found in Thailand. In part the battle was the direct result of the Burmese government telling the Shan farmers that there would be no punishment for growing opium, since Rangoon itself wanted part of the harvest to offset against its crumbling economy. The country's grim economic plight resulted from the decision of Western nations to cut back on aid following the military suppression of the popular uprising during September and October 1988. Farther south, 1200 Karens fought a bloody battle with 3000 government forces during May when several Karen strongholds were destroyed. In the first five months of the year the government claimed that more than 600 Karen guerrillas had been killed for 177 government soldiers, while both sides suffered many hundreds of wounded. The government succeeded in overrunning one of the most important Karen bases at Wangkha; this was a centre of the cross-border smuggling trade upon which the Karen economy depends.

By 1990 it had become plain that Rangoon was primarily concerned to contain the Karens since to defeat them would require more money and bloodshed than the government is either able or willing to spend. But such a policy assumes that the warfare will continue indefinitely.

Estimated costs and casualties

No accurate figures exist, but casualties over 40 years of fighting must run into many tens of thousands dead. The costs of this debilitating war for Burma as a country have been disastrous: what was one of the richest nations in Asia is now officially one of the poorest, while people live in fear of a regime whose *raison d'être* is to fight a running war that it appears incapable of winning. The various insurgents are also fighting a war – or series of wars – that they cannot win. The prospects for the 1990s appear gloomy.

CHINA: CIVIL WAR 1945–1949

Background

The civil war of 1945–9 which brought the Communists to power in China was the culmination of the long-drawn-out death throes of an imperial system which had lasted for more than two thousand years. During the second half of the nineteenth century the major Western powers began to move into China with their demands for trade concessions or an 'open door' policy, as they established their spheres of influence against a background of steadily collapsing central power. This Western impact came close to a colonial carve-up; Chinese intellectuals, who also provided the ruling class, realized that China could not survive unless it learnt from the West and industrialized and modernized its society to enable it to compete on equal terms.

In 1900 a nationwide anti-foreign movement known as the Boxer Rebellion erupted all over China; it was fundamentally nationalist in its origins and, while harnessed by the dying Manchu dynasty for its own ends, was aimed as much at the corruption and ineffectiveness of the imperial system as at foreigners (although they were seen as the symbols of China's degradation). The First Republic was established in the revolution of 1911, which, like the Boxer Rebellion, was as much a revolt against the corruption of the Manchu dynasty as it was a revolution for radical change. But though the Manchu Empire had finally been brought to a close, another 40 years of chaos, revolt and counter-revolution, strife between warlords, Japanese invasion and then full-scale civil war between Nationalists and Communists was to follow before China regained a single central government – that of Mao Zedong – whose writ would run throughout the land.

In 1921 Mao Zedong and others created the Chinese Communist Party (CCP) at a time when the Kuomintang was the revolutionary party in China. After 1924, however, the Kuomintang admitted Communists to its ranks. Sun Yat-sen, the hero figure and real leader of the First Republic, died in 1925 to be succeeded in 1927, after a period of political manoeuvring, by Chiang Kai-shek as leader of the Nationalists.

The Japanese invasion and the Second World War 1931–1945

The Japanese invasion of Manchuria in 1931 inaugurated 15 years of Japanese involvement on the Chinese mainland. At first the Japanese confined their activities to the huge province of Manchuria (now called Dongbei). Meanwhile, quarrels between the Nationalists under Chiang Kai-shek and the rapidly developing Communist Party under Mao Zedong culminated in the Nationalist attempt to destroy the Communists and their retreat in their famous Long March (1934–5) from Kiangsi (now spelled Jianxi) to Shensi (Shaanxi), where they settled in Yenan (Yan'an).

In 1937 the Japanese were ready to take on all China and launched a massive military campaign from Manchuria in the north and against Shanghai in the south. A year later (July 1938) the Japanese controlled most of eastern China, 1 million Chinese and Japanese lives had been lost and 10 million Chinese had become refugees. The war escalated steadily, and it became plain that it was likely to go on indefinitely. The Japanese had the advantage of equipment and training; the Chinese, of numbers.

In the 10 years before the Second World War Chinese industry expanded and many Western-trained Chinese reached positions of authority; Western nations – especially the USA and Britain – favoured a strong China and believed this could best be promoted by supporting Chiang Kai-shek, who for his part managed to persuade the West both to back his Nationalist China aspirations and at the same time to relinquish their Western privileges.

By supporting China, however, the West succeeded in losing Japan. Western support, especially its large financial input into Nationalist China, led Japan to believe that it was being abandoned by the West (and especially by Britain). Japan's strategy was to prevent China from becoming a great power – this lay behind Japan's all-out attack on China in 1937.

During the Second World War Chiang Kai-shek became an important figure as an ally of the Western powers, and his Nationalist forces received massive aid in the form of military equipment from the USA. During the war an uneasy truce was maintained between the Nationalists and the Communists while the Japanese remained in the country, but as the war drew to its conclusion it was apparent to all that a civil war could not be avoided.

The Communists became highly effective as guerrillas working behind the Japanese lines, and by 1944 they had tied down 22 Japanese divisions (64 per cent of their forces in China), which were obliged to operate behind the regular front against the Communists. In addition to the regular Japanese troops, the puppet Chinese army of 750,000 men under Wang Ching-wei (also spelled Wang Jingwei) was also deployed against the Communists. Although few fixed battles took place, the Communists claimed that in the 12 months to June 1944 they accounted for 200,000 Japanese and Chinese troops. The tide of war turned against the Japanese in 1943 and they began to retreat. By then the population in northern China, which was organized to pay taxes to the Communists, had risen from 50,000,000 to 80,000,000. In the three years 1941–4 the Japanese lost to the Communists 13,000 forts guarding strategic points. In the first six months of 1944 the Communists recaptured 24 cities and subsequently were able to retain control over a third of them.

The Communist performance against the Japanese was consistently better than that of the Nationalist Chinese. The Communists claimed that only they had been effective behind the enemy lines and that, while there had been 1 million central government (Nationalist) troops behind the Japanese lines in 1941, by 1944 the number had dwindled to 30,000, while many had deserted to the enemy. None the less, the Communists were hampered throughout the war by their lack of ammunition, a situation that was created by Chiang Kai-shek who blockaded the Communist areas. Yet in 1944, despite or because of these handicaps, the Communists were able to claim two things: that China required immediate democratic reforms in order to function properly; and that they had been far more effective against the Japanese than the Kuomintang. By this time, when no kind of accommodation between the Communists and the Kuomintang seemed possible, it had become obvious that civil war was likely to follow the collapse of the Japanese. By then the Communists were in control of north China and there was little likelihood that the Kuomintang could dislodge them.

The line-up in 1945

Observers of the Communist headquarters at Yenan during the Second World War remarked on the enthusiasm and idealism of its leaders, and these qualities were now to prove of fundamental importance in the coming struggle. The USA had been concerned to build up China as a base for the final onslaught on Japan, although the explosion of the atom bombs at Hiroshima and Nagasaki later made this unnecessary. By the time the Americans sent a military mission to the Communists at Yenan in 1944 and learnt something of their quality, it was too late to assist the Nationalist government in Chungking (now spelled Chongqing) to win the coming civil war.

Moscow appeared not to realize the Communist potential in China until very late: in 1945, for example, the Nationalists concluded secret agreements with Moscow (at Yalta) which gave them control of Outer Mongolia and equal rights with the Soviet Union in Port Arthur (now Lushun) and Dairen (Luta).

When the Sino-Japanese conflict came to an end in August 1945 the Kuomintang army of 500,000 troops (among the best Nationalist forces) under the command of General Hu Tsung-nan, which had been deployed to encircle the Communists in Yenan since 1940, now went on to the offensive. At the same time a brutally oppressive action by the Nationalists at Kunming, when shortly after the Japanese surrender students were massacred (and a leading educationalist, Li Kung-po, and a professor of classics, Wen-I-to, were assassinated), demonstrated that the Nationalists had learnt nothing and ensured that the students united with the peasants against Chiang Kai-shek.

In the north the Nationalist General, Hu Tsung-nan, captured a number of Communist bases, and Communist–Nationalist conflicts began to erupt wherever the two groups were in contact. In September 1945 Mao Zedong flew to Chungking to negotiate with Chiang Kai-shek, and they agreed (10 October) that a conference should be held between the main political parties (there were five) in order to solve differences. But before the conference could be mounted the Nationalists launched attacks on Communist bases in Hopei (now spelled Hebei), Chekiang (Zhejiang), Kwangtung (Guangdong), Shensi (Shaanxi), Honan (Henan), Anhwei (Anhui) and Hupeh (Hubeh). The USA then threw its support behind the Nationalist onslaught on the Communists by allowing its transports to be used to land their forces at Chingwangtao (now spelled Ch'inhuangtao) so as to enable them to destroy the Communist bases in Manchuria and Hopei.

At that time the Soviets were about to withdraw (according to treaty) from Manchuria (6 September), but Chiang Kai-shek asked them to remain for an additional three months to provide him with time to move troops there before the Communists did so. The Soviets were happy to oblige. On 4 November a large Communist force captured Kweisui, the capital of Sulynan province; 10 days later government forces were sent to Tsingtao (now spelled Ch'ingtao) to drive the Communists out of Shantung (Shandong). Both sides were shaping up for a full-scale confrontation, but at that point they agreed a truce.

1946

The civil war which had been brewing between the Communists and the Kuomintang finally burst in 1946, and yet, though greatly feared, it turned out to be neither as destructive nor as long-lasting as most observers had predicted. It became apparent at an early stage in the war that the Communists were set to win: their troops were highly disciplined and fought well, while those of the Kuomintang had little will to fight and plundered whenever they had the opportunity. By this time, moreover, the Kuomintang stood for nothing that anyone wanted. Despite enjoying massive superiority in arms (mainly from the USA) as well as having total air superiority and vastly greater numbers, their armies were to be routed within three years.

The war developed gradually during the first half of 1946, and by the summer both sides were busy probing and testing one another preparatory to an all-out struggle. At Chungking in February all parties had agreed to form a coalition government, and at this time the Communists still claimed to trust Chiang Kai-shek personally even if not those around him, while his government too protested its readiness to reach an accommodation. Then in mid-1946 Nationalist forces launched attacks on the Communists in Kiangsu (Jiansu) north of the Yangtse (or Chang Jiang) and in Manchuria. They were able to use US lendlease weapons, including destroyer escorts and aircraft. In August the Nationalists reached and attacked the Communist capital at Yenan. Later that month the Communists attacked the railway in Manchuria between Mukden (now Shenyang) and Changchun, forcing the Nationalists to rush in reinforcements to save it. The year was one of ominously developing crisis. Chiang Kai-shek still welcomed American mediation in the (apparent) hope that a Council of State could be formed as the basis of the coalition government that had been agreed at the Chungking meeting of February: the Council would consist of 40 members, half from the Kuomintang and the rest from the other parties. Had this come into being, it would have marked the end of Kuomintang dictatorship and the beginning of democracy.

1947

At the end of 1946 and into 1947 the Americans, led by General George C. Marshall, attempted to mediate between the two sides at a time when Nationalist forces were threatening the Communists in Manchuria at both Harbin and Kirin (now spelled Jilin). By the end of January Marshall abandoned his mediation attempts as hopeless, blaming extremists on both sides for the failure. The Communists blamed the Kuomintang for going back on the political accord of April 1946, but in fact the basic distrust between the two sides was fundamental. On 17 February at Nanking (now spelled Nanjing) the Nationalist government introduced a series of harsh economic austerity measures and wartime controls, and Chiang Kai-shek warned that China's survival as a nation was at stake. In March the central government announced that its forces had captured the Communist capital, Yenan, but since the Communists had left, taking anything of importance with them, the victory was a hollow one.

Communist strength at this time lay in the obvious attractions offered by its practice of government as opposed to what had long happened under the Nationalists, whose corruption was by then notorious. The Nationalists now made the mistake of launching a major offensive against the Communists in the north of China, employing the same indifferent and corrupt generals while doing nothing to put their own house in order. In July the Chinese State Council decreed total mobilization while also banning the Democratic League (liberal intellectuals) and admitting their growing dependence on the USA for military aid: it was not a winning combination. The year 1947 was perhaps the last chance for the National-ists to reform, although with the passing of every month it seemed less and less likely that they would even attempt to do so. The USA, by supporting Chiang, was seen to be encouraging him to eliminate the Communists; and the Kuomintang demonstrated that it had no real intention of implementing any of the reforms which had been agreed at the Joint Political Consultative Conference of April 1946, upon which many of China's foreign supporters had placed their hopes. The Communists had been careful not to denounce the 1946 accord, but the Kuomintang and its allies – the Youth Party and the Democratic Socialists – had abandoned any pretence at conciliation.

Relying on US aid, Chiang Kai-shek went for a quick military victory in the first half of 1947. But the Communists put to good use the tactics they had developed so successfully against the Japanese: they had already won the support of the rural populations in the north, and now they avoided major conflicts, keeping their forces intact, while they attacked Nationalist lines of communication. In the process they inflicted heavy casualties on the Kuomintang. During the second half of 1947 the Nationalists experienced a growing number of military setbacks. In Manchuria the fighting was heavy with the Nationalists constantly struggling to reopen or keep open the railways. In Shantung large Communist forces managed to elude encirclement to move into Kiangsu. Elsewhere the Communists advanced steadily: they overran Honan, Anhwei and east Hupeh and then reached the north bank of the Yangtse. By the end of the year the Communists were everywhere on the offensive. They crossed the Yellow River (now called the Huang He) to spread into west Honan, and they took the northern section of the Tientsin–Pukow (Tianjin–P'ukou) railway as well as the Peking–Paoting (Beijing–Baoding) corridor, so that they controlled the Peking–Paoting–Tientsin triangle even if they did not hold the three cities. By the end of the year the Nationalists had abandoned most of Manchuria.

1948

By 1948 the economy of China was in chaos, while its people, who had suffered non-stop warfare since 1930, wanted only peace and a strong government, two conditions which the Communists seemed more and more likely to provide. The year was to see rice riots in both west and central China and growing disobedience to the central government. Moreover, by the end of the year there was no evidence that the government was making any efforts to check the widespread corruption prevalent throughout its members or to tax the wealthy in order to pay for the war. The inefficient at the top, including the generals conducting the war, were never punished. Foreign trade was collapsing, government monopolies were everywhere increasing and no economic plan appeared to exist. This general chaos, as well as manifest Nationalist corruption, worked to the advantage of the Communists at least as much as victories in the field.

Early in 1948 the Communists attacked the Peking–Mukden railway, which they put out of action, and then captured two key ports to the south of Mukden – Liaoyang and Panshan – so that Mukden was now isolated. By March the Communists controlled all Shansi and most of Honan except for the area of Chengchow (now spelled Chengchou). Their grip on Manchuria was everywhere tightened and the railway virtually destroyed. They took north-east Hupeh, cut the Hankow–Ichang (Wuhan–Ichang) waterway and began to advance westwards.

The USA now (but far too late) attempted to persuade Chiang Kai-shek to democratize, so he summoned the National Assembly, whose members had been elected or appointed by him in 1936. He was elected President, but his candidate was not made Vice-President. At most Chiang Kai-shek was putting on a democratic front that no one believed any more. The Communists, on the other hand, were formidably strong in terms of organization and ideological appeal – if not military equipment, for the Nationalists always had more and better arms supplied by the USA. Communist strength came from the enthusiasm and discipline of their leaders, the high degree of discipline of their armed forces and their mastery of guerrilla tactics. The Communists' appeal to the Chinese masses at this stage was derived from the promise of economic reforms and the support they had carefully won and fostered from the peasants, who contrasted it favourably with the dreadful years of Nationalist rule.

In October Communist troops broke into Mukden, which soon fell with the surrender of a powerful Nationalist army. This was seen as a turning point in the war. After the fall of Mukden the Communists turned on the remaining Nationalist strongholds in the north of China, and these fell to them one after another. The Nationalist collapse in the north was now swift, assisted by plummeting morale as well as bad generalship. Thus, shortly before the fall of Mukden, a garrison of 80,000 at Changchun refused to continue fighting and surrendered. In the Peking–Tientsin corridor seven Nationalist divisions gave up and surrendered. Such behaviour became contagious. The Nationalist commander for the whole north, General Fu Tso-yi, now had to hold an enormous front with only 300,000 men. For their part the Communists had obtained huge additions of good weapons and ammunition from these surrendering forces, and their morale was greatly boosted. They began to advance southwards towards Nanking. The government position, which was becoming increasingly desperate, was made worse by food riots in both Nanking and Shanghai, and on 11 November martial law was declared in Shanghai.

At the end of November, after weeks of confused fighting, the 250,000-strong Nationalist garrison of Hsuchow (now spelled Xuzhou) abandoned the city on orders from Nanking and moved to relieve the Twelfth Army Group of 140,000 men, which was encircled at Suhsien (now Suxian). Other groups had so far failed to relieve it, and some 30,000 casualties had resulted. On 10 December Chiang Kai-shek extended martial law to all of China still under his command, except for the west and the island of Formosa (Taiwan). By mid-December the Communist general, Lin Piao (Lin Biao), was closing in on Peking (Beijing). Government forces which had abandoned Hsuchow now fell back on a new defensive line to guard Nanking.

1949: Communist victory

The fall of Hsuchow really spelled the end of effective Nationalist resistance to the Communist onslaught. On 15 January 1949 the People's Liberation Army (PLA) took Tientsin. In Nanking Chiang Kai-shek called a military conference to which hardly any of his commanders came, and on 21 January he was forced to resign by the Sun Fo/Li Tsung-jen faction. The Vice-President, Li Tsung-jen, now became acting president and Sun Fo became Premier. In an attempt to earn some independent credibility Li disbanded the secret police, but they were all loyal to Chiang Kai-shek and refused to be disbanded; at the same time Li ordered the freeing of political prisoners with the effect that many were killed instead by the police. Back in the north the PLA besieged Peking and, after two weeks of negotiations, Fu Tso-yi handed it over to the Communists without further fighting on 31 January.

The Nationalist position became even more stark in March when Li Tsung-jen sent a delegation to Peking to discuss terms with the Communists and instead its members simply joined them. In April the government removed itself to Canton (now Guangzhou) under the Premier, Sun Fo, although the acting President, Li Tsung-jen, remained in Nanking. On 20 April the PLA crossed the Yangtse in force, and on 23 April it entered Nanking, formally ending Chiang Kai-shek's 22-year rule. The Governor of Suiyuan now changed sides, to be followed by other provinces in north-west China. This example was followed by Hunan and Yunnan in the south. The Kuomintang troops now fled, often in panic rout, from Shanghai and the coastal regions to Formosa (Taiwan) and Hainan. In these final stages of the war Chiang Kai-shek used his US aircraft for indiscriminate bombing of civilians as the Communists advanced, one more of many acts which helped to drive people into the Communists camp. From May onwards the march south of the victorious PLA met less and less opposition. The Nationalist government moved to Chungking but found that no one any more rallied to its standard. On 1 October 1949 the Chinese People's Republic was proclaimed in Peking, by which time the rump of the Nationalist government and army had withdrawn to Formosa with Chiang Kai-shek once more in command.

Estimated costs and casualties

The Chinese Communist Party membership had grown from 40,000 in 1937 to 1,200,000 in 1945, while over the same period Communist armed forces had increased from 92,000 to 910,000. In the year following the end of the war against Japan (1945–6) the USA tried to prevent the growing confrontation in China by bringing the Communists and Nationalists together, but in March 1946 it sent a military advisory group to assist Chiang Kai-shek and by this act threw its weight behind the Nationalists. Most of $500 million of US aid to the United Nations Relief and Rehabilitation Administration (UNRRA) at this time was channelled into Nationalist-held areas of China, and in August 1946 the USA sold $900 million worth of arms to the Nationalists for only $175 million. By the end of 1947, when the fighting was in full swing, there were an estimated 2,700,000 Nationalist troops facing 1,150,000 Communists. During the Manchuria campaign of 1948 the Communists under Lin Piao had about 600,000 men. By November the Nationalists had lost 400,000 men as casualties, prisoners or defectors. During the crucial struggle for Hsuchow (November 1948 to January 1949) both sides mustered approximately the same numbers – 600,000 men – and both were well-armed, although the Nationalists had the added advantgage of air control. However, poor leadership, a defensive mentality and collapsing morale led to a unnecessary defeat for the Nationalists. By the time Hsuchow fell on 10 January 1949 the Nationalists had lost 500,000 men and their equipment.

Despite the huge numbers involved in these sieges of cities, the war in fact was fought mainly in the countryside where the CCP had mobilized the peasants, who provided both intelligence and logistic support for the advancing Communists.

Huge numbers of the Nationalists surrendered or deserted and faded away, and although tens of thousands were killed, for a war involving such vast armies not very many were actually killed in battle. The Kuomintang were defeated largely as a result of their own indiscipline and the corruption of their leaders. After decades of suffering the peasants were ready to accept the disciplined CCP as opposed to the Kuomintang who plundered wherever they went. There was huge damage to property and in the final stages of the war an increasing amount of indiscriminate bombing by the Kuomintang air force.

Results: immediate and longer term

Meeting in Peking from 21 to 30 September 1949, the Chinese People's Political Consultative Conference drew up a Common Programme and elected Mao Zedong as Chairman of the People's Republic of China, which was formally proclaimed on 1 October. Recognition followed quickly from the USSR and other Communist countries and from a number in the West, including Britain but excluding the USA. The subsequent unity and central control that the Communists under Mao were able to exercise was all the more impressive when set against the record of Chiang Kai-shek, who had disappointed every hope that he would implement a revolution of modernization as envisaged by Sun Yat-sen. Between 1927 and the full Japanese onslaught in 1937, there were only three months in which Chiang was not at war with other warlords. He forced all other parties underground and showed little interest in anything except personal power.

With his defeat China, the world's most populous country, was suddenly united and freed of foreigners after 150 years of decline and growing chaos. The Communist victory remains one of the half-dozen most important events of the twentieth century. For the Chinese there was to follow a period of internal peace and the elimination for the first time in memory of absolute poverty, while development, even if disastrously handled as in the Great Leap Forward in the late 1950s, none the less became a primary objective of government.

On the international plane the emergence of a united Communist China changed world strategies on almost every front. In Cold War terms the addition of Communist China to the existing Soviet bloc created what then appeared to be a monolithic Communist empire stretching from East Germany to Hong Kong. Chinese intervention in the Korean War in 1950 (see Part II, pp. 135–141), reinforced this view, as did its later interventions in countries on its periphery (see Part III, pp. 246–254). The masterly role played by China's Premier, Zhou Enlai, at the Bandung Conference of 1955 which formalized the concept of non-alignment demonstrated the possibility of China's becoming a model for Third World countries desirous of rejecting both the Western and Soviet approaches to development. This influence reached its highest point in Africa during the late 1960s and the first half of the 1970s when China was responsible for the largest aid project on the continent, the TANZAM railway from Dar es Salaam in Tanzania to Kapiri Mposhi in Zambia. For the USA the defeat of its protégé, Chiang Kai-shek, was politically traumatic; it led to a hardening of American Cold War attitudes and a refusal of Washington to recognize the Beijing government for more than 20 years until President Nixon finally accepted the *fait accompli*. More generally, since 1949 China has been treated as a putative superpower, even though it is economically still part of the developing Third World.

INDIA: PARTITION AND COMMUNAL STRIFE

Introduction

The huge subcontinent of India, the most populous region on earth after China, had been brought under British control by means of a series of wars and treaties during the eighteenth and nineteenth centuries to form the most significant possession in Britain's world-wide empire. Agitation for a greater say in politics – eventual self-rule – had been growing for years, but in 1919 there occurred an event which changed the nature of the struggle. At Amritsar in the Punjab the local British commander, General Dyer, ordered his troops to fire on a crowd of 10,000 unarmed men, women and children; his object was to instil fear into the people and therefore to restore order after a riot in Amritsar protesting at British repression. Some 400 people were killed and 1200 were wounded. The Amritsar Massacre, as it became known, was a turning point in the history of British India; thereafter, many moderate Indians who had been supporters of the British now became revolutionaries. From that time forwards, slowly and painfully, the British were forced to make one concession after another to Indian demands for self-rule and then independence. The Government of India Act of 1919 devolved authority into Indian hands, but was already overshadowed by Amritsar. From 1920 onwards Mahatma Gandhi embarked on his campaigns of non-cooperation.

At the same time as pressures for independence mounted, so too did age-old conflicts between Hindus and Muslims become more acute, at times encouraged by British policies of divide and rule. Through the 1920s and 1930s the main pressures on Britain were maintained through the Congress Party; but at the end of 1920 Mohammed Ali Jinnah, the leader of India's Muslims, had split from Congress, and from that time onwards Hindu and Muslim agitated on increasingly separate platforms, resulting in partition to create a separate state of Pakistan for the Muslim community.

In 1930 the Viceroy of India, Lord Irwin, said that the ultimate aim for India was dominion status (full self-government). A round-table conference to discuss the next political advance was held in London in 1930. Then in 1935 the Government of India Act created an elaborate federal structure for India, although Jawaharlal Nehru and his Congress Party condemned it. Even so there was a real measure of progress and co-operation between the British and Indians from 1935 until the beginning of the Second World War. But then the Viceroy, Lord Linlithgow, declared war on Germany without first consulting national leaders and lost at a stroke the advances of the previous years. All members of Congress resigned from their various government (state) positions, and then, in 1940, the Muslim League under Jinnah demanded a separate state of Pakistan.

Britain's overriding concern was now to fight the Hitler war, and it had great need to carry India with it. In 1942 the Cripps mission went to India and in essence said: support the British war effort and after it is over a Constituent Assembly will be created to work out the details of independence. Congress, however, adopted its 'Quit India' slogan, and many of its leaders, including Gandhi and Nehru, were imprisoned.

In 1945 the Labour Party under Clement Attlee won the British general election. Attlee made plain his determination to give independence to India; he was in any case recognizing an event he could hardly hold back. In 1946 most people still thought that Jinnah and the Muslims were bluffing about a separate state as a way of obtaining maximum concessions for Muslims inside an independent India, and up to the last moment Gandhi and Nehru resisted the idea of partition. But in the run-up to independence communal violence between Hindu and Muslim increased, and during 16–20 August 1946 the 'Great Calcutta Killing' took place in which 4000 people died: it became increasingly clear that partition could not be avoided.

The partition of India

In February 1947 Field Marshal Lord Wavell was replaced as Viceroy by Admiral Lord Louis Mountbatten, and although his brief was to maintain the Union of India, Mountbatten realized soon after his arrival that this would not be possible. Thereafter, he steamrollered both independence and partition through, with the majority of the princely states, more or less willingly, joining India. On 14 August 1947 British rule in India came to an end, and partition created the two successor states of India and Pakistan. Civil war between Hindus and Muslims followed: there were communal riots in many parts of the subcontinent, but especially in those areas where the changeover took place. At a conservative estimate about 5,500,000 Hindu refugees moved from West Pakistan into India, while a similar number of Muslims moved from India into West Pakistan. On the other side of the continent 1,250,000 Hindus moved from East Pakistan into west Bengal.

Estimates of the numbers killed in this mass movement have varied enormously. At the lower end of the scale it is thought that 200,000 of the moving refugees – Hindu and Muslim – were killed while on the move. Upper estimates indicate that the number was more like 500,000, and perhaps as many as 1 million. The result was to be years of bitterness both between the two new states and among the communities of each religion who remained behind in either state. The casualties might have been reduced had the British army, then still in India, been allowed to restore order, but the suggestion was vetoed by Nehru. When Mahatma Gandhi was assassinated in January 1948 the shock throughout India had the effect of ending the communal violence which had continued until then.

Communal problems

India is so vast and complex a country, and made up of so many different communities, that periodic communal violence or demands for greater autonomy have become an accepted part of political life. Since independence communal massacres or separatist movements have accounted for thousands of deaths. During the early 1980s, for example, there was severe communal violence in Assam and north-east India against Bengali immigrants from Bangladesh, formerly East Pakistan (see above, pp. 465–468), leading to bomb outrages, murders, strikes and non-cooperation campaigns in which hundreds lost their lives. Most, though by no means all, violence in India tends to be communal in nature. Secessionist movements have usually had their teeth drawn by the expedient of granting full statehood to the region. By the 1980s the most important communal violence (see below) concerned the demand of the Sikhs in Punjab for secession. Meanwhile, Hindu–Muslim violence erupts fairly consistently from time to time.

Nagaland

Following independence in 1947, a strong nationalist movement attempted to bring unity to the disparate Naga tribes of the extreme north-east of India; the Nagas claimed that they should constitute a separate state of their own, and a small armed resistance army was organized. After 10 years of desultory violence negotiations took place between the central government and the Nagas in 1957; a measure of agreement was reached among the Nagas, and Nagaland was placed under central government administration. But unrest and non-cooperation continued, with rebels defying and attacking Indian army units and carrying out sabotage. In 1960, however, the Naga People's Convention agreed that Nagaland should become a full state, and it entered the Indian Union as such in 1963.

Dissidents refused to accept this state solution and rebel actions against central authority continued, although sometimes these were no more than acts of banditry or tribal rivalry as between different Naga groups. The result was an increased Indian presence in Nagaland. Another ceasefire was agreed with the dissidents and operated from June 1966 to March 1969, but the resulting series of talks also broke down and more clashes followed. At least some Nagas by this time were thought to have received training in China. From the early 1970s separatist agitation again developed and the Nagas formed their Naga Federal Army (NFA). In 1974 300 members of the NFA went into China for training. The NFA also harassed the Assamese people on the borders of Nagaland. Later in the 1970s another secessionist movement, the Naga Nationalist Council, became active, and this too attacked Assamese settlers in Nagaland. However, Naga agitation, though continuing, was low key through the 1980s.

The Naxalites

Various extreme leftist, Marxist groups active during the 1960s and 1970s and ready to resort to violence came to be called collectively the Naxalites. They never won significant support. They began with the far left of the Indian Communist Party and were later joined by other hard-left groups. An early violent incident (1966) involving some of these extremists in west Bengal at Naxalbari gave them the name which was applied thereafter to similar extremists. In February 1969 the Naxalites adopted what became known as the 'annihilation tactic', which was to attack the larger landholders.

The height of the Naxalite campaign, known as the Red Terror, came in the period 1970–2 in Calcutta when the Naxalites resorted to terrorist tactics against their right-wing targets. However, they were largely broken up by successful police counter-measures. Since that time, though various leftist groups have proliferated, they have not posed any threat to the central government. During the 1975–7 state of emergency thousands of Naxalites were arrested; then in 1977, in an effort to win them over, the Janata government released those Naxalites who renounced violence. By 1978, however, there was a resurgence of Naxalite violence.

The Naxalites proved remarkably unsuccessful, given the poverty of India and the poor masses that they ought to have been able to target for followers. They failed because they underestimated the strength of both religious and caste barriers and the hold these had on poor people. Periodically, the Naxalites surface with acts of violence. Thus, in late December 1987 the Indian government had to despatch 400 élite commandos to the south-eastern state of Andhra Pradesh to rescue seven state officials kidnapped by Naxalites, who offered to release their hostages in exchange for eight Naxalites who had been captured over the previous two weeks. The Naxalites were generally strong in the region and still pursuing their Maoist policy of inciting peasant rebellion. But despite such incidents, by the later 1980s they had come to be regarded as little more than bandits.

Other communal and secessionist movements

Since 1951 an increasing number of foreigners – Bengalis mainly from Bangladesh – had entered Assam. A crisis erupted in the early 1980s with demands that such incomers should be detected and deported. The Prime Minister, Indira Gandhi, resorted to direct rule, but that failed to solve the problem. There were many disturbances and riots during 1980, but gradually in 1981 the state returned to normal, although continuing talks did not solve the problem of 'foreigners'. Agitation against these incomers continued through 1982 and was used to prevent polling for the elections, leading to another period of President's rule. When elections were finally held in 1983 Congress won, but increased violence followed Hindu agitation against the immigrants and an estimated 1300 people were killed. In 1985 (15 August) a settlement was finally reached: foreigners who had entered Assam since 24 March 1971 were to be expelled.

Similar resentments at the influx of Bangladeshis occurred in Tripura state to the east of Bangladesh in 1978–9 when immigrants began to outnumber the local people. When the local people attempted to repossess themselves of land that the newcomers had occupied, the latter resisted under the banner of Amra Bengali: many were killed and others were rendered homeless. In June 1980 an estimated 550 people were killed.

The Mizo National Front (MNF), from the little territory of Mizoram between Bangladesh and Burma, was formed in 1966; it was another secessionist movement which indulged in fitful guerrilla action for the next 20 years. Various attempts by the central government to bring about ceasefires failed. The MNF imposed levies on the local population and attacked those refusing to pay. In 1975 members of the MNF assassinated three senior police officers with the result that the government mounted a major security drive against the Front. Its leader, Lal Mian, and about 100 other leading MNF were arrested, and the MNF was then compelled to move to Chittagong in Bangladesh. At that time its guerrillas numbered about 850. The following year the MNF held talks with the government and agreed to work within the constitution, and many of its members – though not all – laid down their arms. Sporadic violence was to occur subsequently, but in 1986 the insurgency came to an end when the Mizo National Front signed an agreement with the Delhi government: Mizoram was to become a full state and the insurgents laid down their arms. Lal Denga, the Mizo leader who had been in exile in London for 20 years, returned to become Chief Minister of the new state.

The Sikh question

In the Punjab in 1960 the Sikhs launched a mass campaign for a Sikh state – one in which they would be in a majority. The Prime Minister, Nehru, refused their demand, yet six years later under his successor, Indira Gandhi, the former Punjab was divided into Punjab, which did have a Sikh majority, Haryana and the Union territory of Chandigarh. This might have satisfied the Sikh demand, but in fact failed to do so.

During the 1980s India faced militant and growing agitation from the Sikhs for an autonomous Sikh state; their party, Akali Dal, demanded the creation of Khalistan. At the beginning of 1982 the Akali Dal rejected the Prime Minister's award for the sharing of the waters of the Ravi and Beas between the states of Punjab, Haryana and Rajasthan. In the course of the year the Sikhs put forward a number of demands: for Amritsar to be declared a holy city; for an all-India Act safeguarding Sikh temples to be passed; for Sikhs to be allowed the right to carry daggers on aircraft; and for Chandigarh to be transferred to the Punjab. They also demanded the acceptance of the 1973 resolution by their own Anand pur Sahib that the Sikhs should be a separate nation. Failing to obtain these demands, the Sikhs launched a campaign of defiance during which 25,000 were arrested, although later (October) they were released. A Sikh march on Delhi on 19 November (planned to coincide with the Asian Games) had little impact owing to tight policing.

In 1983 the Akali Dal decided on a campaign of defiance of the law (*morcha*); this led to violence against Hindus. The demands for an autonomous state became more shrill, leading the central government to place Punjab and Chandigarh under a proclamation that made them 'disturbed areas'.

The year 1984 was to be a time of crisis when the smouldering Sikh anger exploded into violence. There were anti-Sikh outbursts in Haryana, and Prime Minister Indira Gandhi, having outmanoeuvred the moderate Akali Dal party, merely found herself facing extremists and their demands. A small minority of Sikhs demanded total independence – Khalistan. Most wanted a settlement of their grievances. By May 1984 differences between Sikhs and Hindus were steadily polarizing the two groups, and Sikh terrorists were responsible for killing hundreds of people. Then the extremist Sikh leader, Jarnail Singh Bhinranwale, with his followers turned the Sikh Golden Temple in Amritsar into a terrorist stronghold where they collected arms. Prime Minister Gandhi found herself under increasing pressure to do something about Sikh provocation. On 2 June Gandhi said she wanted a peaceful solution to the Sikh problem, but that if necessary the army would assist the civilian power to keep order. On 5 June the army entered the Golden Temple; the Sikhs in control resisted for two days and when the fighting was over there were 554 civilian and terrorist dead (including Bhindranwale) and 121 injured, and 92 soldiers dead and 287 injured. The storming of the temple brought about the death of leading Sikh terrorists, but it did not solve anything. Sikh cadets in army training centres deserted and other Sikh organizations continued their demand for a separate Sikh state.

In July 1984 Sikh terrorists hijacked an Air India plane, which they forced to fly to Lahore in Pakistan. In August they hijacked another plane to Dubai in the Gulf. Then, in an effort at reconciliation, President Zail Singh (India's first Sikh President) visited the Golden Temple (27 September) after Sikh priests had lifted the ban they had placed upon him. On 31 October two of her Sikh bodyguards assassinated Mrs Gandhi, plunging India into a crisis. There followed anti-Sikh riots throughout India in which more than 1000 lives were lost. The rioting was quickly brought under control.

During 1985 the new Prime Minister, Indira's son Rajiv, worked for reconciliation, while at the same time Sikh extremists maintained their terrorist campaigns with murders and bomb outrages through the year. On 10 May some 80 people were killed by simultaneous bomb explosions in New Delhi and elsewhere. On 23 June an Air India plane crashed off Ireland, killing 329 people; the cause was later shown to have been a bomb, believed to be the work of Sikh extremists. Various moves by the Prime Minister culminated in an agreement of 24 July between the President of Akali Dal (Sant Harchand Singh Longowal) and Gandhi whereby Chandigarh would be joined to Punjab, while certain Hindu areas would be separated from Punjab and joined to neighbouring Haryana. Following these boundary adjustments, elections were held on 25 September and went off peacefully. The Akali Dal won 73 of 117 seats, but meanwhile Longowal had been assassinated.

The level of violence continued steadily into 1986, and in the year ending 31 October 1986 418 people were killed in Punjab, including 69 terrorists and 35 policemen, while 1322 terrorists were arrested. On 24 November 1986 Sikh terrorists stopped a bus and massacred 22 Hindus, sparking off a new round of riots in New Delhi and elsewhere.

Violence continued in 1987 with evidence that Sikh ministers were involved with the extremists, and in May the government of Punjab was dismissed, to be replaced by presidential rule. In October Sikh gunmen sprayed a crowd in New Delhi with bullets, killing 10, during the festival of Kali; the ultra-militant Bhindranwale Tigers Force claimed responsibility. The group claimed that police provocations had led to the killing of innocent Sikh youths. More than 1000 people were killed during the course of the year.

Terrorist activity continued through 1988, although police action was stronger and better co-ordinated. In February the Khalistan Commando Force (one of the Sikh extremist groups) used home-made bombs against courts, and by 24 February deaths had already reached 210 for the year. In April (299 people had been killed in March) the Prime Minister announced new moves in an attempt to contain Sikh violence. India closed the Punjab border with Pakistan, which was indirectly accused of supplying the Sikhs with arms; the border was to be fenced and the state's intelligence wing of 2000 was to be screened for Sikh sympathizers. By mid-May deaths from Sikh terrorist activities had reached 800 for the year; a second confrontation took place at the Golden Temple where troops and sharpshooters moved in to deal with between 80 and 100 militant Sikhs armed with automatic weapons.

In 1988, after six years of violence in Punjab, the Prime Minister, Rajiv Gandhi, attempted a new initiative. He announced the release of Sikh separatists who had been held without trial for four years, lifted travel restrictions in the state and suspended police emergency powers. Moderate Sikhs welcomed the government moves but claimed they did not go far enough, and the violent incidents and killings continued. Between May 1987 and March 1989 an estimated 3000 people lost their lives in Punjab as a result of Sikh violence. By this time there were 15 extremist groups operating in Punjab and demanding an independent Khalistan.

At the beginning of the 1990s no solution appeared in sight: the violence continued to erupt in murders and shootings, and the extremists continued to demand Khalistan.

INDONESIA: IRIAN JAYA

Background

When the Dutch withdrew from their East Indian Empire after the Second World War (see Part I, pp. 93–96) they retained control of West New Guinea (West Irian or Irian Jaya), people of which in any case were ethnically totally different (Melanesian) from those of the majority of the Indonesian islands. The new state of Indonesia called on the UN to exert pressure on the Netherlands, but the UN remained neutral, as did the USA, although the Indonesians attempted to involve them in their claim. In December 1957, in order to force the Netherlands to accede to their claim on Irian Jaya, the Indonesians carried out a number of punitive measures against the Dutch still in Indonesia: they ordered strikes against Dutch-owned businesses, refused landing rights to Dutch Airlines, banned the distribution of Dutch publications and expelled a number of Dutch citizens. They also seized Dutch holdings and property. As a result, some 40,000 Dutch people left Indonesia.

Talks brought no solution and so the Dutch built up their military forces in West New Guinea while the Indonesians obtained armaments (principally warships) from the USSR. Then in 1962 Indonesian paratroopers were landed in Irian Jaya and alongside rebel guerrillas fought the Dutch who were still the colonial authority. It now appeared that a full-scale war would erupt at a time when Cold War antagonisms meant that the whole region was delicately poised between the two ideological sides, so the USA and the UN decided to intervene in order to prevent hostilities getting out of hand. The result of their intervention was an agreement (15 August 1962) between the two combatants whereby the Netherlands would transfer sovereignty of its territory (West New Guinea) to the UN, and then the UN (in 1963) would transfer the territory to Indonesia. And this is what happened.

Separatism: the Free Papua Movement

For some years after 1963 the Free Papua Movement (OPM) sustained a series of small guerrilla campaigns against the Indonesian authorities. In 1969 the Indonesians carried out a plebiscite under which the people of Irian Jaya voted to become fully integrated with Indonesia, but this referendum helped spark off the emergence of a number of guerrilla groups calling for independence for Melanesians instead of their integration with Indonesians. The 1970s then witnessed a state of near warfare – if low key – between these groups and the government.

A new impetus for independence from Indonesia came in 1975 when the neighbouring territory of Papua New Guinea (the eastern half of the island) became independent. The OPM not only found sympathizers in Papua New Guinea, but was able to set up camps there and operate across the border from relatively safe havens. Even so, the OPM probably only ever numbered about 500 men and these were not well-equipped or trained. They were nationalists whose sympathies lay with some form of Melanesian rather than Indonesian nationalism. They attempted to cash in on the prevalent mood of Pan-Africanism in Africa by, for example, opening an office in Senegal. The movement, however, now split between a more radical (socialist) section under Yacob Prai and a more moderate section under Zeth Rumkoren.

In May 1977 the OPM, which wished to unite Irian Jaya with Papua New Guinea, led an uprising against Indonesian central authority. On 16 May the OPM seized seven prominent Indonesians as hostages, including two military commanders and the Chairman of the Provincial Parliament. (These were later all released unharmed.) Later, in response to this uprising, Indonesia sent a substantial military force to Irian Jaya to conduct a campaign against the OPM rebels (mid-1978). The result of this was to create fear in Papua New Guinea that Indonesia was contemplating a takeover of its neighbour. However, the two countries worked out a new border agreement in December 1979.

The 1980s

The OPM never really looked like achieving its objective, although it did have the capacity to act as an irritant to the Indonesian government. Prai, the more militant of the OPM leaders, was imprisoned as an illegal immigrant while in Papua New Guinea and was later deported to Sweden, which granted him political asylum. But although the movement appeared to have lost its momentum after the events of 1977–8, it continued frequent if sporadic guerrilla activities for some years. In October 1981 its forces attacked a lumber firm and abducted 50 of its workers, while other attacks were launched against the prison at Abepura and the airport north of Jayapura.

In January 1984 the Indonesian government decided to crack down on OPM activities and this led to fighting in Jayapura, the capital of Irian Jaya. As a result, some 10,000 refugees crossed the border into Papua New Guinea. Indonesian troops followed them across the border, while Indonesia's planes violated that country's air space and led to a crisis in relations between Indonesia and Australia (the ex-colonial power) as well as Papua New Guinea. But in October 1984 a new border agreement (to last five years) was reached between the two countries, and they set up a joint border security committee.

The secession demands remain, as do border problems, but they represent a minor irritant rather than anything more dangerous.

LAOS: LEFT AGAINST RIGHT, RIGHT AGAINST LEFT

Introduction

Laos was always a turbulent area of mixed tribes subject to pressures from its more powerful neighbours – Cambodia (recently also known as Kampuchea), China, Thailand and Vietnam. Colonized by the French during the nineteenth century, Laos became part of French Indo-China; the French established their capital at Vientiane, while the royal capital was at Luang Prabang. There was little unity in Laos under French rule. French Indo-China was invaded by the Japanese during the Second World War, and the Laotians were encouraged to declare independence at the end of the war as the Japanese retreated. During the years 1946–54 the Viet Minh (Communists) from Vietnam worked in harness with the Vietnamese minority in Laos to found the Pathet Lao (left-wing nationalist group) in 1953. That year France recognized the independent kingdom of Laos. But the Communists from exile had established a People's Liberation Army, and they proclaimed a liberation government under Prince Souphanouvong. By April 1953 the Viet Minh had established control over the two northern provinces of Laos, which they handed over to the Pathet Lao. When the Geneva Conference of 1954 brought an end to the first Vietnam War (see Part II, pp. 142–153) it was agreed that Laos should become a 'buffer' state between Thailand and Vietnam. This agreement by the major powers participating in the Geneva Conference did not, however, reflect internal left–right divisions inside Laos.

Prelude to civil strife 1954–1962

The Geneva Conference of 1954 effectively brought an end to French domination of Laos and the peninsula as a whole, and in the succeeding years (1954–8) the Pathet Lao established village cells throughout the country and built up their forces, which numbered about 6000 by 1958. For its part the government attempted to maintain a neutral position (1955–8), and Prince Souvanna Phouma, the Prime Minister, brought Pathet Lao members into the government. Following the elections of 1958, however, when the Pathet Lao made significant gains, the right wing forced Prince Souvanna Phouma out of office and replaced him with Phoui Sananikone. In 1959 the new right-wing government imprisoned Prince Souphanouvong (leader of the Pathet Lao), although he escaped a year later. It also accepted both financial and military aid from the USA. This precipitated the civil war between left and right; subsequent fighting between the two sides was conducted mainly on the Plain of Jars.

In 1960 Souvanna Phouma returned to power and once more pursued his neutralist policies, attempting to achieve a balance between the right and the Pathet Lao. But by this time the armed forces were becoming increasingly politically important, and in August 1960 they mounted a coup which forced Souvanna Phouma into exile in Cambodia. There was some bloody fighting in the capital, Vientiane, and a right-wing government came to power, in part a reaction against the left-wing influences of North Vietnam. Phoui Sananikone, who had begun to move towards the political centre, was replaced by Phoumi Nosavan; he in turn was temporarily ousted by Kong Le (a military paratroop commander) in August 1960, but then restored by US and Thai intervention. The West, principally the USA, now provided increased backing for the Nosavan government, which had the support of and controlled the army.

The civil war really began in 1960. Another big power attempt to resolve the problem (following Kennedy's presidential election victory in the USA and renewed support in Washington for a neutral Laos) led to another Geneva Conference in 1961–2, which produced a neutral government under Prince Souvanna Phouma once more. Meanwhile, in 1961 the Pathet Lao under Prince Souphanouvong had agreed a ceasefire, and his faction joined the new Souvanna Phouma government. Each of the three factions – right, neutralist and left – maintained its own armed forces.

From this time onwards Laos was to be drawn inexorably into the Vietnam War: the North Vietnamese supplied the Pathet Lao with arms, and the USA supported the Phouma government. The Ho Chi Minh trail, which was crucial to the Viet Cong, passed through the mountains of Laos, and from 1962 onwards the Pathet Lao intensified their struggle against the government.

1963–1973

From 1963 events in Laos became more and more influenced by those in Vietnam. The Pathet Lao supported the Viet Cong and ensured its use of the Ho Chi Minh trail; the USA supported the government in Vientiane. Warfare between the two sides was to be continuous through to 1973. From 1964 onwards the USA increased its involvement on the government side. That year the right forced Souvanna Phouma out of office, claiming it was not sufficiently represented in the government, so in retaliation the Pathet Lao left the government and its forces invaded the Plain of Jars. By 1966, when Phoumi Nosavan had been forced into exile and his forces had been integrated in the Royal Laotian Army, the war became synonymous with that between North Vietnam and the USA. At that time US estimates suggested that as many as 70,000 North Vietnamese were fighting alongside the Pathet Lao, and gradually during the second half of the decade the Pathet Lao occupied the greater part of eastern, southern and northern Laos. Despite overwhelming US air support, the government continued to lose ground to the Pathet Lao, while the USA relied on air power to bomb the Ho Chi Minh trail and, through the CIA, created special anti-Communist ground forces such as that of the Meo tribe. The Pathet Lao relied on guerrilla tactics. Laos was crucial to the Viet Cong war effort, which explains the latter's readiness to support the Pathet Lao.

The Pathet Lao launched a major offensive at the end of 1967, resulting in the capture of Nam Boc (20 January 1968) only 56 km (35 miles) from the royal capital of Luang Prabang. The government mounted a series of counter-offensives in 1970–2. In February–March 1971 South Vietnamese forces supported by the USA invaded Laos, captured Techepone, but then had to retreat in disorder. Vientiane was in no position to control such activities and had to allow the USA a free hand to bomb the Ho Chi Minh trail. Some of the fiercest fighting of the war took place over the years 1969–73. Then in February 1973 (with the end of Vietnam War in sight) the two sides agreed to a ceasefire and yet another compromise, neutralist government was arranged (5 April 1974), which included the Pathet Lao: Souvanna Phouma was Prime Minister, and Souphanouvong was deputy. Following the ceasefire, the Pathet Lao had moved some 2500 of their troops into the two capitals – Vientiane and Luang Prabang. The Pathet Lao were now poised to take complete power into their hands.

The Pathet Lao come to power 1973–1975

The government of unity formed in 1974 when the King signed a decree to establish the new coalition was clearly of a fragile nature. Souvanna Phouma remained as Prime Minister, while Souphanouvong became head of the joint National Political Council, which he was later to use as the instrument for his Communist takeover. With the final victory of the Communists in Vietnam in 1975 the coalition fell apart. In April Pathet Lao forces advanced on Vientiane. On 10 May right-wing members of the government resigned and many right-wing politicians and their supporters fled to Thailand. Anti-American demonstrations followed, and by August 1975 the USA had ended all its aid to Laos. The Pathet Lao 'celebrated' the liberation of Vientiane and now took full control, abolishing the monarchy and coalition government and replacing them (3 December 1975) by the Lao People's Democratic Republic.

Estimated costs and casualties

Ten years of civil war, including Vietnamese incursions and the use of massive US airpower, meant many thousands of casualties (possibly above 100,000) although no precise figures exist. The longer-term cost was simply to perpetuate a sense of factionalism and a tradition of rebellion against whatever government is in power in the centre (see below). In the period since 1975 more than 50,000 dissidents and government forces have been killed.

Results: immediate and longer term

The immediate result following the end of the civil war was the abolition of the monarchy when King Savang Vathura abdicated and the Lao People's Democratic Republic was established. Laos joined the Communist world and was thereafter to maintain exceptionally close relations with Moscow and commensurately poor ones with Beijing. More immediately important, it became heavily dependent on Vietnam and a junior partner in the affairs of Indo-China, which were now to be dominated by a united, Communist Vietnam.

Other results became clear over the following years. Many Laotians fled to Thailand and then the new government found it had to face dissidence from right-wing and ethnic minority groups. Thus, in 1977 royalists – the Meo tribesmen – launched an anti-Communist guerrilla war in Xieng Khonang province, while the

Hmong minority group, with support from China, which did not wish to see Vietnam dominate the region, also launched an anti-government insurrection (see Part III, pp. 251–254). By this time there were an estimated 45,000 Vietnamese troops in Laos in support of the government. Resistance to the government increased during the latter years of the 1970s and included desertions from the government side by people opposed to the growing influence and control over events exercised by the Vietnamese, so by 1978 the government faced guerrilla war on several fronts. China supported rebels in the north; in the southern Mekong there appeared the Lao National Liberation Front (LNLF), operating with units of between 10 and 50 men. This was a collection of poorly organized disparate resistance fighters opposed to the government for a variety of different reasons. They had limited success; the Vietnamese troops had ensured that government had control over the villages where the rebels might have recruited followers.

Guerrilla and border activities during the 1980s

By the beginning of the 1980s the number of Vietnamese troops had increased to about 50,000 and included Soviet advisers to assist the government to confront its rebels. This foreign presence was increasingly resented, for by 1980, for example, several thousand Laotians including government officials had been arrested for what were described as anti-Vietnamese activities. Laos now found itself a very junior partner in the Indo-China grouping headed by Vietnam. Tensions with Thailand mounted, and there were shooting incidents along the border. Vietnam backed Laos in suggesting that Thailand was plotting a war to destabilize the countries of Indo-China. The year 1981 also witnessed several small battles along the Laos–China border.

The Third National Congress of the Lao People's Revolutionary Party (LPRP) met in 1982 to confirm the leadership of Kaysone Phomvihan, who had led the party since 1955. Laos maintained its close ties with Vietnam, and at the Congress Kaysone hailed the special relationship with Vietnam while describing China as 'the most dangerous enemy'. Relations with Thailand remained strained because it continued to provide sanctuary on its territory for rebels against the Laos government. The former right-wing Prime Minister, Phoumi Nosavan, who had been living in exile in Thailand since 1965, announced the formation of a United Front of Lao People for the Liberation of Laos and claimed it had 40,000 supporters in the country.

In 1983 there were as many as 45,000 Vietnamese troops in Laos, and rebel groups (some assisted by China) increased their anti-government activities, including a series of attacks against Vietnamese army posts. Refugees crossed into Thailand at a slower rate than previously (1355 in the first five months of the year, as opposed to 2068 in the same period for 1982) but there was a sharp rise in the number of Hmong tribesmen fleeing from Laos to Thailand, up from 1234 in 1982 to 1785 in 1983. A major dispute with Thailand over three border villages erupted in 1984. Vietnam accused China of training dissident Loatians in China and then sending them back into Laos to disrupt the government. In May 1984 right-wing rebels killed 40 Vietnamese troops in south-east Laos.

The border row with Thailand continued during 1985 and was the cause of something like 120 armed encounters, with constant claims; counter-claims and accusations being made by both sides. The main cause of the Laos–Thailand enmity was the presence of something like 280,000 Laotian refugees in Thailand who had fled there since the Communists came to power in 1975. There were now something like 8000 Vietnamese and 1600 Soviet advisers in Laos. Yet opposition to the government was an irritant rather than a threat. The minority tribes, such as the Hmong, Yao and Khmu, were poorly co-ordinated and faced a Loatian army now reinforced with as many as 50,000 Vietnamese troops.

The row with Thailand continued through to 1988, but after fighting broke out early that year the two countries agreed a ceasefire and relations then began to improve. Guerrilla activity, on the other hand, was small-scale if still active. Then China agreed to end its assistance to the guerrilla groups. As a result of these agreements, the government was able to ask Vietnam to reduce its troop presence from 50,000 to 25,000. By the end of the decade the world-wide liberalization in the Communist countries and elsewhere seemed as if it might spell an accommodation between the central government and the various dissident groups.

THE PHILIPPINES: COMMUNIST INSURGENCY AND MUSLIM SEPARATISM

Introduction

At the end of the nineteenth century the Philippines passed from Spanish colonial control to that of the USA. During the 1920s there was a growth of Communist and socialist aspirations in Luzon, the main island of the Philippines group, based on general poverty and peasant land-hunger. During the Second World War the Philippines were invaded and occupied by the Japanese (1942) and Filipinos formed anti-Japanese guerrilla groups – the Hukbalahap (People's Anti-Japanese Army), or Huks as they came to be called. During the occupation they killed thousands of Japanese, and Filipino collaborators. When the war came to an end the Huks gained control of large estates in central Luzon; they set up their own regional government, which collected taxes and adminstered law. The returning Americans had planned immediate independence for the Philippines (4 July 1946) and elections for the new successor government were held in April of that year. The Huks took part in the elections and one of their candidates was elected, but when he (and other Communists who had been elected) was not allowed to take his seat in the assembly the Huks withdrew to their jungle hideouts and launched a civil war against the new government. This was the beginning of a series of insurrections against the central government which, with varying degrees of intensity, have troubled the Philippines ever since. They include the Huk rebellion of the early years after independence; the Communist rebellion which got under way in 1968; and the Muslim secessionist movement in the south.

The Huk rebellion

The Huks were joined after the war by a considerable number of sympathizers, and the government was unable to bring them under control. The Huks were sponsored or supported by the Communists, although there was a strong element of nationalism in their movement as well. In the immediate post-war era the Communists, who had resisted the Japanese, now built upon the existing resistance structures and were able remarkably quickly to gain control (in the late 1940s) of the rice bowl areas of Luzon as well as provincial capitals. In 1950 the Huks were about to launch an attack on the capital, Manila, when their leaders were all caught at their secret headquarters in the city. This led to the abandonment of the plan to attack, and from this point onwards the tide turned in favour of the government.

The USA now began to equip the Philippines army and security forces, which then became more effective against the insurgents. Between 1951 and 1954 the government was able to reverse the situation, and by the latter year the Communist–Huk rebellion had been broken and its leader, Luis Taruc, had surrendered. The man principally responsible for the defeat of the Huks was the Minister of Defence from 1950 onwards, Ramon Magsaysay; he employed a classic 'carrot and stick' approach which he characterized as 'all-out force and all-out friendship', and it worked. He prompted rural rehabilitation for those Huk rebels who surrendered.

In 1953 Magsaysay was elected President of the Philippines, and by his reforms he largely eradicated the grievances that had led to the Huk rebellion in the first place. He was killed in an air crash in 1957.

General and growing opposition to government

Growing dissatisfaction with the Marcos regime (Ferdinand Marcos became President of the Philippines in 1965) erupted in anti-government violence in 1969: both the Communists and the Muslims in Mindanao revolted, and violence was to escalate over the next few years. In September 1972 – major floods were the occasion – Marcos declared martial law at a time when ineffective military action against the guerrillas was, if anything, making the general situation worse. He then tried a more conciliatory approach, offering an amnesty to anyone who handed in his weapons. The declaration of martial law owed less to any perceived threat from the guerrillas than to general rising disorders – student dissatisfaction and growing urban crime – and considerations of Marcos's own power and how to perpetuate it. None the less, martial law made it easier to deal with the Communist insurgency. Thousands of government opponents were arrested, Parliament was suspended, the media were taken under government control, firearms had to be registered and a curfew was imposed.

Martial law and its accompanying offer of an arms amnesty were at least partially successful, for within months 500,000 weapons of all kinds had been turned in; it did seem, for a time at least, that the Communist offensive had been brought to a standstill. From 1973, however, Marcos assumed virtually dictatorial powers. For the balance of the 1970s and through the 1980s the government was to face insurgency from two main sources: the Moro National Liberation Front (MNLF), which developed into a Muslim secessionist movement and was based on the Muslim community of south Mindanao; and the New People's Army, which superseded the outlawed Communist Party of the Philippines. Later there were to be other rebellions against the government.

The Communist insurrection

The Communists did not become a threat until the mid- to late 1960s, when they revived their activities. In 1968 the New People's Army (NPA), whose traditional base was in central Luzon, broke away from the Communist Party of the Philippines (CPP) to operate on its own. Over the succeeding years it was to increase its size and improve its organization until it operated in quite large units, which would move into the towns from the countryside where its support lay. In 1969 the CPP split along pro-Soviet and pro-Chinese lines.

During the early 1970s the NPA operated mainly in Nueva Vizcaya and Isabela provinces, where it gained substantial successes. By July 1972 the NPA had become a sufficient threat to government to cause the latter to launch a major campaign against it at Diogo Bay in northern Luzon. At that time it became clear that the NPA was receiving support from China. However, following the declaration of martial law that year and the offer of amnesty, many Communists in fact turned in their weapons; in 1973 a number of local NPA leaders surrendered and announced their support for Marcos. During 1974 and 1975 the combination of martial law and the operation of the amnesty paid dividends, as did political reforms and improved conditions in the army. The NPA appeared to be losing its attraction and its capacity to do damage. The Soviet-oriented branch of the CPP brought its insurgency to an end in 1974 when it turned instead to orthodox politics after its leader had been captured.

In 1976 two of the leading members of the NPA, Bernabe Buscayno and Victor Corpus, were arrested (another leader, José Maria Sison, was arrested in 1977), and by the end of the year the NPA was split by internal dissension and in further trouble since the Chinese had withdrawn their support. As a result, in 1977, the NPA attempted to link up with the Moro National Liberation Front (MNLF) – the Muslims – in the south. This union led to something of a revival in NPA fortunes, and by 1979 it claimed to control large areas of the island of Samar and could field up to 100 men (in conjunction with the MNLF) for a particular engagement.

The 1980s: a Communist resurgence

By the mid-1980s the NPA was to claim a membership of 30,000 (although other estimates suggested between 10,000 and 12,000) and to be operating in two-thirds of the Philippines' 73 provinces. It was especially strong in north-east and south-east Luzon and in eastern Mindanao. During the decade the NPA derived growing support from rural populations where widespread poverty, rising unemployment and lack of government concern or programmes to ameliorate the situation made people turn to the alternative.

But at the beginning of the decade, after numerous setbacks in the 1970s, the NPA faced years of struggle. The hardest task was the initial process of making contact with villagers and hoping that they would not betray its cadres to the security forces, while also beginning their political education and military organization. In 1980 the NPA had perhaps 4000 guerrillas. In 1981 it was responsible for a grenade attack in the cathedral at Davao City in which 13 people were killed, and during the year it came to be seen as more of a threat than the MNLF. The

NPA cause was assisted during 1982 by the poor state of the Philippines economy, and by the end of that year it was estimated that 20 per cent of villages in the country as a whole either were then or soon would be under NPA control. The government had begun a programme of village relocation to frustrate the NPA, but later abandoned it. The group made further strides in remote rural areas during 1983. Occasionally major attacks would make the headlines, such as on 29 September when an ambush near Zamboanga resulted in the deaths of 39 soldiers and seven civilians, but generally guerrilla activity was low level as it had been for the previous 10 years.

In 1984, however, the NPA widened its guerrilla activities, leading President Marcos to claim that it had 6800 armed insurgents (the USA estimated 10,000). In 1985 it again escalated its campaigns; in December Marcos claimed that 10,000 'innocent civilians' had been killed by the NPA in the course of the year, while the NPA now claimed a membership of 30,000. What had become plain was the fact that the Communists were steadily growing in strength; the US Defense Department warned that the NPA might achieve parity of strength with the security forces by 1988. Continuing economic distress in the country assisted this growth of NPA appeal.

President Aquino and the Communist threat

Corazon Aquino replaced Marcos as President of the Philippines in 1986. On 5 August she initiated peace talks with the NPA, and on 27 November a 60-day truce was agreed. Between these two dates left-wingers, led by founders of the banned Communist Party and the NPA, launched the People's Party in the first organized, legal bid for power in 40 years. It therefore looked as though President Aquino's softer approach to the NPA might be highly successful. However, Aquino's softer line did not meet with the approval of all her cabinet, the army or the USA. At the time these peace talks were going on it was revealed that the guerrilla war had forced 100,000 primary and high school students to abandon classes in the countryside, where guerrilla activity was affecting 64 out of 73 provinces. By late October the cabinet had split on the Communist issue between hardliners led by Defence Minister Juan Ponce Enrile and the softliners who supported President Aquino's approach. The ceasefire agreement was reached and signed on 27 November but it looked precarious since the rebels appeared increasingly to be in a position to negotiate from strength, with their forces reaching parity with those of the government.

The ceasefire in fact collapsed in 1987 and the NPA then stepped up its activities, carrying out constant ambushes and sometimes sending its guerrillas to attack targets in the towns; the NPA's estimated 25,000 guerrillas then controlled 20 per cent of the country's 42,000 villages. In some parts of the country where government was weak anti-Communist vigilantes played an increasingly important role. The truce ended on 8 February and by 2 March the Armed Forces Chief of Staff, General Fidel Ramos, claimed that in the intervening period 181 people had been killed and that an average of eight clashes a day were taking place. The offer of an amnesty was rejected as a farce by the NPA. Yet by the end of the year analysts believed that membership of the New People's Army had peaked and that the greatest threat to the Aquino government came from the right and the military rather than the Communists. The NPA, deprived of any outside backer, was finding the task of providing weapons and maintaining a struggle by living entirely off the countryside increasingly difficult to sustain.

By mid-1988 President Aquino was confident enough to say in her state of the nation address (25 July) that 1988 'may be remembered as the year the insurgency was broken'. In part her assurance came from the capture earlier in the year of eight leading members of the NPA and the revelation of how the group used foreign bank accounts to purchase weapons abroad. Even so, a military report of May that year suggested that the NPA rather than the army was most likely to gain tactical initiatives when the two sides engaged. Revelations of NPA terror tactics – the discovery of a mass grave in Leyte province of people murdered for refusing to help the NPA – did not assist its cause.

During 1989 a witchhunt among the NPA for informers led to many being killed, while others defected; the government increased the size of rewards offered for captured Communists to $45,000 and this had an immediate impact. Both sides were accused of using terrorist tactics. The NPA, which accused the USA of assisting the Aquino government against it, now targeted US servicemen or other Americans in the Philippines. None the less, the group was clearly on the defensive by the end of the 1980s, although it was too early to judge whether the long insurrection was in fact coming to its close.

The Muslim secessionist war

Parallel with the war against the Communists a second war had to be waged against Muslim secessionists, principally to be found in the southern island of Mindanao, the main centre of the Muslim population. Although governments in the post-war period attempted to restrain anti-Muslim tendencies among the largely Christian population – a habit that had developed during the long years of Spanish occupation and had not been lessened during the American occupation – the success was only partial and became less as Muslim hardliners insisted on a separate Muslim state. A history of discrimination was the root cause of the Muslim separatist movement, and unfortunately such legacies are not easy to forget or overcome. Even in Mindanao, where the majority of Filipino Muslims are to be found, they remain a minority of roughly a third of the island's population, whose majority is Christian. Muslim grievances and rural poverty played on each other to promote a recourse to violence. In the 1970s, moreover, during the great boom in Arab influence which followed the explosion of oil prices in 1973, the Muslims in the Philippines could, for a time, obtain backing from Libya, Saudi Arabia and Egypt. At one point Libya was to act as mediator between the Muslim secessionists and the Manila government.

Christian immigration into the south was seen as an added threat to the Muslims, and in 1971 a series of riots erupted in Mindanao. The army restored order, but by May 1972 there had occurred 111 clashes in which 121 Muslims and 123 Christians had been killed. The original Muslim Independence Movement (MIM) was to be replaced by its armed branch, the more forceful Moro National Liberation Front (MNLF), in 1972, and when President Marcos declared martial law in September 1972 this led to an immediate challenge to the government by the MNLF and the beginning of civil war. The MNLF ignored the arms amnesty offered at this time, and instead about 50,000 Muslim insurgents took control of large areas of Zamboanga and the Sulu Chain (Basilan and Jolo islands), where the army was badly mauled and suffered heavy casualties.

Nur Misuari assumed the leadership of the MNLF in 1972, and by 1973 he was presiding over a widespread revolt; his forces captured most of the towns in Cotabato province. Sulu was the centre of the insurgency; the archipelago lies close to Sabah, which is mainly Muslim, and the rebels received support from Sabah's chief minister, whom the government of Malaysia in Kuala Lumpur found hard to control. By 1973 the MNLF numbered 15,000 and was able quite often to overwhelm government positions held by up to 500 men. In February 1974 the MNLF launched a major operation with 800 of its troops to capture the air force headquarters at Jolo Town and occupy Notre Dame College. It took government forces three days of bombardment from ships at sea and aerial attacks before they recaptured the town and forced the rebels to withdraw. The town was reduced to a shambles and the government was obliged to increase the number of security forces in the area to 35,000. This was the high point of the early Muslim insurrection, for not only did the army suffer heavy casualties, but it also ran short of equipment and was obliged to turn to the USA for assistance. As a result, however, it was able to retrieve many of its losses during 1974.

It was MNLF policy to stage a major attack shortly before an Islamic international conference as a means of attracting support from the international Islamic community. After the attack on Jolo Town the Muslim question in the Philippines was to appear regularly on the agenda of Islamic Foreign Ministers' Conferences. However, the attempt to obtain outside support was, in part, counter-productive since moderate Filipino Muslims did not wish to internationalize their grievances or establish a separate state. At the same time the appeal to Muslims outside the country made the government more determined to resist Muslim demands. By 1974 the MNLF leader, Misuari, had established a Central Committee (the Committee of 13), and most of these resided in Tripoli since Libya had become the most important external source of support.

In 1976 Libya acted as mediator, and talks in Tripoli between the MNLF and the Manila government appeared to have resolved the quarrel: a ceasefire was arranged for 23 December 1976. The Marcos government now proposed to establish an autonomous region to comprise the 13 southern provinces, which would have its own legislative assembly, executive council and Sharia courts. It also proposed a mixed security force (government and Muslim troops). In return the MNLF was to drop its secessionist demands. The settlement subsequently foundered when it was submitted to a referendum on 17 April. A clear majority voted against what in essence would have been a Muslim state – there was a 75 per cent turnout despite an MNLF boycott.

The MNLF ignored the results of the referendum and advanced new, even more radical demands, but when these new negotiations broke down in May 1977 Nur Misuari demanded total independence once more. As a result, civil war returned to Mindanao and Sulu. The referendum, however, represented a huge setback for the MNLF. The movement was now split by internal dissension: Hashim Salamat challenged Misuari for the leadership and won the contest, but Misuari established himself in Tripoli and Salamat in Cairo. Clashes between the MNLF and the security forces continued spasmodically until the 1980s. The government made another conciliatory gesture in 1979 when it held elections in Mindanao in an attempt to bring into being at least a form of regional autonomy.

The 1980s

Although regional legislative councils had been established in west and south Mindanao, hostilities were resumed early in 1981 when the struggle against the Muslims entered its ninth year. Martial law was lifted in January 1981, yet on 12 February 119 troops were killed on Pata island and during the year an estimated 2000 people were killed in the southern provinces. From this time onwards Misuari employed his supporters in small-scale actions against soft targets. During 1982 sporadic actions by the MNLF resulted in considerable loss of life; at the same time the movement found that it had little support outside the Philippines.

In June 1984 a military spokesman claimed – somewhat prematurely – that the separatist struggle of the MNLF for a Moro homeland was almost over. Further disjointed fighting took place during 1985. Then in September 1986 an unprecedented meeting was arranged between the newly installed President Aquino and Nur Misuari at which it was agreed to negotiate an end to the 14-year civil war. Peace talks were scheduled for later that year in Jeddah (Saudi Arabia); Mrs Aquino also tried to persuade the breakaway Moro Islamic Liberation Front led by Hashim Salamat to join the talks. The MNLF now took the line that it would drop its demand for independence if the majority of Muslims favoured an autonomy solution inside the Philippines. Unfortunately, these peace efforts came to nothing and by 1987 fighting was taking place in the south once more. On 8 September Nur Misuari claimed that his MNLF would establish its own provisional government within the year.

For the time being, at any rate, the secessionist war had deteriorated into a spasmodic, on–off affair that could either peter out or flare up into something more dangerous again.

Estimated costs and casualties

By 1986, when Aquino attempted to reach a settlement with the Muslim secessionists, the war had resulted in more than 60,000 deaths. That figure could be doubled to take account of deaths in the Communist civil war. In fact casualties might be considerably higher and a reasonable estimate of casualties by 1990 would be around 150,000 altogether. Between 1972 and 1981, largely in response to the Muslim and Communist threats, the government increased the size of the armed forces from 60,000 to 200,000 men, which placed a major economic burden on the country and created other problems, such as those associated with military coup attempts against the civilian authorities. Destruction of property from time to time (as in the attack on Jolo Town) has been substantial. The extent to which development has been retarded is impossible to estimate since in both cases (the Communist and the Muslim revolts) lack of government effort to develop or answer the needs of the rural poor was a principal reason for revolt.

Results: continuing

By the beginning of 1990 the Aquino government was in deep trouble, faced by army mutinies, a resurgence of the Communist insurgency and continuing Muslim activities. Thus, in 1987 there had been three military coup attempts against the government and Marcos's successor, Corazon Aquino, emphasizing the perceived weakness of her position; on the third attempt (28 August) 50 people were killed. One of the justifications put forward by disgruntled military for these coup attempts was that Aquino was too soft on the Communist rebels. Another coup attempt against Aquino – 1–7 December 1989 – resulted in 98 deaths and 500 wounded.

Although the fortunes of the insurgents vary widely from year to year they have not been defeated and nor do they appear ready to come to terms with the government. There is, therefore, every prospect that the Philippines will continue to face debilitating insurgency for years to come.

SRI LANKA: SINHALESE NATIONALISM AND TAMIL SEPARATISM

Introduction

Ceylon (now Sri Lanka) was first colonized by the Portuguese, from whom it was taken by the Dutch; in their turn the British took it from the Dutch during the Napoleonic Wars, and it remained part of their empire until it achieved independence in 1948. The original Sinhalese people form about 74 per cent of the total population of Sri Lanka. The Tamils have come into the country from India as immigrants over the centuries to settle in the north-west and north-east of the country, and now form about 18 per cent of the population. The Tamils can be divided between those (Ceylon Tamils) who have been settled in the country for several centuries or more, and those (Indian Tamils who still tend to see India as their homeland) brought in by the British during the nineteenth century to work on the tea plantations. The Tamils began to make separatist demands in 1965, and from 1975 onwards these demands have been accompanied by increasing violence. The racial, cultural and religious distinctions between the Sinhalese and Tamils appear to be fundamental, so the (Marxist) Liberation Tigers (Tamils) have little in common with the (also Marxist) People's Liberation Front (Sinhalese). The problem is made worse by Sinhalese fears of Indian territorial ambitions since the Tamils come originally from the Indian state of Tamil Nadu in the southern tip of that country, which now has a population of more than 50 million Tamils. This connection has provided India with an excuse to interfere in the affairs of Sri Lanka.

Following independence in 1948 there was a growth of Sinhalese nationalism; this was led by S. W. R. D. Bandaranaike, whose Sri Lanka Freedom Party (SLFP) won the 1956 elections and at once began to implement Sinhalese nationalist aims by making Sinhalese the sole official language and enacting other measures to enhance Buddhism and Sinhala culture. Bandaranaike was assassinated in 1959, but his widow, Sirimavo Bandaranaike, continued with his policies until her political defeat in 1965. By that time Ceylon's growing economic problems were more important and Sinhala nationalism appeared to be in retreat – for the time being.

The Sinhalese insurrection of 1971

The moderate leader, D. S. Senanayake, and his United National Party came to power in 1965 to concentrate on economic problems. It was now that extreme Sinhalese nationalists formed the People's Liberation Front (Janata Vimukthi Peramuna, JVP) under the leadership of Rohana Wijeweera. At this time (1965) it was committed to socialism by peaceful means and drew its membership mainly from former members of the pro-Chinese Communist Party. Towards the end of the 1960s, however, the JVP turned to armed struggle; it found few recruits among the peasants and had to rely on students (often those whose career expectations had been disappointed). In the elections of 1970 the SLFP in alliance with Marxist groups made a political comeback and Mrs Bandaranaike once more became Prime Minister. However, once in power she soon lost the support of radical youth groups and so was faced with the uprising of 1971, which was a reaction partly to apparently insoluble problems of poverty and partly to extremist nationalist (Sinhalese) demands.

There was to be a brief JVP insurrection in April which, although it inflicted considerable harm on the country, did not attract widespread support and was quickly suppressed. On 5 and 6 April squads of between 25 and 30 JVP insurgents attacked 90 police stations across the country, capturing quantities of arms and ammunition. The rising was confined to the south and centre of the country. In places communications were cut or badly interrupted, and the rebels took control of two towns for a brief period; they also tried to take over Colombo. The JVP took the government almost completely by surprise, but by the end of April the security forces had regained control in all the urban areas and the insurrection was brought to an end, although fighting continued in rural and jungle areas until June.

The government appealed for outside help and received military aid from a number of countries, including the USSR, India, Pakistan and Britain. The JVP was now banned and its leaders imprisoned. In 1977, however, when its leaders renounced violence, the party was again legalized, and it was to enjoy something of a resurrection in the late 1980s. In the immediate aftermath of the uprising (1972) the Bandaranaike government carried out a number of reforms: the name of the country was changed from Ceylon to Sri Lanka; it became a republic (it had been a dominion since 1948, recognizing the British sovereign as head of state); and a new constitution emphasized Sinhalese dominance. Thus restraints of the law were removed so that Buddhism (the religion of most of the Sinhalese) was given the 'foremost place' in the country.

The economy of the country worsened through the 1970s. In 1977 the United National Party (UNP) under J. R. Jayawardene returned to power, and in 1978 he modified the constitution by making Tamil as well as Sinhalese a national language, although Sinhalese remained the official language.

Tamil separatism

Increasingly after 1948 the Tamils came to foster ideas of separatism; periodically, outbursts of communal violence were to erupt between Tamils and the majority Sinhalese. The Tamil Hindu community is largely confined to the north-west of the island, although increasing numbers are found elsewhere in the country as well. The narrow straits separating Sri Lanka from the state of Tamil Nadu in India make communication between the two easy, so it is difficult to prevent Indian involvement in the Tamil affairs of Sri Lanka. During the 1970s growing numbers of Tamils began to think in separatist terms, and discussed the creation of an independent state of Eelam in the north-west of the island.

In 1977 the extremist (Marxist) Liberation Tigers emerged as the spearhead of Tamil separatism; they were prepared to use violent terrorist tactics. There already existed the more moderate Tamil United Liberation Front (TULF), which also demanded a separate Tamil homeland. The first targets of the Tigers were moderate Tamil politicians, whom they attempted to assassinate; then they turned to murdering police. The Tigers were motivated by both Tamil nationalism and Marxist ideology, and in this latter regard the extensive poverty of the country provided, or ought to have provided, a rich recruiting ground. In the early days of their activity (1977–80) the Tamil Tigers were few in number – perhaps 100 – operating in four groups round the town of Jaffna, which is the centre of the Tamil community in the north-west of the country. They recruited their members mainly from the student community, robbed banks and attacked members of the security forces. When pressed the Tigers were able to retreat across the straits into Tamil Nadu.

By the beginning of the 1980s Tamil unrest and demands for an autonomous state were mounting, as was the violence. Then in 1981 an explosion of violence occurred between the Sinhalese and Tamils, and that August serious clashes led to many casualties and damage to property, which prompted the government to impose a state of emergency. In September, when the violence had ended, the government set up a committee of cabinet and TULF members to resolve ethnic differences and look at one of the principal causes of the disturbances: poverty. During 1982 a separate cause of violence arose with clashes between the Sinhalese majority and the island's Muslim community in which three people were killed and more than 100 hurt. It was not until 1983, however, that the violence really escalated.

Escalation of violence

Major Sinhalese–Tamil communal violence erupted in July 1983: in the Tamil stronghold of Jaffna 13 government soldiers were killed, an event which was followed by widespread rioting that included the capital, Colombo, and resulted in 387 deaths (mainly of Tamils), while 79,000 people were rendered homeless. The extent of the troubles and the high number of Tamil casualties led to deteriorating relations between India and Sri Lanka, but the two countries hastily sent envoys to each other and patched up their differences (Indian concern was, however, indicative of pressures to come). On 5 August the government amended the constitution to outlaw any group which advocated separatism. As a result, TULF was outlawed and its 18 members of the Assembly were expelled, leading to by-elections.

The year 1984 was dominated by the Tamil issue, with violent clashes between Tamil separatists and security forces taking place in March, April, August, November and December, resulting in more than 400 deaths. President Jayawardene tried to promote peace talks with TULF, but had little success because TULF claimed that government devolution proposals were inadequate to satisfy Tamil demands. At the same time other political parties in Sri Lanka were opposed to the idea of Tamil autonomy. The government created a special Ministry of National Defence (March), which was intended to deal with Tamil separatism. At the same time Sri Lanka accused India of training Tamil guerrillas in Tamil Nadu; in April, therefore, the government set up patrols in the Palk Straits, which separate Sri Lanka from India.

The emergency continued for the third year running through 1985, by which time the Tamil campaign for a separate state was 10 years old. The first half of the year saw a number of clashes between Tamils and the security forces (which were mainly Sinhalese). On 18 June several Tamil groups agreed to a ceasefire, which was to last until mid-September while they searched with government for a solution. These talks were held under Indian auspices at Thimphu in Bhutan, but they broke down in mid-August when the six Tamil groups taking part walked out. Meanwhile, in July there had been an assassination attempt on President Jayawardene. In September the government none the less extended the ceasefire unilaterally in a bid to maintain peace moves, and agreed to enlarge the multi-racial committee responsible for monitoring the ceasefire. The troubles were having a crippling impact on the economy: defence costs had risen to $600,000 a day; tourism, which had long been a major source of foreign exchange, had been drastically curtailed; there was constant disruption of communications; and there were growing fears of an exodus of Sri Lankans (many with abilities the country could ill afford to lose) who did not wish to remain in a permanent state of civil war.

In 1986 Sri Lanka again accused India of allowing Tamil bases in Tamil Nadu state and of providing guerrilla training there. Growing international concern at the problem was matched by the increasing sophistication of Tamil guerrilla training, with the Liberation Tigers of Tamil Eelam (their full title) the most militant and best trained. In August 1986 a breakthrough did appear possible when moderate Tamil leaders discussed government devolution plans in Colombo, yet by mid-September fighting between the security forces and the Tamil separatists had escalated so badly in and around the town of Batticoloa on the east central coast as to produce 10,000 refugees. New peace talks were held in Delhi during October, and in November the government offered part of the eastern province as well as the northern province to the Tamils, but the Liberation Tigers rejected this plan.

In an apparent change of tactics the police in Tamil Nadu rounded up more than 1000 rebel guerrillas in and around Madras; they were photographed and then released, while large quantities of arms were seized. At the same time the Indian government of Rajiv Gandhi was exerting pressure on that of Sri Lanka to improve its offer to the Tamils. By the end of the year there was fighting between rival Tamil groups, from which the Tamil Tigers emerged victorious and stronger than ever. Even so, there were some 35 Tamil groups fighting the Sri Lankan army.

The Indian attempt to pressurize Sri Lanka into a solution had broken down, and the government in Colombo once more looked to a military solution to the 11-year conflict. None the less, some progress appeared to have been made, with the Tamil Tigers showing a readiness to drop their demand for independence in exchange for full autonomy within a federal Sri Lanka. By this stage neither side was strong enough to crush the other. The insurgents could muster about 5000 guerrillas, often better armed than government forces. The Sri Lankan army was being expanded and had reached 23,000 (as opposed to 11,500 18 months earlier), while defence now represented nearly half of total government expenditure. Talks at the very end of 1986 did not reach any solution; the Tamils demanded the release of 3000 of their members then in prison and also wanted Indian involvement in any settlement. By then an estimated 4500 people had lost their lives in the conflict.

The war escalated further during 1987, and by mid-year combined casualties had passed the 6000 mark. Tamil claims that they were discriminated against had the backing of 50 million Tamils in India, and this was the year when India became far more deeply involved in the conflict. On 29 July President Jayawardene met India's Prime Minister, Rajiv Gandhi, and they agreed as follows: that hostilities were to be ended within 48 hours and that the Tamil militants should surrender their arms; that the northern and eastern provinces were to be made within three months into a single unit which was to have its own administration; that there should be an amnesty for all Tamils; that Tamil and English should become official languages with Sinhala; and that India would cease to permit its territory to be used for training. About 130,000 Tamils were to be repatriated to India, and 10,000 Indian troops would be sent to help implement the agreement. From Colombo's (nationalist) point of view it was a settlement of desperation, and both Sri Lankan Tamils and Sinhalese opposed the agreement. Some Tamils did surrender their arms, but more refused to do so. There was another attempt on Jayawardene's life in August, and the arrival of the Indian troops signalled an increase in violence. In September the Sri Lankan government attempted to save the peace accord when it recognized the Liberation Tigers of Tamil Eelam as the key group in both north and east, but the violence continued. The Indian troops now found themselves to be targets as they attempted to keep order. On 12 November the Sri Lanka Assembly passed two bills which gave increased autonomy to the northern and eastern provinces as envisaged in the July agreement, but this only led to increased Tamil–Sinhalese violence.

The war continued unabated in 1988, and now the militant Sinhalese JVP stepped up its violence and assassinations. The accord between Sri Lanka and India rapidly soured, for there were too many fears in Colombo about India's intentions in the country. The Liberation Tigers concentrated their attacks on the Indian troops, whose numbers were increased to about 50,000. India, like many other powers which send peace-keeping forces into foreign lands, rapidly found that it was far easier to become involved than to disengage. By May Sri Lanka and India had agreed to a phased withdrawal of the Indian forces, whose presence in the country was inflaming Sri Lankan nationalism at least as much as it was helping to solve the Tamil question. Many Sinhalese felt that the pact with India had made too many concessions to the Tamils, and the revitalized JVP was waging a violent campaign against the government. By the end of the year, when presssures for the Indians to withdraw had steadily grown, one Sri Lankan assessment was that Tamil terrorism would continue for 20 years. By the end of 1988 Sri Lanka was in general chaos.

At the beginning of 1989, according to Amnesty International, deaths of Tamils, Sinhalese and police were averaging 1000 a month. President Jayawardene was succeeded by President Ranasinghe Premadasa; the General Secretary of the moderate TULF, Appapillai Amirthalingam, was assassinated. Relations with India continued to deteriorate as a result of the continuing presence of its troops in Sri Lanka, with the Liberation Tigers attacking the Indian troops and refusing to accept the 1987 agreement. In July security forces mounted a big campaign to round up more than 10,000 anti-government militants of the JVP, which none the less had great popular support for its demand that all Indian troops should be withdrawn from the island. At that time the bulk of the Sri Lankan army, which had been increased to about 45,000 in strength, was being used in the south of the country against the Sinhalese extremists of the JVP rather than against the Tamils in the north. In September, under intense pressure, India finally agreed to withdraw all its troops (then estimated at 42,000) by 31 December; they had suffered more than 1000 dead. The Tamil Tigers appeared as strong as ever despite casualties, and about 5000 people were thought to have been killed during the year. In November Rohana Wijeweera, leader of the JVP, was killed in curious circumstances.

The Indian withdrawal went slowly and a new deadline was fixed for March 1990. As the last Indian troops prepared to depart, the Tamil Tigers prepared to move in to the eastern part of Trincomalee. By March 1990 the Tigers controlled most of the Tamil districts of the north and east of Sri Lanka, and with the Indian departure they seemed set to become the dominant Tamil force in the country.

The Indian presence in Sri Lanka altered the normal alignments by causing an explosion of extremist Sinhalese violence against the government. As a result, Colombo did a deal with the Tamils. President Premadasa could only quell the Sinhalese rebellion by sending the Indian troops home, and Delhi would only agree to their withdrawal if a solution to the Tamil question was found. The Tamil Tigers therefore agreed to drop the demand for an independent state, while the government promised much greater (though as yet unspecified) autonomy. In Colombo it was generally felt that, if the government and the Tamils failed (during 1990) to resolve the question of Tamil autonomy, this would give India an excuse to return.

Estimated costs and casualties

In 1989 the official estimate was that 11,000 people had been killed in the fighting since July 1983, including 1000 Indian troops, although other estimates (for example that of Amnesty International) put the death toll much higher. In addition a further 5000 Sinhalese had been killed in the clashes between the JVP and government that took place in the south of the country over the two-year period beginning in July 1987. Many thousands had been rendered homeless, between 100,000 and 200,000 Tamils had fled as refugees to Tamil Nadu, great damage had been done to property, and the economic costs to an already poor country had been staggering.

Results: continuing

Early in 1990 the situation was precarious and hopes were pinned on the understanding between the government and the Tamils lasting once the Indian presence had been removed from the country. By the middle of the year (June) these hopes had been dashed when some of the fiercest fighting since the beginning of Tamil separatism erupted. Up to 100,000 people fled the fighting in the north-east between the Tamil Tigers and the Sri Lankan army. At the beginning of the year, when the Indians left, the Tigers had about 2000 armed men; by June 1990 they had trained another 3000. They changed their tactics and made full-scale assaults on army camps and barracks. Despite the ferocity of the renewed fighting, India made plain that it would not intervene again, despite its sympathy for the Tamil cause (India had burnt its fingers badly with the previous intervention). By mid-1990 it had become clear that the Tiger strategy had been to wait for India's withdrawal before once more launching an all-out attempt to create an independent region. The fighting and massacres in July and August 1990 reached a new ferocity.

THAILAND: COMMUNIST INSURGENCY

Introduction

Thailand managed to evade incorporation into one of the European empires and learnt over a long period of time how to survive as an independent state when those around it were becoming colonies. It therefore developed a tradition of neutrality coupled with a readiness to work closely with the dominant power of the time. In the first part of the century it veered towards Britain; then Japan; and in the 1960s (during the Vietnam War) towards the USA. None the less, such leanings towards the big powers represented no more than its determination to remain independent, 'neutral' and Buddhist. It has, more or less, managed to do all three. As a neutral 'ally', Thailand avoided occupation by the Japanese; between 1944 and 1945, when it was plain that Japan was losing the war, Thailand reversed its stand, threw out the pro-Japanese government and replaced it with a pro-Western one.

In the post-war years Thailand suffered a fair degree of dissent, internal violence and insurgency: poverty, ethnic minorities and violent warfare in neighbouring territories each had their effect, while the coming to power of the Communist regime in neighbouring China ensured that Thailand's own Communists had a powerful ally near at hand. In the extreme south of the country, bordering on Malaya where the people are Muslim and Malay rather than Thai, there developed a degree of separatism, although this never became very violent.

The Communist Party of Thailand (CPT) began as a branch of the Chinese Communist Party in 1942 and was only formally constituted in 1952. It always worked to bring about a people's revolution in the rural areas. During the late 1940s with Burma in chaos, the Cold War rapidly escalating and growing Communist insurgency in neighbouring Indo-China, Thailand took a firm anti-Communist line which proved an attraction to the USA, then preparing to take on its world role of containing Communism. In 1954 Thailand became a founder member of the South-East Asia Treaty Organization (SEATO). By the late 1950s the Thai Communists were beginning to train their members in guerrilla warfare tactics; they were sent to China, North Vietnam and Laos for this. Then in 1961 the CPT decided on armed struggle and began to set up a guerrilla structure. During the 1960s, when the Vietnam War was at its height and its effects spilled over into both Cambodia and Laos, Thailand provided rear bases for the USA and some of its troops served in South Vietnam. As a *quid pro quo* (and to serve strategic needs) the USA provided aid for the construction of major highways in Thailand, and this was to have an impact – not always favourable – on the lifestyle of the rural peasants.

The Communists organize 1965–1970

Communist insurgency began in 1965, although it was often at a low level of intensity. Late that year the Communist guerrillas attacked government forces in the north-east of the country. The Communists gained support from various ethnic minorities which had grievances of their own against the government in Bangkok: these were especially strong in the north-east of the country. The CPT adopted Maoist principles and mounted a rural guerrilla struggle. From 1965 until the late 1980s it was to be a permanent destabilizing factor for government, though rarely did its activities become a real threat to the system. When it launched its guerrilla war the CPT had the backing of both China and North Vietnam, and it quickly developed insurgency at various levels in the north (where it had the support of the hill tribes), in the north-east (where it had the support of the Thai-Isan, who were related to the Laotians, and where the threat posed by the Communists was to be greatest) and in the extreme south (where it obtained support from the Malay Muslims).

When it became plain that there was a substantial Communist insurgency threat the government responded by creating what it called a Communist Suppression Operation Command. It adopted tactics that had already been used successfully in British Malaya (see Part I, pp. 97–103), setting up village defence units and attempting to win the hearts and minds of the villagers. The government also withdrew 12,000 troops from South Vietnam (the Black Leopards) to use them as a counter-insurgency division. In 1969 the CPT established its military wing, the Thai People's Liberation Armed Force (TPLAF), which by 1971 had an estimated force of 5000 guerrillas. TPLAF tactics were to assassinate government officials and provincial chiefs and to attack road construction and timber workers. The TPLAF emphasized that it was fighting against corruption, lack of justice for the poor and inadequate educational or health facilities. Where it was able to do so the TPLAF forced peasants to work on its behalf so as to involve them in the struggle. By 1970 most provinces in the country were subject to some degree of destabilization from Communist insurgency activities.

Insurgency during the 1970s

The CPT was to achieve its greatest growth during the first half of the decade when it drew its support from the ethnic minorities and was fully backed by the Chinese. It was already a sufficient threat for the government to mount a major campaign against the TPLAF in the north-eastern provinces during 1971. Guerrilla camps were also found in the south of the country (Surat Thani) in September of that year, and the extent of Communist activity there became clear. In October 1971 government forces captured a guerrilla camp with both Chinese and Vietnamese instructors operating in it, so revealing the extent of the international backing for the CPT.

The TPLAF greatly increased its activities in 1972 and expanded its membership; with training by both Laotian and Vietnamese guerrillas (the first foreign guerrillas to fight inside Thailand) it also improved its tactics and became more effective in the field. It was from this time onwards that the TPLAF concentrated many of its attacks on government targets or construction camps. At the same time it was also successfully winning the support of the ethnic minorities: for example, Mio tribesmen were prepared to join it as guerrillas. That year the TPLAF established bases in the centre of Thailand. The war of insurgency had become sufficiently serious to force the government to declare seven areas in the north-east 'off limits' because of guerrilla activities. The great length of the joint Thai–Laos border, which the government did not have the resources to close, meant that the TPLAF could always obtain support or retreat across it if hard pressed. But government anti-insurgency tactics were also improving, and during the year it managed to destroy a CPT drugs ring and seize quantities of arms.

By 1973 TPLAF numbers had increased to about 7700 in the north and north-east of the country, and by the end of the year their insurgency operations were being carried out in 43 of 71 provinces. Their headquarters, however, remained in Laos. During 1974 the TPLAF began to set up village militias, and (as in Malaya) these acted as suppliers to the guerrillas and were sources of intelligence about government movements. The militant Communists emphasized the primary need to mobilize the masses and employ effective propaganda.

Meanwhile, Thailand suffered from increasing violence between left and right during the democratic rule of 1973–6 (the unpopular military regime of Thanom-Praphat collapsed in 1973 under pressure of rural unrest). In October 1976, however, the right and the military came back to power under Thanin Kraivichien in a bloody coup which was especially aimed at left-wing students, 100 of whom were killed. As a result of this bloodshed, many students fled to the jungle and joined the Communists. Thus the TPLAF became considerably stronger at this time, linking up with left-wing student movements in the towns. By this year the TPLAF had about 10,000 guerrillas in the north and east of the country and another 1500 in the far south. For the two years 1976–8 the TPLAF was probably at its strongest and a major threat to government. However, at the end of 1978 the CPT received a major setback when Vietnam invaded Kampuchea (Cambodia) (see Part III, pp. 262–273): the TPLAF found that its bases in both Kampuchea and Laos were closed to it, and the Chinese-led CPT in those countries was expelled because the CPT had sided with China in its quarrel with Vietnam.

The Thai government took advantage of these Communist quarrels and offered amnesties to the Thai Communists, many of whom were to return to their home and surrender over the next few years. Another complicating factor during the 1970s had been the influx of refugees into Thailand from Burma but still more from Kampuchea and Laos, and so in 1979, with help from international relief agencies, Thailand set up a number of huge refugee camps along the Kampuchea border.

The 1980s: the insurgency declines

Gravely weakened by the events of 1979, TPLAF activity markedly declined although clashes involving small units continued. By the 1980s most counter-insurgency activity by government was in the hands of the paramilitary police rather than the military. None the less, clashes between government and the TPLAF were to continue through the 1980s. TPLAF numbers in 1980–1 stood at 13,000, with 5000 in the north-east, 3000 in the south and 5000 in the north. In 1982 the TPLAF controlled about 450 villages.

During the 1980s the government had to contend with a series of border problems with its eastern neighbours. Thus in 1981 (June) the new government of General Prem Tinuslanond had to cope with border incursions by Vietnamese forces from Kampuchea which occupied three villages; as a result, Thailand opposed the UN seat of Kampuchea being given to the Heng Samrin government. By 1982 the government's amnesty policy for the Communists was beginning to pay dividends as an increasing number of guerrillas came out of the jungle to surrender. Also in 1982 the government mounted a major campaign in the Golden Triangle against the Shan United Army of the drug baron Khun Sa.

Government pressure on the guerrillas was even more rewarding in 1983 when an estimated 5000 guerrillas accepted the amnesty terms; by then many of them were disillusioned with the faction splits in the Communist leadership. The amnesty included offers of land to incoming guerrillas and payment for surrendered guns. The government launched a second attack on the drug barons of the Golden Triangle this year in conjunction with Burma. In December 1983, at a ceremony broadcast nation-wide, 5000 members and supporters of the CPT formally surrendered. The Communists continued to surrender through 1984, and these too received similar amnesty terms to those who had come in earlier. On 3 July 1984 the government had a stroke of luck when it arrested 16 leading members of the CPT in Bangkok.

During 1985 and 1986 insurgency was low key and did not represent any real threat to the government. Early in 1987 there was a fierce engagement between the Thai army and the Vietnamese in the border region where Thailand, Laos and Kampuchea converge. Later in the year (August) there were further border incidents with Laos. However, the Communist insurgency continued to decline; in the south during March and April 540 guerrillas surrendered, while 18 leading members of the CPT were also captured in April.

By 1988 the insurgency appeared to be dying, while the whole nature of the Communist world was changing rapidly as the effects of Moscow's new policies worked their way through. As the 1990s began it was too early to say whether the insurgency had definitely come to an end, although the signs were that it probably had.

Estimated costs and casualties

Although the insurgency never really looked as though it would overthrow the government, it was a running sore for 15 years and on occasion provoked substantial military campaigns against it. Even so, the army never deployed more than 20 per cent of its forces against the TPLAF and usually was more concerned with the threatening situation along Thailand's borders with Cambodia and Laos. Casualties over these years must have run into many thousands.

THE AMERICAS

ARGENTINA: THE DIRTY WAR

Introduction

In a society dominated by military and middle-class values, a clash between revolutionary left and hard right is always a distinct probability. Argentina politics for many years after 1945 were dominated by Juan Perón: first as President, then by his legacy when he was for 18 years in exile, and finally by the developments set off by his return in 1973. A populist dictator greatly aided by his beautiful wife Eva (Evita), Perón was forced into exile by a right-wing army in 1955 for his 'socialist' policies. Growing economic problems over the succeeding years polarized Argentinian classes, so that by the end of the 1960s younger 'Peronists' turned increasingly to violent revolutionary tactics to gain their ends. A number of left-wing guerrilla groups were formed, of which the Montoneros became the most effective and notorious. In 1970 the former President, General Pedro Aramburu, was kidnapped and murdered, an act calculated to polarize further the two extremes of Argentinian society.

The early 1970s saw growing political anarchy until in 1973 President-General Lanusse decided to hold elections and allow the discredited yet powerful Peronists to take part. Perón was not allowed to return to the country during the election, but his representative or proxy, Héctor Cámpora, was elected President in May. Cámpora allowed the release of left-wing guerrillas then in detention before he invited Perón to return to take over the presidency in September. Perón (aged 78) returned to a political situation that was already explosive – under Cámpora there had been a number of kidnappings of businessmen for ransom – and Perón himself, although he had returned preaching social reform, soon moved to the political right and in the process lost the support of the more radical left.

By this time a number of extreme political groups had developed into active guerrilla organizations. They included the Argentine Anti-Communist Alliance, Armed Forces of Liberation, Armed Peronist Forces, Armed Revolutionary Forces, Montoneros, National Liberation Army, National Liberation Movement, People's Guerrilla Army, People's Revolutionary Army, and Red Brigades of Worker Power. Castroism, then perhaps at its most influential, also had a following in Argentina. A number of these groups, whose fortunes waxed and waned, coalesced in the early 1970s to support Perón on his return. The Armed Peronist Forces (FAP) began operations in 1969 but later merged into the Montoneros, who became by far the best known of the left-wing guerrilla organizations.

The Montoneros first came to prominence in 1970 when they kidnapped ex-President Aramburu, who had been responsible for putting down a Peronist plot in 1956. The Montoneros were prepared to work with other organizations and

515

grew in importance and influence during this period. In part they financed themselves by kidnapping wealthy businessmen for ransom. Under Cámpora's brief presidency the Montoneros were legalized in all but name by government. Most other groups had little influence except that their appearance symbolized general disaffection with the political process. But this was not true of the People's Revolutionary Army (ERP), which was the military wing of the Argentine Trotskyist Workers' Revolutionary Party (PRT) that came into being in 1969. In late 1970 the People's Revolutionary Army began its activities round Rosario (its hero was the charismatic Che Guevara, who came from Argentina). The People's Revolutionary Army reached its zenith in 1975 when its cells were operating in many parts of the country; that year it carried out the spectacular kidnapping of Victor Samuelson, the Esso manager, to obtain a ransom of $12 million.

By 1975 these extremist organizations, whose policy of deliberate confrontation was designed to provoke the right – and the military – into action, had caused thousands of deaths and posed a major threat to government.

Perón's return and the escalation of violence 1973–1976

When Perón did return to Argentina in September 1973 he was faced with more extremism than he was able to control, although at least some of these forces – the Armed Peronist Forces (FAP) – were in response to his own overt encouragement. Other groups, such as the Trotskyist People's Revolutionary Army led by Roberto Santucho, went their own way determined to bring about a left–right confrontation. Their excesses bred a counter-reaction from the right, and the Argentine Anti-Communist Alliance (AAA) began operations against targets from the left in 1973. Those of its members responsible for terrorist actions were thought to be either from the police or the security services. The AAA had death lists published in the press, and at least some 'proscribed' targets were able to flee the country to escape death.

The Armed Revolutionary Forces (FAR) were a rural guerrilla group which was prepared to stop its operations when Perón returned to the country. However, when it became clear that he had rejected the left they joined the Montoneros and reverted to terrorist violence. Perón denounced the Montoneros, who in consequence became increasingly militant and the dominant influence of the left-wing groups. On 6 September 1973 the leader of the Montoneros, Mario Firmenich, said that the organization would revert to its terrorist tactics of arson, murder and the conduct of a popular war. During the years 1974–6 the Montoneros led attacks on the government by means of assassinations and kidnappings; their main targets included the Federal Police Chief, the US Consul and two generals.

Perón had returned with his third wife, Isabelita, who was an incompetent woman, but when the old man died in July 1974 she succeeded him as President. There was a rapid growth of left–right violence and the emergence of right-wing death squads, which may have had the connivance of some ministers. In any case the government seemed unable to control the situation. During 1974 and 1975 the People's Revolutionary Army achieved its maximum effectiveness with spectacular attacks on the Azul military garrison 240 km (150 miles) south of Buenos Aires in 1974 and on the barracks at Monte Chingolo in December 1975. In 1976, however, its leader, Santucho, and his deputy were killed, and during that year and 1977 the movement was largely destroyed. The inefficient and corrupt rule of Isabelita (María Estela Perón) led the military to intervene (there is little evidence that they were loath to do so) in March 1976 when they deposed her and took power once more. By that time Argentina was subject to brutal left–right terrorism.

The military and the dirty war 1976–1980

In February 1976 the military took over responsibility for counter-insurgency operations (they were in any case coming increasingly to dominate the government) and established a Council of Security under which they placed the police. The capital and seven provinces were placed under the control of this Council. War councils were empowered to hand down sentences, and the death sentence was decreed for anyone over 16 who attacked members of the military. In December 1975 Quieto, who was the joint head of the Montoneros (with Firmenich), was captured. During 1976 about 1600 Montoneros were killed, and another 500 followed in the first half of 1977, effectively destroying the organization.

Many people welcomed the military takeover of March 1976, which brought a three-man junta to power under General Jorge Rafael Videla, as the only way to deal with the growing menace of terrorism. Following their coup, the military banned political activity and trade unions, and forbade the press to report political violence. At the same time they instituted a ruthless campaign against liberals, leftists and terrorists. From this time onwards right-wing paramilitary activity – death squads – against the left became a normal part of the new order, and in the course of the next few years about 10,000 people were to be murdered (often in brutal circumstances after torture) or disappeared. The death squads were composed of military or police personnel. People were subjected to a form of military terror with arbitrary arrest, kidnapping and torture as the norm; there were no trials and nor was there any pretence at legality. By 1976 the left-wing ERP and Montoneros had been fatally reduced by massive state terrorism as more and more of their personnel had been killed, fled into exile or were imprisoned.

Back to civilian rule: the Falklands factor 1980–1983

The growing unpopularity of the military and demands for a return to civilian rule persuaded the military to lay down a condition in 1980 that (under a civilian government) there should be 'no revision of what had happened during the fight against terrorism'. By then both Argentinian and international pressures were mounting to force the military to explain the death or disappearance of 10,000 people in the 'dirty war'. A US report on human rights (5 February 1980) demonstrated that since its takeover in 1976 the military had embarked on terrorist tactics that included torture, arbitrary arrest, invasion of homes, kidnapping and suspension of rights, and that such measures had been used against anyone considered to be subversive. Reports of the numbers of disappearances gave figures of between 10,000 and 15,000 (Amnesty International put one estimate at 20,000). On 14 August 1980 a huge demonstration took place by the Madres de

Plaza Mayo (Mothers of the Plaza of Mayo) in Buenos Aires, which included relatives of the disappeared ones.

Against a background of mounting disquiet and increasingly overt opposition the military – now headed by General Galtieri – embarked on the Falklands invasion in 1982. This was calculated to appeal to nationalist sentiment, which it did, and like all such ventures was done at least in part as a diversion from pressure against a regime the popularity of which had long been exhausted. When the invasion of the Falklands (Malvinas) took place (2 April 1982) Galtieri hoped to regain at least some of the military's lost popularity and prestige, but (see Part I, pp. 000–000) he did not believe that Britain would mount a full-scale expeditionary force to recover the islands. The surrender of Argentinian forces to the British on 14 June spelt catastrophe for the junta.

Despite the diversion of the Falklands War, the issue of the 10,000 'disappeared ones' would not go away: during October and November, for example, about 1000 unidentified bodies (believed to be the victims of the 1976–9 killings) were discovered in six cemeteries. The military made matters worse in 1983 (they had already agreed to hand power back to the civilians in January 1984) when they published a document in which they said that the disappeared persons should be considered dead. This led to international outrage. Then on 23 September 1983 (shortly before civilian elections were due) the military passed a law which granted amnesty to military personnel who had committed crimes in the anti-guerrilla campaigns (it also covered 'subversives'). By then the military reputation had fallen so low that the great majority of Argentinians were simply waiting for their departure.

Estimated costs and casualties

Between 1976 and 1981 an estimated 6000–15,000 people disappeared. In addition several thousands of people had died in the preceding period of violence (1970–6). Apart from the loss of life, Argentina's reputation was done appalling damage by this dirty war in which human rights were so blatantly violated and disregarded. The behaviour of the military led US President Carter to stop military aid to Argentina, an action which had some effect because a number of prominent prisoners were then released and permitted to leave the country. International outrage undoubtedly played a part in persuading the military to bring the Dirty War to an end.

Return to civilian rule

In 1983 Galtieri was replaced by the retired general Bignone, who called elections for 30 October. The Radical Civic Union led by Raúl Alfonsín swept to power, and he became President formally on 10 December 1983. During his campaign Alfonsín had promised to repeal the law of 23 September, and on 13 December, three days after assuming power, Alfonsín announced plans to prosecute nine members of the former military junta, including three ex-Presidents – Generals Videla, Viola and Galtieri. In the first months of his rule Alfonsín did his best to reorganize the military, retiring some 70 senior personnel, repealing the law of 23 September and bringing the junta to trial. In the course of the year revelations of what had been done under the military shocked Argentina, and more than 800 private prosecutions were brought against them over human rights violations. More mass burial sites were unearthed, revealing that in many cases the hands of victims had been cut off to prevent subsequent identification.

In September 1984 a report on 8960 disappearances gave details of secret prisons and torture chambers established by the military, and named 1200 military personnel implicated in the terror. Alfonsín tried to make the military purge themselves, but they repeatedly refused to take the guilty to courts-martial, so in October it was announced that the nine members of the junta already designated would stand trial in civil courts. That month Brazil extradited Mario Firmenich, the former head of the Montoneros, to stand trial in Argentina, which enabled the government to argue that it was prosecuting the terrorists of the left as well as the military. Public hearings against the nine members of the junta were to be held throughout 1985. The military showed no remorse and argued that they had acted to save the state from subversion. In the end ex-President Videla and the naval commander, Admiral Ermilio Massera, were sentenced to life imprisonment while other members received lesser terms. Trials continued in 1986, but towards the end of that year the government wanted to bring the process to an end, having dealt with the leaders and made its point about human rights. It introduced a 'final stop' bill to set a date for making charges so that the lengthy series of trials could be brought to a close.

There was a resurgence of left-wing violence in January 1989 when ultra-left guerrillas attacked a military barracks and the army showed itself to be increasingly restive under civilian rule. Many of the problems that the left–right clashes of the 1970s brought into the open have yet to be resolved.

BOLIVIA: RIPE FOR REVOLUTION?

Introduction

Averaging slightly more than one coup a year over a period of 150 years, Bolivia has had a deeply troubled history. The army, which has frequently exercised its power to intervene, has done so, at least in theory, to check corruption and force civilian governments back to a reasonable level of responsibility. During the 1940s dissidents began to form opposition parties and an apparently new tradition of popular uprising erupted in 1946 against the right-wing government of Gualberto Villarroel, who was overthrown after several days of bloody fighting. Villarroel was hanged from a lamp-post by the mob outside the presidential palace. A left-wing revolutionary party ruled Bolivia until early 1950 when it was replaced by the Bolivian Communist Party, but elections in 1951 brought to power the National Revolutionary Movement (MNR), which was Fascist; then, once more, the army intervened in order to rectify the situation between left and right.

The events of 1952

In April 1952, in several days of fighting, the military was forced out of power and a reformed MNR came back. The army was almost destroyed in this bloody conflict, in which it fought against workers and peasants. This was the beginning of a remarkable Bolivian national revolution, which turned out to be one of the most far reaching in Latin America. The measures which were enacted over the next few years included nationalization of the tin mines, widespread land reform and the application of universal suffrage, with the Indian population for the first time being given full rights and then also being armed by the government so that they became a new political factor in the country. In 1956, however, the revolutionary President, Víctor Paz Estenssoro, was replaced by Hernándo Siles Zuazo and the revolutionary period came to an end, to be followed by consolidation and growing conservatism.

The 1960s: the Guevara intervention

During the 1960s the power of the army was revived with US assistance. In 1967 the Vice-President, General René Barrientos, seized power in a coup; he was to rule until his death two years later. His policy was to deprive all the popular groups of any influence or power – except for the peasants, who had been promoted to a different status for the first time in the revolution of 1952. He created a situation that invited anti-government guerrilla activity, but although Barrientos's policy was to exaggerate the extremes that already existed in Bolivian society and seemed to set the scene for another revolution, none came.

Ernesto 'Che' Guevara, the Argentinian doctor and revolutionary who had already achieved fame in Cuba, believed that Bolivia was 'ripe for revolution' – a revolution, moreover, that would sweep through the continent – although other revolutionaries in Cuba did not agree with his assessment. He conceived the idea of a guerrilla campaign in Bolivia during the Tricontinental Conference which was held in Havana in 1966, and subsequently he contacted the Communist Party of Bolivia, which agreed to assist his efforts (though in the event it did little). Guevara obtained backing and in late 1966 with 15 'trained' followers he went to Brazil, where he set up headquarters at Nancahuazu in a remote part of the country. In early 1967 his small force (his National Liberation Army, ELN) entered Bolivia, but their attempts to mobilize the peasants met with failure. Usually when the guerrillas had brushes with the military it was the former who won the engagements. In April Guevara sent two emissaries, one of whom was the French left-wing thinker Régis Debray, to publicize their exploits; instead they were captured by the Bolivian authorities before they could leave the country, and their capture (the other man was an Argentinian) was used as a nationalist propaganda ploy to damn the Guevara revolution as foreign inspired.

In July 1967 the army discovered Guevara's camp and supplies, and nine of his small band were killed. Yet such was the fame of Guevara that the army sent several thousand men to the jungle region in which he was operating, including American-trained counter-insurgency units. By September 1967 Guevara and 16 followers were on the run in the jungle pursued by 1500 troops; they were run down eventually at the Yuro river on 8 October when most of the men were killed. Guevara himself was wounded and captured, to be shot dead the following day.

Guevara's romantic foray into the Bolivian jungle was doomed from the start: his men were ill adapted to jungle conditions, the peasants refused to rise at their bidding, they were cheated out of their money by one of their number, and they had to seek food and medicine in rural villages where army spies were waiting to plot their movements. A score or more soldiers were killed in encounters over a few months before the inevitable end came. Had this little guerrilla war been led by an unknown, probably no one would have heard of it. But such was Guevara's fame that it obtained publicity out of all proportion to what it achieved – or failed to achieve – and Guevara's death turned him into a cult figure for more than a generation.

Aftermath

It was both ironical and inglorious that the most famous revolutionary of his generation failed so dismally to rouse the downtrodden of Bolivia. After his death there was sporadic guerrilla activity for a while: in 1970, for example, 70 guerrillas raided a goldmine to take two West German engineers hostage and use them to bargain for the release of 10 guerrillas. In October 1970, however, when Oswaldo Peredo, who had succeeded Guevara as the leader of the ELN, was captured the movement began to disintegrate. It did, however, make an impact in urban activity for a little while longer in La Paz and Cochamba, receiving support from the Soviet Embassy. The 1970s were subsequently to witness a period of right-wing authoritarianism and repression.

BRAZIL: THE FALL OF GOULART

Introduction

The elections of 1960 brought Jânio Quadros of the conservative National Democratic Union to power as President, while João Goulart, an authoritarian left-winger seen as the heir to the long-lasting President Vargas (who had committed suicide in 1954), became Vice-President. It was an odd combination. Quadros was arbitrary and dictatorial in his actions and began to move the country away from its traditional close relations with the USA to a stance of non-alignment. Suddenly in August 1961 he resigned, sparking off a constitutional crisis since many factions and interests were determined to prevent Goulart from succeeding Quadros as President, although he was the person designated to do so according to the constitution. Both the military and a wide range of conservatives regarded Goulart as too radical to be President, but others insisted on his constitutional right to take over; indeed, sections of the military in the south of the country supported Goulart. The crisis lasted from 1961 to 1963, with a manoeuvre to adopt the parliamentary system that would give executive power to a Prime Minister and leave the President – Goulart – as a figurehead. The crisis was finally resolved, if only temporarily, in January 1963 by a plebiscite in which Goulart was voted full presidential powers by a margin of five to one. His subsequent period of presidential office, which only lasted a year, was characterized by massive inflation and economic stagnation as well as right-wing and military plotting to get rid of him.

The coup of 1964

The powerful business community, with military backing, saw Goulart as too left wing and wanted a pretext to depose him; they feared his populism and the ability to manipulate organized labour from which he derived his main support. This included the Sailors and Marines Association, and it was their members, ironically, who provided Goulart's opponents with their change to take action against him. As the possibilities of a coup became more obvious, Goulart, with the help of his brother-in-law, Leonel Brizola, who was then a Deputy, prepared to resist a possible takeover by attempting to mobilize the Peasant Leagues, the Groups of Eleven and organized labour. The Groups of Eleven consisted of 11-man cells that had been established originally by Brizola in the state of Rio Grande do Sul; their object was to defend left-wing political initiatives or the revolution when it came.

On 25 March 1964 1400 sailors and marines seized control of a trade union building in protest at the arrest of the president of their association. They held the building for two days and refused to surrender to the Minister for the Navy. Troops were then sent to restore order; the 1400 surrendered and were immediately pardoned for their action. The military hierarchy expressed its shock and accused Goulart of failing to support them and undermining their position. The President backtracked at least to the extent that he agreed to investigate the amnesty, but from his viewpoint the damage was already done – he had provided his opponents with the pretext they had been seeking. On 31 March the Fourth Military Region revolted against the President; their example was copied by other military regions. In Rio de Janeiro a small number of troops defended Goulart, but they were soon overcome by the garrison. Although in reaction to the military takeover the General Confederation of Workers called a general strike and began to disrupt life in Rio, this was not enough to stop the military takeover. Apart from the call for a general strike, the support groups that Goulart and his brother-in-law had tried to mobilize against a coup proved ineffective when the military took action, and Goulart and Brizola fled to Uruguay.

The army then began arresting leftists and Communists, while later it undertook to purge both Congress and the Labour Party, which had supported Goulart.

Left-wing opposition to government 1964–1970

The coup was led by General Humberto Castelo Branco, and he subsequently inaugurated a policy of economic rectitude, tackling inflation, promoting foreign investment and assisting private enterprise, as well as denationalizing the mining industry and other industries which had previously been taken under state control. These policies had a devastating effect on the poorest sections of the community and produced a great deal of suffering as well as sowing the seeds of future revolt.

The result was an outbreak of guerrilla and terrorist anti-government activity. Two further, non-economic factors fuelled the radical opposition to the military: the Cuban example, then at its most potent throughout Latin America; and the emergence in 1966 of the Organization for Latin American Solidarity (OLAS), which was backed by Havana and supported revolution. Other radical groups also emerged during the 1960s, including the National Liberation Action (ALN) led by the Communist Carlos Marighella (who was to be killed in 1969).

The ALN made headlines during 1968 when its members abducted the US Ambassador to Brazil, Charles Burke Eldbrick, to exchange him later for 15 guerrilla prisoners. The ALN subsequently abducted the West German Ambassador and exchanged him for 40 prisoners, and then the Swiss Ambassador who was rated at 70 prisoners. Marighella was the most successful of the hard-left leaders and enjoyed the support of Cuba. He wrote a brief *Minimanual of the Urban Guerrilla*, but when he was killed in a gun battle with the police (1969) the ALN soon fell apart. Other left-wing guerrilla groups at this time included the Revolutionary Popular Vanguard (VPR), which worked with the ALN and attacked military installations, and the National Revolutionary Movement (MNR).

However, these left-wing movements did not survive the campaign of terror, including mass arrests and torture, which was launched against them. At the same time the right produced its own anti-left death squads during the middle and late 1960s, and these took the law into their own hands. They included the Commando for Hunting Communists (CCC) and the Anti-Communist Movement (MAC). These guerrilla activities had largely died out by the early 1970s.

CHILE: THE FALL OF ALLENDE

Introduction

Social measures carried out in Chile under President Eduardo Frei of the Christian Democrats during the years 1964–70 radicalized the peasants: 5 million hectares (12.4 million acres) of land had been expropriated on their behalf by 1970, so politics as a whole moved to the left, the peasants became a new, much more forceful factor and the middle classes became frightened. One consequence was that the various parties of the left united in 1969 to form the Popular Unity coalition. One of its principal aims was to end the domination of the mining sector (mainly copper) by foreign interests – which meant the USA.

Meanwhile, radical groups were becoming increasingly active. The Movement of the Revolutionary Left (MIR) had been established in 1965 by radical socialist students; by 1967 its members were raiding banks for funds and it had to go underground. The Miristas then began to infiltrate poor squatter quarters on the outskirts of Santiago in order to politicize the people. Subsequently when Salvador Allende Gossens won his presidential election in 1970, MIR decided to remain outside mainstream politics – the government – for it believed that civil war was bound to come and that its chance would then arise. Its tactics, therefore, were to seize small factories or farms which had not been affected by Allende's new socialist laws and force the government to accept the expropriation. Though Allende in power condemned such actions, he did nothing about them. At times

MIR had the backing of the more radical members of Allende's government and so was able to set the pace for radical reform.

Allende rules 1970–1973

In the presidential elections of 1970 Allende had defeated his opponent Alessandri by 39,000 votes out of 3,539,000 to become Chile's first democratically elected Marxist head of state; in his election campaign he had stressed his intention of establishing socialism within a democratic system. In the three years of his rule it was his methods of government as much as his measures which created unnecessary enemies for his regime. Thus he bypassed the Legislature on the issue of using the State Development Corporation to buy out industries which were to be national-ized, and allowed the government to incite radical groups to seize factories or estates. Early on he froze prices and raised wages, nationalized the US-owned copper mines as well as other heavy industries, and broke up large plantations to distribute more land to the peasants. Rapid political polarization took place, as well as an increasing incidence of street violence between factions of left and right. The growth of violence and increasing chaos as radical groups seized small factories or farms was matched by a growth of inflation and a decline in economic production. Foreign aid was curtailed, while open hostility to his regime from the USA fuelled opposition to Allende in Chile. By the summer of 1973 the rate of inflation had risen to 500 per cent, and the world price for copper had fallen by 50 per cent since 1970.

Government inefficiency undoubtedly contributed to the eventual downfall of the Allende government, while doctrinaire decisions made enemies without achieving compensating advantages. Thus the political quota system introduced to control government appointments and to prevent any party from dominating any branch of the public service merely acted as a major threat to the bureaucracy. At the same time Allende's socialist measures created many foreign enemies (which really meant American enemies), while also turning the upper and most of the middle classes against his government. The economy deteriorated steadily and this resulted in food shortages, while a series of strikes made the position worse. During 1973 trucking industry owners held a two-month strike in protest at plans to nationalize them, and this nearly brought the country to a standstill. Foreign banks also refused to furnish much-needed loans.

Possibly most daunting to Chileans was the appearance on the streets of paramilitary militias carrying arms; the most formidable and dangerous of these was MIR, and since it had close ties to Allende and his family it escaped censure and appeared to have presidential protection. The main opposition to the government came from the National Party, which feared the growing ties between Chile and Cuba; from April 1973 onwards the National Party advocated civil disobedience against the government. The far-right Fatherland and Liberty Move-ment, led by Dr Pablo Rodríguez Grez and Walter Roberto Thieme, provoked street battles with members of MIR. (The Fatherland and Liberty Movement had been established shortly after Allende came to power, but was broken up by the government several months before the coup of September 1973.)

By August 1973 the situation was clearly getting out of control, and on 22 August Congress passed a motion of censure on the government and appealed to the armed forces to 're-establish the constitution and the law'. At the beginning of September professional workers such as teachers and doctors went on strike with the avowed aim of bringing down the government. Other violent groups of both right and left operated at this time. In an attempt to mollify the opposition Allende invited members of the military to join his government, but they refused to do so.

The coup of September 1973

Chile appeared to be on the verge of civil war when on 11 September 1973 the armed forces – army, navy, air force and paramilitary police – intervened and carried through a *coup d'état*. President Allende either was killed or committed suicide during an attack on the presidential palace, and thousands of his supporters were killed, arrested or sent into exile. Resistance to the coup when it came was in fact weak and ineffective; the total killed throughout the country came to about 1000. On assuming power, General Pinochet suspended Congress. The CIA was thought to be involved in both the planning and the financing of the coup. In the event MIR, the principal left-wing group, proved unable to offer any meaningful resistance to the military takeover, and a year later (October 1974) its leader, Miguel Enríquez, was killed in Santiago. Leadership of MIR was then taken over for a while by Allende's son, Andries Pascal, but he later fled. Although MIR continued with some terrorism, it soon faded out.

The aftermath

The constitution was suspended and Chile now passed under direct military rule by a four-man junta headed by General Augusto Pinochet Ugarte. Pinochet's policy was to eliminate Marxism and then – slowly – to return the country to democracy. The military set about suppressing all leftist opposition, and while the Christian Democratic, National and Radical Democracy parties were 'recessed', other parties of the far left, such as the Communists and Socialists, were proscribed. In 1977 the traditional political parties were dissolved. Then in 1980 a new constitution was voted on under a carefully controlled plebiscite which gave Pinochet another eight-year term as head of state. Under Pinochet Chile turned to private enterprise as its political–economic creed.

Despite the authoritarian, repressive methods and brutality of the Pinochet regime, he enjoyed substantial support since many people and particularly the middle classes preferred this to the chaos which had been developing under Allende. The regime was to remain one of the most isolated in the world under Pinochet, who became a hate figure for the international left. At the end of the 1980s, bowing to increasing pressures, Pinochet agreed to a plebiscite (5 October 1988) to determine who should be the next presidential candidate; although his name went forward, the voters turned him down by 55 to 43 per cent. In the elections of December 1989 Patricio Aylwin became president, so bringing the Pinochet era to an end.

COLOMBIA: PERMANENT CIVIL STRIFE

Introduction

Colombia has a long tradition of civil violence, and there were major civil disturbances in the years 1839–41, 1851, 1854, 1859–61, 1876–7, 1885, 1895 and 1899–1903; the period of the 1860s and 1870s was known as the epoch of civil wars. The Conservatives replaced the Liberals to dominate politics from 1880 to 1930, and they returned the country to a more rigid adherence to the Roman Catholic Church and the Vatican, as opposed to the greater religious freedom that had been introduced by the Liberals. During the so-called War of 1000 Days (1899–1903) between Conservatives and Liberals, Colombia lost Panama. With assistance from the USA, Panama was able to become a separate state and the Panama Canal was built. During the years 1903 to 1946 there was relative quiet on the civil front and Colombia was the most consistently democratic of Latin American states, yet a tradition of civil violence was never far below the surface.

The Liberals came to power for the years 1930–46. Among their most important measures was the legalization of peasant landholdings, but this was also a period of industralization, so the basis of society changed substantially. In the elections of 1946, however, the Liberals split into two factions, thus allowing the Conservatives to return to power. Under their leader, Mariano Ospina Pérez, they took a series of 'reprisal' measures against the opposition Liberals.

On 9 April 1948 the leader of the left-wing faction of the Liberals, Jorge Eliécer Gaitán, was assassinated in Bogotá, his death sparking off immediate riots in the capital and throughout the country, during which an estimated $570 million worth of damage to property was done. This outburst of riots, the Bogotoza, was a dramatic starting point of the long period of violence that came to be known as La Violencia (1948–62).

Civil violence in Colombia since 1945 may be divided into three kinds: La Violencia; the growing left-wing guerrilla violence against the state (attracting right-wing death squad reprisals), which lasted from the mid-1960s to the present time; and the developing war against the drug barons, which became serious in the 1980s.

There is in relation to Colombia a constant problem of definition. In a country where violence between factions, or between the government and guerrillas, or between the government and drug traffickers appears to be endemic and more or less permanent, at what point should it be defined as civil war? Certainly the level of violence measured by deaths during La Violencia qualifies for this description; the intermittent violence of the 1970s may or may not do so depending upon what criteria are applied; but by the end of the 1980s the growth of violence by both guerrilla groups and the drug traffickers had again brought the country close to civil war.

La Violencia 1948–1962

The country-wide riots which followed the death of Gaitán appeared to represent many different pent-up grievances, and in the succeeding years a terrible violence was to afflict Colombia. Probably the main factor in the violence was sectarianism, which was part of a long tradition that had affected the rural areas in particular during most of the nineteenth century. Although Colombia is Latin America's oldest and most permanent democracy, it has paid a high price for the privilege.

La Violencia had its roots in long-standing political feuds rather than in obvious ideological differences or even in a class war. Both sides treated their opponents with extreme cruelty; between 200,000 and 300,000 people were killed. The beginning of the 1950s saw the worst of the violence when Laureano Gómez was President (1950–3) and attempted to introduce a near-Fascist state. During the violence, the country tended to divide into independent regions or zones under the control of competing power groups, and national law did not operate. Then in 1953 there was a military coup under General Rojas Pinilla, who was to rule until 1957. He offered an amnesty to various of the guerrillas, which about 8000 accepted, and attempted to redress grievances, especially against members of the élite, but his economic policies failed and, following a collapse in world coffee prices, he was replaced in 1957 by a military junta. Then a National Front of Conservatives and Liberals was formed, and under President Alberto Lleras Camargo there was a slow return to normality.

Violence continued, if at a slower pace, until by 1962 it had largely petered out. Colombia was then precariously poised between civil strife and economic recovery. In the presidential elections of that year only about 50 per cent of those eligible to do so voted. Under the dual system Conservative leader, Guillermo León Valencia, was voted in. The National Front gave guarantees to minority groups and it appeared that a more peaceful era was about to follow. From 1958 to the 1980s Liberal and Conservative governments were to alternate and follow essentially middle-of-the-road policies.

Guerrilla movements of the left

The success of the Castro revolution in Cuba (see below, pp. 535–539) undoubtedly had its impact in Colombia as it did elsewhere in Latin America, and some of the guerrilla movements that rose to prominence during the mid-1960s were indebted to it. The government was never at risk from these movements, although the pressures they exerted became greater in the late 1970s and into the 1980s. Guerrilla movements, even the relatively ineffectual ones, were able to persist because they fed on injustice and poverty as well as lack of strong governmental control and were – periodically – supported by forces from outside. The groups which came into being in the 1960s lasted through the 1970s, and two movements at least proved periodically formidable and quite dangerous. These were the April 19 Movement and the Armed Revolutionary Forces of Colombia.

In 1964 the United Front of Revolutionary Action (FUAR) created its own armed wing, the National Liberation Army (ELN), and at the time threatened to overshadow the activities of the Communist Party of Colombia (PCC). To avoid this in 1966 the PCC (which followed the Moscow line) set up as its military wing the Armed Revolutionary Forces of Colombia (FARC) under Manuel Marulanda. To the left of FARC was the Maoist People's Liberation Army (EPL), which came into being in 1967. FARC had some early successes (it claimed to be fighting for a 'people's government'), carried out occasional ambushes of government forces and was to be harried by US-trained counter-insurgency forces; at this time it was never more than 100 to 150 strong. In 1971–2 its forces occupied small villages, but FARC had no real impact until in 1975 it abducted the Dutch Consul in Cali and demanded a ransom of $1 million. During 1977 FARC and the ELN collaborated, and the following year FARC claimed that it was operational in five different districts and by then had become the largest, most effective of the various guerrilla organizations.

The April 19 Movement (M–19) began in 1973, taking its title from 19 April 1970 when dissidents from the National Popular Alliance fared badly in the elections. It was predominantly middle class rather than peasant in origins, and saw itself as new socialist in its politics. Its founders were Carlos Toledo Plata and Jaime Bateman Cayón; the former was to remain active until his capture in 1981, while Jaime Bateman was the organization's main military commander. M–19 established cells in the main cities, each operating independently, and looked for inspiration to groups in other countries such as Argentina and then Cuba. It launched its terrorist tactics in 1976 with the kidnapping of a trade union official, whom it later killed. In 1977 it sabotaged oil pipelines, and in 1978 it launched attacks on business, government and police. In 1979 it was responsible for some spectacular kidnappings.

There were also other groups of the left, such as the Popular Liberation Army (EPL), the Revolutionary Liberal Movement (MRL) the Workers' Self-Defence Movement (MAO) and the Workers', Students' and Peasants' Movement (MOEC).

During the 1970s these left-wing groups attempted to foment left–right civil war, and by 1976 they had become sufficient of a threat to force the government to undertake a major campaign to eradicate them, although this attempt failed. In 1978 the government passed a security statute to curtail individual liberties (it was opposed by the Liberals and the press). Then, on 1 January 1979, M–19 guerrillas captured about 5000 weapons from the main military arsenal in Bogotá. This led to a government crackdown and the arrest of hundreds of leftists, who were imprisoned; some, it is alleged, were tortured. At the same time FARC stepped up its anti-government activities, carrying out attacks on government targets. The basically right-wing government survived these left-wing threats, although it appeared generally quite incapable of putting an end to the guerrilla movements; at the same time the poverty and injustice which had led to the formation of such organizations in the first place continued.

The 1980s: a violent decade

The 1980s became increasingly violent, with growing terrorism from the left-wing guerrilla groups and mounting warfare between the government and the drug traffickers. The M–19 guerrillas executed a spectacular coup on 27 February 1980 when they occupied the Embassy of the Dominican Republic during a reception, taking 15 ambassadors as well as other people hostage; a two-month siege followed before a total of 57 hostages were released at the end of April for a $2.5 million ransom. At the time of the siege President Julio Turbay Ayala sought to speed up the trial of 219 M–19 guerrillas then held by government, while an Amnesty report suggested the lifting of the state of emergency which had operated intermittently in Colombia for 30 years. Also at this time terrorists hijacked a plane with 65 passengers to Cuba.

In a violent shoot-out between police and M–19 in March 1981 a number of the guerrillas were killed and some of their leaders captured. Even so, the year saw the steady escalation of terrorist activity by both FARC and M–19, as well as the growth of right-wing death squads resorting to reprisal terror against the left. However, there was a split in M–19 ranks when its members shot an American Bible translator, Chester Bitterman, in the belief that he was a member of the CIA. The President offered an amnesty to guerrillas, but very few took any notice of it. On 23 March 1981 Colombia broke diplomatic relations with Cuba, accusing it of training Colombian guerrillas.

The presidential elections of 1982 brought the Conservative Belisario Betancur Cuartas to power, and his victory appeared to signal yet another increase in left–right violence. Betancur attempted to treat with the guerrillas. The amnesty he offered was valuable in that it lessened the guerrillas' impact and diminished the mystique which surrounded them when some guerrillas took advantage of it, but it was unpopular with the military, who favoured increasing their counter-insurgency operations. None the less, as a result of direct talks between government and M–19, the latter agreed in September 1982 to cease all armed activity. During 1983 the amnesty which had come into effect in November 1982 brought in about 1000 guerrillas, and at the time had the approval of both M–19 and FARC. Despite this, however, other groups maintained their terrorist tactics and both kidnappings and bank robberies continued. The military, which did not approve of the amnesty, increased the intensity of its counter-insurgency operations. The right-wing death squad, MAS (Death to Kidnappers), which had been formed in 1981, was active through the year. The leader of M–19, Jaime Bateman Cayón, was killed in an ambush and succeeded by Ivan Marino Ospira.

Growing antagonism between Betancur and the military came into the open in January 1984 when the President insisted in the National Security Council that he would continue to pursue a policy of reconciliation with the guerrilla groups. As a result, a number of top-ranking officers resigned. The drug trade became prominent in April 1984 when the Minister of Justice, Rodrigo Lara Rovilla, was assassinated because of his crackdown on the drug traffic (12 tons of drugs had been seized), but his successor vowed to continue the fight. Once more the President placed the entire country under a state of siege. The policy of reconciliation with the guerrillas brought dividends when in March 1984 FARC agreed to implement a ceasefire. FARC, which represented the peasants, was perhaps the most truly ideological and national of the various guerrilla movements. But violence was constantly sparked off by one or other of the active groups: in August, for example, a leading member of M–19, Carlos Toledo Plata, was assassinated by right-wing gunmen; M–19 retaliated with an attack on the town of Yumbo in which 42 people lost their lives. Even so, at the end of August 1984, the government still managed to sign a ceasefire with M–19 and two smaller guerrilla groups.

During 1985, despite the gains of the previous years, there was a general resurgence of terrorist activity fuelled in part by a state of high unemployment. FARC kept the ceasefire, but M–19, having used it to reorganize, broke it. Both FARC and M–19 spent time during 1985 establishing new bases for themselves in rural and urban areas respectively. M–19 claimed that the army was breaking the terms of the ceasefire and so began attacking the army again in June, while the

EPL, which operated in the ranching areas of the north-west, also increased its killings. On 6 November 1985 M–19 seized the Palace of Justice in Bogotá and took a number of people hostage, but this time there was no siege and the next day troops stormed the building. About 100 people were killed, including the Supreme Court President and 10 judges. The government also stepped up its anti-drugs campaign during 1985, causing some drug traffickers to flee the country while others began to enter into alliances of convenience with the guerrillas.

In May 1986 presidential elections brought Virgilio Barco Vargas to power. Violence generally had increased as a reaction to the policies of Betancur, both in relation to the guerrillas and to control the drug business. By 1986 FARC had been rehabilitated – its members had taken part in the elections as part of the Patriotic Union party – but other groups, including M–19, which had refused to take part in dialogue were in danger of being marginalized. Although the attack on the drug trade had sent traffickers underground, both the trade and the violence associated with it increased. Then a number of FARC (Patriotic Union) members were assassinated while, provocatively, the army held manoeuvres in FARC-dominated areas. The army was also accused of using torture in its fight against terrorism, and of being responsible for disappearances. The director-general of the criminal court system (Alvaro Duque Alvárez) described 1986 as a year of 'dirty war'. In the first half of the year at least 600 people were seized and killed by troops, police or gunmen working with them, while army chiefs who alone have the power to prosecute army or police staff for human rights violations refused to do so. In Cali more than 350 killings took place between January and June; the Army's Third Brigade dropped leaflets from the air urging citizens to identify the 'violent and subversive'.

President Barco had no obvious anti-guerrilla policy, but met each incident on an *ad hoc* basis. A number of guerrilla movements came together in 1987 to form the Coordinatora Nacional Guerrillera. At the end of 1986 the newspaper *El Espectador* published a series of articles exposing the Medellín drug cartel; in December 1986 the paper's editor was assassinated, prompting the new government early in 1987 to launch an anti-drugs campaign, one result of which was the extradition to the USA of Carlos Lehder Rivas, a major dealer. Meanwhile, the truce with FARC began to break down and clashes took place between FARC guerrillas and army units. Then, on 11 October 1987, Jaime Pardo Leal, the leader of the Patriotic Union, was assassinated and FARC promised to exact vengeance. At the time of his death more than 470 members of his Patriotic Union had been killed since its founding as the legal political arm of FARC. There were immediate protest riots by the left and shooting at police: two police and five civilians were killed and 20 wounded.

It became increasingly plain during 1988 that the government was losing control over the violence, which increased markedly during the mayoral elections in March. The guerrilla groups caused increasing economic problems and were often in the news. On 29 May M–19 guerrillas abducted the former Conservative presidential candidate, Alvaro Gómez Hurtado; they released him six weeks later, having used his kidnapping to draw attention to the dirty war which they claimed was being waged by the military. The Defence Minister, General Rafael Samudio, demanded more powers and a larger budget to enable his forces to fight the guerrillas effectively; he estimated their strength at 7500 and argued that the biggest mistake had been to negotiate with them. In the rural areas there was an escalation of partisan violence, which included massacres of peasants in Uratu and the Eastern Plains regions, forcing the government to declare the region a war zone in October. The governor of one department (Antioquia) claimed that guerrillas had burnt down 38 farms and 20 banana-packing plants, blown up dozens of electric pylons and destroyed four bridges and 16 vehicles. Guerrillas of the EPL controlled the two banana workers' unions. Similar violence took place in the west of the country on the Venezuelan border, this time by the ELN. More people disappeared.

The growth of guerrilla violence in 1988 was paralleled by the drug war. In January drug traffickers murdered the Attorney-General, Carlos Mauro Hoyas. By November the war betwen rival drug traffickers in Medellín and Cali had accounted for an increasing toll of dead as they battled for control of foreign distribution areas; they worked closely with the right-wing death squads. At the same time the army had to fly three extra battalions to the coastal region of Uraba, where rebels had stormed several towns. The police estimated that 18,000 people had been killed in the course of the year, and many of the dead were left-wing sympathizers killed by right-wing paramilitary groups or the hitmen who worked for the drug traffickers. In October the army had to be mobilized to confront a general strike, which coincided with an increase in guerrilla attacks and sabotage as well as with peasant protest marches. Nineteen eighty-eight was called 'the year of the massacres', and yet the economy did well despite the country's appearing to be on the brink of anarchy.

By 1989 it was increasingly difficult to determine who was responsible for which killings and massacres. Many victims were peasant supporters of FARC and the ELN rebels, trade union leaders or officials fighting the drug business, and although the guerrillas were more active than for many years, so too were the right-wing paramilitary death squads. As the government cracked down on the drug business, the traffickers responded with more terror killings. On 18 August they assassinated Luis Carlos Galan (Liberal presidential candidate for 1990). The government declared a new state of emergency and renewed its drug extradition arrangement with the USA; the drug gangs then increased their killing in Bogotá, Medellín and Cali, and announced that they would kill 10 judges for every trafficker extradited to the USA. Washington increased its anti-drug assistance with the supply of military equipment, trained personnel and $65 million. Following the murder of judge Carlos Ernesto Valencia (who had upheld an arrest warrant against a Medellín drug trafficker), all the country's judges went on strike. No target seemed safe: newspapers and banks were attacked, as were many prominent citizens, and a plane crashed after a bomb believed to have been planted by a drug gang exploded, killing 107. While peace negotiations with FARC and M–19 had some success, the ELN maintained attacks on targets in the country's oil- and gold-bearing regions.

In March 1990 another presidential candidate, Bernardo Jaramillo of the Patriotic Union, was assassinated; the killing was blamed on the drug trafficker Pablo Escobar, who in April declared total war on the police in Medellín, offering a reward of £2500 for every police agent killed. A major hunt for him was met by massive warfare reprisals and more bloodshed, bringing the drug war in Medellín to one of its bloodiest phases ever. By the end of April 1990 it was estimated that since 1985 the security forces had lost 2000 dead with a further 3300 wounded in fighting the drug traffickers. At the same time a number of public figures had been assassinated, including three presidential candidates. Yet despite police confiscation of huge drug hauls, the trade seemed undiminished.

The May 1990 presidential elections were constantly marred by violence and threats to candidates, so protection of politicians stretched the police to the limit. Early in May, while Pablo Escobar threatened to kill any remaining presidential candidates, President Barco said he could not guarantee their safety. The strength of the drug business can be gauged by the fact that it earns Colombia £5 billion a year, and the cartels of Medellín and Cali have huge power as a result; they use it to kill their enemies, and in many parts of Colombia government writ simply does not run. In Medellín during the election campaign huge car bombs were used by the drug cartels, dozens of police were murdered and violence continued unabated up to polling day; the candidates were invisible to the public for reasons of survival, making it one of the oddest elections anywhere. When the elections were finally held at the end of May, the country was in a state of siege and its entire armed forces and police (210,000) were on duty. The Liberal winner faced a country wracked by civil turmoil.

Estimated costs and casualties

Perhaps 300,000 people were killed during La Violencia between 1948 and 1962; damage to property over the same period was estimated at $1 billion. Violence from that date to the end of the 1970s was relatively low key. Then from 1978 it increased sharply, and casualties for the 1980s must run into many thousands, perhaps as high as 100,000. Large numbers of weapons have been channelled through to Colombia from a variety of sources, so the country has a vast storehouse of arms for use by its various guerrilla and drug factions. Major damage has been done to estates, oil pipelines and business premises, although, ironically, the economy improved substantially in the second half of the 1980s despite all the violence. During the election of 1990 the idea was mooted that cocaine should be legalized, thus destroying the basis for drug trafficking.

Results: ongoing

It is not possible either to quantify or to predict results from a situation where there is little indication of change or of any end to the violence. The astonishing thing is that in many respects Colombia survives well and continues to be a democracy – even while a range of guerrilla movements from the left fight to overthrow the government, the death squads from the right fight to destroy the guerrillas of the left, and the drug cartels fight anyone who stands in their way.

COSTA RICA: A BREAK IN TRADITION

Introduction

One of the most stable countries in Central America, Costa Rica has faced only two major upheavals in the whole of the twentieth century. The first of these took place in 1917 when the elected President was ousted by Federico Tinoco. Between that date and 1948 Costa Rica enjoyed democratic rule and was blessed by the absence of an ambitious and dominant military establishment seeking power. Costa Rica has also been fortunate in that it has lacked an obvious oligarchy or élite controlling the country's wealth. The result has been an absence of extreme and a correspondingly greater general readiness to accept democracy.

The events of 1948

The presidential elections of February 1948 witnessed considerable violence, including a 15-day general strike. The opposition National Union candidate for President, Otilio Ulate Blanco, won convincingly, but the government candidate, Rafael Calderón, who was standing for the Communists, and his followers refused to recognize the result, which the government-controlled Congress then nullified on 1 March. Civil war between the two sides followed. The anti-government forces included members of the Caribbean Legion (composed of exiles from several Central American countries) and were led by a rich planter, José Figueres Ferrer. Calderón received help from President Anastasio Somoza of Nicaragua and President Tiburcio Carías Andino of Honduras. The fighting was to last for six weeks until on 28 April Figueres and his forces entered the capital, San José, and ousted the government.

On 8 May Figueres established a ruling junta over which he was to preside for a year and a half. A month after they took the capital Figueres' forces arranged a truce with the defeated side and Santos León Herrera was made interim President. The constitution was abolished and the junta introduced a number of revolutionary changes, for the opponents of the Communists were populist socialists rather than conservatives. These changes included the abolition of the army, the outlawing of the Communist Party, the nationalization of the banks and the reform of the civil service. At the end of 1948 elections were held for a Constituent Assembly, which met in January 1949 to draw up a new constitution.

Invasion from Nicaragua

The Costa Rican army was abolished on 1 December 1948, but 10 days later (10 December) Figueres was obliged to call for general mobilization when supporters of the ousted President, Calderón, invaded the country from neighbouring Nicaragua where they had taken refuge. Initially they seized La Cruz and then turned inland to take Liberia, but they proved no match for Figueres and his mobilization, which was popular and successful. Following complaints by Figueres the Organization of American States (OAS) sent a commission to investigate Somoza's interference in the affairs of Costa Rica; then, on 21 February, representatives of Costa Rica and Nicaragua meeting in Washington agreed a peaceful settlement of their dispute. Also during February the new Constituent Assembly confirmed the earlier election of Ulate as President and drew up a new constitution. On 8 November 1949 Figueres and his junta stepped down and Ulate became President.

Map 20 Central America

Replay 1955

In 1953 Figueres, a moderate socialist, was elected President in succession to Ulate and so was in control when a renewed challenge came from Rafael Calderón, who had been in Nicaragua since 1949. In January 1955, with the support of President Somoza who claimed in justification that Figueres was plotting against him, Calderón led a band of his supporters into Costa Rica. They seized the border town of Villa Quesada and some heavy fighting followed in several towns before the invaders were driven back into Nicaragua. Then, after the OAS had verified that Calderón's war materials had been supplied by Somoza, Nicaragua withdrew its support. During this crisis the USA supported Figueres and sold his government four fighter planes. The following year (1956) the two countries agreed to carry out joint surveillance of their common border.

CUBA: THE CASTRO REVOLUTION

Introduction

Cuba won its independence from Spain by war at the end of the nineteenth century; it was greatly assisted in this by American intervention, and thereafter American influence was to dominate Cuban affairs until the Castro revolution at the end of the 1950s. The country's prosperity depended on sugar, American tourism and gambling, but only a relatively small élite prospered while the great majority of the people remained both poor and oppressed by successive regimes, which all too easily won a reputation for corruption. Fulgencio Batista y Zaldívar was to dominate Cuban politics – sometimes as the power behind the government and sometimes as President – from the early 1930s until his fall at the hands of Castro. He governed by a mixture of force, bribery and assassination.

There were several phases to the Castro revolution: the first attempt to overthrow the regime in 1953 was a disaster; the second attempt in 1956 fared little better, but thereafter Castro and his followers gradually won support in the countryside until their victory at the beginning of 1959. Other crises were to follow as Cuba turned to Moscow at the height of the Cold War: these included the Bay of Pigs fiasco of 1961 and the missile crisis of 1962 that might have sparked off the Third World War. Subsequently (to 1990), Castro was to remain one of the world's most enduring revolutionary figures.

26 July 1953

On 26 July 1953 Fidel Castro and about 200 young men attacked the army barracks at Moncada in Santiago in an effort to begin the overthrow of the dictator Batista. The attempt was a failure and most of the attackers were killed. Fidel and his brother Raúl escaped, but after several months on the run they gave themselves up in order to prevent a campaign of persecution against anti-government plotters then being carried on by the police in Santiago. At his trial Castro used what was to become a famous phrase – 'History will absolve me' – and was sentenced to 15 years in prison. However, he and his brother were pardoned under a general amnesty after serving only 11 months and went into exile in Mexico. Although 26 July was a military disaster, by giving himself up and then with his defence speech Castro turned himself into a national hero. (Subsequently, he produced a political manifesto titled *History Will Absolve Me*.)

In December 1956 Castro returned to Cuba, this time with 81 followers including Ernesto 'Che' Guevara, but their landing was opposed, most of the 82 were killed and a second disaster loomed. Castro with 12 survivors fled to the hills of the Sierra Maestra. There, unmolested by Batista's forces (at first because he was thought to have been killed and later because the little band of guerrillas was too difficult to find), Castro built up a following and prepared for the next phase of his attack on the Batista government. By that time Batista faced other opponents aparts from Castro, including the Directorio Revolucionario, which consisted of young intellectuals. The Directorio launched an attack on the presidential palace in 1957. The attack failed, but from that time onwards Batista became more and more erratic and violent in his behaviour, and alienated the middle classes. After that failure Castro became the focus of opposition.

The guerrilla war

For two years after the December 1956 landing Castro and his small band carried out a guerrilla war from the Sierra Maestra; the police and military were unable to dislodge them, and gradually Castro's following increased until he was leading a band of several hundred men. From time to time they raided military targets and destroyed property, and late in 1957 the rebellion began to take off. There was a general strike in April 1958 in another attempt to overthrow Batista, but it came to nothing. In the summer of 1958, however, Batista's forces launched an offensive against the Castroites. Raúl took a number of American hostages and this led to US pressures on Batista; the hostages were released unharmed. Opposition to Batista came increasingly into the open as Castro called for total war and then, in the autumn of 1958, moved out of the mountains to take the offensive. Economic factors made Cuba ripe for revolutionary change: the average rural worker earned only $91 a year; foreign interests (mainly American) owned 75 per cent of the arable land and controlled 90 per cent of essential services and 40 per cent of sugar production.

From June 1958 onwards the Batista regime began to collapse: its violent methods alienated the middle classes and the USA cut off supplies of arms. In the autumn Castro left the mountains and began to advance on Havana. Batista held an election, but at the end of December he was ousted by the army. On 31 December the Castroites captured Santa Cruz, the capital of Las Villas province, and opposition then collapsed. Batista and his family fled to the Dominican Republic, and Castro and his supporters entered Havana to enthusiastic acclaim. Most of the army welcomed the rebels. Castro at once unified the military groups and incorporated what remained of the Directorio Revolucionario under his own banner. In effect he took absolute power to himself.

The implementation of the revolution

When Castro entered Havana in January 1959 he had fewer than 1000 followers and he and his lieutenants had only vague ideas at that time as to what sort of government they should establish. However, he had the enthusiastic support of the peasants, urban workers and the idealistic young, such as students. A new provisional government was formed with Castro as Premier. Since nationalization of foreign assets was among the first measures he took, Castro was soon facing strong US opposition, including a boycott of Cuba's principal export commodity, sugar; the urgent need to find an immediate market for this was probably the most important single factor that turned him to Moscow – ideological conviction was to come later. The Communist Party of Cuba (PCC), which had been founded in 1925, now became the vehicle which Castro used to implement his revolution and so the dominant political force in Cuba, which became the first and only Communist–Marxist state in the Americas.

Many middle-class Cubans left the country following Castro's victory and fled to the USA. During the period 1959–61 Cuba established close ties with the USSR and confiscated private property; the USA imposed an economic embargo and broke off diplomatic relations. The dismantling of capitalism was now carried out and a series of new institutions such as the Confederation of Cuban Workers (CTC) were created, while wide-ranging agrarian and industrial reforms were introduced. It was the nationalization of US property and private business worth several hundred million dollars that created such bitter and hostile American reaction to the new government. The next few years saw several plots to assassinate Castro. Three factors led to Cuba's isolation: its adoption of Communism; the exodus of thousands of middle-class Cubans, who became articulate enemies of the regime in the USA and elsewhere; and Cuba's readiness to support revolutionary movements in other Latin American countries.

The Bay of Pigs

Florida in the USA became a centre for exiled Cubans opposed to Castro, and some of these requested US support for an invasion of Cuba in order to overthrow Castro. In 1960 the American CIA began to train Cuban exiles in Guatemala. Then on 17 April 1961 some 1400 exiles landed in the Bay of Pigs in southern Cuba. They were at once routed by the Cuban army (20 April) with the majority of them being taken prisoner. At first the fiasco of the Bay of Pigs, which did enormous damage to president Kennedy's reputation, was blamed on inadequate American back-up for the operation; in fact the project had little chance of success, and the CIA operation in Guatemala had been known in Havana since its inception. The invasion itself was poorly planned and badly carried out. Its principal results were to exacerbate already bad relations between Cuba and the USA and to allow Castro to humiliate the USA by demanding ransom money for the 1113 invaders who were taken prisoner. Between 1962 and 1965 ransoms totalling $53 million were raised in the USA by private means, and the prisoners were then allowed to return to the USA. The Bay of Pigs represented a great propaganda victory for Castro.

The missile crisis of 1962

The next warlike crisis came close to sparking off the Third World War. In May 1960, after Castro had aligned his country with Moscow, the USSR promised to defend Cuba. Then in 1962 the Soviet Leader, Nikita Khrushchev, assumed (though on what basis is not clear) that the USA would not intervene if the USSR sited medium- and intermediate-range missiles in Cuba. In July 1962 Washington learned that the USSR was shipping missiles to Cuba, and by August was aware of the construction of missile bases on Cuba as well as the presence there of Soviet technicians; on 14 October it was known that Soviet ballistic missiles were in Cuba. In response to this missile build-up President Kennedy announced a quarantine of Cuba on 22 October, and this was sanctioned the next day by the OAS. President Kennedy announced an 800 km (500 mile) exclusion zone. After a tense week for the world as the two superpowers confronted one another, Khrushchev climbed down and subsequently withdrew his missiles. Castro was not consulted and was furious at his treatment, yet remained in the Communist camp thereafter. The crisis almost certainly played a part in the subsequent fall of Khrushchev two years later (see also Part II, pp. 154–156).

Results: immediate and longer term

The immediate result of the Castro revolution was to end a corrupt dictatorship and replace it by a socialist egalitarian regime. The regime did much to spread literacy and health care throughout the population, but soon also became a full-blooded Communist one. As the only Communist government in the Americas, established moreover at the height of the Cold War, Cuba inevitably called down upon itself the full antagonism of the USA. Much of the country's subsequent history was concerned with relations – or the absence of relations – with the USA. In the longer term Cuba took on an importance out of all proportion to its real potential: as the only left-wing regime in the Americas it became an inspiration (as well as a source of support with arms and training) of left-wing guerrilla movements in various parts of the continent (for example, see above, pp. 519–521, 526–532). Then in the 1970s Cuban military assistance to Ethiopia following the Ogaden War of 1977, and still more important its military assistance to Angola from 1975 to 1990, were crucial to developments in those two countries.

After consolidation (1960–5) the Cuban revolution went through a radical phase from 1965 to 1970 and Castro became a major figure of the left in the Third World. He was always also a figure of controversy: thus, when the Non-Aligned Conference was held in Havana in 1979 a number of Third World countries claimed he jeopardized the concept of non-alignment by his overt support for the Soviet Union and its policies.

In 1980 Cuba lifted emigration restrictions and huge numbers of Cubans immediately fled the country to the USA or Peru; among approximately 120,000 Cubans who went to the USA by boats were a number of criminals released from the prisons as well as mentally ill from the hospitals, and the subsequent question of their repatriation to Cuba became one more problem that constantly soured Cuban–US relations. A further cause of antagonism arose at the time of the US invasion of Grenada in 1983, when a number of Cubans working on that island were killed in the fighting. By 1990, when a settlement had finally been reached in southern Africa leading to Namibia's independence, Cuba finally began to withdraw its estimated 50,000 troops from Angola. In the age of *glasnost* and *perestroika* Castro, still in charge in Havana, appeared an outdated leftover from a bygone age.

EL SALVADOR: A DECADE OF CIVIL WAR (ONGOING)

Introduction

Like other Latin American countries, El Salvador is subject to political extremes, with the great majority suffering terrible poverty while the minority form an economic élite that is opposed to major change. The economy is largely dependent on coffee and cotton exports; the political process is dominated by the military, either as a part of the current government or threatening intervention in the background. Earlier in the century land-hunger, unemployment and overpopulation led 300,000 Salvadoreans to migrate to neighbouring Honduras where they occupied unused land; subsequently, the treatment received by some of them led to the Soccer War of 1969 between the two countries (see Part III, pp. 275–277). At the time of the Soccer War an extreme right-wing terrorist group, the National Democratic Organization (ORDEN), was set up in El Salvador with the object of intimidating those in favour of reform or political change.

The 1970s were to witness a process of polarization as previously orthodox politicians such as Cayetano Carpio turned from party politics to guerrilla action. A number of extreme left-wing guerrilla groups were formed during the decade. At the same time the military veered between repression and concession. Moderates attempted to mediate from the middle ground, and they were most likely to become the victims of the right or left as these battled for supremacy. In the 1972 elections the pro-reform vote supporting José Napoleón Duarte gave the Christian Democrats a majority, but fraud and the intervention of the military brought Colonel Arturo Amanda Molina and the National Conciliation Party (PCN) to power instead. Many believed that Duarte ought to have become President, and he then took part in an unsuccessful coup attempt and was obliged to leave the country for a time as a result.

The idea that a revolution from the left was now essential gained ground, and 1973 witnessed the creation of various left-wing groups reacting to what they saw as an election result manipulated by the right-wing the previous year. Their resort to guerrilla tactics and violence was to be matched by comparable activities – death squads – on the right. Molina tried to damp down the demands of the left with a new agricultural wage in 1974; in 1976 he announced agrarian reforms which would affect 250 of the big landowners. The army, however, undermined these efforts by attacking the peasants and raiding their illegal associations, creating antagonism between army and Church since priests had encouraged the peasant associations as one way of helping them deal with their poverty.

René Cruz had established a People's Revolutionary Army (ERP), and with Cuban support this set out to politicize the masses. In 1975, however, ideological differences led to a split, and the Armed Forces of National Resistance (FARN) broke away from the ERP. Other revolutionary groups appeared. Backed by Cuba, the various groups of the left came together under a single umbrella – Frente Farabundo Marti di Liberación Nacional (FMLN) – which also boasted a political wing, the Frente Democrático Revolucionario, and by the end of the 1970s these presented a formidable challenge to government. Facing them from the right were such groups as ORDEN and the White Fighting Union (UGB).

The presidential elections of 1977 brought a right-wing conservative government of the Party of National Conciliation (PCN) to power, headed by General Carlos Romero. His reaction to left-wing pressures was to allow free rein to the right-wing death squads. These death squads selected as their targets Jesuit priests or nuns, labour leaders, peasant leaders, suspected Communists – in fact anyone who advocated reform – and in the last years of the decade left–right violence escalated rapidly. The left was encouraged by the victory of the Sandinistas in neighbouring Nicaragua, and this, with Cuban encouragement, fuelled a revolutionary situation. The Archbishop of San Salvador, Oscar Romero, now emerged as the champion of the poor and therefore as a target for elimination.

The civil war gets under way 1979–1980

In January 1979 the Inter-American Commission on Human Rights accused the Romero government of using torture and murdering its political opponents. Guerrilla violence from left and right escalated during the year into civil war proportions, with kidnappings, assassinations, arbitrary arrests and torture by the security services becoming more and more frequent. On 15 October the military moved in to oust Romero, who had lost all credibility, and set up a junta which called on both left and right to lay down their arms. It raised no response. The junta promised agrarian reform, free elections and respect for human rights, and on this platform appealed for American aid. The Christian Democrats were prepared to join the government.

On 10 January 1980 three left-wing guerrilla groups united under the banner of the Frente Democrático Revolucionario. During the year the junta, which represented a middle-of-the-road approach to the country's problems, just succeeded in retaining popular support and was able to survive a right-wing coup attempt. In March 1980 the junta made Duarte of the Christian Democrats a member. The left, however, launched a full-scale civil war against the government during 1980, while the USA, following the change of President from Carter to Reagan, increased its military assistance to the El Salvador government to make it effective against the Communism of the left.

On 24 March Archbishop Oscar Romero, who had come to be regarded as the champion of human rights, was assassinated by right-wing terrorists while officiating at mass. At his funeral 31 people in the crowd were killed by bomb explosions or sniper fire and a further 200 were injured. By this time El Salvador was engulfed by civil war. Towards the end of the year (4 December) three US nuns and a laywoman were murdered, and in response the USA temporarily cut off aid. The left-wing guerrillas, working mainly in the countryside, obtained assistance from both Cuba and Nicaragua; periodically they made strikes in towns and raided police stations or military posts to obtain arms. The junta was controlled by Colonel Jaime Abdul

Gutiérrez and Colonel Adolfo Arnoldo Majana Ramos, who tried to follow a middle path and succeeded in antagonizing both left and right. It was a year of extreme violence in which an estimated 22,000 people were killed. The Partido Demócrata Cristiano (PDC) or Christian Democratic Party (CDP) split between left and right factions, with the left forming a new Social Democrat Party and the right remaining as the CDP, which supported the junta. At the end of the year the junta ousted Majana from the leadership and appointed Duarte civilian President. The newly formed FMLN announced a stepped-up campaign against the junta.

The 1980s

During 1981 the USA provided financial and military aid as well as counter-insurgency advisers; it saw this as essential to the defence of the West and in order to contain international Communism. There was a general intensification of the civil war, which spread to the northern regions of the country. Right-wing violence was now aimed at the government as much as against the left, and it helped to reduce the credibility of the junta, which was increasingly seen as incapable of containing the violence. The junta's main support came from the Christian Democrats, the military and the USA. Indeed, US aid had by this time become an essential prop for the government, which veered uneasily between political and military solutions. The left-wing guerrillas sometimes obtained Cuban arms through Nicaragua, but they were just as likely to get them by attacking the military. A number of international efforts to negotiate between the two sides were unsuccessful; on 16 December 1981 the UN General Assembly passed a resolution calling on the junta to negotiate with the guerrillas.

The civil war did increasing damage to the economy as businessmen were kidnapped, crops burnt, electricity pylons blown up. A spectacular guerrilla success (15 October) was the destruction of the Golden Bridge across the Leapa river, which cut communications with the eastern third of the country.

Elections to the Legislative Assembly were held early in 1982 (the Frente Democrático Revolucionario refused to take part), resulting in a right-wing coalition which forced Duarte to resign as President; he was replaced by Álvaro Magaña Borjo. A majority of the international community did not regard the elections as fair. The civil war continued unabated, and the tactics of the death squads became increasingly brutal. There were moves in the US Congress to hold the level of aid to El Salvador, which President Reagan wished to increase.

The military undertook an increased role in the war during 1983 when they attempted to eliminate anyone suspected of providing support for the left-wing guerrillas. The Salvadorean economy was only able to keep going with massive injections of American aid as well as assistance provided through the International Monetary Fund (IMF) and the Inter-American Development Bank. Washington appealed to the government to put an end to the right-wing death squads, which it claimed were the surest way to recruit left-wing guerrillas, but the appeal had little effect. In November 1983 about 100 men, women and children were massacred by newly US-trained troops. By this time in the civil war the National Guard had become the largest, most feared of the three security organizations. The guerrillas had a successful and sometimes spectacular year, at different times overrunning important towns such as Berlin (January) and San Miguel (September). Further attempts at negotiation between government and guerrillas came to nothing. A new constitution was published in December and presidential elections were set for May 1984; these were won by the Christian Democrats, and Duarte returned as President. The FMLN, which had not taken part in the elections, claimed that it had prevented balloting in a total of 89 constituencies.

Duarte offered dialogue to the guerrillas and then direct talks. The two sides met on 15 October 1984 at La Palma in Chalatenango province and expressed optimism about a possible solution, but later the talks bogged down and came to nothing. The guerrillas concentrated increasingly on targets such as bridges and pylons as well as military garrisons, while the army began an attempt to win the hearts and minds of peasants in the villages. President Duarte issued a more humane code of conduct to the military; three colonels who were suspected of involvement in death squad activities were posted overseas. In May 1984, after a long delay, five National Guardsmen received 30-year sentences for the killing of three US nuns and a laywoman in 1980. Duarte's efforts to curb human rights abuses as well as his readiness to talk with the guerrillas made him increasingly unpopular with the right.

By the middle of the decade it had become clear that the government was increasingly dependent for its survival on American aid, and relied on American pressure to prevent the military seizing power. Negotiations with the FMLN in 1983 and 1984 had made little progress, the FMLN insisting that it should be given a share of power in a reconstituted government before it ended the civil war; a war that by 1985 had cost at least 50,000 lives. The government position was that the FMLN could only earn power by participating in open elections. Duarte and the CDP did well in the elections of 1985. Guerrillas, however, abducted Duarte's daughter and a friend, forcing the President into six weeks of negotiations before his daughter, her friend and 23 mayors were released in return for 22 guerrillas and free passage abroad for another 96 disabled guerrillas. Government forces turned to aerial bombardment of guerrilla targets and the relocation of civilians who supported them. In August 1985 the guerrillas unified their political and military wings and concentrated on urban warfare, while government forces concentrated on the rural areas. In October the FMLN attacked a military base at La Union, killing 42 soldiers and wounding 68. The USA greatly increased its military assistance during 1985, but nothing seemed to make any difference to the intensity of the civil war.

During 1986 Duarte came under pressure from the army, the political right and USA to continue the war, although his own instinct was to negotiate; he lost ground as a result. The USA made it clear that the continuation of aid depended on maintaining the war against the left. The strategy of the two sides changed: when the army was successful against the guerrillas in the field these retaliated by launching attacks on economic targets such as electricity pylons. A new series of negotiations due to be held in September 1986 were cancelled by the guerrillas when the government refused either to withdraw troops from Sesori, the proposed meeting place, or to agree to a temporary ceasefire. Duarte then insisted on going to Sesori alone in the hope of demonstrating that left-wing rebels only wanted a 'dialogue of conflict'. The town, which had once had a population of 25,000, had dwindled to 6000 through fear, for it was in the centre of a war zone. By the end of 1986 the army high command at the head of 60,000 men insisted that it was winning the seven-year-old civil war against an estimated 6000 guerrillas, but there was little evidence that this in fact was the case.

The nature of the left–right problem was amply demonstrated at the beginning of 1987 when President Duarte attempted to raise $30 million in taxes from the wealthier sections of the community in order to prosecute a war which was supposedly to their advantage. His taxes were designed to make 'the rich pay their fair share of the war'. The right reacted with predictable anger, and after strikes the government was forced to drop the tax. The old business oligarchy looked upon Duarte as a dangerous Communist who had only lasted as long as he had because of US pressure to maintain a middle-of-the-road government that had some sort of appeal to the international community.

In early April 1987 the guerrillas launched a devastating attack on military headquarters at El Paraíso, killing 69 and wounding more than 100. One of the dead was a US Special Forces sergeant, one of 55 US military advisers officially in the country. The base was supposedly one of the most secure in the country. It became clear at this time that US and government predictions that the war could be ended in two years were over-optimistic, and that what was happening in the countryside bore little relation to government pronouncements in San Salvador. The FMLN claimed that no military position was safe and that while they knew where to find the army the reverse was not true. US diplomats conceded that it might take another eight years to win the civil war. In mid-1987 the right-wing death squads, which had been relatively quiescent, made a disturbing comeback to increase dramatically the number of killings attributed to them.

Duarte signed the Central American Peace Plan drawn up by five Presidents in Guatemala, but it was rejected by the FMLN. The guerrillas agreed to new talks with the government in October – but later in the month the FMLN rejected both the amnesty and the ceasefire offered by government and the war continued. Meanwhile Duarte accused the extreme right-wing Major Roberto D'Aubuisson of the Arena Party of responsibility for the assassination of Archbishop Romero in 1980.

By this time El Salvador had become the biggest per capita recipient of US aid in the world, and US assistance accounted for 80 per cent of the budget. Yet Central America's bloodiest civil war continued unchecked, while deep resentment of American penetration of the politics and economics of the country had grown in proportion to the increase in American aid and military involvement. By November 1987 it was estimated that the death toll for eight years of civil war had risen to 63,000. Ironically, by the end of 1987 both left and right had come to regard Duarte as a tool of the USA. At the same time the two sides agreed to 'humanize' the war, with the FMLN ceasing to lay mines that killed civilians as well as troops, and the army giving up its aerial bombardments. They also agreed to prisoner exchanges and casualty evacuations from war zones.

There was a further increase in right-wing death squad activity during 1988; the guerrillas, meanwhile, launched a campaign against the municipal and Legislative Council elections of March, and FMLN activity succeeded in keeping private traffic off the roads as well as depriving most areas of proper electricity supplies. The year saw at least twice as many political assassinations as 1987. The right-wing National Republic Alliance (Arena) won 30 of 60 seats, the CDP 23 and the Partido de Conciliación Nacional (NCP) 7, but the presidential elections were not scheduled for another year so Duarte carried on, although he was known to be suffering from terminal cancer. The army became increasingly critical of Duarte's handling of the civil war.

In the run-up to the presidential elections of March 1989 complicated proposals for negotiations were advanced by the guerrillas, but these were one more ploy in an endless political game that alternated with warfare. American aid had become crucial to government survival. The presidential elections gave 54 per cent of the vote to the right-wing Arena Party, and Alfredo Cristiani replaced Duarte as President. The FMLN, whose proposals for negotiations had included postponing the elections, mounted attacks on 20 towns during the elections, and no more than 50 per cent of voters turned up at the polls. The FMLN vowed to make the country ungovernable. The incoming President attempted to negotiate with the FMLN, but although talks were held in October, they were broken off when the Labour Federation offices were bombed. Shortly afterwards (11 November) the FMLN launched its biggest offensive ever and carried the fighting into the suburbs of San Salvador. After four days of fighting about 650 people had been killed. On 16 November six Jesuit priests as well as their cook and her daughter were first tortured and then killed during a right-wing raid on the university; the killings by uniformed men destroyed the government claim to be a reforming democracy and once more ended any prospects of peace. The rebels held a large part of the capital for two weeks before they withdrew. This guerrilla offensive resulted in another 2000 deaths altogether.

Although early in 1990 the government announced that it had found members of the army responsible for killing the six Jesuits, few believed that this was a genuine attempt at 'house-cleaning'; rather, it was thought to be a desperate bid by President Cristiani to ensure that the flow of American Aid continued. By March a major row was brewing in Washington as evidence accumulated that US military personnel in El Salvador knew of the activities of the right-wing death squads and may even have been accomplices in their activities. The Roman Catholic Church claimed that victims of the death squads were as many as 35,000 – half of all the casualties of the civil war to 1990.

In May 1990 the two sides met again for more talks, this time in Venezuela, but the demands of the guerrillas for electoral reform, a reduction of the military from 56,000 to its pre-war strength of 12,000, the separation of the police from military control and an end to human rights abuses were unlikely to be met easily or quickly – if at all.

Estimated costs and casualties

Throughout the 1980s the USA committed itself deeply to supporting the government of El Salvador in its fight against left-wing rebels, yet the extent of US aid did not appear to have brought an end to the war or victory for the government any closer. Half-way through the decade (1985) deaths were estimated at 50,000, though no year saw a repeat of the slaughter that had occurred between October 1979 and October 1980 when 22,000 people died. The fortunes of the war constantly see-sawed, but at any given time the left-wing rebels controlled 30 per cent or more of the countryside. Periodically, they attacked and briefly held towns as well. Apart from the killed and maimed, several hundred thousand people have been displaced as refugees either inside the country or across its borders into neighbouring lands. Economic losses for the three years 1979–82 were estimated at $600 million, while GDP fell by 25 per cent, export earnings dropped by 33 per cent and per capita income dropped from $670 to $470. Over the same period guerrilla damage to the electricity grid (pylons) came to $40 million, and to bridges, power plants or other targets a further $100 million. By 1990 estimates for the dead came to about 75,000, the economy and the army were almost totally dependent on US handouts, and the war seemed no nearer to any conclusion.

Results: continuing

At the beginning of the 1990s there seemed every likelihood that the war would continue indefinitely; one American estimate suggested that on existing performance (as far as government and military were concerned) it would continue to the end of the century. Eleven years of terrible brutality had polarized the two sides – the far right and extreme left – so that there seemed little prospect of either an early or an enduring settlement being reached.

GUATEMALA: A PERMANENT STATE OF CIVIL WAR

Introduction

In a country beset by familiar regional problems of extremes of wealth and poverty, civil strife in Guatemala consists essentially of an endless fight between representatives of power – landowners and the wealthy or relatively wealthy – on the right, and the rural Indians and peasants on the left. There is, too, a problem of definition. There have been many years in which left–right killing, violence, kidnapping and assassination have become an integral part of the political scene, with apparently little chance that such activities will bring about any basic alteration to the country's overall structure. At what point and at what degree of intensity do such activities constitute a civil war?

From 1931 to 1944 President Jorge Ubico was in essence a dictator who represented the status quo of wealth, but in 1944 a general strike which became something of a popular uprising forced him to resign; in October 1944 Juan José Arévalo was elected President. The events of 1944 saw the emergence of organized labour as an important new factor in the politics of Guatemala. Moreover, the Communist Party was now to be allowed to operate without hindrance, so for the decade of 1944–54 there was a considerable move to the left, which included the introduction of a labour code and a social security system. Although Arévalo was not pro-Communist as such, he derived much of his support from the Communist Party. The elections of 1950 brought the liberal colonel Jacobo Arbenz Guzmán to the presidency. He adopted a policy of agrarian reform backed by the Communists and expropriated the unused land of major landowners, including land belonging to the US-owned United Fruit Company, for redistribution to the landless. By 1954 right-wing opposition to the government, including exiles in Honduras, centred on Carlos Castillo Armas; he and his followers had the support of the American CIA.

The reaction of the right 1954

The move towards a more equitable society during the decade to 1954 brought its inevitable reaction from the right. In March 1954 the USA, in conjunction with several Latin American countries, condemned the move towards Communism in Guatemala and a 'mini' arms race followed: the Guatemala government received a shipload of arms from Poland and the USA sent arms for 'defence' to neighbouring Honduras and Nicaragua. On 18 June 1954 a 2000-man anti-Communist army under Lt.-Col. Carlos Castillo Armas (backed by the USA – and the United Fruit Company – which by then regarded the Guzman regime as Communist) invaded Guatemala from Honduras. The Guatemalan government called on the UN Security Council and the USSR for assistance, and the Organization of American States (OAS) began an investigation. By 28 June, however, before any results could be obtained, the Arbenz government had collapsed. Arbenz fled to Mexico, while Armas occupied Guatemala City and established a ruling junta. When the invasion came the army had not been prepared to fight on behalf of Arbenz.

Left and right

The period 1954 to 1966 was one of political instability during which the social gains of the previous years were in danger of being reversed. The result was a trend towards violence between the two extremes of Guatemalan society. The elections of 1966 brought a would-be reformer to power as President, but Julio César Méndez Montenegro in fact was dependent on army goodwill, so little reform occurred. Instead the government found itself increasingly involved in fighting urban terrorism and rural guerrillas. During the years 1966–70, under the military leader Colonel Carlos Araña Osorio, the rural guerrilla threat was tackled and more or less eliminated – or so the military believed at the time.

In fact the 1960s saw a general radicalization of the left. Already by 1963, for example, the Guatemalan Labour Party (PGT) had become involved in armed warfare alongside two other radical groups – MR–13 (the Revolutionary Movement Alejandro de León of 13 November), which was Trotskyite, and FAR (Rebel Armed Forces) established in 1962, which was Castroite. A leading left-wing figure at this time was the intellectual César Montes, who had a Labour Party background and then led FAR. After the destruction of FAR he was to re-emerge in 1975 as the leader of the Guerrilla Army of the Poor (EGP). MR–13 and FAR were largely destroyed by the American-aided counter-insurgency activities of Colonel Araña in the later 1960s.

A number of other groups, such as the student Twelfth of April Revolutionary Movement (1962) and the Twentieth of October Front, rose and fell over these years. On the right there emerged from the counter-insurgency campaign of 1966 MANO or the White Hand, which specialized in assassinations. Towards the end of the 1970s an extreme right-wing group – Secret Anti-Communist Army (ESA) – was formed in 1977, while on the left another group – Revolutionary Organization of the People under Arms (ORPA) – was formed in 1979. During the 1960s left-wing and right-wing revolutionary and counter-insurgency violence became a habit.

The growing civil war of the 1970s

Araña Osorio won the elections of 1970 and embarked on a policy of 'pacification' in line with the counter-insurgency for which he had been responsible in the latter half of the 1960s. His policy of pacification included the extermination of habitual criminals and leftist guerrillas; but, in addition, the assassination of opposition leaders of all kinds indicated Araña's determination to crush any opposition to himself. The 1974 elections gave a majority to the Progressive, Ríos Montt, but the result was overthrown and the right brought Laugerud García to power instead. As a result, there was a renewal of left-wing violence, which in turn sparked off increased government repression. In 1976 Guatemala suffered from a devastating earthquake, described as one of the worst-ever disasters in Latin America, which exacerbated existing problems of poverty, although the discovery of oil in the north of the country gave promise of an improved economy. In 1977 the USA curtailed its aid to Guatemala because of continuing abuses of human rights. In 1978 General Lucas García came to power after another coup and inaugurated a new reign of anti-left terror.

The basis of the conflict between left and right lies in the question of land ownership, with the great majority of the rural – Indian – population without land and outside the structure of society. By the beginning of the 1980s, after a decade of government repression and growing anger from the left, the country was ready for a new and more violent stage of civil war.

The violent 1980s

The 1980s witnessed a constant state of civil war: a messy, long-standing guerrilla war against the government was waged by guerrillas of the left, mainly in the rural areas, while the government retaliated with counter-insurgency warfare backed by right-wing terror tactics – death squads – which were often tacitly and sometimes actively connived at by the government. There were constant deaths and disappearances, especially in the north of the country, which produced a steady flow of refugees into Mexico.

In 1980 there was a rapid increase of left–right conflict with the right-wing extremists making targets of trade union and student leaders as well as members of the guerrilla movements. At the end of January Indian peasants from the Quiché region occupied the Spanish Embassy as a protest against repression. The government sent the police to storm the building – against the wishes of the Ambassador – and 39 people were killed as the result of a firebomb. Spain subsequently broke diplomatic relations with Guatemala. In May left-wing opposition groups united under the umbrella of the Patriotic Liberation Front. In September the Vice-President, Francisco Villagrán Kramer, resigned in protest at his own government's violation of human rights.

By 1981 the Guerrilla Army of the Poor presented the greatest challenge to the military government. There was an upsurge in rebellion and greater co-operation between the various left-wing organizations. Amnesty International accused the government of President Fernando Roméo Lucas García of carrying on a pro-gramme of murder and torture against its political opponents. As guerrilla and counter-insurgency activities escalated, it was estimated that as many as 30 political murders were taking place every day. Despite this, relations with the USA improved during the year and the USA provided Guatemala with military vehicles.

In February 1982 four organizations of the left – the EGP, Partido Guatemalteco del Trabajo (Guatemalan Labour Party, PGT), FAR and ORPA – announced a unified command, the Guatemalan National Revolutionary Union (URNG). Elections in March which brought a moderate general to power were overthrown later in the month by the military under General Ríos Montt, who subsequently dismissed the junta of which he was a part to declare himself sole leader (9 June). Montt promised to disband the by now notorious death squads of the right and bring an end to the civil war; but although there was a temporary lull in urban violence, in the rural areas violence actually increased, so many more peasants were forced to flee to Mexico. Montt established special military courts empowered to hand down death penalties to guerrillas and terrorists. A rural campaign to win over peasants and Indians (the 'beans and guns' campaign) merely frightened these people and caused many to flee the country. Amnesty reported the death of 2600 Indians and peasant farmers between March and July.

The widely unpopular Montt, under whose presidency human rights violations had markedly increased, was replaced in 1983, following another military coup, by General Óscar Humberto Mejía Víctores. However, although Mejía abolished the secret military courts, the situation did not improve and the general violence continued to escalate. During 1984 the policy of the National Liberal Movement (MLN) was to purge the rural areas of 'Communistoids', as those of the left were dubbed, so violence increased. By the middle of the decade, however, protests at military rule were becoming increasingly vociferous from all sections of society, forcing a return to civilian rule. Elections of December 1985 gave a clear majority to the Christian Democrat leader Marco Vinicio Cerezo Arevalo, and the return to civilian rule was generally welcomed. Political problems were made worse by the deteriorating condition of the economy.

The military handed power back to the civilians on 14 January 1986 after 16 years of military rule, and President Cerezo abolished the secret police unit, which was generally believed to be behind the political assassinations. Unfortunately 1986 was another bad year economically, making it impossible for the new civilian government to satisfy popular demands for better living standards. The result, predictably, was a return to and escalation of left–right violence, although by the autumn the left-wing guerrillas indicated to government their willingness to enter into talks.

There was no let-up in 1987: murders and disappearances by the right were matched by periodic guerrilla attacks on the military. Cerezo found he was a prisoner of the military with little room in which to embark on policies of which they did not approve. In the first six months of his rule a total of 700 dead and 120 'disappeared' people were dismissed by the government as being the result of common crimes, while two massacres in the rural areas by the army showed how it was maintaining its counter-insurgency operations. Indeed, it seemed clear that the army had allowed the return to civilian rule (which it obviously controlled) in order to divert international pressure from its human rights record, which by the mid-1980s had become the worst in the hemisphere. In the rural areas peasants had to serve in the paramilitary patrols, and refusal was tantamount to seeking death at the hands of the military or the death squads. Travel outside villages required permission of local army commanders, and to be picked up without a patrol identity card resulted in being labelled a subversive.

Cerezo was unwilling to confront the army. He refused repeatedly to prosecute army officers for crimes committed under earlier regimes, and resisted calls by the Mutual Support Group (GAM) of relatives of the disappeared to investigate such disappearances. He did, however, manage to obtain substantial EEC aid by making Guatemala neutral in the Nicaraguan 'Contra' war (see below, pp. 551–559). In October the government held talks with the guerrillas in Madrid without any result; further talks in November produced the offer of an amnesty.

There were several unsuccessful coup attempts during 1989 as a result of military dissatisfaction with the anti-insurgency measures mounted by the Defence Minister, General Héctor Gramajo. Government talks due to take place with the guerrilla group – Guatemalan National Revolutionary Union – were postponed from May to August; as in other similar situations (see above, pp. 526–532), government–guerrilla talks had become part of a pattern of manoeuvre and manipulation that seemed to make little difference to the civil war, although from time to time such talks might provide one or both sides with a breathing space in which to reorganize. President Cerezo purchased fresh arms and helicopters for the army's counter-insurgency operations, but although the government claimed that active membership of the guerrilla organizations was falling, this claim was not reflected in any abatement of the fighting. The right-wing death squads increased their activities and further repression helped limit union and press freedoms. At the end of 1988 the armed forces launched a major anti-guerrilla campaign, although it did not appear to make much impression on the guerrillas.

Cerezo's performance did not encourage the belief that democracy had much of a future in Guatemala, although it has to be said in his favour that he inherited a country with a long history of bloodshed and on the verge of economic collapse. He did manage some economic successes and reduced the rate of inflation from 35 per cent to 12 per cent; but little real achievement is possible in a country where fear and violence have become the norm and where the President is constantly forced to appease a hard right composed of army and business interests. A new right-wing death squad emerged during 1989 – 'Jaguar of Justice' – which claimed responsibility for a number of killings. Human rights groups said that of 220 deaths in February at least 82 were political. Some candidates who registered for the 1990 elections received death threats, and violence escalated through 1989 so that monthly estimates of killings ranged between 40 and 200. Little effort was apparently made by the government to prevent the right-wing terrorist killings of unionists, journalists, Church and human rights activists; on the left the Guatemala National Revolutionary Unity guerrillas extended their operations to more than half the countryside. During the year President Cerezo accused the hard-right leader of Arena in neighbouring El Salvador, Roberto d'Aubuisson, of supplying arms to right-wing groups in Guatemala. The year turned out to be one of the most violent of the decade.

Estimated costs and casualties

Casualties for such a war are notoriously difficult to apportion accurately, but a UNRG estimate of 1990 put the dead since 1962 at 100,000 and the missing at 50,000. Between 1981 and 1985 the army's 'scorched Communists' campaign against the guerrillas was responsible for the total destruction of 440 Indian villages; it also produced 100,000 orphans as well as economic depression and rural poverty on a dramatic scale. The worst casualties of such a long-lasting state of constant civil conflict are the living rather than the dead, for it produces a level of brutality and indifference to death on both sides that is impossible to quantify and that even with peace will take a long time to eradicate as a habit of behaviour.

Results: ongoing

In June 1990 Guatemalan rebels and nine national political parties met in Madrid and agreed on moves to end 28 years of armed conflict. The Guatemalan National Revolutionary Union (UNRG) is to join the political parties in an assembly during 1991 in order to revise the country's constitution. The ruling Christian Democrats of President Vinicio Cerezo agreed that the paramilitary Civil Self-Defence Patrols should be disbanded and that the armed forces should be put under increased political control. The guerrillas for their part, while pledging not to interrupt the general elections scheduled for November, did not agree to a general ceasefire. Whether these accords are allowed to work, or whether hardline elements on either or both sides upset them, remains to be seen.

GUYANA: THE REVOLT OF THE RANCHERS 1969

Guyana has a population of under three-quarters of a million in a land the size of the British Isles, and the great majority of these people live in the coastal areas. The huge region in the interior known as the Rupununi depends on ranching for its economy and, apart from the ranch-owners, is sparsely populated by Wapisiana Indians. Governments in Georgetown on the coast have never shown much concern for this remote area, but are always sensitive to possible threats from neighbouring Venezuela, which has long disputed the joint border of the two countries and claims the Essequibo district of Guyana.

In January 1969 the ranchers of the Rupununi, joined by rebels from over the border – Venezuelans who had cut across part of Brazil to enter southern Guyana – seized the small centres of Lethem and Annai on the edge of the Rupununi Plateau in an apparent bid for independence. The government of President Forbes Burnham sent troops and police from the coast, and after a few days of manoeuvres and fighting in which a handful of policemen and others lost their lives order was restored. The origins of the revolt remain obscure. It may have been sponsored by Americans who owned cattle ranches in the region and aimed to establish a separate state. It was a diversion rather than a serious revolt, and the only really threatening aspect of the affair was the extent of Venezuelan involvement, which remained unclear.

NICARAGUA: THE SANDINISTA REVOLUTION AND THE CONTRA WAR

Introduction

From 1934 to 1979 the politics of Nicaragua were dominated by the Somoza family, whose repression and corruption brought the country to revolution. In 1934 Anastasio Somoza García, the head of the National Guard, was responsible for the assassination of the Liberal leader, César Augusto Sandino; Somoza then ran unopposed for the presidency in 1936. Somoza was to rule Nicaragua until 1956; he did so blatantly on behalf of his family and supporters. He was succeeded (after his assassination) by his son, Luis Somoza Debayle, who died in office in 1967. Meanwhile, in 1962 opponents of what had become a Somoza dictatorship, led by the Marxist Carlos Fonseca Amader, founded the Frente Sandinista de Liberación Nacional (National Sandinista Liberation Front, or simply the Sandinistas), who were named after César Augusto Sandino. In 1967 Luis Somoza was succeeded by his brother, Anastasio Somoza Debayle.

In 1972 Nicaragua was devastated by an earthquake which killed 6000 and rendered a further 300,000 homeless; the Somoza government diverted much of the international relief aid to its own coffers or those of its supporters, thus greatly increasing public hostility and hatred. According to the constitution Somoza could not be re-elected President in 1972, so instead he became Commander of the National Guard. From about this time onwards the Sandinista guerrillas began sporadic actions against government targets. Their tactics included kidnapping for ransom or to obtain the release of imprisoned guerrillas. The corrupt misuse of aid at the time of the earthquake helped to crystallize opposition to the government; this came not only from the Sandinistas but also from other non-marxist groups, one of whose most important figures was Pedro Joaquín Chamorro, the editor of the newspaper *La Prensa*. Following the earthquake, the Roman Catholic Church condemned the Somoza government for its behaviour. In 1974, however, a new constitution made it possible for Somoza to run again for President and he was re-elected. From 1974 onwards both the Sandinistas and the Union Democrática de Liberación (Democratic Union of Liberation, UDEL) under Pedro Joaquín Chamorro became prominent in anti-government activities.

During 1975 and 1976 civil war developed between the Sandinistas and the National Guard; many non-combatants were killed in the escalating strife, and a number of atrocities were committed. The Sandinistas suffered a major setback in 1976 with the death of Fonseca and other leaders. In 1977 the Sandinistas split into factions: they continued to favour a continuation of the war against the Somoza regime, but also advocated democratic elections. Also that year the US State Department accused the Somoza regime of human rights violations, while the Roman Catholic Church accused the government of using torture and executing civilians in its anti-Sandinista campaigns. In 1978 Chamorro was assassinated. Thereafter, an anti-Somoza alliance of the Sandinistas and UDEL as well as others was set to launch an all-out campaign against the government.

The revolution of 1978–1979

The assassination of Chamorro on 10 January 1978 set off widespread anti-government rioting and calls for Somoza to resign. Opposition to the government mounted through the year. On 22 August the Sandinistas seized the national palace and took more than 1000 hostages, including deputies of the lower assembly, whom they held for two days until they obtained the release of 59 hostages and their safe conduct out of the country. The insurrection spread, a general strike was called and the Sandinistas began to take control of towns throughout the country. In September the Sandinistas called for a general insurrection, and although this failed to overthrow the government immediately, 5000 people were killed and about 16,000 were injured. Despite the failure of this premature attempt at overthrowing the government, the Sandinistas had won much support outside the country, including from Venezuela, Panama and Costa Rica. Even so, at the end of 1978 there were perhaps no more than 1500 active Sandinistas.

During 1979 the uprising became widespread. The Sandinistas reunited their three factions and the USA put pressure on Somoza and his National Guard to seek exile. Many of the middle classes now supported the Sandinistas, so the Somoza family and its hitherto loyal National Guard found themselves increasingly isolated. On 29 May Sandinista exiles in Costa Rica invaded Nicaragua and seven weeks of fighting against the Somoza National Guard followed. On 6 June Somoza declared a state of siege, but by the end of the month the capital, Managua, was under siege. Then, on 17 July Somoza fled to the USA (a year later he was assassinated in Asunción, Paraguay) and the long period of Somoza dominance was brought to an end.

The revolution of 1979 was broadly based and one of the most popular in Latin America. By the time it was over between 40,000 and 50,000 people had lost their lives. In June the Sandinistas formed a five-person junta which included Chamorro's widow, Violetta. The Sandinistas now formed a government and embarked on a collectivist approach, which was soon to antagonize the USA. They constrained the press and limited the exercise of democracy, thereby losing the backing of some of their own original supporters.

Immediately, the new government abrogated the 1974 constitution, dissolved the bicameral National Congress and replaced the discredited and disbanded National Guard with the Sandinista People's Army. The government seized the huge properties of the Somoza family and nationalized banks and insurance companies as well as mineral and forest resources. Perhaps most important as far as future relations with the USA were concerned, the government established close diplomatic relations with Cuba and the USSR. In 1981 the junta reduced its number to three. But the Sandinistas had inherited a country in chaos, with an estimated 500,000 people homeless as a result of the earthquake and the preceding years of civil strife, while inflation was running at 60 per cent.

The USA and the Contras

By 1981 about 2000 former members of the Somoza National Guard (many of whom retained their loyalty to the Somoza family), now in bases across the border in Honduras, began to launch raids into Nicaragua. They were organized as the Fuerzas Democráticas Nicaragüenses (FDN), known as the Contras, and before long were receiving covert support from the CIA (by 1985 their numbers had grown to 10,000).

The Sandinistas did themselves considerable damage by their handling of the Miskito Coast Indians (see below) and their confrontation with the Roman Catholic Church. But their greatest difficulties arose from American attitudes towards their revolution, for increasingly Washington came to treat it as an extension of the Cold War between East and West. After the events of 1979 Washington becamed antagonistic to the Sandinista government, principally because of its close and developing relations with Cuba and the USSR and its support for insurgents in neighbouring El Salvador. More generally, the Marxist nature of the government on the USA's back doorstep was anathema to Washington. In its turn the Sandinista government reacted by claiming that its increased militarization was a response to the threat of aggression posed by the exiled National Guard and the possibility of direct US aggression. Throughout the 1980s, therefore, a total lack of trust on both sides led the Sandinistas to turn increasingly to the Soviet bloc countries for arms, while the USA stepped up its support for the Contras.

In any case the 1980s were a time of violence throughout most of Central America, with varying degrees of civil strife occurring in El Salvador, Guatemala, Honduras and Costa Rica. In October 1980 the People's Revolutionary Union announced an armed struggle in Honduras even as pro-Somoza exile groups established themselves in Honduras and Guatemala. Early in the 1980s a number of anti-Sandinista groups (not all of them associated with the Somoza regime) began to organize themselves to oppose what they saw as a left-wing Marxist government. A feature of US support for these opposition groups through the decade was the growing opposition of Congress to such aid; the US President (Ronald Reagan) was constantly clashing with Congress about his policy of support for the Contras.

The Contra war of the 1980s

During its first year of power the Sandinista government carried out a programme of nationalization, forbade foreign-owned banks to accept local currency deposits and imposed controls on food imports and exports, including coffee and cotton (two principal foreign exchange earners). It also passed a Statute of Rights which assured basic rights and freedoms. It was a crucial year, in which the government overtly turned to the left. By 1981 opposition groups were becoming organized across the border in Honduras. The Nicaraguan Armed Revolutionary Forces (FARN) were formed from among exiled Nicaraguans who had fled the Sandinista government, which they regarded as Marxist. At first the members of FARN came predominantly from the discredited National Guard, but later they were joined by other opponents of the Sandinistas who did not believe the Sandinistas would provide the kind of alternative government to the Somoza regime which they had hoped to see emerge from the 1979 revolution.

Although at first the Sandinistas were left-wing but not overtly ideological, by 1981 Daniel Ortega Saavedra, co-ordinator of the ruling junta, was moving towards Marxism-Leninism, at least in the sense that his regime was coming to rely more and more on Cuba for assistance. This predictably antagonized the USA, but it also lost the support of business interests in Guatemala which had – just – come to support the anti-Somoza revolution. Original members of the Sandinistas became alienated. Among these was Edén Pastora, who resigned from the government, retreated to Costa Rica and then in April 1982 took up arms against the Sandinista regime because he regarded it as undemocratic, under Marxist-Leninist control and increasingly dependent on aid from Cuba and the USSR. A year earlier the USA had suspended economic aid to Nicaragua at a time when it needed massive help if it was to tackle its problems of post-war reconstruction effectively. Thereafter, Washington began to allot funds to the exiled National Guard, who came to be called the Contras, and with CIA assistance these embarked on destabilization tactics. Relations between the two countries deteriorated still further when it became known that 600 Nicaraguan exiles were receiving military training in Florida; the USA justified this training by accusing the Sandinista government of arming the El Salvador guerrillas. In October 1981 there was a border clash with Honduras, and the government in Managua called for mobilization because of the threat posed by an estimated 4000 exiled National Guardsmen. By 1984 the CIA was assisting the FDN to mine Nicaragua's ports.

Nicaraguan–US relations worsened during 1982. The USA promised not to assist opponents of the Sandinista regime provided Nicaragua ceased supplying arms (from Cuba) to the rebels in El Salvador. The Sandinista government, however, insisted that the USA should stop its military build-up in Honduras, where it had established a base only 12 miles from the Nicaraguan border. By this time Ortega believed that war with Honduras was becoming probable if that country continued to assist the exiled Nicaraguan National Guardsmen. It was at this stage that the Sandinistas fell foul of Nicaragua's Miskito Indian community. In order the more easily to defend the border against incursions from Honduras, the government moved some 10,000 Miskito Indians from the area along the Coco river which formed the border. However, before the Indians could be moved heavy fighting took place: some of the Miskitos joined the Somocistas (followers of Somoza shortly thereafter to be referred to as the Contras), although others of the Indians joined the Alianza Revolucionario Democrático, which was also anti-Sandinista but not composed of former supporters of Somoza. Everything pointed to a burgeoning civil war. Essentially the Miskitos did not want to be moved from their traditional area. Some of the Miskitos had already fled into Honduras, and the Sandinista forces made the mistake (January 1982) of crossing into Honduras to attack some of their camps, killing as many as 100 of them. This action and other Sandinista pressures on the Miskitos lost the government a good deal of support as well as driving the Indians into the arms of its opponents.

American pressures on Nicaragua were substantially increased during 1983 when, for example, US forces began a series of military exercises (Big Pine) with the Honduran army; the result of such a threat was to make the Sandinistas turn still more towards the Eastern bloc countries for support. The Contras took to raiding across the border into Nicaragua, and in September and October they hit a number of economic targets, such as bridges, fuel tanks or depots and industrial sites, doing considerable damage and helping to worsen an already deteriorating economic situation. In reaction the government was obliged to ration fuel and increase internal security operations; neither action added to its popularity. When they attempted purely military confrontations the Contras were usually worsted. In the south of the country the other anti-Sandinista rebels under Eden Pastora Gómez were not very successful and failed to co-ordinate their activities with other groups. They also lacked money.

The USA now admitted that the CIA was involved in Nicaragua, but justified such intervention on the grounds that it was preventing the Sandinistas from exporting revolution to neighbouring states. This CIA activity, however, led to a developing political row in Washington with the House of Representatives voting to end covert US operations in Nicaragua, although the Senate, with a Republican majority, overrode these objections. Even so, the Senate was only prepared to approve $19 million out of $50 million in aid requested by President Reagan. Daniel Ortega accused the USA of waging an undeclared war against his country in an attempt to destroy the Sandinista revolution. Nicaragua appealed to the UN to intervene but got no satisfaction, and relations with Honduras and Costa Rica deteriorated since both were prepared to allow Contra raids to be mounted from their territories. But Nicaragua did manage to achieve a substantial international breakthrough when it obtained greatly increased aid from the European Community and was elected on to the UN Security Council.

In the elections which they held in November 1984 the Sandinistas won 67 per cent of the votes cast and 61 out of 96 seats, but the right-wing Nicaraguan Democratic Co-ordinating Board (CDN) refused to take part and claimed that the government would not guarantee rights of opposition parties. The USA described the elections as a sham. In the south of the country the anti-government Democratic Revolutionary Alliance under Gómez split. The Contras, however, received substantial aid from private American sources as well as the CIA, whose role was greatly criticized in the USA. CIA assistance included a manual of destabilization. The Contadora Group of Latin American countries – Venezuela, Mexico, Colombia and Panama – worked through the year to find a peaceful solution. The continuing effects of the war forced the Sandinista government to continue rationing and pursue a general policy of austerity as well as holding down wages.

The escalation of US involvement

In 1985 the International Court at The Hague upheld Nicaragua's complaint against the USA for mining its ports. Washington refused to accept the judgment. None the less, this helped to persuade Congress to delay any further aid for the Contras. In May, after a congressional vote against further aid, President Reagan announced a total trade ban on Nicaragua while abrogating the 27-year-old US–Nicaraguan treaty of friendship. Then in June Congress reversed its position and voted $27 million of 'humanitarian' aid to the Contras, which led the Sandinista government to abandon its promise not to seek further weapons and advisers from Eastern countries. The Contadora group continued what then appeared a fruitless search for a peace formula. Meanwhile, the Sandinistas had launched cross-border attacks on the Contra bases in Honduras; they had already moved 10,000 of their own people from the border region so as to prevent them giving aid to the Contras. Although the Contras made periodic attacks into Nicaragua, they were unable to hold on to the positions which they captured. Broadly, economic problems were causing far greater difficulties for the government than the activities of the Contras.

The intensity of the war escalated in 1986 even though the government was always able to contain the Contra threat, but in August the US Congress approved $100 million in military aid to the Contras, which was believed to be enough to enable them to establish military bases inside Nicaragua. A major incident followed the shooting down of a US supply plane and the capture by the Sandinistas of an American citizen, Eugene Hasenfus, who was put on trial in Managua. In his trial he confirmed that the CIA was helping the Contras. He was sentenced to 30 years in prison, but later President Ortega pardoned him and allowed him to return to the USA. There he became involved in investigations into allegations that secret US arms shipments to Iran had been diverted to the Contras – the beginning of the Irangate scandal. Meanwhile, in Costa Rica a high-ranking official admitted that a large clandestine airstrip near the Nicaraguan border had been built with US aid to assist the Contras. By November 1986 the USA found its policy in Nicaragua under attack from more than half its allies in the UN, where the General Assembly adopted a measure urging the Reagan administration to abandon its policy of supporting the Contras. In Nicaragua perhaps the real triumph of the Contras was the abandonment by the Sandinista government of its programme to develop co-operative farms. Since coming to power it had redistributed some 1.5 million hectares (4 million acres) of cultivated land to peasant farmers on condition that they reorganized in co-operatives. However, the pressures of war and economic decline, as well as the conservatism of the peasants and Contra propaganda that under such a system the peasants would not be the true owners of the land, forced the government to give up this ambitious programme.

By the end of 1986 the conflict along the Nicaragua–Honduras border was fierce, and the Honduran army of 15,000 simply stood back from a situation that it was unable to contain; of 18,000 estimated Contras, three-quarters were inside Honduras. There were, however, direct clashes between Honduran and Sandinista forces after the latter had attacked Contra positions across the border. In San Salvador the government of President Duarte refused to acknowledge that US Contra supply flights operated out of Ilopango airport, although the existence of such flights was revealed during the trial of Eugene Hasenfus. Nicaragua ended the year facing an escalating Contra threat with greatly increased US support from across the Honduran border, together with deeply worsening economic conditions inside the country. With 45 per cent of government spending now devoted to fighting the Contra war, the economic demands of the ordinary population were neglected, a fact that risked long-term support for the Sandinistas.

The Irangate scandal

The Irangate scandal erupted in Washington during 1987. In essence it was revealed that the US administration had secretly sold arms to Iran, which it condemned publicly as a terrorist state (for its involvement in hostage-taking activities), and had then channelled the profits from such sales to the Contras as a means of funding them and evading a congressional veto. In this way $15 million of funds were diverted illegally to the Contras, outraging Congress and doing immense damage to the credibility of the Reagan administration as well as to a number of important administration figures – the National Security Adviser, Robert C. McFarlane, his successor, Vice-Admiral John M. Poindexter, and Lt.-Col. Oliver North.

Meanwhile, the Contra war, waged mainly along the Honduras border region, intensified. In April the Contras launched a major offensive; this turned into a disaster with the Contras losing 477 killed, compared to 131 Sandinistas. Despite massive US support, the Contra position suddenly looked far bleaker in mid-1987. The breaking of the Irangate scandal made the Contra position precarious since it threatened further US aid. Furthermore, after long and tortuous negotiations, on 7 August the Sandinista government signed the Contadora Central American Peace Plan; this called on external powers (essentially the USA and USSR) to cease aid to insurgents in Central America. At the same time the Sandinista government relaxed pressures on the opposition parties, allowed La Prensa (which had been closed down) to operate again, and permitted expelled Roman Catholic priests to return to the country. Such liberalizing moves cut much of the ground from under the feet of the Contras and their US backers. By the end of the year growing pressures from other Latin American leaders were forcing the Sandinistas into a compromise with the Contras. At the same time the Contras launched their biggest offensive in six years to coincide with pressures for a ceasefire and direct talks between the Sandinista government and the Contras. Talks were finally undertaken in December. The economy then faced inflation of 1500 per cent as well as further price rises resulting from the Soviet decision to reduce its oil supplies to Nicaragua.

In January 1988 Ortega reversed his earlier stands and held direct talks with the Contras; at the same time he lifted the six-year state of emergency and promised to hold elections in 1990. But the peace effort ran into almost immediate problems, with Nicaragua accusing Washington of unwillingness to co-operate and the White House signalling that it wanted $270 million of aid for the Contras during the year. When Ortega met with the other Contadora Presidents in San José he found himself to be largely isolated, for the others were clearly antagonistic to everything for which the Sandinistas stood. But it was Ortega who made the concessions and the prime reason he did so was because of the effectiveness of Reagan's support for the Contras: not that they had been militarily successful (they had not), but they had so disrupted the economy of Nicaragua that peace had become essential for survival.

The year was to witness on–off Sandinista–Contra talks and further military clashes. The USA, pressing its advantage, sent 3200 troops to Honduras for exercises; in fact their presence served to force the pace of talks, although these broke down again in June. But the USA also cut off aid to the Contras and by May they were dividing into factions. It was a messy and long-drawn-out end to the war. During the second half of 1988 relations between Nicaragua and the USA became even worse than usual: Ortega expelled the US Ambassador, Richard Melba, and seven other diplomats for inciting revolt, and Washington retaliated in like manner. Thereafter, deadlock between the Sandinista government and the Contras continued to the end of the year. With the approaching end of the Reagan presidency the Sandinista government saw a good chance of ending the Contra war quickly and, thereafter, of establishing better relations with the USA. By December 1988, following Mikhail Gorbachev's call at the UN for peace, the Sandinista government said it would reduce its army of 70,000 by 40 per cent in stages. At least it seemed that US President-elect George Bush would be prepared to follow a less belligerent policy towards Nicaragua than his predecessor.

Finally, an accord was reached in February 1989 at Tesoro Beach in El Salvador: the Contras were to disband, and municipal, legislative and presidential elections were to be held in Nicaragua in February 1990. However, after the agreement the Contras said they would only disband when they were sure the Sandinista government was carrying out its part of the agreement – a return to full democracy. In March, as part of the agreement, the government released 1900 National Guards from prison and passed new laws guaranteeing press freedom. In August a new agreement was worked out in Honduras – the Tela Agreement – under which the Contras would voluntarily disband and an international commission would be responsible for collecting their weapons and monitoring their return to Nicaragua, or their relocation elsewhere, as well as the dismantling of their bases in Honduras and Costa Rica. Many of the Contras were afraid that the agreement gave them no proper guarantees and therefore wished to keep their arms, so the future of the agreement – and the peace – remained precarious at the end of 1989.

Estimated costs and casualties

The revolution of 1979 which brought an end to the Somoza dictatorship came after years of violence and fighting which cost between 40,000 and 50,000 lives. The economy which the Sandinistas inherited was near to ruins: economic damage was estimated at $2 billion and foreign debts at $1.3 billion, while 32 per cent of the working population was unemployed. The defeated Somocistas (supporters of the ousted Somoza family), who were mainly members of his National Guard, then settled in bases in Honduras and from 1981 onwards waged a desultory and not very successful campaign across the border into Nicaragua. The crucial factor in this Contra campaign was US backing: it is at least doubtful that the Contras would ever have been able to sustain their war had it not been for the quiescence of the Honduran authorities (under pressure from Washington) and the determination of the Reagan administration to fight Communism in Nicaragua by means of the Contras. Even so, for much of the time President Reagan was only able to support the Contras by bypassing Congress. As late as 1986 Congress voted $100 million for the Contras. In February 1987 the Sandinista government claimed that in five years of fighting to 1986 a total of 5066 government soldiers and civilians and 14,914 Contras had been killed. By the end of the war (December 1989) the figure for the dead might have risen to about 25,000. Many thousands more were maimed for life, and many thousands of children were orphaned. Perhaps more than anything else the war demonstrated the determination of Washington not to allow a Latin American country to follow its own course if that course was too far to the left; the extent of Washington's involvement not only was crucial to the course of events, but also did considerable damage to the international reputation of the USA, which was seen as a bully supporting the most dubious allies (the thugs of the discredited Somoza regime), while the Irangate scandal damaged the very concept of democracy that US actions were supposedly designed to defend.

Results

The outcome of the February 1990 elections in Nicaragua, which brought defeat to the Sandinistas and Ortega, was as much the result of the American 'big stick' policy of the previous decade which had destabilized the Sandinista regime as it was the result of the workings of democracy. The National Opposition Union (UNO) led by Violeta Chamorro won the elections, but as she soon discovered her victory was precarious and she faced a long hard process of integrating the Contras and dealing with an economy in chaos. It became clear that her performance would depend substantially on Sandinista goodwill, for they still represented the largest party in the country. In May 1990 President Chamorro declared Nicaragua bankrupt and asked the USA for aid. By early June 6843 Contras out of 13,000 had handed in their weapons, so it seemed the peace process was being implemented. There remained a long way to go.

PARAGUAY: REPRESSION WORKS

Introduction

All the ingredients for civil war – extremes of wealth and poverty, a harsh repressive regime, corruption – existed in Paraguay as in many other parts of Latin America in the decades after the Second World War. Yet after the brief civil war of 1947, an easily crushed invasion by dissidents in 1959–60 and subsequent occasional explosions of peasant anger, Paraguay under General Alfredo Stroessner managed to avoid the endless left–right bloodshed that has characterized the political life of so many countries in Central and South America. Under Stroessner repression worked.

During the 1930s Paraguay fought the Chaco War with Bolivia and was largely successful in holding on to the greater part of the Chaco region. In February 1936 there was a brief military revolt (the officer group responsible came to be called the Febreristas), but this did not last long. In 1939 José Félix Estigarribia was elected President, but he died a year later in a plane crash and was succeeded by General Higinio Morínigo. There were two main political parties, both dating from 1887: the Liberals and the Colorados. Morínigo relied on the Colorados for his popular support and persecuted the Liberals. Morínigo was only concerned with personal power; he suspended the constitution and acted as a dictator backed by the military. During his period of rule (1940–8) Paraguay was subject to frequent disturbances in the form of labour disputes or student riots, but opposition was put down ruthlessly by the military, to whom about 45 per cent of budgetary expenditure was applied. Under mounting pressure Morínigo allowed a return to two-party politics in 1946 and formed a cabinet drawn from the Colorados and the Partido Revolucionario Febrerista (PRF). But after a short while Morínigo excluded the PRF from the government, precipitating a crisis in 1947.

The civil uprising of 1947

Growth of political opposition to the right-wing government of Morínigo had persuaded him to agree to a coalition between the Colorados and the PRF, but when Morínigo expelled the PRF from his government they joined with the Liberal and Communist opposition. In March 1947 a brief civil war erupted between the two sides (it lasted until August); the opposition groups obtained help from the government of Péron in Argentina. It was a short but bloody conflict in which several thousand people died. The Colorados won with the help of the army, and subsequently exacted vengeance against their opponents throughout the country, causing many to flee into Argentina as refugees.

In 1948 the Colorados turned against President Morínigo, who was deposed. Over the next six years Paraguay suffered from half a dozen coups and a succession of weak Presidents the most important – or long-lasting – of whom was Federico Chaves (1949–54). He was re-elected in 1953 but then overthrown the following year by General Alfredo Stroessner.

The Stroessner years

General Stroessner seized power on 5 May 1954 with the support of the army and the Colorados; he had no difficulty in overthrowing the Chávez government and thereafter ran unopposed for the presidency. He instituted a policy of public works and imposed a harsh system of law and order. He ruled the country with an iron fist for 35 years and none of the attempts to overthrow him in the early years succeeded. All opposition was ruthlessly put down, and his adversaries either ended up in prison or fled the country. Over the years Stroessner provided Paraguay with a kind of stability.

The Cuban revolution of 1959 had its repercussions in Paraguay as elsewhere in Latin America, and in January 1959 dissident liberals belonging to the Movimento 14 de Mayo began to launch anti-government guerrilla attacks, while other attacks came from the Communists. These movements had a short period of activity during 1960 and 1961, but they never constituted any real threat to the government and were dealt with without difficulty. Many of Stroessner's political opponents took refuge across the border in Argentina where they set up bases from which they hoped to strike back and topple the Stroessner government.

By September 1959 the threat from the dissidents in Argentina was sufficiently irritating that Stroessner had the border closed. Then in December 1959 about 1000 rebels crossed from Argentina into Paraguay; they penetrated a few miles into the country, but were then defeated and driven to flight by the military. Stroessner declared a state of siege. There were half a dozen further cross-border incidents before the attempts ended with Stroessner in full control.

Later in the 1960s the Agrarian Peasant Leagues were formed; these were grass roots groups and had the support of the Catholic Church in challenging the existing system of land tenure. By 1969 they had a membership of about 20,000 rural peasants. During the 1970s there was violence in the rural areas when the Agrarian Peasant Leagues posed a threat to the Colorado Party's supremacy. Another revolutionary movement of the 1970s was the First of March Organization; this was formed in 1974 by radical Catholic students. It had its first and main clash with the authorities in 1976 when five policemen and 30 guerrillas were killed. Later about 1500 suspects were rounded up. In March 1980 came the most serious threat to Stroessner after a quarter of a century in power when 1000 troops had to be deployed against Agrarian Peasant Leagues in the Caaguazu department; altogether about 95 people were killed.

Repression works

The harsh repression of the Stroessner years produced its discontent and periodic guerrilla or other outbursts, but none of these posed any meaningful threat to Stroessner, and his government was never at risk. In the end, however, the military turned against the old dictator. On 3 February 1989 General Andrés Rodríguez led a military coup in which several scores of people were killed before Stroessner was overthrown after 35 years in power.

The story of Paraguay since 1945 illustrates the problem of definition: the uprising of 1947 was bloody and led to several thousand deaths, and may be classified as a civil war; but subsequent anti-government violence perhaps had no more than the potential for civil war, while Stroessner was able to demonstrate that harsh repression can work over a long period of time.

PERU: THE SHINING PATH

Introduction

Like its counterparts elsewhere on the continent, the guerrilla movement in Peru is the product of poverty and neglect. Over many years successive governments in Lima paid little attention to the needs or just claims of the Indian peasants; eventually their grievances were crystallized in guerrilla activity against the central government. It is a familiar pattern. There were various left-wing guerrilla movements during the 1960s, all on the political left and influenced by the Castro revolution in Cuba; they showed great daring but had little effective impact. One obvious reason for the failure lay in the fact that guerrilla leaders spoke Spanish rather than the Indian languages of the peasants. Land reforms instituted by the military junta that came to power at the end of the 1960s did not work, but at least they raised expectations among the peasants as to what might happen. Differences in lifestyles and expectations between the towns and the countryside remained huge: people in Lima, for example, could expect to live 20 years longer than the rural peasants. The failure of rural reforms produced anti-government revolt in 1973 and 1975, but little came of it.

Different guerrilla groups such as the Front for the Revolutionary Left, the Movement of the Revolutionary Left (MIR), the National Liberation Army and the Peruvian Communist Party (Red Flag) had brief spells of prominence, but only at the beginning of the 1980s did more permanent and effective guerrilla opposition to government emerge in the form of the Maoist Shining Path or Sendero Luminoso, which was to become a formidable force during the decade. A second smaller movement, the Revolutionary Movement Tupac Amaru (MRTA), which was Marxist-Leninist and drew its inspiration from Che Guevara, also operated through the 1980s but was mainly active in jungle regions. At the end of the 1980s a third, right-wing paramilitary organization, the Rodrigo Franco Commandos, emerged; it operated death squads and made the leaders of the left its targets.

In 1981 Peru faced a brief border war with Ecuador over the long-standing and conflicting claims that the two countries had dating back to the Protocol of Rio de Janeiro of 1942. Further skirmishes took place in 1982 and 1983, but these really served only as a diversion for a government increasingly taken up by the challenge presented by the Shining Path guerrillas. It took several years before the nature of the guerrilla threat posed by the Shining Path had become apparent or was fully appreciated by the government, but by 1984 about 5000 people had been killed and 2000 were 'missing'. Guerrilla activity in the 1980s emphasized the other growing problem that the government had to face: an economy in deepening recession that was less and less able to cope with the demands made upon it. As the decade passed, guerrilla attacks on economic and strategic targets posed the most persistent and difficult threat that the government had to face: the Shining Path, for example, regularly attacked electricity pylons to cause shortages of power in Lima.

The emergence of the Shining Path 1980

Over the 1970s the military junta became increasingly right wing, but in 1980 there was a return to civilian government and the elections were won by the Popular Action Party of Fernando Belaúnde Terry. It was the first time that votes were given to illiterates (who made up 13 per cent of the electorate) and to 18–20-year-olds. At the time the Peruvian economy was on a moderate upsurge, but neither this nor Belaúnde's victory made any difference to the plight of the rural Indian peasants as opposed to those of Spanish or mixed blood who dominate Peruvian affairs.

In July 1980 the Shining Path emerged as an active guerrilla movement. Its leadership had rectified the mistakes of earlier guerrilla movements; although they were the product of the University of Ayacucho, they had learnt the local (Indian) languages and at once recruited Indians to their ranks. Their inspiration came from a former philosophy professor, Abimael Guzmán. The movement embarked on rural sabotage and bomb attacks in the cities; it was to be most active in Ayacucho region, which had suffered years of poverty and neglect, and in Lima. Principal guerrilla targets were electricity pylons and railways. Anti-terrorist legislation was passed in March 1980, though at the time the government was not certain as to the character of the guerrilla enemy it was about to face. Early on in the Belaúnde administration it became plain that the government had little effective policy in relation to the guerrillas, and initiatives came more and more from the army, which waged an anti-guerrilla war of great brutality. However, the army had to face awkward economic factors: with the rural population either quiescent or supporting the guerrillas, the soldiers often unpaid for months at a time and even generals receiving no more than $65 a month, army morale remained low and the soldiers preferred to stay in the towns rather than venture into the more dangerous rural areas.

The Shining Path cadres are grouped in small cells of between five and seven members, and these have proved remarkably efficient and difficult for the authorities to penetrate. Tactics have been ruthless but effective. Thus they instruct the peasants under threat of death only to produce enough food to feed themselves; there must be no surplus to support the masses in the towns. This way urban discontent can be accelerated. Similarly, aid workers have been forced to leave or threatened with death. The strategy has been to create liberated zones in the rural areas of the mountains where the Indians live; they see Peru as a more or less feudal society and the peasants as a natural starting point for a revolution. Broadly, the objective of the Shining Path has been to deny the poor any hope until desperation forces them to rebel. This policy has had the interesting side-effect of increasing co-operation among members of the urban poor for their own survival.

Probably a majority of the people reject the rigid attitudes and hardline violence of the Shining Path; at the same time they are opposed to the poverty and structural violence which appear to be their lot under the system that currently exists. The Shining Path is critical of outside Communist leadership in China, Cuba and the USSR, and so has not established ties of dependency with those parties, a fact which adds to its strength inside Peru. Basic Shining Path policy is to redistribute the land of the wealthy to the peasants either in the form of individual plots or for them to work in co-operatives.

In January 1981 the government was diverted from the Shining Path by the eruption into a mini-border war of its long-standing dispute with Ecuador over the Cordillera del Cóndor, the area which provides access to the Amazon Basin. This had been awarded to Brazil under the terms of the Rio de Janeiro Protocol of 1942. A ceasefire was agreed after a few days of hostilities, and the border between the two countries was reopened in April. Further clashes took place at the beginning of 1982 and again in early 1983.

Meanwhile, the first phase of Shining Path activity covered the period 1980–2 when the guerrillas became increasingly effective. The police were unable to master the guerrilla movement, and liberated zones were established in the Ayacucho region. There was a steady escalation of guerrilla activity during 1982. In March about 150 members of the Path attacked the prison in Ayacucho to release 250 inmates, while bomb attacks became frequent over much of the country and the government was obliged to declare a state of emergency in a number of provinces. During July and August there was an upsurge of guerrilla activity with assassinations of local politicians or community leaders in Ayacucho region and a night of violence in Lima and the port of Callao when pylons were sabotaged. In December, with the police admitting their inability to control the guerrillas, President Belaúnde declared Ayacucho to be an emergency zone; he suspended constitutional rights in the region and sent in the army. But the army was no more successful than the police at ferreting out the guerrillas; instead it fell back on scorched-earth policies and worked on the assumption that if a number of peasants were killed some at least would be guerrillas. The army now began to create 'strategic hamlets' where whole populations were moved so that their activities could be monitored and the guerrillas could be isolated. They also created peasant civil defence groups.

The mid-1980s: a developing pattern

The Shining Path responded to these army tactics by widening the area of conflict so as to disperse the army's efforts. They began to recruit in the shanty towns of the big cities. In the new areas of the countryside into which they moved the Shining Path employed the same tactics, either executing or ordering the big landlords to leave as well as killing or punishing government representatives and criminals. The movement copied the tactics of Mao in the China of the 1930s and 1940s, establishing a 'People's Republic of New Democracy', or rather a number of them in different liberated areas.

The nature of the terrorist war was demonstrated in January 1983 when eight journalists visiting the village of Uchuraccay were killed by the inhabitants, who claimed they thought they were members of the Shining Path (Senderistas). The army had told the people to take the law into their own hands. Later in the year the Path exacted revenge by killing 70 villagers in reprisal. In May 1983 the guerrillas cut off Lima's electricity supply and destroyed the chemical factory of Bayer International. Later they bombed the headquarters of the Action Party, killing two and wounding 33. President Belaúnde asked for the death penalty for terrorism, and a state of emergency was applied to five provinces in the Ayacucho region. Amnesty International argued that Peru's counter-insurgency methods were leading to an unacceptably high number of deaths, but no change followed. Economic recession, meanwhile, was adding to the government's problems as inflation reached a level of 115 per cent.

During the first six months of 1984 there were more than 500 guerrilla-related deaths, while about 1000 people awaited trial for guerrilla activities. In June of that year the Shining Path launched a major offensive, leading President Belaúnde to hand overall responsibility for counter-insurgency from the police to the army. The discovery of a mass grave of army victims with evidence that they had been tortured highlighted the growing abuse of military power. The drug business – cocaine farming – now became an increasingly important factor in the guerrilla war. In 1984 a US-funded anti-cocaine growing project near Tingo Maria, north of Ayacucho, had to be abandoned under attack from the Shining Path, and the army moved into the area.

By 1985, when elections were due, the Belaúnde government had lost its popularity to a significant degree because of its inability to defeat the guerrilla movement; as a result, the centre-left American Popular Revolutionary Alliance (APRA) under Alan García Pérez came to power. He at once faced the problem of the guerrillas, but also that of military abuses of power, which he attempted to curb. Thus one of his early actions was to dismiss three high-ranking soldiers for their part in a peasant massacre. By then something like 1000 people were missing after being detained by the security forces, another familiar Latin American pattern.

By 1986 the Shining Path represented the biggest continuing problem faced by the government. An attempt to negotiate with the guerrillas came to nothing and they increased their activities. By this year 19 provinces had been placed under a state of emergency with suspension of civil rights. In February 1986 the Path mounted a number of attacks in Lima and Callao. In May the government announced that 7307 people had been killed in six years of fighting. President García made valiant but increasingly unsuccessful efforts to insist that human rights be observed in the fight against terrorism.

During June, when the Socialist International held its world congress in Lima, the Shining Path mounted one of its most spectacular dramas when prisoners in three prisons mutinied simultaneously (18–19 June). García ordered the army to restore order, but they did so with great and unnecessary brutality, killing 250 prisoners, including 100 after they had surrendered. Subsequently, some of the Republican Guard involved in these killings were put on trial for murder, the Justice Minister and other officials implicated resigned, and General Jorge Rabanal, who had been in command of the action, was arrested.

In the second half of 1986 the Shining Path began to escalate their operations in a new part of the country – Puno plateau in the far south of Peru. Most of this department lies more than 4000m (13,000 feet) above sea level around Lake Titicaca near the Bolivian border, and is among the most backward regions of Peru. The key to government or Shining Path success lay with President García's plans to redistribute 1.9 million hectares (4.6 million acres) of land to 400 peasant communities. As so often appears to be the case, the offer of reform came after violence had escalated rather than before it had the chance to develop.

A battle between the drug traffickers and the Shining Path was waged during 1987 in the south of the Huallaga valley; the guerrillas won, immensely strengthening their hold on the region, and the drug traffickers came to terms with them, promising to pay taxes in return for the right to operate. Increased guerrilla activity in the capital, Lima, now appeared to have become a permanent feature of the guerrilla war, while the government faced a growing and apparently intractable problem of fighting the guerrillas while also forcing the army to observe human rights. Attacks on government officials increased through the year, and a military protest against government was mounted when the Air Force General, Luis Abram Cavellerino, was dismissed for organizing protests at the merger of the three armed services.

Applying their policy of 'selective terror', the Shining Path were gunning down a policeman somewhere in Peru every other day or so, and there was no sign of abatement in a war apparently designed to destroy all existing social structures. According to captured documents, the aim of the Shining Path is to maintain a 'prolonged popular war' into the next century, when Lima would be encircled and a peasant–worker revolution would become possible. Meanwhile, the Shining Path used four main tactics: selective terror, sabotage, armed propaganda and full-scale guerrilla warfare. During 1987 the government became increasingly concerned that, despite apparent successes against the guerrillas, the level of incidents continued unabated – at about 3000 a year. Growing army brutality, incidents in which only dead were reported and an increasing 'gloves off' approach by the military did not appear to lessen Shining Path activity, which by the end of 1987 had, if anything, become more widespread and effective than ever.

Estimates of guerrilla strength are always difficult, but in the late 1980s the Shining Path were believed to have about 3000 political cadres and 4000 guerrillas, with many more sympathizers. It is an austere movement whose ruthless tactics ensure that it is feared. In January 1988, for example, about 50 peasants were massacred in the Ayacucho region, probably because they were members of the army-organized civilian patrols which have been set up in areas most affected by the guerrillas. Further similar massacres were carried out later in the year. These civilian patrols are seen as collaborators by the guerrillas. Other massascres were carried out by the army, yet the government was unwilling to take any action against it, despite massive evidence of human rights violations. By this time 37 of Peru's 172 provinces were under emergency military control.

The year 1988 was disastrous for the economy, with three general strikes (supported by the Shining Path). As the guerrillas appeared to gain ground, so there were increasing signs that the military and the right would turn to dirty war tactics. The right-wing Commando Rodrigo Franco (named after its first leader, who had been killed by Shining Path guerrillas) emerged to assassinate left-wing politicians and trade union leaders. It operated in the emergency zones and was believed to have close links with the García government, or at least sections of it. By this time the cocaine trade, centred on the Huallaga valley, had become a major part of the war as well as fuelling a great part of Peru's economy.

New austerity measures were announced by the government in November 1988, as many parts of the country faced power cuts from sabotage of electricity pylons by the guerrillas and Lima was plunged into chaos. At the end of the year the armed forces, with morale low and their campaigns against the guerrillas unsuccessful, attempted to mount a coup, but they were informed that the USA would not support the result and so desisted. The government then tripled military wages and purchased a new fleet of helicopters for them. In December another eight provinces were put under a state of emergency, bringing a quarter of the country under such regulations. Yet despite tough new anti-terrorist measures by government, the military did not believe they went far enough. Generally 1988 was one of the worst years yet for violence, with no sign that the government was even remotely mastering the guerrilla threat. The Shining Path held its first Congress during the year, when it stated its aims as the destruction of the old state, the creation of solid bases for taking power and the elimination of the United Left, which is seen as opportunist and revisionist. There is nothing half-hearted about the Shining Path.

By 1989 an estimated 15,000 people had been killed in the guerrilla war since 1980. The Shining Path had control of the upper Huallaga valley and collected taxes from the drug traffickers. The Path denounces drug use, but allows and encourages the trade for three reasons: the crop provides the peasants with a better income than any other crop; the guerrillas take taxes with which they buy arms or other necessities; and the sufferers from the drug trade are 'imperialists' in the rich North. Over five years (1984–9) the guerrillas had killed 300 policemen and 33 (drug) eradication workers, while at the same time organizing the peasant coca growers to demand higher prices from the dealers.

Senderista power increased through the year. In February, for example, the Shining Path guerrillas laid siege to the Puno district town of Azangaro with a population of 45,000. By this time, while the army was badly demoralized and convinced it could not defeat the guerrillas, the Shining Path controlled an area 800km (500 miles) long, was in charge of much of the drug business and was able, periodically, to threaten Lima either by cutting off electricity supplies or by eruptions of sabotage and bombings. There seemed less and less will or ability on the part of the government to deal effectively with the guerrillas. By April 1989 the Shining Path virtually controlled the Junín mining area, which was described as 'convulsed by terrorism', while only a tenth of the district authorities remained. The region, with its capital Huancayo, is one of the richest agricultural areas and supplies Lima with much of its food; it has, therefore, become a major focus for guerrilla activity. The people in the middle are subject to Senderista threats or executions on the one hand, and then counter-threats and torture from the military or the right-wing Commando Rodrigo Franco on the other. Following the death of a left-wing Congressman, Erberto Arroyo, in Lima, a huge sweep of the capital led to more than 6000 arrests. A British tourist was murdered in May apparently to discourage the tourist trade and so deepen the country's economic crisis.

In October 1989 the guerrillas launched a savage campaign of intimidation to sabotage the local elections due for November. Mayors were particular targets for assassination and the count has been a grim one: 60 mayors have been murdered in five years, while 260 have abandoned their posts. When the elections came large numbers of people did turn out to vote, not least as a protest at intimidation. About 10,000 Peruvians a month were emigrating as the state of the economy and security became progressively worse.

The first months of 1990 were taken up with the election campaign for President. In late March the Shining Path brought Lima to a standstill with a general strike as part of its campaign to sabotage the elections. The USA provided the first significant military aid since the 1960s when it gave $35 million for 1990 as part of its anti-drugs operation, but it will also provide counter-insurgency training and assistance with the Shining Path as the primary target. In a possible major blow to the Shining Path, police raided what appeared to be their headquarters in Lima (five safe houses) during May, capturing large quantities of documents. The raid came at a time when the position of the Shining Path in its traditional Andean strongholds seemed to be weakening as the system of peasant self-defence groups at last appeared to be working, at least to some extent, against the guerrillas. The presidential election was won, surprisingly, by the outsider candidate, Japanese-Peruvian Alberto Fujimori, backed by the newly formed Change 90 party and Protestant evangelical sects. His election represented a massive loss of confidence by the electorate in the established political order, which for a decade had presided over developing chaos. His first task was to come to grips with the guerrilla war.

Estimated costs and casualties

The costs have been formidable in deaths, terror and disruption. Between 1980, when the guerrilla war was launched, and 1990 about 18,000 people were killed. In Ayacucho province about 3200 people have simply disappeared after being arrested by the security forces. Assassinations of government personnel such as mayors have become normal practice, and by 1990 the toll of mayors was well above 200. Many more killings simply go unrecorded. The costs of damage (pylons blown up, etc.) have been estimated in excess of $10 billion over the decade, and by 1990 a third of the country was under a permanent state of emergency.

The cocaine trade has become a part of the wider violence, and by the mid-1980s coca took up to 200,000 hectares of farmland, accounted for 45 per cent of export revenues and provided employment for 300,000 peasants. The drug business now accounts for about 9 per cent of Peru's GDP; the country produces two-thirds of the world's supply, and 95 per cent of it is produced illegally. Coca leaves are worth $900 million to Peruvian farmers – a farmer may earn $4500 from growing 1 hectare (2.5 acres) of cocaine, but only $600 from growing coffee, cacao or beans – but by the time the cocaine reaches New York it is worth $76,000 million. So far US efforts to tackle the drug trade at source (in Peru, for example) have proved disastrous, and intensified campaigns against coca farmers have not stopped the trade; rather, they have driven the traffickers into alliance with the Shining Path guerrillas.

Results: continuing

The prospects facing the new President (Alberto Fujimori) after his surprise victory in May 1990 were daunting, and he lacked both experience and a party structure to back him up. His election did, however, represent a conscious choice, a turning away from the politicians who had led the country for 10 increasingly disastrous years, and so it was possible that he would achieve a new breakthrough. Meanwhile, there was no sign of any let-up in the guerrilla war.

SURINAME: REVOLT OF THE BUSH NEGROES

Introduction

Suriname became independent from the Netherlands in 1975; in 1980 there was a military takeover and in December 1982 the former Sergeant-Major Desi Bouterse emerged as the ruler of a 'left-wing' government. During 1982 Bouterse was responsible for the execution of 15 trade union and opposition leaders, an act which cost him most of the popular support he had enjoyed until then, as well as causing the Netherlands to suspend all aid in protest. In 1985 the National Military Council (NMC) agreed with the three main political parties, which broadly represent the three racial divisions (Hindus, Creoles and Javanese), that they should sit on a council to prepare the way for a return to civilian rule. The Bush Negroes (descendants of former runaway slaves or Maroons), who number about 50,000, felt themselves excluded from these proceedings and discriminated against by the army, and so they launched a revolt. Racial antagonisms play an important part in the political life of Suriname, and many thousands of people fled the country before and after independence in order to escape racial strife. The Bush Negroes demanded a return to democracy, but along non-racial lines.

The bush rebellion

The bush rebels were led by Ronnie Brunswijk, who had been Bouterse's bodyguard; he subsequently demonstrated a flair for guerrilla warfare, which he launched against the government in the second half of 1986. He had been dismissed from the army and had carried out a series of bank robberies, distributing the money among the Maroons. When he organized a force of about 100 men to attack government targets he achieved a significant following. Part of the money required to finance the rebellion came from exiles in the Netherlands desirous of overthrowing the Bouterse regime; this probably paid for the half-dozen British mercenaries who joined the rebels. The guerrillas operated from the tropical rain forest, which covers 80 per cent of the country.

The guerrillas launched their campaign in July 1986, when they attacked three military posts on the same night, including the main army camp at Albina where they seized weapons, ammunition and vehicles. They also took 12 soldiers prisoner, and 10 of these promptly joined their ranks. When in response the army sent in its élite Echo company to find and destroy the rebels, the commander (Sergeant-Major Henk van Randwijk) was captured; he too changed sides. In a few weeks of guerrilla action Brunswijk's Bush Negroes successfully besieged and set fire to a border town, trapping 500 government soldiers who were garrisoned in it; raided a state-run palm oil plantation, causing heavy damage; and ambushed an army patrol 50 km (30 miles) from the capital, Paramaribo. Thereafter, the rebels made army posts their targets, and while the government admitted to seven soldiers killed, the Dutch press put the casualties much higher. Brunswijk's status was far from clear: despite the fact that he enjoyed a significant following among the Bush Negroes, government officials claimed that he was a pawn of the exile movement in the Netherlands.

The government was obliged to evacuate civilians from the border areas near French Guiana ready for a major offensive against the rebels. After four months of activity government forces had failed to inflict any significant defeat on them, while the rebels had a string of successes to their credit: they had hijacked planes, kidnapped a minister's son and closed factories, roads and an airport as well as capturing army posts and soldiers.

The guerrilla war and the suspension of Dutch aid forced Bouterse to seek a compromise with the politicians and to abandon his earlier stand, which was to vest all power in the army alone. At the time of the coup Bouterse had adopted a revolutionary stance and made overtures to Cuba, a move that lost him a great deal of support both inside and outside the country. Eventually, however, he had to ask the Cubans to reduce the numbers of their personnel in Suriname as the condition for receiving urgently needed aid from Brazil. He then turned to Libya for aid, but this was no more popular than had been his flirting with Castro's Cuba. By the end of 1986, after a string of guerrilla successes, Bouterse was facing possibly greater danger from his own army as discontent grew and it continued to lose engagements against the rebels.

At the end of 1986 (a week after declaring a state of emergency on 2 December) the Suriname Foreign Minister, Hendrik Herrenberg, accused the French of massing troops in French Guiana ready for an invasion of Suriname; at the same time the government evacuated villages near the border in order to deny support to the rebels and in preparation for an offensive against them. The French replied that they were merely posting troops along the Moroni river for 'humanitarian reasons', to help look after an estimated 4500 refugees who at that time had fled to escape the conflict between the rebels – then thought to number 200 – and the Suriname army of 1000. By that time casualties from the rebellion had reached a figure of at least 250 dead. The rebels suffered a first setback when the army retook a mining town they had captured. The Dutch government accused the Bouterse regime of massacres and announced a plan to evacuate the 6000 Dutch passport holders if it should become necessary to do so.

Although the rebellion was apparently insignificant, it threatened to grow into something considerably larger. By mid-December 1986 the Suriname Cabinet Director, Henk Heidweiller, claimed that 500 French and US mercenaries had collected in French Guiana ready to invade Suriname. At the same time the US Secretary of State, George Shultz, was questioned about reports that Suriname had signed a new military agreement with Libya (which already had a presence in Suriname). Washington saw a Libyan presence as the basis for regional destabilization, although sources in both the Netherlands and Paramaribo claimed that there were no more than 60 Libyans in Suriname altogether. In mid-December Bouterse announced that his army had recaptured all areas of economic importance which the rebels had seized and that he was ready to deal with the 500 mercenaries said to be standing by in French Guiana. The war then reached a stalemate. Government officials admitted that they could not easily capture or defeat the rebels; in any case, after years of ostracism by the West for its left-wing stand, the government was forced to come to terms with the politicians. The rebels, meanwhile, were seeking aid in the West largely through the 200,000 Suriname exiles in the Netherlands.

A return to civilian government

In January 1987 Suriname asked the UN to send observers to monitor the fighting, and ordered out the Dutch Ambassador after accusing him of spreading false information about human rights violations. The rebels then claimed to control about 65,000 square kilometres (25,000 square miles) of territory bordering on French Guiana, though it was almost all jungle. A new twist to the rebellion occurred in April 1987 when Henk Chin-A-Sen, the former President of Suriname, was reported to have returned to the country to declare a free state in the rebel-held territory; earlier he had visited the State Department in Washington to ask for assistance, arguing that this would make possible a rebel victory in a 3–5-day offensive. The French in neighbouring French Guiana allowed free passage to Brunswijk or his agents as well as the passage of arms to the rebels. But though there were comic-opera aspects to the affair, the guerrilla campaign had had the effect, by early 1987, of crippling an economy that had already been brought low by the loss of Dutch aid.

As a result, Colonel Bouterse produced a timetable for a return to constitutional rule; a referendum was to be held in September 1987 for a new political charter, to be followed by elections for a National Assembly in November. The elections were duly held and brought an end to seven years of military rule when the three principal opposition parties combined in a Front for Democracy and Development and defeated Bouterse's National Democratic Party. It was clear, however, that the army retained significant power.

The new civilian government took power in January 1988, but made no immediate gestures of reconciliation towards the Bush Negro guerrillas. Later in the year (27 June) talks between the government and the guerrillas were held across the border in French Guiana, but these were soon deadlocked. A year of stalemate followed. Then in June 1989 the Speaker of the new National Assembly, Jaggernath Lachman, and Ronnie Brunswijk agreed the terms of a truce. The Suriname army was to withdraw from the traditional regions of the Bush Negroes, which Brunswijk's forces would police. The government of President Ramsewak Shankar ratified the agreement, and on 21 July 1989 a peace treaty was signed at Kourou in French Guiana. However, the army as well as other groups in Suriname were unhappy with the agreement, which they claimed threatened their interests.

Estimated costs and casualties

About 250 people were killed during the first most important phase of the rebellion at the end of 1986; figures for subsequent casualties are confused. The rebellion had the effect of crippling an economy already in decline as a result of the withdrawal of Dutch aid; it caused more than $75 million of damage, including the shutdown of the vital aluminium (bauxite) industry for more than a year; and it sent about 12,000 Surinamese as refugees across the border into French Guiana.

Results

The most important result of the rebellion was to force Bouterse to return to civilian rule, although the army retained an ambivalent and powerful role in the new civilian system. It also reasserted the special place of the Bush Negroes in Suriname's life. But the troubles rumbled on; in September 1989 the rebels occupied the bauxite town of Moengo 100 km (60 miles) east of Paramaribo and held it through to June 1990, when the army under Bouterse retook the town.

INDEX OF NAMES

DATE D

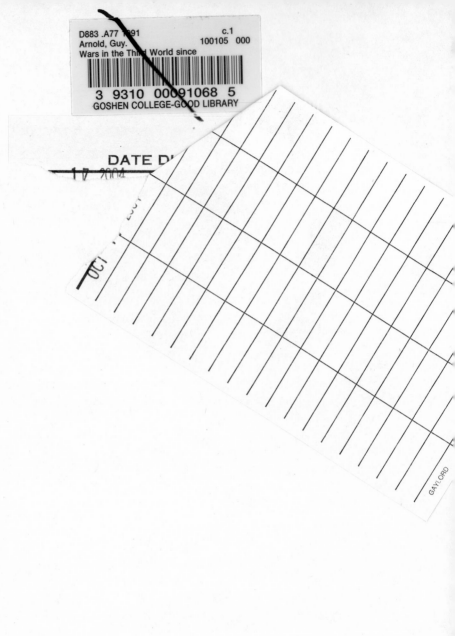

GAYLORD